lonely planet

WITHDRAWN

Andalucía

Huelva
Province
p90

Sevilla
Province
p48

Córdoba
Province
p200

Jaén
Province
p225

Granada
Province
p251

Almería
Province
p292

Cádiz
Province &
Gibraltar
p110

Málaga
Province
p159

Isabella Noble,
Gregor Clark, Duncan Garwood, John Noble, Brendan Sainsbury

Contents

TRIANA, SEVILLE P63

HOLBOX/SHUTTERSTOCK ©

MEZQUITA, CÓRDOBA P204

BILL PERRY/SHUTTERSTOCK ©

Contents

UNDERSTAND

SURVIVAL GUIDE

SPECIAL FEATURES

Welcome to Andalucía

The scent of orange blossom, the swish of a flamenco dress, the glimpse of a white village perched atop a crag: memories of Andalucía linger.

The Essence of Spain

Immortalised in operas and vividly depicted in 19th-century art and literature, Andalucía often acts as a synonym for Spain as a whole: a sun-dappled, fiesta-loving land of guitar-wielding troubadours, reckless bullfighters, operatic heroines and Roma singers wailing sad laments. While this portrait might be outdated, stereotypical and overly romantic, it does carry an element of truth. Andalucía, despite creeping modernisation, remains a spirited and passionate place where the atmosphere sneaks up and envelops you when you least expect it – perhaps as you're crammed into a buzzing tapas bar or lost in the depths of a flamenco performance.

A Cultural Marinade

Part of Andalucía's appeal springs from its peculiar history. For eight centuries it sat on a volatile frontier between two faiths and ideologies, Christianity and Islam, and underwent a cross-fertilisation that threw up a slew of cultural colossi: ancient mosques transformed into churches; vast palaces replete with stucco work; a cuisine infused with North African spices; *hammams* and *teterías* (teahouses) evoking the Moorish life-style; and lofty white towns that dominate the craggy landscape, from Granada's tightly knotted Albayzín to the hilltop settlements of Cádiz province.

Wild Andalucía

It takes more than a few golf courses to steamroll Andalucía's diverse ecology. Significant stretches of the region's coast remain relatively unblemished, especially on Cádiz' Costa de la Luz and Almería's Cabo de Gata. Inland, you'll stumble into villages where life barely seems to have changed since playwright Federico García Lorca created *Bodas de sangre* (Blood Wedding). Thirty per cent of Andalucía's land is environmentally protected, much of it in easy-to-access parks, and conservation measures are showing dividends. The Iberian lynx is no longer impossibly elusive; the ibex is flourishing; even the enormous lammergeier (bearded vulture) is soaring above Cazorla's mountains.

Duende

One of Andalucía's most intriguing and mysterious attractions is the notion of *duende*, the elusive spirit that douses much of Spanish art, especially flamenco. *Duende* loosely translates as a moment of heightened emotion that takes you out of yourself, experienced during an artistic performance, and it can be soulfully evoked in Andalucía if you mingle in the right places. Seek it out in a Lorca play at a municipal theatre, an organ recital in a Gothic church, the hit-or-miss spontaneity of a flamenco *peña* (club) or Málaga's remarkable art renaissance.

Why I Love Andalucía

By Isabella Noble, Writer

I grew up in the whitewashed Málaga province mountain village of Cómpeta, performing flamenco at local *ferias*, picking up a lifelong *malagueño* accent, tackling meat-mad menus as a vegetarian and studying maps of Andalucian peaks, parks and rivers, then later lived in Cádiz province. Tarifa remains my favourite place in the world (though Vejer de la Frontera is creeping up behind) and, while Cádiz, Málaga, Córdoba and Seville are all fabulous, there's no city quite like magical Granada. Andalucía will always be my home, and I love the *andaluz* zest for life, from late-night tapas crawls to full-family beach expeditions.

For more about our writers, see p384

Above: Baños de Doña María de Padilla (p57), Real Alcázar, Seville

Andalucía

ELEVATION

	2000m
	1500m
	1000m
	500m
	200m
	100m
	0

Córdoba
Christian and Islamic architecture
spanning 1000 years (p201)

Seville
Gothic Cathedral meets
Mudéjar palace (p50)

Badajoz

Mérida

SPAIN
BADAJOZ
(EXTREMADURA)

CÓRDOBA

Santa
Eufemia

Pozoblanc

Peñarroya-
Pueblonuevo

Río Guadiato

La Capitana
(959m)

Guadalcanal

Rosal
de la
Frontera

**Parque Natural
Sierra de Aracena
y Picos de Aroche**

Cazalla de
la Sierra

**Parque Natural
Sierra de
Hornachuelos**

Beja

PORTUGAL

Jabugo Castaño
(960m)
Cortegana
Almonaster Aracena
la Real Alájar Linares de
la Sierra

**Parque Natural
Sierra Norte
de Sevilla**

Constantina

Córdoba

Palma
del Río

Zalamea la Real

HUELVA

Río Odiel

SEVILLA

Lora
del Río

Río Huéznar

Écija

Río Genil

Río Tinto

Seville

Carmona

Río Guadalquivir

Monte
Francisco

Almonte

Marchena

Osuna

Ayamonte
Isla
Cristina

Lepe

Huelva

Coria del Río

Utrera

Río Corbones

Punta
Umbría

37°N

Golfo de
Cádiz

Matalascañas

**Parque
Nacional
de Doñana**

Coripe

Olvera

MÁLAG

El Chorro

Parque Nacional de Doñana
Island of biodiversity in the
Río Guadalquivir delta (p97)

**Parque Natural
de Doñana**

Trebujena

Embalse de
Bornos

Villamartín Zahara de
la Sierra

El Burgo

Ronda

Torrecill
(1918m)

Sanlúcar de
Barrameda

Grazalema

Jerez de la Frontera
Cradle of sherry,
horses and flamenco (p121)

Jerez
de la Frontera

Arcos de la
Frontera

El Torreón
(1648m)

El Bosque

Úbrique

**Parque
Natural Sierra
de las Nieves**

Bahía
de Cádiz

CÁDIZ

Gaucín

Arcos de la Frontera
The most spectacular of
Cádiz' white towns (p134)

Cádiz

San Fernando

**Parque Natural
Sierra de
Grazalema**

San Marbe
Pedro
de Alcántar

Medina
Sidonia

Cádiz
Dive into the riotous fun of
Europe's oldest city (p111)

Conil de la Frontera
Los Caños de Meca

Vejer de la
Frontera

Barbate

**Parque
Natural Los
Alcornocales**

La Línea
de la Concepción

Gibraltar (UK)

Algeciras

Costa de la Luz
Kitesurfing and undeveloped
blonde-sand beaches (p142)

Costa de la Luz

Zahara
de los Atunes

Bolonia

36°N

Tarifa

ATLANTIC
OCEAN

Strait of Gibraltar

Ceuta

Tangier

MOROCCO

Tarifa
Andalucía's windsurfing and
kitesurfing capital (p146)

Ronda
Clifftop town in dramatic
mountain setting (p181)

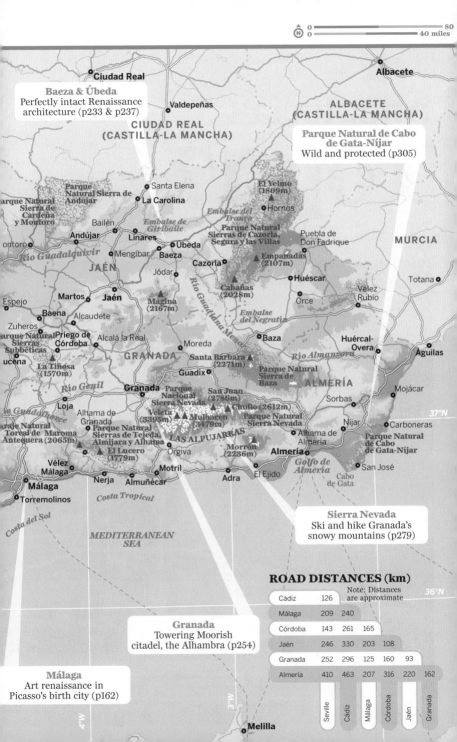

0 / 80
0 / 40 miles

Baeza & Úbeda
Perfectly intact Renaissance
architecture (p233 & p237)

**Parque Natural de Cabo
de Gata-Níjar**
Wild and protected (p305)

Ciudad Real

Valdepeñas

**CIUDAD REAL
(CASTILLA-LA MANCHA)**

**ALBACETE
(CASTILLA-LA MANCHA)**

Albacete

Santa Elena
La Carolina

Parque
Natural Sierra de
Andújar

El Yelmo
(1809m)

Hornos

Embalse del
Tranco

arque Natural
Sierra de
Cardeña
y Montoro

Bailén

Embalse de
Giribaille

Parque Natural
Sierras de Cazorla,
Segura y las Villas

Puebla de
Don Fadrique

MURCIA

ontoro

Andújar

Linares

Mengíbar

Úbeda

Baeza

Río Guadalquivir

JAÉN

Jódar

Cazorla

Empanadas
(2107m)

Huéscar

Vélez
Rubio

Totana

Río Guadiana Menor

Cabañas
(2028m)

Espejo

Martos

Jaén

Magina
(2167m)

Orce

Embalse
del Negratín

Baena

Alcaudete

GRANADA

Santa Bárbara
(2271m)

Baza

Huércal-
Overa

Río Almanzora

Águilas

Zuheros

arque Natural
Sierras
Subbéticas

Priego de
Córdoba

Alcalá la Real

Moreda

Parque Natural
Sierra de
Baza

ALMERÍA

ucena

La Tiñosa
(1570m)

Guadix

Mojácar

Río Genil

Granada

Parque
Nacional
Sierra Nevada

San Juan
(2786m)

Chullo (2612m)

Sorbas

Loja

Veleta
(3395m)

Mulhacén
(3479m)

Parque Natural
Sierra Nevada

Níjar

Carboneras

a Guadalhorce

Alhama de
Granada

Parque Natural
Sierras de Tejeda,
Almijara y Alhama

LAS ALPUJARRAS

Alhama de
Almería

Parque Natural
de Cabo
de Gata-Níjar

raje Natural
Torcal de Maroma (2065m)
Antequera

El Lucero
(1779m)

Órgiva

Morrón
(2236m)

Almería

Vélez
Málaga

Nerja

Almuñécar

Motril

Adra

El Ejido

Golfo de
Almería

San José

Málaga

Torremolinos

Costa Tropical

Cabo
de Gata

Costa del Sol

**MEDITERRANEAN
SEA**

37°N

Sierra Nevada
Ski and hike Granada's
snowy mountains (p279)

36°N

ROAD DISTANCES (km)

		Note: Distances			
Cádiz	126	are approximate			
Málaga	209	240			
Córdoba	143	261	165		
Jaén	246	330	203	108	
Granada	252	296	125	160	93
Almería	410	463	207	316	220	162
	Seville	Cádiz	Malaga	Córdoba	Jaén	Granada

Granada
Towering Moorish
citadel, the Alhambra (p254)

Málaga
Art renaissance in
Picasso's birth city (p162)

3°W

4°W

Melilla

Andalucía's
Top 17

1

Granada's Alhambra

1 If the Nasrid builders of Granada's Alhambra (p254) proved one thing, it was that – given the right blend of talent and foresight – art and architecture can speak far more eloquently than words. With the snow-dusted Sierra Nevada as a backdrop, this towering, hilltop Moorish citadel has been rendering visitors of one kind or another speechless for a millennium. The reason: its harmonious architectural balance between humankind and the natural environment. Fear not the dense crowds: the Alhambra is an essential pilgrimage, and lively Granada is an equally evocative place to explore. Below left: Patio de los Arrayanes (p259)

Seville's Catedral & Alcázar

2 The 15th-century constructors of Seville's cathedral (p50) wanted to create a church so big that future generations would think they were mad. They gloriously succeeded. Only a bunch of architectural geniuses could have built a Gothic masterpiece this humongous: it's the largest in the world. Offering greater subtlety and more intricate beauty is the adjacent Alcázar, still a palace for the Spanish royal family, and a spectacular blend of Christian and Mudéjar architecture. The two buildings sit either side of the Plaza del Triunfo in ironic juxtaposition.

MARQUES/SHUTTERSTOCK ©

MARGARET STEPIEN/LONELY PLANET ©

Córdoba's Mezquita

3 One of the world's great works of Islamic architecture, Córdoba's magnificent mosque (p204) is a grand symbol of the time when Islamic Spain was at its cultural and political peak, and Córdoba, its capital, was western Europe's largest, most cultured city. In the Mezquita's interior, mesmerising rows of horseshoe arches stretch away in every direction. The most intricate surround the gold-mosaic-decorated portal of the *mihrab* (prayer niche). While most Córdoba visitors rightly make a beeline for the Mezquita, you'll find the old city that grew up around it just as fascinating.

Sierra Nevada

4 The lofty, white-peaked Sierra Nevada (p279) backs one of Europe's most striking cityscapes, Moorish Granada, and hosts Andalucía's only ski resort. Much of this mountain range is protected by the 859-sq-km Parque Nacional Sierra Nevada, a high-altitude world best uncovered on hikes that include the chance to scale mainland Spain's highest peak, 3479m Mulhacén. The white villages beautifying the mountains' southern slopes are known as Las Alpujarras and are famous for their craft-making, agricultural fertility, hiking and horse-riding opportunities, and Berber-style houses.

CASILDO CATEDRAL - CORDOB

Parque Nacional de Doñana

5 A figurative biodiversity 'island' in the Río Guadalquivir delta, the Parque Nacional de Doñana (p97) is one of only two national parks in Andalucía (and 15 in Spain). Along with its abutting *parque natural*, it forms one of Europe's largest, most important wetland sites. Long a blueprint for eco-management, the park's assertive environmental policies have set precedents on balancing the wonders of the natural world with tourism and agriculture. Aside from offering multiple nature excursions, the park is a precious sanctuary for deer, wild boar, migrating waterfowl and endangered Iberian lynx (pictured left).

Cádiz

6 The *gaditanos* (citizens of Cádiz) are Spain's great laughers and jokers. Here in the southern city (p111) of ancient *barrios* (districts) and the nation's greatest Carnaval, nothing is taken too seriously. Even the locally concocted brand of flamenco, known as *alegrías,* is uncharacteristically joyful and upbeat. Sitting like a great unlaunched ship on a peninsula that juts out into the Atlantic, Cádiz also sports the region's most romantic sea drive, its most expansive municipal beaches, a buzzing food scene and an unbelievable stash of ancient sights.

Kitesurfing in Tarifa

7 If Andalucía has a hallmark outdoor activity, it's kitesurfing, a daredevil white-knuckle sport given extra oomph by the stiff winds that enliven the choppy waters off the Strait of Gibraltar. The activity has lent a boho-cool vibe to the Costa de la Luz and its wind-battered southern nexus Tarifa (p146), a whitewashed coastal town that often feels more Moroccan than Spanish. Windsurfing and kitesurfing outlets proliferate along nearby beachfronts, tempting the adventurous into the water, while, a little northwest, El Palmar has Andalucía's best board-surfing waves.

Flamenco

8 Like all great anguished music, flamenco has the power to lift you out of the doldrums and stir your soul. It's as if by sharing the pain of innumerable generations of dispossessed misfits you open a door to a secret world of musical ghosts and ancient Andalucian spirits. On the other side of the coin, flamenco culture can also be surprisingly jolly, jokey and tongue-in-cheek. There's only one real proviso: you have to hear it live, preferably in its Seville–Jerez–Cádiz heartland. Above: costumed dancer, Seville (p50)

Tapas

9 Spanish cuisine might have gone molecular in recent years, but there's no getting away from the basics. Tapas define Spain's *style* of eating as much as its *type* of cuisine – a long, drawn-out smorgasbord of tasting and savouring that can go on well into the night. Seville (p50) claims Andalucía's most creative tapas, although Málaga, Granada, Cádiz and Vejer de la Frontera might beg to differ. Granada, Almería and almost every bar in Jaén province are some of the few places in Spain that still serve recession-busting free tapas with every drink.

Cabo de Gata

10 For a cherished memory of what the Spanish coastline used to look like before megaresorts gatecrashed the Costa del Sol, seek out Cabo de Gata (p305) in Almería province, a wild, rugged, golf-course-free zone, where fishing boats still reel in the day's catch and bold cliffs clash with the shimmering azure Mediterranean. Considering it's one of the driest areas of Europe, the *cabo* has abundant feathered fauna and scrubby vegetation. It's also a protected *parque natural*, ideal for hassle-free biking and hiking, and home to some of Andalucía's most pristine beaches.

11

Costa de la Luz Beaches

11 Habitual Costa del Sol–goers may not have heard of Tarifa, Bolonia (pictured above) or Zahara de los Atunes, but Andalucía's wind-lashed Atlantic coast is wilder, blissfully less developed and far less crowded than the southern Mediterranean littoral. Kitesurfers, horse riders and happy wanderers abound on the Costa de la Luz (p142), though there's plenty of room to laze on broad sweeps of fine blonde sand with Morocco fading into the background. The coastline's towns – activity-mad Tarifa and whitewashed Vejer de la Frontera – are a Morocco-flavoured delight.

Ronda

12 Spectacular Ronda (p181) teeters atop sheer-sided cliffs amid the brawny mountainscapes of Málaga province's Serranía de Ronda. This forever-popular white town has an embattled history infested with bandits, smugglers, warriors and rebels, and a weighty bullfighting legacy. Then there's its famous artistic connections with self-styled 'rugged' Hollywood types Ernest Hemingway and Orson Welles, along with a newly invigorated flamenco scene and some truly excellent restaurants serving up hearty mountain cuisine and locally produced wines. Or just dust off your mountain boots and hike out into the hills.

Málaga's Art Renaissance

13 There's no stopping Málaga (p162) and its art renaissance. Until 2003 the city lacked even a museum devoted to native son Picasso; now it's becoming an art heavyweight to rival Madrid or Barcelona. Recent openings include a gallery dedicated to locally born painter Jorge Rando, and the long-awaited re-launch of the Museo de Málaga, exhibiting important Spanish works unseen for decades. Málaga has also developed its own free art space, Soho, embellishing a formerly rundown area near the port with giant murals and graffiti. Bottom right: Museo Picasso Málaga (p162)

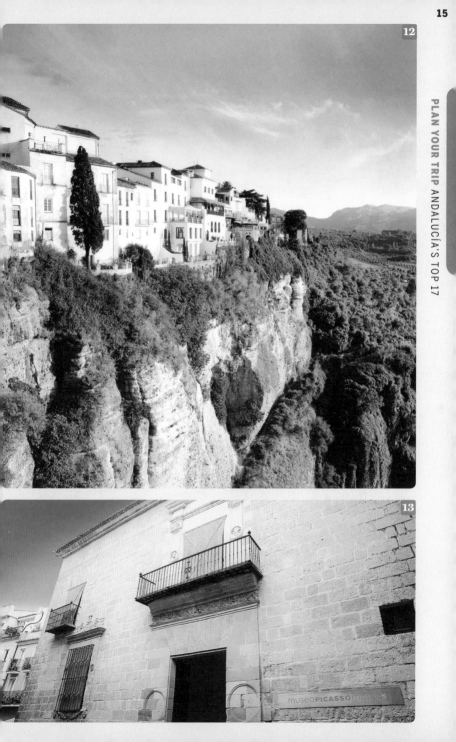

Renaissance Baeza & Úbeda

14 These two outposts among the olive groves of Jaén province look more Italian than Spanish; it's the perfectly intact Renaissance architecture. Local nobility remodelled these towns in the 16th century, commissioning local architect Andrés de Vandelvira to design monumental, beautifully proportioned mansions, churches and civic buildings that helped to introduce Renaissance ideas to Spain. In 2003 Baeza (p233) and Úbeda (p237) joined the great monuments of Granada, Córdoba and Seville as Andalucian Unesco World Heritage sites, yet they get far less foot traffic. Top: Sacra Capilla de El Salvador (p238), Ubeda

The White Towns

15 Choosing your favourite *pueblo blanco* (white town) is like choosing your favourite Beatles album: they're all so good, it's impossible to decide. Pressured for an answer, most people hunt down the classic calling cards: a thrillingly sited location, an evocative old town, a plush *parador* (luxurious state-owned hotel) and a volatile frontier history. The best examples lie dotted all over Andalucía, with two heavy concentrations: one in northeastern Cádiz province and the other in the mountainous Alpujarras. Tour them by bike, car or bus, or on foot. Bottom: Pampaneira (p283)

Semana Santa in Seville

16 Only the *sevillanos* (citizens of Seville) could take the themes of grief and death and transform them into a jaw-dropping spectacle. Many cities around the world mark the Catholic feast of Holy Week (p68), but none approach it with the verve and outright passion of Seville. Watch nightly processions led by various *hermandades* (brotherhoods; the oldest dating back to 1340), including hooded *nazarenos* (penitents), shoulder elaborately decorated floats through the city streets in an atmosphere doused in emotion and religious significance.

Sherry Tasting

17 In the sun-dappled vineyards of western Cádiz province, fortified white wine has been produced since Phoenician times, enjoyed by everyone from Christopher Columbus to Francis Drake. A distinctly Spanish product made for British tastes, sherry is often considered a drink for mildly inebriated English grannies. But it's making a comeback and wine-lovers can dig deeper with tours, tastings, sherry-pairing menus and more. Savour its oaky essence in the feisty Sherry Triangle towns of Jerez de la Frontera (p121), El Puerto de Santa María and Sanlúcar de Barrameda.

Need to Know

For more information, see Survival Guide (p351)

Currency
Euro (€), Gibraltar pound (£)

Languages
Spanish (Castilian), English in Gibraltar

Visas
Generally not required for stays of up to 90 days per 180 days (visas are not required at all for members of EU or Schengen countries). Some nationalities need a Schengen visa.

Money
ATMs widely available. Credit cards accepted in most hotels, restaurants and shops.

Mobile Phones
Local SIM cards widely available and can be used in European and Australian mobile phones. Not compatible with many North American or Japanese systems.

Time
Central European Time (GMT/UTC plus one hour)

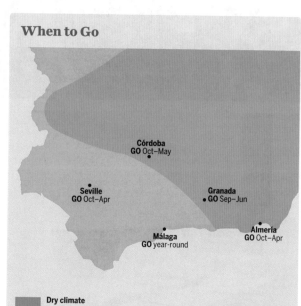

When to Go

Córdoba
GO Oct–May

Seville
GO Oct–Apr

Granada
GO Sep–Jun

Málaga
GO year-round

Almería
GO Oct–Apr

Dry climate
Warm to hot summers; cold winters

High Season
(Jul–mid-Sep)

➡ Temperatures soar, and the climate is very dry.

➡ Most Spaniards holiday in July and, especially, August; expect crowds and traffic jams, particularly along the coast.

➡ Many hotels hike up prices by up to 50%; book ahead.

Shoulder
(Apr, May & mid-Sep–Oct)

➡ Hotel prices can triple during Semana Santa and local ferias.

➡ Ideal weather: warm but not too hot (great for hiking).

➡ Spring brings a colourful cavalcade of Andalucian festivals.

Low Season
(Nov–Mar)

➡ The coastal climate remains warm and relatively dry; it's cooler and rainier inland.

➡ Sierra Nevada ski season.

➡ Hotel bargains available (though some shut down).

➡ Most sights operate reduced hours.

Useful Websites

Turismo Andalucía (www.anda lucia.org) Encyclopaedic official Andalucía tourism site.

Spain (www.spain.info) Official Spanish tourist-board site.

Andalucia.com (www. andalucia.com) One of the most interesting and comprehensive guides to the region.

Lonely Planet (www.lonely planet.com/spain/andalucia) Destination information, hotel bookings, traveller forum and more.

Iberianature (www.iberiana ture.com) Devoted to Spain's natural world.

Ventana del Visitante (www. ventanadelvisitante.es) Down-loadable hiking info and maps for Andalucía's natural parks.

Important Numbers

Telephone numbers in Spain don't use area codes; simply dial the nine-digit number.

Country code	☑34
International access code	☑00
Ambulance	☑061
Emergency	☑112
National police	☑091

Exchange Rates

Australia	A$1	€0.66
Canada	C$1	€0.68
Japan	¥100	€0.76
Morocco	Dh1	€0.09
New Zealand	NZ$1	€0.60
UK	UK£1	€1.13
US	US$1	€0.86

For current exchange rates, see www.xe.com.

Daily Costs

Budget: Less than €75

➡ Budget-hotel double room: €30–65

➡ Meal at traditional tapas bar: €2–4 per tapa

➡ Free sights, tours and shows

➡ Bus transport: €23–29 (Seville–Granada)

Midrange: €75–175

➡ Boutique-hotel double room: €65–140

➡ Car hire: from €20

➡ Meal at local restaurant: €20–45

➡ Admission to monuments, museums and attractions: €3–20

Top end: More than €175

➡ Room at *parador* or upmarket boutique hotel: from €140

➡ Meal at top-end restaurant: from €40

➡ Flamenco show with dinner: €50–70

➡ Car hire: from €20

Opening Hours

Opening hours have local and seasonal variations. (Gibraltar businesses don't take a siesta: restaurants usually open 8am–8pm and shops 10am–6pm; most shops close after lunch Saturday and reopen Monday.)

Banks 8.30am–2pm Monday–Friday, 9am–1pm Saturday

Cafes 8am–11pm

Night-time bars and clubs 10pm–4am

Post offices 8.30am–8.30pm Monday–Friday, 9am–1.30pm Saturday

Restaurants 1pm–4pm and 8pm–midnight

Shops 9am–1.30pm and 5pm–9pm Monday–Saturday

Supermarkets 9am–9pm Monday–Saturday

Arriving in Andalucía

Seville Airport A bus (€4) leaves every 20 to 30 minutes through the day to the city centre (fewer on Sunday). Taxis cost €21 to €31 and take 15 to 20 minutes.

Málaga Airport A train (€1.80) leaves every 20 minutes and takes 12 minutes to the city centre. Bus A leaves for the city centre (€3, 20 minutes) every 20 minutes from outside the main arrivals hall at Terminal 3. Direct buses from the airport go to Granada, Marbella and Torremolinos. A taxi to the city centre costs €20 to €25.

Granada Airport A bus runs to the city centre (€2.90) at 6am and then at least hourly between 9.15am and 11.30pm. A taxi costs around €20 to €24.

Getting Around

Car Andalucía has an excellent road system. Having your own vehicle enables you to make the most of your time, as bus services to smaller villages rarely operate more than once a day and there are often no weekend services. Make rental-car arrangements before you leave home.

Bus With a more extensive net-work than trains, buses travel to even the smallest villages. Alsa (p173) runs the best intercity routes. Various other companies service remoter areas. Buses are usually cheaper than trains over equivalent distances.

Train High-speed AVE trains serve Seville, Córdoba and Málaga. Slower but cheaper regional trains link most other main towns and cities but aren't much use for getting around Cádiz or Huelva provinces. Reserve ahead on AVE trains.

For much more on **getting around**, see p362 ➡

What's New

Museo de Málaga

Relaunched in December 2016 in Málaga's neoclassical customs house, Andalucía's largest museum combines archaeological artefacts with the city's fabulous fine-arts collection, much of which had been locked away since the 1990s. (p166)

Vie Ferrate Fever

These fixed-protection climbing routes pioneered in WWI Italy are soaring in popularity in Spain, with some of the best climbs in Málaga province. Organise guided excursions in Ronda, Gaucín, El Chorro, El Torcal and Comares, plus the Sierra de Grazalema (Cádiz) and Cazorla (Jaén). (p39)

World Heritage Dolmens

Unearthed in the 1900s, Antequera's Dolmen de Menga and Dolmen de Viera, some of Europe's most exceptional neolithic monuments, were inscribed on Unesco's World Heritage list in 2016. (p190)

Cathedral Bell Tower

The Catedral de Cádiz' neoclassical 56m-tall Torre del Reloj (Clock Tower) opened to visitors in mid-2015 after five decades out of action. (p111)

Jerez' Tabancos

In Andalucía's sherry capital, traditional, early-20th-century *tabancos* (humble taverns serving sherry from the barrel) have burst back into life, reinvigorated under keen new ownership. (p126)

Boutique-Hotel Bliss

Gone are the days of dreary *hostales*: boutique hotels are blossoming all over Andalucía. Particularly stylish stays now abound in Málaga, Seville, Granada, Vejer de la Frontera, Córdoba, Tarifa, Sanlúcar de Barrameda, Úbeda and Estepona. (p352)

Palacio de Las Dueñas

The 19th Duque de Alba threw open the doors to Seville's 15th-century Palacio de Las Dueñas in March 2016. Explore the late *duquesa*'s collections in the palace where poet Antonio Machado was born (1875). (p61)

Ronda Guitar Festival

Since 2016, Ronda has celebrated Spain's favourite instrument with a five-day June festival (p185) of concerts, wine-tastings and guitar-maker exhibitions at also-new Ronda Guitar House. (p187)

Game of Thrones

The hit TV series continues its love affair with Andalucía in seasons Seven and (rumouredly) Eight. New star filming locations are Córdoba's Castillo de Almodóvar, Roman Itálica (p224) and Seville's Reales Atarazanas. (p80)

The Alhambra's New Baths

Intricate restoration works saw the opening of part of the Alhambra's 14th-century Baño Real del Palacio de Comares, one of the Western world's most perfectly preserved *hammams*, in December 2017. Keep an eye out for temporary annual openings. (p254)

Mamarracha (Seville)

Fashionable Mamarracha is a welcome addition to the bar scene in one of Seville's most touristy areas, with creative tapas served in the shadow of the colossal cathedral. (p72)

For more recommendations and reviews, see lonelyplanet.com/andalucia

If You Like...

Moorish Architecture

Alhambra (Granada) The high point of Moorish architecture was reached in the 1350s under Sultan Mohammed V. (p254)

Alcázar (Seville) With 10th-century roots, this is just a few smidgens down from the Alhambra on the brilliance scale. (p56)

Mezquita (Córdoba) One of the greatest mosques ever built, an early Al-Andalus gem, is today a Christian church. (p204)

Alcazaba (Almería) A magnificent hilltop fort lording it over the city skyline. (p293)

Giralda Now a belfry, this Moorish minaret stands out from the Gothic mass of Seville's cathedral. (p50)

Beaches

Costa de la Luz Bleach-blonde Cádiz province beaches with kitesurfing action and Morocco shimmering on the horizon. (p142)

Cabo de Gata This super-dry, protected corner of Almería has easy-access sandy strands and secluded coves. (p305)

Nerja A lively Málaga province beach town with the right balance between tourism and authenticity. (p197)

Mojácar Broad sands with dozens of easygoing beach bars. (p310)

Fine Arts

Málaga A stash of galleries and museums embellish Andalucía's fast-developing cultural powerhouse. (p162)

Seville The Museo de Bellas Artes is the obvious draw; Golden Age masterpieces adorn the cathedral. (p50)

Cádiz Impressive art at the Museo de Cádiz takes in important works by Andalucian masters. (p111)

Granada Art hides in Granada's holy buildings, including the Capilla Real and Monasterio de San Jerónimo. (p254)

Bodegas Tradición A standout private art collection concealed in a Jerez de la Frontera sherry bodega. (p121)

Hiking

Sierra de Grazalema Vigorous hikes among orchids and flying vultures, through Cádiz' mountain ruggedness. (p139)

Sierra Nevada Tick off mainland Spain's highest peak, Mulhacén (3479m), or the easier, slightly lower Veleta (3395m). (p279)

Las Alpujarras Ancient paths link white villages on the south-facing slopes of Granada's Sierra Nevada. (p282)

Sierra de Aracena This lost world in Huelva is a jigsaw of pastoral paths punctuated by time-warped villages. (p106)

Cabo de Gata Some 50km of trails snake along this vertiginous Almería stretch of Andalucía's coast. (p305)

Parque Natural Sierras de Cazorla, Segura y Las Villas Beautiful walks to Jaén mountaintops and along scenic valleys in Spain's biggest protected area. (p245)

Parque Natural Sierras Subbéticas Not-too-demanding hiking among canyons, craggy hills, and white villages southeast of Córdoba. (p219)

Great Local Food

Granada Free tapas, Moroccan-influenced cooking, and fresh vegetables plucked straight from the surrounding countryside. (p254)

Seville The Andalucian capital's plentiful, varied tapas bars span the food spectrum from down-to-earth to gourmet. (p50)

Sanlúcar de Barrameda Fantastic fish moulded into inventive tapas is washed down with dry, one-of-a-kind *manzanilla*. (p132)

Sierra de Aracena Created from black acorn-fed pigs, Spain's luxury ham is best sampled in rural Huelva province. (p106)

Cádiz *Pescaíto frito* (fried fish) is one of Andalucía's favourite offerings. (p111)

Málaga Try grilled sardines and *tinto de verano* (similar to sangría) at a *chiringuito* (beach shack). (p162)

Vejer de la Frontera Sherry, *almadraba* tuna and local veg fuel traditional, experimental and Moroccan-fusion Costa de la Luz cooking. (p142)

Úbeda Small Jaén town of superb Renaissance architecture, with creative eateries. (p237)

Hill Towns

Arcos de la Frontera The quintessential Cádiz white town, with castle, church and centuries-old houses clinging to a crag. (p134)

Vejer de la Frontera Cavernous restaurants, ornate tiled fountains, esoteric festivals, luxury boutique hotels and a magical timelessness. (p142)

Capileira A perfect white Las Alpujarras village, from where hikers strike out for the Sierra Nevada. (p285)

Zahara de la Sierra Wander sunbleached, bougainvillea-wrapped streets below a crag-top Moorish castle, in prime Cádiz province mountain-hiking country. (p138)

Zuheros Lesser-known white town in Córdoba province overlooking olive-striped countryside crisscrossed by gentle hiking trails. (p219)

Segura de la Sierra Steeply stacked Jaén province village with medieval castle amid the mountains of Andalucía's largest protected area. (p249)

Cómpeta One of Málaga province's most popular whitewashed hill towns, with good walking and excellent restaurants. (p195)

Top: Real Alcázar (p56), Seville

Bottom: Zahara de la Sierra (p138)

Month by Month

January

The year starts quietly, but *romerías* (religious pilgrimages) and saints' days up the ante by the month's end. The average Málaga temperature is 12°C, sometimes rising to 17°C. Ski season in the Sierra Nevada is well under way.

⭐ Día de los Reyes Magos

Three Kings' Day, on 6 January, is the highlight of any Spanish kid's calendar, with present-giving and family celebrations. Three local personalities dress up as the three wise men on the evening of 5 January and parade around throwing sweets in the Cabalgata de Reyes.

February

Cádiz' Carnaval and Jerez' flamenco festival lure people from far and wide. Andalucía's coolest month, February's also the best month for skiing in the Sierra Nevada. Accommodation gets booked out months ahead in festival areas.

⭐ Carnaval

Cádiz throws mainland Spain's largest Carnaval, with parades, fancy dress and a spectacle more famous for its wit and satire than its grandeur, best embodied by scathingly humorous *chirigotas*. The 10-day party ends the Tuesday 47 days before Easter Sunday, sometimes running into March. (p114)

⭐ Festival de Jerez

The self-styled *cuna* (cradle) of flamenco hosts what is claimed to be the world's most esteemed flamenco festival, over two weeks in late February or early March. (p124)

March

The best time to visit Andalucía starts now, with the arrival of spring and warmer weather, especially in years when Easter falls early.

April

Possibly the best month to visit, April promises fine (but not sweltering) weather, Semana Santa parades and exuberant festivals headlined by the big one in Seville. Hotel prices shoot up (and availability dwindles) when festivals arrive.

⭐ Semana Santa

There are few more elaborate manifestations of Catholic Holy Week than in Seville, where hooded *nazarenos* (penitents) carry huge floats through the streets in ghostly solemnity. It's also spectacularly celebrated in Málaga, Granada, Córdoba and Arcos de la Frontera. The event can also fall in March.

⭐ Feria de Abril

Seville's legendary week-long spring fair, in the second half of April, is Andalucía's biggest fair. It proceeds something like this: *sevillanos* dress up in traditional gear, drink sherry, parade on horseback, dance *sevillanas* (flamenco-influenced folk dances) and stumble home in the early hours. (p69)

★ Romería de la Virgen de la Cabeza

One of Spain's largest, most passionate religious events sees a small statue of the Virgin Mary carried around on the last Sunday in April, at Jaén province's Santuario de la Virgen de la Cabeza, 31km north of Andújar town. It attracts tens of thousands. (p232)

May

The mountain slopes are strewn with wild blooms, the sun is out, and Andalucía buzzes in anticipation of *romerías* or summer fiestas. If Easter is early, the Romería del Rocío (Pentecost weekend) falls in May.

★ Feria del Caballo

Jerez hogs many of Andalucía's best festivals, including its famous one-week horse fair, which dates back to medieval times and involves plenty of parades, music, dancing, competitions and makeshift bars serving the best local sherry. (p124)

★ Feria de la Manzanilla

Head to unheralded Sanlúcar de Barrameda (p133) for some alfresco tapa tasting and manzanilla swilling in this great, fish-biased culinary town. Neighbouring El Puerto de Santa María also has a late-April/early-May sherry festival celebrating the local *fino*. (p129)

★ Fiesta de los Patios de Córdoba

Everything happens in Córdoba in May, from a flower festival to a spring fair. In this homage to the city's gorgeous patios, homeowners open up 50 or more private courtyards (hidden away the rest of the year) to compete for the title of 'best patio'. (p213)

June

The summer fiesta season has fully kicked off, with temperatures rising and every town and village in Andalucía hosting its own particular shindig. Good hiking weather.

★ Romería del Rocío

The greatest of all pilgrimages, centred on Pentecost (Whitsunday) weekend, attracts over a million people to venerate the Virgin in Huelva province's El Rocío. They arrive in colourful parades on foot and horseback, by carriage and boat. Dates: 9 June 2019, 31 May 2020, 23 May 2021. (p101)

★ Noche Blanca del Flamenco

A night-long, top-class flamenco blowout, starring leading artists of the genre in free performances at picturesque venues around Córdoba, on a Saturday night around 20 June. (p213)

★ Ronda Guitar Festival

Ronda's new five-day guitar fiesta, launched in 2016, celebrates all kinds of playing (not just flamenco) with concerts, conferences, wine-tastings and exhibitions. (p185)

★ Corpus Christi

Another movable Catholic feast, celebrated eight-and-a-half weeks after Easter, Corpus Christi is particularly significant in Granada, where, despite the underlying solemnity, it has long been fused with the annual feria. Sometimes falls in May. (p267)

July

Exiles from Northern Europe hit the Mediterranean beaches, and it gets hot. Linger by the coast, or escape to the mountain villages for (slightly) cooler air. The Spanish holiday season starts mid-month; reserve well ahead.

★ Festival Internacional de Música y Danza

Top-notch contemporary and classical performances take place in the Alhambra and other historical settings around Granada during the city's three-week June-and-July international music and dance festival. (p267)

★ Festival de la Guitarra de Córdoba

Flamenco is a highlight of this two-week guitar festival held in early July in the (by then) sizzling city of Córdoba, but you'll also hear live classical, rock and blues performances. (p213)

August

It's hot. Seriously hot. Hit the beaches for sea breezes and Málaga's mid-month feria. If you're on the *costas*, half of Spain (and much of Europe) will be joining you. Book ahead!

✨ Feria de Málaga

In mid-August, Málaga hosts Andalucía's second-most-famous party after Seville's April fair. Celebrations are awash with all the usual calling cards: lights, dancing, sherry and fireworks. Mysteriously, relatively few Costa del Sol tourists show up. (p168)

September

At last, a little relief from the heat (though certainly not everywhere!). September promises great hiking weather and is harvest time for grapes. Jerez and Montilla both have wine festivals.

☆ Bienal de Flamenco

Seville shares this prestigious biennial flamenco festival with Málaga; Seville hosts in even-numbered years. Top-notch artists have been gracing the stages since 1980 to perform at the 30-day event. (p69)

✨ Fiestas de la Vendimia

Jerez' two-week September fair honours the grape harvest with horse riding, sherry drinking, *bulerías*-oriented flamenco and the traditional treading of the first grapes on the steps of the city's cathedral. (p125)

October

Autumn brings the harvest, an alluring stash of food festivals and milder temperatures (good for hiking).

November

A big month for agriculture, with peak olive harvests and, traditionally, pig slaughters. It's also the start of low season and, potentially, the Sierra Nevada ski season, though Seville still registers nearly 200 hours of sunshine.

December

The Andalucians save energy for one last hurrah: Navidad (Christmas), with the festive season spilling into January. Otherwise, chilly December is low-key, apart from some ski action and a long weekend early in the month.

✨ Navidad (Christmas)

Families come together for feast-like dinners on 24 December. Many now celebrate Navidad, with Papá Noel bringing presents for kids, though Three Kings' Day (6 January) is the traditional present-giving celebration.

☆ Fiesta Mayor de Verdiales

On 28 December, Málaga organises a competition of fandango-like folk dances known as *verdiales* in Puerto de la Torre. Groups of singers and dancers called *pandas* dress in ribboned costumes and are accompanied by guitars and violins.

Itineraries

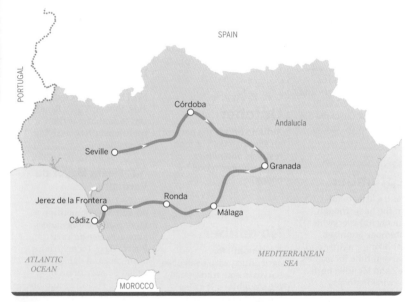

 Andalucía Highlights

You'd need months to poke into every corner of Andalucía, but two weeks will pack in the highlights. This greatest-hits itinerary is ideal for first-timers or those with a limited time ration.

The best starting point is exceptional **Seville**, deserving of three days, where the Gothic cathedral and Mudéjar Alcázar stand side by side in surreal juxtaposition. Travel 150km northeast by train and several centuries back in time to **Córdoba**, site of flower-filled patios and the resplendent Mezquita. Free tapas, shadowy tea rooms and the incomparable Alhambra beckon southeast in **Granada**, where you could fill at least three days reclining in Moorish-style bathhouses, wandering the Albayzín and deciphering the Lorca legend. Easily reached by bus, **Málaga** is understated by comparison; spend a couple of days enjoying the galleries, museums and fresh seafood. To the west (by bus or car), mountain-ringed **Ronda** is a dramatic contrast, doused in rebel-rousing history. West again, **Jerez de la Frontera** is famous for its flamenco, festivals, horses and sherry bodegas. A 45-minute train trip southwest, **Cádiz** has an abundance of free sights, including a fine city museum and a romantic *malecón* (sea drive), plus a majestic cathedral, buzzy beaches and an aficionados' flamenco club.

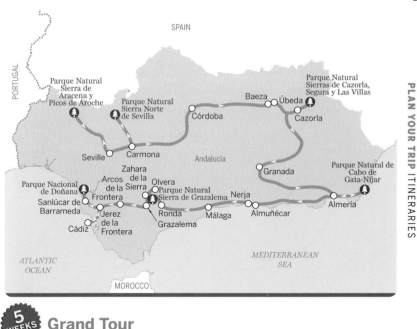

5 WEEKS Grand Tour

To understand every nuance of Andalucía, take a four- to five-week 'grand tour' of all eight provinces. This busy, expansive itinerary will see you staggering home with a virtual PhD in Andalucian culture but also gives you freedom to pick and choose.

Start in **Seville**, visiting the famous (the cathedral, the Alcázar) and less obvious (Casa de Pilatos, Triana) sights. Westward sorties lead into Huelva province; there's prime hiking in the province's north, between the sleepy villages and gentle hills of the **Sierra de Aracena**. Passing back through Seville, head east, stopping in history-rich **Carmona** before escaping north into the **Parque Natural Sierra Norte de Sevilla**. For week two, head to **Córdoba**, marvelling at its labyrinthine streets, hidden patios, Roman relics and splendid Islamic architecture. Tracking east into Jaén province takes you through a land of olive groves and weighty Renaissance architecture. The latter is concentrated in the twin towns of **Baeza** and **Úbeda**. Further east, **Cazorla** is the gateway to Andalucía's largest protected area, the **Parque Natural Sierras de Cazorla, Segura y Las Villas**.

Granada, at the start of week three, has a classic allure, loaded with exotic majesty and guarded by the marvellous Alhambra. To visit all eight provinces, consider circumnavigating the Sierra Nevada to reach **Almería** (with its impressive Alcazaba) and the protected **Cabo de Gata**. Hit the coast at the unadulterated Spanish town of **Almuñécar** and follow it west, dropping in at delightful **Nerja**, to **Málaga**, a provincial capital with a booming art, museum and food scene. Start week four in white-town 'capital' **Ronda**; with its plunging gorge, it's been on most itineraries since Hemingway visited. The white towns continue west across the border in Cádiz province; choose between **Olvera**, **Grazalema** and **Zahara de la Sierra** (or visit them all!), and hike through the surrounding **Parque Natural Sierra de Grazalema**. Tracking west, **Arcos de la Frontera** reels visitors in with its spectacular cliff-top setting, whitewashed alleys and down-to-earth tapas bars.

Spend your final week delving into Andalucian culture in **Jerez de la Frontera** and **Cádiz**, two ancient cities packed with history, flamenco, sherry and a stash of worthwhile sights. Finally, hop across the Río Guadalquivir from **Sanlúcar de Barrameda** to explore the wilds of the ethereal **Parque Nacional de Doñana**.

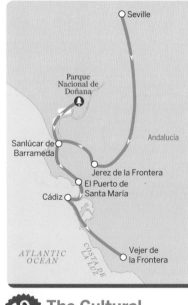

10 DAYS — The Cultural Triangle

If you had to pick a smaller region-within-a-region that best sums up Andalucía's essence, it would probably be the triangle of territory between Seville, Cádiz and Jerez de la Frontera.

Seville is your best starting point. Lap up the Moorish-meets-Gothic architecture and seemingly limitless festivals for a day or two. Fast trains forge south to **Jerez de la Frontera**, first stop on the Sherry Triangle, where you can spend two days mixing bodega tours with horse shows, *tabanco* tapas, authentic flamenco and a *hammam* session. Continuing west (easily by bus) to **Sanlúcar de Barrameda** allows you to compare *fino* with *manzanilla* and savour some of Spain's finest seafood tapas. This is also a good base for forays into Huelva's biodiverse **Parque Nacional de Doñana**. Buses link Sanlúcar with **El Puerto de Santa María**, home of more bodegas, festivals and fish restaurants. A catamaran ride across the bay, ancient, sea-surrounded **Cádiz** feels like the edge of Europe. The blonde beaches here are famously broad and beautiful, continuing southeast along the Costa de la Luz. Explore them from **Vejer de la Frontera**, a dramatically perched white town with a fashionable feel.

2 WEEKS — The West in Detail

Already seen the Alhambra and hiked the Sierra Nevada? Then go west to the self-styled cradle of Andalucian culture.

Start in Huelva province's **Parque Nacional de Doñana**, arguably Andalucía's finest natural attraction. **Seville** has a wealth of well-known sights, while its hinterland is less heralded. Visit **Carmona**, with its Alcázar, and **Osuna**, with its grand palaces. South, rugged **Ronda** is on the tourist map, though most visitors don't stay overnight; if time allows, sidestep west to white towns **Zahara de la Sierra** and/or **Grazalema**. Exciting stops en route east from Ronda could be **El Chorro** gorge (home to the Caminito del Rey) or ancient **Antequera**. Lively **Málaga** has great seafood and excellent galleries and museums. With time, you can head southwest to Cádiz province's less-trodden spots, including **Jimena de la Frontera**, a good base for hiking in the **Parque Natural Los Alcornocales**. To the south, **Gibraltar** lures Brits missing roast beef. Track southwest and stay in cool **Tarifa**, before checking out the Costa de la Luz and overnighting in **Vejer de la Frontera**. Save time for culturally intense **Cádiz**, with a detour to **Jerez de la Frontera**.

The Coast

3 WEEKS

Lapping five of its eight provinces, the Andalucian coastline is one of the region's delights. Empires were built here, though more recently resorts have colonised the shore. Most coastal towns are linked by bus.

Start with Almería's protected **Cabo de Gata**, a spectacular combination of cliffs, salt flats and sandy beaches. Tracking west, **Almería** is worth a stop for its Moorish Alcazaba. Granada's Costa Tropical is precipitous and authentic: **Almuñécar** makes a great base and low-key **La Herradura** offers water sports. Further west, Málaga province's **Nerja** has tempered its development, and excellent inland hiking beckons in **La Axarquía**. **Málaga** deserves three days; its international reputation has skyrocketed thanks to its fine gastronomy and growing art and museum scene. **Marbella** is the most interesting stop on the touristed Costa del Sol, though **Mijas** merits a day trip. Southwest, British-owned **Gibraltar** guards the jaws of Europe. Extending northwest from kitesurfing capital **Tarifa**, Cádiz' Costa de la Luz offers water sports, coastal hikes, Roman ruins, beaches and great cuisine. Stay in **Vejer de la Frontera**, visiting **Zahara de los Atunes** and **Los Caños de Meca**, before a grand two-day finale in **Cádiz**.

The East in Detail

2 WEEKS

Spend three days in each of the two big-hitter cities, then branch out (you're best off with your own wheels).

Córdoba is an unmissable city graced by one of the finest mosques ever built. To the southeast, **Granada** has the dazzling Alhambra, Albayzín and Moorish-style bathhouses. Beyond the cities, Córdoba province's wilderness includes the **Parque Natural Sierras Subbéticas**, while Granada offers the **Parque Nacional Sierra Nevada** and **Las Alpujarras**, the village-dotted valleys on the Sierra's southern slopes. Granada-province detours might include **Guadix**, with its inhabited caves, and coastal **Almuñécar**, a slice of domestic seaside bliss North from Granada, **Jaén** provides fine tapas bars, while **Baeza** and **Úbeda** are unique for their Renaissance architecture. Continue east to the **Parque Natural Sierras de Cazorla, Segura y Las Villas** for rugged mountain scenery, hilltop castles and abundant wildlife.

In Almería province, beachy **Mojácar** promises a both boho and glitzy vibe; **Cabo de Gata** is the region's most unspoiled coastal stretch; and **Almería**, with its formidable Moorish Alcazaba (fortress), is a kind of Granada-on-the-sea.

Plan Your Trip

Eat & Drink Like a Local

Dining in Andalucía isn't just about what you eat; it's about how you eat, too. The culinary culture revolves around light breakfasts, leisurely lunches and late dinners spent grazing slowly from a selection of small tapas plates. If you're a visitor, adjust your body clock to a quintessentially Spanish groove.

The Year in Food

Andalucía is unusual in Europe in that, due to the balmy climate and extensive use of giant greenhouses, fruit and vegetables can be grown year-round, especially in Almería province and on Granada's Costa Tropical.

April–August

Spring and summer bring rice dishes and gazpacho, Andalucía's signature chilled soup, with regional variations such as *salmorejo* (Córdoba) and *ajo blanco* (Málaga).

August–October

The grape harvest ushers in a number of wine festivals, most notably Jerez de la Frontera's Fiestas de la Vendimia in September – the perfect opportunity to pair your *finos* and *manzanillas* with tapas.

November–March

November is traditionally the start of the pig *matanza* (slaughter) and its accompanying pork-heavy feasts. The olive-tree harvest is also under way. Winter is the time for hot roast chestnuts sold by street vendors, especially in mountainous areas. Huelva's strawberry season peaks from January to April.

Food Experiences

Meals of a Lifetime

La Brunilda (p73) Seville's best tapas bar, bar none.

La Fábula Restaurante (p273) Granada's top fine-dining experience.

Aponiente (p130) Andalucía's first triple-Michelin-starred restaurant, in El Puerto de Santa María.

Café Azul (p150) Best breakfasts in Andalucía.

El Jardín del Califa (p144) Moroccan-Andalucian cooking in a beautiful Moroccan-styled maze of a restaurant.

Misa de 12 (p241) Small Úbeda bar with a big culinary reputation.

El Mesón de Cervantes (p171) Fabulous octopus and meats at an Argentine-run Málaga gem.

Óleo (p171) A partnership between a *malagueño* chef and a Japanese sushi master.

Palacio de Gallego (p237) Superb meat and fish dishes in a 16th-century Baeza house.

Restaurante Arrieros (p107) Innovative mountain-sourced slow food in Huelva's Sierra de Aracena.

El Bar de Fede (p273) Creative tapas and a feel-good vibe in a buzzing Granada bar.

Cheap Treats

Free tapas Granada, Jaén and Almería provinces are all known for serving free tapas with every drink.

Chiringuitos Semipermanent shack-restaurants that specialise in fried seafood, often (not always) by the beach. The staples – *espeto de sardinas* (sardine skewers) and *boquerones fritos* (fried anchovies) – are best washed down with beer or *tinto de verano* (red wine with lemonade). Some *chiringuitos* only operate in summer.

Desayuno A typical Andalucian *desayuno* (breakfast) consists of a small strong coffee and a toasted roll topped with olive oil and/or crushed tomato, and rarely costs more than €2.50. *Bocadillos* (filled rolls) are also cheap and tasty.

Menú del día Three-course, excellent-value restaurant lunch usually served with bread and wine. All-inclusive prices start at €10.

Dare to Try

Ortiguillas Croquette-sized sea anemones deep-fried in olive oil. Their intense seafood flavour is considered a delicacy in the Cádiz area.

Callos A traditionally cheap leftover dish of tripe stew, particularly popular in Seville; it's recently been given a modern makeover by some of Andalucía's cutting-edge chefs.

Carrilleras de cerdo Pork cheeks, grilled or in a sauce as a delicacy.

Jabalí Wild boar is common on menus throughout rural parts of Jaén and Córdoba provinces. It can come plain-grilled or in sauces or stews.

Cooking Courses & Food Tours

Annie B's Spanish Kitchen (p143) Popular cooking courses and classes in Vejer de la Frontera, often incorporating tapas, food and sherry tours.

Cooking Holiday Spain (☑637 802743; www.cookingholidayspain.com) Cooking classes in the mountains near Gaucín, plus tapas, wine and olive-oil tours.

Taller Andaluz de Cocina (p67) Combines cooking courses, tastings and food-market tours in Seville's Triana district.

Mimo Sevilla (p68) Wine tastings and food tours, including to Jerez.

All Ways Spain (www.allwaysspain.com) Six- to nine-day gourmet-food tours with cooking classes.

Local Specialities
Sevilla Province

As well as its extraordinarily varied tapas (in traditional or experimental form), Seville also produces some excellent sweets. *Polvorones* are small, crumbly shortbreads that traditionally come from the town of Estepa. *Tortas de aceite* are sweet biscuits made from olive oil. *Huevos a la flamenca* is an ancient savoury dish of *morcilla* (blood sausage), garlic, onions and tomatoes topped with baked eggs. Seville's

JAMÓN

Unlike Italian prosciutto, Spanish *jamón* is a bold, deep red, well marbled with buttery fat. At its best, it smells like the forest and the field. Like wine and olive oil, Spanish *jamón* is subject to a strict series of classifications. *Jamón serrano*, which accounts for around 90% of cured ham in Spain, refers to *jamón* made from white-coated pigs introduced to Spain in the 1950s. Once salted and semidried by the cold, dry winds of the Spanish sierra, most now go through a similar process of around a year's curing and drying in a climate-controlled shed.

Jamón ibérico, also called *pata negra* (black leg), is more expensive and comes from a black-coated pig indigenous to the Iberian peninsula and a descendant of the wild boar. Considered to be the best *jamón* of all is the *jamón ibérico* of Jabugo, in Andalucía's Huelva province, which comes from pigs free-ranging in the Sierra Morena oak forests. The best Jabugo hams are graded from one to five *jotas* (Js). *Cinco jotas* (JJJJJ) hams come from pigs that have never eaten anything but acorns (*bellotas*). If the pig gains at least 50% of its body weight during the acorn-eating season, it can be classified as *jamón ibérico de bellota*, the most sought-after designation for *jamón*.

VEGETARIANS & VEGANS

Throughout Andalucía, fruit and vegetables are delicious and fresh, and eaten in season, but local cuisine still indisputably revolves around meat, fish and seafood. There's only a handful of specifically vegetarian or vegan restaurants in the region, though numbers are growing, and many regular restaurants now offer a vegetarian option (this is less so in rural areas). A word of warning: 'vegetable' dishes may not be meat-free (eg beans sprinkled with bits of ham).

Vegetarians will find that salads are a good bet (specify *'sin atún'* – 'without tuna'), as are gazpacho (chilled tomato soup) and *ajo blanco* (a white gazpacho made from almonds and garlic). Another reliable dish is *pisto* (ratatouille), especially good when eaten with bread; or try *espárragos trigueros* (thin wild asparagus) and *tagarninas* (thistles, popular in Cádiz), either grilled or in *revueltos* (scrambled eggs cooked with fried garlic). Tapas without meat include *pimientos asados* (roasted red peppers), *aceitunas* (olives), *alcachofas* (artichokes), *garbanzos con espinacas* (chickpeas with spinach; may contain meat stock) and *queso* (cheese; rarely fully vegetarian, however).

Tarifa (p150), Vejer (p144), Granada (p272), Córdoba (p214) and Málaga (p170) are some of Andalucía's better spots for vegetarians and vegans, while Las Alpujarras' L'Atelier (p286) is a wonderful vegetarian-vegan restaurant in a meat-mad region.

bitter oranges are primarily used to make marmalade.

Huelva Province

Two gastronomic words define Huelva province: strawberries (the region grows 90% of the Spanish crop) and *jamón ibérico*. Huelva's famous *jamón* is the champagne of Spain's cured meats, produced from black Iberian pigs that roam freely in the Sierra de Aracena feeding mainly on acorns. Sweeter and nuttier than the more ubiquitous *jamón serrano,* it is served sliced wafer thin and is notoriously expensive. *Chocos* (cuttlefish) are another local speciality, so much so that Huelva residents are known as *choqueros*.

Cádiz Province

Cádiz' Atlantic coast and river estuaries support different types of fish from the Mediterranean. Tuna headlines on the Costa de la Luz, often caught using the ancient *almadraba* method; the town of Barbate claims the best catches. Prawns are similarly fabulous along the coast, and Moroccan-influenced cooking is popular, too.

Pescaíto frito (fried fish) is a Cádiz staple (though you'll also find it in Granada). There are few products of the sea that

don't get the deep-fry treatment, but the more common ones include *chipirones* (baby squid), *cazón en adobo* (dogfish or shark that feed on shellfish, producing a strong, almost sweet flavour) and *tortilla de camarones*, a delicious, crispy frittata embedded with tiny shrimps that are a Sanlúcar de Barrameda favourite.

Cádiz province is also the home of sherry. Jerez de la Frontera and El Puerto de Santa María produce the best *fino* (dry) and *oloroso* (sweet, dark) varieties, while Sanlúcar de Barrameda makes its own unique *manzanilla*.

Typical Cádiz cheeses include Manchego-like Grazalema, made from ewe's milk, and Cádiz, a strong goat's cheese from the countryside around Cádiz.

Málaga Province

The Mediterranean is all about fish, notably *boquerones* (anchovies) and *sardinas* (sardines) in Málaga. An *espeto de sardinas* is sardines grilled on a skewer, best eaten on the beach at a *chiringuito*. *Ajo blanco* is Málaga's take on chilled gazpacho soup; it's the same basic recipe but with the tomatoes replaced by almonds, giving it a creamy white colour, and grapes floating on top. *Porra antequerana* is Antequera's popular, thicker version of gazpacho. Málaga's grapes have a long history of producing sweet dessert wines (white and red), which have recently come back into fashion.

Andalucians love cheese, and although most are imported from elsewhere in Spain, there are exceptions, including Málaga goat's cheese preserved in olive oil.

Córdoba Province

Landlocked Córdoba grows copious chickpeas and olives, while its grapes are made into Montilla wines, including the golden-amber, nutty-flavoured *amontillado* (not to be confused with *amontillado* sherry). Pedroches is a strong semicured sheep's-milk cheese from the Pedroches region in the north of the province. Córdoba menu specialities include *salmorejo* (a thick gazpacho-like soup usually topped with boiled eggs and cured ham) and *flamen-quín* (pork loin wrapped around *jamón serrano,* then coated in breadcrumbs and deep-fried).

Jaén Province

Jaén is the olive-oil capital of the world, the province alone accounting for 17% of global production. Quality is understandably high; classic Jaén oils are bitter but fruity. The mountainous area of the Parque Natural Sierras de Cazorla, Segura y Las Villas has a strong hunting fraternity and is famous for its game, including partridge, venison and wild boar. Among Cazorla's local delicacies you'll find *rin-rán,* a mix of salted cod, potato and dried red peppers.

Granada Province

Few cuts of *jamón serrano* are better than those left to mature in the fresh mountain air of the village of Trevélez in Las Alpujarras. The mountains are also home to rabbit stews and the classic *plato alpujarreño,* a meat-heavy stomach-filler with eggs and potatoes. Meanwhile, down on the flat plains of La Vega, beans and asparagus grow in abundance. Granada is Spain's most strongly Arabic-influenced city, with fine tagines, couscous and *tete-rías* (Moroccan-style teahouses).

Almería Province

Rather than deep-frying its fresh coastal fish, Almería tends to cook it *a la plancha* (on a metal grill). Then there are those ubiquitous greenhouses filled with fruit and vegetables soaking up the southern sunrays. Almería is rightly famous for its plump year-round tomatoes.

SHERRY & FOOD PAIRINGS

Sherry, aside from being one of the world's most unappreciated wines (though it's now making a bit of a comeback), is also one of its most versatile, particularly the *fino* and *man-zanilla* varietals. You'll find strong sherry-pairing menus, along with bodega tours, in Jerez de la Frontera, Sanlúcar de Barrameda and El Puerto de Santa María.

TYPE OF SHERRY	SERVING TEMPERATURE	QUALITIES	FOOD PAIRINGS
Manzanilla	well chilled	dry, fresh, delicate, slightly salty essence	tapas, almonds, sushi, olives
Fino	chilled	very dry & pale	aperitif, tapas, soup, white fish, shellfish, prawns, oysters, a counterpoint for cheeses
Amontillado	cool but not chilled	off dry	aperitif, blue cheeses, chicken & white meat, cured cheese, foie gras, rabbit, consommé, rice dishes, asparagus, artichokes
Oloroso	cool but not chilled	dry, nutty, dark	red meat & game, mature cheeses
Pale Cream	room temperature	sweetened *fino*	fresh fruit, blue cheese
Cream	room temperature	sweet	dried fruit, cheesecake
Pedro Ximénez	room temperature	very sweet	dark chocolate, biscotti

CHURROS

Supposedly invented by Spanish shepherds centuries ago, churros are long, thin, doughnut-like strips deep-fried in olive oil and then dipped in thick hot chocolate. In Andalucía churros are enjoyed for breakfast, during the early-evening *merienda* (snack) or as you stumble home from a night out. Good *churrerías* (churro cafes) abound across the region, though Granada is often held up as Andalucía's churros capital, in particular Plaza Bib-Rambla and its eponymous cafe (p273). Casa Aranda (p170) in Málaga is another legendary churros spot. The *tejeringo* is a distinctively Andalucian version of the churro: a lighter, fluffier dough-nut strip rolled into a large wheel.

procured at around 10am, often a *tostada* (toasted bread) drizzled with olive oil and topped with crushed tomatoes. Your first tapas window comes at 1pm, when you can *picar* (graze) your way through a few small plates as a prelude to a larger *almuerzo* (lunch) at around 2pm. Some favour a full-blown meal with starter and main; others just up the ante at the bar and order a selection of *medias raciones* (half-plate tapas servings) or *raciones* (full-plate servings).

Next comes the siesta. If you're up again by 5pm, consider having a revitalising *merienda,* a quick round of coffee and cakes. It's not impolite to start on tapas again around 8pm, or closer to 9pm in summer. *Cena* (dinner) rarely happens before 9pm and is usually less substantial than lunch, especially if you've warmed up with some tapas first. It's almost a faux pas to hit the sack before midnight. At weekends many people party until dawn.

How to Eat & Drink

Like a lot of things in life, eating in Andalucía is all about timing, etiquette and a little insider knowledge.

When to Eat

Tip number one: get into the groove and feast on Spanish time. A typical Andalucian eating day transpires something like this. Wake up to a strong coffee accompanied by a light, sweet pastry, preferably taken standing up in a cafe. A more substantial *desayuno* (breakfast) can be

Where to Eat

As elsewhere in Spain, Andalucía's bars are places to eat and socialise as much as drink, but they come in many guises. These include bodegas (traditional wine bars), *cervecerías* (beer bars), *tascas* (tapas bars), *taperías* (tapas bars) and *tabernas* (taverns). At many you can eat tapas at the bar, but there's often a *comedor* (dining room) for sit-down meals, too. You'll usually save 10% to 20% by eating at the bar rather than a table.

Restaurantes are more formal places where you sit down to eat. A *mesón* is a

OLIVE OIL

Andalucía's statistics are impressive: there are over 100 million olive trees in Andalucía; it is the world's biggest producer of olive oil; a remarkable 17% of the world's olive oil originates in Jaén province, which produces more olive oil than Greece; and Jaén's more than 4500 sq km of olive trees are, it is sometimes claimed, the world's largest human-made forest. The seemingly endless olive groves of Córdoba, Jaén and Sevilla were originally planted by the Romans, but the production of *az-zait* (juice of the olive) – from which the modern generic word for olive oil, *aceite,* is derived – was further developed by the Muslims.

The best olive oils are those classified as 'virgin' (which must meet 40 criteria for quality and purity) and 'extra virgin' (the best olive oil, with acidity levels no higher than 1%). Accredited olive-oil-producing regions receive the designation Denominación de Origen (DO, which indicates the unique geographic origins, production processes and quality of the product). DO regions in Andalucía include Baena and Priego de Córdoba in Córdoba, and Sierra de Segura and Sierra Mágina in Jaén.

THE ORIGINS OF TAPAS

There are many stories concerning the origins of tapas. One holds that in the 13th century, doctors to King Alfonso X advised him to accompany his sips of wine between meals with small morsels of food. So enamoured was the monarch with the idea that he passed a law requiring all bars in Castilla to follow suit. Another version attributes tapas to bar owners who placed a saucer with a piece of bread on top of a sherry glass either to deter flies or to prevent the punter from drinking on an empty stomach and getting too tipsy.

As for the name, *tapa* (which means 'lid') is said to have attained widespread usage in the early 20th century, when King Alfonso XIII stopped at a beachside bar in Cádiz province. When a strong gust of wind blew sand in the king's direction, a quick-witted waiter rushed to place a slice of *jamón* (cured ham) atop the king's glass of sherry. The king so much enjoyed the idea (and the *jamón*) that, wind or no wind, he ordered another – and the name stuck.

simple restaurant with homestyle cooking, while an *asador* specialises in roasted meats. A *venta* is a roadside inn (where food *can* be delicious and inexpensive). A *marisquería* is a seafood restaurant, and a *chiringuito* is a semi-open-air bar or kiosk, usually (not always) fronting the beach.

Ordering Tapas

Tapeando (going out for tapas) is a favourite Andalucian pastime and, while it may serve as the prelude to lunch, it's often also the main event in the evening, when Andalucians drag out their meal with tapas and drinks.

Tapas can draw on the gastronomic peculiarities of their region. In Huelva, it would be a culinary crime to order anything but the local *jamón ibérico,* while in Granada North African tagine tapas reflect the city's days as the historical capital of Al-Andalus. In Cádiz province, seafood tapas are the real luxury.

A few *bar de tapas* tips:

➡ The best tapas times are from 1pm to 3pm and from 8pm onwards (9pm in summer).

➡ Tapas bars are often clustered together, enabling bar-hopping between bites.

➡ Be prepared to elbow your way to the bar.

➡ That massive crowd at the bar usually means something. Good tapas places aren't always fancy, but they're invariably crowded.

➡ Don't worry about all those discarded serviettes on the floor – it's the Andalucian way to brush them off the table.

➡ Granada, Almería and Jaén all offer a free *tapa* with every drink. Almería goes one better and allows you to choose which free *tapa* you would like.

➡ You can also eat tapas as *medias raciones* (half-platters) or *raciones* (full platters).

Menu Decoder

➡ Always ask for the house-special tapa/s.

➡ Andalucian paella is often made with almonds, sherry, chicken and sausages, as well as seafood.

➡ Olives (typically green) and a bread basket accompany most meals.

➡ Gazpacho is usually only available in spring and summer.

➡ Not that many Spaniards actually drink sangría; *tinto de verano* is a popular substitute.

➡ Andalucians rarely drink sweet sherry; they prefer *fino* or *manzanilla*, especially with tapas.

Hiking to Mulhacén (p282), Sierra Neva

Plan Your Trip

Activities

One of the most epiphanic Andalucian experiences is discovering that most of the region remains traditional, untouristed and bursting with outdoor-adventure opportunities. Ancient walking trails lead to time-worn villages, and cycling paths wind past ruined castles. Try diving, kitesurfing, horse riding, snowboarding and even paragliding, or go searching for emblematic wildlife.

Best Walking

Best Mountain Hikes
Sierra Nevada; Parque Natural Sierra de Grazalema

Best Hike-up Peaks
Mulhacén (Sierra Nevada); El Torreón (Parque Natural Sierra de Grazalema)

Best for Thrill-Seekers
Málaga province's unique Caminito del Rey

Best for Wildlife Spotting
Parque Natural Sierras de Cazorla, Segura y Las Villas

Best for Birdwatching
Parques Nacional and Natural de Doñana; Parque Natural Sierras de Cazorla, Segura y Las Villas; Parque Natural Sierra de Grazalema

Best Pastoral Hikes
Sierra de Aracena; Parque Natural Sierra Norte de Sevilla

Best Coastal Hikes
Parque Natural de Cabo de Gata-Níjar; Parque Natural de la Breña y Marismas del Barbate

Best Long-Distance Hikes
GR7 trail in Las Alpujarras; GR247 trail around Parque Natural Sierras de Cazorla, Segura y Las Villas

Walking

Walking in Andalucía gets you to where 95% of visitors never go. If you're after some alone time while exercising your way through unblemished rural bliss, hit the *senderos* (footpaths).

All of Andalucía's *parques naturales* (natural parks) and *parques nacionales* (national parks) are criss-crossed by numerous well-marked day-walk trails, ranging from half-hour strolls to full-day mountain ascents. The scenery is rarely less than lovely and often majestic. You can sometimes string together day walks into a multiday treks, sleeping along the way in

a variety of hotels, *hostales* (budget hotels) and campgrounds, or the occasional mountain refuge.

Maps and signage are steadily improving but are often still iffy. The best markers are in the *parques naturales* and *nacionales*, and on major routes such as the GR7, identified by red-and-white paint splashes.

The two main categories of marked walking route in Spain are *senderos de gran recorrido* (GRs; long-distance footpaths) and *senderos de pequeño recorrido* (PRs; shorter routes of a few hours or one or two days).

When To Go

The best months for walking are generally May, June, September and October. July and August are ideal for the high Sierra Nevada but unbearably hot elsewhere; some trails close due to fire risk.

Information

The *parques naturales* and *nacionales* offer detailed walking information (sometimes in Spanish only) at their official visitor centres, and online at www.ventana delvisitante.es. Local tourist offices can be helpful.

Numerous English-language guides to localised regions are available. Among the best maps are those of Editorial Alpina (www.editorialalpina.com) to the Grazalema, Cabo de Gata, Sierra Nevada and Cazorla parks, in English and Spanish.

Cycling

Andalucía has more and more bike-hire opportunities, increasingly well-maintained and signposted touring and off-road trails, and a growing number of urban bike-sharing schemes and cycle paths – most notably in Seville (p69).

Beware of hot weather, particularly in July and August.

Where to Go

The safest, flattest and most family-friendly paths for cyclists are the *vías verdes* (greenways; p38) fashioned out of old railway lines.

Mountain-biking hot spots include the El Chorro and Ronda/Grazalema areas, the Parque Natural Sierras de Cazorla, Segura y Las Villas, and Las Alpujarras. The

Parque Natural Sierra Nevada maintains 12 mountain-bike trails, of which the king is the 450km Ruta Cicloturística Trans-nevada, which circles the entire mountain range between 1500m and 2000m.

Diving & Snorkelling

It's not quite the Caribbean, but Andalucía has some worthwhile spots for underwater exploration. Most establishments offer PADI or NAUI courses, plus dives for qualified divers and introductory 'baptisms'. A single dive with full equipment costs around €50; three-hour 'baptisms' are about €70.

Where to Go

The Atlantic coast, with its strong currents, is best avoided (aside from some interesting wrecks around Gibraltar), and the western part of Andalucía's Mediter-ranean coast is of similarly limited interest to divers and snorkellers. This leaves the coast of eastern Andalucía:

Cabo de Gata, Almería (p307) Andalucía's top diving and snorkelling spot, with clear protected waters and a varied seabed of seagrass, sand and rock dotted with caves, crevices, canyons and a wreck.

Costa Tropical, Granada (p289) Multicoloured fish, octopuses, corals and crustaceans, plus (relatively) warm waters make for excellent year-round diving and snorkelling; the gentle, shallow sea off La Herradura (p291) is ideal for beginners.

Horse Riding

Beautiful horses define Andalucía as much as feisty flamenco, and an ever-growing number of *picaderos* (stables) offer guided rides or classes across the region. Many of the horses are Andalucian or Andalucian-Arab crosses – medium-sized, intelligent, good in traffic and usually easy to handle.

Typical ride or lesson prices are €20 to €30 per hour, €30 to €60 for two hours, and €60 to €80 for a half-day. Most stables cater to all levels, offering beginner lessons alongside challenging trail rides.

Where to Go

The hub of Andalucía's horse culture is Jerez de la Frontera (Cádiz), home of the famous Real Escuela Andaluza del Arte Ecuestre (p127) and Feria del Caballo (p124). The nearby Yeguada de la Cartuja – Hierro del Bocado (p127) breeding centre offers a fascinating insight into Andalucía's equestrian world. Horse-riding highlights:

➡ Beach and dune rides outside Tarifa (p149) on Cádiz' Costa de la Luz.

➡ Mountain trails around Lanjarón (p282) in Las Alpujarras.

➡ Woodland rides around Doñana (p100).

➡ Estepona's renowned Escuela de Arte Ecuestre Costa del Sol (p180).

Kitesurfing, Windsurfing & Surfing

Thanks to the stiff winds that batter the Strait of Gibraltar, Cádiz' Costa de la Luz plays host to Europe's liveliest windsurfing and kitesurfing scene. Windsurfing, the original favourite, kicked off in the early 1980s. Kitesurfing, the newer, cooler, more extreme younger sibling, is equally popular.

Be warned: the choppy seas off the Costa de la Luz aren't always beginners' territory. May, June and September are

---

GREENWAYS

Spain's *vías verdes* (greenways; www.viasverdes.com) are disused railway lines that have been transformed into designated paths for cyclists, walkers and other non-motorised transport, including wheelchairs. Since 1993, 2100km of Spain's 7500km of abandoned railway track has been converted into *vías verdes*. Andalucía currently has 23 (totalling 500km), with the Vía Verde de la Sierra (p141) (Cádiz) usually considered the finest. Two more leading lights are the Vía Verde de la Sierra Norte (p87) (Sevilla) and the Vía Verde del Aceite (p229) (Jaén and Córdoba). *Vías verdes* have relatively slight gradients, and preserve many original engineering features. They're well marked with kilometre posts and equipped with maps, lookouts, picnic spots, and old stations reimagined as cafes or rural hotels that rent bikes.

ALTERNATIVE ACTIVITIES

Fancy some fun beyond the usual hiking, diving, biking, kitesurfing, horse-riding and wildlife-watching? Here are some great, lesser-known ideas for active pursuits.

Vie Ferrate

Climbers might tackle Andalucía's increasingly popular vie ferrate – a form of fixed protection climbing using routes that are equipped with ladders, cables, bridges and, sometimes, ziplines. There are good beginner routes in Ronda and other more advanced routes in El Torcal, El Chorro and Comares, plus further options in the Sierra de Grazalema and near Cazorla. Several companies offer guided trips; try Al Andalus Activa (p185) or Andalucia Aventura (p189) in Málaga province, Tierraventura (p244) in Jaén province, and Horizon (p138) in Cádiz province.

Paragling & Hang-Gliding

Parapente (paragliding) and, to a lesser extent, *ala delta* (hang-gliding) are also popular in Andalucía. Little-known Algodonales, on the edge of Cádiz' Parque Natural Sierra de Grazalema, is among Andalucía's top free-flying centres. Locally based Zero Gravity (p140) offers one-week learn-to-fly paragliding courses (€990).

El Yelmo, in Jaén's Parque Natural Sierras de Cazorla, Segura y Las Villas, is another major paragliding spot, attracting thousands of people with its June free-flying fair, the Festival Internacional del Aire (p250). Granada's Sierra Nevada has some of Andalucía's highest launch sites.

Canyoning

Exciting Andalucian destinations for careering down canyons include Cádiz' Sierra de Grazalema with Zahara Catur (p139) or Horizon (p138), Granada's Las Alpujarras with Nevadensis (p284), Jaén's Parque Natural Sierra de Cazorla, Segura y Las Villas with Tierraventura (p244), or Málaga's La Axarquía region with Salamandra (p195).

Other Activities

Along Andalucía's beautiful coastline, beachside operators enable you to paddle off in a kayak, try stand-up paddleboarding (SUP) and wobble you way through SUP yoga. Join a class, take a course, or simply hire the gear and go!

Or laze away an evening with a blissful *hammam* session, inspired by Andalucía's Moorish heritage – Granada (p266), Córdoba (p212), Málaga (p168), Almería (p297) and Jerez (p124) are top *hammam* spots.

usually the best months (calmer water, fewer people). There are over 30 schools in and around Tarifa. Typical prices:

Kitesurfing Full-day equipment hire €90; six-hour beginner course €140.

Windsurfing Half-day equipment hire €60; six-hour group lesson €130.

Surfing Two-hour group class €28; full board and wetsuit hire €25.

Where to Go

Tarifa (p147) Europe's windsurfing and kitesurfing capital.

Los Caños de Meca (p145) Another surfing/kitesurfing hot spot, northwest of Tarifa.

El Palmar (p145) Andalucía's best board-riding waves.

Rock Climbing

Mention Andalucía to rock-climbing enthusiasts and they'll reply 'El Chorro'. This sheer limestone gorge above the Río Guadalhorce, 50km northwest of Málaga, contains hundreds of climbing routes, from easy to ultra-difficult. Many of them start in the vicinity of the infamous Caminito del Rey (p189), a notoriously narrow (and recently reopened) path that clings to the rock face.

Other climbable limestone crags are El Torcal de Antequera (Málaga) and Los Cahorros gorge (Sierra Nevada).

Information

For El Chorro, you can organise rock-climbing trips and classes through Finca La Campana (p189) or Andalucia Aventura (p189). The season is October to April.

A good climbing guidebook is *Andalucía* by David Munilla (2007).

Skiing & Snowboarding

The Sierra Nevada (p281) is Europe's most southerly ski area. Although its slopes lack the mega-steep, off-piste action of France or Switzerland, their skiing potential is fantastic. These are the highest mountains in Europe outside the Alps and the Caucasus, with cross-country routes, over 100km of runs and a top skiing elevation of 3300m. Snow can fall as early as November and linger until early May; the slopes are well suited to beginners and families, along with advanced skiers.

Information

One-day adult ski passes cost between €36 and €48. Add €25 for equipment rental. Six hours of group classes with a ski school cost around €60. Peak season is between Christmas and New Year, and from early February to early March.

The small settlement of Pradollano at the base (2100m) is an ugly, purpose-built ski resort for the Sierra Nevada; it's linked to the mightier attractions of Granada, about 30km away, by three daily buses (four at weekends).

WILDLIFE SPOTTING

Bounding deer, majestic sea mammals, flocks of migrating birds, the elusive Iberian lynx – Andalucía plays host to a fantastic array of wildlife (p338). A number of local companies run wildlife-spotting and birdwatching trips in the most popular areas.

Andalucía's famously endangered lynx population, now totalling around 400, is split between the Parques Nacional and Natural de Doñana, and the Sierra Morena in and around the Sierra de Cardeña y Montoro, Sierra de Andújar and Despeñaperros natural parks. Local operators run 4WD trips into the Parque Natural Sierra de Andújar (Jaén province) and the Parques Nacional and Natural de Doñana, which are your best bet for spotting lynxes (though chances remain low).

PLACE	ANIMAL	TOUR OPERATOR
Parques Nacional & Natural de Doñana (p40)	Wild boar, Spanish imperial eagles, red & fallow deer, greater flamingos, waterbirds	Cooperativa Marismas del Rocío (p40), Doñana Reservas (p40), Doñana Nature (p40)
Parque Natural Sierras de Cazorla, Segura y Las Villas (p40)	Ibexes, red & fallow deer, wild boar, mouflons, red squirrels, bearded vultures, black vultures, golden eagles, peregrine falcons	Turisnat (p40)
Sierra Nevada (p40)	Andalucía's largest ibex population, wild boar, golden eagles, Bonelli's eagles, griffon vultures, kestrels	Nevadensis (p40)
Parque Natural Sierra de Andújar (p40)	Ibexes, red & fallow deer, wild boar, mouflons, black vultures, black storks, Spanish imperial eagles, Iberian lynxes	IberianLynxLand (p40), Iberus Birding&Nature (p40)
Parque Natural Sierra de Grazalema (p40)	Ibexes, griffon vultures	Independent visits recommended
Strait of Gibraltar (p40)	Marine mammals (Apr-Oct), over 300 species of migrating bird	FIRMM (p40), Aviantours (www.aviantours.net)
Laguna de Fuente de Piedra (p40)	Birds, especially greater flamingos (Feb-Aug)	Centro de Visitantes José A Valverde (p40)
Peñón de Zaframagón (p40)	Griffon vultures	Independent visits recommended

Plan Your Trip

Travel with Children

Andalucía's facilities, climate and attractions are ideal for families. The region's culture revolves around the (extended) family, and children are welcomed at all but the most formal restaurants, as well as at bars and most hotels. To get the most of what's on offer, plan ahead.

Andalucía for Kids

The Andalucian basics – beaches and fabulous climate – are pretty good raw ingredients for starters. Add to this water sports, museums, parks, boat rides and loads of ice cream and it becomes serious spoil-them-rotten time. Note that the majority of theme parks and entertainment for children are in Málaga province, especially along the Costa del Sol.

Away from the coast, you may not find so many dedicated kids' attractions, but every town will have at least one good-sized children's playground. Public spaces, such as town and village plazas, also morph into informal play spaces, with children kicking a ball, riding bikes and playing while parents enjoy a drink and tapas in one of the surrounding terrace bars. Many Andalucian towns also have municipal swimming pools – ideal in the summer.

Eating & Drinking

Whole families, often including several generations, sitting around a restaurant or bar table eating and chatting is a fundamental element of the lifestyle here, and it's rare to find a restaurant where children are not welcome. Even if restaurants do not advertise children's menus (and few

Best Regions for Kids

Málaga Province

Parents may balk, but the theme parks around Torremolinos and Benalmádena on the Costa del Sol have undeniable appeal for children, while beaches with shallow waters and boat rides should have the whole family smiling.

Almería Province

And now for something completely different: the Wild West shoot-'em-up shows in desert film locations are bound to knock kids' socks off (not literally, you understand...).

Seville

Seville has great leafy parks, boat trips and an amusement park on the former Expo site.

Cádiz Province & Gibraltar

Older kids will love the kite- and windsurfing in Tarifa, which is one of the major destinations for the sport in Europe. You can also hop on a ferry to Morocco for the day.

do), they will normally be willing to prepare a small portion for your child or suggest a suitable tapa or two.

High chairs in restaurants are increasingly common but by no means universal, and nappy-changing facilities are rare.

Favourite Foods

It's perhaps not the healthiest of snacks, but you can't go wrong with ordering your child a churro (or two). These thick, tubular doughnuts are irresistible to children – and to children at heart.

Discerning young diners may like to ease themselves into Andalucian cuisine by tasting various tapas; this will allow them to sample new flavours gradually and on a small scale. *Tortilla de patatas* (potato omelette), *albóndigas* (meatballs) and, of course, chips (or French fries) are a good bet. You can also find kebabs or *shwarmas* in places with a large North African population – essentially a hot chicken wrap, kebabs are tasty (and messy) enough to be a big hit with most youngsters.

You can generally find freshly squeezed orange juice in most bars. Other popular choices for children are Cola Cao and Nesquik, chocolate drinks served hot or cold with milk.

BEFORE YOU GO

➡ You can hire car seats for infants and children from most car-rental firms, but you should always book them in advance.

➡ No particular health precautions are necessary. Sun protection is essential but can be purchased locally.

➡ Plan which activities, theme parks, museums and leisure pursuits you want to opt for – and, more importantly, can afford – early on in the holiday.

➡ English books can be hard to find, so if your child enjoys reading or you have a bedtime-story routine, be sure to bring a couple of books from home.

Discounts

Children pay two-thirds of the fare on the high-speed AVE train, but full price on most buses and ferries. There are generally discounts for admission to sights, and those under four generally get in free.

Children's Highlights

Museums

Museo Lara, Ronda (p182) Vast private museum; includes exhibitions on witchcraft and torture instruments that kids with an interest in the macabre will doubtless enjoy!

Casa Museo de Mijas, Mijas (p177) Folk-themed museum with models, artefacts and a donkey made from esparto grass.

Museo del Baile Flamenco, Seville (p62) Includes daily flamenco performances at the family-friendly time of 7pm.

Museo Picasso Málaga (p162) An unmissable, colourful introduction to Málaga's great artist.

Caves, Caverns & Castles

Cueva de Nerja, Nerja (p197) Full of spooky stalactites and stalagmites.

St Michael's Cave, Gibraltar (p155) A huge natural grotto with a lake and atmospheric auditorium.

Gruta de las Maravillas, Aracena, Huelva (p103) Explore 12 caverns here, including stunning underground pools.

Centro de Interpretación Cuevas de Guadix, Guadix (p278) Cave museum re-creating typical cave life for a family.

Cueva de la Pileta, Benaoján, Ronda (p189) Fascinating, uncommercial caves with narrow, low walkways, lakes and cave paintings.

Castles Jaén, Segura de la Sierra (p250), Alcalá La Real, Almodóvar del Rio and Málaga (p163) have castles with displays designed to amuse children as well as adults.

Wildlife

Selwo Aventura, Estepona (p180) Wild-animal park with an African theme and animals including rhinos, giraffes, hippos and cheetahs.

Dolphin-watching, Gibraltar (p156) The strait of Gibraltar is home to several species of dolphin. Whales can occasionally be spotted, too.

Mariposario de Benalmádena, Benalmádena (p175) A butterfly park with several reptiles, including iguanas and a giant tortoise.

Centro de Fauna Silvestre Collado del Almendral, Cazorla (p246) Kids can take a mini train on a 5km ride around a 1-sq-km enclosure and see wild boar, mouflon, ibex and deer, as well as rescued birds recovering in cages.

Parque Nacional de Doñana (p97) Families can look for deer, wild boar and elusive Iberian lynx in Spain's favourite national park.

Whale-watching, Tarifa (p148) Spot whales and dolphins in one of the best places in Europe for this.

Theme Parks

Isla Mágica, Seville (p67) Plenty of rides, including a roller coaster, plus pirate shows, bird-of-prey displays and more.

Oasys Mini Hollywood, Desierto de Tabernas (p301) Wild West shows, stagecoaches, can-can dancers and a zoo at this former film set for westerns.

Aventura Amazonia, Marbella (p178) Adventure theme park with ziplines.

Other Sights & Activities

Fairs & fiestas Annual fairs are held in every Andalucian town and village and always include a funfair with rides for kids.

Rowing boats Rent a rowing boat to paddle along the moat at Seville's Plaza de España (p64) or a four-wheel bike to explore the park further.

Windsurfing & kiteboarding Older children can take courses in both sports at Tarifa (p147) on the Cádiz coast.

Trip to Morocco Take a speedy ferry (p151) from Tarifa to Tangier for the day.

LATE NIGHTS

Local children stay up late and at fiesta time it's commonplace to see even tiny kids toddling the streets at 2am. Visiting children will invariably warm to this idea but can't always cope with it quite so readily.

Planning

This is an easygoing, child-friendly destination with little advance planning necessary.

When To Go

July and August can be very busy with Spanish families, as well as foreign tourists, in the main tourist resorts, and some hotels are block-booked by tour companies. May, June, September and October are good times to travel with young children: the weather's still warm enough for paddling in the sea but hasn't yet reached serious sizzle. The theme parks and attractions are also not too crowded – aside from the Easter holidays, that is.

Accommodation

Most hotels and even *hostales* (budget hotels) will be able to provide an extra bed or cot for a child or baby. However, always check and reserve in advance as there will be a limited number available. You will sometimes be charged a supplement for this. When selecting a hotel, check whether it has a kids club, activities geared to youngsters and/or babysitting facilities.

What's Available

You can buy baby formula in powder or liquid form, as well as sterilising solutions such as Milton, at *farmacias* (pharmacies). Disposable nappies are widely available at supermarkets and *farmacias*.

Regions at a Glance

Sevilla Province

Festivals
Architecture
Music

Spring Events

No other city changes its personality from one festival to another so radically as Seville, where the constrained mourning of Semana Santa erupts into the carefree celebrations of the Feria de Abril.

Catedral, Alcázar & More

You can walk from lively, geometric Mudéjar to dark, atmospheric Gothic in less than 200 paces in central Seville, where the Alcázar and Catedral sit side by side. Indeed, the cathedral itself is a Moorish-Christian hybrid. Beyond the capital, architectural jewels await in Osuna, Carmona and Écija.

Flamenco

Seville has the largest, most varied stash of flamenco venues in Andalucía. Triana is the best haunt for intimate *peñas* (clubs), while the Barrio de Santa Cruz hosts authentic *tablaos* (choreographed flamenco shows). During the raucous Feria de Abril, *sevillanas* (flamenco-influenced folk dances) are de rigueur.

p48

Huelva Province

Wildlife
Hiking
History

Delta Dwellers

The Parque Nacional de Doñana is one of Spain's – and Europe's – finest protected areas. In the Río Guadalquivir delta, the park treats visitors to sightings of rare birds and mammals, including deer, wild boar and, if you're lucky, Iberian lynx.

Pastoral Trails

Walks are an obvious draw in the Parque Nacional de Doñana, but Huelva province's north harbours the contrasting topography of the Parque Natural Sierra de Aracena y Picos de Aroche, an ancient pastoral region criss-crossed by easy walking trails between sleepy villages.

Columbus et al

Huelva province is often bracketed as being 'on the way to Portugal', but it conceals some surprising historical heirlooms, including Christopher Columbus paraphernalia, the walled Almohad town of Niebla, and Almonaster la Real with its *mezquita*.

p90

Cádiz Province & Gibraltar

Beaches
White Towns
Music

Hilltop Settlements

They're all here, the famous white towns, with ruined hilltop castles, geranium-filled balconies, twisting alleys and somnolent churches. Arcos, Vejer, Zahara, Olvera, Jimena...the ancient sentinels on a once-volatile frontier that divided Muslim and Christian Spain.

Font of Flamenco

With a little help from Seville, Cádiz province's towns essentially created modern flamenco. Look no further than the flamenco songs – the *bulerías* of Jerez or the *alegrías* of Cádiz – still performed in local *tablaos* and *peñas*. Sherry, made from local grapes, is the perfect accompaniment.

White-Sand Wonders

The sandy blonde beaches that sweep along Cádiz' wind-blown Costa de la Luz, between Tarifa and the provincial capital, are some of Andalucía's most beautiful and pristine. Go kitesurfing in Tarifa, sunsoak beside Roman ruins in Bolonia and lounge in mellow Los Caños de Meca.

p110

Málaga Province

Beaches
Art
Food

Coastal Resorts

Málaga's popular beaches bag more tourist euros than the rest of the region put together. Choose according to your style and budget between Estepona, Marbella, Fuengirola, Torremolinos, Málaga and Nerja.

Picasso & Beyond

So what if Picasso left Málaga when he was only 10 years old? The birthplace of the great master continues to branch out, launching a slew of exciting new galleries and museums and proving that it may just have outdone Seville and Granada as Andalucía's 'art capital'.

Regional Dishes

Along Málaga's coastline, simple beachside *chiringuitos* (beach bars) stand next to Michelin-starred restaurants specialising in fish. Inland, Antequera has fine soups and desserts, while Ronda is the home of mountain stews and meat specialities.

p159

Córdoba Province

Architecture
Castles
Natural Areas

Córdoba Caliphate

Córdoba, the 10th-century caliphate, pretty much defined Islamic architecture 1000 years ago. You can see it in all its glory in the famous Mezquita (Grand Mosque) or elegantly ruined at Medina Azahara just outside the city limits.

Border Fortifications

In the Middle Ages this was a frontier area between the Muslim- and Christian-ruled parts of Spain, hence the castles and towers that crown the high points of the undulating landscape – from picturesquely perched little Castillo de Zuheros to massive, nine-towered Castillo de Almodóvar.

Off the Beaten Track

The southern Parque Natural Sierras Subbéticas encompasses memorably beautiful emerald-green mountains riven by deep ravines and caves and surrounded by handsome white villages. North of Córdoba city stretch the boundless horizons of the Los Pedroches region in the remote Sierra Morena.

p200

Jaén Province

Natural Areas
Wildlife
Architecture

Andalucian Wilderness

Jaén province safeguards one of Europe's largest protected areas, the Parque Natural Sierras de Cazorla, Segura y Las Villas, as well as some lesser-known but no less beautiful wild tracts, such as the unsullied Parque Natural Sierra de Andújar.

Rare Fauna

Lynx, wild boar and mouflon are hardly ubiquitous in Andalucía. Your best chance of seeing these rare animals is probably in the quieter corners of Jaén province, where protected parks and mountains break the never-ending expanse of olive groves.

Renaissance Towns

Renaissance architecture makes a cameo appearance in Andalucía courtesy of Jaén province's two Unesco-listed pearls – Úbeda and Baeza – plus its less-heralded provincial capital Jaén (the city), whose grandiose cathedral is worthy of Granada or Seville.

p225

Granada Province

Architecture
White Towns
Hiking

Historical Eras

A celebrated Nasrid palace-fortress, a hilltop Moorish quarter, the charming Realejo (a district adjacent to the Alhambra that was the old Jewish quarter) and a baroque-Renaissance cathedral: Granada is a magnificent 'mess' of just about every architectural style known to European building.

Alpujarras Villages

Matching Cádiz province's white towns for spectacular beauty, Granada's villages are certainly higher, perched above the steep valleys of Las Alpujarras. They're notable for their artisan crafts, hearty mountain food and large communities of British expats.

Hill Walking

The mighty peaks of the Sierra Nevada and the lower slopes of Las Alpujarras set an epic stage for exhilarating hiking. A network of well-established trails meanders across the area, providing walks for enthusiasts of all ages and fitness levels.

p251

Almería Province

Coastal Scenery
Film Sets
History

Protected Coast

Forgotten, lucky or perhaps just too arid to develop, Cabo de Gata has escaped Costa del Sol–style bulldozer treatment and is now protected as a natural park, guarding the most precious flora and marine life in the southern Mediterranean.

Mini Hollywood

Hmm...doesn't that dusty desert backdrop look familiar? Hang on. Isn't that where Sergio Leone shot Clint Eastwood in the spaghetti westerns and where 'the Doctor' faced a cyborg in *Doctor Who?* Come to Oasys Mini Hollywood and relive the Wild West.

Moorish Heritage

Often overlooked by Alhambra pilgrims, the city of Almería has plenty of stories to tell, many of them hailing from the pre-Christian era. Check out the old town and Alcazaba before treating yourself to a soothing bath at a *hammam*.

p292

On the Road

Sevilla Province

Best Places to Stay

➡ Hotel Casa 1800 (p70)

➡ Las Navezuelas (p87)

➡ El Rincón de las Descalzas (p82)

➡ Hotel Palacio Marqués de la Gomera (p84)

➡ Hotel Amadeus (p70)

Best Places to Eat

➡ Bar-Restaurante Eslava (p76)

➡ La Brunilda (p73)

➡ Agustina (p87)

➡ Ágora (p86)

➡ Mamarracha (p72)

Why Go?

From Moorish palaces and Roman ruins to sun-baked plains and bosky river valleys, Sevilla province boasts some of Andalucía's greatest hits and least-known treasures. At its heart is the region's charismatic capital, Seville. A gregarious, flamboyant city famed for its artistic and architectural riches, flamenco clubs and teeming tapas bars, this heady riverside metropolis provides a fabulous introduction to the region. But if you can break its spell you'll discover there's plenty to admire in the surrounding province.

Just outside Seville, the wonderfully preserved ruins of Itálica make for one of southern Spain's most remarkable Roman sites. To the east, the vast, shimmering plains of La Campiña are punctuated by a string of handsome towns, most notably Carmona, Écija and Osuna, whilst to the north, you can explore the wooded hills of the little-visited Parque Natural Sierra Norte de Sevilla.

Driving Distances

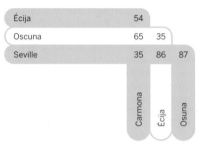

	Écija	Carmona	Écija	Osuna
Écija	54			
Oscuna	65	35		
Seville	35	86	87	

Sevilla Province Highlights

1 **Real Alcázar** (p56) Revelling in the astonishing Mudéjar decor of Seville's royal palace complex.

2 **Catedral & Giralda** (p50) Admiring artistic masterpieces at the world's largest Gothic cathedral.

3 **Hospital de los Venerables Sacerdotes** (p61)

Contemplating paintings by Seville's Golden Age maestro Diego Velázquez.

4 **Itálica** (p80) Roaming through the ruins of this ancient Roman city.

5 **Museo Histórico Municipal** (p85) Marvelling at magnificent Roman mosaics at Écija's history museum.

6 **Colegiata de Santa María de la Asunción** (p84) Browsing the baroque art treasures in Osuna's landmark church.

7 **Carmona** (p81) Strolling a delightful historic centre, an attractive hilltop enclave of Moorish forts and Mudéjar churches.

SEVILLE

POP 690,570

Some cities blast you away, others slowly win you over. Seville disarms and seduces you. Its historic centre, lorded over by a colossal Gothic cathedral, is an intoxicating mix of resplendent Mudéjar palaces, baroque churches and winding medieval lanes. Flamenco clubs keep the intimacy and intensity of this centuries-old tradition alive whilst aristocratic mansions recall the city's past as a showcase Moorish capital and, later, a 16th-century metropolis rich on the back of New World trade.

But while history reverberates all around, Seville is as much about the here and now as the past. It's about eating tapas in a crowded bar or seeing out the end of the day over a drink on a buzzing plaza. The *sevillanos* have long since mastered the art of celebrating and the city's great annual festivals, notably the Semana Santa and Feria de Abril, are among Spain's most heartfelt.

History

According to legend Seville was founded by the Greek demigod Hercules. More plausibly, it probably started life as an Iberian town before growing to become an important Roman port (Hispalis). But it was under a succession of Islamic rulers that the city really came into its own. It enjoyed a heyday in the late 11th century as a major cultural centre under the Abbadid dynasty, and then again in the 12th century when the Almohads took control and built, among other things, a great mosque where the cathedral now stands. Almohad power dwindled after the disastrous defeat of Las Navas de Tolosa in 1212, and in 1248, the city fell to Castilla's King Fernando III (*El Santo*; the Saint).

Some 240-odd years later, the discovery of the Americas paved the way for another golden era. In 1503 the city was awarded an official monopoly on Spanish trade with the new-found continent. The riches poured in and Seville blossomed into one of the world's largest, richest and most cosmopolitan cities.

But it was not to last. A plague in 1649 killed half the city's population, and as the 17th century wore on, the Río Guadalquivir became more silted and difficult to navigate. Then, in 1717 the Casa de la Contratación (Contracting House), the government office controlling commerce with the Americas, was transferred to Cádiz. The city went into decline.

The beginnings of industry in the mid-19th century saw a spate of major building projects. Notably, the first bridge across the Guadalquivir, the Puente de Triana (or Puente de Isabel II), was built in 1852, and in 1869 the old Almohad walls were knocked down to let the city expand. The city's hosting of the 1929 Exposición Iberoamericana led to further building projects.

The Spanish Civil War saw the city fall to the Nationalists in 1936 shortly after the outbreak of hostilities, despite strong resistance in working-class areas (which brought savage reprisals).

More recently, the city has undergone something of a roller-coaster ride. It was made capital of the autonomous Andalucía region in 1982, and in 1992 it hosted Expo's world fair. By the early 2000s, its economy was on the up thanks to a mix of tourism, commerce, technology and industry. But then the 2008 financial crisis struck and despite the continuation of projects such as the Metropol Parasol, the economy tanked, reaching rock bottom in 2012. Recent years have seen growth returning to the Spanish economy but unemployment, particularly youth unemployment, remains a worrying issue.

◉ Sights

Seville's centre is relatively compact and most sights are concentrated in the area between Parque de María Luisa, the city's showcase park to the south, the Macarena district to the north, and the Río Guadalquivir to the west. Distances are not great and walking is generally the best way of getting around.

◉ Cathedral & Around

★ **Catedral de Sevilla & Giralda**   CATHEDRAL
(Map p58; ✆954 21 49 71; www.catedraldesevil la.es; Plaza del Triunfo; adult/child €9/free, rooftop tours €15; ⊙11am-3.30pm Mon, to 5pm Tue-Sat, 2.30-6pm Sun) Seville's immense cathedral is awe-inspiring in its scale and majesty. The world's largest Gothic cathedral, it was built between 1434 and 1517 over the remains of what had previously been the city's main mosque. Highlights include the Giralda, the mighty bell tower, which incorporates the mosque's original minaret, the monumental tomb of Christopher Columbus, and the Capilla Mayor with an astonishing gold altarpiece.

The history of the cathedral goes back to the 15th century but the history of Christian worship on the site dates to the mid-13th century. In 1248, the Castilian King Fernando III captured Seville from its Almohad rulers and transformed their great 12th-century mosque into a church. Some 153 years later, in 1401, the city's ecclesiastical authorities decided to replace the former mosque, which had been damaged by an earthquake in 1356, with a spectacular new cathedral: 'Let's construct a church so large future generations will think we were mad', they quipped (or so legend has it).

The result is the staggering cathedral you see today, officially known as the Catedral de Santa María de la Sede. It's one of the world's largest churches and a veritable treasure trove of art with notable works by Zurbarán, Murillo, Goya and others.

➜ **Exterior**

From close up, the bulky exterior of the cathedral with its Gothic embellishments gives hints of the treasures within. Pause to look at the **Puerta del Perdón** (now the cathedral's exit) on Calle Alemanes. It's one of the few remaining elements from the original mosque.

➜ **Sala del Pabellón**

Selected treasures from the cathedral's art collection are exhibited in this room, the first after the ticket office. Much of what's displayed here, as elsewhere in the cathedral, is the work of masters from Seville's 17th-century Golden Age.

DON'T MISS

SEVILLE IN FIVE WORKS OF ART

A leading player in the Golden Age of Spanish art, Seville reveals a lot through its paintings. Here are five not-to-be-missed masterpieces and the stories behind them.

Visión de San Antonio (*Vision of St Anthony*, 1656) This giant Murillo painting in the cathedral was the victim of a notorious art theft in 1874 when an opportunistic thief cut the figure of the kneeling St Anthony from the canvas and absconded with it to America. Miraculously, the figure turned up several months later in New York. It was spotted by a savvy art dealer who bought it for $250 and sent it back to Seville where it was skillfully reinserted into the canvas.

Misericordia (*Mercy*, 1666–70) In the 1660s, Murillo was commissioned to complete a series of six paintings on the theme of mercy for Seville's newly inaugurated Hospital de la Caridad, a task he completed with his customary aplomb. In 1810 four of the series were stolen by a French general, Jean de Dieu Soult, when Napoleon's army occupied Seville. The paintings were never returned – they remain scattered around museums in Paris, London and Canada – meaning four of the 'Murillos' on show in the hospital are 21st-century copies.

Santa Rufina (*St Rufina*, 1629–32) One of only a handful of canvases by Diego Velázquez on display in his native city, this rendering of Santa Rufina (a 3rd-century Christian martyr) was bought by the local Focus-Abengoa Foundation in 2007 with the aim of bringing the artist 'home'. The painting cost a hefty €12.4 million and is now on display in the Hospital de los Venerables Sacerdotes.

Inmaculada concepción (*Immaculate Conception*, 1650) Debate over the Immaculate Conception obsessed Spanish artists in the 16th and 17th centuries and you'll see it depicted in artworks across the city – Murillo alone painted more than a dozen versions of it. One of his most notable renditions lights up a restored chapel in the Museo de Bellas Artes. A more sober rendering by Zurbarán can be seen in the Hospital de los Venerables Sacerdotes.

Virgen de los mareantes (*Madonna of the Seafarers*, 1531–36) Hung in the Sala de Audiencias in the Real Alcázar, a chapel where sailors went to pray before sailing for the Indies, Alejo Fernández' masterpiece was painted sometime between 1531 and 1536 and is generally reckoned to be the oldest known depiction of the discovery of the New World. It depicts Columbus, Amerigo Vespucci, Charles V and a cluster of indigenous Americans sheltering beneath the Virgin Mary's outstretched cape.

Seville

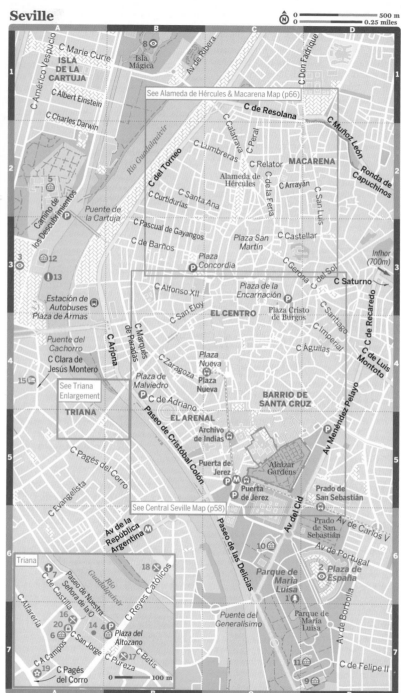

N 0 — 500 m
0 — 0.25 miles

ISLA DE LA CARTUJA

C Marie Curie
C América Vespucio
C Albert Einstein
C Charles Darwin

Isla Mágica
Av de Ribera
C Don Fadrique

See Alameda de Hércules & Macarena Map (p66)

C de Resolana
C Muñoz León
Ronda de Capuchinos

Río Guadalquivir
C del Torneo
C Calatrava
C Peral
C Relator
MACARENA
C de la Feria
C Arrayán
C San Luis

Alameda de Hércules
C Lumbreras
C Santa Ana
C Curtidurías

C Pascual de Gayangos
C de Barnos
Plaza San Martín
C Castellar

Puente de la Cartuja
Camino de los Descubrimientos

Plaza Concordia
C Gerona
C del Sol
C Saturno

Infhor (700m)

Estación de Autobuses
Plaza de Armas

C Alfonso XII
Plaza de la Encarnación
C San Eloy
EL CENTRO
Plaza Cristo de Burgos
C Santiago
C de Recaredo

Puente del Cachorro
C Clara de Jesús Montero

C Arjona
C Marqués de Paradas
C Zaragoza
C Imperial
C Águilas
C de Luis Montoto

See Triana Enlargement

TRIANA

Plaza de Malviedro
C de Adriano
Plaza Nueva

Plaza Nueva
BARRIO DE SANTA CRUZ

Paseo de Cristóbal Colón
EL ARENAL
Archivo de Indias

Av Menéndez Pelayo

Puerta de Jerez
Alcázar Gardens
Prado de San Sebastián

Puerta de Jerez

See Central Seville Map (p58)

Av de la República Argentina

Paseo de las Delicias
Av del Cid
Prado de San Sebastián
Av de Carlos V

Parque de María Luisa
Av de Portugal
Plaza de España

C Pagés del Corro
C Evangelista

Puente del Generalísimo
Parque de María Luisa
Av de Borbolla

Triana
C Reyes Católicos
C de Castilla
Paseo de Nuestra Señora de la O
Río Guadalquivir

C Alfarería
C A Campos
C San Jorge
Plaza del Altozano
C Pureza
C Betis
C de Felipe II

C Pagés del Corro

0 — 100 m

Seville

➡ Tomb of Christopher Columbus

Once inside the cathedral proper, head right and you'll see the tomb of Christopher Columbus (the Sepulcro de Cristóbal Colón) in front of the **Puerta del Príncipe** (Door of the Prince). The monument supposedly contains the remains of the great explorer, but debate continues as to whether the bones are actually his.

Columbus' remains were moved many times after his death (in 1506 in Valladolid, northern Spain), and some claim his real bones lie in Santo Domingo. Certainly his bones spent time in the Dominican Republic after they were shipped to Spanish-controlled Hispaniola from their original resting place, the Monasterio de la Cartuja (p66), in 1537. However, they were later sent to Havana and returned to Seville in 1898.

DNA testing in 2006 proved a match between the bones supposed to be Columbus' and bones known to be from his brother Diego. And while that didn't conclusively solve the mystery, it strongly suggested that the great man really is interred in the tomb that bears his name.

➡ Sacristía de los Cálices

To the right of Columbus' tomb are a series of rooms containing some of the cathedral's greatest masterpieces. First up is the Sacristy of the Chalices, where Francisco de Goya's painting of the Sevillan martyrs, *Santas Justa y Rufina* (1817), hangs above the altar.

➡ Sacristía Mayor

Next along is this large room with a finely carved stone cupola, created between 1528 and 1547: the arch over its portal has carvings of 16th-century foods. Pedro de Campaña's 1547 *El descendimiento* (Descent from the Cross), above the central altar at the southern end, and Francisco de Zurbarán's *Santa Teresa*, to its right, are two of the cathedral's most precious paintings. Also look out for the *Custodia de Juan de Arfe*, a huge 475kg silver monstrance made in the 1580s by Renaissance metalsmith Juan de Arfe.

➡ Sala Capitular

The circular chapter house, also called the Cabildo, features a stunning carved dome and a Murillo masterpiece, *La inmaculada*, set high above the archbishop's throne. The room was built between 1558 and 1592 as a venue for meetings of the cathedral hierarchy.

➡ Capilla Mayor

Even in a church as spectacular as this, the Capilla Mayor (Main Chapel) stands out with its astonishing Gothic retable, reckoned to be the world's largest altarpiece. Begun by Flemish sculptor Pieter Dancart in 1482 and finished by others in 1564, this sea of gilt and polychromed wood holds more than 1000 carved biblical figures. At the centre of the lowest level is a tiny 13th-century silver-plated cedar image of the *Virgen de la sede* (Virgin of the See), patron of the cathedral. West of the Capilla is the Choir into which is incorporated a vast organ.

➡ Southern & Northern Chapels

The chapels along the southern and northern sides of the cathedral hold more artistic treasures. The Capilla de San Antonio, at the western end of the northern aisle, houses Murillo's humongous 1656 depiction of the vision of St Anthony of Padua. The painting was victim of a daring art heist in 1874.

Seville Cathedral

THE HIGHLIGHTS TOUR

In 1402 the inspired architects of Seville set out on one of the most grandiose building projects in medieval history. Their aim was to shock and amaze future generations with the size and magnificence of the building. It took until 1506 to complete the project, but 500 years later Seville Cathedral is still the largest Gothic cathedral in the world.

To avoid getting lost, orient yourself by the main highlights. Directly inside the southern (main) entrance is the grand ❶ **Tomb of Columbus**. Turn right here and head into the southeastern corner to uncover some major art treasures: a Goya in the Sacristía de los Cálices, a Zurbarán in the ❷ **Sacristía Mayor**, and Murillo's shining *La inmaculada* in the Sala Capitular. Skirt the cathedral's eastern wall past the often closed ❸ **Capilla Real**, home to some important royal tombs. By now it's impossible to avoid the lure of the ❹ **Capilla Mayor** with its fantastical altarpiece. Hidden over in the northwest corner is the ❺ **Capilla de San Antonio** with a legendary Murillo. That huge doorway nearby is the rarely opened ❻ **Puerta de la Asunción**. Make for the ❼ **Giralda** next, stealing admiring looks at the high, vaulted ceiling on the way. After looking down on the cathedral's immense footprint, descend and depart via the ❽ **Patio de los Naranjos**.

TOP TIPS

➡ Don't try to visit the Alcázar and cathedral on the same day. There is far too much to take in.

➡ Take time to admire the cathedral from the outside. It's particularly stunning at night from the Plaza Virgen de los Reyes, and from across the river in Triana.

➡ Skip the line by booking tickets online or buying them at the Iglesia Colegial del Divino Salvador on Plaza del Salvador.

Capilla de San Antonio
One of 80 interior chapels, you'll need to hunt down this little gem notable for housing Murillo's 1656 painting, *The Vision of St Anthony*. The work was pillaged by thieves in 1874 but later restored.

Patio de los Naranjos
Inhale the perfume of 60 Sevillan orange trees in a cool patio bordered by fortress-like walls – a surviving remnant of the original 12th-century mosque. Exit is gained via the horseshoe-shaped Puerta del Perdón.

Puerta del Perdón

Iglesia del Sagrario

Puerta del Bautismo

Puerta de la Asunción
Located on the western side of the cathedral and also known as the Puerta Mayor, these huge, rarely opened doors are pushed back during Semana Santa to allow solemn processions of Catholic *hermandades* (brotherhoods) to pass through.

Giralda

Ascend, not by stairs, but by a series of 35 ramps to the pinnacle of this 11th-century minaret topped by a Gothic-baroque belfry. Standing 104m tall, it has long been the defining symbol of Seville.

El Giraldillo

Capilla Mayor

Behold! The cathedral's main focal point contains its greatest treasure, a magnificent gold-plated altarpiece depicting various scenes in the life of Christ. It constitutes the life's work of one man, Flemish artist Pieter Dancart.

Capilla Real

The atmospheric, but often closed, Royal Chapel is dedicated to the Virgen de los Reyes. In a silver urn lie the hallowed remains of the city's Christian conqueror Fernando III and his son, Alfonso the Learned.

③

④   ②

Sacristía Mayor

Art lovers will adore this large domed room containing some of the city's greatest paintings, including Zurbarán's *Santa Teresa* and Pedro de Campaña's *Descendimiento*. It also guards the city key captured in 1248.

①

Main Entrance

Tomb of Columbus

Buried in Valladolid in 1506, the remains of Christopher Columbus were moved four times before they arrived in Seville in 1898 encased in an elaborately carved catafalque.

ⓘ CATEDRAL TICKETS

To avoid queueing for tickets at the cathedral (p50), you have two choices: you can either book through the Spanish-language website or you can buy tickets at the Iglesia Colegial del Divino Salvador (p62). There are rarely queues at this church, which sells combined tickets covering admission to the church, the cathedral and the Giralda.

➡ **Giralda**

In the northeastern corner of the cathedral you'll find the entry to the Giralda. The climb to the top involves walking up 35 ramps, built so that the guards could ride up on horseback, and a small flight of stairs at the top. Your reward is sensational rooftop views.

The 104m decorative brick tower was the minaret of the mosque, constructed between 1184 and 1198 at the height of Almohad power. Its proportions, delicate brick-pattern decoration and colour, which changes with the light, make it perhaps Spain's most perfect Islamic building. The topmost parts – from bell level up – were added in the 16th century, when Spanish Christians were busy 'improving on' surviving Islamic buildings. At the very top is *El Giraldillo*, a 16th-century bronze weathervane representing 'faith', that has become a symbol of Seville.

➡ **Patio de los Naranjos**

Outside the cathedral's northern side, this patio was originally the mosque's main courtyard. It's planted with 66 *naranjos* (orange trees), and has a small Visigothic fountain in the centre. Look out for a stuffed crocodile hanging over the courtyard's doorway – it's a replica of a gift the Sultan of Egypt gave Alfonso X in around 1260.

⭐ **Real Alcázar**   PALACE

(Map p58; ☑954 50 23 24; www.alcazarsevilla .org; Plaza del Triunfo; adult/child €9.50/free; ⊙9.30am-7pm Apr-Sep, to 5pm Oct-Mar) A magnificent marriage of Christian and Mudéjar architecture, Seville's Unesco-listed palace complex is a breathtaking spectacle. The site, which was originally developed as a fort in 913, has been revamped many times over the 11 centuries of its existence, most spectacularly in the 14th century when King Pedro added the sumptuous Palacio de Don Pedro, still today the Alcázar's crown jewel. More recently, the Alcázar featured as a location for the *Game of Thrones* TV series.

The Alcázar started life in the 10th century as a fort for the Cordoban governors of Seville but it was in the 11th century that it got its first major rebuild. Under the city's Abbadid rulers, the original fort was enlarged and a palace known as Al-Muwarak (the Blessed) was built in what's now the western part of the complex. Subsequently, the 12th-century Almohad rulers added another palace east of this, around what's now the Patio del Crucero. The Christian king Fernando III moved into the Alcázar when he captured Seville in 1248, and several later monarchs used it as their main residence. Fernando's son Alfonso X replaced much of the Almohad palace with a Gothic one and then, between 1364 and 1366, Pedro I created his stunning namesake palace.

➡ **Patio del León**

Entry to the complex is through the **Puerta del León** (Lion Gate) on Plaza del Triunfo. Passing through the gateway, which is flanked by crenellated walls, you come to the Patio del León (Lion Patio), which was the garrison yard of the original Al-Muwarak palace. Off to the left before the arches is the **Sala de la Justicia** (Hall of Justice), with beautiful Mudéjar plasterwork and an *artesonado* (ceiling of interlaced beams with decorative insertions). This room was built in the 1340s by the Christian King Alfonso XI, who disported here with one of his mistresses, Leonor de Guzmán, reputedly the most beautiful woman in Spain. It leads to the pretty **Patio del Yeso**, part of the 12th-century Almohad palace reconstructed in the 19th century.

➡ **Patio de la Montería**

Dominated by the facade of the Palacio de Don Pedro, the Patio de la Monteria owes its name (The Hunting Courtyard) to the fact that hunters would meet here before hunts with King Pedro. Rooms on the western side of the square were part of the **Casa de la Contratación** (Contracting House), founded in 1503 to control trade with Spain's American colonies. The **Salón del Almirante** (Admiral's Hall) houses 19th- and 20th-century paintings showing historical events and personages associated with Seville. The room off its northern end has an international collection of beautiful, elaborate fans. The **Sala de Audiencias** (Chapter House) is hung with tapestry representations of the shields of Spanish admirals and Alejo Fernández' celebrated 1530s painting *Virgen de los mareantes* (Madonna of the Seafarers).

➡ Cuarto Real Alto

The Alcázar is still a royal palace. In 1995 it hosted the wedding feast of Infanta Elena, daughter of King Juan Carlos I, after her marriage in Seville's cathedral. The **Cuarto Real Alto** (Upper Royal Quarters), the rooms used by the Spanish royal family on their visits to Seville, are open for guided tours (€4.50; half hourly 10am to 1.30pm; booking required). Highlights of the tours, which are conducted in either Spanish or English, include the 14th-century **Salón de Audiencias**, still the monarch's reception room, and Pedro I's bedroom with marvellous Mudéjar tiles and plasterwork.

➡ Palacio de Don Pedro

This palace, also known as the Palacio Mudéjar, is Seville's single most stunning architectural feature.

King Pedro, though at odds with many of his fellow Christians, had a long-standing alliance with the Muslim emir of Granada, Mohammed V, the man responsible for much of the decoration at the Alhambra. So when Pedro decided to build a new palace in the Alcázar in 1364, Mohammed sent many of his top artisans. These were joined by others from Seville and Toledo. Their work, drawing on the Islamic traditions of the Almohads and caliphal Córdoba, is a unique synthesis of Iberian Islamic art.

Inscriptions on the palace's facade encapsulate the collaborative nature of the enterprise. While one, in Spanish, announces that the building's creator was the 'highest, noblest and most powerful conqueror Don Pedro, by God's grace King of Castilla and León', another proclaims repeatedly in Arabic that 'there is no conqueror but Allah'.

At the heart of the palace is the sublime **Patio de las Doncellas** (Patio of the Maidens), surrounded by beautiful arches, plasterwork and tiling. The sunken garden in the centre was uncovered by archaeologists in 2004 from beneath a 16th-century marble covering. To the north of the patio, the **Alcoba Real** (Royal Quarters) feature stunningly beautiful ceilings and wonderful plaster-and tilework. Its rear room was probably the monarch's summer bedroom.

Continuing on brings you to the covered **Patio de las Muñecas** (Patio of the Dolls), the heart of the palace's private quarters, featuring delicate Granada-style decoration; indeed, plasterwork was actually brought here from the Alhambra in the 19th century, when the mezzanine and top gallery were added for Queen Isabel II. The **Cuarto del Príncipe** (Prince's Suite), to its north, has an elaborate gold ceiling intended to recreate a starlit night sky.

The most spectacular room in the Palacio, and indeed the whole Alcázar, is the **Salón de Embajadores** (Hall of Ambassadors), south of the Patio de las Muñecas. This was originally Pedro I's throne room, although the fabulous wooden dome of multiple star patterns, symbolising the universe, was added later in 1427. The dome's shape gives the room its alternative name, Sala de la Media Naranja (Hall of the Half Orange).

On the western side of the Salón, the beautiful **Arco de Pavones**, named after its peacock motifs, leads onto the **Salón del Techo de Felipe II**, with a Renaissance ceiling (1589–91) and beyond, to the **Jardín del Príncipe** (Prince's Garden).

➡ Palacio Gótico

Reached via a staircase at the southeastern corner of the Patio de las Doncellas is Alfonso X's much remodelled 13th-century Gothic palace. Interest here is centred on the **Salones de Carlos V**, named after the 16th-century Spanish King Carlos I who was also the Holy Roman Emperor Charles V, and the **Salone de los Tapices**, a huge vaulted hall with a series of vast tapestries.

➡ Patio del Crucero

Beyond the Salone de los Tapices, the Patio del Crucero was originally the upper storey of a patio from the 12th-century Almohad palace. Initially it consisted only of raised walkways along its four sides and two cross-walkways that met in the middle. Below grew orange trees, whose fruit could be plucked at hand height by the lucky folk strolling along the walkways. The patio's lower level was built over in the 18th century after it suffered earthquake damage.

➡ Gardens & Exit

On the other side of the Salone de los Tapices are the Alcázar's gardens. Formal gardens with pools and fountains sit closest to the palace. From one, the **Jardín de la Danza** (Garden of the Dance), a passage runs beneath the Salones de Carlos V to the photogenic **Baños de Doña María de Padilla** (María de Padilla Baths). These are the vaults beneath the Patio del Crucero – originally the patio's lower level – with a grotto that replaced the patio's original pool.

The gardens' most arresting feature is the **Galería de Grutesco**, a raised gallery with porticoes built in the 16th century out of an Islamic-era wall. There is a fun hedge maze,

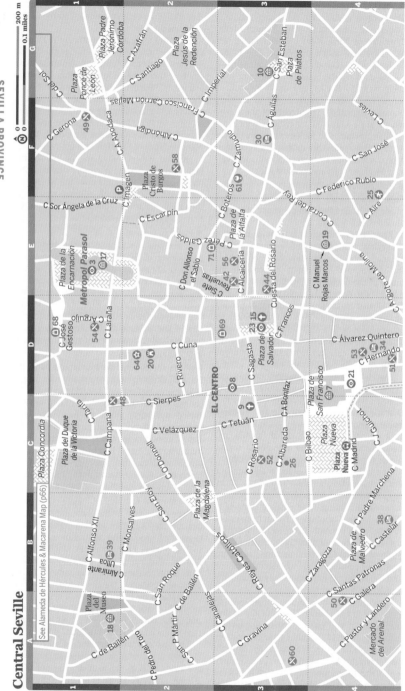

Central Seville

See Alameda de Hércules & Macarena Map (p66)

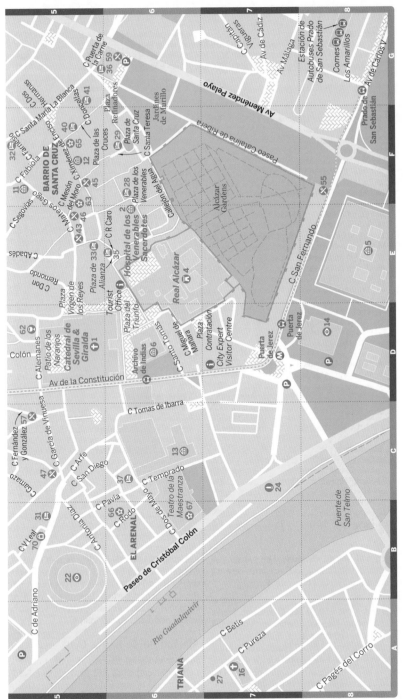

TRIANA

EL ARENAL

BARRIO DE
SANTA CRUZ

Río Guadalquivir

Paseo Cristóbal Colón

Av de la Constitución

Catedral de
Sevilla & Giralda

Real Alcázar

Alcázar Gardens

Paseo Catalina de Ribera

Av Menéndez Pelayo

Jardines
de Murillo

Estación de
Autobuses Prado
de San Sebastián

Prado de
San Sebastián

Puerta
de Jerez

Puente de
San Telmo

Archivo
de Indias

Hospital de los
Venerables
Sacerdotes

Patio de los
Naranjos

Plaza
Virgen de
los Reyes

Plaza del
Triunfo

Plaza de
Contratación

Plaza del
Cabildo

Plaza de
San Francisco

Plaza de las
Cruces

Plaza de los
Venerables

Plaza de
Santa Cruz

Plaza
Refinadores

Colón

C Alemanes

C Fabiola

C Dos
Hermanas

C Santa María La Blanca

C Mateos Gago

C Mesón
del Moro

C Ximénez de Enciso

C Santa Teresa

Callejón del Agua

C San Fernando

C Puerta de
la Carne

C Doncellas

C Segovias

C Don
Remondo

C Abades

C R Caro

C Santo Tomás

C Miguel de Mañara

C Tomás de Ibarra

C Arfe

C San Diego

C Pavía

C Dos de Mayo

C Antonia Díaz

C García de Vinuesa

C Fernández
y González

C Temprado

C Teatro de la
Maestranza

C Gamazo

C Vidal

C de Adriano

C Betis

C Pureza

C Pagés del Corro

C Capitán
Vigueras

Av de Cádiz

Av Málaga

Comes
Los Amarillos

Av de Carlos V

Tourist
Office

City Expert
Visitor Centre

Puerta
de Jerez

Puerta
de Jerez

32
11
62
57
47
31
70
22
66
37
13
24
67
16
27
1
6
4
14
5
55
2
35
33
46
63
45
12
65
40
41
36 59
29
28
43

Central Seville

which will delight children. The gardens to the east, beyond a long wall, are 20th-century creations, but no less heavenly for it.

Archivo de Indias   MUSEUM
(Map p58; ☎954 50 05 28; Calle Santo Tomás; ☺9.30am-5pm Mon-Sat, 10am-2pm Sun) FREE
Occupying a former merchant's exchange on the western side of Plaza del Triunfo, the Archivo de Indias provides a fascinating insight into Spain's colonial history. The archive, established in 1785 to house documents and maps relating to Spain's Ameri-

can empire, is vast, boasting 7km of shelves, 43,000 documents, and 80 million pages dating from 1492 to the end of the empire in the 19th century. Most documents are filed away but you can examine some fascinating letters and hand-drawn maps.

◎ Barrio de Santa Cruz

Seville's medieval *judería* (Jewish quarter), east of the cathedral and Real Alcázar, is today a tangle of atmospheric, winding streets and lovely plant-decked plazas perfumed with orange blossom. Among its most characteristic plazas is Plaza de Santa Cruz, which gives the *barrio* (district) its name, and the wonderfully romantic Plaza de Doña Elvira.

★ Hospital de los Venerables Sacerdotes · MUSEUM

(Map p58; ☑954 56 26 96; www.focus.abengoa.es; Plaza de los Venerables 8; adult/child €8/4, 1st Thu of month to 2pm free; ☺10am-2pm Thu-Sat summer, to 6pm Thu-Sat rest of year) This gem of a museum, housed in a former hospice for ageing priests, is one of Seville's most rewarding. The artistic highlight is the Focus-Abengoa Foundation's collection of 17th-century paintings in the Centro Velázquez. It's not a big collection but each work is a masterpiece of its genre – highlights include Diego Velázquez' *Santa Rufina*, his *Inmaculada Concepción*, and a sharply vivid portrait of *Santa Catalina* by Bartolomé Murillo. Elsewhere, you can admire the Hospital's ornately decorated chapel and delightful patio – a classic composition of porticoes, ceramic tiles and orange trees arranged around a sunken fountain.

Casa de Salinas · HISTORIC BUILDING

(Map p58; ☑618 254498; www.casadesalinas.com; Calle Mateos Gago 39; guided tour €6; ☺10am-6pm Mon-Fri mid-Oct–mid-Jun, to 2pm mid-Jun–mid-Oct) If you've already seen the Alcázar, check out this little-known micro version nearby in Santa Cruz, with no queues. Like Casa de Pilatos, Palacio de Lebrija and Palacio de Las Dueñas, it's privately owned, with the family still occupying the mansion (the redoubtable nonagenarian chatelaine with three of her 12 sons). You'll see 16th-century patios with a stunning Mudéjar plasterwork arches and a Roman mosaic of Bacchanalian shenanigans, original ceramic tiles, and the family's winter and summer drawing rooms with exquisite painted wooden ceilings.

Centro de Interpretación Judería de Sevilla · MUSEUM

(Map p58; ☑954 04 70 89; www.juderiadesevilla.es; Calle Ximénez de Enciso 22; adult/reduced €6.50/5; ☺11am-7pm) Dedicated to Seville's Jewish history, this small, poignant museum occupies an old Sephardic house in the higgledy-piggledy Santa Cruz district, the one-time Jewish neighbourhood that never recovered from a brutal pogrom and massacre in 1391. The events of the pogrom and other historical happenings are catalogued inside, along with a few surviving mementoes including documents, costumes and books. The museum also offers guided walks of Seville's Jewish sites (€22). Minimum two people. Call ahead.

◉ El Centro

As the name suggests, this is Seville's central district, and the densely packed zone of narrow streets and squares north and east of Plaza Nueva, centred on Calles Sierpes and Tetuán/Velázquez, is the heart of Seville's shopping world, as well as home to some excellent bars and restaurants. On the north-eastern edge is the Metropol Parasol, aka *Las Setas*, a modern complex of vast wooden parasols with a rooftop walkway.

★ Metropol Parasol · LANDMARK

(Map p58; ☑606 635214; www.metropolsevilla.com; Plaza de la Encarnación; €3; ☺10am-10.30pm Sun-Thu, to 11pm Fri & Sat) Since opening in 2011, the opinion-dividing Metropol Parasol, known locally as *las setas* (the mushrooms), has become something of a city icon. Designed as a giant sunshade by German architect Jürgen Mayer-Hermann, it's said to be the world's largest wooden structure, and it's certainly a formidable sight with its 30m-high mushroom-like pillars and undulating honeycombed roof. Lifts run up from the basement to the top where you can enjoy killer city views from a winding walkway.

The building, six years in the making, covers a former dead zone in Seville's central district once filled with an ugly car park. Roman ruins discovered during its construction have been cleverly incorporated into its foundations and are now on show at the Museo Antiquarium (☑955 47 15 81; €2.10; ☺10am-8.30pm Tue-Sat, to 2pm Sun) in the basement below the plaza. The structure also houses the local neighbourhood market, a panoramic cafe and a concert space.

Palacio de Las Dueñas · PALACE

(Map p66; ☑954 21 48 28; www.lasduenas.es; Calle Dueñas 5; adult/child €8/6; ☺10am-8pm Apr-Oct, to 6pm Nov-Mar) This 15th-century palace was the favourite home of the world's most titled noble, the late Duchess de Alba, who owned mansions, castles and estates all over Spain. Marvel at the pretty lemon-tree-filled garden, gorgeous arcaded courtyard, paintings and tapestries, as well as her collection of Semana Santa, bullfighting and football memorabilia (she was a Betis fan). Inherited by her eldest son, Carlos, the 18th Duke of Alba, the palace opened to the public in March 2016.

Casa de Pilatos
HISTORIC BUILDING

(Map p58; 954 22 52 98; www.fundacion medinaceli.org; Plaza de Pilatos; ground fl €8, whole house €10; 9am-7pm Apr-Oct, to 6pm Nov-Mar) The haunting Casa de Pilatos, which is still occupied by the ducal Medinaceli family, is one of the city's most glorious mansions. Originally dating to the late 15th century, it incorporates a wonderful mixture of Mudéjar, Gothic and Renaissance decor, with some beautiful tilework and *artesonados*. The overall effect is like a mini-Alcázar.

The staircase to the upper floor has the building's finest tiles, and a great golden *artesonado* dome above. Visits to the upper floor, still partly inhabited by the Medinacelis, are guided. Of interest are several centuries' worth of Medinaceli portraits and a small Goya bullfighting painting.

Palacio de la Condesa de Lebrija
PALACE

(Map p58; 954 22 78 02; www.palaciodeleb rija.com; Calle Cuna 8; ground fl €6, whole bldg €9, ground fl free 10am & 11am Mon; 10.30am-7.30pm Mon-Fri, 10am-2pm & 4-6pm Sat, to 2pm Sun Sep-Jun, 10am-3pm Mon-Fri, to 2pm Sat Jul & Aug) This aristocratic 16th-century mansion, set around a beautiful Renaissance-Mudéjar courtyard, boasts an eclectic look that incorporates a range of decorative elements, including Roman mosaics, Mudéjar plasterwork and Renaissance masonry. Its former owner, the late Countess of Lebrija, was an archaeologist, and she remodelled the house in 1914, filling many of the rooms with treasures from her travels.

Ancient Rome was the countess' specialty, so the library is full of books on antiquity and there are plenty of remains from Roman Itálica, including some marvellous mosaics. If you want to see the top floor, with its Arabic, baroque and Spanish rooms, you'll have to join a guided tour, but it's worth it.

Museo del Baile Flamenco
MUSEUM

(Map p58; 954 34 03 11; www.museoflamenco .com; Calle Manuel Rojas Marcos 3; adult/reduced €10/8; 10am-7pm) The brainchild of *sevillana* flamenco dancer Cristina Hoyos, this museum makes a noble effort to showcase the mysterious art with sketches, paintings and photos of erstwhile (and contemporary) flamenco greats, as well as a collection of dresses and shawls. Even better than the displays are the fantastic nightly performances (7pm and 8.45pm; €20) staged in the on-site courtyard.

Classes and workshops can also be organised, and there's an interesting shop with unique books and garments.

Museo de Bellas Artes
MUSEUM

(Fine Arts Museum; Map p58; 955 54 29 42; www. museodebellasartesdesevilla.es; Plaza del Museo 9; EU citizens/other free/€1.50; 9am-8pm Tue-Sat, to 3pm Sun mid-Sep–mid-Jun, 9am-3pm Tue-Sun mid-Jun–mid-Sep) Housed in the beautiful former Convento de la Merced, Seville's Fine Arts Museum provides an elegant showcase for a comprehensive collection of Spanish and Sevillan paintings and sculptures. Works date from the 15th to 20th centuries, but the onus is very much on brooding religious paintings from the city's 17th-century *Siglo de Oro* (Golden Age).

Works are displayed here in chronological order, with the Golden Age masterpieces clustered in *salas* V to X. The most visually arresting room is the convent's former church (*sala* V), hung with paintings by masters of the Sevillan baroque, above all Murillo. His *Inmaculada concepción grande* (1650) at the head of the church displays all the curving, twisting movement so central to baroque art. Other artists represented include Pacheco (teacher and father-in-law of Velázquez), Juan de Valdés Leal, Zurbarán (look for his deeply sombre *Cristo crucificado,* c 1630–35) and sculptor Juan Martínez Montañés. Also of note is El Greco's portrait of his son Jorge Manuel (c 1600–05), Velázquez's *Cabeza de apóstol* (1620), and a portrait by Goya in *sala* XI.

Plaza del Salvador
SQUARE

(Map p58) This plaza, a popular early evening drinking hang-out, was once the forum of the ancient Roman city of Hispalis. It's dominated by the Iglesia Colegial del Divino Salvador (www.iglesiadelsalvador.es; €4, incl cathedral & Giralda €9; 11am-6pm Mon-Sat, 3-7.30pm Sun Sep-Jun, 10.30am-5.30pm Mon-Sat, 3-7pm Sun Jul & Aug), a handsome baroque church built between 1674 and 1712 on the site of Islamic Ishbiliya's main mosque.

Plaza de San Francisco
SQUARE

(Map p58) Plaza de San Francisco has been Seville's main public square since the 16th century. Forming its western flank is the city's historic city hall, the Ayuntamiento (Casa Consistorial; www.visitasayto.sevilla.org; guided tour Mon-Thu €4, Sat free; tours 7pm & 8pm Mon-Thu, 10am Sat), the southeastern walls of which boast some lovely Renaissance carvings from the 1520–30s.

Calle Sierpes   STREET

(Map p58) Pedestrianised Calle Sierpes, heading north from Plaza de San Francisco, and the parallel Calle Tetuán/Velázquez form the heart of Seville's main shopping district. Lined with chain stores, family-run shops, the occasional independent boutique, and frozen drinks outlets, they're busiest between 6pm and 9pm.

Capilla de San José   CHURCH

(Map p58; ☑ 954 22 32 42; Calle Jovellanos; ⏰ 9.30am-12.30pm & 6.30-8.30pm) FREE For a blast of full-on baroque bling, pop into this small church hidden away on a side street between Calles Sierpes and Tetuán. Behind its 18th-century facade, it boasts some startlingly lavish decor, culminating in an extraordinary gold alterpiece centred on a sculpture of San José.

◉ El Arenal & Triana

Hugging the Río Guadalquivir to the west of Santa Cruz, the compact El Arenal district boasts plenty of lively bars and the city's historic bullring. In times past, this was where colonising *caballeros* made rich on New World gold stalked the streets, watched over by Spanish galleons offloading their American booty. The legendary *barrio* of Triana sits on the west bank of the Río Guadalquivir. This atmospheric quarter, famous for its ceramic tiles, was once home to many of Seville's most quintessential bullfighting and flamenco characters and it still hosts some of its most poignant sights.

Plaza de Toros de la
Real Maestranza   BULLRING, MUSEUM

(Map p58; ☑ 954 22 45 77; www.realmaestranza.com; Paseo de Cristóbal Colón 12; tours adult/child €8/3; ⏰ half hourly 9.30am-9pm, to 3pm bullfight days) In the world of bullfighting, Seville's bullring is the Old Trafford and Camp Nou. In other words, if you're selected to fight here, you've made it. In addition to being regarded as a building of almost religious significance to fans, it's also the oldest ring in Spain (construction began in 1758) and it was here, along with the bullring in Ronda, that bullfighting on foot began in the 18th century. A visit here is a way to learn about this deep-rooted tradition without witnessing a bullfight.

Hospital de la Caridad   MUSEUM

(Map p58; ☑ 954 22 32 32; www.santa-caridad.es; Calle Temprado 3; €5; ⏰ 10.30am-7.30pm Mon-Sat, 10.30am-1pm & 2.30-7.30pm Sun) The Hospital de la Caridad, a large sturdy building one block east of the river, was established in the late 17th century as a hospice for the poor and elderly. It was founded by Miguel de Mañara, by legend a notorious libertine who supposedly changed his ways after seeing a vision of his own funeral procession.

The Hospital's headline act is its gilded chapel, decorated with works by several Golden Age painters and sculptors, most notably Murillo and Roldán.

The hospital was famously pillaged by Napoleon's troops in 1810 when a kleptomaniac French officer named General Soult helped himself to several of the Murillo paintings on the chapel's walls. The paintings were never returned, though copies were made and hung up in place of the originals in 2008. See if you can spot the fakes.

Torre del Oro   TOWER, MUSEUM

(Map p58; Paseo de Cristóbal Colón; adult/reduced €3/1.50, Mon free; ⏰ 9.30am-6.45pm Mon-Fri, 10.30am-6.45pm Sat & Sun) One of Seville's signature landmarks, this 13th-century riverside watchtower was the last great building constructed by the Muslims in the city. Part of a larger defensive complex, it supposedly had gilded tiles, hence its name, 'Tower of Gold', although some dispute this, claiming the name is a reference to the fact that conquistadors returning from Mexico and Peru used the tower to store booty they'd siphoned off colonial coffers. Today, it hosts a small maritime museum and a rooftop viewing platform.

Castillo de San Jorge   MUSEUM

(Map p52; ☑ 954 33 22 40; Plaza del Altozano; ⏰ 11am-5.30pm Tue-Sat, 10am-2.30pm Sun) FREE Adjacent to the Isabel II bridge in Triana, the Castillo de San Jorge is steeped in notoriety for it was here that the infamous Spanish Inquisition had its headquarters from 1481 to 1785. When the Inquisition fires were finally doused in the early 19th century, the castle was destroyed and a market built over the top. Its foundations were rediscovered in 1990, and what's left of the castle today houses a museum charting the Inquisition's activities and life in the *castillo*.

Centro Cerámica Triana   MUSEUM

(Map p52; ☑ 954 34 15 82; Calle Antillano Campos 14; €2.10; ⏰ 11am-5.30pm Tue-Sat, 10am-2.30pm Sun) Opened in 2014, this smart Triana museum is an attempt to rekindle the flames that once lit the kilns of the neighbourhood's erstwhile ceramic industry. It cleverly mixes the methodology and history of ceramic

SEVILLA PROVINCE SEVILLE

LOCAL KNOWLEDGE

TRIANA: SEVILLE'S OUTSIDER NEIGHBOURHOOD

To fully understand the modern montage that makes up Seville, there are several essential pilgrimages. Arguably, the most important is to Triana, the neighbourhood on the west bank of the Río Guadalquivir, a place whose past is littered with stories of sailors, ceramicists, bullfighters, flamenco artists, religious zealotry and a strong working-class identity.

Triana's 'outsider' reputation was first cemented in the Middle Ages when it was labelled *extramuros* (outside the walls) by Seville's authorities, a place where 'undesirables' were sent to live and factories were built. In 1481 the Catholic Church set up the Inquisition Court in the Castillo de San Jorge and began trying suspected religious deviants (ie. non-Catholics) for heresy. The outsider myth burgeoned in the 15th century as itinerant Roma people drifted in from the east and started to put down roots, an influx that gave Triana much of its musical personality. By the 19th century, Triana's interlinked Roma families were producing the finest bullfighters and flamenco singers of the age.

From Roman times, but especially from the 14th century, the neighbourhood was also famous for its pottery and *azulejo* (ceramic tile)-making using thick clay dug out of the river banks. Most of the neighbourhood's Roma were resettled in Seville's new suburbs in the 1960s, a move that altered the demographics of Triana, but not its essence. Unlike the more sanitised Santa Cruz quarter, Triana has kept much of its authenticity. Its outdoor summer living room is the bar-filled Calle Betis overlooking the river, while its kitchen is the Mercado de Triana. The district's religious devotion can be glimpsed in a series of churches, most notably the Gothic-Mudéjar Iglesia de Santa Ana, Triana's so-called 'cathedral', and the baroque Iglesia de Nuestra Señora de la O (Map p52; Calle de Castilla 30; ⊙ 10am-1pm & 6-9pm Tue-Sun) **FREE**.

production with the wider history of Triana and its people.

Iglesia de Santa Ana   CHURCH
(Map p58; Calle de la Pureza 80; €2; ⊙ 10.30am-1.30pm & 4.30-6.30pm Mon-Fri) This salmon-orange church, nicknamed the cathedral of Triana, is one of the oldest in Seville, dating to around 1280. Architecturally, it's Gothic-Mudéjar in style with a high vaulted interior and a wealth of religious imagery.

⊙ South of the Centre

South of Santa Cruz and El Centro, the city opens out into expansive parks and broad boulevards that in recent years have been reclaimed by trams, bikes and strollers. The chief attraction here is the Parque de María Luisa, the city's main park, and the extravagant Plaza de España.

★ Parque de María Luisa   PARK
(Map p52; ⊙ 8am-10pm Sep-Jun, to midnight Jul & Aug; 🖼 🖼) A delightful oasis of green, the extensive Parque de María Luisa is a lovely place to escape the noise of the city, with duck ponds, snoozing *sevillanos* and shady paths snaking under the trees.

If you'd rather continue your cultural exploration than commune with the flowers, the park contains several notable drawcards. Chief among them is Plaza de España, the

most extravagant of the building projects completed for the 1929 Exposición Iberoamericana. A vast brick-and-tile confection, it features fountains, mini-canals, and a series of gaudy tile pictures depicting historical scenes from each Spanish province. You can hire row boats to pootle around the canals for €6 (for 35 minutes).

In the south of the park, the Museo Arqueológico (☎ 955 12 06 32; Plaza de América; EU citizens/other free/€1.50; ⊙ 9am-8pm Tue-Sat, to 3pm Sun mid-Sep–mid-Jun, 9am-3pm Tue-Sun mid-Jun–mid-Sep) has some wonderful Roman sculptures, mosaics and statues – many gathered from the nearby site of Itálica. Opposite is the Museo de Artes y Costumbres Populares (☎ 955 54 29 51), with the same fee and opening hours, dedicated to local customs, costumes and traditions.

The park is a great place for children to let off steam and families to bond over a bike ride – four-person quad bikes are available to hire for €12 per half-hour.

Antigua Fábrica de Tabacos   HISTORIC BUILDING
(Map p58; ☎ 954 55 10 00; Calle San Fernando; ⊙ 8am-9pm Mon-Fri, to 2pm Sat, free tours 11am Mon-Thu) **FREE** Now home to the University of Seville, this massive former tobacco factory – workplace of Bizet's fictional heroine, Carmen – was built in the 18th century and is said to be the second-largest building in

Spain after the El Escorial monastery complex. You can wander in at will or join a free tour. Meet in the main lobby.

Hotel Alfonso XIII   LANDMARK

(Map p58; Calle San Fernando 2) As much a local landmark as an accommodation option, this striking, only-in-Seville hotel – conceived as the most luxurious in Europe when it was built in 1928 – was constructed in tandem with Plaza de España for the 1929 world fair. Ring-fenced by towering palm trees, it sports a classic neo-Mudéjar look complete with glazed tiles and terracotta bricks.

Museo Casa de la Ciencia   MUSEUM

(Map p52; ☑ 954 23 23 49; www.casadelaciencia .csic.es; Pabellón de Perú, Avenida de María Luisa, Parque de María Luisa; museum €3, incl planetarium €5; ◉ 10am-9pm Tue-Sun) Housed in the Peruvian Pavilion from the 1929 Exposición |Iberoamericana, complete with carved condors and llamas, this excellent, hands-on science museum has several permanent exhibitions and a planetarium, plus two temporary exhibitions. The cetaceans room has models of whales and dolphins, common in the Straits of Gibraltar, with information in English. Temporary exhibitions (Spanish only) are interactive and family-friendly. No cafe, but there are refreshment vending machines and tables to sit at.

◉ Alameda de Hércules & Around

To the north of El Centro, the Alameda de Hércules area is one of the city's most vibrant districts. Until fairly recently, it was largely a no-go neighbourhood, the preserve of shady characters. But it has undergone a 'Soho makeover' and these days it's crammed with trendy bars, chic shops and popular eateries. It's also Seville's main gay hang-out.

San Luis de los Franceses   CHURCH

(Map p66; ☑ 954 55 02 07; www.dipusevilla.com/ sanluisdelosfranceses; Calle San Luis 27; €4, audio guide €3, free 4-8pm Sun; ◉ 10am-2pm & 4-8pm Tue-Sun) The finest example of baroque architecture in Seville, San Luis is a former 18th-century Jesuit novitiate dedicated to King Louis IX of France. Designed by Leonardo de Figueroa, its unusual circular shape features four extravagantly carved and gilded altarpieces inset with paintings (Louis' image is topped by a huge crown), with a central cupola. You can also visit the chapel decorated with macabre reliquaries (saints' bones) in glass boxes, and the crypt.

This (deconsecrated) church was closed for decades, and only reopened after a major refurbishment in 2017. Don't miss the beautiful ceiling murals, which carry messages defending the Jesuits against criticisms – unsuccessfully, as they were expelled from Spain soon after the church was completed in 1731. The main cupola's decoration – use the cleverly angled mirror to study it, saving your neck – has the theme of continuity of worship: the old is represented by the Jewish Ark of the Covenant and seven-branched candlestick, and the new by the angels.

Alameda de Hércules   SQUARE

(Map p66) Flanked by bars, cafes and eateries, this tree-lined plaza is a popular evening hang-out, as well as a focus of the city's gay scene. It was originally laid out in the late 16th century and became a fashionable promenade during the 17th-century Golden Age. The two Roman columns at its southern end are 2000-year-old originals, topped by statues of Hercules and Julius Caesar.

Palacio de los Marqueses
de la Algaba   PALACE, MUSEUM

(Map p66; ☑ 955 47 20 97; Plaza Calderón de la Barca; ◉ 10am-2pm & 6-9pm Mon-Fri, to 2pm Sat Apr-Oct, reduced hours Nov-Mar) FREE One of Seville's classic Mudéjar-style palaces, complete with lovely central courtyard, this historic mansion houses the Centro de la Interpretación Mudéjar, a small museum showcasing Mudéjar relics from the 12th to the 20th centuries. Though the collection gets a little lost in the wonderfully restored mansion, the captions (in Spanish and English) do a good job of explaining the nuances of the complex Mudéjar style.

Basílica de La Macarena   BASILICA

(Map p66; ☑ 954 90 18 00; Calle Bécquer 1; basilica/museum free/€5; ◉ 9am-2.30pm & 6-9.30pm Mon-Sat, 9am-2pm & 6-9pm Sun) This basilica is home to Seville's most revered religious treasure, the *Virgen de la Esperanza Macarena* (Macarena Virgin of Hope), popularly known as the Macarena. This magnificent statue, a star of the city's fervent Semana Santa (Holy Week) celebrations, stands in splendour behind the main altarpiece, adorned with a golden crown, lavish vestments and five diamond-and-emerald brooches donated by the famous 20th-century matador Joselito El Gallo. The church also has a small museum containing further treasures relating to the Virgin. Across the street from the basilica is the longest surviving stretch of Seville's 12th-century Almohad walls.

Alameda de Hércules & Macarena

◉ Isla de la Cartuja

This former island on the Río Guadalquivir takes its name from the on-site monastery, the Monasterio de la Cartuja de Santa María de Las Cuevas. It was connected to Seville's west bank in 1992 to incorporate the city's Expo '92 site. Monastery apart, most of the buildings here are modern, including the impossible-to-miss Cajasol tower completed in 2015.

Centro Andaluz de Arte
Contemporáneo   MUSEUM
(Map p52; ☏ 955 03 70 70; www.caac.es; Camino de los Descubrimientos; temporary exhibition €1.80, complete visit €3, 7-9pm Tue-Fri & all day Sat free; ⊙11am-9pm Tue-Sat, 10am-3.30pm Sun) This historic but offbeat site was once a monastery, then a ceramics factory, and is today the Centro Andaluz de Arte Contemporáneo, Seville's shrine to modern art with temporary exhibitions set alongside some truly bizarre permanent pieces. You can't miss *Alicia*, by Cristina Lucas, a massive head and arm poking through two old monastery windows that was supposedly inspired by *Alice in Wonderland*. You could be forgiven for walking obliviously past Pedro Mora's *Bus Stop*, which looks exactly like...well, a bus stop.

The original monastery, Monasterio de la Cartuja de Santa María de Las Cuevas, was founded in 1399 and became the favourite Sevillan lodging place for Christopher Columbus, who prayed in its chapel before his trip to the Americas and whose remains lay here from his death in 1506 to 1537.

In 1839 the complex was bought by an enterprising Englishman, Charles Pickman, who turned it into a porcelain factory, building the tall bottle-shaped kilns that stand rather incongruously beside the monastery. The factory ceased production in the 1980s and in 1992 the building served as the Royal Pavilion during the Expo.

Alameda de Hércules & Macarena

CaixaForum Sevilla ARTS CENTRE
(Map p52; ☑ 955 65 76 11; http://agenda.obra
social.lacaixa.es/es/caixaforum-sevilla; Calle Jeroni-
mo de Aguilar; exhibition €4, family workshops/exhi-
bitions/concerts €2/4/6, under 16yr free; ☺10am-
8pm) CaixaForum Sevilla is an underground
(literally) cultural centre that opened in
March 2017. Situated on the Isla de la Cartuja, it's home to two temporary contemporary
art exhibitions (one inaugural show featured
Cindy Sherman and Jean-Michel Basquiat),
with integrated children's activities. It also
puts on concerts, movies, discussions and
conferences, as well as family workshops.

Pabellón de la Navegación MUSEUM
(Map p52; ☑ 954 04 31 11; www.pabellondela
navegacion.es; Camino de los Descubrimientos 2;
adult/child €4.90/3.50; ☺11am-8.30pm Tue-Sat,
to 3pm Sun Sep-Jun, 10am-3.30pm daily Jul & Aug;
⊞) This boxy concrete-and-glass pavilion on
the banks of the Río Guadalquivir revived a
previous navigation museum that had been
here from the 1992 Expo until 1999. Its permanent collection is split into four parts
– navigation, mariners, shipboard life and
historical views of Seville – and although
its exhibits are interactive and kid-friendly,
they might be a little underwhelming for an
adult. The ticket includes a ride up the adjacent **Torre Schindler** (adult/child €4.90/3.50).

Note that only temporary exhibitions are
open on Mondays in July and August.

Isla Mágica AMUSEMENT PARK
(Map p52; ☑ 902 16 17 16; www.islamagica.
es; Camino de los Descubrimientos; adult/child

€29/21; ☺11am-10pm mid-Jun–Aug, shorter hours
Sep-Nov, closed Dec-Mar; ⊞) This Disney-goes-
Spanish-colonial amusement park provides
an action-packed day out for kids and thrill
seekers with an array of white-knuckle rides,
shows and swimming pools. Hours vary by
season – see the website for details. Buses C1
and C2 both stop near the park.

🏃 Activities

Aire Baños Árabes HAMMAM
(Map p58; ☑ 955 01 00 24; www.beaire.com; Calle
Aire 15; bath/bath with massage from €33/49;
☺10am-10pm Sun-Thu, to midnight Fri & Sat)
These smart, Arabic-style baths win prizes
for tranquil atmosphere, historic setting (in
the Barrio de Santa Cruz) and Moroccan
riad-style decor. Various bath and massage
packages are available – see the website for
details – for which it's always best to book a
day or so in advance.

🎓 Courses

Seville is a great city in which to learn a new
skill. Many visitors take a Spanish-language
course and there are dozens of schools offering lessons. Alternatively, you could release
your inner performer at one of the city's
flamenco and dance schools or brush up on
Spanish cuisine on a cookery course.

Taller Andaluz de Cocina COOKING
(Map p52; ☑ 672 162621; www.tallerandaluzde
cocina.com; Mercado de Triana, Plaza del Altozano;
courses €35-55) In Triana market, this cooking school offers a range of hands-on courses

SEVILLE FOR CHILDREN

Seville is a kid-friendly city with a largely pedestrianised centre and numerous parks and free play areas. Kids get into many sights free, though age limits vary – the Catedral (p50) is free for under-15s; the Real Alcázar (p56) for under-17s. Both are accessible with strollers. Children under three travel free on city buses.

Other kid-friendly sights and activities include the following:

Parque de María Luisa (p64) Seville's main park. Rowboats are available for hire in the park at Plaza de España.

Isla Mágica (p67) Big amusement park targeted at kids over 10.

Museo Casa de La Ciencia (p65) Science museum with hands-on displays.

Pabellón de la Navegación (p67) Has interactive exhibits illustrating Seville's maritime history.

covering classic Spanish cuisine and tapas as well as tastings and guided market tours. Check the website for further details.

Fundación Cristina Heeren de Arte Flamenco
DANCING

(Map p58; ☑ 954 21 70 58; www.flamencoheeren .com; Calle Pureza 76; workshops €60-80) Seville's best-known flamenco school offers a range of courses and workshops in singing, dancing and guitar playing. Reckon on €60 to €80 for a 90-minute workshop; €2000 for an intensive summer course.

Taller Flamenco
DANCING, LANGUAGE

(Map p66; ☑ 954 56 42 34; www.tallerflamenco .com; Calle Peral 49) Offers flamenco dance courses, singing and guitar lessons, and language classes with the possibility of being taught in groups or on a one-to-one basis. A one-week semi-intensive language course costs €102; for a one-week flamenco course for beginners reckon on €259.

CLIC
LANGUAGE

(International House; Map p58; ☑ 954 50 21 31; www. clic.es; Calle Albareda 19) A well-established language centre headquartered in a pleasant house with a good social scene and adjacent bookshop. Courses are available for children and adults, with prices starting at €190 for a week-long course of 20 lessons. Accommodation can also be arranged.

👉 Tours

⭐ Pancho Tours
TOURS

(☑ 664 642904; www.panchotours.com) 🆓 Runs excellent free tours, although you're welcome to tip the hard-working guide who'll furnish you with an encyclopedia's worth of anecdotes, stories, myths and theories about Seville's fascinating past. Tours kick off daily, normally at 11am – check the website for

exact details. Pancho also offers bike tours (€25), skip-the-line cathedral and Alcázar visits (€15) and nightlife tours (€10 to €15).

Mimo Sevilla
FOOD

(Map p58; ☑ 854 55 68 00; www.sevilla.mimo food.com/en; Calle San Fernando 2; tours €60-285) This professional set-up, based at the Hotel Alfonso XIII (p65), offers wine tastings, cooking classes, tapas tours and day trips, including to the sherry city of Jerez. Bank on €95 for a three-hour tapas tour, €60 for two hours of wine tasting. The shop has excellent gourmet products such as extra-virgin olive oil, squid ink and dehydrated caviar.

Past View
TOURS

(Map p58; ☑ 954 32 66 46; www.pastview.es; Plaza de la Encarnación; tours €15; ⊙ 10.30am Tue-Sun, 8pm Wed, Fri & Sat Jun-Sep, 11am Tue-Sun, 4.30pm Wed, Fri & Sat Oct-May; 🐾) This ingenious augmented-reality video tour takes you on a guided walk using 3D video glasses that recreate scenes from the past in the actual locations they happened. The ticket office and starting point is in the Metropol Parasol (p61) and the two-hour walk (with a guide) proceeds through Seville's main sights to the Torre del Oro (p63).

🎎 Festivals & Events

Semana Santa
RELIGIOUS

(www.semana-santa.org; ⊙ Mar/Apr) Seville's Holy Week celebrations are legendary. Every day from Palm Sunday to Easter Sunday, large, life-size *pasos* (sculptural representations of events from Christ's Passion) are solemnly carried from the city's churches to the cathedral, accompanied by processions of marching *nazarenos* (penitents). Adding to the sombre atmosphere are the white robes and sinister conical hats the penitents wear – a look that was incongruously copied by America's Ku Klux Klan. The processions, which culminate in the *madrugada* (early hours) of Good Friday, are organised by more than 50 different *hermandades* or *cofradías* (brotherhoods, some of which include women). Schedules are widely available during Semana Santa, or on the Semana Santa website. Arrive near the cathedral in the early evening for the best views.

Feria de Abril FERIA

(www.turismosevilla.org; ⊙Apr) The largest and most colourful of all Andalucía's *ferias* (fairs), Seville's week-long spring fair is held in the second half of the month (sometimes edging into May) on El Real de la Feria, in the Los Remedios area west of the Río Guadalquivir. For six nights, *sevillanos* dress up in elaborate finery, parade around in horse-drawn carriages, eat, drink and dance till dawn.

Bienal de Flamenco DANCE

(www.labienal.com; ⊙Sep) The big names of the flamenco world descend on Seville for this major flamenco festival. Held in September in even-numbered years, it features a comprehensive program of events including performances, exhibitions and workshops.

🛏 Sleeping

Expect high season rates March to June and in September and October. Rates also skyrocket during Semana Santa and the Feria de Abril, for which you'll have to book well in advance.

🛏 Cathedral & Around

EME Catedral Hotel DESIGN HOTEL €€€

(Map p58; ✆954 56 00 00; www.emecatedral hotel.com; Calle de los Alemanes 27; d €180-411, ste €274-609; ❄@🕾≈) Marrying contemporary design with a fabulous location and stunning close-ups of Seville's mammoth Gothic cathedral, the EME impresses on all

fronts. The hotel occupies the shell of 14 fine old Sevillan houses, offering 60 slick modern rooms, the best with cathedral views, and fine facilities including a rooftop bar, pool, wellness centre and several restaurants.

🛏 Barrio de Santa Cruz

Pensión San Pancracio PENSION €

(Map p58; ✆954 41 31 04; Plaza de las Cruces 9; tr €75, q €85-90, with shared bathroom s €25, d €30-40, tr €45.50, q €85-90; ❄🕾) A cheap-as-chips budget option in Santa Cruz, this old, rambling family house has plenty of room options (all cheap) and a pleasant flower-bedizened patio-lobby. Don't expect frills, just friendly staff and basic, spartan rooms. Note that only the triples and quads with private bathrooms have air-con; all other rooms have fans.

Casual Sevilla Don Juan Tenorio HOTEL €€

(Map p58; ✆955 54 44 16; www.casualhoteles. com/hoteles-sevilla/casual-don-juan-tenorio; Plaza de los Venerables 5; d €77-155; ❄🕾) At this cheerful hotel, in the heart of Barrio Santa Cruz, each room is themed after a character from *Don Juan Tenorio*. Although it's only two-star, the hotel has excellent wi-fi, hydromassage showers and wall-mounted TVs; the mobile-phone pack features router, battery charger and selfie stick to loan. The hotel's theme draws on the 19th-century play by José Zorrilla, which tells the story of legendary lothario Don Juan, a fictional literary figure possibly based on a 17th-century nobleman of Seville. The restaurant downstairs, **Hosteria del Laurel**, features in the play.

Hostal Plaza Santa Cruz HOTEL €€

(Map p58; ✆954 22 88 08; www.hostalplazasanta cruz.com; Calle Santa Teresa 15; d €40-95; ❄@🕾) Offering decent value and a lovely location in the Barrio de Santa Cruz, this modest outfit has rooms spread over several sites. Those in

---

CYCLING SEVILLE

Since the inauguration of the **Sevici** (✆900 900722; www.sevici.es) bike-sharing scheme in 2007, cycling in Seville has taken off in a big way. The scheme has been a major success and it remains one of the largest of its kind in Europe with 2500 bikes and 250 docking stations.

Most of Sevici's users are locals, but visitors can use bikes by getting a seven-day subscription for around €14 (plus a €150 returnable deposit). To register, go to a Sevici docking station and follow the on-screen instructions. Seville has 130km of bike lanes (all painted green and equipped with their own traffic signals) and the first 30 minutes of usage are free. Beyond that, it's €1.03 for the first hour and €2.04 an hour thereafter.

Alternatively, a number of operators offer bike tours, including Pancho Tours.

the main hotel, just off Plaza Santa Cruz, are unflashy with laminated parquet floors and the occasional blast of colourful wallpaper, whilst those in its nearby apartments are slightly more upmarket with tiles, artworks and heavy wooden furniture.

★ **Hotel Amadeus**   BOUTIQUE HOTEL €€€
(Map p58; ☑954 50 14 43; www.hotelamadeus sevilla.com; Calle Farnesio 6; d €92-185, tr €121-325, q €180-355; P ❄ ⚹) A musical oasis in the heart of the old *judería* (Jewish quarter) district, this elegant hotel exudes a sense of calm with its ceramic-tiled lobby, white walls, period furniture and artfully displayed musical instruments. Rooms, named after composers, are equally stylish and there's a small panoramic terrace offering views over to the Giralda. Other perks include in-room classical CDs and a rooftop terrace with a jacuzzi. Composers and Mozart lovers will be suitably impressed.

★ **Hotel Casa 1800**   LUXURY HOTEL €€€
(Map p58; ☑954 56 18 00; www.hotelcasa 1800sevilla.com; Calle Rodrigo Caro 6; d €120-650; ❄ @ ⚹) A short hop from the cathedral in the heart of Santa Cruz, this stately *casa* (house) is positively regal. Setting the tone is the elegant, old-school decor – wooden ceilings, chandeliers, parquet floors, and plenty of gilt – but everything about the place charms, from the helpful staff to the rooftop terrace and complimentary afternoon tea.

Un Patio en Santa Cruz   HOTEL €€€
(Map p58; ☑807 31 70 70; www.patiosantacruz. com; Calle Doncellas 15; s €55-185, d €70-200; ❄ ⚹) Feeling more like a gallery than a hotel, this place has stark white walls hung with bright works of art and lofty pot plants. The summery rooms, complete with parquet and dashes of purple, are good looking and comfortable, staff are friendly, and there's a cool rooftop terrace with Moroccan-mosaic tables.

Hotel Palacio Alcázar   BOUTIQUE HOTEL €€€
(Map p58; ☑954 50 21 90; www.hotelpalacio alcazar.com; Plaza de Alianza 12; s €65-180, d €75-195; ❄ @ ⚹) Soothing, white minimalism in the lush *barrio* of Santa Cruz, Palacio Alcázar sparkles in Seville's oldest quarter. It sports 12 lovely rooms, each in white and pearl grey with small oil paintings providing a dash of colour. Up top, there's a panoramic rooftop bar where you call the waiter by ringing a bell on your table.

Hotel Puerta de Sevilla   HOTEL €€€
(Map p58; ☑954 98 72 70; www.hotelpuertade sevilla.com; Calle Puerta de la Carne 2; s €40-155,

d €45-195; ❄ @ ⚹) This superfriendly – and superpositioned – hotel is a great mix of chintz and style. In the lobby there's an indoor water feature lined with superb Seville tilework while rooms reveal a rustic look with flower-patterned textiles, wrought-iron beds and pastel wallpaper. There's also an unbeatable people-watching roof terrace.

🛏 El Centro

Oasis Backpackers' Hostel   HOSTEL €
(Map p58; ☑955 26 26 96; www.oasissevilla. com; Calle Almirante Ulloa 1; dm €13-40, d €45-150; ❄ @ ⚹ ⚏) A veritable oasis in the busy city-centre district, this welcoming hostel is set in a palatial 19th-century mansion. There are various sleeping options ranging from mixed 14-person dorms to doubles with ensuite bathrooms, and excellent facilities, including a cafe-bar, kitchen and rooftop deck with a small pool. Breakfast, not included in most rates, is available for €3.50.

★ **Hotel Casa de Colón**   BOUTIQUE HOTEL €€
(Map p58; ☑955 11 78 28; www.hotelcasadecolon. com; Calle Hernando Colón 3; d €65-180; ❄ @ ⚹) This small, family-owned hotel stands out for its superbly central location between the cathedral and city hall, warm, friendly service and quirky architectural and decorative features: white cast-iron pillars in the bright patio, cobalt-blue stained-glass in the neo-Mudéjar windows. Some rooms have exposed-brick walls and side views of the cathedral; top-floor *aticos* have private terraces. Continental breakfast is available for €8.

Hotel Abanico   HOTEL €€
(Map p58; ☑954 21 32 07; www.hotelabanico.com; Calle Águilas 17; s €47-95, d €47-125; ❄ ⚹) From the beautiful, vaulted lobby to the distinctive tilework, wrought-iron balconies and radiant religious art, this welcoming hotel has Seville written all over it. Rooms are simple affairs with pronounced colours and modest, old-school furniture.

Hotel Boutique Doña Lola   BOUTIQUE HOTEL €€
(Map p66; ☑954 91 52 75; www.donalolasevilla. com; Calle Amor de Dios 19; s €36-63, d €40-135; ❄ ⚹) Ensconced in an ordinary-looking tenement in El Centro, gay-friendly Doña Lola is a little haven of modernity and well positioned for sorties pretty much everywhere. From the lobby, complete with a coloured chequered floor, stairs lead to guest rooms which, although small, are modern and spotless.

🛏 El Arenal & Triana

⭐ La Banda
HOSTEL €

(Map p58; 📞955 22 81 18; www.labandahostel.com; Calle Dos de Mayo 16; dm €18-38; ❄️📶) Run by a young, energetic crew, this Arenal hostel ticks all the boxes. Its mixed dorms are clean and tidily furnished, communal areas are relaxed and inviting, and best of all, it has a great **rooftop bar**. Evening meals are available at 9pm and a weekly program of events ensures there's always something going on.

Hotel Adriano
HOTEL €€

(Map p58; 📞954 29 38 00; www.adrianohotel.com; Calle de Adriano 12; s €70-80, d €80-150; 🅿️❄️📶) In the Arenal neighbourhood near the bullring, the three-star Adriano scores across the board with friendly staff, traditional, individually styled rooms and a lovely coffee shop, Pompeia, on the ground floor. Garage parking is available for €18 per day.

Hotel Monte Triana
BUSINESS HOTEL €€

(Map p52; 📞954 34 31 11; www.hotelesmonte. com; Clara de Jesús Montero 24; s €51-110, d €62-130; 🅿️❄️@📶) In the Triana neighbourhood over the river from the centre, the business-like Monte Triana offers spacious, modern rooms and decent facilities including a fitness room, bar, cafe and garage (€14 per night). You can even choose your own pillow stuffing – latex, feather or viscoelastic.

Mercer Sevilla
BOUTIQUE HOTEL €€€

(Map p58; 📞954 22 30 04; www.mercersevilla. com; Calle Castelar 26; d €400-531, ste €504-1657; ❄️📶🏊) Opened in late 2016, Seville's second five-star GL (Gran Lujo, or Grand Luxe) hotel combines a sensitively converted period building with modern European furniture and faultless service. Twelve superbly appointed rooms feature Nespresso machines and Japanese-style shower toilets. A chic bar, innovative contemporary Andalucian restaurant, and rooftop terrace with pool complete the hotel, in a discreetly elegant class of its own.

🛏 Alameda de Hércules & Around

Corner House
HOTEL €€

(Map p66; 📞954 91 32 62; www.thecornerhouse sevilla.com; Alameda de Hércules 31; d €45-100; ❄️📶) Opened in 2016, this friendly newcomer sits well with the buzzing bars and cafes on the Alameda de Hércules. Modern in look and upbeat in vibe, it offers sun-filled rooms with minimal, low-key decor and wet-room style bathrooms. To eat and drink, there's a ground-floor restaurant, El Disparate, and, up top, a chilled rooftop bar (p77).

Hotel San Gil
HOTEL €€

(Map p66; 📞954 90 68 11; www.hotelsangil.com; Calle Parras 28; d €65-180; ❄️📶🏊) Shoehorned at the northern end of the Macarena neighbourhood, San Gil's slightly out-of-the-way location is balanced by its proximity to the nightlife of the Alameda de Hércules. Behind the mustard-yellow colonial facade, an ostentatiously tiled lobby fronts plain but modern rooms with large beds and ample space.

Hotel Sacristía de Santa Ana
BOUTIQUE HOTEL €€€

(Map p66; 📞954 91 57 22; www.hotelsacristia.com; Alameda de Hércules 22; d €95-250; ❄️📶) This delightful hotel, superbly positioned for the buzzing bars and eateries on the Alameda de Hércules, makes a fabulous first impression. On entering you're greeted by a splendid red-tiled courtyard centred on a small fountain and overlooked by carved wooden balustrades. Up from here, hallways lead to old-fashioned rooms furnished with arty bedsteads, beamed ceilings and cascading showers.

🍴 Eating

It's not hard to eat well in Seville. The city is brimming with bars, cafes, restaurants and markets ranging from centuries-old watering holes serving traditional tapas to hip gourmet joints cooking up innovative contemporary dishes. Bar hot spots include the Barrio de Santa Cruz, the streets around Plaza de la Alfalfa and the Alameda de Hércules. Note that some restaurants close for part of August.

🍴 Barrio de Santa Cruz

Bodega Santa Cruz
TAPAS €

(Map p58; 📞954 21 86 18; Calle Rodrigo Caro 1; tapas €2; ⏰8am-midnight) This is as old-school as it gets, a perennially busy bar staffed by gruff waiters and frequented by locals and visitors alike. Its fiercely traditional tapas are best enjoyed alfresco with a cold beer as you watch the passing armies of Santa Cruz tourists traipse past.

Vinería San Telmo
TAPAS €€

(Map p58; 📞954 41 06 00; www.vineriasantelmo. com; Paseo Catalina de Ribera 4; tapas €2.90-5.80, medias raciones €6.90-15; ⏰10.30am-4.30pm &

8-11.30pm) San Telmo's own brand of innovative tapas has proved a hit with diners, and tables in the salmon-orange and brick interior are a prized commodity. Bag one, for which you'll either have to wait or book, and you'll be sitting down to the likes of crispy bread-crumbed prawns with soy mayonnaise or foie gras with vanilla oil and caramelised peanuts.

Casa Tomate
TAPAS €€

(Map p58; ☑954 22 04 21; Calle Mateos Gago 24; tapas €3-4.50, raciones €8.50-17; ☺noon-midnight) Hams swing from ceiling hooks, old posters are etched with art-nouveau and art-deco designs, and outdoor blackboards relay what's cooking in the kitchen of Casa Tomate. It's a touristy spot, but don't let that put you off what is a fine tapas bar serving the likes of fried aubergine sticks sweetened with honey and succulent grilled calamari with pesto.

Café Bar Las Teresas
TAPAS €€

(Map p58; ☑954 21 30 69; www.lasteresas.es; Calle Santa Teresa 2; tapas €3.50, mains €8-14; ☺10am-1am) The hanging hams look as ancient as the bar itself, a sinuous wraparound affair with a cheerfully cluttered interior and wonky wooden tables outside. Not surprisingly, the menu is highly traditional, featuring staples such as fried *bacalao* (salted cod) and hearty *salchichón ibérico* (sausage).

✖ El Centro

Sal Gorda
ANDALUCIAN €

(Map p58; ☑955 38 59 72; www.facebook.com/SalGordaSevilla; Calle Alcaicería de la Loza 23; tapas €2.50-8.50; ☺1-4.30pm & 8-11.30pm Wed-Mon) Incongruously located in an old shoe shop – you sit in the plate glass window – this tiny, low-key place serves innovative takes on Andalucian dishes – strawberry gazpacho with pistachios, and a first-class version of the ubiquitous tuna *tataki*. Chicken kimchi is a firm favourite, and the wine list features good local whites such as El Mirlo Blanco from Constantina.

Bolas
ICE CREAM €

(Map p58; ☑954 22 74 11; www.bolashela dosartesanos.com; Cuesta del Rosario 1; €2.50-4.40; ☺1pm-midnight) If you're wilting in the summer heat, or even if you're not, an ice cream from Bolas makes for a refreshing treat. Choose from a selection of classic fruit flavours or opt for something more exotic – perhaps La Medina, a sorbet of orange, ginger and cinnamon, or the strange sounding goat's cheese and quince jelly.

El Rinconcillo
TAPAS €

(Map p58; ☑954 22 31 83; www.elrinconcillo.es; Calle Gerona 40; tapas €2.20-3.50, raciones €5.50-13; ☺1pm-1.30am) The blueprint for centuries' worth of imitators, this is the oldest bar in Seville – and some say, Spain – dating to 1670. Over the years, it's become pretty touristy, but it's managed to retain a gnarled sense of authenticity and its woody, tiled interior sets a memorable backdrop for classic tapas.

laCava.bar
TAPAS €

(Map p58; ☑954 53 16 52; www.lacava.bar; Calle Hernando Colón 12; tapas €3.50-12; ☺12.30pm-midnight Sun-Thu, to 1am Fri & Sat) Original tapas, a relaxed, unpretentious atmosphere and a prime central location, laCava is one of the better options in the city's touristy centre. It gets very busy at lunchtime but bag a perch and you'll be rewarded with a choice of classic tapas staples and more creative efforts such as strawberry gazpacho and herbed fish ceviche.

★ Mamarracha
TAPAS €€

(Map p58; ☑955 12 39 11; www.mamarracha.es; Calle Hernando Colón 1-3; tapas €2.20-8, mains €6.50-16; ☺1.30pm-midnight) Ideal for a lunch after a morning visit to the cathedral, this is a fine example of the modern tapas bars that Seville so excels at. Its interior is a handsome mix of blond wood, bare cement surfaces and exposed ducts, whilst its menu reveals some adventurous combos, including a terrific foie gras and orange dish.

★ La Azotea
FUSION, ANDALUCIAN €€

(Map p66; ☑955 11 67 48; www.laazoteasevilla.com; Calle Conde de Barajas 13; tapas €3.75-6.50, raciones €11-19; ☺1.30-4.30pm & 8.30pm-midnight Tue-Sat) Fashionable and much recommended by locals, Azotea is one of Seville's stable of modern eateries with culinary ambitions. Its pearl-grey Scandi-inspired interior sets the scene for artfully plated tapas and contemporary creations such as tomato, *burrata* and lemon sorbet salad. Note there are three other branches across town, including one near the cathedral at Calle Mateos Gago 8.

Bar Europa
TAPAS €€

(Map p58; ☑954 21 79 08; Calle Siete Revueltas 35; tapas €3.50-4.80, media raciones €6.50-15; ☺8.30am-4.30pm & 7.30pm-12.30am) An old-school bar with a classic tiled interior and a few alfresco tables, Bar Europa has been knocking out tapas since 1925. Notwithstanding, it isn't afraid to experiment and it serves some excellent modern creations such as grilled mackerel with a strawberry and radish tartar and sweet nut bread with foie gras, mushrooms and crunchy ham.

Lobo López
MEDITERRANEAN €€

(Map p58; ☑854 70 58 34; http://facebook.com/LoboLopezRestaurante; Calle Rosario 15; tapas €4.20-7, mains €8-11; ☺8am-12.30am Mon-Fri, to 1am Sat & Sun; ✴☎🖉🖶) From the hip-yet-historic decor (concrete-cast art, vertical garden, exposed brick arches) to the cheeky waiters, this place rocks a cool vibe. The food doesn't disappoint, with a short but well-chosen menu: standouts are the lobster (hot) dog and the vegan coconut salsa taco. Unusually, it's open all day, so this is also an ideal mid-afternoon cake-and-smoothie stop.

Perro Viejo
FUSION €€

(Map p58; ☑955 44 00 30; www.equipompuntor.com/perro-viejo; Calle Arguijo 3; tapas €4, mains €9-19; ☺1.30-4.30pm & 8pm-midnight) Fusing the lively buzz of a Seville tapas bar with an upbeat New York loft vibe, this three-storey emporium has well-priced Asian and Andalucian dishes, plus decent local craft beer and wine. Pork dumplings, marinaded sardines and ceviche are among the perennial crowd pleasers. Perfectly placed on a quiet side street for post-shopping lunch, complete with a sun-soaker's outdoor terrace.

Taberna Coloniales San Pedro
ANDALUCIAN €

(Map p58; ☑954 50 11 37; www.tabernacoloniales.es; Plaza Cristo de Burgos 19; tapas €2-4, mains €9-13; ☺12.30pm-midnight) It might not look like much from the outside, but ever-popular Los Coloniales is the business with quality tapas, alfresco tables and cheerful, helpful staff. Stand-out choices include the classic *solomillo al whisky* (pork tenderloin in a whisky-flavoured sauce) and *crujiente de berenjenas con miel* (crunchy aubergines in honey). There's a second, more touristy, **branch** (Map p58; ☑954 22 93 81; Calles Fernández y González 36-38; tapas €2.10-3.90, mains €8.75-12.80; ☺12.30pm-midnight) near the cathedral.

Confitería La Campana
PASTRIES €

(Map p58; ☑954 22 35 70; www.confiterialacampana.com; Calle Sierpes 1-3; pastries from €2.10; ☺8am-10pm) A patisserie and cafe with the word 'institution' stamped all over it, La Campana has been heaving with sugar addicts since 1885. Join the mixed crowd in its elegant interior for a *yema* (soft, crumbly biscuit cake wrapped like a toffee), or a delicious *nata* (custard cake).

🍴 El Arenal & Triana

★ La Brunilda
TAPAS €

(Map p58; ☑954 22 04 81; www.labrunildatapas.com; Calle Galera 5; tapas €3.20-7.50; ☺1-4pm & 8.30-11.30pm Tue-Sat, 1-4pm Sun) A regular fixture on lists of Seville's best tapas joints, this backstreet Arenal bar is at the forefront of the city's new wave of gourmet eateries. The look is modern casual with big blue doors, brick arches and plain wooden tables and the food is imaginative and good looking. The word is out, though, so arrive promptly or expect to queue.

★ Manu Jara Dulcería
PASTRIES €

(Map p52; ☑675 873674; Calle Pureza 5; pastries €1.15-2.80; ☺10am-3pm daily & 6-9.30pm Mon-Fri, 4-9.30pm Sat) Tradition, history, flamenco – forget all that. The real reason to cross the river to Triana is to visit this exquisite patisserie and stock up on heavenly cakes. These mini-masterpieces are laid out in ceremonial splendour in the traditional wood and tiled interior, just demanding to be eaten. Try the creamy *milohajas* (millefeuille, aka vanilla slice) with chantilly cream.

Mercado Lonja del Barranco
INTERNATIONAL €

(Map p52; www.mercadodelbarranco.com; Calle Arjona; snacks from €2; ☺10am-midnight Sun-Thu, to 2am Fri & Sat) 🍴 A food court in a handsome glass-and-wrought-iron pavilion near the Isabel II bridge, with stalls serving everything from seafood salads and avocado wraps to tortillas, cakes and craft beer. Browse through, load up and then tuck in at one of the shared tables. Out back, you can enjoy cocktails and soothing riverside breezes.

Casa Cuesta
TAPAS €

(Map p52; ☑954 33 33 35; www.casacuesta.net; Calle de Castilla 1; tapas €3, medias raciones €7.50-10; ☺8am-12.30am Mon-Fri, 9am-12.30am Sat, 12.30pm-12.30am Sun) Plate-glass windows look out onto a crowded Triana plaza, mirrors artfully reflect bullfighting and flamenco memorabilia, and gleaming beer pumps furnish a wooden bar shielding bottles that look older than most of the clientele. In keeping with its looks, the food is traditional with a good selection of tapas, rice dishes, and meat and fish *raciones*.

Zoko
ANDALUCIAN €€

(Map p58; ☑954 96 31 49; www.facebook.com/zokosevilla; Calle Marqués de Paradas 55; tapas from €4.50; ☺1-4pm & 8pm-midnight) The fishing town of Zahara de los Atunes on the Cádiz coast is famed for its superb sustainably

Seeing Flamenco

The intensity and spontaneity of flamenco have never translated well onto studio recordings. Instead, to ignite the goosebumps and inspire the powerful emotional spirit known to aficionados as *duende*, you have to be there at a performance, stamping your feet and passionately yelling '*ióle!*'.

Peñas

Peñas are private local clubs run by enthusiasts determined to preserve flamenco in its traditional form. To find an appropriate *peña* ask in flamenco bars or tourist offices, check posters and use your ears to follow any interesting sounds you might hear in the street. Not surprisingly, *peñas* present some of the most authentic and passionate shows in Spain. They also incorporate flamenco's oft-overlooked fourth component, the *jaleo* (audience participation).

1. Peña La Platería (p274), Granada 2. Tablao El Arenal (p78), Seville 3. Flamenco dresses drying in the sun, Málaga (p162)

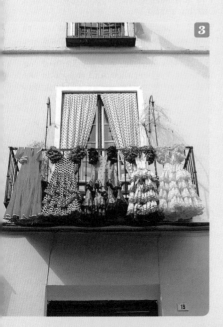

Tablaos

Tablaos are well-rehearsed flamenco shows that display the art in a highly professional and choreographed way. Unlike *peñas, tablao* shows are held in venues where drinks and sometimes dinner are included in the price of the ticket. While the artistic talent at these events is of a high standard, *tablaos* are sometimes derided by flamenco experts for lacking the spit and sawdust that makes the music so unique.

Cultural Centres

A few cultural centres in Andalucía's bigger cities offer a more authentic and intimate alternative to *tablaos*. Cultural centres are sometimes attached to museums and attract small, savvy audiences who shout encouraging '*olés*' from the sidelines, willing the show to a soulful climax. Food and drink are rarely available.

caught bluefin tuna *(atun de almadraba)* – this is the Seville outpost of one of its top restaurants, Zokarra. As well as the tenderest tuna, which comes in tacos, *tataki* and empanadas, the prawn satay has a bite unusual in spice-averse Spain.

Cinco Jotas TAPAS €€
(Map p58; ☎954 21 07 63; www.cincojotas.es; Calle Castelar 1; tapas €3-3.95, raciones €10-14; ☺8am-midnight Mon-Thu, to 1am Fri, noon-1am Sat & Sun) Cinco Jotas is one of Spain's best-known *jamón* producers, famous for its Ibérico ham from the small village of Jabugo in southern Andalucía. Not surprisingly, ham features heavily on the menu at this, its elegant Arenal bar-restaurant.

✕ South of the Centre

Restaurante Oriza BASQUE €€€
(Map p58; ☎954 22 72 54; www.restauranteoriza.com; Calle San Fernando 41; tapas €2.80-4.80, mains €24-46; ☺bar 1-5pm & 8pm-1am Mon-Thu, 1pm-1am Fri & Sat, restaurant 1.30-5.30pm & 8.30pm-1am Mon-Sat) The fabulous flavours of the Basque Country come to town at this upmarket eatery near the Parque de María Luisa. For the full-on à la carte experience, book at the restaurant; for a more casual meal, head to the in-house Bar España, which serves tapas and a €12.50 weekday lunch menu comprising starter, main course, dessert, coffee and drink.

✕ Alameda de Hércules & Around

Mercado de Feria MARKET €
(Lonja de Feria; Map p66; www.lonjadeferia.com; Plaza Calderón de la Barca; tapas €3, mains €8; ☺1pm-midnight Mon-Sat, to 6pm Sun) For a casual, great-value meal in atmospheric surrounds, head up to this Macarena market, said to be the oldest in Seville. Tapas and mountainous mains, mostly fresh seafood but not exclusively so, are dished out in a cool, white food hall set around a large central island. To order, buy a ticket then hand it in to one of the cheerful staff skilfully working the counters.

Dúo Tapas TAPAS €
(Map p66; ☎955 23 85 72; Calle Calatrava 10; tapas €3-4.50, medias raciones €8-12; ☺12.30-4.30pm & 8.30pm-midnight) Missed by the masses who rarely wander north from the Alameda de Hércules, Duo Tapas is a casual, 'new school' tapas bar. But what it lacks in *azulejo* (tiles) and illustrious past patrons, it makes up for

with inventive tapas with an Asian twist such as noodles with veggies and shrimp spring rolls.

★conTenedor ANDALUCIAN €€
(Map p66; ☎954 91 63 33; www.restaurantecontenedor.com; Calle San Luis 50; mains €9-21; ☺1.30-4pm & 8.30-11.30pm Mon-Thu, 1.30-4.30pm & 8.30pm-midnight Fri-Sun, closed Aug) This slow-food restaurant in the boho Macarena district prides itself on using local, organic produce. The atmosphere is arty and relaxed, with an open kitchen, mismatched furniture and colourful contemporary paintings by co-owner Ricardo. Try the duck rice, justly famous for its perfect taste and texture, or the venison *tataki* with chard, mushrooms and sweet potato.

★Bar-Restaurante Eslava FUSION, ANDALUCIAN €€
(Map p66; ☎954 90 65 68; www.espacioeslava.com; Calle Eslava 3; tapas €2.90-4.20, restaurant mains €15-22; ☺bar 1-4.30pm & 7.30-11.30pm Tue-Sat, 1.30-4.30pm Sun, restaurant 1.30-4pm & 9-11.30pm Tue-Sat, 1.30-4pm Sun) A hit with locals and savvy visitors, much-lauded Eslava shirks the traditional tilework and bullfighting posters of tapas-bar lore in favour of a simple blue space and a menu of creative contemporary dishes. Standouts include slow-cooked egg served on a mushroom cake, and memorable pork ribs in a honey and rosemary glaze. Expect crowds and a buzzing atmosphere.

Kök Tu Cocina BREAKFAST €€
(Map p66; ☎609 232598; www.koktucocina.com; San Luis 46; set menus €15-20, dishes €4-6.50; ☺10am-4pm Tue-Sun; ❄☑⊞) Centred on an open kitchen, this brunch spot in the Macarena buzzes. Set menus are beautifully presented, with homemade breads and jams, cheese, cold meat, eggs, fish, fresh fruit, yoghurt and muesli; vegan and vegetarian options are available. Vintage dial phones, food tins and weighing machines, coupled with red gingham tablecloths, lend a quirky, homely feel.

Arte y Sabor TAPAS €€
(Map p66; ☎954 37 28 97; www.arteysabor.es; Alameda de Hércules 85; tapas €2.90-4.50, raciones €7.50-14; ☺1pm-midnight; ☑) People-watching and eating go hand in hand at this casual eatery on the Alameda de Hércules. Grab a table – you'll need to come early – and go vegetarian with classic North African–inspired dishes such as tabouli and felafel or stick to traditional Spanish staples such as pork loin with *serrano* ham.

🍷 Drinking & Nightlife

Popular drinking areas include Calle Betis in Triana, Plaza de Salvador, Barrio de Santa Cruz, and the Alameda de Hércules, host to a lively scene and the city's gay nightlife. In summer, dozens of *terrazas de verano* (open-air bars) pop up on the river's banks.

Bars' evening hours vary but are typically from around 5pm to midnight or 2am on weekdays, or later on weekends. Drinking and partying generally get going late, around midnight on Friday and Saturday nights (daily when it's hot), upping the tempo as the night goes on.

★ El Viajero Sedentario   CAFE
(Map p66; ☎ 677 535512; www.elviajeroseden tario.jimdo.com; Alameda de Hércules 77; ☺ 9am-2pm & 6pm-2am) With its bright murals, shady courtyard and tiny book-stacked interior, this boho book cafe is a lovely place to hang out. From breakfast to the early hours people stop by, and it's not uncommon to find people dancing to low-key jazz tunes on sultry summer nights.

Rooftop Bar EME Catedral   ROOFTOP BAR
(Map p58; www.emecatedralhotel.com; Calle de los Alemanes 27; ☺ noon-1am Sun-Thu, to 2am Fri & Sat) Enjoy spectacular cathedral close-ups and classic cocktails (€14) at the chic roof terrace bar of the five-star EME Catedral Hotel (p69). To experience it at its most glamorous stop by on Friday or Saturday night when DJs spin tunes to the elegant crowd.

Maquila   MICROBREWERY
(Map p66; ☎ 955 18 23 20; www.maquilabar.com; Calle Delgado 4; ☺ 1-4.30pm & 8pm-midnight Tue-Sun) Craft beer is big in Seville, so why not try a microbrewery? The six different beers on tap here change monthly – three in-house Son beers, which might include fruity numbers made from pineapple and coconut, or blackberry, plus guest brews from the US and Europe. To accompany them there are decent tapas, including crunchy, smoky *patatas bravas* (roasted potatoes in a spicy tomato sauce).

Gallo Rojo   CAFE, BAR
(Map p66; ☎ 628 056489; http://gallorojo.es; Calle Madre Maria de Purisima 9; ☺ 5pm-midnight Tue-Thu & Sun, to 2am Fri & Sat) A bar, cafe, gallery, co-working space and cultural centre, Gallo Rojo is a lively yet laid-back spot near Calle Feria that has events every night, from concerts to poetry readings. Settle into a vintage leather sofa and try the house craft beers, Zurda golden ale and Pallaksch IPA; more

Sevillan brews are on offer, plus homemade cakes and empanadas.

El Garlochi   BAR
(Map p58; Calle Boteros 4; ☺ 9pm-3am) There surely can't be many weirder places to drink than this dark temple of kitsch. Decked out in ultracamp religious decor, it's dedicated entirely to the iconography, smells and sounds of the Semana Santa (Holy Week). To get into the mood, try its signature cocktail, a Sangre de Cristo (Blood of Christ), made from grenadine, pink champagne and whisky.

Corner House Roof Terrace Bar   ROOFTOP BAR
(Map p66; ☎ 954 91 32 62; www.thecornerhouse sevilla.com; Alameda de Hércules 31; ☺ 5.30pm-1am Wed-Sun winter, from 8.30pm summer) With its wooden decking, handmade tables and grandstand views over the vibrant, tree-lined plaza below, the laid-back rooftop terrace at the Corner House (p71) is a top spot to kick back and enjoy a cool evening drink.

☆ Entertainment

★ Casa de la Memoria   FLAMENCO
(Map p58; ☎ 954 56 06 70; www.casade lamemoria.es; Calle Cuna 6; adult/child €18/10; ☺ 10.30am-10.30pm, shows 6pm & 9pm) Housed in the old stables of the Palacio de la Condesa de Lebrija (p62), this cultural centre stages authentic, highly charged flamenco shows. On nightly, they are perennially popular and as space is limited, you'll need to reserve tickets a day or so in advance by calling or visiting the venue.

Naima Café Jazz   JAZZ
(Map p66; ☎ 653 753976; Calle Trajano 47; ☺ 8pm-3am) Popular, laid-back and mellow, this bar is an evergreen favourite for live jazz and blues, staged most nights. Drinks are reasonably priced and its tiny interior – you could easily find yourself squeezed in next to the drummer with a hi-hat crashing inches from your nose – ensures a humming vibe.

Teatro de la Maestranza   CONCERT VENUE
(Map p58; ☎ 954 22 33 44; www.teatrodelamaes tranza.es; Paseo de Cristóbal Colón 22; concerts €8-20, opera €46-125) Home to Seville's Royal Symphony Orchestra, this modern theatre, inaugurated in 1991, stages a rich program of classical music concerts, opera and ballet by top Spanish and international performers. Check the website for upcoming dates.

Casa de la Guitarra   FLAMENCO
(Map p58; ☎ 954 22 40 93; www.flamencoen sevilla.com; Calle Mesón del Moro 12; adult/child €17/10; ☺ shows 7.30pm & 9pm) This is a tiny

flamenco-only venue in Santa Cruz (no food or drinks served). Its two evening shows are intimate affairs with three on-stage performers and the audience squeezed into a small seating area flanked by display cases full of guitars. To guarantee a place, it's best to book ahead.

La Casa del Flamenco
FLAMENCO

(Map p58; ☑954 50 05 95; www.lacasadelflamencosevilla.com; Calle Ximénez de Enciso 28; adult/child €18/10; ⊙ shows 7pm autumn & winter, 8.30pm spring & summer) This beautiful patio in an old Sephardic Jewish mansion in Santa Cruz is home to La Casa del Flamenco. Shows, performed on a stage hemmed in by seating on three sides, are mesmerising.

Casa Anselma
FLAMENCO

(Map p52; ☑606 162502; Calle Pagés del Corro 49; ⊙11.45pm-late Mon-Sat) True, the music is often more folkloric than flamenco, but this characterful Triana spot is the antithesis of a touristy flamenco *tablao* (choreographed show), with cheek-to-jowl crowds, zero amplification and spontaneous outbreaks of dancing. Beware: there's no sign of life until the doors open at around 11.45pm.

Fun Club
LIVE MUSIC

(Map p66; ☑636 669023; www.funclubsevilla.com; Alameda de Hércules 86; €5-12; ⊙midnight-late Thu-Sat, from 9.30pm concert nights) Positively ancient by nightlife standards, the iconic Fun Club has been entertaining the nocturnal Alameda de Hércules crowd since the late 1980s. It still packs them in, hosting club nights and regular gigs – indie, rock, hip-hop.

Tablao El Arenal
FLAMENCO

(Map p58; ☑954 21 64 92; www.tablaoelarenal.com; Calle Rodo 7; show with drink/tapas/dinner €58/60/72; ⊙shows 7.30pm & 9.30pm) Of all the venues offering flamenco 'dinner shows', this is one of the best. With a seating capacity of 100 in an old-school tavern, it lacks the grit and – invariably – *duende* (flamenco spirit) of the *peñas* (small flamenco clubs), although you can't fault the skill of the performers. Skip the food, though.

🛍 Shopping

Seville's main shopping district is centred on Calles Sierpes, Velázquez/Tetuán and Cuna, north of Plaza Nueva. For a more alternative choice of shops, head for 'Soho Benita', the area around Calle Pérez Galdós and Calle

Regina; also Calles Amor de Dios near the Alameda de Hércules.

Over the river, Triana is the place to shop for ceramic ware.

Cerámica Triana
CERAMICS

(Map p52; ☑954 33 21 79; Calle San Jorge 31; ⊙10am-9pm Mon-Fri, to 8pm Sat, 11am-6pm Sun) Seville specialises in distinctive *azulejos* (ceramic tiles) and they are best seen in the Triana neighbourhood, the historic hub of the city's ceramic industry. Cerámica Triana (previously called Cerámica Santa Ana) has been around for more than 50 years and its tiled shopfront is famous locally. Inside, you can browse shelves laden with decorative crockery, tiles, signs, crucifixes and figurines.

Caotica
BOOKS

(Map p58; ☑955 54 19 66; www.facebook.com/espaciocaotica; Calle José Gestoso 8; ⊙10am-2pm & 5-9pm Mon-Sat) Downstairs in this multilevel bookstore you can have a coffee, fresh juice, or healthy breakfast of yoghurt with muesli and fruit; upstairs are endless shelves of tomes, from literary and popular novels, to comics, travel, art and architecture titles. The children's section has a gallery above a wooden tree, so they're up in their own world. Also quirky gifts.

Tarico
FOOD & DRINKS

(Map p66; ☑954 02 68 03; www.facebook.com/TiendaTarico; Calle Amor de Dios 14; ⊙10am-2.30pm & 6.30-10pm) A pleasant, light-filled space near the Alameda, packed with (mostly) Andalucian) craft beer, wine, cheese, olive oil, cold meats, pâté, honey and other foods made by small producers. Look out for goat's milk cheese from Huelva; award-winning Supremo extra-virgin olive oil from Jaén; and a kit for cooking rice with goose, complete with meat preserve and stock.

Un Gato en Bicicleta
BOOKS

(Map p58; ☑955 29 56 51; www.facebook.com/ungatoenbicicleta; Calle Pérez Galdós 22; ⊙9am-9pm Tue-Sun, 4.30-9pm Mon) Relocated from hip Calle Regina to its fellow creative patch Soho Benita, this all-day bookshop/gallery/cafe/ceramics studio is a hub for Seville's artistic community. Look out for painter Agustín Israel's irreverent takes on *nazarenos*, the hooded Holy Week penitents, while tomes cover cinema, fashion and architecture. Ceramics classes take place most afternoons; the cafe serves breakfast and cakes.

Padilla Crespo
ACCESSORIES, CLOTHING

(Map p58; ☑ 954 21 29 88; Calle de Adriano 18B; ⊙ 10am-9pm) If you're in the market for a wide-brimmed hat and beautiful leather bag – all the rage during the Feria de Abril – this long-standing Arenal shop is the place for you. Specialising in traditional wardrobe staples, it also stocks fans, espadrilles and classic Panama hats.

Libelula Shop
CLOTHING

(Map p58; ☑ 954 22 28 19; www.libelulashop. com; Calle Cuna 45-49; ⊙ 10am-9pm Mon-Sat) A large fashion emporium spread over two floors and several houses, Libelula offers clothing and accessories for men, women and children. From kids pyjamas to fringed manta shawls, fine knits to sparkly tops, over 20 different designers cover all styles and tastes. The layout makes it inviting to browse, with rails suspended by ropes, and traditional light-filled courtyards.

Record Sevilla
MUSIC

(Map p66; ☑ 954 38 77 02; Calle Amor de Dios 17A; ⊙ 10am-2pm & 5-9pm Sun-Fri, 5-9pm Sat) Fancy mixing flamenco with house? Then grab your vinyl at this music shop full of new and used records – covering everything from folk to indie and hard rock – CDs, DVDs, posters and T-shirts. Staff are knowledgeable about the local music scene.

ℹ Information

Airport Tourist Office (☑ 954 78 20 35; www. andalucia.org; Seville Airport; ⊙ 9am-7.30pm Mon-Fri, 9.30am-3pm Sat & Sun)

Centro de Salud El Porvenir (☑ 954 71 23 23; Calle Porvenir; ⊙ 8am-3pm Mon-Fri) Public clinic with emergency services.

Hospital Virgen del Rocío (☑ 955 01 20 00; www.huvr.es; Avenida de Manuel Siurot) Seville's main hospital, 1km south of Parque de María Luisa.

Tourist Office (Map p58; ☑ 954 21 00 05; www.turismosevilla.org; Plaza del Triunfo 1; ⊙ 9am-7.30pm Mon-Fri, 9.30am-7.30pm Sat & Sun)

Train Station Tourist Office (☑ 954 78 20 02; www.andalucia.org; Estación Santa Justa; ⊙ 9am-7.30pm)

There are also private City Expert offices providing information and booking services in the **centre** (Map p58; ☑ 673 289848; www. cityexpert.es; Avenida de la Constitución 21B; ⊙ 9.30am-8pm) and at the **train station** (www. cityexpert.es; Estación Santa Justa; ⊙ 9.30am-6pm Mon-Sat, to 2.30pm Sun).

ℹ Getting There & Away

AIR

Seville Airport (Aeropuerto de Sevilla; ☑ 902 404704; www.aena.es; A4, Km 532), 7km east of the city, has flights to/from Spanish cities and destinations across Europe including London, Paris, Amsterdam, Dublin, Frankfurt and Rome.

It's served by international airlines such as Ryanair, EasyJet and Vueling airlines.

BUS

Estación de Autobuses Plaza de Armas (Map p52; ☑ 955 03 86 65; www.autobuses plazadearmas.es; Avenida del Cristo de la Expiración) Seville's main bus station. From here, **ALSA** (☑ 902 422242; www.alsa.es) buses serve Málaga (€18.50 to €23.50, 2¾ hours, seven daily), Granada (€23 to €29, three hours, eight daily), Córdoba (€12, two hours, seven daily) and Almería (€37 to €45, 5½ to 8½ hours, three daily). **Damas** (☑ 902 114492; www.damas-sa.es) runs buses to Huelva province and **Eurolines** (☑ 902 405040; www. eurolines.es) has international services to Germany, Belgium, France and beyond.

Estación de Autobuses Prado de San Sebastián (Map p58; Plaza San Sebastián) has services to smaller towns in western Andalucía. Operators include **Los Amarillos** (Map p58; ☑ 902 210317; http://losamarillos.autobusing. com), which serves towns in the provinces of Sevilla, Cádiz and parts of Málaga, and **Comes** (Map p58; ☑ 956 29 11 68; www.tgcomes.es), which runs to various regional destinations including Cádiz and some of the harder-to-reach *pueblos blancos* (white towns) in Cádiz province.

TRAIN

Seville's principal train station, **Estación Santa Justa** (Avenida Kansas City), is 1.5km northeast of the centre.

High-speed AVE trains go to/from Madrid (€60, 2½ to 3¼ hours, 14 daily) and Córdoba (from €21, 45 minutes to 1¼ hours, 25 daily). Slower trains head to Cádiz (€16 to €23, 1¾ hours, 13 daily), Huelva (€12, 1½ hours, four daily), Granada (€30, 3½ hours, four daily) and Málaga (€24 to €44, two to 2½ hours, 10 daily).

ℹ Getting Around

TO/FROM THE AIRPORT

The **EA Bus** (☑ 955 010010; www.tussam.es; one way/return €4/6) connects the airport to the city centre, running to/from Plaza de Armas bus station via Santa Justa train station, Prado de San Sebastián bus station and the Torre del Oro.

Departures from the airport are every 20 to 30 minutes between 5.20am and 12.45am; from

Plaza Armas between 4.30am and midnight. Note that services are reduced slightly on Sundays, very early in the morning and late in the evening.

Taxis charge set fares: €22 (daytime Monday to Friday); €25 (weekends and night-time Monday to Friday); €31 (night-time Easter and the Feria de Abril). On top of this, there's a €0.49 surcharge for each bag over 10kg.

BUS

Seville's buses are operated by **Tussam** (☎ 955 01 00 10; www.tussam.es).

Buses run from around 6am to 11.30pm. Night buses (buses A1 to A8 and N29) operate out of Prado de San Sebastián (p79) between midnight and 2am from Sunday to Thursday and until 5am on Friday and Saturday.

Useful routes include the following circular lines:

C1 and C2 External route around the centre.
C3 and C4 Internal route around the centre.
C5 Runs through the centre.

Tickets can be bought on buses, at stations and at kiosks next to stops. A standard ticket is €1.40 but a range of passes are also available, including 1/3 day passes for €5/10.

CAR & MOTORCYCLE

Traffic restrictions are in force and the small streets of Seville's historic centre are not car friendly. Parking can be hard to find.

For car hire, there's **Avis** (☎ 902 110283; www.avis.com; Estación Santa Justa; ◷ 8am-midnight) or **Enterprise** (☎ 954 41 26 40; www.enterprise.es; ◷ 7.30am-11pm) at Santa Justa train station, and all the normal brands at the airport.

METRO

Seville's single metro line, run by the **Metro de Sevilla** (☎ 900 92 71 72; www.metro-sevilla.es), connects Ciudad Expo with Olivar de Quinto. It's not that useful for visitors.

A single ticket costs €1.35 to €1.80 depending on how far you go. A one-day travel card costs €4.50.

TAXI

Taxis are common and a journey across the city centre during daylight hours will cost around €8.

TRAM

Operated by Tussam, Seville's tram service has a single line. T1 runs between Plaza Nueva and San Bernado via Avenida de la Constitución, Puerta de Jerez and San Sebastián.

The standard ticket is €1.40 but a range of passes is available if you're likely to use it a lot.

AROUND SEVILLE

Santiponce

POP 8440

Some 9km northwest of Seville, the small town of Santiponce is home to Andalucía's most thrilling Roman site, Itálica, as well as a grand Gothic-Mudéjar monastery. Just off the A66 and well served by buses from Seville, it makes for a fantastic day trip.

★ Itálica   ROMAN SITE

(☎ 600 141767; www.museosdeandalucia.es; Avenida de Extremadura 2; EU/non-EU citizens free/€1.50; ◷ 9am-9pm Tue-Sat, 8am-3pm Sun Apr-Jun, reduced hours Jul-Mar; P) The evocative Roman ruins of ancient Itálica are impressive and wonderfully maintained. Broad paved streets lead to the remains of houses set around beautiful mosaic-laid patios and, best of all, a stunning 20,000-seat amphitheatre, one of the largest ever built. Itálica, founded in 206 BC and later the birthplace of emperors Trajan and Hadrian (he who built the wall across northern England), enjoyed a golden age in the 2nd century AD, when many of its finest buildings were constructed. Highlights include the Casa de los Pájaros (House of the Birds), the Edificio del Mosaico de Neptuno (Building of the Neptune Mosaic), and the Casa del Planetario (House of the Planetarium), with a mosaic depicting the gods of the seven days of the week.

Monasterio de San Isidoro del Campo   MONASTERY

(☎ 955 962 44 00; Avenida de San Isidoro del Campo 18; ◷ 10am-3pm Tue-Thu, to 7pm Fri & Sat, to 2.30pm Sun Sep-Jun, 10am-3pm Tue-Sat, to 2.30pm Sun Jul & Aug; P) FREE At the southern end of Santiponce, this fortified former monastery was founded in 1301 by Guzmán El Bueno (hero of the 1294 battle at Tarifa). Over the centuries it has hosted a succession of religious orders, including the hermetic Hieronymite monks, who embellished the Patio de Evangelistas with some striking 15th-century murals and Mudéjar-style floral and geometric patterns. The monastery also enjoys celebrity as the place where the Bible was first translated into Castilian (in 1569).

Among the monastery's impressive Spanish art collection is a wonderful altarpiece by 17th-century Sevillan sculptor Juan Martínez Montañés.

ℹ️ Getting There & Away

From Seville's Plaza de Armas bus station, bus M172 runs to Santiponce (€1.55, 25 minutes, at least half-hourly), making its final stop at the entrance to the archaeological site.

LA CAMPIÑA

Carmona

POP 28,600

Rising above a sea of golden, sun-baked plains 35km east of Seville, Carmona is a delight. Its hilltop old town sparkles with noble palaces, majestic Mudéjar churches and two Moorish forts; nearby, a haunting Roman necropolis recalls its ancient past.

The strategically sited town flourished under the Romans, who laid out a street plan that survives to this day: Via Augusta, running from Rome to Cádiz, entered Carmona by the eastern Puerta de Córdoba and left by the western Puerta de Sevilla. The Muslims subsequently built a strong defensive wall but in 1247 the town fell to Fernando III. Later, Mudéjar and Christian artisans constructed grand churches, convents and mansions.

◉ Sights

Most of Carmona's sights are in the walled old town, accessible on foot through the Puerta de Sevilla.

★**Necrópolis Romana**   ROMAN SITE
(Roman cemetery; ☎ 600 143632; www.museos deandalucia.es; Avenida de Jorge Bonsor 9; EU/ non-EU citizens free/€1; ☺ 9am-6pm Tue-Sat, to 3pm Sun Apr–mid-Jun, reduced hours mid-Jun–Mar) This ancient Roman necropolis, on the southwestern edge of town, is considered one of the most important of its kind in Andalucía. Hundreds of tombs, some elaborate and many-chambered, were hewn into the rock in the 1st and 2nd centuries AD. Most of the inhabitants were cremated: in the tombs are wall niches for the box-like stone urns. You can enter the huge Tumba de Servilia, the tomb of a family of Hispano-Roman VIPs, and climb down into several others.

The site also features an interesting museum displaying objects found in the tombs. Across the street is the 1st-century-BC Anfiteatro Romano.

Alcázar de la Puerta de Sevilla   FORTRESS
(Plaza de Blas Infante; adult/child €2/1, free Mon; ☺ 9am-3pm Mon-Fri, 10am-3pm Sat & Sun sum-mer, reduced hours winter) Carmona's signature fortress is a formidable sight. Set atop the Puerta de Sevilla, the imposing main gate of the old town, it had already been standing for five centuries when the Romans reinforced it and built a temple on top. The Muslim Almohads added an *aljibe* (cistern) to the upper patio, which remains a hawk-like perch from which to admire the typically Andalucian tableau of white cubes and soaring spires.

Prioral de Santa María de la Asunción   CHURCH
(☎ 954 19 14 82; Plaza Marqués de las Torres; €3; ☺ 9.30am-2pm & 6.30-8pm Tue-Fri, 7-8.30pm Sat, 10am-noon & 7-8.30pm Sun summer, reduced hours winter) This splendid church was built mainly in the 15th and 16th centuries on the site of Carmona's former mosque. The Patio de los Naranjos, through which you enter, has a Visigothic calendar carved into one of its pillars. The interior, capped by high Gothic vaults, is centred on an altar detailed to an almost perverse degree with 20 panels of biblical scenes framed by gilt-scrolled columns.

Museo de la Ciudad   MUSEUM
(☎ 954 14 01 28; www.museociudad.carmona. org; Calle San Ildefonso 1; adult/child €2.50/1.20, free Tue; ☺ 10am-2pm & 6.30-8.30pm Mon-Fri, 9.30am-2pm Sat & Sun summer, reduced hours winter) Explore the town's fascinating history at the city museum, housed in an aristocratic 16th-century palace. The sections on the Tartessians and their Roman successors are highlights: the former includes a unique collection of large earthenware vessels with Middle Eastern decorative motifs, the latter several excellent mosaics.

Convento de Santa Clara   CONVENT
(☎ 954 14 21 02; www.clarisasdecarmona.word press.com; Calle Torno de Santa Clara; adult/child €2/1; ☺ 11am-2pm & 5-7pm Thu-Mon summer, reduced hours winter) With its Gothic ribbed vaulting, carved Mudéjar-style ceiling and dazzling altarpiece – a shining example of Sevillan baroque – the Santa Clara convent appeals to both art and architecture buffs. Visits start with a spiral ascent of the tower, an 18th-century addition. Don't miss the pretty, arch-lined cloister out back.

Iglesia de San Pedro   CHURCH
(☎ 954 14 12 70; www.sanpedrocarmona.es; Calle San Pedro; €1; ☺ 9.30am-3pm Sun & Mon) West of Puerta de Sevilla, the 15th-century Iglesia de San Pedro has a rich baroque interior and a tower modelled on Seville's Giralda (p50).

Alcázar del Rey Don Pedro
RUINS

(Calle Extramuros de Santiago) The stark, ruined Alcázar on the southeastern edge of Carmona was an Almohad fort that Pedro I turned into a country palace in the 13th century. It was brought down by earthquakes in 1504 and 1755 and its ruins now provide a memorable backdrop to the luxurious Parador de Carmona hotel, which occupies a building next door.

Ayuntamiento
HISTORIC BUILDING

(☑954 14 00 11; Calle El Salvador; ⊙8am-3pm Mon-Fri) **FREE** Carmona's 17th-century town hall, originally a Jesuit convent, contains an impressive Roman mosaic depicting the head of the gorgon Medusa surrounded by figures representing the four seasons. Visible in the central courtyard, it was unearthed in the historic centre.

🛏 Sleeping

Hostal Comercio
HOSTAL €

(☑954 14 00 18; hostalcomercio@hotmail.com; Calle Torre del Oro 56; s €35, d €40-50, tr €70, q €90; ❄️🖥) A warm welcome awaits at this long-standing, family-run *hostal* just inside the Puerta de Sevilla. Its 14 rooms, set around a plant-filled patio with Mudéjar-style arches, are modest and simply furnished with brick floors and heavy wood furniture.

⭐ El Rincón de las Descalzas
BOUTIQUE HOTEL €€

(☑954 19 11 72; www.elrincondelasdescalzas.com; Calle de las Descalzas 1; incl breakfast s €52-62, d €64-112, ste €134-175; ❄️🖥) Elegantly sited in a revamped 18th-century townhouse, this rambling hotel offers 13 colourful rooms and a picturesque patio. Each room is different, and some are better than others, but all sport a refined period look with carved-wood beds, exposed brick and sandstone, timber arches and the occasional fireplace.

Posada San Fernando
BOUTIQUE HOTEL €€

(☑954 14 14 08, 666 907788; www.posadasan fernando.es; Plaza de San Fernando 6; s/d/tr €55/65/100; ❄️🖥) This excellent-value hotel enjoys a prime location on Carmona's main square. It's a cosy affair with characterful and tastefully designed rooms ensconced in a 16th-century building. Expect antique furnishings, hand-painted bathroom tiles and, in some rooms, balconies overlooking the palm-lined plaza.

Parador de Carmona
HISTORIC HOTEL €€€

(☑954 14 10 10; www.parador.es/en/paradores/parador-de-carmona; Alcázar del Rey Don Pedro, Calle Extramuros de Santiago; s €100-210, d €130-240; 🅿️❄️@🖥🏊) With jaw-dropping views of the surrounding valley, Carmona's luxurious *parador* (top-end state-owned hotel) occupies the 13th-century Alcázar del Rey Don Pedro. Most of its smart, terracotta-floored rooms overlook the plains, as does its divine terrace, where you can stop by for a coffee or cocktail. There's also a dining room serving high-end Andalucian fare.

🍴 Eating

Mingalario
ANDALUCIAN €€

(☑954 14 38 93; Calle El Salvador; tapas €2-4.50, raciones €6-18; ⊙1-4pm & 7.30pm-midnight Wed-Mon) This small restaurant with hams hanging from the rafters, kitschy religious paintings and upturned barrels to eat off is the very picture of an old-school tapas bar. Dishes are listed on blackboards and include many regional favourites, such as *solomillo al whisky* (steak served in a whisky sauce), *presa ibérica* (Iberian pork) and spinach with chickpeas (a Carmona speciality).

Molino de la Romera
ANDALUCIAN €€

(☑954 14 20 00; www.molinodelaromera.es; Calle Sor Ángela de la Cruz 8; tapas €2.50-4, mains €11-20; ⊙1-4pm & 8.30pm-midnight Mon-Sat) Housed in a cosy, 15th-century olive-oil mill with a terrace and wonderful views across the *vega* (valley), this popular restaurant serves hearty, well-prepped meals with a splash of contemporary flair. For a taste of traditional Carmona cuisine, there's *alboronías* (a kind of ratatouille); for something more international try the fig and *burrata* salad.

Cervecería San Fernando
ANDALUCIAN €€

(☑661 654960; Plaza de San Fernando 18; tapas €2.50, mains €10-17; ⊙noon-5pm & 8pm-midnight Tue-Sun) With ringside seating on Carmona's vibrant central square, friendly service and fine food, Cervecería San Fernando hits all the right notes. The menu, which lists tapas and *raciones*, covers multiple bases, with everything from fried fish to scrambled eggs and steaks. Particularly good is the artichoke capped by *jamón* and a sweet-wine reduction.

Casa Curro Montoya
SPANISH €€

(☑657 903629; Calle Santa María de Gracia 13; tapas €1.50-6, raciones €8.50-17; ⊙1.15-5pm & 8.15pm-midnight) This friendly, family-run eatery near the Convento de Santa Clara occupies a narrow, high-ceilinged hall full of memorabilia, topped by a formal dining room. A low-key jazz soundtrack sets the mood for the likes of smoked-tuna tapas and

Carmona

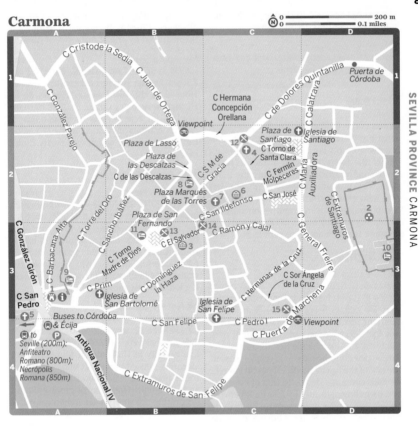

raciones of *morcilla* (black pudding) with rice and raisins.

ℹ️ Information

Tourist Office (☎954 19 09 55; www.turismo.carmona.org; Alcázar de la Puerta de Sevilla; ⊗9am-3pm Mon-Fri, 10am-3pm Sat & Sun)

ℹ️ Getting There & Around

BICYCLE

To explore the surrounding countryside, consider hiring a bike at **Carmona Bike Tours** (www.carmonabiketours.com; Calle Mimosa 15; bicycle hire per day €12; ⊗9.30am-2pm Mon-Sat & 5.30-8.30pm Mon-Fri).

BUS

Casal (☎954 99 92 90; www.autocarescasal.com) runs buses to Seville (€2.80, one hour, at least seven daily) from the stop on Paseo del Estatuto. **ALSA** (☎902 42 22 42; www.alsa.es) has three daily buses to Córdoba (€9.70,

Carmona

◎ Sights

1 Alcázar de la Puerta de Sevilla	A3
2 Alcázar del Rey Don Pedro	D2
3 Ayuntamiento	B3
4 Convento de Santa Clara	C2
5 Iglesia de San Pedro	A3
6 Museo de la Ciudad	C2
7 Prioral de Santa María de la Asunción	C2

🛏 Sleeping

8 El Rincón de las Descalzas	B2
9 Hostal Comercio	A3
10 Parador de Carmona	D3
11 Posada San Fernando	B3

🍴 Eating

12 Casa Curro Montoya	C2
13 Cervecería San Fernando	B3
14 Mingalario	B3
15 Molino de la Romera	C3

1½ hours) via Écija (€4.70, 35 minutes) leaving from a stop near the Puerta de Sevilla.

CAR & MOTORCYCLE
There's 24-hour underground parking on Paseo del Estatuto (€13 per 24 hours).

Osuna

POP 17,740

Osuna is the unlikely setting for a cache of artistic and architectural treasures. Set in an otherwise empty landscape of vast, billowing plains, the town boasts an attractive white centre and a series of grand baroque mansions. Capping everything is a mighty, art-rich Renaissance church. Most of the town's notable buildings were commissioned by the fabulously wealthy dukes of Osuna and built between the 16th and 18th centuries.

◉ Sights

★**Colegiata de Santa María de la Asunción**   CHURCH
(☑954 81 04 44; Plaza de la Encarnación; guided tours €4; ◷tours hourly 9.30am-1.15pm Tue-Sun plus 7pm & 9pm Thu summer, hourly 10.15am-1.15pm plus 4pm & 5pm Tue-Sun winter) Lording it over the town, this formidable Renaissance structure – two churches above a crypt – sits on the site of the town's medieval parish church. Its halls contain a rich collection of baroque art, including paintings by José de Ribera (El Españoleto) and a fine sculpture by Juan de Mesa. Visits are by Spanish-language guided tours, which take in the grand underground sepulchre, created in 1548 as the family vault for the Dukes of Osuna.

Monasterio de la Encarnación   MUSEUM
(Plaza de la Encarnación; €3; ◷9.30am-2.30pm Tue-Sun & 7-9pm Thu summer, reduced hours winter) This former monastery is now Osuna's museum of religious art. Its church boasts baroque sculpture and art, while the cloister features some wonderful 18th-century Sevillan tilework depicting various biblical,

hunting, bullfighting, monastic and seasonal scenes. Entry is by guided tour only (in Spanish), led by one of the resident nuns.

Museo de Osuna   MUSEUM
(☑954 81 57 32; Calle Sevilla 37; €2; ◷9.30am-2.30pm Tue-Sun summer, reduced hours winter) Housed in the 18th-century Palacio de los Hermanos Arjona y Cubas, Osuna's museum displays an eclectic mix of local relics, as well as exhibits dedicated to the TV show *Game of Thrones*, which was partly filmed in Osuna.

🛏 Sleeping

Five Gates Hostal   HOSTAL €
(☑626 620717, 955 82 08 77; www.fivegates.es; Calle Carrera 79; s €30-35, d €50-55; ✳🖲) A friendly, modern *hostal* on the main strip through Osuna's historic centre. It has 14 comfortable, uncluttered rooms decorated in tasteful, low-key style, with colourful walls and blond-wood floors. There's also a big lounge with games and DVDs.

★**Hotel Palacio Marqués de la Gomera**   HISTORIC HOTEL €€
(☑954 81 26 32; www.hotelpalaciodelmarques.es; Calle San Pedro 20; s €72.50, d €85; ✳🖲) Live like nobility at this palatial four-star hotel, elegantly housed in one of Osuna's finest baroque mansions. Tiled floors and sandstone arches remain from the original building, decorating the sumptuous arched courtyard and spacious, individually styled rooms. There's even an ornate private chapel, as well as a smart restaurant and peaceful back patio. Rates include breakfast.

🍽 Eating

Confitería Santo Domingo   PASTRIES €
(☑954 81 03 72; Calle Carrera 63; pastries from €1; ◷10am-10pm Wed-Mon) A historic address on Osuna's main throughfare, this centuries-old *pastelería* – it opened its doors in 1750 – is where locals come for their Sunday treats. Speciality of the house is its *aldeanas:*

GAME OF THRONES IN OSUNA

In late 2014 Osuna sprang into the spotlight as an unlikely filming location for the fifth season of hit TV show *Game of Thrones* (*Juego de Tronos* in Spanish). Osuna's 100-year-old bullring, the **Plaza de Toros** (Calle Lantejuela; €2; ◷10am-2pm Sat & Sun & 7-9pm Thu summer, 10am-2pm & 4-7pm Sat & Sun winter), starred as the Great Pit of Daznak, the fighting pit of Meereen, and around 600 *osunense* extras jumped in as battling slaves and spectating nobles. Photos of cast members, who stayed at the Hotel Palacio Marqués de la Gomera and ate at Casa Curro , are a feature of local decor, whilst the Museo de Osuna has a permanent exhibition dedicated to the series.

DON'T MISS

OSUNA'S BAROQUE MANSIONS

Lined with pristine white buildings, the streets west of Calle Carrera, Osuna's central spine, are sprinkled with aristocratic mansions and florid baroque facades. Many are strung along two roads: Calle Sevilla, which leads west off central Plaza Mayor, and Calle San Pedro, a few blocks to the north. As a rule, the buildings are closed to the public, but even viewed from outside they are a mesmerising sight.

One of the most impressive mansions is the late 18th-century **Palacio de los Cepeda** (Calle de la Huerta 10; ⊘ closed to the public). Now Osuna's courthouse, it boasts rows of churrigueresque columns topped by stone halberdiers holding the Cepeda family coat of arms. Other standouts include the 18th-century **Palacio de Govantes y Herdara** (Calle Sevilla 44; ⊘ closed to the public), characterised by twisted pillars encrusted with grapes and vine leaves, and the 1773 **Cilla del Cabildo Colegial** (Calle San Pedro 16; ⊘ closed to the public), whose flamboyant facade features a sculpted version of Seville's famous bell tower, the Giralda (p50). A short walk away, **Palacio del Marqués de la Gomera** (Calle San Pedro 20) features elaborate pillars on its facade, with the family shield at the top; it's now a hotel.

Twinkie-like pastries filled with a vanilla custard-cream.

Casa Curro TAPAS €€
(☑ 955 82 07 58; www.facebook.com/restaurante casacurro; Plazuela Salitre 5; tapas €3, mains €9-15; ⊘ noon-4pm & 8pm-midnight Tue-Sun) For an authentic dining experience join locals at this vivacious bar-restaurant, one of Osuna's most popular. It looks the part with its long polished bar, cluttered walls and blackboard menus, and the tapas (and *raciones*) are reliably good: pork cheeks cooked in rich Pedro Jimenez wine, tuna with peppers and lemon, Iberian 'secret' (sliced pork) in a quince sauce.

Restaurante Doña Guadalupe ANDALUCIAN €€
(☑ 954 81 05 58; Plaza Guadalupe 6-8; mains €11-21; ⊘ noon-5pm & 7pm-midnight Mon-Fri) Discreetly tucked away in a white porticoed courtyard between Calles Quijada and Gordillo, this starched, formal restaurant serves up quality Andalucian cooking accompanied by premium Spanish wines.

ℹ Information

Oficina Municipal de Turismo (☑ 954 81 57 32; www.osuna.es; Calle Sevilla 37; ⊘ 9.30am-2.30pm Tue-Sun summer, reduced hours Tue-Sat winter) Helpful office in the Museo de Osuna.

ℹ Getting There & Away

Osuna is 91km southeast of Seville, off the Granada–Seville A92.

The **bus station** (Avenida de la Constitución) is 1km southeast of Plaza Mayor. **Autocares Valenzuela** (☑ 954 98 82 22; www.grupovalen

zuela.com) runs at least seven daily buses (four on Sunday) to/from Seville (€8.05, 1½ hours).

By train, **Renfe** (☑ 912 32 03 20; www.renfe. com) services run to/from Seville (€11.10, 70 minutes, 10 daily) and Málaga (€13.55, 1½ hours, five daily) from the **train station** (Avenida de la Estación), 1km west of Plaza Mayor.

Écija

POP 40.270

Écija, the least known of the Campiña towns, is something of an underrated star. Many travellers overlook it, perhaps put off by its reputation as *la sartén de Andalucía* (the frying pan of Andalucía) – in July and August temperatures can reach a suffocating 45°C. But avoid high summer and you'll find it a fascinating town rich in architectural and historic interest.

Its compact centre is riddled with Gothic-Mudéjar palaces, churches and baroque towers – hence a second nickname, *la ciudad de las torres* (the city of towers) – while Roman ruins tell of its past as a wealthy Iberian centre. Then known as Colonia Augusta Firma Astigi, it flourished in the 1st and 2nd centuries supplying olive oil to markets across the Roman Empire.

◉ Sights

Écija's compact old town centres on cafe-lined Plaza de España, otherwise known as El Salón (the parlour).

★ **Museo Histórico Municipal** MUSEUM
(☑ 954 83 04 31; http://museo.ecija.es; Plaza de la Constitución 1; ⊘ 10am-1.30pm & 4.30-6.30pm Tue-Fri, 10am-2pm & 5.30-8pm Sat, 10am-3pm Sun)

DON'T MISS

ÉCIJA'S CHURCHES & BELL TOWERS

Nicknamed *la ciudad de las torres* (the city of towers) Écija is famous for its spire-studded skyline. A series of baroque towers rises above the town's rooftops, most dating to the late 18th century, when many churches were rebuilt following a devastating earthquake in 1755. One of the town's finest towers belongs to the **Iglesia de Santa María** (Plaza de Santa María; ⊙ 9.30am-1.30pm & 5.30-8.30pm Mon-Fri, 9.30am-1.30pm & 5-30-7.45pm Sat, 10am-1pm Sun), an 18th-century church just off Plaza de España. A few blocks to the northeast, the striking baroque belfry of the **Iglesia de San Juan** (Plaza de San Juan; tower €2; ⊙ 10.30am-1.30pm & 4.30-7.30pm Tue-Sat, 10.30am-1.30pm Sun) is the only tower in town you can actually climb. Nearby, the Gothic-Mudéjar **Iglesia de San Pablo y Santo Domingo** (Plaza de Santo Domingo; ⊙ 6.30-7.30pm Tue-Fri, 7-8pm Sat, 11.30am-12.30pm & 7-8pm Sun) features an 18th-century brick tower.

Fronting a pretty plaza in the north of the old town, the **Parroquia Mayor de Santa Cruz** (Plazuela de Nuestra Señora del Valle; €1; ⊙ 9am-1pm & 5-9pm Mon-Sat, 9am-1pm & 6-10pm Sun summer, 10am-1pm & 4-8pm Mon-Sat, 10am-1pm & 6-8pm Sun winter) was once Écija's principal mosque and still has traces of Islamic features and some Arabic inscriptions. Beyond the roofless atrium, which retains a series of impressive Gothic arches from the original 13th-century church, the interior is crammed with sacred paraphernalia and baroque silverwork.

FREE Écija's history museum, housed in the 18th-century **Palacio de Benamejí**, is an authentic gem. It has rooms dedicated to the area's prehistory and protohistory, but its chief drawcard is its fabulous collection of local Roman finds. These include a graceful sculpture of a wounded Amazon (a legendary female warrior) and a series of stunningly preserved mosaics, mostly unearthed in and around the town. A particular highlight is the *Mosaico del Triunfo de Baco* depicting the 'birth' of wine.

Palacio de Peñaflor   PALACE
(Calle Emilio Castelar 26) The huge, 18th-century 'Palace of the Long Balconies', 300m east of Plaza de España, is Écija's most iconic image. The palace's interior is off limits, but you can still admire its curved facade complete with ornate, columned portal, wrought-iron balconies and traces of flamboyant frescoes.

🛏 Sleeping & Eating

**Hotel Palacio de
los Granados**   HISTORIC HOTEL €€
(☑ 955 90 53 44; www.palaciogranados.com; Calle Emilio Castelar 42; d/ste incl breakfast €99/145; P🌀❄🗤🏊) This charming palace, sections of which date to the 15th century, has been lovingly restored by its architect owner. The rooms, which are all slightly different, have a stately look with wood-beamed ceilings, Mudéjar arches, 18th-century floors and even the occasional fireplace. Adding to the romance is a tiny courtyard where pomegranate trees grow over a tiny plunge pool.

★**Ágora**   TAPAS €
(☑ 955 31 70 77; Calle Barquete 38A; tapas €1.50-2.50, raciones €9.50-12.50; ⊙ 11am-4pm Mon, to 11pm Wed & Thu, to midnight Fri, noon-midnight Sat, noon-11pm Sun) This friendly tapas joint run by a young, energetic crew is one of Écija's favourite bars. Its outdoor tables, overlooked by a gnarled olive tree, are much sought after – particularly at weekends, when crowds of locals pour in to dine on decadently seasoned scrambled eggs and slow-cooked pork cheeks in wine sauce.

Hispania   SPANISH €€
(☑ 954 83 26 05; www.hispaniacafe.com; Pasaje Virgen de Soterraño; tapas €3-8, mains €10-18; ⊙ noon-3am Tue-Sun) Stylish, friendly and packed with *ecijanos,* this popular side-street operation ensures a full house with its contemporary approach to Spanish cooking. In line with the modern decor, dishes are creative and forward-looking, with everything from Iberian pork-burgers to wok-fried rice combos. Book ahead Thursday to Saturday.

ℹ Information

Tourist Office (☑ 955 90 29 33; www.turismo ecija.com; Calle Elvira 1; ⊙ 10am-2pm & 4.30-6.30pm Mon-Sat, 10am-2pm Sun)

ℹ Getting There & Away

Écija is 53km east of Carmona on the A4 between Córdoba and Seville. From the **bus station** (Avenida del Genil; ⊙ 7am-10.30pm), ALSA (p136) buses connect with Carmona (€4.70, 35 minutes, three daily), Córdoba (€5, one hour, six daily) and Seville (€7.30, 1¼ hours, at least four daily).

PARQUE NATURAL SIERRA NORTE DE SEVILLA

Cazalla de la Sierra

POP 4930 / ELEV 582M

This attractive little *pueblo blanco* (white town), spread around a hilltop 85km northeast of Seville, sits in the heart of the Parque Natural Sierra Norte, making it the ideal base for exploring the area.

There are some lovely walks in the surrounding woods; in town the action is focussed on Plaza Mayor, the town's central square, which is overshadowed by the Iglesia de Nuestra Señora de la Consolación.

Activities

Sendero de Las Laderas HIKING

This 8.5km hiking trail leads down from Cazalla to the Huéznar valley, passing through typical Sierra Norte evergreen-oak woodlands, olive groves and small cultivated plots, as well as the odd chestnut wood and vineyard. It's rated as medium difficulty and is hard work in places with some steep stretches. Allow about three hours to complete it. The first leg starts at El Chorrillo fountain at the foot of Calle Parras - a sign on Paseo El Moro directs you here. The path leads down to the Puente de los Tres Ojos bridge on the Río Huéznar, from where you follow the western bank of the river. Finally, head west under the Puente del Castillejo railway bridge to return to Cazalla on the **Camino Viejo de la Estación** (Old Station Track).

Vía Verde de la Sierra Norte CYCLING

(www.viasverdes.com) This 18km cycling (and walking) route is one of the most popular of Andalucía's 23 *vías verdes* (greenways). Running along a disused mining railway, it leads north through the Huéznar valley below Cazalla to the village of **San Nicolás del Puerto** and on south to the old **Cerro del Hierro mines**. Bike hire is available at **Bicicletas Verde Vía** (☏955 49 01 04; www.bicicletasverdevia.com; Carretera A455, Km 8; per day adult/child €10/6; ☺9am-8pm) at the start of the *vía*, 8km east of Cazalla on the A455.

Sleeping

Paraíso del Huéznar COTTAGE €

(☏955 49 01 04; www.paraisodelhueznar.com; Carretera A455, Km 8; cottages per person incl breakfast €30; P🅿🛜🏊) Some 8km down the windy A455 east of Cazalla (towards Constantina), the Paraíso has five comfortable, country-style *casitas* (cottages). Sleeping from two to 12 people, these come with fully equipped kitchens, log fires and hydromassage showers. There's also handy on-site cycle hire.

La Plazuela CASA RURAL €

(☏954 42 14 96; www.apartamentos-elpua.es; Calle Caridad 4; s €42-55, d €60-75; ❄🛜) With a prime central location just off Cazalla's main pedestrian drag and spacious rooms, this modest guesthouse makes a convenient base. Its nine rooms are individually decorated in neo-rustic style with brightly coloured walls, decorative tiled floors and functional wooden furniture.

★**Las Navezuelas** CASA RURAL €€

(☏954 88 47 64; www.lasnavezuelas.com; Carretera A432, Km 43.5; s/d/ste incl breakfast €50/70/88, 4-person apts €140; ☺late Feb-Dec; P🅿🛜🏊) 🏅 Once you've made it to this blissful rural retreat - signposted off the A432, 3km south of Cazalla - you may be tempted to never leave. Immersed in silence, it's housed in a 16th-century *cortijo* (farmhouse) and offers rustic, thick-walled rooms and three self-catering apartments. Outside, you can lounge by the pool and wander through the olive groves and vines that flourish in the extensive grounds.

Italian owner Luca and family prepare wonderful meals (hotel guests only; €18) using organic ingredients grown on their farm. Their heating system is powered by solar and geothermal energy.

Eating

★**Agustina** ANDALUCIAN €€

(☏954 88 32 55; Plaza del Concejo; mains €8-15; ☺1-5pm & 8pm-midnight Wed-Mon) With its urban modern interior and alfresco seating on a pretty stone plaza, Agustina brings a dash of contemporary style to Cazalla. The food reflects this, with updated takes on traditional Sierra dishes such as *queso de cabra con miel* - grilled goat's cheese in a moat of melted honey - and wonderful, tender *carrillada* (slow-cooked pork cheeks).

Cortijo Vistalegre ANDALUCIAN, ITALIAN €€

(☏954 88 35 13; www.cortijovistalegre.es; Carretera Real de la Jara, Km 0.5; mains €8-20;

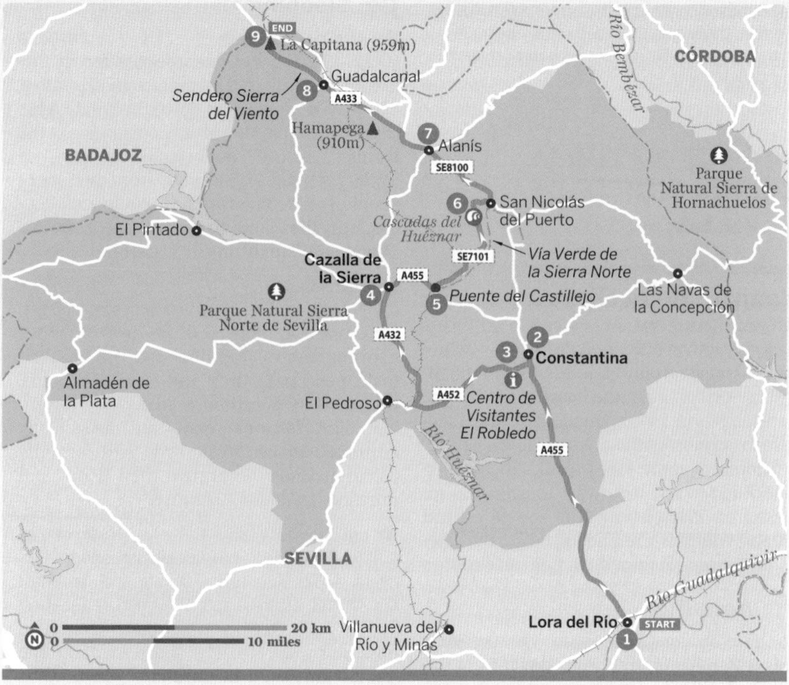

Driving Tour
Parque Natural Sierra Norte de Sevilla

START LORA DEL RÍO
END LA CAPITANA
LENGTH 105KM; TWO DAYS

Head up to the Parque Natural Sierra Norte de Sevilla for a taste of life in the slow lane and some wonderfully scenic driving. From Seville, follow the A4 and the A457 to ❶ **Lora del Río**, then pick up the A455 for the climb up to ❷ **Constantina**, the park's largest town. Stop off to explore its attractive old town and landmark castle before continuing west on the A452 to the ❸ **Centro de Visitantes El Robledo**, where you can pick up walking maps and wander the botanical garden. Push on along the A452 as it winds through the hilly countryside, mists clinging to the mountains as they recede into the distance. Shortly after crossing the Río Huéznar, where you can see part of an old aqueduct, turn right onto the A432 and drive 12km north to ❹ **Cazalla de la Sierra** (p87). Lunch on inventive tapas at Agustina (p87), then spend the afternoon investigating the

town's charming streets and nearby walking trails. Overnight at Las Navezuelas (p87), 3km to the south.

Next morning, pick up the A455 back towards Constantina. This road crosses the Río Huéznar just east of the Cazalla-Constantina train station. A bumpy 1km track leads downstream from here to the ❺ **Puente del Castillejo** railway bridge. Next, follow the SE7101 as it parallels the river for 13km on the way to San Nicolás del Puerto. Just before getting to the village, take a moment for a quick detour to the powerful ❻ **Cascadas del Huéznar** (waterfalls). From riverside San Nicolás del Puerto, take the SE8100 northwest, ploughing on through the increasingly dramatic landscape to ❼ **Alanís**, topped by a medieval castle. Keep going on the A433, along the edge of the park, to remote, windswept ❽ **Guadalcanal**. North of town, leave your car and hit the hiking trail: the 5km (two-hour) Sendero Sierra del Viento follows a ridge to ❾ **La Capitana**, the park's highest peak (959m) and the perfect point to wrap up your tour.

⊙12.30-4.30pm & 8.30pm-12.30am Wed-Fri, 12.30pm-12.30am Sat & Sun) Italian pastas and pizzas star alongside Andalucian hams and steaks at this smartly rustic *cortijo,* just off the A450 on the southwestern edge of town. Colourful wall hangings, candle-lit tables and an open log fire set the indoors scene, or you can dine on the huge outdoor terrace.

ℹ️ Information

Tourist Office (☎ 954 88 35 62; www.cazalla.org; Plaza Doctor Nosea 1; ⊙10am-2pm Tue-Sat, 4-6pm Thu & 4-7pm Fri & Sat, 11am-1pm Sun) Offers maps and information on walks in the area.

ℹ️ Getting There & Away

Autocares Valenzuela (p85) runs buses between Cazalla de la Sierra and Seville (€6.74, 1¾ hours) four times daily Monday to Friday, and twice daily on Saturdays and Sundays.

Constantina

POP 6120 / ELEV 552M

Constantina, the Sierra Norte's largest town and unofficial capital, is a charming spot set amidst the rolling, tree-clad hills of the Huéznar valley. Narrow medieval lanes weave through its compact white centre lined with handsome 18th-century mansions and traditional cafes.

◉ Sights & Activities

Castillo Árabe   RUINS
(⊙9am-9pm) FREE Topping the western side of town, Constantina's ruined Almoravidera Islamic fort is worth the climb for the views alone. Below, you'll see the distinctive Mudéjar bell tower of the Iglesia de Santa María de la Encarnación towering above the huddled white houses of the Barrio de la Morería.

Sendero Los Castañares   HIKING
The 5.5km Sendero Los Castañares trail takes you up through thick, peaceful chestnut woods to a hilltop viewpoint, then loops back to Constantina (about two hours total). It's signposted from Paseo de la Alameda at the north of town.

🍴 Eating

Asador Los Navarro   ANDALUCIAN €€
(☎ 954 49 63 61; www.asadorlosnavarro.com; Paseo de la Alameda 39; tapas €2.50, raciones €8-15; ⊙9am-11.45pm) Attractively positioned at the head of the tree-lined Paseo de la Alameda, this coffee-coloured bar-restaurant is a cheerful local haunt, appreciated for its barbecued meats and quality local wines.

ℹ️ Information

Centro de Visitantes El Robledo (☎ 610 663214; Carretera Constantina-El Pedroso, Km 1; ⊙9am-2pm & 4-6pm Apr-Jun, hours vary rest of year) The park's main visitor centre, 1km west of Constantina off the A452, with hiking information and a botanical garden.

Oficina Municipal de Turismo (☎ 955 88 12 97; Avenida de Andalucía; ⊙10am-2pm Tue-Sun) On the main southern approach to town.

ℹ️ Getting There & Away

Autocares Valenzuela (p85) runs buses from Seville to Constantina (€7.35, 1¾ hours) four times daily Monday to Friday, twice on Saturday and three times on Sunday.

El Pedroso

A pleasant village of broad cobbled streets, El Pedroso lies 16km south of Cazalla de la Sierra on the A432 Seville road. There's little to detain you in the village itself but there's fine walking on the Sendero del Arroyo de las Cañas.

Sendero del Arroyo de las Cañas   HIKING
The Sendero del Arroyo de las Cañas is a waymarked 10km (3½-hour) circuit through the flattish countryside west of El Pedroso. One of the prettiest walks in the area, it traverses a landscape strewn with boulders and, in spring, gorgeous wildflowers. The start point is opposite Bar Triana on the western side of the village.

Hotel Entreolivos   HOTEL €€
(☎ 954 88 98 95; www.hotelentreolivos.es; Avenida de la Estación 15; s/d €60/80; ※ 🐕 🏊) If you decide to sleep over in El Pedroso, this welcoming, family-run hotel ticks all the boxes. Its summery white rooms are clean and simply attired, and it has a small (but very welcoming) swimming pool. There's also a restaurant serving traditional regional food (mains €10 to €12).

ℹ️ Getting There & Away

Autocares Valenzuela (p85) buses run to El Pedroso from Seville (€5.53, 1¼ hours) four times daily Monday to Friday, and twice daily on Saturdays and Sundays.

Huelva Province

Best Places to Stay

➡ Posada de San Marcos (p107)

➡ Finca La Fronda (p108)

➡ Molino Río Alájar (p108)

➡ Hotel Toruño (p100)

➡ Hotel Convento Aracena (p105)

Best Places to Eat

➡ Jesús Carrión (p106)

➡ Restaurante Arrieros (p106)

➡ Casa Padrino (p108)

➡ Azabache (p93)

➡ Restaurante Toruño (p101)

Why Go?

Andalucía's most westerly, end-of-the-line destination packs in a mix of historical intrigue, natural beauty and sun worship, but still remains largely off the beaten track for foreign visitors. Here you'll find sleepy mountain villages, relics from Columbus' voyages of discovery, endless stretches of untainted coastline and Spain's most beloved national park.

Southeastern Huelva province shelters the marshes, dunes, beaches and woodlands of the Parque Nacional de Doñana, as well as the enchanting whitewashed town of El Rocío, where tens of thousands of pilgrims converge every spring during the boisterous Romería del Rocío festival. West to Portugal runs the Costa de la Luz, an attractive yet relatively undiscovered coastline, quite unlike the packaged chaos further east. Northwest, towards Extremadura, rises the enchanting Sierra de Aracena, dotted with cobblestoned villages, criss-crossed by some of Andalucía's finest walking trails, and home to some of the Iberian Peninsula's most prized pork products.

Driving Distances

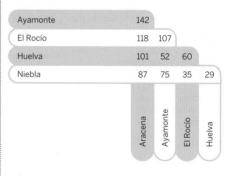

	Aracena	Ayamonte	El Rocío	Huelva
Ayamonte	142			
El Rocío	118	107		
Huelva	101	52	60	
Niebla	87	75	35	29

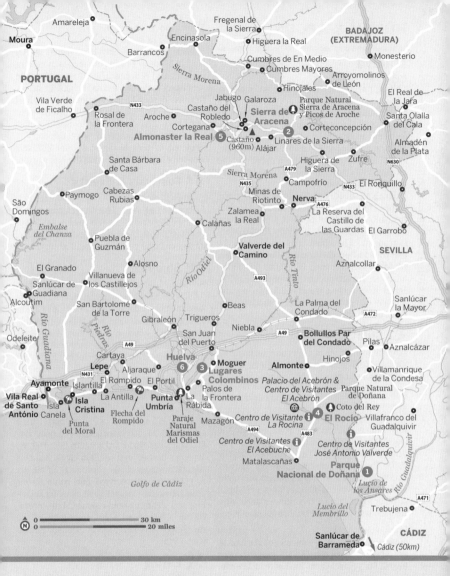

Huelva Province Highlights

1 **Parque Nacional de Doñana** (p97) Exploring the wilderness of Europe's largest nature reserve.

2 **Sierra de Aracena** (p106) Hiking from one enchanted village to the next and tasting creative regional cooking in this off-the-radar rural hideaway.

3 **Lugares Colombinos** (p94) Retracing the historic steps of Christopher Columbus in La Rábida, Palos de la Frontera and Moguer.

4 **El Rocío** (p99) Feeling the festive fervour and delighting in the pageantry of Spain's largest religious pilgrimage.

5 **Almonaster la Real** (p109) Checking out 9th-century Islamic architecture in this remote mountain village.

6 **Huelva** (p92) Trawling for tapas and getting a taste of local life in the pedestrianised streets surrounding Plaza de las Monjas.

HUELVA & AROUND

Huelva

POP 147,000

The capital of Huelva province is a modern, unpretentious industrial port set between the Odiel and Tinto estuaries. Despite its unpromising approaches and slightly grimy feel, central Huelva is a lively enough place, and the city's people – called *choqueros* because of their supposed preference for the locally abundant *chocos* (cuttlefish) – are noted for their warmth.

Huelva's history dates back 3000 years to the Phoenician town of Onuba. Onuba's river-mouth location made it a natural base for exporting inland minerals to the Mediterranean. The town was devastated by the 1755 Lisbon earthquake, but later grew when British company Rio Tinto developed mines in the province's interior in the 1870s. Today Huelva has a sizeable fishing fleet and a heavy dose of petrochemical industry (introduced in the 1950s by Franco).

◉ Sights

More a scene than a collection of dazzling sights, Huelva nevertheless offers a few worthwhile stops.

Muelle-Embarcadero de
Mineral de Río Tinto   HISTORIC SITE
An odd legacy of the area's mining history, this impressive iron pier curves out into the Odiel estuary 500m south of the port. It was designed for the Rio Tinto company in the 1870s by British engineer George Barclay Bruce. Equipped with boardwalks on upper and lower levels, it makes for a delightful stroll or jog to admire the harbour and ships. It's 1km southwest of Plaza de las Monjas.

Museo de Huelva   MUSEUM
(☑959 65 04 24; www.museosdeandalucia.es; Alameda Sundheim 13; EU/non-EU citizens free/€1.50; ☉9am-3pm Tue-Sun mid-Jun–mid-Sep; 9am-8pm Tue-Sat, 9am-3pm Sun rest of year) **FREE** This wide-ranging museum is stuffed with history and art. The permanent ground-floor exhibition concentrates on Huelva province's impressive archaeological pedigree, with interesting items culled from its Roman and mining history; upstairs houses a collection of Spanish painting spanning seven centuries. Don't miss the stunning ancient Roman *noria* (waterwheel), the best preserved of its kind anywhere in the world.

Santuario de Nuestra
Señora de la Cinta   CHAPEL
(Avenida de la Cinta; ☉9am-1pm & 4-7pm; [P]) Of Gothic-Mudéjar origins but reconstructed in the 18th and 19th centuries, this pretty white sanctuary looks out across the Odiel estuary from its peaceful hillside spot 3km north of the centre. Columbus allegedly promised to pray here upon returning to Spain across the turbulent Atlantic in 1493; the story is depicted in tiles by artist Daniel Zuloaga. Take city bus 6 from outside the bus station.

☆ Festivals & Events

Fiestas Colombinas   CULTURAL
(☉late Jul/early Aug) Huelva celebrates Columbus' departure for the Americas (3 August 1492) with this six-day festival of music, dance, cultural events and bullfighting.

⨋ Sleeping

Senator Huelva Hotel   BUSINESS HOTEL €
(☑959 28 55 00; www.senatorhuelvahotel.com; Avenida Pablo Rada 10; r from €60; ✴☎) Catering to the business set, this impeccably maintained hotel is definitely your best bet in Huelva. Bright-red banisters draped in greenery liven up the lobby, and staff are charmingly efficient. All 162 rooms are smartly outfitted with dark-wood desks and crisp white sheets, and Huelva's central square is only a five-minute walk away.

Hotel Familia Conde   BUSINESS HOTEL €
(☑959 28 24 00; www.hotelfamiliaconde.com; Alameda Sundheim 14; s/d from €55/65; ✴@☎) True, it's housed in a soulless block, but this central business-class operation is efficiently run with friendly service, and some rooms have attractive features such as wood panelling and gleaming bold-coloured bathrooms. It's on a busy road a few steps east of the cafe-lined Avenida Martín Alonso Pinzón (Gran Vía).

✕ Eating

In a salty city such as Huelva it's no surprise that seafood stars on most menus. Busy tapas bars line Avenida Pablo Rada, just north of the centre, and pedestrianised Calle Vázquez López to the south.

Restaurante Juan José   ANDALUCIAN €
(☑959 26 38 57; Calle Villa Mundaka 1; tapas €2-2.50, raciones €7.50-11.50; ☉7.30am-5pm & 8pm-12.30am Mon-Sat) Locals regularly pack into this humble, friendly neighbourhood restaurant 1.5km northeast of Plaza de las

Huelva

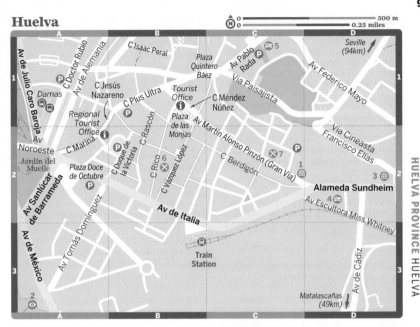

Monjas for its fabulously gooey *tortilla de patatas* (potato-and-onion omelette). The tuna (fresh from Isla Cristina) and *carne mechada* (meat stuffed with pepper and ham) are tasty, too. Arrive before 2pm to snag a lunch table.

Catch bus 6 from the city bus station to Plaza Huerto Paco; walk one block south down Avenida de las Adoratrices and turn left on Calle Villamundaka.

★ **Azabache**   TAPAS €€
(☑ 959 25 75 28; www.restauranteazabache. com; Calle Vázquez López 22; raciones €7-18; ⊘ 8.30am-midnight Mon-Fri, to 4pm Sat) After a taste of traditional Huelva? Squeeze into this narrow tiled tapas bar where busy, helpful waiters are quick to deliver cheese and *jamón* (ham) platters, scrambled *gurumelos* (local wild mushrooms), fried *chocos* (cuttlefish) and fresh fish specials. Beyond the front bar area is a more formal restaurant serving a rather pricey set menu (€36 including wine, dessert and coffee).

La Mirta   SPANISH, GREEK €€
(☑ 959 28 36 57; www.lamirta.com; Avenida Martín Alonso Pinzón 13; raciones €7-17; ⊘ noon-5pm & 8pm-midnight Mon-Sat, noon-5pm Sun) This popular restaurant/wine bar on the bubbly Gran Vía specialises in local flavours blended with

Huelva

◉ Sights
1 Casa Colón C2
2 Muelle-Embarcadero de
   Mineral de Río Tinto........................ A3
3 Museo de Huelva D2

⊜ Sleeping
4 Hotel Familia Conde D2
5 Senator Huelva Hotel C1

⊗ Eating
6 Azabache B2
7 La Mirta.. C2

contemporary flair. *Chocos* get served with everything from linguine to four-cheese fondue; other creative temptations include mushrooms stuffed with goat's cheese and *pisto* (Spanish ratatouille), or salads of fruit and smoked fish with Greek yoghurt vinaigrette, all accompanied by hot crispy bread.

ⓘ Information

Regional Tourist Office (☑ 959 25 74 67; www.turismohuelva.org; Calle Jesús Nazareno 21; ⊘ 9am-7.30pm Mon-Fri, 9.30am-3pm Sat & Sun) Helpful for the whole province.

Tourist Office (☑ 959 54 18 17; Plaza de las Monjas; ⊘ 10am-2pm Mon-Sat, plus 5-8pm Mon-Fri)

ⓘ Getting There & Around

BUS

Most buses from the **bus station** (Calle Doctor Rubio) are operated by **Damas** (☑ 902 11 44 92; www.damas-sa.es; Calle Doctor Rubio). Destinations include Almonte (for El Rocío, €4, 1¼ hours), Aracena (€10.85, 2½ to three hours), Isla Cristina (€4, one to 1¼ hours), La Rábida (€1.65, 20 minutes), Moguer (€1.65, 45 minutes), Matalascañas (€4, 1¼ hours), Palos de la Frontera (€1.65, 30 minutes), Seville (€8.65, 1¼ to two hours) and Faro, Portugal (€16, 2½ hours). Frequency is reduced on Saturday, Sunday and public holidays.

CAR & MOTORCYCLE

There's metered street parking around town (Monday to Saturday), indicated by blue and orange lines, and a useful parking lot off Calle Duque de la Victoria.

TRAIN

From Huelva's **train station** (Avenida de Italia), just south of the centre, **Renfe** (☑ 912 43 23 43; www.renfe.com; Avenida de Italia) runs three services to Seville (€12.25, 1½ hours) and one direct high-speed ALVIA train to Córdoba (€38, 1¾ hours) and Madrid (€38 to €73, 3¾ hours) daily. A new station adjacent to Huelva's century-old original is slated to open in 2018, though Renfe's promised high-speed AVE service remains in limbo at the time of research.

Lugares Colombinos

The 'Columbian Sites' are the three townships of La Rábida, Palos de la Frontera and Moguer, along the eastern bank of the Tinto estuary. All three played a key role in Columbus' preparation for his journey of discovery and can be visited in a fun day trip from Huelva, Doñana or Huelva's eastern coast. As the countless greenhouses suggest, this is Spain's main strawberry-growing region (Huelva province produces 90% of Spain's crop).

La Rábida

POP 500

◉ Sights

Monasterio de la Rábida   MONASTERY
(☑ 959 35 04 11; www.monasteriodelarabida. com; Paraje de la Rábida; adult/student €3.50/3; ⊙ 10am-1pm & 4-7pm Tue-Sat, from 10.45am Sun; ℗) In the pretty, peaceful village of La Rábida, don't miss this 14th- and 15th-century Franciscan monastery, visited several times by Columbus before his great voyage of discovery. Highlights include a chapel with a 13th-century alabaster Virgin before which Columbus prayed, and a fresco-lined Mudéjar cloister, one of the few parts of the original structure to survive the 1755 earthquake.

It was here that Columbus met Abbot Juan Pérez, who was instrumental in helping him gain backing from the Spanish Crown for his ambitious plans to cross the Atlantic. Fine early 20th-century frescoes by Huelvan cubist painter Daniel Vázquez Díaz detail Columbus' adventures.

Muelle de las Carabelas   HISTORIC SITE
(Wharf of the Caravels; €3.60; ⊙ 10am-9pm Tue-Sun mid-Jun–mid-Sep; 9.30am-7.30pm Tue-Sun rest of year; ℗) On the waterfront below the Monasterio de la Rábida is this pseudo 15th-century quayside, where you can board life-size replicas of the *Niña*, the *Pinta* and the *Santa María* – the three ships used by Columbus in his initial trans-Atlantic expedition. A single ticket grants access to all three ships and the attached museum, which features excellent bilingual (English-Spanish) displays tracing the history of Columbus' voyages. Here you can see instruments of navigation and get a glimpse of the indigenous experience at the time of the Spaniards' arrival.

ⓘ Getting There & Away

Damas (www.damas-sa.es) runs frequent buses from Huelva to La Rábida (€1.65, 20 minutes). Buses continue northeast from here to Palos de la Frontera (€1.30, 10 minutes) and Moguer (€1.65, 25 minutes).

Palos de la Frontera

POP 5300

It was from the port of Palos de la Frontera that Columbus and his merry band set sail into the unknown. The town provided the explorer with two of his ships, two captains (brothers Martín Alonso Pinzón and Vicente Yáñez Pinzón) and more than half his crew.

Casa Museo Martín Alonso Pinzón   MUSEUM
(☑ 959 10 00 41; Calle Colón 24; adult/concession €1/0.50; ⊙ 10am-2pm & 5-8.30pm Mon-Fri) The former home of the Pinzón brothers (captains of the *Niña* and the *Pinta*) now houses a permanent exhibition on Palos' crucial contribution to Columbus' famous first expedition.

Iglesia de San Jorge   CHURCH
(Calle Fray Juan Pérez; ⊙ variable) Towards the northern end of Calle Colón is this 15th-century Gothic-Mudéjar church, where Co-

lumbus and his sailors took Communion before embarking on their great expedition. Water for their ships came from La Fontanilla well nearby.

El Bodegón ANDALUCIAN €€
(☎959 53 11 05; Calle Rábida 46; mains €12-25; ⊙noon-4pm & 8.30-11.30pm Wed-Mon) This atmospheric brick-floored grotto of a restaurant specialises in meat, fish and vegetables cooked to perfection over an oak-fired grill.

Getting There & Away

Damas (www.damas-sa.es) runs frequent buses from Palos de la Frontera to La Rábida (€1.30, 10 minutes), Moguer (€1.30, 15 minutes) and Huelva (€1.65, 30 minutes).

Moguer

POP 14,300

The sleepy whitewashed town of Moguer, 8km northeast of Palos de la Frontera on the A494, is where Columbus' ship, the *Niña*, was built. The main Columbus site in town is the 14th-century Monasterio de Santa Clara. Moguer's other claim to fame is as the birthplace and home town of Nobel Prize-winning poet Juan Ramón Jiménez (p96).

Monasterio de Santa Clara MONASTERY
(☎959 37 01 07; www.monasteriodesantaclara.com; Plaza de las Monjas; guided tours adult/concession €3.50/2.50, free Sun; ⊙tours 10.30am, 11.30am, 12.30pm, 5.30pm & 6.30pm Tue-Sat, 10.30am & 11.30am Sun) Columbus spent a night of vigil and prayer at this 14th-century monastery on returning from his first voyage in March 1493. Highlights of the 45-minute guided visit include a Mudéjar cloister, a 14th-century kitchen, the whitewashed Claustro de las Madres, illuminated manuscripts and a one-of-a-kind 14th-century Nasrid choir stall bearing images of Alhambra-inspired lions, columns and Arabic capitals.

Hotel Plaza Escribano HOTEL €
(☎959 37 30 63; www.hotelplazaescribano.com; Plaza Escribano 5; s/d €39/56; P❄🛜) This friendly hotel in Moguer's historic core offers modern, pastel-hued rooms surrounding a central patio with potted plants; there's a small library and lounge area for guests' use.

Mesón El Lobito ANDALUCIAN €€
(☎959 37 06 60; www.mesonellobito.com; Calle Rábida 31; mains €7-16; ⊙noon-4pm & 8.30pm-midnight) About 300m southwest of the central Plaza del Cabildo, Mesón El

THE FOUR VOYAGES OF CHRISTOPHER COLUMBUS

In April 1492 Christopher Columbus (Cristóbal Colón to Spaniards) finally won the Spanish royal support of the Reyes Católicos (Catholic Monarchs; Fernando and Isabel) for his proposed westward voyage of exploration to the spice-rich Orient. This proposal was to result in four great voyages and a fabulous golden age for Spain, though some historians now argue that Columbus' captains, the Pinzón brothers, really deserve the credit for finding the New World.

On 3 August 1492 Columbus embarked from Palos de la Frontera with 100 men and three ships. After a near mutiny as the crew despaired of finding land, they finally made landfall on the Bahamian island of Guanahaní on 12 October, naming it San Salvador. The expedition went on to discover Cuba and Hispaniola, where the *Santa María* sank. The *Niña* and the *Pinta* made it back to Palos on 15 March 1493.

Columbus – with animals, plants, gold ornaments and six Caribbean Indians – received a hero's welcome on his return, as all were convinced that he had reached the fabled East Indies (in fact, his calculations were some 16,000km off). Martín Alonso Pinzón died on arrival in Spain, supposedly having failed to beat Columbus back with the big news.

Columbus made further voyages in 1493 and 1498, discovering Jamaica, Puerto Rico, Trinidad and the mouth of the Orinoco River. But he proved a disastrous colonial administrator, enslaving the indigenous peoples and alienating Spanish settlers. Eventually he was arrested by a Spanish royal emissary and sent home in chains. In an attempt to redeem himself, Columbus embarked on his fourth and final voyage in May 1502. This time he reached Honduras and Panama, but then became stranded for a year in Jamaica, having lost his ships to sea worms.

Columbus died in 1506 in Valladolid, northern Spain – impoverished and apparently still believing he had reached Asia. His remains were eventually returned to the Caribbean, as he had wished, before being brought back to Seville (p50). Or were they? The story of Columbus' posthumous voyages has become quite the saga itself.

DON'T MISS

MOGUER & JUAN RAMÓN JIMÉNEZ

Moguer has its own charming flavour of Andalucian baroque, and its sunny beauty was fulsomely expressed by local poet laureate Juan Ramón Jiménez (1881–1958), who won the Nobel Prize for literature in 1956. The **Casa Museo Zenobia y Juan Ramón Jiménez** (☑ 959 37 21 48; www.fundacion-jrj.es/servicios/visita-a-la-casa-museo; Calle Juan Ramón Jiménez 10; adult/concession €3.50/2.50; ☉ 10am-2pm & 4-8pm Tue-Fri, 10am-2.30pm Sat & Sun mid-Jun–mid-Sep, reduced hours rest of year), the old home of the poet and his writer wife, Zenobia Camprubí, is open for visits. As you wander around town, keep an eye out for tiled quotes marking key locations from Jiménez' most famous poem *Platero y yo* (Platero and I), which was inspired by his beloved donkey Platero and celebrated its centenary in 2014, and for sculptures of Jiménez' well-known characters.

Lobito dishes up huge, good-value clay platters of traditional country fare in a cavernous bodega; grilled meats and fish are cooked over an open log fire.

ⓘ Information

There's an excellent **tourist office** (☑ 959 37 18 98; Calle Andalucía 17, Teatro Municipal Felipe Godínez; ☉ 10am-2pm & 5-7pm Tue-Sat) inside the Teatro.

ⓘ Getting There & Away

Damas (www.damas-sa.es) runs frequent daily buses (14 on weekdays, seven on weekends) from Moguer to Palos de la Frontera (€1.30, 15 minutes), La Rábida (€1.65, 25 minutes) and Huelva (€1.65, 45 minutes).

HUELVA'S COSTA DE LA LUZ

Huelva province's modestly developed Costa de la Luz consists of beautiful broad white sands backed by dunes and pine trees. West of Huelva, the main beach hot spots are Punta Umbría, Flecha del Rompido, Isla Cristina and Ayamonte. All are friendly, unpretentious places, more popular with Spanish holidaymakers than with foreign visitors.

The Costa de la Luz continues southeast from Huelva, along almost the entire coastline of neighbouring Cádiz province (p142).

Flecha del Rompido   BEACH

Possibly the most spectacular beach on Huelva's Costa de la Luz, this 8km-long sand bar along the mouth of the Río Piedras can be reached only by ferry, which keeps the crowds away, even in midsummer. The waters on the inland side remain calm, while the south side faces the open sea. Part of the Río Piedras wetlands reserve, it's a place of great ornithological and botanical interest.

From April to October, hourly **Flechamar** (☑ 959 39 99 42; www.flechamar.com; return €4; ☉ Apr-Oct) boats go to the Flecha from the port at the western end of El Rompido (23km southwest of Huelva). At least two daily buses go from Huelva to El Rompido (€2.35, 50 minutes).

Isla Cristina

POP 18,500

Founded after the 1775 earthquake, Isla Cristina is first and foremost a bustling fishing port with a 250-strong fleet. Besides the tuna and sardines, it's famous for its lively **Carnaval** (☉ Feb). To the south of town lies a pair of long sandy beaches popular with Spanish holidaymakers.

◎ Sights

Playa Central   BEACH

Along the rear of Playa de la Gaviota, a boardwalk trail heads east to Playa Central, the main tourism zone with a few hotels and restaurants. The beach here is a long unbroken swath of sand, popular for sunbathing and swimming in warm weather. Further east a nature trail winds through forested marshlands, with good birdwatching opportunities.

Sala Muestra del Carnaval   MUSEUM

(☑ 959 33 26 94; Tourist Office, Calle San Francisco 12; ☉ 10am-2pm) **FREE** If you can't make it to Carnaval, pop into this small museum attached to the tourist office, which hosts a permanent display of prize-winning costumes. From here, the Ruta Turística del Carnaval walking route leads to several other Carnaval-related sights.

ⓘ Sleeping & Eating

Hotel Sol y Mar   HOTEL **€€**

(☑ 959 33 20 50; www.hotelsolymar.org; Paseo Maritimo, Playa Central; s/d €75/120; ☉ early Jan-

Oct; P ✶ 🛜) Possibly the best-value hotel on this coast, with perfect balconies overlooking a broad swathe of beach and little else. It has plenty of style, and welcome extras such as rain showers and friendly service. The on-site restaurant (mains €12-15; ⊗12.30-11.30pm) serves mostly seafood on a lovely beachfront terrace.

Hermanos Moreno   SEAFOOD €
(☑959 34 35 71; Avenida Padre Mirabent 39; raciones €6-10; ⊗noon-4pm & 8pm-midnight Apr-Sep, noon-4pm Oct-Mar) Beloved for its friendly service and reasonably priced daily specials, Moreno is one of several busy seafood spots on this square on the peninsula's northwest tip. It's opposite the seafood auction market, where you can watch restaurant buyers from across Spain bid for the day's catch. *Chocos, castañuelas* (small cuttlefish), *chipirones* (squid), stuffed tuna – it just doesn't get any fresher.

❶ Information

Tourist Office (Calle San Francisco 12; ⊗10am-2pm) A block inland from the fishing port.

❶ Getting There & Away

Damas (www.damas-sa.es) runs at least five daily buses between Isla Cristina's **bus station** (Calle Manuel Siurot) and Huelva (€4, one to 1¼ hours).

Ayamonte

POP 15,800

Staring across the Río Guadiana to Portugal, Ayamonte has a cheerful border-town buzz. The riverside strip between the tourist office and the port makes for a pleasant stroll, as does the adjoining town centre. The old town, between Paseo de la Ribera and the ferry dock (400m west), is dotted with attractive plazas, old churches, cafes, boutiques and restaurants.

Casa Luciano   SEAFOOD €€
(☑959 47 10 71; www.restaurantecasaluciano.es; Calle La Palma del Condado 1; tapas €3, mains €10-22; ⊗1-4.30pm & 9pm-midnight Tue-Sat, 1-4.30pm Sun) Of Ayamonte's many seafood restaurants, Casa Luciano is a worthy favourite. Everything on your plate is freshly cooked, minutes out of the water. Its version of tuna, particularly prized along this stretch of coast, is excellent; the *tortilla de patatas, salpicón de gambas* (shrimp salad) and paella tapas are equally popular.

❶ Information

Tourist Office (☑959 32 07 37; Plaza de España; ⊗9am-8pm Mon-Fri, 10am-2pm Sat Mar-Oct, 9am-3pm Mon-Fri, 10am-2pm Sat Nov-Feb)

❶ Getting There & Away

There are no customs or immigration checks when crossing the Spain–Portugal border here, by road or ferry.

BUS

From the **bus station** (Avenida de Andalucía), four daily buses go to Isla Cristina (€1.65, 25 minutes), six to Huelva (€5.30, 1¼ hours) and one to Faro (Portugal; €15, 40 minutes).

FERRY

Portugal-bound romantics can skip the fast, modern A49 motorway and enjoy a slower 15-minute ferry trip across the Guadiana to Portugal's Vila Real de Santo António with **Transporte Fluvial del Guadiana** (☑959 47 06 17, 652 525168; www.rioguadiana.com; Avenida del Muelle de Portugal; adult/child/bicycle/motorcycle/car €1.90/1.20/1.20/3.50/5.50; ⊗half-hourly departures 9.30am-9pm Jul–mid-Sep, hourly departures 10am-7pm mid-Sep–Mar, to 8pm Apr-Jun). The same operator runs cruises up the Guadiana, one of Spain's longest rivers, to Sanlúcar de Guadiana (nine hours). Check timings and buy tickets at the kiosk facing the ferry dock.

PARQUE NACIONAL DE DOÑANA & AROUND

The World Heritage–listed Parque Nacional de Doñana is a place of haunting natural beauty and exotic horizons, where flocks of flamingos tinge the evening skies pink above one of Europe's most extensive wetlands (the Guadalquivir delta), huge herds of deer and boar flit through *coto* (woodlands), and the elusive Iberian lynx battles for survival. Here, in the largest roadless region in Western Europe, and Spain's most celebrated national park, you can experience nature at its most raw and powerful.

The 542-sq-km national park extends 30km along or close to the Atlantic coast and up to 25km inland. Much of the perimeter is bordered by the separate Parque Natural de Doñana, under less strict protection, which forms a 538-sq-km buffer for the national park.

The national park and its surrounding natural park together provide a refuge for 360 bird species and 37 types of mammal, including endangered species such as the

Iberian lynx (p100) and Spanish imperial eagle (nine breeding pairs). It's also a crucial habitat for half a million migrating birds.

Since its establishment in 1969, the national park has been under pressure from tourism operators, farmers, hunters, developers and builders who oppose the restrictions on land use. Ecologists, for their part, argue that Doñana is increasingly hemmed in by tourism and agricultural schemes, roads and other infrastructure that threaten to deplete its water supplies and cut it off from other undeveloped areas.

Access to the interior of the national park is restricted, although anyone can walk or cycle along the 28km Atlantic beach between Matalascañas and the mouth of the Río Guadalquivir (which can be crossed by boat from Sanlúcar de Barrameda in Cádiz province; p132), as long as they do not stray inland.

The towns of El Rocío (p99) and Matalascañas (p102), both with good accommodation and restaurants, are Huelva province's main bases for adventures into the Parques Nacional and Natural de Doñana.

◎ Sights & Activities

Four-hour, land-based trips in eight- to 30-passenger all-terrain vehicles are the only way to get inside the national park from the western side. Bookings can be made directly with various accredited agencies, including Doñana Nature (p100), Cooperativa Marismas del Rocío and Doñana Reservas (p100) – several of these are based in El Rocío. Especially in the larger vehicles, the experience can feel a bit theme park–like, but guides have plenty of in-depth information to share.

During spring, summer and holidays, book as far ahead as possible, but otherwise a week or less is usually sufficient notice. Bring binoculars (if you like), drinking water and mosquito repellent (except in winter). English-, German- and French-speaking guides are normally available if you ask in advance.

You can pretty much count on seeing deer, wild boar and numerous bird species. Serious ornithologists may be disappointed by the strict limits on access to the heart of the park, and you'd be very lucky to spot a lynx.

Playa del Parador BEACH

This stunning 6km stretch of cliff-backed sands at the western edge of Parque Natural de Doñana is one of the prettiest beaches in Huelva province. Access is from the Parador de Mazagón, just off the A494 about 25km west of Matalascañas.

Cooperativa Marismas del Rocío WILDLIFE

(☑ 959 43 04 32, 648 762914; www.donanavisitas. es; Centro de Visitantes El Acebuche; tours €30) Runs four-hour tours of the national park in 20- to 30-person all-terrain vehicles, with one morning and one afternoon departure daily from the Centro de Visitantes El Acebuche. Tours traverse 75km of the southern part of the park and cover all the major ecosystems – coast, dunes, marshes and Mediterranean forest. Trips start with a long beach drive, then head inland.

❶ Information

The park has seven information points. The most important four for visitors accessing the park from Huelva province are as follows:

DOÑANA: LIFE CYCLES

The many interwoven ecosystems that make up the Parque Nacional de Doñana give rise to fantastic diversity. About 380 sq km of the park consists of *marismas* (marshes). These are almost dry from July to October, but in late autumn they fill with water, eventually leaving only a few islets of dry land. Hundreds of thousands of waterbirds arrive from the north to winter here, including an estimated 80% of Western Europe's wild ducks. As the waters sink in spring, greater flamingos, herons, storks, spoonbills, avocets, hoopoes, bee-eaters and albatrosses arrive for the summer, many of them to nest. Fledglings flock around the *lucios* (ponds) and, as these dry up in July, herons, storks and kites move in to feast on trapped perch.

Between the marshlands and the park's 28km-long beach is a band of sand dunes, pushed inland by the wind by 2m to 5m per year. When dune sand eventually reaches the marshlands, rivers carry it back down to the sea, which washes it up on the beach – and the cycle begins again.

Elsewhere in the park, stable sands support 144 sq km of *coto* (woodland and scrub). *Coto* is the favoured habitat of many nesting birds and the park's abundant mammal population – 37 species including red and fallow deer, wild boar, wildcats and genets.

DON'T MISS

DOÑANA WALKS

The walking trails near the park's visitor centres are easy enough to be undertaken by most. The March–May and September–November migration seasons are the most exciting for birdwatchers. The isolated, pond-side Centro de Visitantes José Antonio Valverde has particularly good birdwatching.

Sendero Lagunas del Acebuche From the Centro de Visitantes El Acebuche, the two Senderos del Acebuche (Acebuche Paths; 1.5km and 3.5km round trip) lead to bird-watching hides overlooking nearby lagoons (though these can get quite dry).

Sendero Charco de la Boca At the Centro de Visitantes La Rocina, the Sendero Charco de la Boca is a 3.5km return walk along a stream, then through a range of habitats, passing four birdwatching hides.

Raya Real The Raya Real, one of the most important routes used by Romería pilgrims on their journeys to and from El Rocío (p101), can be accessed from the northeastern edge of that village by crossing the Puente del Ajolí and following the track into the woodland.

Centro de Visitantes La Rocina (☑ 959 43 95 69; A483; ⏱ 9am-3pm & 4-7pm) Beside the A483, 1km south of El Rocío. Has a national park information desk and walking paths.

Centro de Visitantes El Acebrón (☑ 671 593138; ⏱ 9am-3pm & 4-7pm) Located 6km along a minor paved road west from the Centro de Visitantes La Rocina, this centre offers a Doñana information counter and an ethnographic exhibition on the park inside a palatial 1960s residence, plus walking paths.

Centro de Visitantes El Acebuche (☑ 959 43 96 29; ⏱ 8am-3pm & 4-9pm May–mid-Sep, to 7pm mid-Sep–Mar, to 8pm Apr) Twelve kilometres south of El Rocío on the A483, then 1.6km west, El Acebuche is the national park's main visitor centre. It has paths to birdwatching hides and a live film of Iberian lynxes at its breeding centre.

Centro de Visitantes José Antonio Valverde (☑ 671 564145; ⏱ 10am-8pm Apr-Sep, to 7pm Mar & Oct, to 6pm Nov-Feb) The remote Centro de Visitantes José Antonio Valverde, on the eastern edge of the park, is generally an excellent birdwatching spot as it overlooks a year-round *lucio* (pond). The easiest way to reach the centre is by authorised tour from El Rocío; the alternative is to drive yourself on rough roads from Villamanrique de la Condesa or La Puebla del Río to the northeast.

ⓘ Getting There & Away

You cannot enter the national park in your own vehicle, though you can drive to the four main visitor centres. **Damas** (www.damas-sa.es) runs eight to 10 buses daily between El Rocío and Matalascañas, which stop at the El Acebuche turn-off on the A483 on request. Some tour companies will pick you up from Matalascañas with advance notice.

El Rocío

POP 1340

El Rocío, the most significant town in the vicinity of the Parque Nacional de Doñana, surprises first-timers. Its sand-covered streets are lined with colourful single-storey houses with sweeping verandahs, left empty half the time. But this is no ghost town: these are the well-tended properties of 115 *hermandades* (brotherhoods), whose pilgrims converge on the town every Pentecost (Whitsunday) weekend for the Romería del Rocío (p101), Spain's largest religious festival.

Beyond its uniquely exotic ambience, El Rocío impresses with its striking setting in front of luminous Doñana *marismas* (wetlands), where herds of deer drink at dawn and, at certain times of year, flocks of flamingos gather in massive numbers.

Whether it's the play of light on the marshes, an old woman praying to the Virgin at the Ermita, or someone passing by in a flamenco dress, there's always something to catch the eye on El Rocío's dusky, sand-blown streets.

◎ Sights & Activities

The marshlands in front of El Rocío, which have water most of the year, offer some of the best bird- and beast-watching in the entire Doñana region. Deer and horses graze in the shallows and you may be lucky enough to spot a big pink cloud of flamingos wheeling through the sky. Pack a pair of binoculars and stroll the waterfront promenade.

Ermita del Rocío   CHURCH
(Calle Ermita; ⏱ 8am-9pm Apr-Sep; to 7pm Oct-Mar) A striking splash of white at the heart of

DOÑANA'S IBERIAN LYNX

For wildlife watchers, the Iberian lynx is Doñana's most prized, yet elusive, animal. Lynx numbers in the Doñana area now fluctuate between 70 to 100 individuals (the official figure in 2016 was 74, down from a peak of 93 in 2013, but still up significantly from 41 in 2002). A disastrous slump in Doñana's population of rabbits (the lynx's main prey) has recently prompted park authorities to introduce 10,000 new rabbits into the area. There's also an increasingly successful captive breeding program – with Doñana's five breeding lynx pairs in 2017–18 expected to add 10 to 12 new cubs to the resident population (check out www.lynxexsitu.es). The Centro de Visitantes El Acebuche (p99) streams a live video of lynxes in its nearby breeding centre, which makes for pretty exciting viewing even when they're just stretching, yawning and grooming themselves – but you can't visit them. Some resident lynxes have been run over attempting to cross roads around Doñana (the park lost five lynxes in road accidents in 2016, which offers a compelling incentive to heed the posted speed limits).

the town, the Ermita del Rocío was built in its present form in 1964. This is the permanent home of the celebrated Nuestra Señora del Rocío (Our Lady of El Rocío), a small wooden image of the Virgin dressed in long, jewelled robes, which normally stands above the main altar. People arrive to see the Virgin every day of the year, and especially on weekends, when El Rocío's brotherhoods often gather for colourful celebrations.

**Francisco Bernis
Birdwatching Centre** BIRDWATCHING

(☑959 44 23 72; www.seo.org; Paseo Marismeño; ◷9am-2pm & 4-6pm Tue-Sun) FREE About 700m east of the Ermita along the waterfront, this birdwatching facility backs on to the marshes. Flamingos, glossy ibises, spoonbills and more can be observed through the rear windows or from the observation deck with high-power binoculars (free). Experts here can help you identify species and inform you about visiting migratory birds and where to see them.

👉 Tours

Doñana Nature WILDLIFE

(☑630 978216, 959 44 21 60; www.donana-nature.com; Calle Moguer 10; tours per person €28) Runs half-day, small-group (eight- to 15-person) tours of the Parque Natural de Doñana (p97) twice daily (one morning and one afternoon departure; binoculars provided). Specialised ornithological and photographic trips are also offered. English-speaking guides available on request.

Doñana Reservas WILDLIFE

(☑959 44 24 74, 629 060545; www.donanareservas.com; Avenida de la Canaliega; tours per person €28) Runs four-hour tours in 20- to 30-person all-terrain vehicles, focusing on

the marshes and woods in the northern section of the park, and including a stop at the Centro de Visitantes José Antonio Valverde (p99) – usually an excellent birdwatching spot. There's one morning and one afternoon departure daily.

Doñana a Caballo HORSE RIDING

(☑674 219568; www.donanaacaballo.com; Avenida de la Canaliega; per 1/2hr €20/30, half day €50) Guided horse rides for all levels through the Coto del Rey woodlands east of El Rocío.

🛏 Sleeping

Hotels get booked up to a year ahead for the Romería del Rocío.

Pensión Cristina PENSION €

(☑959 44 24 13; pensioncristina@hotmail.com; Calle El Real 58; s/d incl breakfast from €40/55; ❄🛜) Just east of the Ermita, Cristina provides comfy, colourful rooms around a cheerful tile-lined patio with lots of plants (sadly, no marsh views). The attached restaurant (mains €12-18; ◷1-4pm & 8-11pm) serves a varied menu of meat and seafood dishes.

Hotel Toruño HOTEL €€

(☑959 44 23 23; www.toruno.es; Plaza Acebuchal 22; s €35-59, d €50-80, all incl breakfast; 🅿❄🛜) About 350m east of the Ermita, this brilliantly white villa stands right by the *marismas* (wetlands), where you can spot flamingos going through their morning beauty routine. Inside, tile murals continue the wildlife theme – from otters to ibises – even in the showers! Interior rooms are rather bland and uninspiring, especially on the ground floor; request one overlooking the marshes if available. Better yet, splurge on room 302 (the Imperial Eagle, €80 to €150), a corner eyrie with whirlpool tub and stupendous marsh views from its high arched windows.

Breakfast (always included) is in the wonderful restaurant, opposite.

Hotel La Malvasía   HOTEL €€
(☎959 44 27 13; www.hotellamalvasia.com; Calle Sanlúcar 38; s €100-110, d €110-150, ste €160-190; ✳🗺) This idyllic hotel occupies a grand *casa señorial* (manor house) overlooking the marshes at the eastern end of town. Rooms have rustic tiled floors, vintage El Rocío photos and floral-patterned iron bedsteads. The top-floor sun terrace makes a spectacular bird-viewing perch, as does the suite, with its front-facing views of the lagoon.

🍴 Eating & Drinking

⭐**Restaurante Toruño**   ANDALUCIAN €€
(☎959 44 24 22; www.toruno.es; Plaza Acebuchal; mains €13-25; ⊗1-4pm & 8-11pm; 🅟) With its traditional Andalucian atmosphere, authentically good food and huge portions, this is El Rocío's one must-try restaurant. A highlight on the menu is the free-range *mostrenca* calf, unique to Doñana; for non-carnivores, the huge *parrillada* (grilled assortment) of vegetables is fantastic. Dine in front of the restaurant by the 1000-year-old

acebuche (olive) tree or out back overlooking the wetlands.

Aires de Doñana   ANDALUCIAN €€
(La Choza; ☎959 44 22 89; Avenida la Canaliega 1; mains €9-22; ⊗1-11pm Tue-Sun) Affectionately nicknamed La Choza (the Hut), this thatched-roofed, whitewashed local institution has one big thing going for it: knockout views of La Ermita framed by horse pastures and bird-thronged wetlands. The food, which includes everything from local Mostrenca beef to seafood, is hit or miss, but you can't go wrong sipping drinks on the terrace here at sunset.

ℹ Information

Tourist Office (☎959 44 23 50; www.almonte.es/es; Calle Muñoz Pavón; ⊗9.30am-2pm) Inside the town hall.

ℹ Getting There & Away

Damas (www.damas-sa.es) buses run from Seville's Plaza de Armas to El Rocío (€6.30, 1½ hours, two daily), continuing to Matalascañas (€1.30, 25 minutes). From Huelva, take a Damas bus to Almonte (€4, 1¼ hours, one to four daily), then another to El Rocío (€1.30, 20 minutes, eight daily).

DON'T MISS

SPAIN'S GREATEST RELIGIOUS PILGRIMAGE: ROMERÍA DEL ROCÍO

Every Pentecost (Whitsunday) weekend, seven weeks after Easter, El Rocío transforms from a quiet backwater into an explosive mess of noise, colour and passion. This is the culmination of Spain's biggest religious pilgrimage, the Romería del Rocío, which draws up to a million joyous pilgrims. The focus of all this revelry is the tiny image of Nuestra Señora del Rocío (Our Lady of El Rocío), which was found in a marshland tree by a hunter from Almonte village back in the 13th century. When he stopped for a rest on the way home, the Virgin magically returned to the tree. Before long, a chapel was built on the site of the tree (El Rocío) and pilgrims started arriving.

Solemn is the last word you'd apply to this quintessentially Andalucian event. Participants dress in their finest Andalucian costume and sing, drink, dance, laugh and romance their way to El Rocío. Most belong to the 115 *hermandades* (brotherhoods) who arrive from towns all across southern Spain on foot, horseback and in colourfully decorated covered wagons.

The weekend reaches an ecstatic climax in the very early hours of Monday. Members of the Almonte *hermandad,* which claims the Virgin as its own, barge into the church and bear her out on a float. Violent struggles ensue as others battle for the honour of carrying La Paloma Blanca (the White Dove). The crush and chaos are immense, but somehow the Virgin is carried round to each of the *hermandad* buildings before finally being returned to the church in the afternoon. Upcoming dates: 9 June 2019, 31 May 2020 and 23 May 2021.

In recent years, Spaniards' rising concern for animal rights, spearheaded by animal-welfare political party PACMA (https://pacma.es), has drawn attention to mistreatment and neglect of animals, particularly horses and mules, during the Romería del Rocío festivities, and, despite the presence of voluntary veterinary services, 10 horses and one ox died during the 2017 *romería*.

Matalascañas

Abutting the Parques Nacional and Natural de Doñana, 50km southeast of Huelva, Matalascañas is a modern, purpose-built tourist resort (much like Mazagón to its west). Thanks to national park regulations, development is confined to a 4km by 1km space. The beachhere is simply gorgeous.

Playa de Matalascañas   BEACH
Matalascañas's long sandy beach stretches for 4km along the south edge of town, merging at either end into the wilder beaches of Parque Nacional de Doñana. To reach the best part of the beach, follow the main road east to a trail leading down along the edge of the park. From a control post on the beach below the Gran Hotel del Coto, a 1.5km boardwalk trail snakes through the dunes, here dotted with umbrella pine and maritime juniper.

Parque Dunar   PARK
(Km 52, A494; ☺8am-9pm) On the western edge of Matalascañas, the Parque Dunar is a 1.3-sq-km expanse of high, pine-covered dunes laced with a maze of sandy pathways and boardwalk trails.

Hotel Doñana Blues   HOTEL **€€**
(☏959 44 81 32; www.donanablues.com; Sector I, Parcela 129; s/d from €88/99; ☺mid-Mar–Oct; ✻@🛜❄) Not blue but mustard yellow (it's named after a tune the owner composed), this flower-filled compound is in the suburban maze of central Matalascañas. Decor is standard rural kitsch, but lovingly done, and you get your own terrace/balcony amid the jasmine, roses, bougainvillea and ivy. There's a cool blue pool out back.

❶ Getting There & Away

Damas (www.damas-sa.es) runs two to three buses daily from Matalascañas to Seville (€7.70, two hours), plus twice-daily service Monday to Friday to Huelva (€4, 1¼ hours).

NORTHERN HUELVA PROVINCE

North of Huelva, straight highways are replaced by winding byways and you enter a more temperate zone, up to 960m higher than the coast. The rolling hills of Huelva's portion of the Sierra Morena are covered with a thick pelt of cork oak and pine, punctuated by winding river valleys, enchanting stone-and-tile villages, and the bustling 'capital' of the area, Aracena.

Word is slowly getting out about this still little-discovered rural world, threaded with walking trails. Most of the area lies within

---

OFF THE BEATEN TRACK

NIEBLA

Thirty kilometres east of Huelva on the A472 to Seville (4km north of the A49), the brilliantly preserved medieval town of Niebla makes a fascinating stop. Encircled by 2km of dusty-orange Moorish-era walls and with five original gates plus 46 towers, Niebla's old town and its narrow streets simmer with history. Damas (www.damas-sa.es) runs three to five daily buses to Niebla from Seville (€6, 1½ hours) and three to seven daily buses from Huelva (€3, 30 minutes). From El Rocío, there's no direct bus service to Niebla, but it's an easy 35-minute drive if you've got your own wheels.

Castillo de los Guzmán (☏959 09 12 23; Calle Campo del Castillo; admission €2.50; ☺10am-6pm) Niebla's main attraction is the majestic 15th-century Castillo de los Guzmán, probably of Roman origins but built up into a palace fortress under Moorish rule. It's set around two open patios; in the dungeon below there's a spine-chilling torture museum. Also here is Niebla's **tourist office** (☏959 09 12 23; www.turismoniebla.com; Calle Arrabal 36; ☺10am-6pm).

Iglesia de Santa María de Granada (Plaza de Santa María; ☺mass 7pm Mon-Sat, noon Sun) On the central Plaza de Santa María, the beautiful Iglesia de Santa María de Granada was originally a Visigothic cathedral before becoming a 9th-century mosque, and then a Gothic-Mudéjar church in the 15th century.

Iglesia de San Martín (Plaza de San Martín; ☺mass 9am Fri) Just inside the Puerta del Socorro, the main gate into the old town, you'll find the remains of this Gothic-Mudéjar church, built on the site of a former synagogue and mosque, and now split in two by a plaza.

the 1870-sq-km **Parque Natural Sierra de Aracena y Picos de Aroche**, Andalucía's second-largest protected zone.

Minas de Riotinto

POP 3260 / ELEV 420M

Tucked away on the southern fringe of Huelva's Sierra Morena is one of the world's oldest mining districts; King Solomon of Jerusalem is said to have mined gold here for his famous temple, and the Romans were digging up silver by the 4th century BC. The mines were then left largely untouched until the British Rio Tinto company made this one of the world's key copper-mining centres in the 1870s (leading, incidentally, to the foundation of Spain's first football club). The mines were sold back to Spain in 1954, and the miners clocked off for the last time in 2001. Nowadays it's a fascinating place to explore, with a superb museum, and opportunities to visit the old mines and ride the mine railway. The Río Tinto itself rises a few kilometres northeast of town, its name ('red river') stemming from the deep red-brown hue of its iron- and copper-infused waters.

◉ Sights & Activities

Museo Minero MUSEUM
(☑ 959 59 00 25; www.parquemineroderiotinto.es; Plaza Ernest Lluch; adult/child €5/4; ⊙ 10.30am-3pm & 4-7pm; ℗) Riotinto's mining museum is a figurative goldmine for devotees of industrial archaeology. Displays take you through the area's unique history from the megalithic tombs of the 3rd millennium BC to the Roman and British colonial eras, then the 1888 *año de los tiros* (year of the gunshots) upheaval and finally the closure of the mines in 2001. The tour includes an elaborate 200m-long recreation of a Roman mine.

Peña de Hierro MINE
(☑ 959 59 00 25; www.parquemineroderiotinto.es; adult/child €8/7; ⊙ 10.30am-3pm & 4-7pm) These are old copper and sulphur mines 3km north of Nerva (6km east of Minas de Riotinto). Here you see the source of the Río Tinto and a 65m-deep opencast mine, and are taken into a 200m-long underground mine gallery. There are three guaranteed daily visits but schedules vary, so it's essential to book ahead through the Museo Minero (by phone or online).

Ferrocarril Turístico-Minero RAIL
(☑ 959 59 00 25; www.parquemineroderiotinto.es; adult/child €11/10; ⊙ 1.30pm & 5.30pm mid-Jul-mid-Sep, 1.30pm mid-Sep-mid-Jul, closed Mon-Fri Nov-mid-Feb) A fun way to see the area (especially with children) is to ride the old mining train, running 22km (round trip) through the surreal landscape in restored early 20th-century carriages. The train parallels the river for the entire journey, so you can appreciate its constantly shifting hues. It's mandatory to book ahead, either at the town's museum or the railway station.

Trips along the rust-red Río Tinto start at the old railway repair workshops 4km east of Minas de Riotinto off the road to Nerva. Commentary is in Spanish (with English-language handouts).

❶ Getting There & Away

Damas (www.damas-sa.es) runs three to five daily buses between Minas de Riotinto and Huelva (€6.85, 1¾ hours).

Aracena

POP 6700 / ELEV 730M

Sparkling white in its mountain bowl, the thriving old market town of Aracena is an appealingly lively place that's wrapped like a ribbon around a medieval church and ruined castle. With a stash of good places to eat and sleep, it makes an ideal Sierra de Aracena base.

◉ Sights

★**Gruta de las Maravillas** CAVE
(Cave of Marvels; ☑ 663 937876; www.aracena.es/es/municipio/gruta; Calle Pozo de la Nieve; tours adult/child €9/6.50; ⊙ 10am-1.30pm & 3-6pm) Beneath the town's castle hill is a web of caves and tunnels carved from the karstic topography. An extraordinary 1.2km, 50-minute loop takes you through 12 chambers and past six underground lakes, all beautifully illuminated and filled with weird and wonderful rock formations, which provided a backdrop for the film *Journey to the Center of the Earth*.

Tours are in Spanish, with optional English-language audioguides available for €1.50. Frequency of departures varies according to demand. Tickets can sell out in the afternoons and on weekends when busloads of visitors arrive.

Museo del Jamón MUSEUM
(Gran Vía; adult/child €3.50/2.50; ⊙ 10.45am-2.30pm & 3.45-6.30pm) The *jamón* for which the sierra is famed gets due recognition in this modern museum. You'll learn why the

Aracena

acorn-fed Iberian pig gives such succulent meat, about the importance of the native pastures in which they are reared, and about traditional and contemporary methods of slaughter and curing. Displays are in Spanish, with free audio guides available in four other languages. Afterwards, the museum shop invites visitors to 'pig' out with a free tasting of local *bellota* ham.

⊙ Old-Town Aracena

The handsome, cobbled Plaza Alta was originally the centre of the town. Here stands the elegant 15th-century Cabildo Viejo, the former town hall, with a grand Renaissance doorway (and a natural park information centre). From Plaza Alta, Calle Francisco Rincón descends the hill back towards town, passing a series of narrow streets attractively lined with humble whitewashed houses, before finally entering the main Plaza del Marqués de Aracena, a lively square fronted by a few cafe-restaurants.

Castillo   CASTLE

(Cerro del Castillo; guided tour adult/child €2.50/1) Dramatically dominating the town are the tumbling, hilltop ruins of the *castillo*, built by the kingdoms of Portugal and Castilla in the 12th century atop the ruins of an earlier Islamic settlement. Directly adjacent is the

Gothic-Mudéjar Iglesia Prioral de Nuestra Señora del Mayor Dolor (Plazoleta Virgen del Mayor Dolor; ⊙10am-5pm, to 7.30pm Jul & Aug). Both are reached via a steep lane from Plaza Alta; guided tours grant access to the castle's interior, though it's honestly more impressive from the outside.

🏃 Activities

The hills and mountains around Aracena offer some of the most beautiful, and least known, walking country in Andalucía. Any time of year is a good time to hike here but spring (April and May), when the meadows are awash with wildflowers and colourful butterflies, is the best time to hit the trails. The Centro de Visitantes Cabildo Viejo (p106) can recommend walks of varying difficulty and give you basic maps; the tourist office (p106) sells a good map with dozens of suggested hikes.

Linares de la Sierra Walk   HIKING

This sublime and fairly gentle 5km, two-hour ramble takes you down a verdant valley to beautifully sleepy Linares de la Sierra (p106). The signposted path (PRA48) is easy to find off the HU8105 on the southwestern edge of Aracena, 500m beyond the municipal swimming pool. You can extend the walk to Alájar (4km, 1½ hours), with the option of

Aracena

returning to Aracena on the 4pm or 4.30pm bus (except Sunday).

Escuela de Equitación
Barquera Alta   HORSE RIDING
(☑959 12 77 11; Finca Valbono, Carretera Aracena-Carboneras Km 1; 2hr rides per person €30) A friendly establishment organising horse rides through the countryside surrounding Aracena, plus classes. It's 1km northeast of town.

☞ Tours

★ **Jamones Eíriz Jabugo**   FOOD & DRINK
(www.rutadeljamondejabugo.com; Calle Pablo Bejarano 43, Corteconcepción; per person incl tasting €40) For a first-hand understanding of Denominación de Origen Calificada (DOC) Iberian ham production, nothing beats the two- to three-hour tours offered by this award-winning, fourth-generation, family-run operation. After an hour mingling with acorn-crazed pigs in their little patch of paradise under the oak trees, decamp to the maze of salting and curing chambers, where you'll witness hundreds of dangling hams developing their prized flavour. All tours must be booked in advance. It's 6km northeast of Aracena.

🛏 Sleeping

Molino del Bombo   BOUTIQUE HOTEL €
(☑689 471675; www.molinodelbombo.com; Calle Ancha 4; s/d from €38/55; ❄🛜) Though of recent vintage, the top-of-town Bombo has a rustic style that blends in with Aracena's time-worn architecture. Bright rooms have wonderfully comfy, pillow-laden beds, plus frescoes and exposed stone and brick designs; some bathrooms are done up as pic-

turesque grottoes. The cosy salon and courtyard with trickling fountain are perfect for lounging. The lone downside: reception is occasionally less than friendly.

★ **Hotel Convento**
Aracena   HISTORIC HOTEL €€
(☑959 12 68 99; www.hotelconventoaracena.es; Calle Jesús y María 19; d €98-149, ste €173-234; 🅿❄🛜🏊) Glossy, modern rooms contrast with flourishes of original Andalucian baroque architecture at this thoughtfully converted 17th-century convent, Aracena town's finest lodging. Enjoy the on-site spa, sierra cuisine and year-round saltwater pool, with gorgeous village views and summer bar. Room 9 is fabulously set in the church dome (though be forewarned that it's windowless, save for the skylight in the cupola).

Finca Valbono   HOTEL €€
(☑959 12 77 11; www.fincavalbono.com; Carretera Aracena-Carboneras, Km 1; d €55-70, 2-person apt €65-80, 4-person apt €100-120; 🅿❄🛜🏊) Just 1km northeast of Aracena, this lovingly run farmhouse immersed in greenery offers a splendid mix of country charm and convenient location. It has 20 *casitas* (cottages) set up with log fires, kitchenettes and supplementary sofa beds (perfect for groups or families), plus six rustic rooms. Other standout features include a lovely pool, friendly staff and an on-site riding school.

✕ Eating

★ **Rincón de Juan**   TAPAS €
(Avenida de Portugal 3; tapas €2-3, raciones €7-10; ⊙7.30am-4pm & 6.30pm-midnight Mon-Sat) It's standing room only at this wedge-shaped, stone-walled corner bar, indisputably the top tapas spot in town. Iberian ham is the star attraction and forms the basis for a variety of *montaditos* (small stuffed rolls) and *rebanadas* (sliced loaves for several people). The local goat's cheese is always a good bet.

ℹ **ARACENA DISCOUNT TICKET**

If you're visiting multiple sights in Aracena, save 20% with the **Tarjeta Aracena Turística**, a combo ticket offering admission to the Gruta de las Maravillas (p103), the Museo del Jamón (p103) and the Castillo for €12, vs €15 for tickets bought separately.

★ **Jesús Carrión** TAPAS €€
(☑959 46 31 88; www.jesuscarrionrestaurante.
com; Calle Pozo de la Nieve 35; tapas €6.50-13,
mains €12-25; ☉1.15-4pm Wed-Sun, 8.15-11pm
Thu-Sat; ☎☑) Devoted chef Jesús heads up
the creative kitchen at this wonderful family-run restaurant, which is causing quite
the stir with its lovingly prepared, contemporary twists on traditional Aracena dishes.
Try the Iberian ham carpaccio or the local
boletus-mushroom risotto. Homemade
breads come straight from the oven and
salads are deliciously fresh – not a tinned
vegetable in sight!

❶ Information

Centro de Visitantes Cabildo Viejo (☑959
12 95 53; Plaza Alta; ☉9.30am-2.30pm, opening
days vary) Gives out hiking information and
maps, and has an exhibit on the Parque Natural
Sierra de Aracena y Picos de Aroche.
Tourist Office (☑663 937877; www.aracena.
es; Calle Pozo de la Nieve; ☉10am-2pm &
4-6pm) Opposite the Gruta de las Maravillas;
sells a good walking map.

❶ Getting There & Away

The **bus station** (Calle José Andrés Vázquez)
is 700m southeast of Plaza del Marqués de
Aracena. **Damas** (www.damas-sa.es) runs one
morning and two afternoon buses (one on Sunday) from Seville (€7.40, 1¼ hours), continuing
to Cortegana via Alájar or Jabugo. From Huelva,
there are two afternoon departures Monday
to Friday, and one on weekends (€10.85, 2½ to
three hours). There's also a local service between Aracena and Cortegana via Linares de la
Sierra, Alájar and Almonaster la Real.

Sierra de Aracena

Stretching west of Aracena is one of Andalucía's most unexpectedly picturesque
landscapes, a flower-sprinkled hill country
dotted with old stone villages and imposing
castles. Woodlands alternate with expanses
of *dehesa* (evergreen oak pastures where the
region's famed black pigs forage for acorns).
The area is threaded by an extensive network of well-maintained walking trails, with
ever-changing vistas and mostly gentle ascents and descents, making for some of the
most delightful rambling in Andalucía.

Great hiking routes are particularly thick
in the area between Aracena and Cortegana, making attractive villages such as
Alájar, Castaño del Robledo, Galaroza and
Almonaster la Real perfect bases from which
to set forth.

You can download maps and Spanish-
and English-language hiking information
from www.sierradearacena.com and www.
ventanadelvisitante.es, but ideally you need
a reliable map and walking guide. The best
are Discovery Walking Guides' *Sierra de
Aracena* and its partner *Sierra de Aracena
Tour & Trail Map.*

❶ Getting There & Away

BUS

All buses are operated by **Damas** (www.damas
-sa.es). Morning and afternoon buses travel
the HU8105 daily from Aracena to Cortegana
(€3.30, one hour). From Monday to Saturday,
one daily bus also travels from Aracena to
Linares de la Sierra (€1.15, 10 minutes), Alájar
(€1.15, 30 minutes) and Almonaster la Real
(€2.20, 50 minutes).

TRAIN

There's at least one daily train each way between
Huelva and the stations of Almonaster-Cortegana
(€9.50, 1¾ hours) and Jabugo-Galaroza (€10.55,
two hours). Almonaster-Cortegana station is
1km off the Almonaster–Cortegana road, halfway between the two villages.

Linares de la Sierra

POP 230 / ELEV 505M

Just 7km west of Aracena along the HU8105,
you'll bump into one of the area's cutest
villages, Linares de la Sierra. Surrounded
by a verdant river valley, its cobbled streets
are renowned for their 300-odd *llanos*
(front-patio mosaics) and are lined with
oddly angled, tiled-roof houses. In the centre, behind the 18th-century Iglesia de San
Juan Bautista, a minute bullring plaza is
paved with concentric rings around a shield
of flowers. From the village's fringes, signposted walking paths fan out into the hills
towards Aracena (p105) and Alájar.

There's a little **visitors centre** (☑959 46
37 28; www.linaresdelasierra.com; Calle Iglesia;
☉9am-6pm Tue-Sun) with (limited) information on walks around Linares just south of
the bullring plaza.

★ **Restaurante Arrieros** ANDALUCIAN €€
(☑959 46 37 17; www.arrieros.net; Calle Arrieros
2; mains €14-20; ☉1.30-4pm, closed mid-Jun–
mid-Jul) The art of slow food is taken to the
extreme here with meals normally spinning
out over several lazy hours. The innovative
approach to local pork products and wild

Sierra de Aracena

mushrooms, such as the mushroom-and-apple stuffed *solomillo* (pork sirloin) and *carrilleras* (pig cheeks) in red wine, makes this one of the sierra's top places to eat.

Alájar

POP 800 / ELEV 570M

Five kilometres west of Linares de la Sierra is possibly the region's most picturesque village, Alájar, which retains its narrow cobbled streets and cubist stone houses along with a fine baroque church. Several good walking routes leave from or pass through here.

◉ Sights & Activities

Peña de Arias Montano   HISTORIC SITE
(HU8121; Ⓟ) High above Alájar, this rocky spur provides magical views over the village. The site takes its name from remarkable 16th-century polymath and humanist Benito Arias Montano, who repeatedly visited this spot for retreat and meditation. The *peña*'s 16th-century chapel, the Ermita de Nuestra Señora Reina de los Ángeles, is an important local pilgrimage site.

**Ermita de Nuestra Señora
Reina de los Ángeles**   CHURCH
(HU8121; ⏱11am-sunset) On the Peña de Arias Montano, the 16th-century Ermita de Nuestra Señora Reina de los Ángeles contains a small carving of the Virgin that is considered the patron of the whole Sierra de Aracena. In early September the chapel is the focus of the area's biggest annual religious event, the **Romería de la Reina de los Ángeles**, when people from all around the sierra converge here to honour their Virgin.

Outside the chapel are stalls selling local honey and cheeses, and an **info booth** (☏ 625 512442; HU-8121; ⏱Fri-Sun, hours vary) with displays about the local area.

Castaño del Robledo Walk   HIKING
Starting beside the bus stop on the western edge of Alájar, across the HU8105, this moderately difficult 5km uphill route leads you past the once deserted hamlet of El Calabacino, now an international artist/hippy colony, then on to the beautiful little village of Castaño del Robledo, passing through cork-oak and chestnut forest. Allow two hours.

🛏 Sleeping & Eating

Posada de Alájar   INN €
(☏959 12 57 12; www.posadasalajar.com; Calle Médico Emilio González 2; s/d €40/55; ✸🐾) 𝄖
The lovely English-Spanish owners of this basic one-star inn in the heart of town are keen walkers and have excellent hiking advice and materials. Among the simple rooms, No 6 stands out for its gorgeous *peña* views. For €5, guests here can use the pool at sister establishment Posada de San Marcos.

★ Posada de San Marcos   INN €€
(☏667 906132, 959 12 57 12; www.posadasalajar.com; Calle Colón 12; s/d incl breakfast €70/95; Ⓟ✸@🐾🏊) 𝄖 Hot on sustainability, this brilliantly restored 200-year-old house bordering a stream in the heart of the village runs on geothermal energy, rain harvesting and natural-cork insulation. The six comfortably rustic, airy rooms have big terraces, breakfast is homemade, and welcoming

SIERRA DE ARACENA CUISINE

The hills around Aracena have given rise to some superb, and increasingly innovative, cuisine. Delights include the region's mushrooms; dozens of different varieties pop up out of the ground every autumn. And then there's the ham: the *jamón ibérico* of nearby Jabugo is considered the finest in the entire country; you won't fail to notice the providers of this bounty – contented-looking black pigs foraging in the forests for acorns.

Spanish-English hosts Ángel and Lucy are experts on local hiking. The pool looks across the village to the *peña*.

The owners take pride in sharing Aracena's culture with guests, offering tastings of local olive oil or local goat cheese (per person €40) and comprehensive mini-courses about the region's famous DOC ham, including a carving and tasting session accompanied by local wines (€70). Lucy makes excellent three-course dinners upon request (per person €25, plus €12 per bottle of wine).

★ **Finca La Fronda** HOTEL €€
(☑ 959 50 12 47; www.fincalafronda.com; Carretera Cortegana-Aracena, Km 22; r incl breakfast €115-145; P ✳ 🛜 🌊) Pocketed away amid cork/chestnut forest, La Fronda makes the perfect hillside hideaway. Its modern-rustic beauty comes out in the bright lounge, Mudéjar-inspired patio and huge, flowery rooms with splashes of British character (warm pastels, smart armchairs). Spectacular vistas of Alájar and the Peña de Arias Montano unfold from the rose-fringed pool.

Long-time owner Charles Wordsworth (who is indeed a great-great-grandson of the poet) together with his daughters, can arrange *jamón* tastings, horse riding, live piano concerts and hiking. It's signposted off the HU8105, 2km northeast of Alájar.

★ **Molino Río Alájar** COTTAGE €€€
(☑ 638 081415, 959 50 17 74; www.molinorioalajar.com; Finca Cabeza del Molino; house per day €125-183, per week €850-1275) A labour of love for well-travelled Dutch owners Peter Jan and Monica, these six rental cottages are ideal for families or anybody wanting a self-contained home in the heart of nature. Each unique unit is beautifully constructed of reclaimed wood, brick, stone and tile, equipped with a full kitchen and creative-

ly decorated with vintage furniture, family heirlooms and flea-market finds.

★ **Casa Padrino** ANDALUCIAN €€
(☑ 959 12 56 01; Plaza Miguel Moya 2; mains €10-18; ⊙ 2-4pm & 9pm-midnight Fri & Sat, 2-4pm Sun) With atmospheric dining by a brick-ring fireplace or on a sunny terrace, Casa Padrino serves scrumptious country fare loosely based on old village recipes. The *pencas de acelgas* (Swiss chard stuffed with Iberian pork) is memorable, as is the *lomo ibérico* (Iberian pork loin) in chestnut sauce, broiled to perfection. Desserts include pennyroyal mint ice cream and pine nut flan.

Castaño del Robledo

POP 190 / ELEV 740M

North of Alájar on the minor HU8114 road between Fuenteheridos and Jabugo, little Castaño del Robledo is a truly idyllic spot, surrounded by hazy green olive and cork forests. Its jigsaw of tiled terracotta roofs is overlooked by two large churches (one unfinished), either of which could easily accommodate the entire village population.

🏃 Activities

Castaño del Robledo-Galaroza Loop Walk HIKING
A worthwhile 10km loop (three hours) can be hiked by taking the PRA38 trail from Castaño del Robledo to Galaroza village and returning via the alternative SLA129 riverside route. The walk traverses woodlands interspersed with long-distance panoramas. Wildflowers pop up in spring and you're likely to spot *pata negra* (black leg) pigs of Jabugo fame rooting about for acorns.

Leave via the unsigned path beside the shrine in the Área Recreativa Capilla del Cristo, on the HU8114 road passing along the north of the village. To the left you'll soon see Cortegana and Jabugo, before you fork right, 15 minutes along the track. Your path winds downhill until you cross the Jabugo–Fuenteheridos trail after 10 minutes. About 50m beyond, go right at a fork. In 10 minutes Galaroza comes into view as you pass between its outlying *fincas* (rural properties). Cross a small river on a footbridge and emerge on the N433 road three minutes later. Walk left towards Galaroza, skirting the town along the N433 for around 800m. Just before you reach a palm-studded plaza, leave by a track on the left marked by a 'Sendero Ribera del Jabugo' sign.

Fork right at a green-and-white-striped post one minute from the sign, then turn left at a 'Camino Galaroza-Castaño Bajo' sign five minutes later down to a footbridge over a stream. The path soon starts winding up the Río Jabugo valley, a particularly lovely stretch lined with poplars, willows and alders. Half an hour from the footbridge you'll reach a vehicle track marked 'Camino de Jabugo a Fuenteheridos'. Head right, passing some *cortijos* (farmhouses), to cross the river on a low bridge. Turn left 50m past the bridge, then left at a fork 30m further on. You recross the river by stepping stone. Fifteen minutes from the river, turn left at a red-tile-roofed house and arrowed stump; in 15 minutes (mostly uphill) you're re-entering Castaño del Robledo.

🛏 Sleeping & Eating

Posada del Castaño　　　　CASA RURAL €
(☎959 46 55 02; www.posadadelcastano.com; Calle José Sánchez Calvo 33; s/d incl breakfast €40/50; 🛜) This chilled-out converted village house, with its bendy roof beams, big book collection and colourful throws, has walkers foremost in mind. The British owners (experienced travellers and hikers) are full of information, and offer self-guided walking tours and horse-riding holidays. Weather permitting, homemade breakfast is served on the back terrace overlooking the lush garden.

El Dornillo　　　　ANDALUCIAN €€
(☎619 024630; Plaza del Álamo 5; mains €10-16; ⊙1.30-3.30pm & 8.30-11pm Wed-Mon) Good honest mountain staples – grilled meats, croquettes, *revueltos* (Spanish-style scrambled egg dishes) and salads – rule the menu at this centrally located restaurant run by a friendly couple. On sunny days, the vine-clad outdoor terrace is a delightful place to eat, with its view of orange trees, whitewashed walls and rooftops, and the distant sound of schoolkids playing down the street.

Almonaster la Real

POP 650 / ELEV 613M

Set amid rolling hills covered in cork oak forest, Almonaster la Real is one of the Sierra de Aracena's most picturesque and appealingly authentic towns. Elderly locals loll about the peaceful village centre, while the hillside just above harbours a fabulous gem of Islamic architecture.

◉ Sights & Activities

★ Mezquita　　　　HISTORIC BUILDING
(Mosque; Calle Castillo 10; ⊙9am-dusk) FREE This historic little *mezquita* (mosque) stands above the town about five minutes' walk from the main square. The almost perfectly preserved structure, a rare find in this region, is like a miniature version of Córdoba's great mosque. Despite being Christianised in the 13th century, it retains nearly all its original Islamic features: the horseshoe arches, the semicircular mihrab, an ablutions fountain and various Arabic inscriptions. Even older are the capitals of the columns nearest the mihrab, which are Roman.

The original square minaret adjoins the building. Just below is Almonaster's 19th-century bullring.

Iglesia de San Martín　　　　CHURCH
(Placeta de San Cristóbal; ⊙variable) The Mudéjar Iglesia de San Martín has a 16th-century portal in the Portuguese Manueline style, unique in the region.

Cerro de San Cristóbal Walk　　　　HIKING
From the eastern end of town, this circular hiking route (5.5km, about 2½ hours) leads up to the Cerro de San Cristóbal (912m) for fantastic views across the sierra.

🛏 Sleeping & Eating

Posada El Camino　　　　HOTEL €
(☎959 50 32 40; www.posadaelcamino.es; Carretera Cortegana-Aracena, Km 6.8; s/d/tr €36/50/65; P🅿❄🛜) Popular with Spanish families, this salmon-pink motel-like lodging stands at the bottom of a hill of cork trees, with trails heading off nearby. It has a good **restaurant** (mains €12-18; ⊙9am-midnight Tue-Sat, to 6pm Sun) specialising in regional cuisine. Look for it 500m east of Almonaster, just off the HU8105 to Alájar.

El Rincón de Curro　　　　ANDALUCIAN €€
(☎959 14 31 49, 676 780606; Calle Carretera; mains €12-25; ⊙1.30-4.30pm daily & 8.30-11pm Fri & Sat) Look for this wonderful local restaurant in a whitewashed building on the main road just west of town. Since 2000, Señor Curro has been delighting discerning palates with his fine mountain cuisine. Local pork products get top billing, but plenty of dishes also feature seafood and vegetables – not to mention the deliciously crispy, cumin-y *patatas bravas* offered as a free appetiser.

Cádiz Province & Gibraltar

Best Places to Stay

➡ V... (p143)

➡ La Casa del Califa (p143)

➡ Hostal África (p149)

➡ Riad (p150)

➡ Parador de Cádiz (p115)

➡ Hostal Alcoba (p133)

Best Places to Eat

➡ Aponiente (p130)

➡ El Jardín del Califa (p144)

➡ Café Azul (p150)

➡ Casa Balbino (p133)

➡ Casa Manteca (p115)

➡ Albores (p125)

Why Go?

If you had to pick just one region to attempt to explain Andalucía in its full, complex beauty, it'd probably be Cádiz. Lying in wait across Spain's southernmost province are craggy mountains, olive trees, fortified sherry, festivals galore, flamenco in its purest incarnation, the font of Andalucian horse culture, and a blond-sand coastline, the uncommercial Costa de la Luz, sprinkled with surfer-cool towns like Tarifa. And then – just when you thought you were getting a handle on it – there's the idiosyncratic British anomaly of Gibraltar.

Packed in among all this condensed culture are the expansive Sierra de Grazalema and Los Alcornocales natural parks, an unbroken tract of land from Olvera in the north to Algeciras in the south. The same line once marked the ever-changing frontier between Christian Spain and Moorish Granada, and that ancient border remains dotted with castle-topped, whitewashed towns, many with a 'de la Frontera' suffix that testifies to their volatile history.

Driving Distances

	Cádiz	Jerez de la Frontera	Tarifa	Gibraltar
Jerez de la Frontera	32			
Tarifa	103	113		
Gibraltar	144	113	43	
Arcos de la Frontera	63	32	113	115

CÁDIZ

POP 118,920

You could write several weighty tomes about Cádiz and still fall short of nailing its essence. Cádiz is generally considered to be the oldest continuously inhabited settlement in Europe, founded as Gadir by the Phoenicians in about 1100 BC. Now well into its fourth millennium, the ancient centre, surrounded almost entirely by water, is a romantic jumble of sinuous streets where Atlantic waves crash against eroded sea walls, cheerful taverns fry up fresh fish and salty beaches teem with sun-worshippers. Spain's first liberal constitution (La Pepa) was signed here in 1812, while the city's distinctive urban model provided an identikit for fortified Spanish colonial cities in the Americas.

Enamoured return visitors talk fondly of Cádiz' seafood, sands and intriguing monuments and museums. More importantly, they gush happily about the *gaditanos*, an upfront, sociable bunch whose crazy Carnaval is an exercise in ironic humour and whose upbeat *alegrías* (flamenco songs) warm your heart.

◉ Sights

To understand Cádiz, first you need to befriend its *barrios* (districts). The old city is split into classic quarters: the Barrio del Pópulo, home of the cathedral, and nexus of the once prosperous medieval settlement; Barrio de Santa María, the old Roma and flamenco quarter; Barrio de la Viña, a former vineyard that became the city's main fishing quarter and Carnaval epicentre; and Barrio del Mentidero, centred on Plaza de San Antonio in the northwest. Las Bicis Naranjas (p120) and Urban Bike (p120) run guided bike tours of the old town.

★ **Catedral de Cádiz**   CATHEDRAL
(📞 608 090424; www.catedraldecadiz.com; Plaza de la Catedral; incl Museo Catedralicio & Torre del Reloj adult/child €5/free; ⊙ 10am-9pm Jul & Aug, to 8pm Apr-Jun & Sep, to 7pm Oct-Mar) Cádiz' beautiful yellow-domed cathedral is an impressively proportioned baroque-neoclassical construction, best appreciated from seafront Campo del Sur in the evening sun. Though commissioned in 1716, the project wasn't finished until 1838, by which time neoclassical elements (the dome, towers and main facade) had diluted architect Vicente Acero's original baroque plan. Highlights within are the intricate wood-carved choir and, in the crypt below, the tomb of

renowned 20th-century *gaditano* composer Manuel de Falla.

Tickets include audio guides, the religious treasures of the Museo Catedralicio (⊙ 10am-4.30pm Mon-Sat Jul & Aug, to 3.30pm Apr-Jun & Sep, to 3pm Oct-Mar), just east, and a climb up the cathedral's (eastern) Torre del Reloj, reopened with fabulous wraparound old-city views after half a century off limits.

★ **Museo de Cádiz**   MUSEUM
(www.museosdeandalucia.es; Plaza de Mina; EU citizens/noncitizens free/€1.50; ⊙ 9am-3pm Tue-Sun mid-Jun–mid-Sep, 9am-8pm Tue-Sat, to 3pm Sun mid-Sep–mid-Jun) Admittedly a little dusty, the Museo de Cádiz is the province's top museum. Stars of the ground-floor archaeology section are two Phoenician marble sarcophagi carved in human likeness, along with lots of headless Roman statues and a giant marble 2nd-century Emperor Trajan (with head) from Bolonia's Baelo Claudia (p152) ruins. Upstairs, the excellent fine-art collection displays Spanish art from the 18th to early 20th centuries, including 18 superb 17th-century canvases of saints, angels and monks by Francisco de Zurbarán.

Equally important is the beautifully composed baroque altarpiece from the chapel of Cádiz' Convento de Capuchinas, which cost artist Bartolomé Esteban Murillo his life when he fell from its scaffolding in 1682.

Teatro Romano   ARCHAEOLOGICAL SITE
(Calle Mesón 12; ⊙ 11am-5pm Mon-Sat, 10am-2pm Sun Apr-Sep, 10am-4.30pm Mon-Sat, to 2pm Sun Oct-Mar, closed 1st Mon of month) FREE On the seaward edge of the Barrio del Pópulo is Cádiz' Roman theatre, dating from the late 1st century BC and, originally, with space for 10,000 spectators. The theatre is undergoing renovation works (due for completion in 2020), but you can still access parts of it via its modern interpretation centre, with intriguing English- and Spanish-language displays detailing the theatre's history.

Playa de la Caleta   BEACH
Hugging the western side of the Barrio de la Viña, this small, popular city beach catches the eye with its mock-Moorish, oriental-inspired Modernista *balneario* (bathhouse). It's flanked by two forts: the Castillo de San Sebastián (Paseo Fernando Quiñones; ⊙ 9.30am-5pm) FREE, for centuries a military installation, and the star-shaped Castillo de Santa Catalina (📞 956 22 63 33; Calle Antonio Burgos; ⊙ 11am-8.30pm Mar-Oct, to 7.30pm Nov-Feb) FREE, built after the 1596 Anglo-Dutch sacking of the city and with a 1683 chapel.

Cadiz Province & Gibraltar Highlights

1 Tarifa (p147) Soaking up the kitesurfing, wind-surfing and beach-lazing scenes.

2 Jerez de la Frontera (p121) Unravelling a fashionable world of flamenco, horses, sherry and bodegas.

3 Cádiz (p111) Travelling through 3000 years of history as you wander Cádiz' sea-encircled old city.

4 Vejer de la Frontera (p142) Getting lost in white-town magic, feasting on Andalucian-fusion cooking and slumbering in boutique hotels.

5 Parque Natural Sierra de Grazalema (p139) Hiking the Garganta Verde, or kayaking and canyoning between white villages.

6 Arcos de la Frontera (p134) Wandering around the ultimate cliff-top *pueblo blanco*.

7 Sanlúcar de Barrameda (p132) Tucking into fresh-from-the-ocean fish along Bajo de Guía and venturing into the Parque Nacional de Doñana.

8 Baelo Claudia (p152) Turning back the clock at Bolonia's ruined Roman seaside town.

9 Los Caños de Meca (p145) Sinking into white-sand-beach bliss.

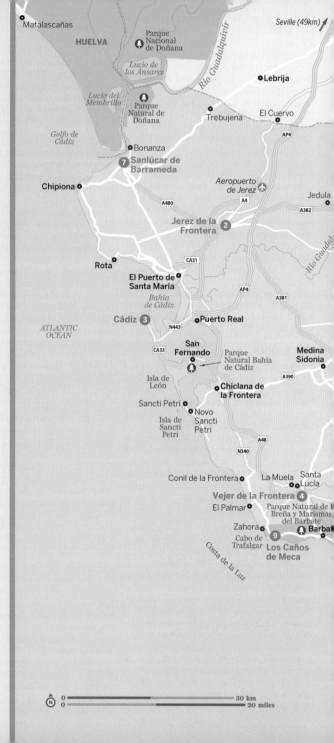

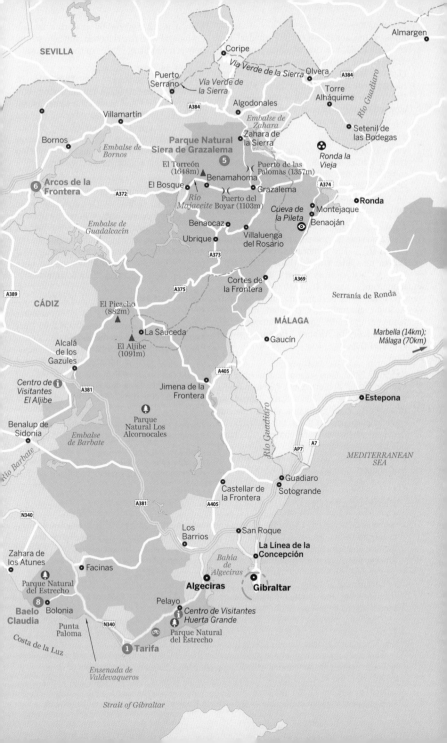

Plaza de Topete SQUARE

About 250m northwest of the cathedral, this triangular plaza is one of Cádiz' most intimate. Bright with flowers, it's usually called Plaza de las Flores (Square of the Flowers). Right beside is the revamped 1837 **Mercado Central de Abastos** (☉9am-3pm), the oldest covered market in Spain, now doubling as a buzzing gastromarket.

Playa de la Victoria BEACH

Often overshadowed by the city's historical riches, Cádiz' beaches are Copacabana-like in their size, feel and beauty. This fine, wide strip of Atlantic sand, with summer beach bars, starts 1km south of the Puerta de Tierra and stretches 4km back along the peninsula.

Museo de las Cortes de Cádiz MUSEUM

(Calle Santa Inés 9; ☉9am-6pm Tue-Fri, to 2pm Sat & Sun) **FREE** The remodelled Museo de las Cortes de Cádiz travels through the city's 18th- to 20th-century history, and is full of memorabilia associated with the revolutionary 1812 Cádiz parliament. The highlight? A huge, marvellously detailed model of 18th-century Cádiz, made in mahogany, silver and ivory by Alfonso Ximénez between 1777 and 1779.

Oratorio de la Santa Cueva CHURCH

(☏956 22 22 62; Calle Rosario 10; adult/child €3/ free, Sun free; ☉10.30am-2pm & 4.30-8pm Tue-Fri, 10.30am-2pm Sat, 10am-1pm Sun) Behind an unassuming door, the Santa Cueva conceals quite the surprise. Of its two superposed neoclassical 18th-century chapels, the bare, pillared subterranean **Capilla de la Pasión** is washed in white. Above is the richly adorned, oval-shaped **Capilla del Santísimo Sacra-** mento, its altar graced by six Corinthian columns, and with five religious canvases strung between its pillars – three of them by Goya.

Puerta de Tierra GATE

(Plaza de la Constitución; ☉9.30am-1.30pm & 3.30-6.30pm Tue-Sat) **FREE** The imposing 18th-century 'Land Gate' guards the southeastern (and only land) entry to the old town. You can wander the upper fortifications and defence tower, where Spanish- and English-language panels detail visible sights and the evolution of Cádiz' complex fortification system.

Torre Tavira TOWER

(www.torretavira.com; Calle Marqués del Real Tesoro 10; adult/child €6/free; ☉10am-8pm May-Sep, to 6pm Oct-Apr) Northwest of Plaza de Topete, the 18th-century Torre Tavira is the highest point in town, opening up dramatic panoramas of Cádiz, and has a camera obscura that projects live, moving images of the city onto a screen (sessions every 20 to 30 minutes).

🍳 Courses

K2 Internacional LANGUAGE

(☏956 21 26 46; www.k2internacional.com; Plaza Mentidero 19) Based in the Barrio del Mentidero, this old-city school offers special courses for long-term students and people over 50 years old, as well as regular classes. An intensive one-week course costs €175. It also organises city tours, accommodation, and flamenco, cooking and even surf courses.

Gadir Escuela de Español LANGUAGE

(☏956 26 05 57; http://gadir.net; Calle Pérgolas 5) About 300m southeast of the Puerta de Tierra, this long-established school has a wide range of classes in small, specialised groups.

CÁDIZ' CARNAVAL

No other Spanish city celebrates **Carnaval** (www.turismo.cadiz.es) with as much spirit, dedication and humour as Cádiz. Here it becomes a 10-day singing, dancing and drinking fancy-dress street party spanning two February weekends. The fun, fuelled by huge amounts of alcohol, is irresistible. Costumed groups of up to 45 people, called *murgas*, tour the city on foot or on floats and tractors, dancing, drinking, singing satirical ditties or performing sketches. The biggest hits are the 12-person *chirigotas* with their scathing humour, irony and double meanings, often directed at politicians. Most of their famed verbal wit will be lost on all but fluent Spanish speakers.

This being carefree Cádiz, in addition to the 300 or so officially recognised *murgas* (who are judged by a panel in the Gran Teatro Falla), there are also plenty of *ilegales* – any singing group that fancies taking to the streets.

The heart of Carnaval, where you'll stumble across some of the liveliest and most drunken scenes, is the working-class Barrio de la Viña, between the Mercado Central de Abastos and Playa de la Caleta, and along Calle Ancha and around Plaza de Topete, where *ilegales* tend to congregate.

If you plan to sleep in Cádiz during Carnaval, book accommodation months ahead.

Sample rates are €170 for a week-long intensive course.

🛏 Sleeping

Casa Caracol   HOSTEL €

(☎ 956 26 11 66; www.casacaracolcadiz.com; Calle Suárez de Salazar 4; incl breakfast dm €22-28, d €43-55, with shared bathroom €40-50; 🗟) 🧖 Mellow Casa Caracol is Cádiz' original old-town backpacker hostel. Cheery as only Cádiz can be, it has colourful, contemporary, locker-equipped dorms for four, six or seven, a sociable communal kitchen, and a roof terrace with hammocks, along with three private doubles (one a duplex-style affair with bathroom). Other perks include home-cooked dinners, yoga, and bike and surfboard rental. No lift.

Hotel Argantonio   HOTEL €€

(☎956 21 16 40; www.hotelargantonio.com; Calle Argantonio 3; incl breakfast s €80-90, d €100-155; ❄@🗟) Rambling across an 18th-century home, this stylishly charming hotel in Cádiz' old quarter sparkles with its hand-painted, wood-carved doors, colourfully tiled floors adorning bedrooms, bathrooms and corridors, and intricate Moorish-style arch and fountain in the lobby. The 1st floor is Mudéjar, the 2nd 'colonial romantic', the 3rd a mix. There's a tucked-away roof-terrace lounge, plus a cafe and good breakfasts.

Hotel Convento Cádiz   HERITAGE HOTEL €€

(☎ 956 20 07 38; www.hotelconventocadiz.com; Calle Santo Domingo 2; r €64-127; ❄🗟) Rest assured that you won't be living like a monk here. A fresh hotel in a 17th-century former monastery, this place has spacious, pared-back rooms with comfortable neutral-toned modern decor, set around a cloistered, check-tiled courtyard made still more soothing by monastic chanting music.

Hotel Patagonia Sur   HOTEL €€

(☎856 17 46 47; www.hotelpatagoniasur.es; Calle Cobos 11; s €86-113, d €89-155; ❄🗟) This glossy Argentine-run gem offers clean-lined modernity and efficient yet friendly management just steps from the cathedral. The 16 rooms, all with tea-and-coffee sets, are smart, bright, fresh and snug. Bonuses include a glass-fronted cafe and sun-filled 5th-floor attic rooms with cathedral views and sun loungers on private terraces.

★ Parador de Cádiz   LUXURY HOTEL €€€

(☎ 956 22 69 05; www.parador.es; Avenida Duque de Nájera 9; incl breakfast d €183-268, ste €200-400; ❄🗟❄) Bold, beautiful and right beside Playa de la Caleta, the so-called Parador Atlántico contrasts with Andalucía's other *paradores* (luxurious state-owned hotels) in that it's super modern and built from scratch. Sultry reds, ocean blues and bright turquoises throw character into the sleek, contemporary rooms with balcony and floor-to-ceiling windows. Soak in four seaview swimming pools, or seek out the spa.

🍴 Eating

Just as the air in Jerez is thick with sherry, Cádiz smells unforgettably of fresh fish. Calle Virgen de la Palma, in the Barrio de la Viña, is the city's go-to fresh-seafood street. Calles Plocia and Sopranis, off Plaza de San Juan de Dios, are upmarket eat streets. There are good options off Plaza de Mina in the Barrio del Mentidero.

★ Casa Manteca   TAPAS €

(☎ 956 21 36 03; www.facebook.com/tabernanmanteca; Calle Corralón de los Carros 66; tapas €2.50; ⏱noon-4pm & 8.30pm-12.30am, may close Sun & Mon evenings Nov-Mar) The hub of the Barrio de la Viña's Carnaval fun, with every inch of its walls covered in flamenco, bullfighting and Carnaval paraphernalia, always-busy Casa Manteca is full of old tapas favourites. Ask the chatty waiters for a tapa of mussels or *chicharrones* (pressed pork dressed with a squeeze of lemon), and it'll fly across the bar on waxed paper.

Rincón Gastronómico   TAPAS €

(Mercado Central de Abastos, Plaza de la Libertad; tapas €2-8; ⏱9am-4pm Mon, 9am-3.30pm & 7pm-midnight Tue-Fri, 9am-4pm & 8pm-1am Sat; 🧖) Cádiz' neoclassical market is the setting for this ultra-buzzy gastromarket, where stalls get packed with lunching *gaditanos*. Sample gloriously simple specialities like *patatas aliñadas*, mountain cheeses and platters of Ibérico ham; pick your fresh fish and have it grilled before your eyes; venture into a plant-based world of vegan tortilla (convincingly delicious!); or hit the sushi stand.

La Candela   TAPAS, FUSION €

(☎956 22 18 22; www.facebook.com/LaCandelaTapasBar; Calle Feduchy 3; tapas €3.50-7, mains €8-12; ⏱1.30-4pm & 8.30-11.30pm; 🗟🧖) Like an arty cafe meets colourful tapas bar, La Candela surprises with floral-stamped windows, rustic-industrial decor and brilliantly original Andalucian-Asian tapas and mains. From the busy open kitchen at the back come bold creations with local inspiration – prawn and sea-bream ceviche, honey-goat's-cheese salad,

Cádiz

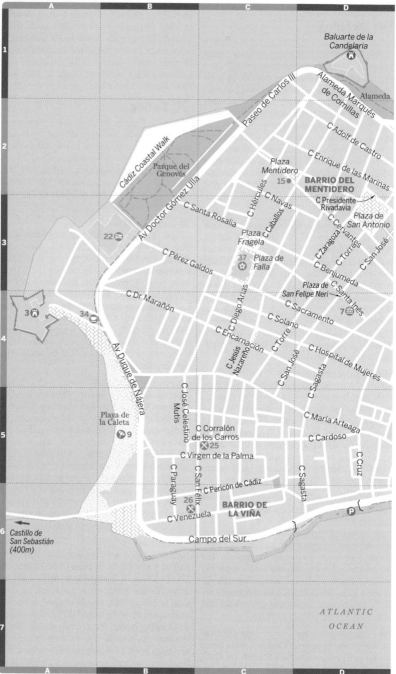

Baluarte de la Candelaria

Alameda Marqués de Cornillas

Alameda

Paseo de Carlos III

C Adolf de Castro

C Enrique de las Marinas

Cádiz Coastal Walk

Parque del Genovés

Plaza Mentidero

15

BARRIO DEL MENTIDERO

C Presidente Rivadavia

Plaza de San Antonio

Av Doctor Gómez Ulla

C Santa Rosalía

C Hércules

C Navas

C Caballos

C Cervantes

C Zaragoza

C Torres

C San-José

22

Plaza Fragela

37 Plaza de Falla

C Pérez Galdos

C Benjumeda

C Santa Inés

Plaza de San Felipe Neri

7

C Dr Marañón

C Diego Arias

C Sacramento

C Solano

3

34

C Encarnación

C Torre

C Jesús Nazareño

C San-José

C Hospital de Mujeres

C Sagasta

Av Duque de Nájera

C María Arteaga

Playa de la Caleta

9

C José Celestino Mutis

C Corralón de los Carros

25

C Cardoso

C Cruz

C Virgen de la Palma

C Paraguay

C San-Félix

C Pericón de Cádiz

C Sagasta

P

26

BARRIO DE LA VIÑA

C Venezuela

Campo del Sur

Castillo de San Sebastián (400m)

ATLANTIC OCEAN

Cádiz

strawberry *salmorejo* with tuna tartare, and scallop tempura with wasabi mayonnaise.

Taberna La Sorpresa　　　　　　TAPAS €
(☏956 22 12 32; www.tabernalasorpresa.com; Calle Arbolí 4; tapas €2.50-5.50; ⊗11.30am-4.30pm & 8.30-11.30pm Tue-Sat, 11.30am-4.30pm Sun) Wood barrels of Pedro Ximénez, *manzanilla* (chamomile-coloured sherry) and *oloroso* (sweet, dark sherry) stack up behind the bar at this buzzy, down-to-earth 1956 tavern. Tapas focus on *almadraba* tuna, but there are plenty of other tasty bites, such as mussels, *chicharrones* and Iberian *bellota* ham, along with other Cádiz-province wines and vermouth on tap.

Freiduría Las Flores　　　　SEAFOOD, TAPAS €
(☏956 22 61 12; Plaza de Topete 4; tapas €1.50, raciones €5-12; ⊗noon-4pm & 7.30pm-midnight) Cádiz' addiction to fried fish reaches new heights at this packed-out spot. If it comes from the sea, it's been fried and dished up at Las Flores as a tapa, *media ración* (larger tapas serving) or *ración* (full-plate serving), or fish-and-chips style in improvised paper cups. If you can't choose, try a *surtido* (mixed fry-up). Don't count on a table.

La Marmita Centro　　　　TAPAS, FUSION €€
(☏956 21 52 27; www.grupolamarmita.com; Calle Buenos Aires 5-7; tapas €4.50-10, 5-course set menu

€25; ⊗1.30-3pm & 8.30-11.30pm; ☏⚲) Courtesy of Cádiz' popular La Marmita Group, this sleekly minimalist old-city spot thrills diners with its wonderfully imaginative, exquisitely presented Andalucian-international tapas. Border-crossing dishes put the focus on local produce, such as Cádiz burgers with *payoyo* cheese or *cucuruchos* (cones) of avocado and red *almadraba* tuna. Veggie-friendly delights include Vietnamese rolls stuffed with avocado, basil and cashew pesto.

Ultramar&nos　　　　ANDALUCIAN, FUSION €€
(☏856 07 69 46; www.ultramarynos.com; Calle Enrique de las Marinas 2; dishes €6-15; ⊗1.30-4pm & 8.30-11pm; ⚲) Busy with travellers and *gaditanos* alike, this expertly reimagined former *ultramarinos* (grocer's shop) radiates stripped-back contemporary styling with recycled materials and long blue-tiled bar. Putting a twist on Cádiz favourites, its inventive seasonal cooking revolves around local produce, featuring a drool-worthy menu of lime-dressed *chicharrones*, zesty vegetable curry, tuna-sashimi salad and king-prawn skewers.

Atxuri　　　　BASQUE, ANDALUCIAN €€
(☏956 25 36 13; www.atxuri.es; Calle Plocia 7; mains €16-25; ⊗1.15-5pm & 9-11.30pm Thu-Sat, 1.15-5pm Sun-Wed) One of Cádiz' most long-standing restaurants, Atxuri fuses

Basque and Andalucian influences into a refined range of flavours. As you'd expect from a place with Basque roots, *bacalao* (cod; perhaps scrambled, in a herby green *salsa verde* or *al pil pil*) and high-quality steaks are recurring themes.

Café Royalty
CAFE, ANDALUCIAN €€€

(☑956 07 80 65; www.caferoyalty.com; Plaza Candelaria; tapas €4.50-14, mains €23-30, set menus €38-55; ☺cafe 11am-11pm Sun-Thu, 9am-midnight Fri & Sat, restaurant 12.30-4pm & 8-11pm) Originally opened in 1912 on the centenary of the 1812 constitution, the Royalty was once a discussion corner for the intellectuals of the day, including *gaditano* composer Manuel de Falla. The cafe closed in the 1930s but, thanks to an inspired renovation project overseen by a local *gaditano* it reopened in 2012, 100 years after its initial inauguration. The frescoed, mirrored, intricately carved interior is – no exaggeration – breathtaking. It's fantastic for brunch, tapas, cocktails, home-baked cakes and elegant updated-Andalucian meals.

El Faro de Cádiz
TAPAS, SEAFOOD €€€

(☑956 21 10 68; www.elfarodecadiz.com; Calle San Félix 15; tapas €2.70-3.50, mains €17-24; ☺1-4pm & 8.30-11.30pm) Ask any *gaditano* for their favourite Cádiz tapas bar and there's a high chance they'll choose El Faro. Seafood, particularly the *tortillitas de camarones* (shrimp fritters), is why people come here, though the *rabo de toro* (oxtail) and *patatas aliñadas* (potato salad) have their devotees. El Faro's upmarket restaurant, decorated with pretty ceramics, gets mixed reviews.

🍸 Drinking & Nightlife

The Plaza de Mina–Plaza San Francisco–Plaza de España triangle is the centre of the old city's late-night bar scene, especially Calle Beato Diego; things get going around midnight, but it can be quiet early in the week. More bars are scattered around the Barrio del Pópulo, east of the cathedral. Punta San Felipe (La Punta), on the northern side of the harbour, has a string of drinks/dance bars packed with a youngish crowd from about 3am to 6am Thursday to Saturday.

Cádiz' other nocturnal haunt, especially in summer, is down along Playa de la Victoria and the Paseo Marítimo, on and around Calle Muñoz Arenillas near the Hotel Playa Victoria (2.5km southeast of the Puerta de Tierra).

Quilla
CAFE, BAR

(www.quilla.es; Playa de la Caleta; ☺11am-midnight Sun-Thu, to 2am Fri & Sat; 🛜) A bookish cafe-bar encased in what appears to be the rusty hulk of an old ship overlooking Playa de la Caleta, with coffee, pastries, tapas, wine, art exhibitions, gratis sunsets and lightly modernised Andalucian dishes (burgers, salads, *tostas*, grilled fish; €7 to €12). Opening hours spill over in summer.

Nahu Centro
BAR

(www.facebook.com/NahuCentro; Calle Beato Diego 8; ☺8pm-3am Tue-Thu, 6pm-4am Fri & Sat; 🛜) Stylish student-oriented cocktail bar with mood lighting, Moroccan lamps and chill-out sofas. At its best when you're perched at the bar, G&T in hand, but good for coffee and wi-fi too. Regular DJ sessions; check the Facebook page.

Taberna La Manzanilla
WINE BAR

(www.lamanzanilladecadiz.com; Calle Feduchy 19; ☺11am-3.30pm & 7-10.30pm Mon-Fri, 11am-3.30pm Sat & Sun; 🛜) Family-run since the 1930s, La Manzanilla is a gloriously time-warped sherry tavern decked with bullfighting posters, on a spot once occupied by a pharmacy. The speciality, of course, is *manzanilla* from the giant oak barrel. Keep an eye out for tastings and other events.

La Clandestina
CAFE

(www.facebook.com/libreriacafe.laclandestina; Calle José del Toro 23; ☺9.30am-2pm & 5.30-9pm Mon-Fri, 10am-2pm Sat; 🛜) A cosy, boho bookshop cafe where you can flick through the day's papers over coffee, homemade cakes, *tostadas* with artisan jams, freshly squeezed orange juice and organic goodies.

☆ Entertainment

★Peña Flamenca La Perla
FLAMENCO

(☑956 25 91 01; www.laperladecadiz.es; Calle Carlos Ollero) Paint-peeled, sea-splashed La Perla, set romantically next to the crashing Atlantic surf off Calle Concepción Arenal in the Barrio de Santa María, hosts flamenco at 10pm most Fridays, more often in spring and summer, for an audience full of aficionados. It's an unforgettable experience.

La Cava
FLAMENCO

(☑956 21 18 66; www.flamencolacava.com; Calle Antonio López 16; €22) Cádiz' main *tablao* (choreographed flamenco show) happens in a rustically bedecked tavern on Tuesday, Thursday and Saturday at 9.30pm. Schedules are reduced November to February.

Gran Teatro Falla
THEATRE

(☑956 22 08 34; www.facebook.com/TeatroFalla; Plaza de Falla) Named for Andalucía's finest classical composer and native *gaditano*

Manuel de Falla, this red-bricked neo-Mudéjar theatre hosts Cádiz' annual Carnaval competitions (p114). The rest of the year it's busy with theatre, dance and music.

El Pay Pay   LIVE PERFORMANCE
(www.cafeteatropaypay.com; Calle Silencio 1; ⊙10am-3am Wed-Sat; 🎵) In the Barrio del Pópulo, this 'cafe-theatre' runs a hugely varied arts program including drama, magic, storytelling, drag shows, stand-up comedy, and live jazz, blues and flamenco.

ⓘ Information

Centro de Recepción de Turistas (☑956 24 10 01; www.turismo.cadiz.es; Paseo de Canalejas; ⊙9am-7pm Mon-Fri, to 5pm Sat & Sun Jul-Sep, 8.30am-6.30pm Mon-Fri, 9am-5pm Sat & Sun Oct-Jun) Near the bus and train stations.

Hospital Puerta del Mar (☑956 00 21 00; www.hupm.com; Avenida Ana de Viya 21) Main general hospital, 2km southeast of the Puerta de Tierra.

Oficina de Turismo Regional (☑956 20 31 91; www.andalucia.org; Avenida Ramón de Carranza; ⊙9am-7.15pm Mon-Fri, 10am-2.45pm Sat & Sun)

Policía Nacional (☑956 29 75 00, emergency 091; Edificio Torre Tavira II, Calle Santa María Soledad 6) National police; 500m southeast of the Puerta de Tierra.

ⓘ Getting There & Around

BICYCLE

Urban Bike (www.urbanbikecadiz.es; Calle Marques de Valdeíñigo 4; bike hire per hour/day €5/14, 2hr bike tours €25; ⊙10am-6pm Mon-Fri, by appointment Sat & Sun) and **Las Bicis Naranjas** (☑956 22 97 25; https://lasbicisnaranjas.com; Calle Antonio López 5; bike hire per hour/day €4/15, 3hr tours €30; ⊙10am-9pm) rent bicycles and run tours of the old town.

BOAT

From Cádiz' **Terminal Marítima Metropolitana** (Muelle Reina Victoria), 17 to 19 daily CMTBC catamarans head to El Puerto de Santa María (€2.70, 30 minutes).

BUS

All out-of-town buses leave from Cádiz' new **bus station** (Avenida de Astilleros), inaugurated in late 2017, on the eastern side of the train station (at the southeastern end of the old city). Most buses are operated by **Comes** (☑902 64 64 28; www.tgcomes.es) or **Los Amarillos** (☑902 21 03 17; http://losamarillos.autobusing.com). The **Consorcio de Transportes Bahía de Cádiz** (CMTBC; ☑955 03 86 65; www.cmtbc.es) runs to/from Jerez airport (p128).

Cádiz has a decent urban bus system, fanning out from Plaza de España. Useful routes include buses 1 and 7 for Playa de la Victoria; bus 7 also goes to Playa de la Caleta. Tickets cost €1.10.

CAR & MOTORCYCLE

There's lots of pricey underground parking, including on Paseo de Canalejas near the port (€25 per 24 hours). There's a cheap supervised car park on Avenida del Descubrimiento, on the northwestern side of the port (€7.75 per 24 hours).

TRAIN

From the train station, next to the bus station on the southeastern edge of the old town, trains go to El Puerto de Santa María (€4.05 to €5.05, 25 to 35 minutes, 28 to 38 daily), Jerez de la Frontera (€4.05 to €6.05, 45 minutes, 33 to 42 daily) and Seville (€16 to €22, 1¾ hours, 12 to 15 daily). Three or four daily high-speed ALVIA trains go to Madrid (€68 to €74, 4½ hours).

BUSES FROM CÁDIZ

DESTINATION	COST	DURATION	FREQUENCY
Arcos de la Frontera	€7.30	1-1½hr	3-8 daily
El Puerto de Santa María	€2.70	45min	every 30-60min
Granada	€34	5¼hr	4 daily
Jerez de la Frontera	€3.80	50min	2-7 daily
Jerez de la Frontera airport	€3.80	1½hr	1-2 daily
Málaga	€28	4½hr	4 daily
Ronda	€16	3¼hr	1-2 daily
Sanlúcar de Barrameda	€5	1hr	5-10 daily
Seville	€13	1¾hr	9-10 daily
Tarifa	€10	1¼-1¾hr	8 daily
La Barca de Vejer (for Vejer de la Frontera)	€5.85	1-1½hr	9-11 daily

THE SHERRY TRIANGLE

North of Cádiz, Jerez de la Frontera, Sanlúcar de Barrameda and El Puerto de Santa María mark the three corners of Spain's famous 'sherry triangle'. Even if Andalucía's unique, smooth wine isn't your cup of tea, you won't want to miss the history, the beaches, the handsome horses, the fabulous food, the feisty flamenco and the evocative environmental marvel that is the Parque Nacional de Doñana (p97).

Jerez de la Frontera

POP 191,550

Stand down, all other claimants. Jerez, as most savvy Hispanophiles know, *is* Andalucía. It just doesn't broadcast it in the way that Seville and Granada do. Jerez is the capital of Andalucian horse culture, stop one on the famed Sherry Triangle and – cue protestations from Cádiz and Seville – the cradle of Spanish flamenco. The *bulería* (flamenco songs), Jerez' jokey, tongue-in-cheek antidote to Seville's tragic *soleá*, was first concocted in the legendary Roma *barrios* of Santiago and San Miguel. But Jerez is also a vibrant modern Andalucian city, where fashion brands live in old palaces and stylishly outfitted businesspeople sit down to distinctly contemporary cuisine between glasses of *fino* at bubbly *tabancos* (p126; simple taverns serving sherry). If you really want to unveil the eternal riddle that is Andalucía, start with Jerez.

Sights & Activities

Jerez (the word even means 'sherry') has around 20 sherry bodegas. Most require bookings for visits, but a few offer tours where you can just turn up. The tourist office (p128) has details.

★ **Bodegas Tradición** WINERY, GALLERY
(956 16 86 28; www.bodegastradicion.com; Plaza Cordobeses 3; tours €25; 9am-5pm Mon-Fri Jul & Aug, reduced hours Sep-Jun) An intriguing, evocative bodega, not only for its extra-aged sherries (at least 20, mostly 30 years old) but also because it houses the **Colección Joaquín Rivero**, a private Spanish art collection that includes important works by Goya, Velázquez, El Greco and Zurbarán. Tours (in English, Spanish or German) require bookings, and are worth splashing out on.

Alcázar FORTRESS
(956 14 99 55; Alameda Vieja; excl/incl camera obscura €5/7; 9.30am-5.30pm Mon-Fri, 9.30am-2.30pm Sat & Sun Jul–mid-Sep, 9.30am-2.30pm daily mid-Sep–Jun) Jerez' muscular yet elegant 11th- or 12th-century fortress is one of Andalucía's best-preserved Almohad-era relics. It's notable for its octagonal tower, a classic example of Almohad defensive forts, reached through Islamic-style **gardens**, past a 12th-century **mosque-turned-chapel** and the 17th- and 18th-century baroque **Palacio Villavicencio**. Fortress hours vary.

You enter the Alcázar via the **Patio de Armas**. On the left is the beautiful *mezquita* (mosque), transformed into a chapel by Alfonso X in 1264, though retaining its fountain and horseshoe arches; it's the only remaining one of 18 mosques that once stood in Jerez. On the right, the Palacio Villavicencio, built over the Almohad palace ruins, displays artwork but is best known for its bird's-eye views of Jerez; the camera obscura inside its tower provides a picturesque panorama of the city. Beyond the Patio de Armas, the peaceful gardens recreate the ambience of Islamic times with geometric flower beds and tinkling fountains. The well-preserved, domed Almohad Baños Árabes (Arabic Baths), with their star-shaped shafts of light, are particularly worth a look.

Catedral de San Salvador CATHEDRAL
(Plaza de la Encarnación; adult/child €5/2.50, 10.30am-12.30pm Sun & 7-9pm Mon free; permanent exhibition 10am-6.30pm Mon-Sat) Echoes of Seville colour Jerez' dramatic cathedral, a surprisingly harmonious mix of baroque, neoclassical and Gothic styles. Standout features are its broad flying buttresses and intricately carved stone ceilings. Behind the main altar, a series of rooms and chapels shows off the cathedral's collection of silverware, religious garments and art (including works by Zurbarán and Pacheco). Across the square, the bell tower is 15th-century Gothic-Mudéjar on its lower half and 17th century at the top.

Bodegas González–Byass WINERY
(Bodegas Tío Pepe; 956 35 70 16; www.bodegas tiopepe.com; Calle Manuel María González 12; tours from €15; tours hourly noon-6pm Mon-Sat, noon-2pm Sun) Home to the famous Tío Pepe brand, González–Byass is one of Jerez' biggest sherry houses, handily located just west of the Alcázar. Three to five daily tours run in Spanish, three to four in English and two to three in German. Basic visits include a two-wine tasting; others have tapas and extra sherries. You can book online, but it isn't essential.

Centro Andaluz de Flamenco ARTS CENTRE
(Andalucian Flamenco Centre; 956 90 21 34, 956 34 92 65; www.centroandaluzdeflamenco.es; Plaza

Jerez de la Frontera

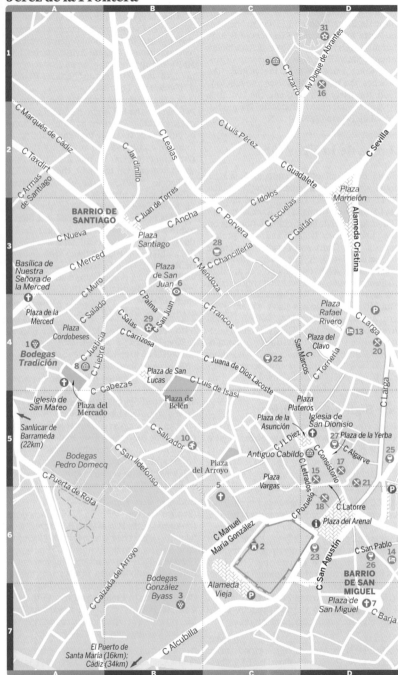

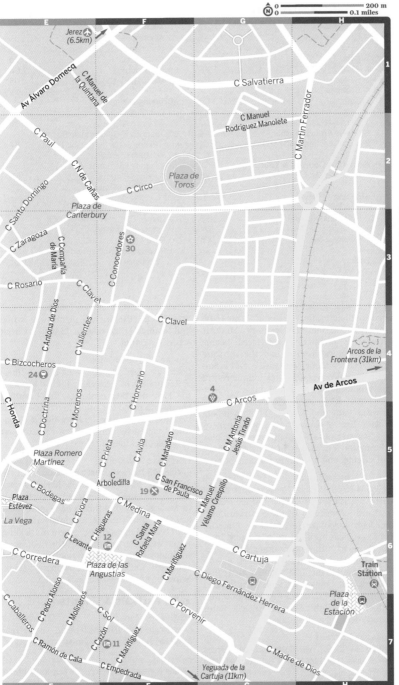

0 ___ 200 m
0 ___ 0.1 miles

Jerez (6.5km)

Av Álvaro Domecq

C Manuel de la Quintana

C Salvatierra

C Manuel Rodriguez Manolete

C Martín Ferrador

C Paul

C N de Cañas

C Circo

Plaza de Toros

C Santo Domingo

Plaza de Canterbury

C Zaragoza

C Compañía de María

C Conocedores

30

C Rosario

C Clavel

C Clavel

C Antona de Dios

C Valientes

C Honsario

C Bizcocheros

24

C Honda

C Doctrina

C Morenos

4

C Arcos

Arcos de la Frontera (31km)

Av de Arcos

Plaza Romero Martínez

C Prieta

C Ávila

C Matadero

C M Antonia Jesús Tirado

C Arboledilla

C San Francisco de Paula

19

C Bodegas

C Évora

C Medina

C Manuel Yélamo Crespillo

Plaza Estévez

La Vega

C Higueras

C Levante

C Santa Rafaela María

12

C Corredera

Plaza de las Angustias

C Martínguez

C Cartuja

Train Station

C Caballeros

C Pedro Alonso

C Molineros

C Sol

C Diego Fernández Herrera

Plaza de la Estación

C Ramón de Cala

C Cazón

11

C Martínguez

C Porvenir

C Empedrada

Yeguada de la Cartuja (11km)

C Madre de Dios

Jerez de la Frontera

de San Juan 1; ◷9am-2pm Mon-Fri) **FREE** At once architecturally intriguing – note the entrance's original 15th-century Mudéjar *artesonado* (ceiling of interlaced beams with decorative inserts) and the intricate Andalucian baroque courtyard – and a fantastic flamenco resource, this unique centre holds thousands of print and musical works. Flamenco videos are screened half hourly between 9am and 1.30pm. Staff members provide lists of flamenco-hosting *tabancos* and 19 local *peñas* (small private clubs), plus information on classes in flamenco dance and singing, and upcoming performances.

Museo Arqueológico   MUSEUM
(📞956 14 95 60; Plaza del Mercado; adult/student €5/1.80; ◷9am-2.45pm mid-Jun–mid-Sep, reduced hours mid-Sep–mid-Jun) In the Santiago quarter, Jerez' revamped archaeology museum houses fascinating local relics ranging from Paleolithic to 20th-century times. Look especially for the 7th-century-BC Greek bronze helmet found in the Río Guadalete, two cylindrical marble Copper Age idols from the 2nd or 3rd century BC, and a fragment of a rare 15th-century Gothic-Mudéjar mural. Rates include detailed audio guides.

Bodegas Lustau   WINERY
(📞956 34 15 97; www.lustau.es; Calle Arcos 53; ◷tours 11am-1pm Mon & Sat, 10.30am-3pm Tue-Fri) Book ahead for excellent-value, English- or Spanish-language tours of the handsome Lustau bodega, founded in 1896. 'Basic' tours (€15) include eight wines, while 'full tastings' (€25) take in 12 wines. Check schedules online.

Iglesia de San Miguel   CHURCH
(Plaza de San Miguel; adult/child €2/free; ◷9.30am-1.30pm Mon-Fri) Built between the 15th and 18th centuries, this beautiful church is a blend of Gothic, Renaissance and baroque architecture. Its three-tiered, elaborately carved baroque bell tower is topped by a colourful tile-patterned roof.

Hammam Andalusí   HAMMAM
(📞956 34 90 66; www.hammamandalusi.com; Calle Salvador 6; baths €25, with 15/30min massage €35/55; ◷10am-10pm) Jerez is full of echoes of its Moorish past, but there's none more magical than this. Incense, essential oils, fresh mint tea and the soothing sound of trickling water welcome you through the door, then you enjoy three turquoise pools (tepid, hot and cold). You can even throw in a massage. Numbers are limited, so book ahead.

🎉 Festivals & Events

Festival de Jerez   DANCE, MUSIC
(www.facebook.com/FestivalDeJerez; ◷late Feb-early Mar) Jerez' biggest flamenco celebration.

Feria del Caballo   FAIR
(◷late Apr-early May) Jerez' week-long horse fair is one of Andalucía's grandest festivals,

with music and dance, and equestrian competitions and parades.

Fiestas de la Vendimia   WINE, MUSIC

(☉Sep) This fiesta celebrates the grape harvest for two weeks or so, with flamenco, horse events and the traditional treading of the first grapes outside the cathedral.

🛏 Sleeping

Nuevo Hotel   HOTEL €

(📞956 33 16 00; www.nuevohotel.com; Calle Caballeros 23; s €25-30, d €40-60; ❋🛜) One of the sweetest family-run hotels in Andalucía, the Nuevo is an ancient home filled with comfortable, simple rooms. But the star is spectacular room 208, replete with Moorish-style stucco work and blue-and-white tiling creeping up the walls; you'll wake thinking you've taken up residence in the Alhambra. Breakfast (€5) is available.

Hostal Fenix   HOSTAL €

(📞 956 34 52 91; www.hostalfenix.com; Calle Cazón 7; incl breakfast s €30-35, d €35-40; ❋🛜🛁) There's nothing flash about this revamped 19th-century home – and that's part of its charm. The 14 characterful, unfussy rooms are impeccably maintained by friendly owners, who'll bring breakfast to your room. Top-floor rooms are bigger and brighter. Moorish-inspired patios are dotted around. The impressive art adorning the walls is by the owner and her cousin.

Hotel Casa Grande   HOTEL €€

(📞956 34 50 70; www.hotelcasagrande.eu; Plaza de las Angustias 3; r/ste €100/165; 🅿❋🛜) This brilliant hotel lives within a beautifully restored 1920s mansion. The 15 smartly classic rooms are set over three floors around a light-flooded patio, where local-produce breakfasts (€12) are served, or beside the fantastic roof terrace with views across Jerez' rooftops. All is overseen by the congenial Monika Schroeder, a mine of information about Jerez.

Hotel Palacio Garvey   HOTEL €€

(📞956 32 67 00; www.hotelpalaciogarvey.com; Calle Tornería 24; incl breakfast s €65-70, d €77-99, ste €105-110; 🅿❋🛜) Jerez' nominal posh hotel is a gorgeous 19th-century neoclassical palace conversion, with part of the ancient city wall visible from the lift. The public areas sport leopard prints, African-themed paintings and low-slung tables, while bold colours, luxurious leather furniture, tiled bathrooms and mirrored Moroccan-inspired bowls feature in the 16 individually decorated rooms.

🍴 Eating

Jerez gastronomy combines Moorish heritage and maritime influences with international touches. Sherry, of course, flavours many traditional dishes such as *riñones al jerez* (sherry-braised kidneys) and *rabo de toro* (oxtail), and there's also a notable turn towards creative contemporary cuisine in many of the city's top restaurants. Some of Jerez' most authentic and affordable eating spots are its *tabancos*.

La Moderna   TAPAS, ANDALUCIAN €

(📞956 32 13 79; Calle Larga 67; tapas €1.80; ☉7am-late) As popular for breakfast *tostadas* as for lunchtime tapas (cod-stuffed peppers, *patatas aliñadas*, *riñones al Jerez*), La Moderna's marble-topped tables are busy all day long. Beyond its hot-red doors, it's built into the city's Islamic-era walls, which you can see out the back.

Bar Juanito   TAPAS, ANDALUCIAN €

(📞956 33 48 38; www.bar-juanito.com; Calle Pescadería Vieja 8-10; tapas €2-3; ☉12.30-4pm & 8-11pm Mon-Sat, 12.30-4pm Sun) With its outdoor tables, rustic red chairs and chequered tablecloths, Bar Juanito is like a slice of village Andalucía in the heart of the city, rustling up scrumptiously simple tapas since the 1940s. Its *alcachofas* (artichokes) are a past winner of the National Tapa Competition, but there's plenty more local cuisine to choose from and it's all served with Cádiz' best wines.

★Albores   ANDALUCIAN, FUSION €€

(📞956 32 02 66; www.restaurantealbores.com; Calle Consistorio 12; tapas €2.50-4.50, mains €8-18; ☉8am-midnight Mon-Sat, noon-midnight Sun) Pitching itself among age-old city-centre favourites, Albores brings a sophisticated, contemporary edge to local flavours with its original tapas and mains combos. If there's one overall highlight it's probably the fish, though the artfully presented goat's-cheese *tosta* is just as delectable. One of Jerez' top breakfast spots. The Albores team is also behind stylish, seafood-starring Jerez restaurant **A Mar** (📞956 32 29 15; www.a-marrestaurante.com; Calle Latorre 8; mains €11-22; ☉noon-4.30pm & 8pm-midnight Tue-Sat year-round, noon-5pm Sun Oct-May, 8pm-midnight Sun Jun-Sep), where fresh fish of the day is served *a la plancha* (grilled), paired with an impressive menu of sherries and other Cádiz wines.

★La Carboná   ANDALUCIAN €€

(📞956 34 74 75; www.lacarbona.com; Calle San Francisco de Paula 2; mains €15-22; ☉12.30-4.30pm

& 8pm-12.30am Wed-Mon) This cavernous, imaginative restaurant occupies an exquisite old bodega set around a suspended fireplace that's oh-so-cosy in winter. Delicately presented specialities, often infused with sherry, include grilled meats, fresh fish, boletus rice jazzed up with razor clams or red *almadraba* tuna tartare with egg-yolk-and-*amontillado* (dry sherry) emulsion, plus outstanding local wines. Or go all-in with sherry-pairing menus (€45).

Albalá ANDALUCIAN, FUSION €€

(📞956 34 64 88; www.restaurantealbala.com; cnr Calle Divina Pastora & Avenida Duque de Abrantes; tapas €2-4, mains €8-15; ⊙noon-4pm & 8.30pm-midnight; 🐟) Slide into blond-wood booths amid minimalist oriental-inspired decor for chef Israel Ramos' beautifully creative contemporary meat, fish and veg dishes fuelled by typical Andalucian ingredients. House specials include *rabo de toro* (oxtail) croquettes and *almadraba* red tuna with Thai-style salad, plus deliciously crispy chunky asparagus tempura dipped in soy aioli. It's 1km north of Plaza del Arenal.

Mesón del Asador SPANISH, GRILL €€

(📞956 32 26 58; Calle Remedios 2; tapas €3, mains €9-20; ⊙12.30-4pm & 8.30-11.30pm) This big-and-busy spot is a carnivore's dream that dishes up generous grilled-meat tapas and full meaty spreads ranging from sizzling pork/beef/chicken brochettes to a two-person

DON'T MISS

JEREZ' GREAT TABANCO REVIVAL

Sprinkled across the city centre, Jerez' famous old *tabancos* are, essentially, simple taverns serving sherry from the barrel. Most date from the early 20th century and, although *tabanco* comes from the fusion of *tabaco* (tobacco) and *estanco* (tobacco shop), the focus is indisputably the local plonk (ie sherry). In danger of dying out just a few years ago, Jerez' *tabancos* have sprung back to life as fashionable modern-day hang-outs, re-invigorated by keen new ownership and frequented by crowds of stylish young *jerezanos* as much as old-timers. Several stage regular flamenco (though you're just as likely to catch an impromptu performance) and some now offer sherry tastings. All are fantastic, cheap, down-to-earth places to get a real feel for Jerez – *fino* in hand.

The tourist office (p128) hands out information on the official Ruta de los Tabancos de Jerez (www.facebook.com/rutadelostabancosdejerez), though there are plenty of other places, too. Suddenly, every other bar is calling itself a *tabanco*!

Tabanco El Pasaje (📞956 33 33 59; www.tabancoelpasaje.com; Calle Santa María 8; ⊙11am-4pm & 8pm-midnight, shows 2pm & 10pm; 🐟) Born back in 1925, Jerez' oldest *tabanco* serves up its excellent sherry selection and pleasantly uncomplicated tapas (€2 to €3) with suitably raw twice-daily flamenco sessions.

Tabanco Plateros (📞956 10 44 58; www.facebook.com/tabanco.plateros; Calle Algarve 35; ⊙noon-4pm & 8pm-midnight) Join the crowds spilling out from this lively drinking house for a glass of *fino*, *oloroso* or *amontillado* glugged alongside ingeniously simple meat and cheese tapas (€2 to €3). There's tortilla at weekends, and sherry tastings sometimes happen, too.

Tabanco El Guitarrón de San Pedro (www.facebook.com/guitarrondesanpedro; Calle Bizcocheros 16; ⊙noon-4pm & 8pm-midnight Mon-Sat, shows 10pm Thu-Sat) Revitalised by sherry-loving owners (who offer pairings and tastings), El Guitarrón hosts regular flamenco dancing (Thursday) and singing (Friday and Saturday), plus art exhibitions – all best enjoyed while feasting on its local-style tapas (€2 to €4) or sipping one of its many sherries.

Tabanco Las Banderillas (www.facebook.com/TabancoLasBanderilla; Calle Caballeros 12; tapas €2.50-3.50; ⊙noon-5pm & 8.15pm-midnight) Decked with bullfighting memorabilia, this yellow-walled *tabanco* is forever popular for its wonderfully simple, meat-heavy tapas, from *chacinas* (cold cuts), *tortillitas de camarones* (shrimp fritters) and *patatas aliñadas* (potato salad, often with tuna) to *riñones al Jerez*. The chalkboard matches sherries with customers' moods.

Tabanco A la Feria (📞663 476542; www.facebook.com/Antoniocontrerascarava; Calle Armas 5; ⊙noon-4pm & 8pm-midnight) One of just a few venues offering daily shows, A la Feria gets taken over by fiery flamenco at 10.30pm each night. Sherries and tapas are a bargain at €1, or arrive early to secure a table for the four-tapa, two-wine *menú flamenco* (€7.50).

JEREZ' FERTILE FLAMENCO SCENE

Jerez' moniker as the 'cradle of flamenco' is regularly challenged by aficionados in Cádiz and Seville, but the claim has merit. This comparatively untouristed city harbours not just one but *two* Roma quarters, Santiago and San Miguel, which have produced numerous renowned artists, including Roma singers Manuel Torre and Antonio Chacón. Like its rival cities, Jerez has concocted its own flamenco *palo* (musical form), the intensely popular *bulería*, a fast, rhythmic musical style with the same *compás* (accented beat) as the *soleá*.

Begin your explorations at the Centro Andaluz de Flamenco (p121), Spain's only bona fide flamenco library. From here, stroll down Calle Francos past a couple of legendary flamenco bars where singers and dancers still congregate. North of the Centro Andaluz de Flamenco, in the Santiago quarter, you'll find dozens of *peñas* known for their accessibility and intimacy; entry is normally free if you buy a drink. The *peña* scene is particularly lively during the February flamenco festival (p124). Jerez' revitalised tabancos are also fantastic for flamenco; some, such as El Pasaje , El Guitarrón de San Pedroand A la Feria host regular performances, while others have more spur-of-the-moment flamenco.

Centro Cultural Flamenco Don Antonio Chacón (☑ 605 858371; www.facebook.com/DAChaconFlamencoJerez; Calle Salas 2) One of the best *peñas* in town (and hence Andalucía), the Chacón, named for the great Jerez-born flamenco singer, often sees top-notch flamenco performers grace its stage. Happenings are usually (but not always) impromptu, especially during the February flamenco festival. For upcoming events, check the Facebook page or contact the Centro Andaluz de Flamenco (p121).

Puro Arte (☑ 647 743832; www.puroarteflamencojerez.com; Calle Conocedores 28; €30, with tapas/dinner €39/50) Jerez' main *tablao* (choreographed flamenco show) stages popular local-artist performances at 10pm daily. Options with drinks, tapas and/or dinner; advance bookings essential.

Damajuana (www.facebook.com/damajuanajerez; Calle Francos 18; ⊗8pm-3am Sun-Thu, to 4am Fri & Sat Jul-Sep, 8pm-3am Tue-Thu, 4pm-3am Fri-Sun Oct-Jun) One of two historic bars on Calle Francos where flamenco singers and dancers have long met and drunk, with varied live music, tapas (€2 to €5.50) and a fun *movida flamenca* (flamenco scene).

---

chuletón de buey (giant beef chop). The *solomillo de cerdo* (pork tenderloin) in Cabrales or Roquefort sauce is highly recommended.

🍷 Drinking & Nightlife

Tucked away on the narrow streets north of Plaza del Arenal are a few wine, beer and *copas* (drinks) bars, while, northeast of the centre, Plaza de Canterbury has a couple of pubs popular with a 20-something crowd. Jerez' tabancos are busy drinking spots.

Tetería La Jaima   TEAHOUSE
(Calle Chancillería 10; ⊗4-11.30pm Tue-Thu, to 2am Fri & Sat, to 9pm Sun & Mon mid-Sep–mid-Jun; 🛜) Recline with a fruity, aromatic brew in the cavernous depths of this atmospherically dark tea room, decked out with breezy curtains and Moroccan lanterns. If you're hungry, try some hummus, a stuffed pitta bread or a vegetable tagine (dishes €4 to €10).

☆ Entertainment

Jerez is home to one of Andalucía's liveliest and most authentic flamenco scenes.

★ Real Escuela Andaluza del Arte Ecuestre   LIVE PERFORMANCE
(☑ 956 31 80 08; www.realescuela.org; Avenida Duque de Abrantes; training sessions adult/child €11/6.50, exhibiciones adult €21-27, child €13-17; ⊗training sessions 11am-1pm Mon, Wed & Fri, exhibiciones noon Tue & Thu) Jerez' renowned Royal Andalucian School of Equestrian Art trains horses and riders. On 'thematic visits', you can watch them going through their paces in training sessions and visit the **Museo del Arte Ecuestre** and **Museo del Enganche** (Calle Pizarro; adult/child €4.50/2.50; ⊗10am-2pm Mon-Fri). The big highlight is the official *exhibición* (show), in which the beautiful horses show off their tricks to classical music. Book tickets online.

Yeguada de la Cartuja – Hierro del Bocado   LIVE PERFORMANCE
(☑ 956 16 28 09; www.yeguadacartuja.com; Finca Suerte del Suero, Carretera Medina–El Portal, Km 6.5; adult €16-22, child €10-16; ⊗11am-1pm Sat) This stud farm is dedicated to improving the fine Cartujano stock. Guided visits are

followed by a spectacular show consisting of free-running colts, demonstrations by a string of mares, and dressage. Book ahead. To get here, take the signposted turn-off from the A2002 5km south of central Jerez; then it's 6.5km southeast.

ℹ Information

Oficina de Turismo (📞956 33 88 74; www.turismojerez.com; Plaza del Arenal; ⊙9am-3pm & 5-6.30pm Mon-Fri, 9.30am-2.30pm Sat & Sun)

ℹ Getting There & Away

AIR

Jerez airport (📞956 15 00 00; www.aena. es; Carretera A4), the only one serving Cádiz province, is 10km northeast of town on the A4.
Iberia (www.iberia.com) To/from Madrid.
Ryanair (www.ryanair.com) To/from Barcelona, London Stansted and Frankfurt–Hahn (seasonal).
Vueling (www.vueling.com) To/from Barcelona, Palma de Mallorca and Bilbao (seasonal).

BUS

The **bus station** (📞956 14 99 90; Plaza de la Estación) is 1.3km southeast of the centre, served by CMTBC (p120), Comes (p120), Los Amarillos (p120) and **Autocares Valenzuela** (📞956 34 10 63; www.grupovalenzuela.com).

TO	COST	DURATION	FREQUENCY
Arcos de la Frontera	€1.95-3.09	30-40min	18-29 daily
Cádiz	€3.75	1hr	3-9 daily
El Puerto de Santa María	€1.65	20min	2-8 daily
Ronda	€13	2¼hr	1-2 daily
Sanlúcar de Barrameda	€1.95	40min	7-14 daily
Seville	€8.85	1¼hr	5-7 daily

CAR & MOTORCYCLE

There's 24-hour parking (€5) under the Alameda Vieja (beside the Alcázar); press the red button.

TRAIN

Jerez' train station is beside the bus station.

TO	COST	DURATION	FREQUENCY
Cádiz	€4.05-6.05	35-45min	29-42 daily
Córdoba	€21-37	1¾-3hr	12 daily
El Puerto de Santa María	€2.70	8min	29-45 daily
Seville	€11	1¼hr	13-16 daily

ℹ Getting Around

TO/FROM THE AIRPORT

Taxis to/from the airport cost €15.

Eight to 10 daily trains run between the airport and Jerez (€2.45, seven minutes), El Puerto de Santa María (€3.65, 15 minutes) and Cádiz (€6.05, 45 minutes).

Local airport buses run three times on weekdays and once daily Saturday and Sunday to Jerez (€1.10, 30 minutes), once on weekdays to El Puerto de Santa María (€1.65, 50 minutes) and once daily to Cádiz (€3.80, 1½ hours).

El Puerto de Santa María

POP 43,890

When you're surrounded by such cultural luminaries as Cádiz, Jerez de la Frontera and Seville, it's easy to overlook the small print; such is the fate of El Puerto de Santa María, despite its collection of well-known icons. Osborne sherry, with its famous bull logo (a highly recognisable symbol of Spain), was founded and retains its headquarters here, as do half a dozen other sherry bodegas. With its abundance of sandy blond beaches, tempting cuisine, sherry wineries and smattering of architectural heirlooms, El Puerto can seem like southern Andalucía in microcosm. It's an easy day trip from Cádiz or Jerez.

⊙ Sights

★**Bodegas Osborne**   WINERY
(📞956 86 91 00; www.bodegas-osborne.com; Calle los Moros 7; tours from €14, tastings €8-30) Creator of the legendary black-bull logo still exhibited on life-size billboards all over Spain (now without the name), Osborne is El Puerto's best-known sherry winery. It was set up by an Englishman, Thomas Osborne Mann, in 1772, and it remains one of Spain's oldest companies run continuously by the same family. The gorgeous whitewashed bodega leads tours with tastings at noon in Spanish, 10am in English and 11am in German. Book ahead.

Castillo de San Marcos   CASTLE
(📞627 569335; servicios.turisticos@caballero. es; Plaza Alfonso X El Sabio; adult/child €8/4, Tue free; ⊙tours hourly 11.30am-1.30pm Tue, 10.30am-1.30pm Wed-Sat, closed Wed & Fri Nov-Apr) Heavily restored in the 20th century, El Puerto's fine castle was constructed over an Islamic mosque by Alfonso X El Sabio after he took the town in 1260. The old mosque inside, now converted into a church, is the highlight. Wednesday-to-Saturday visits end with a five-sherry tasting (the castle is owned by

A VERY BRITISH DRINK

The names give it away: Harvey, Sandeman, Terry, Humbert, Osborne. Andalucía's sherry industry might be Spanish in character, but it's firmly Anglo-Irish in origin. Francis Drake sacked Cádiz in 1587 and greedily made off with over 3000 barrels of local *vino* – and a whole new industry was inauspiciously born.

Thomas Osborne Mann, from Exeter, was among the first to jump on board. Befriending local winegrowers in El Puerto de Santa María in 1772, he set up what is today one of Spain's oldest family firms, Osborne, famous for its imposing black bull logo. George Sandeman, a Scotsman from Perth, founded his fledgling sherry empire in Tom's Coffee House in the City of London in 1790. John Harvey from Bristol began importing sherry from Spain in 1796 and concocted the world's first cream sherry, Harvey's Bristol Cream, in the 1860s. The Terry family, from southern Ireland, founded their famous bodegas in El Puerto de Santa María in 1865. Even Spain's most illustrious sherry dynasty, González–Byass – producers of the trademark Tío Pepe brand – was formed from an 1835 Anglo-Spanish alliance between Andalucian Manuel María González and his English agent Robert Byass.

Bodegas Caballero). All 11.30am sessions are in English; Tuesday tours require bookings.

Bodegas Gutiérrez Colosía — WINERY
(956 85 28 52; www.gutierrezcolosia.com; Avenida de la Bajamar 40; tours €10) No bookings are needed for tours of this intimate, family-run, 1830-founded sherry bodega, right beside the catamaran dock. Visits end with a six-wine tasting, which can include tapas and flamenco on request. Visits run at 11.15am in English and 12.30pm in Spanish Monday to Friday, and at 1pm in both languages on Saturday; additional evening tours happen July to September.

Fundación Rafael Alberti — MUSEUM
(956 85 07 11; www.rafaelalberti.es; Calle Santo Domingo 25; adult/child €4/2; 10am-2pm Tue-Fri, 11am-2pm Sat & Sun) Two blocks inland from Plaza Alfonso X El Sabio, this foundation has interesting, well-displayed exhibits on Rafael Alberti (1902–99), one of Spain's great Generation of '27 poets, in what was his childhood home. Free English, French or Spanish audio guides.

Festivals & Events

Feria de Primavera y Fiestas del Vino Fino — WINE
(Spring Fair; Apr-May) Around 200,000 half-bottles of *fino* (dry, straw-coloured sherry) are drunk during this six-day fiesta.

Sleeping

El Baobab Hostel — HOSTEL €
(956 54 21 23; www.baobabhostel.com; Calle Pagador 37; dm €20-35, d €40-80; mid-Feb–mid-Oct;) In a converted 18th-century building near the bullring, this 10-room hostel is El Puerto's best budget choice, with a homey, friendly feel, simple interiors, and communal kitchen and courtyard. There are private doubles, while fan-cooled, locker-equipped dorms sleep four to eight; half have private bathrooms. Renovations were under way at research time: all rooms should have air-con and bathrooms from 2018.

Palacio San Bartolomé — HERITAGE HOTEL €€€
(956 85 09 46; www.palaciosanbartolome.com; Calle San Bartolomé 21; r €68-200, ste €198-250; closed 2 weeks Jan;) Fancy a room with its own mini swimming pool, sauna, hot tub, bathrobes and deckchairs? It's all yours with the Spa Suite at the deftly designed, welcoming San Bart, set in a luxuriously converted 18th-century palace. If you don't bag the pool room, the 10 others are equally enticing: four-poster beds, giant showers, tile-patterned floors and contemporary elegance.

Eating & Drinking

El Puerto is famous for its seafood and tapas bars. Look along central Calles Luna and Misericordia, Calle Ribera del Marisco to the north, Avenidas de la Bajamar and Aramburu de Mora to the south, and Calle La Placilla near Plaza de España.

Romerijo — SEAFOOD €
(956 54 12 54; www.romerijo.com; Ribera del Marisco 1; seafood per 250g from €5, raciones €4-15; noon-11.30pm) A huge, always-busy El Puerto institution, Romerijo has been going strong since 1952 and has three sections: one boiling seafood, another (opposite) frying it, and the third a *cervecería* (beer bar). Buy seafood by the quarter-kilo in paper cones.

EL PUERTO'S BEACHES

Drawing a predominantly Spanish crowd, El Puerto's white-sand beaches are among southern Spain's more popular coastal escapes. Closest to town is pine-flanked **Playa de la Puntilla**, 1.5km southwest of the centre; walk, or take bus 1 or 2 (€1.10) from **Avenida Aramburu de Mora**. Two kilometres further southwest is the swish **Puerto Sherry** marina, beyond which lie little **Playa de la Muralla** and 3km-long **Playa de Santa Catalina**, this last with beach bars and served by bus 6 from the bullring bus stop. Bus 3 from central Avenida Aramburu de Mora runs 6km northwest to **Playa Fuentebravía** (Playa Fuenterrabía), at the far northwestern end of Playa de Santa Catalina. On the eastern side of the Río Guadalete is popular, built-up **Playa de Valdelagrana**; bus 3 goes here.

Mesón del Asador   SPANISH, BARBECUE €€

(☑ 956 54 03 27; Calle Misericordia 2; tapas €2-4, mains €9-20; ☺1-4pm & 8.15pm-midnight) It's a measure of El Puerto's gastronomic nous that, in such a seafood-oriented town, there's a meat restaurant that could compete with any Buenos Aires steakhouse. The power of the Mesón's delivery is in its deceptively simple chicken brochettes, two-person *parrilladas* (grilled-meat mixes), and chargrilled beef and pork sizzling away on mini barbecues brought to your table.

⭐ **Aponiente**   SEAFOOD, FUSION €€€

(☑956 85 18 70; www.aponiente.com; Molino de Mareas El Caño, Calle Francisco Cossi Ochoa; 21-course menu €205; ☺1-1.30pm & 8-8.30pm Tue-Sat early Mar-early Dec, plus Mon Jul & Aug) Audacious is the word for the bold experimentation of leading Spanish chef Angel León, whose seafood-biased *nueva cocina* has won a cavalcade of awards, transforming Aponiente into Andalucía's first triple-Michelin-starred restaurant. Occupying a design-led 19th-century tide mill, Aponiente splits opinion in traditional El Puerto. Some snort at its pretension, others salivate at the thought of its uber-imaginative 21-course tasting menus.

Aponiente is 1.5km northeast of the centre. For a tapas-sized, town-centre taster of the Aponiente magic, dine at creative sister venture **La Taberna del Chef del Mar** (☑956 11 20 93; Calle Puerto Escondido 6; tapas & raciones €5-17; ☺1.30-4.30pm & 8.30pm-midnight Mon-Sat, 1.30-4.30pm Sun Apr-Oct).

El Faro del Puerto   ANDALUCIAN, SEAFOOD €€€

(☑956 87 09 52; www.elfarodelpuerto.com; Carretera de Fuentebravía, Km 0.5; tapas €5-15, mains €18-27; ☺1.30-4.30pm & 8.30-11pm Mon-Sat, 1.30-4.30pm Sun; ☑) El Faro is worth hunting down for its traditional-with-a-hint-of-innovation take on local seafood, excellent Spanish wine list, and classically smart, multiroom setting inside an old *casa señorial* (manor house). The *almadraba* tuna tartare is a highlight. The bar/tapas menu has some exciting vegetarian and gluten-free choices. It's on the roundabout at the northwestern end of Calle Valdés.

Bodega Obregón   BAR

(☑956 85 63 29; Calle Zarza 51; ☺9am-2pm & 6-11pm Mon-Fri, 9am-late Sat, 10am-2pm Sun) Think sherry is just a drink for grandmas? Come and have your illusions blown to pieces at this family-run, spit-and-sawdust-style bar where its own sweet stuff is siphoned from woody barrels. The Saturday-lunch *guisos* (stews) are a local favourite.

⭐ Entertainment

Peña Flamenca Tomás El Nitri   FLAMENCO

(☑956 54 32 37; Calle Diego Niño 1) This good, honest *peña*, with the air of a foot-stomping, 19th-century flamenco bar, showcases some truly amazing guitarists, singers and dancers in a lively space full of regulars. Shows are usually on Saturday nights; call or ask at the tourist office.

ℹ Information

Oficina de Turismo (☑ 956 48 37 15; www.turismoelpuerto.com; Plaza de Alfonso X El Sabio 9; ☺9am-2.50pm & 5-8pm Mon-Sat, 9am-2pm & 6-8pm Sun Jun-Oct, closed Sun afternoon Nov-May)

ℹ Getting There & Away

BOAT

The **catamaran** (www.cmtbc.es; ☺6.45am-9.10pm Mon-Fri, 9am-2pm & 3.45-9.25pm Sat & Sun) leaves for Cádiz (€2.70, 30 minutes) up to 18 times daily Monday to Friday, and up to 16 times at weekends, from in front of the Hotel Santa María.

El Puerto de Santa María

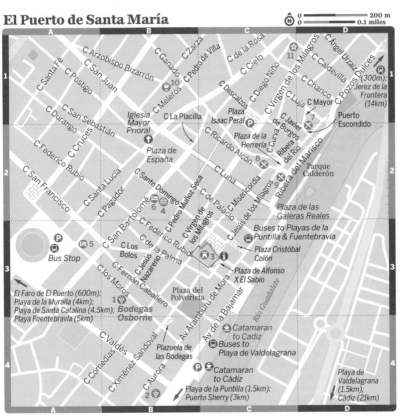

BUS

El Puerto has two bus stops. CMTBC (p120) buses to Cádiz (€2.70, 45 minutes, every 30 to 60 minutes), Jerez de la Frontera (€1.65, 20 minutes, two to eight daily) and Sanlúcar de Barrameda (€1.95, 25 minutes, five to 11 daily) go from the **bus stop** (Plaza Elías Ahuja) outside the bullring. Comes (p120) buses to Seville (€10, 1½ hours, one or two daily) go from outside the train station.

CAR & MOTORCYCLE

There's supervised parking at the bullring and the catamaran dock (€10 per 24 hours). Plaza Isaac Peral has underground car parking (€3.95 per 24 hours).

TRAIN

From the train station at the northeastern end of town, frequent trains go to/from Jerez de la Frontera (€2.70, eight minutes), Cádiz (€5.05, 35 minutes) and Seville (€14, 1¼ hours).

El Puerto de Santa María

◎ Top Sights
1 Bodegas Osborne B3

◎ Sights
2 Bodegas Gutiérrez Colosía B4
3 Castillo de San Marcos C3
4 Fundación Rafael Alberti B2

🛏 Sleeping
5 El Baobab Hostel A3
6 Palacio San Bartolomé B2

⊗ Eating
7 La Taberna del Chef del Mar D2
8 Mesón del Asador C2
9 Romerijo C2

⊜ Drinking & Nightlife
10 Bodega Obregón B1

⊛ Entertainment
11 Peña Flamenca Tomás El Nitri C1

THE SHERRY SECRET

Once sherry grapes have been harvested, they're pressed, and the resulting must is left to ferment in wooden barrels or, more commonly these days, in huge stainless-steel tanks. A frothy veil of *flor* (yeast) appears on the surface at the end of the fermentation, after which wines are fortified with a grape spirit, to 15% for finer wines and 17% or 18% for coarser wines.

Next, wine enters the *solera* (from *suelo*, 'floor') ageing process. The most delicate palomino wines are biologically aged under *flor* (becoming *finos* and *manzanillas*), while coarser palomino wines are matured by oxidation (becoming *olorosos*); an *amontillado* or *palo cortado* is produced by a combination of biological and oxidative ageing. Wine from the sweeter grapes, Pedro Ximénez and muscatel, is matured through oxidation.

In the *solera* system, American-oak barrels, five-sixths full, are lined up in rows at least three barrels high. Those on the bottom contain the oldest wine. From these, about three times a year (more for *manzanilla*), 10% to 15% of the wine is drawn out. This is replaced with the same amount from the barrels directly above, which is then replaced from the next layer – so you'll never know quite how old your sherry is. The wines age for at least three years and may be refortified before bottling.

Sanlúcar de Barrameda

POP 46,100

Sanlúcar is one of those lesser-known Andalucian towns that pleasantly surprise. Firstly, there's the gastronomy: Sanlúcar cooks up some of the region's best seafood on a waterside strip called Bajo de Guía. Secondly, Sanlúcar's unique location at the northern tip of the esteemed Sherry Triangle enables its earthy bodegas, nestled in the monument-strewn old town, to produce the much-admired one-of-a-kind *manzanilla*. Thirdly, plonked at the mouth of the Río Guadalquivir estuary, Sanlúcar provides a quieter, less touristed entry point into the ethereal Parque Nacional de Doñana (p97) than the more popular western access points in Huelva province. As if that weren't enough, the town harbours a proud nautical history. Both Christopher Columbus, on his third sojourn (p95), and Portuguese mariner Ferdinand Magellan struck out from here on their voyages of discovery.

◉ Sights

Many of Sanlúcar's *manzanilla* bodegas are open for guided visits (usually in English or Spanish), including legendary Bodegas Barbadillo. The tourist office (p134) has a list.

★**Bodegas Barbadillo**   WINERY
(🖋956 38 55 21; www.barbadillo.com; Calle Sevilla 6; tours €10; ⊙tours noon & 1pm Tue-Sun, in English 11am Tue-Sun, open Mon Jul & Aug, closed Sun Nov-Mar) With its bodega founded in 1821, Barbadillo was the first family to bottle Sanlúcar's famous *manzanilla* and also

produces one of Spain's most popular *vinos*. Bodega tours end with a four-wine tasting. This 19th-century building also houses the eye-opening **Museo de la Manzanilla** (⊙10am-3pm) **FREE**, which traces the 200-year history of *manzanilla*.

Palacio de los Guzmán   PALACE
(🖋956 36 01 61; www.fcmedinasidonia.com; Plaza Condes de Niebla 1; tours €5; ⊙tours noon Wed & Thu, 11.30am & noon Sun) Just off Calle Caballeros, this rambling palace was the home of the Duques de Medina Sidonia, the aristocratic family that once owned more of Spain than anyone else. The mostly 17th-century house, of 12th-century origin, bursts with antiques, and paintings by Goya, Zurbarán and other Spanish greats. Stop for coffee and home-baked cakes in its old-world **cafe** (cakes €2-3.50; ⊙9am-10pm), with tables amid palm-sprinkled gardens.

Iglesia de Nuestra Señora de la O CHURCH
(Plaza de la Paz; suggested donation €2; ⊙11am-1.15pm, Mass 8pm Mon, Wed & Thu, noon & 8pm Sun) Fronting the old town's Calle Caballeros, this medieval church stands out among Sanlúcar's many others for its elaborate 1360s Gothic-Mudéjar portal and its rich interior embellishment, particularly the Mudéjar *artesonado* (ceiling of interlaced beams). The bell tower was built reusing a tower from the Moorish *alcázar* (fortress) that once stood here.

Castillo de Santiago   CASTLE
(🖋956 92 35 00; www.castillodesantiago.com; Plaza del Castillo 1; adult/child €7/5; ⊙10.15am-3pm & 6.15-9pm Mon & Tue, 10.15am-7.30pm Wed, 10.15am-9pm Thu-Sun approx May-Oct, reduced

hours Nov-Apr) Surrounded by Barbadillo bodegas, Sanlúcar's restored 15th-century castle has sprawling views across the Guadalquivir delta from its hexagonal Torre del Homenaje (keep), and displays military uniforms and weapons. According to legend, Isabel la Católica first saw the sea from here.

Tours

Sanlúcar is a good base for exploring the Parque Nacional de Doñana (p97), which glistens just across the Río Guadalquivir.

Trips are run by the licensed Visitas Doñana (956 36 38 13; www.visitasdonana.com; Centro de Visitantes Fábrica de Hielo, Bajo de Guía; 9am-7pm) whose boat, the *Real Fernando,* chugs up the river for wildlife viewing. Your first option is a 2½-hour boat/jeep combination (€35), which goes 30km through dunes, marshlands and pine forests in 21-person 4WD vehicles, operated in conjunction with Cooperativa Marismas del Rocío (p98), based in El Rocío, Huelva province. There are two trips in the morning and two in the afternoon March to September, and one daily trip November to February. The second (less interesting) option is a three-hour hop-on, hop-off ferry tour with a little walking (adult/child €17/9), which runs with the same frequency. Book at the Centro de Visitantes Fábrica de Hielo (p134). Trips depart from Bajo de Guía; it's best to reserve a week ahead.

Viajes Doñana (956 36 25 40; http://viajesdonana.es; Calle San Juan 20; 10am-2pm & 5-8.30pm Mon-Fri, 10.30am-2pm Sat) agency books the same trips, as well as 3½-hour tours (adult/child €40/24) with the Cooperativa Marismas del Rocío in 21-person 4WDs, which travel 70km into the park. Depending on demand, it can also arrange private five- to six-person jeep tours (€270 per jeep).

Festivals & Events

Romería del Rocío   RELIGIOUS
(7th weekend after Easter) Many pilgrims and covered wagons set out from Sanlúcar bound for El Rocío in Huelva province on Spain's largest religious pilgrimage, the Romería del Rocío (p101).

Feria de la Manzanilla   WINE
(late May/early Jun) A big *manzanilla*-fuelled fair kicks off Sanlúcar's summer.

Sleeping

Hostal Alcoba   BOUTIQUE HOTEL €€
(956 38 31 09; www.hotelalcoba.com; Calle Alcoba 26; s €65-80, d €73-90; P) The stylish 14-room Alcoba, with a slick contemporary courtyard complete with loungers, hammock and lap pool, looks like something that architect Frank Lloyd Wright might have conceived. Skillfully put together (and run), it's a genius white-on-white creation that's wonderfully homey, functional and central (just off the northeastern end of Calle Ancha), all at once. Breakfast (€7) is a good buffet.

La Casa   BOUTIQUE HOTEL €€
(617 575913; www.lacasasanlucar.com; Calle Ancha 84; r €50-90) A friendly young team manages this gorgeously fresh boutique guesthouse. Done up in blues, whites, pinks and turquoises, the eight rooms are loosely inspired by Doñana national park, blending traditional charm (19th-century shutters, marble-effect floors) with contemporary style (see-through showers, geometric lamps, rectangular sinks). Breakfasts feature organic Huelva jams, fresh orange juice and other local goodies.

Hotel Barrameda   HOTEL €€
(956 38 58 78; www.hotelbarrameda.com; Calle Ancha 10; r €80-116; mid-Feb–mid-Dec;) This gleaming, 40-room hotel overlooks the tapas-bar fun on Plaza del Cabildo, and makes an excellent, central choice for its sparkling modern rooms, wood-and-cream decor, ground-floor interior patio, marble floors and efficient service. Among the 12 superior rooms, all with little terraces, four have hot tubs.

Eating

Strung out along Bajo de Guía, 1km northeast of central Sanlúcar, is one of Andalucía's most famous eating strips, once a fishing village and now a haven of high-quality seafood restaurants that revel in their simplicity. The undisputed speciality is *arroz caldoso a la marinera* (seafood rice); the local *langostinos* (king prawns) are another favourite. Plaza del Cabildo is another food hot spot.

Casa Balbino   TAPAS, SEAFOOD €
(956 36 05 13; http://casabalbino.es; Plaza del Cabildo 14; tapas €2-3; noon-5pm & 8pm-midnight, closed first 3 weeks Nov) It doesn't matter when you arrive, Casa Balbino is always overflowing with people, drawn in by its fantastic seafood tapas. Whether you're perched at the bar, tucked into a corner or lucky enough to score an outdoor plaza table, you'll have to elbow your way through and shout your order to a waiter, who'll yell back and provide your dish.

The options are endless, but the *tortillas de camarones* (crisp shrimp fritters), fried-egg-topped *tagarninas* (thistles) and *langostinos a la plancha* (grilled king prawns) are exquisite.

Casa Bigote SEAFOOD €€
(☏956 36 26 96; www.restaurantecasabigote. com; Bajo de Guía 10; mains €12-20; ☺1-4pm & 8-11.30pm Mon-Sat) Classier than its neighbours, Casa Bigote is the most renowned of Bajo de Guía's seafood-only restaurants. House specials include red tuna in raisin-infused Mozarabic sauce or *cococchas de bacalao* (a tender cut of cod) with herby green sauce. Waiters flit back and forth across a small lane to Bigote's permanently packed tapas bar on the corner opposite.

Poma SEAFOOD €€
(☏956 36 51 53; www.restaurantepoma.com; Bajo de Guía 6; mains €12-20; ☺1-4.30pm & 8pm-midnight) You could kick a football on Bajo de Guía and guarantee it'd land on a decent plate of fish, but you should probably aim for Poma, where the *frito variado* (€15) arrives loaded with lightly fried species plucked out of the nearby sea and river. Seafood stews, grilled fish and *arroz a la marinera* for two are also popular.

El Espejo ANDALUCIAN, FUSION €€
(☏651 141650; http://elespejogastrobar.com; Calle Caballeros 11; mains €9-16; ☺8.30-11.45pm Sun-Tue, 12.30-4pm & 8.30-11.45pm Wed-Sat) Flavours from Cádiz collide with international flair in imaginative concoctions at this romantic patio restaurant up in the old town. Tables huddled between palms and geranium pots set the tone for elegantly prepped dishes such as Sanlúcar *langostinos* in red curry, *almadraba* red tuna tartare or slow-poached egg with cheese foam. Good wine-pairing menus, and a smart bar.

ⓘ Information

Centro de Visitantes Fábrica de Hielo (☏956 38 65 77; Bajo de Guía; ☺9am-8pm Apr-Sep, to 7pm Oct-Mar)

Oficina de Información Turística (☏956 36 61 10; www.sanlucarturismo.com; Avenida Calzada Duquesa Isabel; ☺10am-2pm & 5-7pm Mon-Sat, 10am-2pm Sun)

ⓘ Getting There & Away

From Sanlúcar's **bus station** (Avenida de la Estación), Los Amarillos (p120) goes hourly to/ from El Puerto de Santa María (€2.15, 30 minutes), Cádiz (€5.10, one hour) and Seville (€8.77, two hours), less frequently at weekends. Autocares Valenzuela (p128) has hourly buses to/ from Jerez de la Frontera (€1.95, 40 minutes), fewer at weekends.

CÁDIZ' WHITE TOWNS

Arcos de la Frontera
POP 22,350

Everything you've ever dreamed a *pueblo blanco* (white town) could be miraculously materialises in Arcos de la Frontera (33km east of Jerez): a thrilling strategic clifftop location, a swanky *parador,* a volatile frontier history and a soporific old town full of mystery, with whitewashed arches soaring above a web of slender, twisting alleys. The odd tour bus and foreign-owned guesthouse do little to dampen the drama.

For a brief period during the 11th century, Arcos was an independent Berber-ruled *taifa* (small kingdom). In 1255 it was claimed by Christian king Alfonso X El Sabio for Seville and it remained literally *de la frontera* (on the frontier) until the fall of Granada in 1492.

◉ Sights

Plaza del Cabildo SQUARE
Lined with fine ancient buildings, Plaza del Cabildo is the heart of Arcos' old town, its vertiginous *mirador* affording exquisite panoramas over the Río Guadalete. The Moorish-origin **Castillo de los Duques**, rebuilt in the 14th and 15th centuries, is closed to the public, but its outer walls frame classic Arcos views. On the square's eastern side, the Parador de Arcos de la Frontera (p137) is a reconstruction of a grand 16th-century magistrate's house; pop in for coffee.

Basílica Menor de Santa María de la Asunción BASILICA
(Plaza del Cabildo; €2, incl Iglesia de San Pedro €3; ☺10am-12.45pm & 4-6.45pm Mon-Fri, 10am-1.30pm Sat Mar–mid-Dec) This Gothic-baroque creation is one of Andalucía's more beautiful, intriguing small churches, built over several centuries on the site of a mosque. Check out the ornate gold-leaf altarpiece (a miniature of that in Seville's cathedral) carved between 1580 and 1608, the striking painting of San Cristóbal (St Christopher), the restored 14th-century Gothic-Mudéjar mural, the ornate woodcarved 18th-century choir and the lovely Isabelline ceiling tracery. The original

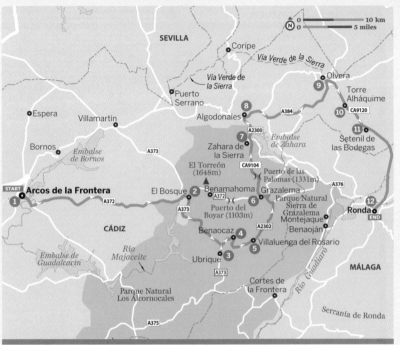

Driving Tour
White Towns

START ARCOS DE LA FRONTERA
END RONDA
LENGTH 147KM; TWO DAYS

Rev up in dramatic ① **Arcos de la Frontera**, a Roman-turned-Moorish-turned-Christian citadel perched atop a sheer-sided sandstone ridge. Head 32km east along the A372 to ② **El Bosque**, the western gateway to Parque Natural Sierra de Grazalema and location of the park's main information centre. The A373 takes you 13km south to leather-making ③ **Ubrique** (supplier to some of the world's top designers), close to the borders of Grazalema and Alcornocales natural parks. Mountains rise quickly as you drive 7km up the A2302 to tiny ④ **Benaocaz**, where several Grazalema park hikes start/finish, then another 7km on to equally tiny ⑤ **Villaluenga del Rosario** with its artisanal-cheese museum. Plying the craggy eastern face of the sierra and then taking the A372 west brings you to ⑥ **Grazalema** (p137), a red-roofed park-activity nexus also famous for its blanket making and honey; the perfect overnight stop. Count the switchbacks on the steep CA9104 as you climb to the 1357m Puerto de las Palomas and, beyond, ⑦ **Zahara de la Sierra** (p138), with its huddle of houses spread around the skirts of a castle-topped crag above a glassy reservoir at the foot of the Grazalema mountains. The A2300 threads 10km north to ⑧ **Algodonales**, a white town on the edge of the natural park known for its guitar-making workshop and hang-gliding/paragliding obsession. Take the A384 19km northeast past the Peñón de Zaframagón (a refuge for griffon vultures) to reach ⑨ **Olvera** (p140), visible for miles around thanks to its Moorish castle but also known for its olive oil and *vía verde* path. Following the CA9106 southeast, you'll pass the little-known white town of ⑩ **Torre Alháquime**. The CA9120 winds 11km southeast towards the border with Málaga province and ⑪ **Setenil de las Bodegas** (p142), a village recognisable for its cave houses. Once used for storing wine, today they offer a shady antidote to the summer heat plus some good tapas bars. Head 17km south and wrap up in beautiful gorge-top ⑫ **Ronda** (p181).

Arcos de la Frontera

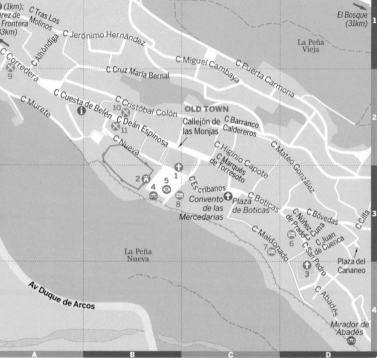

bell tower was toppled by the 1755 Lisbon earthquake; its neoclassical replacement remains incomplete.

Iglesia de San Pedro
CHURCH

(Calle San Pedro 4; €2, incl Basílica Menor de Santa María de la Asunción €3; ⊘10am-12.45pm & 4-6.45pm Mon-Fri, 10am-1.30pm Sat) Containing a 16th-century main altarpiece said to be the oldest in Cádiz province, this Gothic-baroque confection sports what is perhaps one of Andalucía's most magnificent small-church interiors, behind an 18th-century facade, and may have been constructed atop an Almohad-era fortress.

🎇 Festivals & Events

Semana Santa
RELIGIOUS

(⊘Mar/Apr) Dramatic Semana Santa processions see hooded penitents inching through Arcos' narrow streets.

🛏 Sleeping

Casa Campana
GUESTHOUSE €

(☑600 284928; www.casacampana.com; Calle Núñez de Prado 4; r/apt €54/78; ❉🛜) One of several charming guesthouses in old Arcos, Casa Campana has two cosy doubles and a massive five-person apartment with kitchenette that's filled with character, in a house dating back 600 years. The intimate, flower-filled patio is dotted with sun loungers and the rooftop terrace flooded with views. It's expertly run by knowledgeable owners, who supply excellent old-town walking-tour leaflets.

★ La Casa Grande
HERITAGE HOTEL €€

(☑956 70 39 30; www.lacasagrande.net; Calle Maldonado 10; r €90-118, ste €120-135; ⊘closed 6-31 Jan; ❉🛜) This gorgeous, rambling, cliff-side mansion dating to 1729 once belonged to the great flamenco dancer Antonio Ruiz Soler. With each of the seven rooms done in different but tasteful modern-rustic design (most with divine views), it feels more arty

Arcos de la Frontera

home than hotel. Great breakfasts (€10), a well-stocked library, a rooftop terrace, and on-demand massage and yoga complete the perfect package.

Parador de Arcos de la Frontera HERITAGE HOTEL €€
(☑956 70 05 00; www.parador.es; Plaza del Cabildo; r €85-150; ❈@☎) A rebuilt 16th-century magistrate's residence that combines typical *parador* luxury with a splendid setting and the best views in town. Eight of the 24 classic-style rooms have balconies opening onto sweeping cliff-top panoramas; most others look out on Plaza del Cabildo. With its gorgeous terrace, the elegant **restaurant** (mains €13-22; ⊙8-11am, noon-4pm & 8.30-11pm) offers a smart menu rooted in local specialities. Best deals online.

✕ Eating

★**Taberna Jóvenes Flamencos** ANDALUCIAN €
(☑657 133552; www.facebook.com/pg/taberna. jovenezflamencos; Calle Deán Espinosa 11; tapas €2.50-3.50; ⊙noon-midnight Thu-Tue, closed 1 week Oct; ☑) You've got to hand it to this cheerful, popular place, which successfully opened amid the recession. Along with wonderful flamenco/bullfighting decor, tiled floors and hand-painted hot-red tables, it has an enticing menu of meat, fish, vegetarian, scramble and stew tapas and *raciones,* including aubergines and grilled goat's cheese drizzled with local honey. Service is impeccable. Music and dance break out regularly.

Babel MOROCCAN, FUSION €
(☑671 138256; www.restaurantebabel.es; Calle Corredera 11; dishes €5-12; ⊙1-4pm & 7.30-11.30pm Mon-Sat, evenings only Jul–mid-Sep; ☎☑) Arcos' Moroccan-fusion restaurant has tasteful decor (red-washed walls, cushy booths and ornate stools shipped in from Casablanca) and some equally tasty dishes. Choose from perfectly spiced tagines and couscous, zingy hummus, chicken-and-almond *pastela* (a stuffed pastry), or the full Arabic tea treatment with silver pots and sweet pastries. It's a cosy, friendly place. Hours vary.

Bar La Cárcel TAPAS, ANDALUCIAN €€
(☑956 70 04 10; Calle Deán Espinosa 18; tapas €2.50-4, raciones €8-14; ⊙noon-1am Tue-Sun) A *cárcel* (prison) in name only, this welcoming, low-key bar-restaurant offers no-nonsense tapas – honeyed eggplant with goat's cheese, spinach-cheese crêpes, bacon-wrapped prawns – alongside ice-cold *cañas* (small draught beer) and *tinto de verano* (red wine with lemonade and ice). Sample a few different delights with one of the seven-or eight-course tapas tasting menus (€22 to €25).

❶ Information

Oficina de Turismo (☑956 70 22 64; http://turismoarcos.com; Calle Cuesta de Belén 5; ⊙9.30am-2pm & 3-7.30pm Mon-Sat, 10am-2pm Sun)

❶ Getting There & Around

BUS

Buses from Arcos' **bus station** (Calle Los Alcaldes) in the new town (down to the west of the old town), off Avenida Miguel Mancheño, are operated by Los Amarillos (p120), Comes (p120) and/or the Consorcio de Transportes Bahía de Cádiz (p120). Frequency is reduced at weekends. For Seville, it's best to connect in Jerez.

CAR & MOTORCYCLE

There's underground parking below Paseo de Andalucía (€15 for 24 hours), west of the old town. A half-hourly 'microbus' (€1) runs up to the old town from Plaza de España 9am to 7pm Monday to Friday and 9am to 2pm Saturday.

Grazalema

POP 1640 / ELEV 825M

Few white towns are as generically perfect as Grazalema, with its spotless whitewashed houses sporting rust-tiled roofs and wrought-iron window bars, and sprinkled on the steep, rocky slopes of its eponymous mountain range. With hikes fanning out in all directions, Grazalema is the most popular base for adventures into the Parque Natural Sierra de Grazalema (p139). It's also an age-old producer of blankets, honey, cheese and meat-filled stews, and has its own special mountain charm.

◉ Sights

Plaza de España   SQUARE
Grazalema centres on 18th-century Plaza de España, overlooked by the stone-facade Iglesia de la Aurora (⊙11am-12.30pm), begun in 1760 and completed 40 years later, and refreshed by a four-spouted Visigothic fountain.

🏃 Activities

Horizon   ADVENTURE SPORTS
(☑655 934565, 956 13 23 63; www.horizonaventura.com; Calle Las Piedras 1; ⊙10am-2pm & 5-8pm Mon-Sat) Just off Plaza de España, highly experienced Horizon offers all the most exciting activities in the Parque Natural Sierra de Grazalema, including hiking, kayaking, climbing, canyoning, caving, paragliding and vie ferrate, with English-, French- or German-speaking guides. Prices per person range from €13 for a four-hour walk to €90 for tandem paragliding (but may rise for fewer than six people).

El Calvario-Corazón de Jesús   WALKING
A signposted 500m route that eventually splits in two climbs to El Calvario, an 18th-century chapel ruined during the civil war, and to a crag-top statue of Jesus (Corazón de Jésus), both with fine mountain and village views. The path starts on the southern side of the A372, 500m uphill from the car park at the eastern end of Grazalema.

🛏 Sleeping & Eating

La Mejorana   CASA RURAL €
(☑649 613272, 956 13 23 27; www.lamejorana.net; Calle Santa Clara 6; r incl breakfast €62; ❄🐕🐾) An exceptionally welcoming house towards the upper end of Grazalema, La Mejorana has nine comfy rooms in colourful, updated rustic style. Some have private lounges and sky-blue Moroccan-style arches; others balconies, terraces, huge mirrors or wrought-iron bedsteads. There's a spacious sitting room plus a breakfast terrace with gorgeous village views, above a leafy hammock-strung garden surrounding a pool.

Casa de las Piedras   HOTEL €
(☑956 13 20 14; www.casadelaspiedras.es; Calle Las Piedras 32; s/d €35/48, with shared bathroom €15/28; ❄🐾) Mountain air and a homey feel go together like Isabel and Fernando at this rustic-design hotel with a snug downstairs lounge and masses of park activities infor-

mation. Simple, cosy rooms are decorated with Grazalema-made blankets. It's 100m west of Plaza de España.

La Maroma   TAPAS, ANDALUCIAN €€
(☑617 543756; www.facebook.com/gastrobar lamaroma; Calle Santa Clara; tapas €2-6, mains €6-16; ⊙noon-5pm & 7.30-11pm; 🐾) The cooking is significantly more fun and inventive than the rustic check-cloth, beamed-ceiling, bull-festival-inspired decor suggests at this cosy gastrobar, run by a young family team. Creative local-inspired tapas and *raciones* throw mountain ingredients into tasty bites like mushrooms in honey-and-thyme sauce, *huevos rotos* (fried eggs with potatoes), topped *tostas* or *payoyo*-cheese salad with Grazalema-honey dressing.

Restaurante El Torreón   ANDALUCIAN €€
(☑956 13 23 13; www.restauranteeltorreongrazal ema.com; Calle Agua 44; mains €7-18; ⊙1-3.30pm & 7.45-11pm Thu-Tue; 🐾🍴) This cosy, friendly restaurant with a roaring winter fire specialises in traditional mountain cuisine, from local chorizo and cheese platters to *tagarnina* (thistle) scrambles (a Cádiz delicacy) and sirloin in green-pepper sauce. There's a dedicated meat-free Andalucian-style menu (mushroom risotto, *tagarnina* croquettes, spinach scramble and more). Tables spill onto the street when it's sunny.

ⓘ Information

Oficina de Turismo (☑956 13 20 52; www. grazalema.es; Plaza de los Asomaderos; ⊙9am-3pm Tue-Sun Jun-Sep, 10am-2pm & 3-5.30pm Tue-Sun Oct-May) Excellent Parque Natural Sierra de Grazalema walking information, plus last-minute, same-day hiking permits (in person only). Probably the province's most helpful tourist office.

ⓘ Getting There & Away

Los Amarillos (p120) runs two daily buses to/from Ronda (€2.85, one hour); two daily to/from Ubrique (€2.32, 30 to 40 minutes) via Benaocaz (€1.61, 20 to 30 minutes); and one to two daily Monday to Friday to/from El Bosque (€1.45, 30 minutes), where you can change for Arcos de la Frontera.

Zahara de la Sierra

POP 1250 / ELEV 550M

Rugged Zahara, strung around a vertiginous crag at the foot of the Grazalema mountains, overlooking the glittering turquoise Embalse de Zahara (Zahara Reservoir), hums with Moorish mystery. For over 150 years in the

14th and 15th centuries, it stood on the old medieval frontier facing off against Christian Olvera, clearly visible in the distance. These days Zahara ticks all the classic white-town boxes and, with vistas framed by tall palms and hot-pink bougainvillea, its streets invite exploration. It's also a great base for hiking the Garganta Verde (p135), so it's popular. Visit during the afternoon siesta, however, and you can still hear a pin drop.

The precipitous CA9104 road over the ultra-steep 1357m Puerto de las Palomas (Doves' Pass) links Zahara with Grazalema (17km south) and is a spectacular drive full of white-knuckle switchbacks.

Sights & Activities

Zahara village centres on Calle San Juan; towards its western end stands 20th-century **Capilla de San Juan de Letrán** (Calle San Juan; ⊙11am-1.30pm), with a Moorish-origin clock tower, while at its eastern end is the pastel-pink, 18th-century baroque **Iglesia de Santa María de Mesa** (Plaza del Rey; admission by donation; ⊙11am-1.30pm & 3.30-5.15pm).

Castillo CASTLE
(⊙24hr) FREE To reach Zahara's 12th-century castle keep, take the path almost opposite the Hotel Arco de la Villa – it's a steep, steady 10- to 15-minute climb. The castle's recapture from the Christians by Emir Abu al-Hasan of Granada, in a night raid in 1481, provoked the Reyes Católicos (Catholic Monarchs) to launch the last phase of the Reconquista, which ended with the 1492 fall of Granada.

Zahara Catur ADVENTURE SPORTS
(☎657 926394, 656 986009; www.zaharacatur.com) This well-established Zahara-based adventure outfit rents two-person canoes (€18 per hour) and runs canyoning trips (from €34), guided walks in the Grazalema natural park (€13 to €15 per person) and three-hour via ferrata expeditions (€30 per person). Minimum numbers apply to some activities, but you can join other groups.

Sleeping & Eating

★ **Al Lago** ANDALUCIAN, MEDITERRANEAN €€
(☎956 12 30 32; www.al-lago.es; Calle Félix Rodríguez de la Fuente; mains €12-17; ⊙1-4pm & 8-11pm mid-Feb–mid-Nov, closed Wed approx mid-Feb–May & Oct–mid-Nov; 🛜🍽) At the foot of the village, overlooking the reservoir, British-American-run Al Lago serves Andalucian cuisine with an inventive, contemporary slant. Local, seasonal, often-organic ingredients star in creations ranging from beautifully prepared flatbread pizzas, mountain-cheese platters and vegetable tempura to chef Stefan's six-course tasting menus (€42), expertly paired with Spanish wines (including Cádiz and Málaga picks). Excellent vegetarian and gluten-free options. Upstairs are six chic lake-view **rooms** (☎956 12 30 32; incl breakfast s €72-82, d €90-120, f €110-125; ⊙mid-Feb–mid-Nov; ❄🛜), styled by designer-owner Mona.

ℹ Information

Punto de Información Zahara de la Sierra (☎956 12 31 14; Plaza del Rey 3; ⊙10am-2pm Tue-Sun)

ℹ Getting There & Away

Comes (p120) runs two daily buses to/from Ronda (€4.55, one hour) Monday to Friday.

Parque Natural Sierra de Grazalema

The rugged, pillar-like peaks of the Parque Natural Sierra de Grazalema rise abruptly from the plains northeast of Cádiz, revealing sheer gorges, rare firs, wild orchids and the province's highest summits, against a beautifully green backdrop at altitudes of 260m to 1648m. This is the wettest part of Spain – stand aside, Galicia and Cantabria, Grazalema village logs an average 2200mm annually. It's gorgeous walking country (best months: May, June, September and October). For the more intrepid, adventure activities abound. The 534-sq-km park, named Spain's first Unesco Biosphere Reserve in 1977, extends into northwestern Málaga province, where it includes the Cueva de la Pileta (p189).

🏃 Activities

Hiking, caving, canyoning, kayaking, rock climbing, cycling, birdwatching, horse riding, paragliding, vie ferrate – this beautiful protected area crams it all in. For the more technical stuff, go with a guide; Zahara's Zahara Catur and Grazalema-based Horizon are respected adventure-activity outfits.

The Sierra de Grazalema is criss-crossed by 20 beautiful official marked trails. Four of the best – the Garganta Verde (p135), El Pinsapar (p140), **Llanos del Rabel** and El Torreón (p140) paths – enter restricted areas and require (free) permits from the **Centro de Visitantes El Bosque** (☎956 70 97 33; cvelbosque.amaya@juntadeandalucia.es; Calle Federico García Lorca 1, El Bosque; ⊙10am-2pm, closed Mon Jun-Sep). Ideally, book a month or

DON'T MISS

GARGANTA VERDE WALK

The 2.5km path that winds into the precipitous Garganta Verde (Green Throat), a lushly vegetated gorge over 100m deep, is one of the Sierra de Grazalema's most spectacular walks. A large colony of enormous griffon vultures, whose feathers ruffle in the wind as they whoosh by, makes the one-hour descent even more dramatic. The best viewpoint is 30 minutes in. At the bottom of the ravine, you follow the riverbed to an eerie cavern known as the Cueva de la Ermita. Then it's a 1½-hour climb back up.

The trail starts 3.5km south of Zahara de la Sierra, at Km 10 on the CA9104 to Grazalema. You'll need a (free) prebooked permit from the Centro de Visitantes El Bosque (p139) or Grazalema's tourist office (p138) (last-minute permits only). The route is partly off limits 1 June to 15 October.

two ahead. The centre will email permits on request with minimum five days' notice; communication may be in English, but permits are in Spanish only. Additional (leftover) permits are sometimes available on the day; you can ask ahead by phone or email, but you'll have to collect them at the Centro or Grazalema's tourist office (p138) on the day. Some trails are fully or partly off limits from 1 June to 15 October due to fire risk.

The Centro de Visitantes El Bosque, Grazalema's tourist office and the unofficial Punto de Información Zahara de la Sierra (p139) have maps outlining the main walking possibilities. There's downloadable Spanish- and English-language hiking information with maps online at www.ventanadelvisitante.es.

El Pinsapar Walk   HIKING
The 12km Sendero del Pinsapar to Benamahoma starts from a car park 2km uphill (northwest) from Grazalema, 1km along the CA9104 to Zahara de la Sierra. Keep an eye out for the rare dark-green *pinsapo*, a relic of the great Mediterranean fir forests of the Tertiary period, which survives only in southwest Andalucía and northern Morocco. Allow six hours one way. This hike requires a permit from the Centro de Visitantes El Bosque (p139) or Grazalema's tourist office (p138; last-minute permits only); from 1 June to 15 October it's only partly accessible on guided hikes with park-authorised operators.

El Torreón Walk   HIKING
(⊙16 Oct–May) El Torreón (1648m) is Cádiz province's highest peak and, on clear days, from the summit you can see Gibraltar, Granada's Sierra Nevada and Morocco's Rif mountains. The 3km route starts 100m east of Km 40 on the Grazalema–Benamahoma A372, 8km west of Grazalema. It takes about 2½ hours to the summit. You'll need a permit from the Centro de Visitantes El Bosque (p139) or Grazalema's tourist office (p138; last-minute permits only).

Salto del Cabrero Walk   HIKING
Of the park's free-access paths, the most dramatic is the well-signed, 7.2km Sendero Salto del Cabrero between the Puerto del Boyar (reached from Grazalema via the 1.8km Camino de los Charcones) and Benaocaz, traversing the western flanks of the Sierra del Endrinal. The route was closed at the Grazalema end at research time, but it may reopen. Allow three to four hours from Grazalema to Benaocaz. Two daily buses return from Benaocaz to Grazalema at 7.40am and 3.40pm. Despite the route's closure at one end, you can still reach the Salto del Cabrero (Goatherd's Leap) itself, a gaping fissure in the earth's surface, from Benaocaz (about one hour).

Zero Gravity   ADVENTURE SPORTS
(☑615 372554; www.paraglidingspain.es; Avenida de la Constitución 44, Algodonales; 1-week courses €990) Little-known Algodonales, 6km north of Zahara de la Sierra, surprises as a major paragliding and hang-gliding centre of Andalucía. Long-standing Zero Gravity offers an extensive range of beginner and 'refresher' paragliding programs, plus 30-minute tandem flights with instructors (€90).

Olvera
POP 8060 / ELEV 643M

Dramatically topped by a Moorish castle, Olvera beckons from miles away across olive-tree-covered country. Reconquered by Alfonso XI in 1327, this relatively untouristed town was a bandit refuge until the mid-19th century. Most people now come to Olvera to walk or cycle the Vía Verde de la Sierra, but, as a white town par excellence, it's also renowned for its olive oil, two striking churches and roller-coaster history, which probably started with the Romans.

◎ Sights

Castillo Árabe
CASTLE

(Plaza de la Iglesia; incl La Cilla adult/child €2/1; ☉10.30am-2pm & 4-8pm Tue-Sun Jun-Sep, 10.30am-2pm & 4-6pm Tue-Sun Oct-May) Perched on a crag high atop town is Olvera's late-12th-century Arabic castle, which later formed part of Nasrid-era Granada's defensive systems. Clamber up to the tower, with ever-more-exquisite town and country views opening up as you go.

La Cilla
MUSEUM

(Plaza de la Iglesia; incl Castillo Árabe adult/child €2/1; ☉10.30am-2pm & 4-8pm Tue-Sun Jun-Sep, 10.30am-2pm & 4-6pm Tue-Sun Oct-May) The old grain store of the Duques de Osuna, next to the castle, houses the tourist office (p142), the fascinating Museo de la Frontera y los Castillos (devoted to Olvera's turbulent history and the Reconquista), and an exposition on the nearby Vía Verde de la Sierra cycling/hiking path.

Santuario de los Remedios
CHURCH

(CA9106; ☉9am-2pm & 5-8.30pm Mar-Sep, 9am-2pm & 4-7pm Oct-Feb) Three kilometres southeast of Olvera's historic core, en route to Torre Alháquime, this 17th-century sanctuary honours the town's patron saint. Its superposed cloisters have a tropical feel, draped in plants and with muralled ceilings and floral-motif floor tiles. Upstairs is a room crammed with colourful offerings made to the much-revered Virgen de los Remedios.

Iglesia Parroquial Nuestra Señora de la Encarnación
CHURCH

(Plaza de la Iglesia; €2; ☉11am-1pm Tue-Sun) Built over a Gothic-Mudéjar predecessor, Olvera's neoclassical top-of-the-town church was commissioned by the Duques de Osuna and completed in the 1840s.

🛏 Sleeping & Eating

Hotel Estación Vía Verde de la Sierra
HOTEL €

(☎644 747029; www.hotelviaverdedelasierra.es; Calle Pasadera 4; s/d/tr €45/55/65, 2-/6-person apt €90/110; ☉Tue-Sun; P❄️🛜🏊) This unique hotel 1km north of Olvera is the official start of the Vía Verde de la Sierra, Spain's finest *vía verde*. Accommodation is in seven smartly updated rooms for one to four people tucked into the converted station, or in train-wagon-inspired 'apartments' with kitchens, sleeping up to six. Other facilities

---

DON'T MISS

VÍA VERDE DE LA SIERRA

The 36km Vía Verde de la Sierra (www.fundacionviaverdedelasierra.com) between Olvera and Puerto Serrano (to the west) is regularly touted as the finest of Spain's *vías verdes*, greenways that have transformed old railway lines into traffic-free thoroughfares for bikers, hikers and horse riders. It's one of 23 such *vías* in Andalucía, which together total 500km. Aside from the wild, rugged scenery, this route is notable for four spectacular viaducts, 30 tunnels (some with sensor-activated lighting) and three old stations transformed into hotel-restaurants. The train line itself was never actually completed: it was constructed in the late 1920s as part of the abortive Jerez–Almargen railway, but the Spanish Civil War put a stop to construction works. The line was restored in the early 2000s.

The Hotel Estación Vía Verde de la Sierra, 1km north of Olvera, is the route's official eastern starting point. Here, Sesca (☎657 987432, 687 676462; www.sesca.es; Calle Pasadera 4; half-/full-day bike hire €9/12; ☉9am-2pm & 4-6pm) rents bicycles, including tandems, kids' bikes, electric bikes and chariots, and you can check out the Centro de Interpretación Vía Verde de la Sierra (www.fundacionviaverdedelasierra.es; Calle Pasadera 4; adult/child €2/1; ☉9.30am-4.30pm Thu-Mon). Bike hire is also available at Coripe and Puerto Serrano stations (daily October to May, weekends only June to September). Other services include the Patrulla Verde (☎638 280184; ☉8am-3.30pm Sat & Sun Jun-Sep, 9am-5pm Sat & Sun Oct-May), a staff of on-the-road bike experts. Note that hotel-restaurants (but not bike-hire facilities) close Monday in Olvera, Wednesday in Coripe and Tuesday in Puerto Serrano.

A highlight of the *vía verde* is the Peñón de Zaframagón, a distinctive crag that's a prime breeding ground for griffon vultures. The Centro de Interpretación y Observatorio Ornitológico (☎956 13 63 72; www.fundacionviaverdedelasierra.es; Antigua Estación de Zaframagón; adult/child €2/1; ☉9.30am-5.30pm), in the former Zaframagón station building 16km west of Olvera, allows close-up observations by means of a high-definition camera placed up on the crag.

WORTH A TRIP

SETENIL DE LAS BODEGAS

While most white towns sought protection atop lofty crags, the people of Setenil de las Bodegas (pop 2210; 14km southeast of Olvera) burrowed into the dark caves beneath the steep cliffs of the Río Trejo. Clearly, the strategy worked: it took the Christian armies a 15-day siege to dislodge the Moors from their well-defended positions in 1484. Many of the town's original cave-houses remain, some converted into bars and restaurants.

The **tourist office** (☑ 635 365147, 616 553384; www.setenil.com; Calle Villa 2; ☺ 10am-2pm Tue-Sun) is near the top of the town in the 16th-century **Casa Consistorial** (which exhibits a rare wooden Mudéjar ceiling) and runs guided walks around Setenil. Above is the 12th-century **castle** (Calle Villa; ☺ 10.30am-2pm & 5-8pm Mon-Fri, 10.30am-7pm Sat & Sun), captured by the Christians just eight years before the fall of Granada; you can climb the 13th-century tower. Setenil has some great tapas bars that make ideal pit stops while you study its unique urban framework. Start with the cave bar-restaurants built into the rock along Calles Cuevas del Sol and Cuevas de la Sombra, and work your way up to **Restaurante Casa Palmero** (☑ 956 13 43 60; www.facebook.com/RestauranteCasa Palmero; Plaza de Andalucía 4; mains €8-19; ☺ 1am-late Fri-Wed; 🛜 🅿).

Los Amarillos (p120) has one to two daily buses to/from Málaga (€11, two hours). **Autocares Sierra de las Nieves** (☑ 952 87 54 35; http://grupopacopepe.com) runs five weekday buses and three Saturday buses to/from Ronda (€1.80, 45 minutes).

include bike hire (p141), a restaurant and a saltwater pool.

ⓘ Information

Oficina de Turismo (☑ 956 12 08 16; www.olvera.es; Plaza de la Iglesia; ☺ 10.30am-2pm & 4-8pm Tue-Sun Jun-Sep, 10.30am-2pm & 4-6pm Tue-Sun Oct-May)

ⓘ Getting There & Away

Los Amarillos (p120) runs one daily bus to/from Jerez de la Frontera (€9.11, 2½ hours) and Ronda (€5.40, 1½ hours) and one to two daily to/from Málaga (€12, two hours). Comes (p120) has one daily bus Monday to Friday to/from Cádiz (€15, three hours).

SOUTHEAST CÁDIZ PROVINCE & THE COSTA DE LA LUZ

Arriving on the Costa de la Luz from the Costa del Sol is like flinging open the window and breathing in the glorious fresh air. Bereft of tacky resorts, this is a world of flat-capped farmers, grazing bulls and furtive slugs of dry sherry with lunchtime tapas. Throw in beautiful blond, windswept beaches, a buzzing surfing/kitesurfing scene and a string of spectacularly located white towns, and you're unequivocally back in Andalucía. Spaniards, well aware of this, flock to places like Tarifa, Zahara de los Atunes and Los Caños de Meca in July and August. It's by no means a secret, but the stunning Costa de la Luz remains the same old laid-back beachy hang-out it's always been. The Costa de la Luz continues west into neighbouring Huelva province (p96), up to the Portugal border.

Vejer de la Frontera
POP 9260

Vejer – the jaw drops, the eyes blink, the eloquent adjectives dry up. Looming moodily atop a rocky hill above the busy N340, 50km south of Cádiz, this serene, compact white town is something very special. Yes, there's a labyrinth of twisting old-town streets plus some serendipitous viewpoints, a ruined castle, a surprisingly elaborate culinary scene, a smattering of exquisitely dreamy hotels and a tangible Moorish influence. But Vejer has something else: an air of magic and mystery, an imperceptible touch of *duende* (spirit).

◉ Sights

Plaza de España   SQUARE
With its elaborate 20th-century, Seville-tiled fountain and perfectly white town hall, Vejer's palm-studded, cafe-filled Plaza de España is a favourite, much-photographed hang-out. There's a small lookout above its western side (accessible from Calle de Sancho IV El Bravo).

Casa del Mayorazgo   HOUSE
(Callejón de la Villa; admission by donation; ☺ hours vary) If the door's open, pop into this private 18th-century house to find two stunning

flower-filled patios (home to 450 potted plants!) and one of just three original 13th- to 14th-century towers that kept watch over the city, with panoramic views down to Plaza de España and across town.

Castillo
CASTLE

(Calle del Castillo; ⊙10am-2pm & 5-9pm approx May-Sep, 10am-2pm & 4-8pm approx Oct-Apr) **FREE** Vejer's much-reworked castle, once home of the Duques de Medina Sidonia, dates from the 10th or 11th century. It isn't astoundingly impressive, but you can wander through the Moorish entrance arch and climb the hibiscus-fringed ramparts for fantastic views across town and down to the white-sand coastline.

Estatua de la Cobijada
STATUE

(Calle Trafalgar) Just below the castle is a lookout point guarded by this statue of a woman sporting Vejer's cloak-like, all-black traditional dress, the *cobijada*, which covers the entire body except the right eye. Despite its similarities to Islamic clothing, the *cobijada* is believed to be of 16th- or 17th-century Christian origin; it was banned in the 1930s and, after the civil war, few women had managed to hang onto their full outfits. Today it appears only for local festivities.

Iglesia del Divino Salvador
CHURCH

(Plaza Padre Ángel; ⊙Mass 6.30pm Mon, Wed & Fri, 7pm Sat, 10am Sun) Built atop an earlier mosque, this unusual church is 14th-century Mudéjar at the altar end and 16th-century Gothic at the other. In the late afternoon the sun shines surreally through its stained-glass windows, projecting multicoloured light above the altar.

Walls
WALLS

Enclosing the 40,000-sq-m old town, Vejer's imposing 15th-century walls are particularly visible between the Arco de la Puerta Cerrada (of 11th- or 12th-century origin) and the 15th-century Arco de la Segur, two of the four original gateways to survive. The area around the Arco de la Segur and Calle Judería was, in the 15th century, the *judería* (Jewish quarter). Start with the 10th- or 11th-century Puerta de Sancho IV (another surviving gateway) next to Plaza de España and work round.

🍳 Courses

⭐ Annie B's Spanish Kitchen
COOKING

(☑ 620 560649; www.anniebspain.com; Calle Viñas 11; 1-day course €165) This is your chance to master the art of Andalucian cooking with top-notch local expertise. Annie's popular day classes (Andalucian, Moroccan or sea-

food focused) end with lunch by the pool or on the roof terrace at her gorgeous old-town house. She also offers six-day Spanish Culinary Classics courses, plus tapas, food and sherry tours of Vejer, Cádiz, Jerez and more.

🎆 Festivals & Events

Velada de Nuestra Señora de la Oliva
MUSIC, RELIGIOUS

(⊙10-24 Aug) Nightly themed dancing and music in Plaza de España (flamenco, jazz etc).

🛏 Sleeping

⭐ La Casa del Califa
BOUTIQUE HOTEL €€

(☑956 44 77 30; www.califavejer.com; Plaza de España 16; incl breakfast s €92-145, d €106-155, ste €175-230; P❈🐾🛜) Rambling over several floors of labyrinthine corridors, this gorgeous hotel has style and character, and inhabits a building with its roots in the 10th century. Rooms are soothing, with Morocco-chic decor; the top-floor 'Africa' suite is divine. Special 'emir' service (€45) brings flowers, pastries and *cava* (sparkling wine). Breakfast is a delicious spread in the fabulous Moroccan–Middle Eastern restaurant (p144).

⭐ Casa Shelly
BOUTIQUE HOTEL €€

(☑ 639 118831; www.casashelly.com; Calle Eduardo Shelly 6; r €105-140; ⊙Mar-Nov; ❈🛜) All understated elegance and homey Andalucian cosiness, Casa Shelly feels as though it's wandered out of the pages of an old-meets-new interior-design magazine and into the thick of Vejer's old town. Beyond a calming reception lounge and fountain-bathed patio, it has seven exquisitely designed rooms adorned with antique-style tiles, wood-beamed ceilings, shuttered windows and fresh decor in pinks, blues and whites.

La Fonda Antigua
BOUTIQUE HOTEL €€

(☑625 372616; www.chicsleepinvejer.com; Calle San Filmo 14; r incl breakfast €90-150; ❈🛜) A *jerezano* couple with an eye for contemporary-chic interiors runs this boutiquey adults-only bolthole on the fringes of Vejer's old town. In the seven individually styled rooms, antique doors morph into bedheads, mismatched vintage tiles dot polished-concrete floors and include glass-walled showers and, for room 6, a claw-foot tub. The rooftop chill-out terrace opens up sprawling old-town vistas.

⭐ V...
BOUTIQUE HOTEL €€€

(☑956 45 17 57; www.hotelv-vejer.com; Calle Rosario 11-13; r €219-329; ❈🛜) V... (that's V for Vejer, and, yes, the three dots are part of the name) is one of Andalucía's most exquisite creations, a brilliantly run 12-room hotel where contemporary design (luxurious open-plan bathrooms with huge tubs and giant mirrors) mixes with antique artefacts (pre-Columbus doors). On the vista-laden rooftop there's a tiny pool and bubbling hot tub.

✖ Eating

Vejer has quietly morphed into a gastronomic highlight of Andalucía. Restaurants cluster around Plaza de España, Calle de la Corredera and the Mercado de Abastos.

Mercado de Abastos ANDALUCIAN, INTERNATIONAL €
(Calle San Francisco; dishes €2-8; ☺noon-4pm & 7pm-midnight) Glammed up with modern gastrobar design, Vejer's Mercado de San Francisco has become a buzzy foodie hot spot. Grab a *vino* and choose between classic favourites and bold contemporary creations at its wonderfully varied tapas stalls: Iberian ham *raciones, tortilla de patatas*, fried fish in paper cups or hugely popular sushi.

★ El Jardín del Califa MOROCCAN, FUSION €€
(☑956 45 17 06; www.califavejer.com; Plaza de España 16; mains €12-18; ☺1.30-4pm & 8-11.30pm; 🖋) The sizzling atmosphere matches the cooking at this exotically beautiful restaurant, also a hotel (p143) and *tetería* (teahouse). It's hidden in a cavernous house where even finding the bathroom is a full-on adventure. The Moroccan–Middle Eastern menu – tagines, couscous, hummus, falafel – is crammed with Maghreb flavours (saffron, figs, almonds). Book ahead, whether that's for the palm-sprinkled garden or the moody interior. With tables on Plaza de España, **Califa Exprés** (dishes €4-6; ☺12.30-4pm & 7.30-11.30pm, may close Dec-Mar; 🖋) offers a taste of the Califa magic in a simpler setting.

★ Corredera 55 ANDALUCIAN, MEDITERRANEAN €€
(☑956 45 18 48; www.califavejer.com; Calle de la Corredera 55; mains €10-19; ☺noon-11pm; 🖋) This fresh-faced veggie-friendly eatery delivers elegant, inventive cooking packed with local flavours and ingredients. Menus change with the seasons. Try chilled, lemon-infused grilled courgette and goat's-cheese parcels, cauliflower fritters with honey-yoghurt dressing, or *cava*-baked prawn-stuffed fish of the day. Perch at street-side tables (complete with winter blankets!) or eat in the cosily stylish dining room amid Vejer paintings.

Abacería La Oficina ANDALUCIAN €€
(☑655 099911; www.facebook.com/Abaceriala oficina; Paseo de las Cobijadas 1; mains €7.50-14; ☺1-4.30pm & 8.30pm-late Jul-Oct, 8.30pm-late Thu, 1-4.30pm & 8.30pm-late Fri & Sat, 1-4.30pm Sun Nov-Jun) With its chequered floors, vibrant original artwork and deliciously updated Andalucian menu, La Oficina is an atmospheric, laid-back spot for a meal in the depths of old-town Vejer. Dishes such as creamy mushroom-and-truffle risotto, red *almadraba* tuna tartare or entrêcote with Cabrales-cheese sauce are artfully presented on slate slabs, or go for fuss-free tapas at the bar. Restaurant hours vary.

☆ Entertainment

Peña Cultural Flamenca 'Aguilar de Vejer' FLAMENCO
(☑606 171732, 956 45 07 89; Calle Rosario 29) Part of Vejer's magic is its small-town flamenco scene, best observed in this atmospheric bar and performance space founded in 1989. Free shows usually happen on Saturday at 9.30pm; book in for dinner (mains €12 to €23) or swing by for drinks and tapas (€6). The tourist office has schedules.

❶ Information

Oficina Municipal de Turismo (☑956 45 17 36; www.turismovejer.es; Avenida Los Remedios 2; ☺10am-2.30pm & 4.30-9pm Mon-Fri, 10am-2pm & 4.30-9pm Sat, 10am-2pm Sun, reduced hours mid-Oct–Apr) About 500m below the town centre, beside the bus stop and a free car park.

❶ Getting There & Around

From Avenida Los Remedios, Comes (p120) runs buses to Cádiz, Barbate, Zahara de los Atunes, Jerez de la Frontera and Seville. More buses stop at La Barca de Vejer, on the N340 at the bottom of the hill; from here, it's a steep 20-minute walk or €6 taxi ride up to town.

TO	COST	DURATION	FREQUENCY
Algeciras	€7.20	1¼hr	10 daily
Barbate	€1.40	15min	4 daily
Cádiz	€5.70	1¼hr	3-4 daily
Jerez de la Frontera	€7.80	1½hr	1 daily Mon-Fri
La Línea (for Gibraltar)	€9.10	1¾hr	4 daily
Málaga	€22	3¼hr	2 daily
Seville	€16	2¼hr	4 daily
Seville (from Avenida Los Remedios)	€17	3hr	1 daily Mon-Fri
Tarifa	€4.49	40min	8 daily
Zahara de los Atunes	€2.50	25min	2-3 daily

Los Caños de Meca

POP 120

Little laid-back Los Caños de Meca, 16km southwest of Vejer, straggles along a series of spectacular open white-sand beaches. Once a hippie haven, Caños still attracts beach-lovers of all kinds and nations – especially in summer – with its alternative, hedonistic scene and nudist beaches, as well as kitesurfing, windsurfing and board-surfing opportunities.

◉ Sights & Activities

Caños' main beach is straight in front of Avenida de Trafalgar's junction with the A2233 to Barbate. Nudists head to its eastern end for more secluded coves, including Playa de las Cortinas, and to Playa del Faro beside Cabo de Trafalgar. Broad, blond Playa de Zahora extends northwest from Los Caños.

★ Parque Natural de la Breña
y Marismas del Barbate   NATURE RESERVE
(www.ventanadelvisitante.es) ✔ This 50-sq-km coastal park protects important marshes, cliffs and pine forest from Costa del Sol–type development. Its main entry point is a 7.2km (two-hour) walking trail, the Sendero del Acantilado, between Los Caños de Meca and Barbate, along clifftops that rival Cabo de Gata in their beauty. The hike's high point is the 16th-century Torre del Tajo with its tranquil *mirador* perched above the Atlantic. The signposted path starts just behind Hotel La Breña at the eastern end of Los Caños de Meca and emerges by Barbate's fishing port; it can also be accessed from car parks along the A2233 between Caños and Barbate.

Cabo de Trafalgar   LIGHTHOUSE
At the western end of Los Caños de Meca, a side road (often half-covered in sand) leads out to an 1860 lighthouse on a low spit of land. This is the famous Cabo de Trafalgar, off which Spanish naval power was swiftly terminated by a British fleet under Admiral Nelson in 1805.

El Palmar   BEACH
About 7km northwest of Los Caños, lovely, long El Palmar has Andalucía's best board-surfing waves from about October to May. In summer it's busy with surf schools, beach bars, horse riding, yoga and more.

CÁDIZ PROVINCE & GIBRALTAR LOS CAÑOS DE MECA

WORTH A TRIP

MEDINA SIDONIA

An air of dwindling majesty sweeps through the wind-lashed, whitewashed streets of Medina Sidonia (pop 10,280). This strategic hilltop town, 30km north of Vejer de la Frontera, was once the seat of the Duques de Medina Sidonia – one of Spain's most powerful families. Medina Sidonia's hillock has been inhabited since early prehistoric times, and the Phoenicians, Romans and Moors all established settlements here. The town was reconquered for the Christians in 1267 by Alfonso X El Sabio and, from 1445, flourished under the Ducado de Medina Sidonia. Today, history-rich Medina is very much worth exploring, yet remains off southern Andalucía's beaten track. It's an easy day trip from Vejer, Arcos (40km north) or Jerez (35km northwest).

In the historic core, approached through the Moorish Arco de Belén (Calle Cilla), one of three still-standing gates from this era. You'll find the 16th-century Gothic-Renaissance Iglesia Mayor (Plaza de la Iglesia Mayor; €2.50; ◷10.30am-2pm & 5.30-7.30pm Jun-Sep, 10.30am-2pm & 4.30-6.30pm Oct-May); its Renaissance door gives way to a hushed Gothic-Mudéjar cloister, and the interior shines with its 22-image, plateresque main altarpiece, completed in 1584, and its 17th-century Cristo del Perdón (Christ of Forgiveness) carving by Sevillan baroque sculptor Pedro Roldán. Crowning Medina Sidonia is a Roman military fortress turned 11th-century Almoravid *alcázar* turned ruined 15th-century medieval castle (Calle Ducado de Medina Sidonia; €2; ◷10.30am-2pm & 5.30-7.30pm Jun-Sep, 10.30am-2pm & 4.30-6.30pm Oct-May). There's also an excavated Roman *calzada* (road) open for visits in the town centre.

If you fancy staying, British-owned La Vista de Medina (☑690 626360; www.lavista demedina.com; Plaza de la Iglesia Mayor 2; r €70-110) offers six rustic-chic, apartment-like rooms and two soothing pools in hibiscus-filled, fountain-washed gardens, plus an Andalucian-international restaurant (mains €14 to €20) with horizon-reaching views.

Medina Sidonia has CMTBC (p120) buses to/from Cádiz (€5.10, 50 minutes, two to three daily) and Jerez de la Frontera (€2.70, 45 minutes, three daily weekdays).

Escuela de Surf 9 Pies SURFING, YOGA

(⌖620104241; www.escueladesurf9pies.com; Avenida de la Playa; board & wetsuit rental per 2/4hr €12/18, 2hr group class €28) Professional surf school offering board hire and surf classes for all levels, plus yoga sessions (€10) and SUP (stand-up paddleboard) rental (€15 for two hours), towards the northern end of El Palmar beach.

🛏 Sleeping

Casas Karen HOTEL €€

(⌖956 43 70 67, 649 780834; www.casaskaren. com; Camino del Monte 6; d €85-135, q €155-195; 🅿🐕🤖) This eccentric, easygoing Dutch-owned hideaway has rustic rooms and apartments across a flower-covered, pine-sprinkled plot. Options range from a converted farmhouse to thatched *chozas* (traditional huts) and two modern, split-level 'studios'. Decor is casual Andalucian–Moroccan, full of throws, hammocks and colour. It's 1km northeast of Caños' Cabo de Trafalgar turn-off.

🍴 Eating & Drinking

Las Dunas CAFE €

(⌖956 43 72 03; www.barlasdunas.es; Carretera del Cabo de Trafalgar; dishes €4-12; ⊙9am-midnight Sep-Jun, to 3am Jul & Aug; 🤖) Say *hola* to the ultimate relaxation spot, where kitesurfers kick back between white-knuckle sorties launched from the beach outside. Bob Marley tunes, great *bocadillos* (filled rolls), fresh juices, *platos combinados*, a warming winter fire, and a laid-back, beach-shack feel.

Jaima Meccarola LOUNGE, BAR

(Avenida Trafalgar; ⊙1pm-4am May-Sep) This massive, super-popular multipurpose venue is set into the cliffs above Caños' main beach. You can dig into grilled fish in the alfresco beer bar or sip beachy mojitos on the Atlantic-facing cocktail terrace, while the semi-open-air *jaima* (Bedouin tent) lounge-*tetería*, strewn with Moroccan rugs and pouffes, serves fusion meals (€10 or €16). Later on, there's a low-key club-like vibe.

ⓘ Getting There & Away

Comes (p120) has two daily weekday buses from Los Caños de Meca to Cádiz (€6.30, 1½ hours) via El Palmar (€2, 15 minutes). Additional summer services may run to Cádiz and Seville.

Zahara de los Atunes

POP 1090

About 20km southeast of Los Caños de Meca, Zahara de los Atunes fronts a fantastic 12km-long, west-facing sweep of white-gold sand. For years a traditional fishing village famous for its Atlantic bluefin tuna caught using the ancient *almadraba* method, today Zahara is a popular, easygoing summer beach hang-out that's forging its way into the local culinary scene, with two annual gastronomic festivals. Its tiny old core of narrow streets and lively bars centres on the ruined 15th-century Castillo de las Almadrabas (Avenida Hermanos Doctores Sánchez Rodríguez), where the tuna catch was once processed. In summer, *chiringuitos* (beach bars) spill out onto the sand; the rest of the year, things can be *very* quiet. Southeast of Zahara is the more developed resort of Atlanterra.

🛏 Sleeping & Eating

Hotel Avenida Playa HOTEL €€

(⌖956 43 93 38; www.avenidaplayahotel.com; Avenida Hermanos Doctores Sánchez Rodríguez 12; incl breakfast s €90-118, d €100-128; ✳🤖) It's all tasteful rustic design, floral paintings and warm yellow walls at this friendly, family-run eight-room hotel in the heart of Zahara. Best are the two airy top-floor 'suites' with spacious terraces, sun loungers and castle/sea views. There's a good, local-focused restaurant (mains €10 or €20), and the owners rent out six nearby apartments, too.

Restaurante Antonio SEAFOOD €€€

(⌖956 43 95 42; www.restauranteantoniozahara. com; Bahía de la Plata, Km 1, Atlanterra; mains €15-30; ⊙1.30-4pm & 8.30-10.30pm Feb–mid-Dec) Prize-winning Antonio's, 1km south of Zahara, is wildly recommended for its top-quality seafood, brought to you by attentive waiters in crisp white shirts in a sparkly contemporary sea-view setting. *Almadraba* red tuna, of course, is the star, dished up in a million incarnations from *atún encebollado* (tuna stew) to sashimi. The tartare of locally caught tuna is a speciality. It's also a pool-equipped hotel (including breakfast, singles are €77 to €100, doubles €123 to €200).

ⓘ Getting There & Away

Comes (p120) runs two or three daily buses to/from Vejer de la Frontera (€2.50, 25 minutes) and Cádiz (€8.30, two hours), and one daily weekday bus to/from Los Caños de Meca (€2.15, 30 minutes). More buses may run in summer.

Tarifa

POP 13,680

Tarifa's southern-tip-of-Spain location, where the Mediterranean and the Atlantic meet, gives it a different climate and character to the rest of Andalucía. Stiff Atlantic winds draw in surfers, windsurfers and kitesurfers who, in turn, lend this ancient yet deceptively small settlement a refreshingly laid-back international vibe. Tarifa is the last stop in Spain before Morocco, and it's also a taste of things to come. With its winding white-washed streets and tangible North African feel, the walled windswept old town could easily pass for Chefchaouen or Essaouira. It's no secret, however, and, in August especially, Tarifa gets packed (but that's half the fun).

Tarifa may be as old as Phoenician Cádiz and was definitely a Roman settlement. It takes its name from Tarif ibn Malik, who led a Muslim raid in AD 710, the year before the main Islamic invasion of the peninsula.

⊙ Sights

Tarifa's narrow old-town streets, mostly of Islamic origin, hint at Morocco. Wander through the fortified Mudéjar **Puerta de Jerez**, built after the Reconquista, then pop into lively **Mercado de Abastos** (Calle Colón; ⊙8.30am-2pm Tue-Sat) before winding your way past the whitewashed, 18th-century baroque-neoclassical **Iglesia de San Francisco de Asís** (Calle Santísima Trinidad; ⊙10am-1pm & 6.15-8.15pm Mon-Sat, 9.15-11am Sun) to the mainly 16th-century **Iglesia de San Mateo** (Calle Sancho IV El Bravo; ⊙8.45am-1pm Mon, 8.45am-1pm & 6-8pm Tue-Sat, 10am-1pm & 7-8.30pm Sun). Head south along Calle Coronel Moscardó, then up Calle Aljaranda; the **Miramar** (atop part of the castle walls) has spectacular views across to Africa and 851m Jebel Musa, one of the 'Pillars of Hercules' (Gibraltar is the other).

Castillo de Guzmán   CASTLE
(Calle Guzmán El Bueno; adult/child €4/free; ⊙11am-2.30pm & 5-7.30pm Mon-Sat approx Mar-Sep, 11am-2.30pm & 4-6.30pm Mon-Sat approx Oct-Feb, 11am-4pm Sun year-round) Though built in 960 on the orders of Cordoban caliph Abd ar-Rahman III, this restored fortress is named after Reconquista hero Guzmán El Bueno. In 1294, when threatened with the death of his captured son unless he surrendered the castle to Merenid attackers from Morocco, El Bueno threw down his own dagger for his son's execution. Guzmán's descendants later became the Duques de Medina Sidonia, one of Spain's most powerful families. Above the interior entrance, note the 10th-century castle-foundation inscription.

🏃 Activities

Kitesurfing & Windsurfing
Tarifa's legendary winds have turned the town into one of Europe's premier windsurfing and kitesurfing destinations. The most popular strip is along the coast between Tarifa and Punta Paloma, 10km northwest. Over 30 places offer equipment hire and classes, from beginner to expert level. The best months are May, June and September, but bear in mind that the choppy seas aren't always beginners' territory. Some schools also offer SUP sessions.

Gisela Pulido Pro Center   KITESURFING
(☑608 577711; www.giselapulidoprocenter.com; Calle Mar Adriático 22; 3hr group courses per person €70) World champion Gisela Pulido's highly rated kitesurfing school offers year-round group/private courses, including six-hour 'baptisms' (€135) and nine-hour 'complete' courses (€199), in Spanish, French, English

CÁDIZ PROVINCE & GIBRALTAR TARIFA

TARIFA: BEACH BLISS

Jazzed up by the colourful kites and sails of kitesurfers and windsurfers whizzing across turquoise waves, the exquisite bleach-blond beaches that stretch northwest from Tarifa along the N340 are some of Andalucía's (and Spain's) most beautiful. In summer they fill up with sun-kissed beach lovers and chill-out bars, though the relentless winds can be a hassle. If you tire of lazing on the sand, kitesurfing, windsurfing and horse riding await.

Punta Paloma One of Andalucía's most fabulous beaches, Punta Paloma, 10km northwest of Tarifa, is famous for its huge blond sand dune. At its far western end, you can lather yourself up in a natural mud bath.

Playa de Valdevaqueros Sprawling between 7km and 10km northwest of Tarifa, to the great white dune at Punta Paloma, Valdevaqueros is one of Tarifa's most popular kite-surfing beaches, blessed with dusty alabaster-hued sand and aqua waters.

Playa de los Lances This broad snow-white sandy beach stretches for 7km northwest from Tarifa. The low dunes behind it are a *paraje natural* (protected natural area); you can hike across them on the 1.5km **Sendero de los Lances**, signposted towards the northwestern end of Calle Batalla del Salado.

and German. Also rents kitesurfing gear (€70 per day).

ION Club KITESURFING, WINDSURFING
(📞619 340913; www.ion-club.net; Carretera N340, Km 76, Playa de Valdevaqueros; 2hr group kitesurfing/windsurfing class €80/60; ⊙Easter-Dec) Recommended daily group/private windsurfing and kitesurfing classes with multilingual instructors at beginner, intermediate or advanced level, along with kit rental (€90 per day) and paddle-boarding sessions (€25 per hour), 10km northwest of town. Windsurfing is usually from the ION Club's *centre* (📞956 68 90 98; Carretera N340, Km 78; 2hr group kitesurfing/windsurfing class €80/60; ⊙Easter-Dec) at the Hurricane Hotel, 7km northwest of Tarifa.

Spin Out WINDSURFING, KITESURFING
(📞956 23 63 52; www.tarifaspinout.com; Carretera N340, Km 75.5, Playa de Valdevaqueros; 90min windsurfing class per person €59, board & sail rental per hour €30; ⊙10.30am-7pm Apr-Oct) Daily windsurfing classes and five-day courses for beginners, kids and experts, from a switched-

on, multilingual team, 11km northwest of town. There's also a kitesurfing school.

Whale-Watching

The waters off Tarifa are one of the best places in Europe to see whales and dolphins as they swim between the Atlantic and the Mediterranean from April to October; sightings of some kind are almost guaranteed in these months. In addition to striped and bottlenose dolphins, long-finned pilot whales, orcas (killer whales) and sperm whales, you may spot endangered fin whales and common dolphins. Sperm whales swim the Strait of Gibraltar from April to August; the best months for orcas are July and August. Find out more at Tarifa's *Centro de Interpretación de Cetáceos* (www.facebook.com/CICAMTARIFA; Avenida Fuerzas Armadas 17; ⊙Mar-Oct) **FREE** .

FIRMM WHALE WATCHING
(📞956 62 70 08; www.firmm.org; Calle Pedro Cortés 4; 2hr tours adult/child €30/20; ⊙10am-7pm Easter-Oct) 🐋 Among Tarifa's dozens

Tarifa

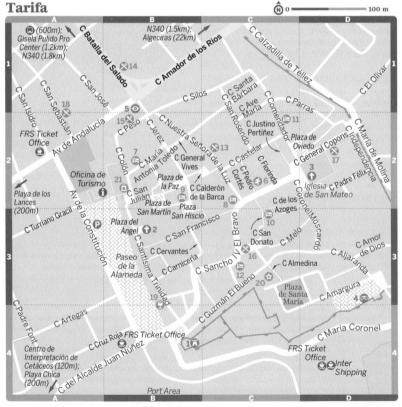

of whale-watching outfits, not-for-profit FIRMM is a good option. Its primary purpose is to study the whales and record data, and this gives rise to environmentally sensitive two- or three-hour tours and week-long whale-watching courses.

Horse Riding

One-hour beach rides along Playa de los Lances cost €30 and two-hour beach-and-mountain rides cost €60, while four-hour rides are €70 to €80. A recommended outfit, with excellent multilingual guides, is **Aventura Ecuestre** (📞956 23 66 32, 626 480019; www.aventuraecuestre.com; Hotel Dos Mares, Carretera N340, Km 79.5), which also offers pony rides for kids (30 minutes €15), private courses (five days €300) and five-hour rides into the Parque Natural Los Alcornocales (€80). **Molino El Mastral** (📞646 964279; www.mastral.com; Carretera Santuario Virgen de la Luz; per hour €30), 5km northwest of Tarifa, is also brilliant.

Yoga

Hotels can put you in touch with local yoga teachers. Tarifa Eco Center (p150) is a major yoga hub, offering classes (€10) to suit most levels and styles.

🎆 Festivals & Events

Feria de la Virgen de la Luz   FAIR
(☉1st week Sep) Tarifa's town fair, honouring its patron, mixes religious processions, handsome horses and typical Spanish fiesta.

🛏 Sleeping

⭐**Hostal África**   HOSTAL €
(📞956 68 02 20; www.hostalafrica.com; Calle María Antonia Toledo 12; s €40-55, d €55-80, tr €80-110; ☉Mar-Nov; 🛜) This mellow, revamped

19th-century house within Tarifa's old town is one of the Costa de la Luz' (and Cádiz province's) best *hostales* (budget hotels). Full of potted plants and sky-blue-and-white arches, it's run by hospitable, on-the-ball owners, and the 13 all-different rooms (including one triple) sparkle with bright colours. Enjoy the lovely roof terrace, with its loungey cabana and Africa views.

Sulok Hostel   HOSTEL €
(📞603 567229; http://suloktarifa.com; Calle Sancho IV El Bravo 23; dm €20-40; ☉may close Dec-Feb; ❄🛜) This contemporary hostel, accessed through a Tarifa-chic old-town boutique, is a welcoming, reliable budget choice. There are three spotless dorms sleeping six, eight or 10 people, plus separate bathrooms for men and women; each capsule-style bunk bed comes with two plugs, a light, a locker and a curtain for privacy.

Hotel Misiana   BOUTIQUE HOTEL €€
(📞956 62 70 83; www.misiana.com; Calle Sancho IV El Bravo 16; s €105-120, d €125-155, ste €235-310; ❄🛜🏊) The Misiana's penthouse suite, with private roof terrace engulfed in wraparound Morocco views, is one of Tarifa's top-choice rooms. But the doubles are lovely, too, with their stylish whiteness, pale greys, driftwood-chic decor, sea-life paintings and desks with tea/coffee sets. Light sleepers might prefer a quieter room at the back. It's predictably popular; book ahead.

Posada La Sacristía   BOUTIQUE HOTEL €€
(📞956 68 17 59; www.lasacristia.net; Calle San Donato 8; r excl/incl breakfast €140/160; ❄🛜🏊) A beautifully renovated 17th-century townhouse hosts this elegant historical-boutique find in the heart of the old town. Attention to detail is impeccable, with 10 stylish rooms

Tarifa

(some sporting four-poster beds) spread over two floors around a central courtyard. Colour schemes keep things tastefully neutral, while, downstairs, there's a sumptuous lounge and a summer Asian-Mediterranean fusion **restaurant** (mains €12-18; ⊘7.30pm-late Easter-Sep).

La Casa de la Favorita HOTEL, APARTMENT **€€**
(📞690 180253; www.lacasadelafavorita.com; Plaza de San Hiscio 4; r €80-115; ❄🔊) This welcoming Tarifa star gets booked up fast. Crisp, white contemporary design sweeps through its uncluttered, impeccable rooms, all with kitchenettes and coffee-makers. The best have balconies and/or terraces, while the suite is a two-level duplex-style affair. A small library, a roof terrace and dynamic, colourful art add to the appeal. No lift.

⭐**Riad** BOUTIQUE HOTEL **€€€**
(📞856 92 98 80; www.theriadtarifa.com; Calle Comendador 10; r incl breakfast €140-210) This seductive hotel is an exquisitely converted 17th-century townhouse. Opening through a polished-concrete lobby punctuated by an ornamental fountain, it's dressed with original architecture: exposed-stone walls, antique doors, red-brick arches and a frescoed facade. The 10 intimate rooms are pocketed away off the patio, styled with *tadelakt* (waterproof plaster) walls, bold reds and blues, and chic Andalucía-meets-Morocco design.

Hotel Dos Mares HOTEL **€€€**
(📞956 68 40 35; www.dosmareshotel.com; Carretera N340, Km 79.5; r incl breakfast €135-255; 🅿❄🔊🏊) Opening onto blinding-white sands 5km northwest of town, Moroccan-flavoured Dos Mares has comfy, bright, tile-floored rooms and bungalows in yellows, blues and burnt oranges, some with sea-facing balconies. Other perks include a sleepy cafe, a gym, a pool, a kitesurfing school, a *chiringuito* (dishes €6 to €11) and an excellent on-site horse-riding school (p149).

✖ Eating

Tarifa is full of good food with a strong international flavour, Italian, Moroccan and Middle Eastern in particular. It's also one of Andalucía's top breakfast spots – time to break out of the *tostada*-and-coffee monotony! Other Tarifa treats are smoothies, fusion food, organic ingredients and wonderful vegetarian/vegan meals.

⭐**Café Azul** CAFE, BREAKFAST **€**
(www.facebook.com/cafeazultarifa; Calle Batalla del Salado 8; breakfasts €2-8; ⊘9am-3pm; 🔊) This long-established Italian-run place with blue-and-white Moroccan-inspired decor whips up the best breakfasts in Tarifa, if not Andalucía. You'll want to eat everything. The fresh fruit salad with muesli, yoghurt and coconut, and the fruit-and-yoghurt-stuffed crêpe are works of art. It also serves good coffee, smoothies, juices, *bocadillos* and cooked breakfasts, with delicious gluten-free and vegan options.

El Francés TAPAS **€**
(Calle Sancho IV El Bravo 21; tapas €2.50-4.80; ⊘12.30pm-midnight Fri-Tue; 🍴) Squeeze into the standing-room-only bar or battle for your terrace table at always-rammed El Francés, which gives Andalucian classics a subtle twist. Tarifa's favourite tapas bar is a buzzing place, serving *patatas bravas* and *tortillitas de camarones* (shrimp fritters) alongside mini chicken-veg couscous or prawn curry. No reservations; pop in on the day to secure a table (dinner from 6.30pm only).

Café 10 CAFE, BREAKFAST **€**
(www.facebook.com/cafe10tarifa; Calle Nuestra Señora de la Luz 10; dishes €2-6; ⊘9am-1am; 🔊) This old-town cafe delivers the breakfast/snack goods in a snug, neo-rustic lounge with pink-cushioned chairs spilling out onto the sloping street. Tuck into homemade cakes, great coffee, fresh juices, sweet and salty crêpes, and *revueltos* (scrambles) and *molletes* (small toasted rolls) in exciting international-themed combinations (avocado, mozzarella). There's even latte art. Later on, the G&Ts and mojitos (€6) come out.

Chilimosa VEGETARIAN **€**
(📞956 68 50 92; www.facebook.com/chilimosa; Calle Peso 6; mains €5-10; ⊘12.30-3.30pm & 7-11pm; 🔊🍴) This cosy, casual vegetarian restaurant at the top of the old town, with just a handful of tables, is Tarifa at its low-key best. The unpretentious home-cooked menu is Middle Eastern with a few international flourishes, turning out such meat-free delights as spiced-vegetable samosas, falafel-hummus wraps, meze platters, tofu burgers and broccoli-and-leek quiche. Takeaway, too.

Tarifa Eco Center VEGETARIAN **€**
(📞956 92 74 56; www.tarifaecocenter.com; Calle San Sebastián 6; mains €8.50-12.50; ⊘9.30am-11.30pm; 🔊🍴) ✐ This relaxed terrace restaurant, co-working space and cocktail/juice bar pulls out all the stops with ultra-enticing, organic vegetarian and vegan cooking. Wholemeal wood-oven pizzas with plant-based toppings are the speciality, or pick from wholesome bites like vegetable curry, soy burgers, pasta specials or 'Verdísima' green salads, many artfully presented in mini paella pans.

La Oca da Sergio
ITALIAN €€

(☑615 686571, 956 68 12 49; Calle General Copons 6; mains €8.50-19; ☺1-4pm & 8pm-midnight Jun-Oct & Dec, reduced hours Jan-May) Amiable Sergio roams the tables Italian style, armed with loaded plates and amusing stories, and presides over genuine home-country cooking at this popular restaurant tucked behind Iglesia de San Mateo (p147). Look forward to *caprese* salads, homemade pasta (try the truffle pappardelle), wood-oven thin-crust pizzas, cappuccinos and after-dinner *limoncello*.

🍷 Drinking & Entertainment

Tarifa has a busy bar scene (especially in summer), plus a few late-night clubs. The after-dark fun centres on the old town's narrow Calles Cervantes, San Francisco and Santísima Trinidad. Summer *chiringuitos* (snack bars) get going with music/DJs on Playa de los Lances and the beaches northwest of town.

Tumbao
LOUNGE, BAR

(www.facebook.com/tumbaotarifa; Carretera N340, Km 76, Playa de Valdevaqueros; ☺5pm-midnight Easter-Sep) The ultimate Tarifa-cool beach hang-out, Tumbao serves up cocktails, *tinto de verano* (cold, wine-based drink similar to sangria) loungey sunset beats on a grassy, beanbag-strewn patch overlooking the kitesurfing action on Playa de Valdevaqueros, 10km northwest of town. The kitchen delivers burgers, salads, nachos, grilled *chuletones* (giant beef chops) and other tasty bites, mostly sizzled up on the open barbecue (mains €7 to €15). The attached ivy-wrapped restaurant does excellent Spanish-international buffet lunches (€11) from 1pm to 5pm.

Tangana
BAR

(☑956 68 51 32; www.tarifaweb.com/tangana; Carretera N340, Km 75.5, Playa de Valdevaqueros; ☺10am-9pm Easter-Oct; ☎) This mellow beach bar is set around a boho-chic boutique and two chill-out lounges, one with deckchairs looking out across the beach, 11km northwest of Tarifa. Turquoise-washed bench-style tables set a lazy-life scene for sipping mojitos and caipirinhas (€6), balanced out by *bocadillos*, burgers, pastas, paella and build-your-own salad bowls (dishes €5 to €12).

La Ruina
CLUB

(www.facebook.com/La-Ruina-Tarifa-97140989180; Calle Santísima Trinidad 2; ☺midnight-3am Sun-Thu, to 4am Fri & Sat) Quite possibly Tarifa's favourite late-night haunt, this old-town ruin turned club amps things up with a steady early-hours diet of electro and house.

Almedina
FLAMENCO

(☑956 68 04 74; www.almedinacafe.net; Calle Almedina 3; ☺8.30pm-midnight; ☎) Built into the old city walls, cavernous bar Almedina squeezes a flamenco ensemble into its clamorous, stone-arched confines for its well-known Thursday sessions at 10.30pm.

ℹ Information

Oficina de Turismo (☑956 68 09 93; Paseo de la Alameda; ☺10am-1.30pm & 4-6pm Mon-Fri, 10am-1.30pm Sat & Sun)

ℹ Getting There & Away

BOAT

FRS (☑956 68 18 30; www.frs.es; Avenida de Andalucía 16; adult/child/car/motorcycle 1 way €41/15/136/33) runs one-hour ferries up to eight times daily between Tarifa and Tangier (Morocco). **Inter Shipping** (☑956 68 47 29; www.intershipping.es; Recinto Portuario, Local 4; adult/child/car/motorcycle 1 way €38/14/100/24) offers up to seven daily one-hour ferries to Tangier. All passengers need a passport.

BUS

Comes (p120) operates from the **bus station** (☑956 68 40 38; Calle Batalla del Salado) beside the petrol station at the northwestern end of town. In July and August, **Horizonte Sur** (☑699 427644; http://horizontesur.es) runs 11 to 14 daily buses Monday to Saturday from here to Punta Paloma via Tarifa's beaches.

TO	COST	DURATION	FREQUENCY
Algeciras	€2.45	30min	13-25 daily
Cádiz	€9.83	1½hr	6 daily
El Puerto de Santa María	€10	2hr	2 daily
Jerez de la Frontera	€11	2½hr	12 daily
La Barca de Vejer (for Vejer de la Frontera)	€4.49	40min	7 daily
La Línea (for Gibraltar)	€4.45	1hr	6 daily
Málaga	€17	2¾hr	3 daily
Marbella	€11	1¾hr	3 daily
Seville	€20	3hr	4 daily

CAR & MOTORCYCLE

There's metered parking on Avenida de la Constitución beside the Alameda (€2 per two hours; free 8pm to 10am Monday to Friday, from 2pm Saturday, all day Sunday).

Bolonia

POP 100

Tiny Bolonia village, signposted off the N340 15km northwest of Tarifa, overlooks a gloriously white beach framed by a large dune, rolling pine-dotted or field-covered hills, and the impressive Roman remains of Baelo Claudia. In July and August, three weekday Horizonte Sur buses run between Bolonia and Tarifa (€2.50, 30 to 40 minutes). Otherwise it's your own wheels.

★ **Baelo Claudia**   ARCHAEOLOGICAL SITE
(🗷956 10 67 96; www.museosdeandalucia.es; EU citizens/noncitizens free/€1.50; ⊙9am-3pm Tue-Sun mid-Jun–mid-Sep, reduced hours mid-Sep–mid-Jun) The ruined town of Baelo Claudia is one of Andalucía's most important Roman archaeological sites. These majestic beachside ruins – with fine views across to Morocco – include the substantial remains of a theatre, a paved forum, thermal baths, a market, a marble statue and the columns of a basilica, and the workshops that turned out the products that made Baelo Claudia famous in the Roman world: salted fish and *garum* (spicy seasoning made from leftover fish parts). There's a good museum. Baelo Claudia particularly flourished during the reign of Emperor Claudius (AD 41–54), but it declined after an earthquake in the 2nd century.

Parque Natural Los Alcornocales

The 1736-sq-km Parque Natural Los Alcornocales is rich in archaeological, historical and natural interest, but it's off Andalucía's beaten track. Stretching 75km north almost from the Strait of Gibraltar to the border of the Parque Natural Sierra de Grazalema and into Málaga province, it's a beautiful jumble of sometimes rolling, sometimes rugged medium-height hills, much of it covered in Spain's most extensive *alcornocales* (cork-oak woodlands), its fringes peppered with white villages. There are plenty of walks and outdoor-activity options; you'll need a car to explore.

🏃 Activities

Of the park's 20 official walking routes, five require (free) permits, including the 3.3km (two-hour) **Sendero Subida al Picacho** up the park's second-highest peak (El Picacho; 882m). You must request permits by phone or email at least three days in advance from the **Oficina del Parque Natural Los Alcornocales** (🗷856 58 75 08; www.ventanadelvisi-

tante.es; Carretera Alcalá-Benalup Km 1, Alcalá de los Gazules; ⊙9am-2pm Mon-Fri); it'll email your permit to you. Last-minute permits may also be available at weekends from the Centro de Visitantes El Aljibe. Downloadable Spanish- and English-language hiking information is online at www.ventanadelvisitante.es.

❶ Information

Centro de Visitantes El Aljibe (🗷685 122686; www.ventanadelvisitante.es; Carretera Alcalá-Benalup, Km 1, Alcalá de los Gazules; ⊙10am-2pm Sat-Wed Mar-Dec, 10am-2pm Wed-Sun Jan & Feb) Off the Jerez–Los Barrios A381, 4km southwest of Alcalá de los Gazules.
Centro de Visitantes Huerta Grande (🗷956 02 46 00; www.ventanadelvisitante.es; Carretera N340, Km 96; ⊙9.30am-2.30pm Tue-Sun) Off the Tarifa–Algeciras N340, at the western end of Pelayo. Walking information and maps, plus a butterfly/bird-observation garden.

Jimena de la Frontera

POP 3020

Tucked away in crinkled hills on the eastern edge of the Parque Natural Los Alcornocales, Jimena sits in prime cork-oak country. Its blanched whiteness and crumbled Nasrid-era castle look out towards Gibraltar and Africa, both magnificently visible. Property-seeking Brits have discovered the town, but, so far, it's retained its Andalucian feel and makes a great base for exploring the park (though it could use a bit more loving care from the municipal maintenance department). The trails here are lovely, including treks along the Tarifa–Andorra GR7 (part of the 10,000km cross-continental E4) path, and forays out to Bronze Age cave paintings at Laja Alta.

◎ Sights

Castillo de Jimena   CASTLE
(⊙9am-10pm Apr-Sep, to 8pm Oct-Mar) 〔FREE〕 Jimena's romantically ruined 13th-century Nasrid castle, built on Roman ruins, once formed part of a defence line stretching from Olvera down through Setenil de las Bodegas, Zahara de la Sierra, Castellar de la Frontera and Algeciras to Tarifa. It was taken by the Christians in 1456.

🛏 Sleeping & Eating

Posada La Casa Grande   APARTMENT, GUESTHOUSE €
(🗷956 64 11 20; www.posadalacasagrande.es; Calle Fuente Nueva 42; r €35-50, apt €60-70; ✳🅯) Spread around plant-dotted patios in an ancient townhouse, La Casa Grande has everything you need for a delightful central-

Jimena stay, including colourfully rustic rooms and two- to four-person apartments, friendly staff and a library/painting studio with wraparound views. It also offers guided walks, and excellent hiking information for Alcornocales natural park.

El Anón MOROCCAN, SPANISH €€

(☑956 64 01 13; www.hostalanon.com; Calle Consuelo 34; mains €12-15; ☺1-3.30pm & 8-11.30pm Thu-Tue; ☎☑) A rambling townhouse full of hidden nooks, tile-topped tables and terraces bursting with flowers and palms is the

ALGECIRAS: GATEWAY TO MOROCCO

The major port linking Spain with Africa is an ugly industrial fishing town famous for producing the greatest flamenco guitarist of the modern era, Paco de Lucía, who was born here in 1947 and died in 2014 in Playa del Carmen, Mexico. The tourist office (☑956 57 12 54, 670 949047; www.algeciras.es; Paseo Río de la Miel; ☺9am-7.30pm Mon-Fri, 9.30am-3pm Sat & Sun) has information on a self-guided Paco de Lucía tour that uncovers local landmarks connected with the great musician. New arrivals usually leave quickly, by ferry to Morocco or bus to Tarifa or Málaga. The bus station (Calle San Bernardo) is opposite the train station; Algeciras is a 600m walk east along Calle San Bernardo.

Buses from Algeciras

DESTINATION	PRICE	DURATION	FREQUENCY
Cádiz	€13	2hr	8-9 daily
Córdoba	€27	6hr	1 daily
Granada	€26-33	3¾hr	4 daily
Jerez de la Frontera	€12	1¼-2½hr	7 daily
La Línea (for Gibraltar)	€2.45	30min	every 30-45min
Málaga	€15-19	1¾-3hr	18 daily
Málaga airport	€17	2hr	2 daily
Seville	€21	2¾hr	11-12 daily
Tarifa	€2.45	30min	13-19 daily

Ferries from Algeciras

Ferries from Algeciras to Tangier drop you in Tangier Med, 40km east of Tangier itself, and are operated by FRS (☑956 68 18 30; www.frs.es), Inter Shipping (☑956 68 47 29; www.intershipping.es) and Trasmediterránea (☑902 45 46 45; www.trasmediterranea.es). Remember your passport when travelling to Tangier; no passport is required for trips to the Spanish Moroccan enclave of Ceuta, although you will need to show identification (such as a passport or national ID card) to board the ferry.

DESTINATION	FERRY COMPANY	PRICE (1 WAY) ADULT/CHILD/CAR	DURATION	FREQUENCY
Ceuta	FRS	€32/18/123	1hr	5 daily
Ceuta	Trasmediterránea	€34/20/114	1¼hr	5 daily
Tangier Med	FRS	€35/15/142	1½hr	6 daily
Tangier Med	Inter Shipping	€25/15/110	1½hr	3 daily
Tangier Med	Trasmediterránea	€32/17/135	1½hr	3 daily

Trains from Algeciras

DESTINATION	PRICE	DURATION	FREQUENCY
Granada	€30	4¼hr	3 daily
Madrid	€44-80	5½hr	3 daily
Ronda	€11-14	1½hr	5 daily

romantic setting for El Anón's incredibly varied, world-roaming menu. Tasty hummus, falafel and vegetable tagines sit alongside spinach-mushroom crêpes, coconut grouper curry and Iberian-pork sirloin doused in Cabrales-cheese sauce.

ℹ Getting There & Away

Jimena's **bus stop** (Avenida de los Deportes), at the bottom of town, has once-daily weekday Comes (p120) services to/from Ronda (€6.44, two hours) and one to three daily weekday buses to/from Algeciras (€4.56, 55 minutes).

Three daily trains go to Algeciras (€5.05, 40 minutes), Granada (€26, 3¾ hours) and Ronda (€7.35, one hour) from the station in Los Ángeles, 1km southeast of Jimena.

GIBRALTAR

POP 32,700

Red pillar boxes, fish-and-chip shops and creaky 1970s seaside hotels: Gibraltar – as British writer Laurie Lee once commented – is a piece of Portsmouth sliced off and towed 500 miles south. 'The Rock' overstates its Britishness, a bonus for pub-grub and afternoon-tea lovers, but a confusing double-take for modern Brits who thought the days of Lord Nelson memorabilia were long gone. Poised strategically at the jaws of Europe and Africa, Gibraltar, with its Palladian architecture and camera-hogging Barbary macaques, makes an interesting break from the white towns of bordering Cádiz province. Playing an admirable supporting role is the swashbuckling local history; the Rock has been British longer than the United States has been American. This towering 5km-long limestone ridge rises to 426m, with cliffs on its northern and eastern sides. Gibraltarians speak English, Spanish and a curiously accented, sing-song mix of the two, swapping mid-sentence. Signs are in English.

See the Directory (p355) for practicalities about visiting Gibraltar.

History

Both the Phoenicians and the ancient Greeks left traces here, but Gibraltar really entered the history books in AD 711 when Tariq ibn Ziyad, the Muslim governor of Tangier, made it the initial bridgehead for the Islamic invasion of the Iberian Peninsula. The name Gibraltar derives from Jebel Tariq (Tariq's Mountain).

The Almohad Muslims founded a town here in 1159 and were usurped by the Castilians in 1462. In 1704 an Anglo-Dutch fleet captured Gibraltar during the War of the Spanish Succession. Spain ceded the Rock to Britain by the 1713 Treaty of Utrecht, but it didn't give up military attempts to regain it until the failure of the Great Siege of 1779–83; Spain has wanted it back ever since.

In 1969, Francisco Franco (infuriated by a referendum in which Gibraltarians voted by 12,138 to 44 to remain under British sovereignty) closed the Spain–Gibraltar border. The same year a new constitution committed Britain to respecting Gibraltarians' wishes over sovereignty, and gave Gibraltar domestic self-government and its own parliament, the House of Assembly (now the Gibraltar Parliament). In 1985, just before Spain joined the European Community (now the EU), the border was reopened.

Gibraltarians believe in their right to self-determination and, in a 2002 vote, resoundingly rejected the idea of joint British–Spanish sovereignty. The issue of the Rock's long-term future still raises its head, with debates recently sparked by the still-unclear effects of the UK's decision to leave the EU.

In the UK's 2016 EU-membership referendum, Gibraltarians voted by 96% against Brexit, a higher pro-Remain percentage than anywhere else in Britain. Some among Spain's centre-right Partido Popular (PP) government see in Brexit a chance to take back Gibraltar (into the EU), and many are concerned Spain could close the border completely. A closed or non-EU Spain–Gibraltar border would, among other things, seriously complicate matters for the 10,000 Spain-based workers who cross into Gibraltar each day.

◉ Sights

◉ Gibraltar Town

Most Gibraltar sojourns start in Grand Casemates Sq, accessible through Landport Tunnel (at one time the only land entry through Gibraltar's walls), then continue along Main St, a slice of the British high street under the Mediterranean sun.

★ **Gibraltar Museum**　　　MUSEUM
(Map p157; ☏20074289; www.gibmuseum.gi; 18-20 Bomb House Lane; adult/child £2/1; ◷10am-6pm Mon-Fri, to 2pm Sat) Gibraltar's swashbuckling history unfolds in this fine museum, which comprises a labyrinth of rooms and exhibits ranging from prehistoric and Phoenician Gibraltar to the infamous Great Siege (1779–83). Don't miss the well-preserved 14th-century Islamic baths, and a 7th-century-BC Egyptian mummy found in the bay in the 1800s.

Gibraltar

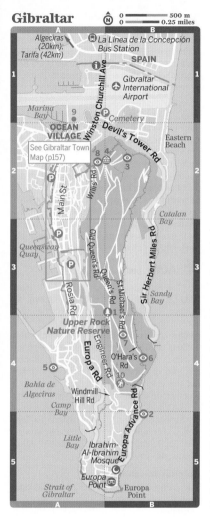

with its graves of British sailors who perished in the town after the 1805 Battle of Trafalgar, and of 19th-century yellow-fever victims.

◉ Upper Rock & Around

★**Upper Rock**
Nature Reserve   NATURE RESERVE
(Map p155; adult/child incl attractions £10/5, vehicle £2, pedestrian excl attractions 50p, combined ticket with cable car adult/child £22/14; ⊙9.30am-6.45pm Apr-Sep, 9am-5.45pm Oct-Mar) ✎ The Rock is one of the most dramatic landforms in southern Europe. Most of its upper sections (but not the main lookouts) fall within the Upper Rock Nature Reserve. Entry tickets include admission to **St Michael's Cave**, the Apes' Den, the **Great Siege Tunnels**, the **Moorish Castle** (Tower of Homage; Willis' Rd), the **Military Heritage Centre** (crn Willis' & Queen's Rds) and Nelson's Anchorage. The upper Rock is home to 600 plant species and is the perfect vantage point for watching bird migration between Europe and Africa.

About 1km (15 minutes' walk) south down St Michael's Rd from the top cable-car station, O'Hara's Rd leads left up to **O'Hara's Battery** (9.2 Gun; adult/child £3/2; ⊙10am-5pm Mon-Fri), a gun emplacement on the Rock's summit (not included in nature-reserve tickets). Slightly further down is the extraordinary St Michael's Cave, a spectacular natural grotto full of stalagmites and stalactites. People once thought the cave was a possible subterranean link with Africa. Today, apart from attracting tourists in droves, it's used for concerts, plays and even fashion shows. For a more extensive look (including a glimpse of the cave's underground lake), take the three-hour guided **Lower St Michael's Cave Tour**

Nelson's Anchorage   LANDMARK
(100-Tonne Gun; Map p155; Rosia Rd; £1, incl Upper Rock Nature Reserve & attractions adult/child £10/5; ⊙9.30am-6.15pm Apr-Sep, 9am-5.45pm Oct-Mar) At the southwestern end of town, Nelson's Anchorage pinpoints the site where Nelson's body was brought ashore from the HMS *Victory* after the Battle of Trafalgar – preserved in a rum barrel, so legend says. A 100-tonne, British-made Victorian supergun (1870) commemorates the spot.

Trafalgar Cemetery   CEMETERY
(Map p157; Europa Rd; ⊙9.30am-sunset) Gibraltar's cemetery gives a poignant history lesson,

(£10); the tourist office (p158) can recommend guides; no children under 10.

A 1.5km (30-minute) walk north (downhill) from the top cable-car station, the Military Heritage Centre occupies the 18th-century Princess Caroline's Battery. From here one road leads down to Princess Royal Battery – more gun emplacements – while another heads 300m up to the Great Siege Tunnels, a complex defence system hewn out of the Rock by the British during the siege of 1779–83 to provide gun emplacements. The **WWII tunnels** (☑ 20071649; Willis' Rd, Hay's Level; tours £8, incl Upper Rock Nature Reserve & attractions £18; ⊙ 10am-4pm Mon-Sat), where the Allied invasion of North Africa was planned, can also be visited, but you'll need to book ahead; you must have a nature reserve ticket to access the tunnels, but they aren't actually included in that ticket. Even combined, the Great Siege and WWII tunnels constitute only a tiny proportion of the Rock's more than 50km of tunnels, most of which remain off limits to visitors.

Gibraltar's Moorish Castle was rebuilt in 1333 after being retaken from the Spanish; it's on the way down to town from Princess Caroline's Battery. A glass-floored **Skywalk** opened atop the Rock in March 2018.

➤ **Apes' Den**

(Map p157) The Rock's most famous inhabitants are the tailless Barbary macaques. Many of the 160 primates hang around the Apes' Den near the middle cable-car station,

as well as at the top cable-car station and the Great Siege Tunnels. Legend has it when the macaques (possibly introduced from North Africa in the 18th century) disappear from Gibraltar, so will the British. Summer is the best time to see newborns, but keep a safe distance to avoid run-ins with protective parents.

Gorham's Cave Complex CAVE
(Map p155) Inscribed on Unesco's World Heritage list in 2016, these four archaeologically rich cliffside caves on Gibraltar's southeastern coast were inhabited by Neanderthals from around 127,000 to 32,000 years ago, making them a key source for modern-day debates about human evolution. Dolphin Adventure runs boat trips to (but not into) the caves on demand, with historical commentary (£25 per person; minimum six people). You can see finds from the caves at the town-centre Gibraltar Museum (p154).

🏃 Activities

⭐ **Mediterranean Steps** HIKING
(Map p155) Not the most well-known attraction in Gibraltar, but surely the most spectacular, this narrow, ancient path with steep steps – many hewn into the limestone – starts at the nature reserve's southern entrance at Jews' Gate and traverses the southern end of Gibraltar before steeply climbing the crag on the eastern escarpment. It emerges on the ridge near O'Hara's Battery.

The views along the way are stupendous; ornithologists won't know where to look first, as birds soar above, below and around you. The 1.5km trail is mildly exposed. Allow 45 minutes to an hour.

Dolphin-Watching

The Bahía de Algeciras has a sizeable year-round population of dolphins (striped, bottlenose and short-beaked common). **Dolphin Adventure** (Map p155; ☑ 20050650; www.dolphin.gi; 9 The Square, Marina Bay; adult/child £25/13) and **Dolphin Safari** (Blue Boat; Map p155; ☑ 20071914; www.dolphinsafari.gi; 6 The Square, Marina Bay; adult/child £25/15) run excellent dolphin-watching trips of one to 1½ hours. Most of the year each usually has two to three daily excursions. Dolphin Adventure also does summer whale-watching trips in the Strait of Gibraltar (adult/child £40/30). Advance bookings essential.

Birdwatching

One of Gibraltar's best views is right above your head. The Strait of Gibraltar is a key point of passage for migrating birds be-

---

ℹ **CABLE CAR–NATURE RESERVE COMBO**

The best way to explore the Rock is to whizz up on the **cable car** (Lower Cable-Car Station; Red Sands Rd; adult one way/return £13/15, child one way/return £6/6, adult/child one way incl nature reserve £22/14; ⊙ 9.30am-7.45pm Apr-Oct, to 5.15pm Nov-Mar) to the **top cable-car station**, then stop off at all the Upper Rock Nature Reserve sights on your way down. You can get special cable car–nature reserve one-way combo tickets for this. Note that the lower cable-car station stops selling these about two hours before the reserve closes. For the Apes' Den, hop out at the **middle station** (⊙ closed Apr-Oct).

Combined dolphin-watching and cable-car tickets (adult/child £30/16) are also available through dolphin-watching companies.

Gibraltar Town

are narrow enough for storks to get into Europe by this method. One is the Bosphorus, between the Black Sea and the Sea of Marmara; the other is the Strait of Gibraltar. White storks sometimes congregate in flocks of up to 5000 to cross the strait. Northward migrations generally occur between mid-February and early June, southbound flights between late July and early November. When a westerly wind is blowing, Gibraltar is good for seeing the birds; when the wind is calm or easterly, the Tarifa area is usually better. The Gibraltar Ornithological & Natural History Society (www.gonhs.org) is an excellent resource.

🛏 Sleeping

Rock Hotel HOTEL €€€
(Map p157; ☎20073000; www.rockhotelgibraltar.com; 3 Europa Rd; incl breakfast r £120-150, ste £145-240; P❋🛜🛉) As famous as the local monkeys, Gibraltar's grand old dame has 86 elegant yet cosy, creamy, wood-floored rooms with fresh flowers, tea/coffee kits, sea views and, for some, private balconies. Tick off gym, pool, welcome drink, writing desks, bathrobes, a sparkling cafe-bar, winter Sunday roasts (£25) and summer poolside barbecues.

O'Callaghan Eliott Hotel HOTEL €€€
(Map p157; ☎20070500; www.eliotthotel.com; 2 Governor's Pde; r £156-342, ste €278-512; ❋🛜🛉) This super-central, four-star establishment was mid-revamp at research time. Best are the brand-new 'Journey' rooms, smartly contemporary and styled in blues, some with capsule-coffee kits. Original rooms are old school in a comforting English way. Bonuses include a pool on the rooftop, where a bar and restaurant are in the works.

tween Africa and Europe; around 315 species (so far) have been recorded in the Gibraltar area. Soaring birds such as raptors, black and white storks and vultures rely on thermals and updraughts for their crossings, and there are just two places where the seas

✕ Eating

Goodbye tapas, hello fish and chips. Gibraltar's food is unashamedly British – and pretty pricey by Andalucian standards. The staples are pub grub, beer, sandwiches, chips and stodgy desserts, though a few international flavours can be found at Queensway Quay, Marina Bay and Ocean Village. There's a cluster of good restaurants on Fish Market Lane, just outside Grand Casemates Sq.

Verdi Verdi   INTERNATIONAL €
(Map p157; ☑20060733; www.verdiverdi.com; International Commercial Centre, Main St 2A; dishes £2-5; ☻8am-3pm Mon-Fri) This energetic kosher espresso bar serves up tasty homemade quiches, crunchy creative salads, soups, hummus, falafel wraps and cakes. Eat in or take away.

Clipper   PUB FOOD €
(Map p157; 78B Irish Town; mains £5-9; ☻9am-10pm Mon-Fri, 10am-4pm Sat, 10am-10pm Sun; ☎) Ask five...10...20 people in Gibraltar for their favourite pub and, chances are, they'll choose the Clipper. Looking sparklingly modern nowadays, the Clipper does real pub grub in traditionally large portions. British faves include jacket potatoes, chicken tikka masala, cheesy chips, Sunday roasts and that essential all-day breakfast (£5.95).

Sacarello's   INTERNATIONAL, CAFE €€
(Map p157; ☑20070625; www.sacarellosgibraltar.com; 57 Irish Town; mains £8-15; ☻8.30am-7.30pm Mon-Fri, 9am-3pm Sat; ☎⚲) A jack of all trades and master of...well...some, Sacarello's offers a great range of vegetarian cooking (pastas, quiches) alongside pub-style dishes in an old multilevel coffee warehouse. There's a good coffee list, plus lots of cakes, a salad bar and daily specials. From 3.30pm to 7.30pm you can linger over cream tea (£6.20).

The Lounge   INTERNATIONAL €€€
(Map p157; ☑20061118; 17A & B Ragged Staff Wharf, Queensway Quay; mains £14-19; ☻noon-4pm & 6-10pm Mon-Sat, noon-4pm Sun) This popular, stylish waterside gastrobar and lounge, just south of the town centre, serves a globetrotting, fresh-produce menu of salads, pastas, risottos, sandwiches, meats, and fish and chips, along with creative, seasonal specials. Starters like gin-cured salmon with beetroot are followed by, say, beer-battered cod or rib-eye steak with *chimichurri* sauce, all overlooking Queensway Quay's mega-yachts.

ℹ Information

Royal Gibraltar Police Headquarters (☑20 072500, emergency 190, 199; www.police.gi; New Mole House, Rosia Rd)

St Bernard's Hospital (☑20079700; www.gha.gi; Harbour Views Rd; ☻24hr) Has 24-hour emergency facilities.

Tourist Office (Map p157; ☑20045000; www.visitgibraltar.gi; Heritage Bldg, 13 John Mackintosh Sq; ☻9am-4.30pm Mon-Fri, 9.30am-3.30pm Sat, 10am-1pm Sun)

Tourist Office (Map p155; ☑20050762; www.visitgibraltar.gi; Customs Bldg, Winston Churchill Ave; ☻9am-4.30pm Mon-Fri) Next to the Gibraltar–Spain border.

ℹ Getting There & Away

AIR

Gibraltar's well-connected **airport** (Map p155; ☑20012345; www.gibraltarairport.gi) is at the northern end of the Rock, next to the Spanish border.

British Airways (www.britishairways.com) To/from London (Heathrow).

EasyJet (www.easyjet.com) To/from London (Gatwick), Bristol and Manchester.

BUS

No buses go directly to Gibraltar, but the **bus station** (Map p155; Avenida de Europa) in La Línea de la Concepción (Spain) is only 400m north of the border. From here, there are regular buses to/from Algeciras, Cádiz, Málaga, Seville and Tarifa.

CAR & MOTORCYCLE

Long vehicle queues at the border and congested streets in Gibraltar make it far less time-consuming to park in La Línea and walk south across the frontier (1.5km to Casemates Sq). To take a car into Gibraltar (free), you need an insurance certificate, a registration document, a nationality plate and a driving licence. Gibraltar drives on the right. In Gibraltar, there are car parks on Line Wall Rd, Reclamation Rd and Devil's Tower Rd (50p per 30 minutes). La Línea has some street parking, but it's easier and safer to use the underground car parks (€21 per 24 hours) just north of Avenida Príncipe de Asturias.

ℹ Getting Around

Bus 5 runs between town and the border every 10 to 20 minutes. Bus 2 serves Europa Point, bus 3 the southern town; buses 4 and 8 go to Catalan Bay. All these buses stop at Market Pl (Map p157), immediately northwest of Grand Casemates Sq. Tickets cost £1.50, or £2.25 for a day pass. Check schedules at www.gibraltarbuscompany.gi/site.

Málaga Province

Best Places to Stay

➡ Claude (p179)

➡ Aire de Ronda (p185)

➡ TRH Mijas (p177)

➡ Molina Lario (p169)

➡ Finca El Cerrillo (p196)

Best Places to Eat

➡ El Mesón de Cervantes (p171)

➡ Almocábar (p186)

➡ El Gato Lounge (p175)

➡ Arte de Cozina (p192)

➡ Farm (p179)

➡ Bar-Restaurante El Acebuchal (p194)

Why Go?

After decades of being pointedly ignored, particularly by tourists to the coastal resorts, revitalised Málaga is now the Andalucian city everyone is talking about. Its 30-odd museums and edgy urban art scene are well matched by contemporary-chic dining choices, a stash of new boutique hotels and a shopping street voted one of the most stylish in Spain. Málaga is at its most vibrant during the annual feria, when the party atmosphere is infused with flamenco, *fino* (dry, straw-coloured sherry) and carafe-loads of fiesta spirit.

Each region of the province has equally fascinating diversity, from the mythical mountains of La Axarquía to the tourist-driven razzle-dazzle of the Costa del Sol. Inland are the *pueblos blancos* (white towns), crowned by spectacularly situated Ronda. There's also the under-appreciated, elegant old town of Antequera, with its nearby archaeological site and fabulous *porra antequera* (thick local soup).

Driving Distances

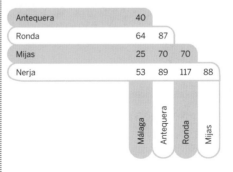

	Málaga	Antequera	Ronda	Mijas
Antequera	40			
Ronda	64	87		
Mijas	25	70	70	
Nerja	53	89	117	88

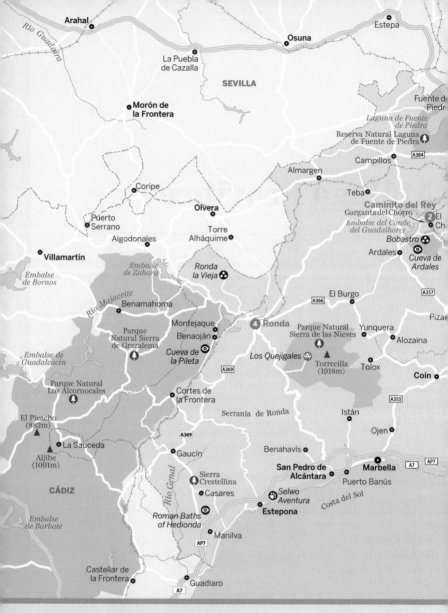

Málaga Province Highlights

1 Málaga (p162) Taking a trip from Picasso to modern graffiti in Spain's ever-evolving art city extraordinaire.

2 Caminito del Rey (p190) Following a narrow 100m-high path through the jaws of El Chorro gorge.

3 Cueva de Nerja (p197) Delving into a surreal subterranean world of stalagmites and stalactites beneath the tourist bustle of Nerja.

4 Ronda (p181) Choosing from a rich cache of impressive historical hotels in this rugged mountain town.

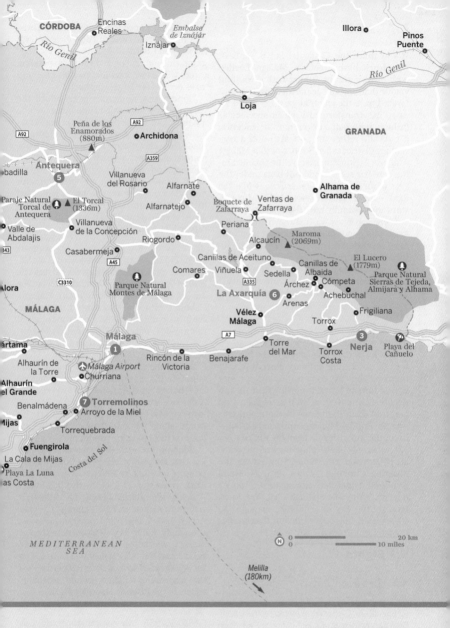

5 Antequera (p190)
Admiring baroque churches, a Moorish fortress and proudly traditional food in this understated crossroads town.

6 La Axarquía (p194)
Finding a rural *finca* to use as a base for walking or horse-riding trips into the steep-sided hills north of Nerja.

7 Torremolinos (p174)
Sitting down to fresh sardines barbecued on a charcoal grill on the busy beachfront at La Carihuela.

MÁLAGA

POP 569,000

If you think the Costa del Sol is soulless, you clearly haven't been to Málaga. Loaded with history and brimming with a youthful vigour that proudly acknowledges its multi-layered past, the city that gave the world Picasso has transformed itself in spectacular fashion, with half a dozen new art galleries, a radically rethought port area and a nascent art district called Soho. Not that Málaga was ever lacking in energy: the Spanish-to-the-core bar scene could put bags under the eyes of an insomniac *madrileño*, while the food culture encompasses both Michelin stars and tastefully tatty fish shacks.

Come for tapas washed down with sweet local wine, and stay in a creative boutique hotel sandwiched between a Roman amphitheatre, a Moorish fortress and the polychromatic Pompidou Centre, while you reflect on how eloquently Málaga has reinvented itself for the 21st century. Look out, Seville.

History

The name Málaga comes from *malaka,* meaning 'to salt': the appellation was given to the city by the Phoenicians in the 8th century BC after their culinary custom of salting fish. The city grew to become a major port in Roman times, exporting olive oil and *garum* (fish paste), as well as copper, lead and iron from the mines in the mountains around Ronda. Málaga continued to flourish under Moorish rule from the 8th century AD, especially as the chief port of the emirate of Granada. The city held out against the invading Christian armies until 1487 and displayed equal tenacity against Franco's fascists during the Spanish Civil War. More recently, the city has, happily, managed to stave off the mass development that typifies the adjacent Costa del Sol.

⊙ Sights

⊙ Historic Centre

⭐ **Museo Picasso Málaga** MUSEUM
(☎952 12 76 00; www.museopicassomalaga.org; Calle San Agustín 8; €7, incl temporary exhibition €10; ⊙10am-8pm Jul & Aug, to 7pm Mar-Jun, Sep & Oct, to 6pm Nov-Feb) This unmissable museum in the city of Picasso's birth provides a solid overview of the great master and his work, although, surprisingly, it only came to fruition in 2003 after more than 50 years of planning. The 200-plus works in the collection were donated and loaned to the museum by Christine Ruiz-Picasso (wife of Paul, Picasso's eldest son) and Bernard Ruiz-Picasso (Picasso's grandson) and catalogue the artist's sparkling career with a few notable gaps (the 'blue' and 'rose' periods are largely missing).

Nonetheless, numerous gems adorn the gallery's lily-white walls. Highlights include a painting of Picasso's sister Lola undertaken when the artist was only 13; sculptures made from clay, plaster and sheet metal; numerous sketches; a quick journey through cubism; and some interesting late works when Picasso developed an obsession with musketeers. The museum, which is housed in the 16th-century Buenavista Palace, has an excellent cafe and holds revolving temporary exhibitions.

⭐ **Catedral de Málaga** CATHEDRAL
(☎952 21 59 17; www.malagacatedral.com; Calle Molina Lario; cathedral & Ars Málaga €6, incl roof €10; ⊙10am-9pm Mon-Fri, to 6.30pm Sat, 2-6.30pm Sun Apr-Oct, closes 6.30pm daily Nov-Mar) Málaga's elaborate cathedral was started in the 16th century on the site of the former mosque. Of the mosque, only the Patio de los Naranjos survives, a small courtyard of fragrant orange trees.

Inside, the fabulous domed ceiling soars 40m into the air, while the vast colonnaded nave houses an enormous cedar-wood choir. Aisles give access to 15 chapels with gorgeous 18th-century retables and religious art. It's worth taking the guided tour up to the *cubiertas* (roof) to enjoy panoramic city views.

Building the cathedral was an epic project that took some 200 years. Such was the project's cost that by 1782 it was decided that work would stop. One of the two bell towers was left incomplete, hence the cathedral's well-worn nickname, La Manquita (The One-Armed Lady). The ticket price includes use of an audio guide as well as entry to the Ars Málaga (www.arsmalaga.es; Plaza del Obispo; €4, incl cathedral €6; ⊙10am-9pm Mon-Fri, to 6.30pm Sat, 2-6.30pm Sun Apr-Oct, closes 6.30pm daily Nov-Mar) museum of religious art and African artefacts in the Bishop's House opposite.

⭐ **Alcazaba** CASTLE
(☎630 932987; www.malagaturismo.com; Calle Alcazabilla; €2.20, incl Castillo de Gibralfaro €3.55; ⊙9.30am-8pm Tue-Sun) No time to visit Granada's Alhambra? Then Málaga's Alcazaba can provide a taster. The entrance is next to the Roman amphitheatre (p163), from where a meandering path climbs amid lush greenery: crimson bougainvillea, lofty palms,

fragrant jasmine bushes and rows of orange trees. Extensively restored, this palace-fortress dates from the 11th-century Moorish period; the caliphal horseshoe arches, courtyards and bubbling fountains are evocative of this influential period in Málaga's history. There are various unlabelled exhibits of Islamic pottery, but the main joys are the building itself, the gardens and the views. The dreamy **Patio de la Alberca** is especially redolent of the Alhambra.

Museo Carmen Thyssen　　　　MUSEUM
(www.carmenthyssenmalaga.org; Calle Compañía 10; €6, incl temporary exhibition €9; ☉10am-8pm Tue-Sun) Located in an aesthetically renovated 16th-century palace in the heart of the city's former Moorish quarter, this extensive collection concentrates on 19th-century Spanish and Andalucian art by painters such as Joaquín Sorolla y Bastida and Ignacio Zuloaga. It's particularly interesting for its almost cartoonish *costumbrismo* paintings that perpetuated a sentimental myth of 19th-century Spain as a place of banditry, flamenco, fiestas, bar-room brawls and bullfighting (and little else). There are also regular temporary exhibitions and a lovely patio cafe.

Castillo de Gibralfaro　　　　CASTLE
(☑952 22 72 30; www.malagaturismo.com; Camino de Gibralfaro; €2.20, incl Alcazaba €3.55; ☉9am-9pm Apr-Sep, to 6pm Oct-Mar) One remnant of Málaga's Islamic past is the craggy ramparts of the Castillo de Gibralfaro, spectacularly located high on the hill overlooking the city. Built by Abd ar-Rahman I, the 8th-century Córdoban emir, and later rebuilt in the 14th century when Málaga was the main port for the emirate of Granada, the castle originally acted as a lighthouse and military barracks.

Nothing much is original in the castle's interior, but the protective walkway around the ramparts affords the best views over Málaga. There is also a military museum, which includes a small scale model of the entire castle complex and the lower residence, the Alcazaba.

The best way to reach the castle on foot is via the attractive Paseo Don Juan de Temboury, to the south of the Alcazaba. From here a path winds pleasantly (and steeply) through lushly gardened terraces with viewpoints over the city. Alternatively, you can drive up the Camino de Gibralfaro or take bus 35 from Avenida de Cervantes.

Casa Natal de Picasso　　　　MUSEUM
(www.fundacionpicasso.malaga.eu; Plaza de la Merced 15; €3, incl Sala de Exposiciones €4;

☉9.30am-8pm) For an intimate insight into the painter's childhood, head to the Casa Natal de Picasso, the house where Picasso was born in 1881. Now a study foundation, the house has a replica 19th-century artist's studio and small quarterly exhibitions of Picasso's work. The personal memorabilia of Picasso and his family make up part of the display. The foundation also owns the small **Sala de Exposiciones** (Plaza de la Merced 13; €3, incl Casa Natal €4; ☉9.30am-8pm) across the square, which shuffles an excellent deck of temporary shows, often including or heavily influenced by Picasso's work.

Roman Amphitheatre　　　　LANDMARK
(☑951 50 11 15; Calle Alcazabilla 8; ☉10am-8pm) **FREE** The story of the unearthing of Málaga's Roman theatre is almost as interesting as the theatre itself. Dating from the time of Augustus (1st century AD), it was rediscovered in 1951 by workers building the foundations for a new Casa de Cultura. Today the theatre sits fully exposed beneath the walls of the Alcazaba. A small interpretive centre next door outlines its history and displays a few artefacts shovelled from its crusty foundations.

Museo de Arte Flamenco　　　　MUSEUM
(☑952 22 13 80; www.museoflamencojuanbreva.com; Calle Franquelo 4; donation €1; ☉10am-2pm Mon-Sat) Fabulously laid out over two floors in the HQ of Málaga's oldest and most prestigious *peña* (private flamenco club), this collection of fans, costumes, posters and other flamenco paraphernalia is testament to the city's illustrious flamenco scene.

Museo Jorge Rando　　　　GALLERY
(☑952 21 09 91; www.museojorgerando.org; Calle Cruz del Molinillo 12; ☉10am-8pm Mon-Sat) **FREE** One of Málaga's newest museums exhibits the work of one of its most contemporary artists. Rando is now in his 70s, and his abstract paintings and sculptures focus, among other topics, on poverty in Africa. It's stirring stuff.

Museo Revello de Toro　　　　GALLERY
(☑952 06 20 69; www.museorevellodetoro.net; Calle Afligidos 5; €2.50; ☉10am-8pm Tue-Sat, to 2pm Sun) Showcases the work of 20th-century Málaga artist Félix Revello de Toro (b 1926) in a 17th-century mansion that was once the workshop of religious sculptor Pedro de Mena.

Museo del Vidrio y Cristal　　　　MUSEUM
(Museum of Glass & Crystal; ☑952 22 02 71; www.museovidrioycristalmalaga.com; Plazuela Santísimo Cristo de la Sangre 2; €6; ☉11am-7pm Tue-Sun)

Málaga

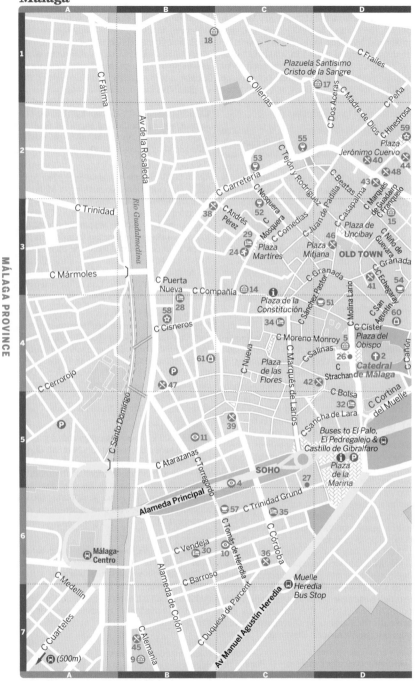

C Frailes

C Fatima

C Ollerias

Plazuela Santísimo
Cristo de la Sangre

17

C Dos Aceras

C Madre de Dios

C Hinestrosa

C Peña

59

Av de la Rosaleda

55

C Tejón y Rodríguez

Plaza
Jerónimo Cuervo

40

48

44

53

C Carretería

C Beatas

43

C Trinidad

Río Guadalmedina

C Nosquera

52

C Andrés
Pérez

38

C
Mosquera

C Comedias

C Juan de Padilla

C Casapalma

C Marqués
de Guadiaro

C Tranquilo

15

Plaza de
Uncibay

46

C Niño de
Guevara

29

Plaza
Martíres

24

Plaza
Mitjana

C Granada

OLD TOWN

C Mármoles

C Puerta
Nueva

C Compañía

14

Plaza de la
Constitución

C Sánchez-Pastor

C Molina Lario

51

C/C Echegaray

41

C San
Agustín

54

60

58

28

C Cisneros

34

C Moreno Monroy

5

C Cañón

C Salinas

26

2

*Catedral
de Málaga*

61

Plaza
de las
Flores

C Nueva

C Marqués de Larios

42

C
Strachan

C Bolsa

C Cortina
del Muelle

32

C sancha de Lara

39

C Santo Domingo

C Cerrorojo

47

11

C Atarazanas

C Torregordo

SOHO

Buses to El Palo,
El Pedregalejo &
Castillo de Gibralfaro

Plaza
de la
Marina

27

4

Alameda Principal

57

C Trinidad Grund

35

Málaga-
Centro

C Vendeja

30

10

C Tomás de Heredia

C Córdoba

36

Muelle
Heredia
Bus Stop

C Medellín

Alameda de Colón

C Barroso

C Duquesa de Parcent

Av Manuel Agustín Heredia

C Cuarteles

C Alemania

45

9

(500m)

18

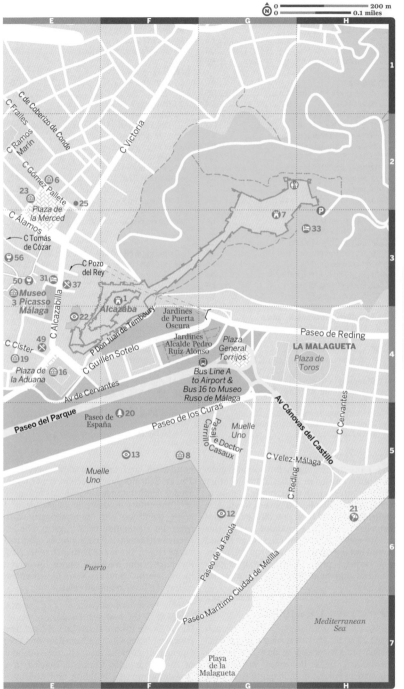

N

0 ———————————— 200 m
0 ———————————— 0.1 miles

E   **F**   **G**   **H**

1

C de Cobertizo de Conde
C Fraíles
C Ramos Marín
C Gómez Pallete

2

6
23
25

Plaza de la Merced
C Álamos
C Tomás de Cózar

C Victoria

7
P
33

56
50 31
37

C Pozo del Rey

3

Museo
3 Picasso
Málaga

C Alcazabilla

1
Alcazaba
22

Jardines de Puerta Oscura

49
C Cister
19

Plaza de la Aduana
16

Jardines Alcalde Pedro Ruiz Alonso

Plaza General Torrijos

Paseo de Reding

LA MALAGUETA

Plaza de Toros

4

P Don Juan de Tembourg
C Guillén Sotelo

Av de Cervantes

Bus Line A to Airport & Bus 16 to Museo Ruso de Málaga

Av Cánovas del Castillo

C Cervantes

Paseo del Parque

Paseo de España

20

Paseo de los Curas

Muelle Uno

C Velez-Málaga

C Reding

5

13
8

Pasaje Doctor Carrillo Casaux

Muelle Uno

21

6

12

Paseo de la Farola

Puerto

Mediterranean Sea

7

Paseo Marítimo Ciudad de Melilla

Playa de la Malagueta

E   **F**   **G**   **H**

Málaga

The more-interesting-than-it-sounds glass museum is housed in a palatial 18th-century house, complete with three central patios, in a charmingly dilapidated part of town. Aesthetically restored by aristocratic owner and historian Gonzalo Fernández-Prieto, this private collection concentrates on glass and crystal but includes antique furniture, priceless carpets, pre-Raphaelite stained-glass windows and huge 16th-century ancestral portraits.

◉ Port Area & Around

Museo de Málaga   MUSEUM
(☑951 29 40 51; Plaza de la Aduana; ◎9am-3pm Tue-Sun mid-Jun–mid-Sep, to 8pm Tue-Sun mid-Sep–mid-Jun) **FREE** Reopened in Málaga's neoclassical Palacio de Aduana in December 2016 following a full renovation, this museum houses art and archaeological collections. The 1st-floor fine-arts collection, kept in storage for nearly two decades, consists primarily of 19th-century Andalucian landscape and genre paintings, plus more modern work from the 'Generation of '27' (p343). The extensive archaeological collection, bequeathed to the city by the noble Loring-Heredia family, ranges from Neolithic shards uncovered in the nearby Cueva de Nerja to a headless statue of a Roman noblewoman.

Centre Pompidou Málaga   MUSEUM
(☑951 92 62 00; www.centrepompidou.es; Pasaje Doctor Carrillo Casaux, Muelle Uno; €7, incl temporary exhibition €9; ◎9.30am-8pm Wed-Mon) Opened in 2015 in the port, this offshoot of Paris' Pompidou Centre is housed in a low-slung modern building crowned by a playful multicoloured cube. The permanent

exhibition includes the extraordinary *Ghost*, by Kader Attia, depicting rows of Muslim women bowed in prayer and created from domestic aluminium foil, plus works by such modern masters as Frida Kahlo, Francis Bacon and Antoni Tàpies. There are also audiovisual installations, talking 'heads' and temporary exhibitions.

Centro de Arte Contemporáneo   MUSEUM
(Contemporary Art Museum; www.cacmalaga. org; Calle Alemania; ⊙9am-2pm & 5-9pm Tue-Sun) FREE The contemporary-art museum is housed in a skilfully converted 1930s wholesale market on the river estuary. The bizarre triangular floor plan of the building has been retained, with its cubist lines and shapes brilliantly showcasing the modern art on display. Painted entirely white, windows and all, the museum hosts temporary shows featuring the work of well-known contemporary artists and has an obvious Spanish bias. It's usually filled with plenty of spectacularly weird exhibits.

Muelle Uno   PORT
The city's long-beleaguered port area underwent a radical rethink in 2013 and was redesigned to cater to the increase in cruise-ship passengers to the city. Wide quayside walkways now embellish Muelle 1 and Muelle 2, which are lined by palm trees and backed by shops, restaurants, bars and a small kid-focused aquarium, the **Museo Alborania** (☑951 60 01 08; www.museoalborania. com; Palmeral de las Sopresas, Muelle 2; adult/child €7/5; ⊙11am-2pm & 5-8pm Jul-10 Sep, 10.30am-2pm & 4.30-6.30pm 11 Sep-Jun; ⊕).

Paseo de España   PARK
(Paseo del Parque; P) Looking like a mini jungle when viewed from the Gibralfaro hill, this palm-lined extension of the Alameda was created in the 1890s on land reclaimed from the sea. The garden along its southern side is full of exotic tropical plants and trees, making a pleasant refuge from the bustle of the city. *Malagueños* stroll and take shelter in the deep shade of the tall palms, and on Sunday buskers and entertainers play to the crowds.

Mercado Atarazanas   MARKET
(Calle Atarazanas; ⊙market 8am-3pm Mon-Sat; P) North of the city's main artery, the Alameda Principal, you'll find this striking 19th-century iron-clad building incorporating the original Moorish gate that once connected the city with the port. The magnificent stained-glass window depicts historical highlights of the city. The daily market here is pleasantly noisy and animated.

◉ Other Areas

Museo Ruso de Málaga   MUSEUM
(☑951 92 61 50; www.coleccionmuseoruso.es; Avenida de Sor Teresa Plat 15; €6, incl temporary exhibitions €8; ⊙9am-8pm Tue-Sun; P) This offshoot of the Russian State Museum in St Petersburg opened on a 10-year lease in 2015 in a former tobacco factory. It is dedicated to Russian art from the 16th to 20th centuries, featuring works by Ilya Repin, Wassily Kandinsky and Vladimir Tatlin, among others, although the main focus seems to be to tell the story of Russian history rather than the art itself. From Málaga's Paseo del Parque, take bus 16 and get off at Avenida de Sor Teresa Prat (€1.35, 10 minutes). Alternatively, take the metro to Princesa-Huelin and walk the last 400m.

Museo Automovilístico Málaga   MUSEUM
(☑951 13 70 01; www.museoautomovilmalaga.com; Avenida Sor Teresa Prat 15; adult €8.50; ⊙10am-7pm Tue-Sun) Fashion and old cars might seem like weird bedfellows, but they're an inspired combo when viewed through the prism of this slightly out-of-the-box museum

MÁLAGA PROVINCE MÁLAGA

DON'T MISS

LA MALAGUETA & THE BEACHES

At the end of the Paseo del Parque lies the exclusive residential district of La Malagueta, situated on a spit of land protruding into the sea. Apartments here have frontline sea views, and some of Málaga's best restaurants are found near the Playa de la Malagueta (the beach closest to the city centre). Head 2km east to reach the fabulous setting of seafood restaurant El Balneario de los Baños del Carmen (p171).

East of Playa de la Malagueta, sandy beaches continue to line most of the waterfront for several kilometres. Next along are Playa de Pedregalejo and Playa el Palo, El Palo being the city's original, salt-of-the-earth fishing neighbourhood. This is a great place to bring children and an even better place to while away an afternoon with a cold beer and a plate of sizzling seafood. To reach either beach, take bus 11 from Paseo del Parque.

in Málaga's erstwhile tobacco factory. The museum juxtaposes cars from the 1900s to the 1960s with haute couture from the same era. Imagine a 1936 Merc lined up next to a mannequin clothed in a Chanel jacket. From Málaga's Paseo del Parque, take bus 16 and get off at Avenida de Sor Teresa Prat (€1.35, 10 minutes). Alternatively, take the metro to Princesa-Huelin and walk the last 400m.

Jardín Botánico Histórico
La Concepción   GARDENS
(⏰951 92 63 80; http://laconcepcion.malaga.eu; Camino del Jardín Botánico 3; €5.20; ⏰9.30am-7.30pm Tue-Sun Apr-Sep, to 4.30pm Tue-Sun Oct-Mar) These exotic gardens were conceived in the mid-19th century by the Loring-Heredia clan, a noble family of railway builders and bankers who bequeathed the city its weighty archaeological collection (now on display in the Museo de Málaga; p166). Laid out in 1855, the hillside grounds were updated by different owners in 1911. The state took over management of the gardens in 1990, and in 1994 they were opened to the public. The gardens are 5km north of Málaga. Bus 2 will get you close, or you can take the five-times-a-day City Tour bus (€1.30) from the train station that'll drop you at the entrance.

🏃 Activities

★ Málaga Bike Tours   CYCLING
(⏰606 978513; www.malagabiketours.eu; Calle Trinidad Grund 1; tours €25; ⏰10am-8pm Apr-Sep, to 7pm Oct-Mar; 👪) 🚲 One of the best tours in town and certainly the best on two wheels. Málaga Bike Tours was a pioneer in city cycling when it was set up a decade ago. Its perennially popular excursions, including the classic City Bike Tour, are available in

---

DON'T MISS

MAUS & SOHO
....

The antithesis of Málaga's prestigious world-class art museums is refreshingly down-to-earth MAUS (Málaga Arte Urbano en el Soho; www.mausmalaga.com), a grassroots movement born out of an influx of street artists to the area. The result is a total transformation of the formerly rundown district between the city centre and the port. Now called Soho, the district has edgy contemporary murals several stories high, as well as arty cafes, ethnic restaurants and street markets.

---

at least five languages, with kids' seats on offer if you're bringing the family.

Daily tours leave from outside the municipal tourist office in Plaza de la Marina at 10am. Reservations are required. Book at least 24 hours ahead. Alternatively, you can rent your own bike from €5 for four hours.

Hammam Al-Andalus   HAMMAM
(⏰952 21 50 18; www.hammamalandalus.com; Plaza de los Mártires 5; baths €30; ⏰10am-midnight) These Moorish-style baths provide *malagueños* with a luxurious marble-clad setting in which to enjoy the same relaxation benefits as those offered by similar facilities in Granada and Córdoba. Massages are also available.

Málaga Adventures   WALKING
(⏰699 756864; www.malagaadventures.com; ⏰11am & noon; 👟) FREE Free walking tours leave daily from the Plaza del Obispo opposite the cathedral (p162). Look out for the tour leaders in red T-shirts with red umbrellas. Tips are appreciated.

🎓 Courses

Instituto Picasso   LANGUAGE
(⏰952 21 39 32; www.instituto-picasso.com; Plaza de la Merced 20) Private language school in Málaga, which runs two-/three-/four-week courses for €330/460/580 starting every fortnight on a Monday. There are four 50-minute lessons a day and the price includes access to cultural activities such as flamenco and cookery courses. Accommodation is also available.

🎉 Festivals & Events

There's a whole host of festivals throughout the year in Málaga province, listed in the booklet *¿Qué hacer?*, available each month from the municipal tourist office (p173).

Semana Santa   HOLY WEEK
Each night from Palm Sunday to Good Friday, six or seven *cofradías* (brotherhoods) bear holy images for several hours through the city, watched by large crowds.

Feria de Málaga   FAIR
(⏰mid-Aug) Málaga's nine-day feria, launched by a huge fireworks display, is the most ebullient of Andalucía's summer fairs. It resembles an exuberant Rio-style street party, with plenty of flamenco and *fino*; head for the city centre to be in the thick of it. At night, festivities switch to large fairgrounds and nightly rock and flamenco shows at Cortijo de Torres, 3km southwest

MÁLAGA'S ARTISTIC REVIVAL

Befitting Picasso's birthplace, Málaga has an art collection to rival those of Seville and Granada, particularly in the field of modern art, where galleries and workshops continue to push the envelope. It wasn't always thus.

Little more than 15 years ago, Málaga's art scene was patchy and understated. The first big coup came in 2003, when, after 50 years of on-off discussion, the city finally got around to honouring its most famous son with the opening of the Museo Picasso Málaga (p162). More galleries followed, some focusing on notable malagueños such as Jorge Rando and Félix Revello de Toro, others – such as the Museo Carmen Thyssen (p163), which shines a light on costumbrismo (Spanish folk art) – taking in a broader sweep of Spanish painting. Then, in 2015, Málaga earned the right to be called a truly international art city when it opened offshoot galleries of St Petersburg's prestigious Russian State Museum and Paris' Pompidou Centre. Around the same time, edgy street artists put forward the idea of MAUS, an urban-renewal project that has fostered a free creative space in the Soho neighbourhood for street and graffiti artists.

The finishing touches to this colourful canvas were added in December 2016: after 20 years in the dark, Málaga's 2000-piece-strong fine-arts collection was reinstated in the city's beautifully restored old customs house (p166) down by the port.

of the city centre; special buses run from all over the city.

🛏 Sleeping

⭐ Dulces Dreams   HOSTEL €

(🖉 951 35 78 69; www.dulcesdreamshostel.com; Plaza de los Mártires 6; r incl breakfast €45-60; ❄🤖) Managed by an enthusiastic young team, the rooms at Dulces (sweet) Dreams are, appropriately, named after desserts; 'Cupcake' is a good choice, with a terrace overlooking the imposing red-brick church across the way. This is an older building, so there's no lift and the rooms vary in size, but they're bright and whimsically decorated, using recycled materials as much as possible. Breakfast is healthy and cosmopolitan, with choices including avocado, cheese, fruit and muesli, plus organic coffee that guests say is the best in town.

Feel Málaga Hostel   HOSTEL €

(🖉 952 22 28 32; www.feelhostels.com; Calle Vendeja 25; d €45, with shared bathroom €35, dm from €16; @🤖) Located within a suitcase trundle of the city-centre train station, the accommodation here is clean and well equipped, with a choice of doubles and shared rooms. The downstairs communal area has a colourful seaside look, with striped deck chairs and mini football; bathrooms sport classy mosaic tiles; the top-floor kitchen has all the essentials for whipping up a decent meal.

⭐ Hotel Boutique
Teatro Romano   BOUTIQUE HOTEL €€

(🖉 951 20 44 38; www.hotelteatroromano.com; Calle Alcazabilla 7; r €117-130; ❄🤖) One in a new wave of plush new boutique offerings

in Málaga, this place overlooks the Roman theatre (p163) and has chocolate-brown corridors leading to sparkling white rooms so clean they look as if they've never been used. The whole place is modern, well managed, and studded with interesting design accents. The healthy breakfasts in the bright on-site cafe are a bonus.

⭐ Molina Lario   HOTEL €€

(🖉 952 06 20 02; www.hotelmolinalario.com; Calle Molina Lario 20-22; r €125-137; ❄🤖🏊) Perfect for romancing couples, this hotel has a sophisticated, contemporary feel, with spacious rooms decorated in a cool palette of earthy colours. There are crisp white linens, soft pillows and tasteful paintings, plus a fabulous rooftop terrace and pool with views to the sea. Situated within confessional distance of the cathedral (p162).

Soho Málaga
Boutique Hotel   BOUTIQUE HOTEL €€

(🖉 952 22 40 79; https://sohomalaga.sohoho teles.com; Calle Córdoba 5; r €86-118; ❄🤖) The renaissance of the Soho neighbourhood is reflected vividly in hotels like this one, which has added slick new rooms to a handsome 19th-century building. Enjoy plush bathrooms and bedside espresso machines alongside older features such as large French windows and cast-iron balconies. Huge photo prints of Málaga are hung in each room, and there's a great little cafe downstairs.

Room Mate Larios   DESIGN HOTEL €€

(🖉 952 22 22 00; www.room-matehotels.com; Calle Marqués de Larios 2; r from €125; ❄@🤖) Part of a small chain of Spanish-run design hotels, this central accommodation is housed in an elegantly restored 19th-century building. Rooms are luxuriously furnished with king-size beds and carpeting throughout; several rooms have balconies overlooking the sophisticated strut of shops and boutiques along Calle Marqués de Larios. The black-and-white rooftop bar comes with a lovely outdoor terrace.

Apartamentos Málaga Picasso APARTMENT €€
(☑633 35 00 71; www.apartamentosmalagapicasso. es; Calle Muro de Puerta Nueva 1; apt €55-95; ☎) A fantastic addition to Málaga's accommodation scene, these four slick apartments (regally classical on the outside, modern and minimalist within) set the bar high. Surgically clean with stainless-steel fittings, flowering orchids, and paint as white as an Andalucian *pueblo blanco* (white town), they come with kitchenettes, tiny pod bedrooms and beer-stocked fridges. The 'old city' location is highly convenient.

Parador Málaga Gibralfaro HISTORIC HOTEL €€€
(☑952 22 19 02; www.parador.es; Castillo de Gibralfaro; r incl breakfast €130-155; 🅿❄☎☔) Perched next to Málaga's Moorish castle (p163) on the pine-forested Gibralfaro, the city's stone-built *parador* (luxurious state-owned hotel) hums with a sultan-like essence. Like most Spanish *paradores*, the kick is more in the setting and facilities than the rooms, which are modern and businesslike. Most have spectacular views from their terraces. You can dine at the excellent terrace restaurant, even if you're not a hotel guest.

✗ Eating

Málaga has a staggering number of tapas bars and restaurants, particularly around the historic centre (over 400 at last count).

Tapeo de Cervantes TAPAS €
(www.eltapeodecervantes.com; Calle Cárcer 8; media raciones €4.50-8, raciones €9-16; ☺1.30-3.30pm & 7.30-11.30pm Tue-Sat, 7.30-11.30pm Sun) The original Cervantes bar-restaurant (there are now four) is a little more boisterous and crowded than the Mesón around the corner, although the menu is almost identical – ie the best in the city.

Dulces Dreams Cafeteria CAFE €
(Plaza de los Mártires 6; breakfast €5-7; ☺8am-10pm) Located in an intimate traffic-free square, one of Málaga's great breakfast spots offers muesli, fruit juice, coffee, and tomato on toast. You might throw all your health commitments aside when you come back for an afternoon *merienda* – it's hard to go past the cake case.

Noviembre BREAKFAST €
(☑952 22 26 54; Calle Álamos 18; sandwiches & salads €8-10; ☺9am-1am Sun-Thu, to 2am Fri & Sat; ☎✐) ✐ With its purposefully aged wood, mismatched furniture, and bearded young men, uber-hip Noviembre offers excellent breakfast choices made with organic eggs, and the Big Apple burger provides a good lunch filler. The later you linger, the trendier the clientele becomes.

Brunchit BREAKFAST €
(www.brunchit.es; Calle Carretería 46; breakfasts €4-6; ☺9am-8.30pm; ☎✐) ✐ Set on Málaga's scruffy but increasingly trendy Calle Carretería, Brunchit, despite the name, is open all day ready to serve freshly made sandwiches, melt-in-your-mouth cakes, pizzas you'll want to order on sight and – of course – healthy breakfasts, in a fresh pine interior that could've been plucked straight from an Ikea catalogue.

Casa Aranda CAFE €
(www.casa-aranda.net; Calle Herrería del Rey; churro €0.45; ☺8am-3pm Mon-Sat; ♿) Casa Aranda is in a narrow alleyway next to the market and, since 1932, has been *the* place in town to enjoy chocolate and churros (tubular-shaped doughnuts). The cafe has taken over the whole street, with several outlets overseen by an army of mainly elderly, white-shirted waiters who welcome everyone like an old friend (and most are). There's another branch open later hours on Calle Santos nearby.

Nuevo y Sur TAPAS €
(☑951 25 44 71; www.nuevoysurmalaga.com; Calle Madre de Dios 22; tapas €3-6; ☺7pm-1am) The delicate range of 'street tapas' with various international influences are as well executed as the whimsical murals at this candlelit cocoon on the cusp of the city centre. Try the Indian-style poppadams with a trio of punchy dips, or the snappy street tacos.

Recyclo Bike Café CAFE €
(www.recyclobike.com; Plaza Enrique García Herrera 16; snacks €1.5-5; ☺9am-midnight Mon-Thu, to 2am Fri & Sat, 10am-midnight Sun; ☎) ✐ Hip cafe with affiliated bike shop where you can enjoy a 'Wiggins' salad, or exceedingly cheap cakes, coffee and breakfasts. Old bikes adorn the walls and ceiling.

MÁLAGA TAPAS TRAIL

The pleasures of Málaga are essentially undemanding, easy to arrange and cheap. One of the best is a slow crawl around the city's numerous tapas bars and old bodegas (cellars).

La Tranca (www.latranca.es; Calle Carretería 93; ⊙12.30pm-2am Mon-Sat, to 4pm Sun) Drinking in this slim, always busy bar is a physical contact sport, with small tapas plates passed over people's heads.

El Piyayo (☎952 22 90 57; Calle Granada 36; raciones €6-11; ⊙12.30pm-midnight) A popular, traditionally tiled bar and restaurant famed for its *pescaitos fritos* (fried fish) and typical local tapas, including wedges of crumbly Manchego cheese, the ideal accompaniment to a glass of hearty Rioja wine.

Uvedoble Taberna (www.uvedobletaberna.com; Calle Císter 15; tapas €2.70; ⊙12.30-4pm & 8pm-midnight Mon-Sat; ☎) If you're seeking something a little more contemporary, head to this popular spot with its innovative take on traditional tapas.

Pepa y Pepe (☎615 656984; Calle Calderería 9; tapas €1.30-2, raciones €3.60-5.50; ⊙12.30-4.30pm & 7.30pm-12.30am) A snug tapas bar that brims with young diners enjoying tapas such as *calamares fritos* (battered squid) and fried green peppers.

Gorki (☎952 22 70 00; www.grupogorki.com; Calle Strachan 6; mains €10-13; ⊙noon-4pm & 8pm-midnight) A tastefully decorated tapas bar for enjoying sophisticated small bites such as mini burgers and sweetbreads encased in light, flaky pastry.

★**El Mesón de Cervantes** TAPAS, ARGENTINE €€
(☎952 21 62 74; www.elmesondecervantes.com; Calle Álamos 11; media raciones €4.50-8, raciones €9-16; ⊙7pm-midnight Wed-Mon) Cervantes started as a humble tapas bar run by expat Argentine Gabriel Spatz but has now expanded into four bar-restaurants (each with a slightly different bent), all within a block of each other. This one is the HQ, where pretty much everything on the menu is a show-stopper – lamb stew with couscous, pumpkin and mushroom risotto, and boy, the grilled octopus! Most things can be ordered as half or full portions, meaning you can taste a rich variety. Cervantes is still humble but now vastly popular. Book ahead.

The newest bar of the quartet, **La Taberna de Cervantes**, sits directly opposite and is often less busy.

★**Óleo** FUSION €€
(☎952 21 90 62; www.oleorestaurante.es; Edificio CAC, Calle Alemania; mains €16-22; ⊙1.15-4.30pm & 8.30pm-midnight Wed-Sat, 1.15-4.30pm Tue & Sun; ☎) Located at the city's contemporary art museum (p167) with white-on-white minimalist decor, Óleo provides diners with the unusual choice of Mediterranean or Asian food, with some subtle combinations such as duck breast with a side of seaweed with hoisin, as well as more purist Asian and gourmet fare such as candied roasted piglet. There's a full-on sushi bar if you really want to play away and plenty of excellent wines. Service is snappy and sharp. Book in advance.

El Balneario de los Baños del Carmen SEAFOOD €€
(www.elbalneariomalaga.com; Calle Bolivia 40, La Malagueta; mains €8-18; ⊙8.30am-1am Sun-Thu, to 2.30am Fri & Sat; P☎) El Balneario is a wonderful place to sit outside on a balmy evening and share a plate of prawns or grilled sardines, along with some long, cold beverages. Built in 1918 to cater to Málaga's bourgeoisie, it's rekindling its past as one of the city's most celebrated venues for socialising.

Batik MODERN SPANISH €€
(☎952 22 10 45; www.batikmalaga.com; Calle Alcazabilla 12; mains €9-16; ⊙12.30-4pm & 8pm-midnight; ☎) With Málaga's Alcazaba (p162) posing like the Alhambra in the background, this classy but not-too-posh restaurant (you can opt for stools rather than chairs) is where *malagueños* come to impress a date. The food is about taste and arty presentation rather than quantity, but it packs a punch: octopus with puréed squash and green *mole* sauce is among the whimsical creations.

Al Yamal MOROCCAN €€
(Calle Blasco de Garay 7; mains €13-16; ⊙noon-3pm & 7-11pm Mon-Sat) Moroccan restaurants aren't as ubiquitous in Málaga as they are in Granada, but, in the heart of the Soho district, this family-run place serves the authentic stuff, including tagines, couscous, hummus and *kefta* (meatballs). The street profile looks unpromising, but the tiny dining room has six cosy booths decorated with vivid Moroccan fabrics and a trickling fountain.

🍷 Drinking & Nightlife

Málaga might not be as big as Madrid, but it's just as much fun. The pedestrianised old town is the main hive, especially around Plaza de la Constitución and Plaza de la Merced.

⭐ La Tetería
TEAHOUSE

(www.la-teteria.com; Calle San Agustín 9; speciality teas €2.50; ⏰9am-midnight Mon-Sat) There are numerous *teterías* in Málaga, but only one *La* Tetería. While it's less Moorish than some of its more atmospheric brethren, it still sells a wide selection of fruity teas, backed by a range of rich cakes. Along with the cafe's location next to the Museo Picasso Málaga (p162), this ensures that the place is usually close to full.

La Madriguera Craft Beer
CRAFT BEER

(📞951 71 62 11; Calle Carretería 73; ⏰noon-4pm & 6pm-1am Mon-Thu, noon-3am Sat & Sun) Craft beer barely registered in Spain a few years ago, but the 'Rabbit Hole', as its name translates, is riding a new wave with daily listings of a dozen ever-changing craft beers and an equal number of more permanent light bites to soak them up. A wall chart honours the feats of punters past – 11 pints appears to be the record.

Bodegas El Pimpi
BAR

(www.elpimpi.com; Calle Granada 62; ⏰noon-2am Mon-Fri, to 3am Sat & Sun; 🛜) This rambling bar is an institution in this town. The interior encompasses a warren of rooms, and there's a courtyard and open terrace overlooking the Roman amphitheatre (p163). Walls are decorated with historic feria posters and photos of visitors past, while the enormous barrels are signed by more well-known passers-by, including Tony Blair and Antonio Banderas. Tapas and meals are also available.

El Último Mono Juice & Coffee
COFFEE

(📞951 39 29 76; Calle Santa María 9; ⏰9am-9pm; 🛜) If you want your coffee dispatched quickly in a takeaway cup and don't really care for Starbucks, head to the 'Last Mon-

key', a super-friendly small cafe with space to perch on a stool and a handful of sweet bites to go with the joe.

Los Patios de Beatas
WINE BAR

(📞952 21 03 50; www.lospatiosdebeatas.com; Calle Beatas 43; ⏰1-5pm & 8pm-midnight Mon-Sat, 1-6pm Sun; 🛜) Two 18th-century mansions have metamorphosed into this sumptuous space where you can sample fine wines from a selection reputed to be the most extensive in town. Stained-glass windows and beautiful resin tables inset with mosaics and shells add to the overall art-infused atmosphere. Innovative tapas and *raciones* (full-plate servings) are also on offer.

Santa Canela
CAFE

(www.santacanelacafe.com; Calle Tomás Heredia 5; ⏰8am-8pm Mon-Fri, 9am-3pm & 5-8pm Sat & Sun; 🛜) This cafe in Soho mixes traditional Spanish touches (table service, alfresco seating and great cakes) with a more modern hipster vibe and an appreciation of micro-roasted coffee. There's a long menu of coffees and you can buy bags of it to take away.

La Casa Invisible
BAR

(www.lainvisible.net; Calle Nosquera 11; ⏰11am-late Mon-Sat; 🛜) Hidden away in the back alleys of Málaga's old town, this patio bar has a young, left-field feel, with plenty of Frank Zappa hairstyles and Che Guevara beards on show. Bright murals add splashes of colour, and a blackboard advertises earnest political discussions and upcoming punk-rock gigs should you get bored with your beer.

⭐ Entertainment

The city has a strong flamenco legacy and its own *palo* (style) called *malagueñas*. There are several longstanding venues and a couple of new ones (though not as many as in Seville or Jerez).

⭐ Kelipe
FLAMENCO

(📞692 829885; www.kelipe.net; Muro de Puerta Nueva 10; €25; ⏰shows 9.30pm Thu-Sat) There are many flamenco clubs springing up all over Andalucía, but few are as soul-stirring as Kelipe. Not only are the musicianship and dancing of the highest calibre, but the talented performers create an intimate feel and a genuine connection with the audience.

Peña Juan Breva
FLAMENCO

(Calle Juan Franquelo 4) You'll feel like a gate-crasher at this private *peña*, but persevere: the flamenco is *muy puro*. Watch guitarists who play as though they've got 24 fingers

---

TINTO DE VERANO

If you're visiting in summer, consider ordering a *tinto de verano* at any local bar. This long, cold drink is made with red wine, local lemonade (not too sweet), lashings of ice and a slice of lemon. It's refreshing, and it shouldn't make your head reel too much on a hot day.

and listen to singers who bellow forth as if their heart was broken the previous night. There's no set schedule. Ask about dates at the on-site Museo de Arte Flamenco (p163).

Teatro Cervantes THEATRE
(www.teatrocervantes.com; Calle Ramos Marín; ☺ Sep–mid-Jul) The handsome art-deco Cervantes has a fine program of music, theatre and dance, including some well-known names on the concert circuit. It also hosts a November jazz festival.

Shopping

The chic, marble-clad Calle Marqués de Larios is increasingly home to designer stores and boutiques. In the surrounding streets are family-owned small shops in handsomely restored old buildings, selling everything from flamenco dresses to local sweet Málaga wine. Don't miss the fabulous daily Mercado Atarazanas (p167).

La Recova ARTS & CRAFTS
(www.larecova.es; Pasaje Nuestra Señora de los Dolores de San Juan; ☺ 9.30am-1.30pm & 5-8pm Mon-Thu, 9.30am-8pm Fri, 10am-2pm Sat) Seek out this intriguing Aladdin's cave of an art, crafts and antique shop selling traditional *sevillana* tiles, handmade jewellery, antique irons, textiles and much more. It also has a small local bar tucked into the corner, handy for enjoying a beer between browsing.

Alfajar ARTS & CRAFTS
(www.alfajar.es; Calle Císter 3; ☺10am-2pm & 5-8pm Mon-Fri, to 2pm Sat) Perfect for handcrafted Andalucian ceramics produced by local artisans. You can find traditional designs and glazes, as well as more modern, arty and individualistic pieces.

Information

Hospital Carlos Haya (☑951 03 01 00; Avenida de Carlos Haya)

Municipal Tourist Office (☑951 92 60 20; www.malagaturismo.com; Plaza de la Marina; ☺9am-8pm Mar-Sep, to 6pm Oct-Feb) Also operates information kiosks at the Alcazaba entrance (Calle Alcazabilla), at the main train station (Explanada de la Estación), on Plaza de la Merced and on the eastern beaches (El Palo and La Malagueta).

Regional Tourist Office (Plaza de la Constitución 7; ☺9.30am-7.30pm Mon-Fri, 10am-7pm Sat, 10am-2pm Sun) Located in a noble 18th-century former Jesuit college with year-round art exhibitions, this small tourist office carries information on all of Málaga province.

Getting There & Away

AIR
Málaga's **airport** (AGP; ☑952 04 88 38; www.aena.es), the main international gateway to Andalucía, is 9km southwest of the city centre. It is a major hub in southern Spain, serving top global carriers as well as budget airlines.

BUS
The **bus station** (☑952 35 00 61; www.estabus.emtsam.es; Paseo de los Tilos) is 1km southwest of the city centre and has links to all major cities in Spain. The main bus lines are **Alsa** (☑952 34 17 38; www.alsa.es) and **Portillo** (☑91 272 28 32; www.avanzabus.com).

Buses to the Costa del Sol (east and west) also usually stop at the more central Muelle Heredia bus stop. Destinations include the following; note that the prices listed are the minimum quoted for the route.

TO	COST	DURATION	FREQUENCY
Almería	€19	4¾hr	8 daily
Cádiz	€27	4hr	3 daily
Córdoba	€12	3-4hr	4 daily
Granada	€12	2hr	18 daily
Jaén	€20	3¼hr	4 daily
Madrid airport	€45	10hr	5 daily
Seville	€19	2¾hr	6 daily

TRAIN
Málaga is the southern terminus of the Madrid–Málaga high-speed-train line.

Málaga María Zambrano Train Station (☑902 43 23 43; www.renfe.com; Explanada de la Estación; ☺5am-12.45am) is near the bus station, 15 minutes' walk from the city centre. Destinations include Córdoba (€27.50, one hour, 18 daily), Seville (€24, 2¾ hours, 11 daily) and Madrid (€80, 2½ hours, 17 daily). Note that for Córdoba and Seville the daily schedule includes fast AVE trains at roughly double the cost.

Getting Around

TO/FROM THE AIRPORT
Bus
Bus Line A to the city centre (€3, 20 minutes) leaves from outside the arrivals hall every 20 minutes, from 7am to midnight. The bus to the airport leaves from the eastern end of Paseo del Parque, and from outside the bus and train stations, about every half-hour from 6.30am to 11.30pm.

Car & Motorcycle
Numerous local and international car-hire agencies have desks at the airport.

Taxi

Taxis from the airport to the city centre cost between €20 and €25.

Train

Trains run every 20 minutes from 6.50am to 11.54pm to María Zambrano station, and Málaga-Centro station beside the Río Guadalmedina. Departures from the city to the airport are every 20 minutes from 5.30am to 11.30pm.

BUS

Useful buses around town (€1.35 for all trips around the centre) include bus 16 to the Museo Ruso de Málaga (p173), bus 34 to El Pedregalejo and El Palo, and bus 35 to Castillo de Gibralfaro, all departing from points on Paseo del Parque.

CAR & MOTORCYCLE

There are several well-signposted underground car parks in town. The most convenient are on Avenida de Andalucía, Plaza de la Marina and Plaza de la Merced.

TAXI

Taxi fares are typically around €6 per 2km to 3km. Fares within the city centre, including to the train and bus stations and Castillo de Gibralfaro, are around €8.

TRAIN

Renfe *cercanías* trains (www.renfe.com) run from central Málaga to Fuengirola (€3.60), via the train station (€1.80), airport (€1.80) and Torremolinos (€2.05). They run every 20 minutes from 5.30am to 11.30pm.

COSTA DEL SOL

Regularly derided but perennially popular, Spain's famous 'sun coast' is a chameleonic agglomeration of end-to-end resort towns that were once (hard to believe) fishing villages. Development in the last 60 years has been far-reaching and not always subtle. Torremolinos is a popular gay resort, Benalmádena plugs theme parks and aquariums, Fuengirola draws families and water-sport lovers, Mijas poses as one of Andaucía's authentic white villages of yore and Marbella is loudly rich, while Estepona maintains a semblance of its former Spanish self.

Torremolinos & Benalmádena

POP 136,000

Once a small coastal village dotted with *torres* (towers) and *molinos* (watermills), 'Terrible Torre' became a byword for tacky package holidays in the 1970s, when it wel-comed tourism on an industrial scale and morphed into a magnet for lager-swilling Brits whose command of Spanish rarely got beyond '*dos cervezas, por favor*'. But Torre has grown up and widened its reach. These days the town attracts a far wider cross-section of people, including trendy clubbers, beach-loving families, gay visitors and, yes, even some Spanish tourists. Waiting for them is an insomniac nightlife, 7km of un-sullied sand and a huge array of hotels.

Benalmádena, Torre's western twin, is more of the same with a couple of added quirks: a large marina (Benalmádena; P) de-signed as a kind of homage to Gaudí and a giant Buddhist stupa.

⊙ Sights & Activities

The centre of Torremolinos revolves around the pedestrian shopping street of San Miguel, from where several flights of steps lead down to the beach at Playamar (there's also a lift). Benalmádena Pueblo has main-tained a smidgen of traditional charm, with cobbled streets, orange trees and simple, flower-festooned houses. There's a magnifi-cent view of the coast from the tiny church at the top of the village.

Casa de los Navajas   HISTORIC BUILDING
(Calle del Bajondillo, Torremolinos; ⊙11am-2pm & 6-8pm) **FREE** Impossible to miss in the concrete jungle of Torremolinos is this neo-Mudéjar beauty, a mini palace that for-merly belonged to a local sugar baron, Antó-nio Navajas. Originally constructed in 1925 in a style not dissimilar to that of Seville's Plaza de España, the house was renovated in 2014 and subsequently opened to the public. While there's no specific museum here, the terraced gardens, detailed architecture and sweeping views from the upstairs balconies are all impressive.

La Carihuela   BEACH
(Torremolinos) La Carihuela, Torremolinos' most western beach, stretching from a small rocky outcrop (La Punta) to Benalmádena, is a former fishing district and one of the few parts of town that hasn't suffered rampant overdevelopment. The beachside prome-nade is lined with low-rise shops, bars and restaurants, and is one of the most popular destinations for *malagueños* to enjoy fresh seafood at weekends.

Playamar   BEACH
(Torremolinos) This long stretch of beach in Torremolinos is lined with reliably good *chi-*

ringuitos (beach bars) and is also extremely family friendly, with playgrounds, and pedalos, sunbeds and parasols for hire. The wide promenade is popular with strollers and joggers, and in midsummer films are often screened.

Mariposario de Benalmádena
BUTTERFLY PARK

(www.mariposariodebenalmadena.com; Calle Muérdago, Benalmádena Pueblo; adult/child €10/ 8.50; ⊙10am-6.30pm; P ⊞) Next to the Buddhist stupa, in a quasi-Thai temple in Benalmádena (get off the train at Torremuelle station), this butterfly park is a delight. There are some 1500 fluttery creatures, including exotic subtropical species, moths and cocoons (in action), along with impressive plants and water features. Two iguanas, a wallaby and a giant tortoise are resident in the park.

Buddhist Stupa
MUSEUM, MONUMENT

(Benalmádena Pueblo; ⊙10am-2pm & 3.30-6.30pm Tue-Sat, 10am-7.30pm Sun; P) `FREE` The largest Buddhist stupa in Europe is in Benalmádena Pueblo. It rises up, majestically out of place, on the outskirts of the village, surrounded by new housing and with sweeping coastal views. The lofty interior is lined with exquisitely executed devotional paintings.

🛏 Sleeping

Hotel Zen
HOTEL €

(☑ 952 37 38 82; www.hotelzen.es; Calle de los Fresnos, Torremolinos; r incl breakfast €53; P ❄ 🛜 🏊) Located between the airport and Torremolinos, this hotel is ideal for travellers, as a free airport shuttle (also to the beach and town centre) is included in the price. There's nothing particularly exotic about the decor, which is beige-on-beige bland, aside from some Buddha motifs and an elephant statue by the pool, which is heated in winter.

★ Hostal Guadalupe
HOSTAL €€

(☑ 952 38 19 37; www.hostalguadalupe.com; Calle del Peligro 15, Torremolinos; s €57-63, d €66-87, 3-/4-/5-person apt €118/144/171; 🛜) At the bottom of the staircases that lead down to Torre's main beach is this nugget of old Spain that sits like a wonderful anachronism amid the concrete jungle. Enter through a delightful tiled tavern and ascend to plain but comfortable rooms, several with terraces overlooking the sea. There's also a couple of apartments with kitchen facilities for longer stays.

🍴 Eating & Drinking

There's no shortage of greasy English-breakfast cafes and fish-and-chip shops, but fear not, Spain-o-philes: Torremolinos has arguably the finest clutch of beachside *chiringuitos* in the nation.

★ El Gato Lounge
SEAFOOD €

(☑951 25 15 09; www.elgatolounge.com; Paseo Marítimo 1; mains €5-10; ⊙10am-late) Gato Lounge tries to be a little different from the other places on the beach, so you won't find the default sardines here. The menu leans towards international dishes with a bit of Asian flair: Thai fish cakes and Japanese carpaccio. The relaxing beach-facing interior has a luxuriant allure, and the cocktails and highly attentive staff mean most people linger.

La Alternativa
TAPAS €

(Avenida de la Constitución, Arroyo de la Miel; tapas from €2.50; ⊙1pm-2am Wed-Mon) Well worth seeking out, this large multiroomed place in an old-fashioned mall that has a year-round feria atmosphere has adorned its walls with flamenco posters, matador pics and the occasional Virgin Mary. It's often packed and the tapas are superb. You can also have larger *raciones* like oxtail and Galician-style octopus.

Yate El Cordobés
SEAFOOD €€

(☑952 38 49 56; Playamar, Torremolinos; mains €12-15; 🛗) One of the better beachside *chiringuitos*, this place attracts a loyal Spanish clientele. Specialities include a delicious *salmorejo* (thick, garlicky gazpacho), the always wonderful barbecued sardines, and *almejas* (clams) in a spicy, paprika-based sauce.

Casa Juan
SEAFOOD €€

(www.losmellizos.net; Calle San Ginés 20, La Carihuela; mains €14-22) The business dates back to the 1950s, but the fish is fresh daily at this, La Carihuela's most famous seafood restaurant, attracting shoals of *malagueños* on Sundays. It's been expanded into four dining spaces, so you can't go wrong provided you order carefully – some fish is sold by weight, so the bill can add up fast.

Cafe Goyesca
CAFE

(Calle San Miguel 40, Torremolinos; ⊙8am-10pm) Finding a piece of old Torremolinos is like looking for a needle in a haystack, but don't pass up a trip to the Goyesca, a traditional Spanish cafe half-hidden along the main shopping street. In operation since 1908, this place has seen a lot of changes and clearly has plenty of staying power. Must be that strong coffee and those delicate cakes.

ℹ Information

The main **tourist office** (☑ 951 95 43 79; https://turismotorremolinos.es; Plaza de Andalucía, Torremolinos; ⊘ 9.30am-6pm) is in the town centre. There are additional tourist kiosks at **Playa Bajondillo** (⊘10am-2pm) and **La Carihuela** (⊘10am-2pm).

ℹ Getting There & Away

BUS

Portillo (p173) runs services to Málaga (€2.50, 25 minutes, 14 daily), Marbella (€5.90, 1¼ hours, 24 daily) and Ronda (€13, 2½ hours, six daily).

TRAIN

Trains run on the Renfe *cercanías* line to Torremolinos (Avenida Palma de Mallorca 53) and Arroyo de la Miel-Benalmádena (Avenida de la Estación 3) every 20 minutes from Málaga (€2.05, 18 minutes) from 5.30am to 10.30pm, continuing on to the final stop, Fuengirola (€2.05, 22 minutes).

Fuengirola

POP 77,500

Fuengirola is a crowded beach town decorated with utilitarian apartment buildings, but, despite half a century of rampant development, it retains a few redeeming qualities. Check out the beach – all 7km of it – adorned with a 10th-century Moorish castle. The town also has a large foreign-resident population, many of whom arrived in the '60s.

🎆 Festivals & Events

Feria   CULTURAL

(⊘6-12 Oct) Arguably the best and biggest on the Costa del Sol, Fuengirola's feria includes a *romería* (religious pilgrimage) during which locals head to the *campo* (countryside) for flamenco, paella and *cerveza* (beer). A flamenco Mass is held in the main church on 6 October, and is followed by drinking and dancing in the street, with most women in traditional flamenco attire.

🍴 Eating

Cafe Fresco   INTERNATIONAL €

(Las Rampas; wraps €4.80, salads €7.50; ⊘10am-4pm Mon-Sat) This breezy restaurant is popular with the health conscious for its menu of homemade soups, salads and wraps (including curried chicken and Greek salad), best accompanied with an energising smoothie. There's a branch in Los Boliches.

★ Arte y Cocina   MEDITERRANEAN €€

(☑952 47 54 41; Calle Cervantes 15; mains €11-20; ⊘7.30-11.30pm Tue-Sun; 🌱) Italian-inflected food here is as fresh as the decor. Expect handmade pasta, and arty renditions of rabbit ravioli and prawn-and-courgette risotto.

La Cepa Playa   SEAFOOD €€

(☑ 692 623296; www.lacepaplaya.com; Paseo Marítimo; raciones €9-15; ⊘10.30am-7pm) In business since the late 1950s, when Fuengirola inhabited a different universe (both politically and economically), La Cepa is a *chiringuito* near the harbour serving a dizzying array of fish. Prawns, anchovies, cuttlefish, swordfish, clams, mussels, squid, sardines and hake are all on show – and there's more! The paella's pretty good, too.

🍷 Drinking & Nightlife

Plenty of tacky disco-pubs line the Paseo Marítimo (promenade), and a cluster of music bars and discos can be found opposite the port.

Café Andino   CAFE

(www.cafeandino.es; Avenida Matias Seánz de Tejada 1; ⊘7.30am-9pm Mon-Fri, 8am-8pm Sat, 9am-3pm Sun) This cosy little cafe roasts its own beans, serves strong, aromatic coffee and does a sideline in homemade cakes. It's right next to the bus station. There's a branch in Málaga.

Colón   BAR
(www.casacolon.es; Plaza de los Chinorros; ⊙6pm-late; 🛜) This is one of a clutch of similar traditional Spanish bars with sprawling terraces behind the main post office. The wines are good, and the weekend ambience has a big-city feel and seems authentically Spanish despite being just a couple of blocks from the banks of sunbeds on the sand.

ℹ Information

Tourist Office (📞 952 46 74 57; Paseo Jesús Santos Rein; ⊙ 9.30am-6pm Mon-Fri, 10am-2pm Sat & Sun; 🛜) One block northeast of the train station.

ℹ Getting There & Away

BUS
Portillo (p173) runs bus services to Málaga (€4.25, 50 minutes, 15 daily), Estepona (€6.70, 1¾ hours, 10 daily) and Marbella (€4.25, 30 minutes, four daily). Fuengirola's bus station is half a block from the train station.

CAR & MOTORCYCLE
A toll road (AP7) connects Fuengirola with Estepona (€14), providing a (costly) alternative to the hazardous N340 coast road.

TRAIN
Trains (Avenida Jesús Santos Rein) on the Renfe *cercanías* line run every 20 minutes to Málaga (€3.60, 45 minutes) from 6.20am to 12.40am, with stops including the airport and Torremolinos.

Mijas

POP 77,750 / ELEV 428M

The story of Mijas encapsulates the story of the Costa del Sol. Originally a humble village, it's now the richest town in the province. Since finding favour with discerning bohemian artists and writers in the 1950s and '60s, Mijas has sprawled across the surrounding hills and down to the coast, yet it's managed to retain the throwback charm of the original *pueblo* (village).

Mijas has a foreign population of at least 40% and the municipality includes Mijas Costa and La Cala de Mijas, both located on the coast southwest of Fuengirola.

◎ Sights & Activities

There are numerous trails leading out from Mijas. Call at the tourist office (p178) for maps. The fit can make for **Pico Mijas** (1151m) on a well-marked route. It's five hours return and a bit of a grunt.

Virgen de la Peña   HISTORIC SITE
(Avenida Virgen de la Peña) If you walk past the *ayuntamiento* (town hall), you will reach this gorgeous grotto where the Virgin is said to have appeared to two children who were led here by a dove in 1586. Within the cliff-top cave is a flower-adorned altar in front of an image of the Virgin, plus some religious chalices and pennants in glass cases. It's a poignant spot despite the barrage of visitors.

Centro de Arte Contemporáneo de Mijas   MUSEUM
(CAC; www.cacmijas.info; Calle Málaga 28; adult/child €3/free; ⊙10am-6pm Tue-Sun) This art museum houses an extraordinary exhibition of Picasso ceramics (the second-largest collection in the world), plus some exquisite Dalí bronze figurines, glassware and bas-reliefs. There are also temporary exhibitions. Note that, despite the name, this museum is not affiliated with Málaga's CAC museum.

Coastal Footpath   WALKING
(Playa La Luna, La Cala de Mijas, Mijas Costa; 🚹🚺) Enjoy a coastal stroll along a wooden promenade stretching 6km from La Cala de Mijas to Calahonda. The meandering walkway passes several beachside *chiringuitos*, coves and rocky headlands. The path is in Mijas Costa, 20km southwest of the hilltop town of Mijas.

🛏 Sleeping

Casa Tejón   APARTMENT €
(📞661 669469; www.casatejon.com; Calle Málaga 15; 2-person apt per day/week €45/300) The small apartments here are cosily kitted out with a happy mishmash of furniture and textiles, and set around a small courtyard decorated with pots of scarlet geraniums. It's bang in the centre of the village, and the owners run a handy bar and restaurant next door.

★TRH Mijas   HOTEL €€
(📞952 48 58 00; www.trhhoteles.com; Plaza de la Constitución; s/d €65/85; 🅿❄🐾) The spectacularly sited TRH offers possibly the best views on the Costa del Sol from its long terrace bar, where the evocative decor recalls the art-deco era with a bit of old empire thrown in. Then there are the orange-tree patio, on-site spa, lovely outdoor pool, head-turning paintings and vintage motorbikes on display in the lobby.

🍴 Eating

Tomillo Limón   TAPAS €
(📞951 43 72 98; Avenida Virgen de la Peña 11; tapas €3.50-5; ⊙noon-5pm & 7pm-midnight Tue-Sun, noon-5pm Sun) Great for a glass of wine and a

tapa or three, the 'Thyme and Lemon' is one of the better options in Mijas' array of mainly tourist-oriented eating stops. It's modern with a country-kitchen-meets-hip-bistro feel, and everything from the prawns *pil-pil* to the mini-burgers is presented creatively on dishes, newspaper, tins or slates.

Aroma
INTERNATIONAL €€

(www.aromacafeandsecretgarden.com; Calle San Sebastián 8; mains €8-16; ☉noon-1am; 🐾) The house dates to 1872, but the real charmer (aside from the Canadian owner) here is the 'secret garden' out the back: a divine dining space under mature orange, fig and olive trees with a well that dates from Moorish times. An Argentine barbecue is served nightly (weather permitting), while other dishes include traditional tapas, crêpes, pasta and pizza.

Lew Hoad
SPANISH €€

(☑952 46 76 73; www.lew-hoad.com; Carretera de Mijas, Km 3.5; mains €11-18; ☉1-5pm & 7.30-11pm; 🅿️🐾) Founded in 1964 by Wimbledon champion Lew Hoad, this elegant restaurant is surrounded by mature gardens, plus tennis and *padel* courts (available for hourly rent). The cuisine befits the setting, with classic dishes such as *zarzuela* (seafood stew) and oxtail, plus lighter snacks for those hoping to play a few sets rather than sink into a siesta.

ℹ️ Information

Mijas Tourist Office (☑958 58 90 34; www.mijas.es; Plaza Virgen de la Peña; ☉9am-8pm Mon-Fri, 10am-3pm Sat) Helpful tourist office with a free map-dispensing machine outside.

ℹ️ Getting There & Away

The quickest way to get to Mijas is the half-hourly M122 bus from Fuengirola bus station (€1.55, 15 minutes). There are four daily Portillo (p173) buses to/from Málaga (€2.30, one hour).

Marbella

POP 140,750

The Costa del Sol's bastion of bling is, like most towns along this stretch of coast, a two-sided coin. Standing centre stage in the tourist showroom is the 'Golden Mile', a conspicuously extravagant collection of star-studded clubs, shiny restaurants and expensive hotels stretching as far as Puerto Banús. But Marbella has other, less ostentatious attractions. Its natural setting is magnificent, sheltered by the beautiful Sierra Blanca mountains, while its surprisingly attractive

casco antiguo (old town) is replete with narrow lanes and well-tended flower boxes.

Long before Marbella started luring golfers, zillionaires and retired Latin American dictators it was home to Phoenicians, Visigoths, Romans and Moors. One of the joys of a visit to the modern city is trying to root out their legacy.

◎ Sights & Activities

Marbella's tightly packed old town is chocolate-box perfect, with pristine white houses, narrow, mostly traffic-free streets and geranium-adorned balconies. You can easily spend an enjoyable morning or evening exploring the cafes, restaurants, bars, designer boutiques, and antique and craft shops.

Plaza de los Naranjos
SQUARE

At the heart of Marbella's *casco antiguo* is the extremely pretty Plaza de los Naranjos, dating back to 1485, with tropical plants, palms, orange trees and, inevitably, overpriced bars.

Museo Ralli
MUSEUM

(www.museoralli.cl; Urbanización Coral Beach; ☉10am-3pm Tue-Sat) FREE This superb private art museum exhibits paintings by primarily Latin American and European artists in bright, well-lit galleries. Part of a nonprofit foundation with four other museums (in Chile, Uruguay and Israel), it has exhibits including sculptures by Henry Moore and Salvador Dalí, vibrant contemporary paintings by Argentinian surrealist Alicia Carletti and Cuban Wilfredo Lam, plus works by Joan Miró, Marc Chagall and Giorgio de Chirico.

The museum is 6km west of central Marbella near Puerto Banús.

Aventura Amazonia
ADVENTURE SPORTS

(☑952 83 55 05; www.aventura-amazonia.com; Avenida Valeriano Rodriguez 1; adult/child €24/20; ☉10am-6pm Tue-Fri, to 7pm Sat & Sun; 🐾) Twenty zip lines are located over six adventure circuits, the longest measuring 240m. Tots are catered to with an adventure playground, and there's even a crèche so that parents who want a quick escape can whiz through the trees.

🛏️ Sleeping

Hostal El Gallo
HOTEL €

(☑952 82 79 98; www.hostalelgallo.com; Calle Lobatas 44; r from €55; 🐾) In expensive Marbella, El Gallo – a traditional Spanish bar with a few rooms upstairs – is what you might call a rough in the diamond. Run by a friendly family, it inhabits a narrow whitewashed street replete with flower boxes and throwback charm, and has all you need for a comfortable but economical stay.

Hotel San Cristóbal
HOTEL €€

(📞952 86 20 44; www.hotelsancristobal.com; Avenida Ramón y Cajal 3; s/d incl breakfast €60/85; 🛜) Not the most 'Marbella' (ie flashy) of Marbella's hotels, the well-located San Cristóbal dates back to the 1960s. However, regular revamps have kept the place looking solidly contemporary: rooms sport tasteful pale-grey and cream decor and smart navy fabrics. Most rooms have balconies.

★Claude
BOUTIQUE HOTEL €€€

(📞952 90 08 40; www.hotelclaudemarbella.com; Calle San Francisco 5; d/ste €265/330; ❄🛜) The former summer home of Napoleon III's wife has updated its regal decor to create a hotel fit for a 21st-century empress. Situated in the quieter upper part of town, the Claude's arched courtyards and shapely pillars successfully marry contemporary flourishes with the mansion's original architecture, while claw-foot bath tubs and crystal chandeliers add to the classic historical feel. With only seven rooms and plenty of exquisite common areas, the Claude also offers great personalised service and attention to detail.

🍴 Eating

Marbella has a veritable Milky Way of restaurants that'd take aeons to sample in its entirety. Restaurants in the historic centre tend to be (over) priced for tourists; an exception is narrow Calle San Lázaro near the Plaza de los Naranjos, which is home to several excellent tapas bars generally frequented by locals.

Boulangerie TradiPan
BAKERY, CAFE €

(📞687 241233; Avenida Puerta del Mar 13; pastries €2-4; ⊙9am-4pm Thu-Tue) Marbella is replete with restaurants of all shapes and sizes, but if you just want a quick fix of something sweet, head to this newcomer bakery just off Avenida del Mar. It sells divine French-style pastries and satisfyingly strong coffee.

El Estrecho
TAPAS €

(Calle San Lázaro; tapas €2.50-3.50; ⊙noon-midnight) More like a pre-Franco-era dive in Almería than an eating joint in 21st-century Marbella, El Estrecho is a place where sitting down is a luxury and the serviettes are bits of paper the size of postage stamps. But the traditional tapas here are as intense as the atmosphere, from *tortilla* (Spanish ome-

lette) to *salmorejo* (Córdoba-style thick gazpacho) to seafood salad.

Lobito del Mar
SEAFOOD €€

(📞951 55 45 54; www.grupodanigarcia.com; Bulevar Príncipe Alfonso de Hohenlohe 178; mains €12-24; ⊙1-4pm & 7.30-11.30pm) *Chiringuito* restaurants are usually on the beach, but if you're a well-known chef called Dani Garcia with several Michelin stars to your name you can break the rules a little and open one on a main road a few blocks away. The sleek bistro-style interior features a wraparound deli counter displaying yesterday's catch nestled on ice.

Garum
INTERNATIONAL €€

(📞952 85 88 58; www.garummarbella.com; Paseo Marítimo; mains €9-18; ⊙11am-11.30pm; 🛜) Finnish owned and set in a dreamy location right on the 'Golden Mile' across from the beach, Garum has a menu that'll especially please those seeking a little gourmet variety. Expect dishes ranging from smoked-cheese soup to Moroccan chicken samosas and red-lentil felafel.

★Farm
SPANISH €€€

(📞952 82 25 57; www.thefarm-marbella.com; Plaza Altamirano 2; 3-course set menus €24-32; ⊙noon-11pm; 🌿♿) ✿ First, it's not a farm but rather an exceptionally pretty restaurant in Marbella's old town consisting of a patio, a terrace and a dining room furnished with modern 'chill-out' flourishes. The food's all farm fresh and there's a brilliant selection of set menus showcasing organic ingredients, including vegetarian and kids' options. Cheap? Not particularly (this is Marbella). Worth it? Absolutely.

Bonus: there are flamenco shows for diners most Tuesdays, Thursdays and Saturdays at 8pm and 10pm.

🍷 Drinking & Nightlife

For the most spirited bars and nightlife, head to Puerto Banús, 7km west of Marbella. In town, the best area is around the small Puerto Deportivo. There are also some beach clubs open only in summer.

Buddha
CLUB

(www.buddhamarbella.net; Avenida del Mar; ⊙7pm-late) As Buddhist statues overlook the heathens on the dance floor, the DJ spins everything from funk and acid jazz to hip hop and rock. The interior is suitably posh: all plush fabrics, moody lighting and comfortable sofas. There are regular theme nights.

MÁLAGA PROVINCE MARBELLA

Tibu
CLUB

(www.tibubanus.com; Plaza Antonio Banderas, Puerto Banús; ⏱11pm-7am) A spirited, sexy nightclub unsubtly advertising itself over the main plaza. There are dancers, acrobats, guest DJs and predictably costly cocktails.

Shopping

Déjà Vu
VINTAGE

(☑952 82 55 21; Calle Pedraza 8; ⏱11.30am-3pm & 5-8.30pm Mon-Fri, noon-3pm Sat) This is the place for designer vintage fashion from 1960s Chanel suits to classic Yves Saint Laurent three-piece suits. Also sells accessories, jewellery and some truly fabulous hats.

Information

Tourist Office (www.marbellaexclusive.com; Plaza de los Naranjos; ⏱9am-8pm Mon-Fri, 10am-2pm Sat) Has plenty of leaflets and a good town map. There are other tourist offices on the Paseo Marítimo and in Puerto Banús.

Getting There & Away

BUS

The **bus station** (☑952 82 34 09; Avenida del Trapiche) is 1.5km north of the old town just off the A7 *autovía*. Portillo (p173) runs buses to Fuengirola (€4.25, 30 minutes, four daily), Estepona (€4.30, one hour, hourly), Málaga (€7.25, 45 minutes, half-hourly) and Ronda (€7.50, 1½ hours, nine daily).

CAR & MOTORCYCLE

Marbella's streets are clogged with traffic and street parking is notoriously difficult to find. The most central underground car park is on Avenida del Mar (€2.20 per hour).

Estepona

POP 66,500

Estepona was one of the first resorts to attract foreign residents and tourists almost 50 years ago and, despite the surrounding development, the centre of the town still has a cosy, old-fashioned feel. There's good reason for that: Estepona's roots date back to the 4th century. Centuries later, during the Moorish era, the town was an important and prosperous centre due to its strategic proximity to the Strait of Gibraltar.

Estepona is steadily extending its promenade to Marbella; at its heart is the pleasant Playa de la Rada beach. The Puerto Deportivo is the focal point of the town's nightlife, especially at weekends, and is also excellent for water sports.

Sights

Orchidarium
GARDENS

(www.orchidariumestepona.com; Calle Terraza 86; adult/child €3/1; ⏱10am-2pm & 5-10pm Tue-Sat, 10am-2pm Sun) FREE The relatively new orchidarium is housed in a unobtrusive modern building set off by a glass dome and surrounded by lush landscaping. There are 1500 species of orchid here, the largest collection in Europe, as well as 5000 subtropical plants, flowers and trees.

Museo Arqueológico
MUSEUM

(Plaza Blas Infante 1; ⏱8am-3pm Mon, to 8pm Tue-Fri, 10am-2pm & 4-8.30pm Sat) FREE A modest collection that testifies to Estepona's 4th-century roots, with many of the displayed pieces dug out of offshore shipwrecks, often by local divers and fisherfolk.

Activities

Escuela de Arte
Ecuestre Costa del Sol
HORSE RIDING

(☑952 80 80 77; www.escuela-ecuestre.com; El Padrón; 45min class €67; ⏱10am-2pm & 5-7pm; ⊞) This British Horse Society–approved riding school offers a range of classes and treks for all ages and levels of ability. It also puts on sporadic shows and has an on-site bar and restaurant. The facility is 6km east of central Estepona.

Selwo Aventura
WILDLIFE

(www.selwo.es; Carretera A7, Km 162.5; adult/child €25/17; ⏱10am-6pm) This popular safari park has more than 200 exotic animal species. You can tour the park by 4WD or on foot and enjoy various adventure activities. It's home to the only Asian elephant born in Spain, and there's even a lodge if you fancy an overnight stay in – erm – Africa.

Buceo Estepona
DIVING

(☑645 610374; www.buceoestepona.com; Puerto Deportivo; dive €25; ⏱10am-2.30pm & 4.30-8pm) A reputable diving outfit offering a wide range of options and courses, including diving trips to Tarifa, Gibraltar and Algeciras.

Sleeping

Hotel Boutique
Casa Veracruz
BOUTIQUE HOTEL €€

(☑951 46 64 70; www.hotelboutiquecasaveracruz.com; Calle Veracruz 22; d/ste €85/125; ☀☎) The 'boutique' label barely does this place justice. With its diminutive courtyard, trickling fountain, stately paintings and stylish antique furniture, it's like a little slice of historic Seville dispatched to the Costa del Sol – and all yours for a very economical sum. Extra touches include Nespresso machines, ample continental breakfasts, and complimentary tea, coffee and sweets available all day.

✗ Eating

Estepona has some good restaurants, particularly in the old town and port. Traditional places are usually the best bet: follow the aroma of fresh-off-the-boat fish and the sound of quick-fire Spanish.

La Escollera SEAFOOD €
(Puerto Pesquero; mains €8-11; ⊙1-4.30pm & 8-11.30pm Tue-Sat, 1-4.30pm Sun) Locals in the know arrive at this port-located eatery in shoals to dine on arguably the freshest and best seafood in town. The atmosphere is no-frills basic, with plastic tables and paper cloths. But when the fish tastes this good and the beer is this cold, who cares?

La Esquina del Arte TAPAS €
(Calle Villa; tapas €2-3; ⊙noon-midnight Mon-Sat; 🛜) This place may be right in the historic centre, but there's nothing old-fashioned about the creative tapas and *pintxos* (Basque tapas). Expect satisfying bites such as prawns wrapped in flaky pastry, pâté with fig jam or peppers stuffed with salt cod. Excellent wines by the glass.

Venta García EUROPEAN €€
(☑952 89 41 91; Carretera de Casares, Km 7; mains €12-18; ⊙noon-10pm Tue-Sat, to 5pm Sun; 🅿) 🖉 Venta Garcia specialises in superbly presented and conceived dishes using local produce, and the countryside views are similarly sublime. There's an emphasis on meat like venison (served with a red fruit sauce) and pork: the Montes de Málaga dish executes a local take on pork served with peppers, fried egg and chips. The word is out, though: reserve at weekends. It's on the road to Casares, around 7km from the centre of Estepona.

🍺 Drinking & Nightlife

The Puerto Deportivo is the best place to head for late-night bars. Beach clubs also swing into action in summer. Check flyers around town to see what's on.

★Siopa CAFE
(80 Calle Real; ⊙9am-late) Stamp-sized Irish-run bar-cafe on a pedestrian street near the historic centre specialising in bottled craft beers. You'll see no clichéd Gaelic-pub motifs here. Instead, you get a blackboard listing more than 40 craft beers and almost as many gins. Several of the beers come from local Estepona brewery Babel. It also serves the best coffee in town.

ℹ Information

Tourist Office (www.estepona.es; Plaza de las Flores; ⊙9am-8pm Mon-Fri, 10am-2pm Sat & Sun) Located on a historical square, this office has brochures and a decent map of town.

ℹ Getting There & Around

The **bus station** (Avenida Litoral) is 2km east of the town centre next to the Palacio de Exposiciones y Congresos. Portillo (p173) buses run over a dozen times a day to Marbella (€4.30, one hour) and Málaga (€9.90, two hours).

Estepona has several well-signposted car parks on Avenida España (per hour €1.50).

THE INTERIOR

Ronda

POP 34,400 / ELEV 744M

Built astride a huge gash in the mountains carved out by the Río Guadalevín, Ronda is a brawny town with a dramatic history littered with outlaws, bandits, guerrilla warriors and rebels. Its spectacular location atop El Tajo gorge and its status as the largest of Andalucía's white towns have made it hugely popular with tourists – particularly notable when you consider its relatively modest size. Modern bullfighting was practically invented here in the late 18th century, and the town's fame was spread further by its close association with American Europhiles Ernest Hemingway (a lover of bullfighting) and Orson Welles (whose ashes are buried in the town).

South of the gorge, Ronda's old town largely dates from Islamic times, when it was an important cultural centre filled with mosques and palaces. Further north, the grid-shaped 'new' town is perched atop steep cliffs, with parks and promenades looking regally over the surrounding mountains.

◉ Sights

La Ciudad, the historic old town on the southern side of El Tajo gorge, is an atmospheric area for a stroll, with its evocative, still-tangible history, Renaissance mansions and wealth of museums. The newer town, where you'll be deposited if you arrive by bus or train, harbours the emblematic bullring, the leafy Alameda del Tajo gardens and armies of visitors. Three bridges crossing the gorge connect the old town with the new.

PARQUE NATURAL SIERRA DE LAS NIEVES

Southeast of Ronda lies the virtually uninhabited Parque Natural Sierra de las Nieves, noted for its rare Spanish fir, the *pinsapo,* large caves, and fauna including some 1000 ibex and various species of eagle. The *nieve* (snow) after which the mountains are named usually falls between January and March. **El Burgo**, a remote but attractive village 10km north of Yunquera on the A366, makes a good base for visiting the east and northeast of the park. The spa town of **Tolox**, 35km southeast of El Burgo, is another good option.

The park is crossed by a network of trails. The most rewarding walk is an ascent of the highest peak in western Andalucía, **Torrecilla** (1918m). Start at the Área Recreativa Los Quejigales, which is 10km east by unpaved road from the A376 Ronda–San Pedro de Alcántara road. The turn-off, 12km from Ronda, is marked by signs. From Los Quejigales there's a steepish 470m ascent by the **Cañada de los Cuernos gully**, with its tranquil Spanish-fir woods, to the high pass of **Puerto de los Pilones**. After a fairly level section, the final steep 230m to the summit rewards you with marvellous views. The walk is five to six hours return, and is easy to moderate in difficulty.

There's a tourist office in **Yunquera** (☎ 663 346620; www.sierranieves.com; Calle del Pozo 17, Yunquera; ☺ 10.30am-2pm & 6-8pm Sat, 10.30am-2pm Sun) and other offices in Tolox and El Burgo. You should also be able to pick up some park information at the tourist office in Ronda (p187). Buses run by Autocares Sierra de las Nieves depart from Ronda's bus station (p187) bound for the villages of El Burgo (€3.40) and Yunquera (€3.40) up to three times a day. The journey takes 45 minutes to an hour.

Plaza de Toros
NOTABLE BUILDING

(Calle Virgen de la Paz; €7, incl audio guide €8.50; ☺10am-8pm) In existence for more than 200 years, the Plaza de Toros is one of Spain's oldest bullrings and the site of some of the most important events in bullfighting history. A visit is a way of learning about this deep-rooted Spanish tradition without actually attending a bullfight. The on-site Museo Taurino is crammed with memorabilia such as blood-spattered costumes worn by 1990s star Jesulín de Ubrique. It also includes artwork by Picasso and photos of famous fans such as Orson Welles and Ernest Hemingway.

Built by Martín Aldehuela, the bullring is admired for its soft sandstone hues and galleried arches. At 66m in diameter, it is also the largest and, therefore, most dangerous bullring in Spain, yet it only seats 5000 spectators – a tiny number compared with the huge 50,000-seat bullring in Mexico City. Behind the Plaza de Toros, spectacular cliff-top views open out from Paseo de Blas Infante and the nearby Alameda del Tajo park.

Puente Nuevo
BRIDGE

(New Bridge; €2; ☺10am-6pm Mon-Fri, to 3pm Sat & Sun) Straddling the dramatic gorge and the Río Guadalevín (Deep River) is Ronda's most recognisable sight, the towering Puente Nuevo, so named not because it's particularly new (building started in 1759) but because it's newer than the **Puente Viejo** (Old Bridge). It's best viewed from the Camino de los Molinos, which runs along the bottom of the gorge. The bridge separates the old and new towns.

Plaza de España
SQUARE

The town's main square was made famous by Ernest Hemingway in *For Whom the Bell Tolls.* Chapter 10 tells how, early in the civil war, the 'fascists' of a small town were rounded up in the *ayuntamiento* (town hall), clubbed, and made to walk the gauntlet between two lines of townspeople before being thrown off a cliff. The episode is based on events that took place here in the Plaza de España. What was the *ayuntamiento* is now Ronda's parador (p186).

Museo Lara
MUSEUM

(www.museolara.org; Calle de Armiñán 29; adult/child €4/2; ☺11am-8pm Jun-Oct, to 7pm Nov-May; 🖐) The museum is the private collection of Juan Antonio Lara Jurado, who has been a collector since the age of 10. Now in his 70s, he still lives above the museum, but his living space is set to shrink, as he wants to expand still further. You name it, it's here: priceless, historic collections of clocks, weapons, radios, gramophones, sewing machines, telephones, opera glasses, Spanish fans, scales, cameras and far, far more.

Iglesia de Santa María La Mayor
CHURCH

(Calle José M Holgado; adult/child €4.50/2; ☺10am-7pm Mon-Sat, 10am-12.30pm & 2-6pm Sun) The city's original mosque metamorphosed into this elegant church. Just inside the entrance is an arch covered with Arabic inscriptions that was part of the mosque's *mihrab* (prayer niche indicating the direction of Mecca). The church has been declared a national monument, and its interior is a riot of decorative styles and ornamentation. A huge central cedar choir stall divides the church into two sections: aristocrats to the front, everyone else at the back.

Museo de Ronda MUSEUM
(Palacio Mondragón, Plaza Mondragón; €3.50; ◷10am-7pm Mon-Fri, to 3pm Sat & Sun) The city museum has artefacts and information related to both Roman and Islamic funerary systems. Of even more interest to some will be the palatial setting. Built for Abomelic, ruler of Ronda in 1314, the palace has retained its fountains and internal Mudéjar courtyard, from where a horseshoe arch leads to a clifftop garden with splendid views.

Baños Árabes HISTORIC SITE
(Arab Baths; Hoyo San Miguel; €3.50, Mon free; ◷10am-7pm Mon-Fri, to 3pm Sat & Sun) Enjoy the pleasant walk here from the centre of town. Backing onto Ronda's river, these 13th- and 14th-century Arab baths are in good condition, with horseshoe arches, columns and clearly designated divisions between the hot and cold thermal areas. They're some of the best-preserved Arab baths in Andalucía. A short video and several explanatory boards help shed some light on their history.

Casa del Rey Moro GARDENS
(House of the Moorish King; Calle Santo Domingo 17; adult/child €5/3; ◷10am-7pm) Several landscaped terraces give access to La Mina, an Islamic stairway of more than 300 steps cut into the rock all the way down to the river at the bottom of the gorge. These steps enabled Ronda to maintain water supplies

when it was under attack. It was also the point where Christian troops forced entry in 1485. The steps are not well lit and are steep and wet in places. Take care.

Museo Joaquín Peinado GALLERY
(☑952 87 15 85; www.museojoaquinpeinado.com; Plaza del Gigante; €4; ◷10am-5pm Mon-Fri, to 3pm Sat) Native Ronda artist Joaquín Peinado was an amigo and contemporary of Picasso's, a fact reflected in his work, with its strong abstract lines, flirtations with cubism and seeming obsession with female nudes. It's all on show in a most typical Andalucian gallery: a historic building that's been fitted with a plush minimalist interior.

🏃 Activities

Spa-Hammam Aguas de Ronda HAMMAM
(☑654 221577; www.hammamaguasderonda.com; Hoyo San Miguel 12; baths €18, incl massage €23; ◷10am-10pm) Joining numerous other Andalucian cities, Ronda has recently opened its own Moorish-style hammam. Book a two-hour slot at 10am, noon, 4pm, 6pm or 8pm. Massages also available.

Hiking
Eight well-marked hikes, ranging in distance from 2.45km to 9.1km, leave from the city limits. If you only have time for one, try Los Molinos, which takes you down to the mouth of the gorge and offers classic views back up to the Puente Nuevo. A board outside the tourist office (p187) maps out the walks and you can ask for more information inside.

Climbing
The Serranía de Ronda has developed over half a dozen vie ferrate (fixed-protection climbing routes). The two most popular are on the cusp of the town. The Tajo de

MÁLAGA PROVINCE RONDA

RONDA'S FIGHTING ROMEROS

Ronda can claim to be the home of bullfighting – it proudly boasts the Real Maestranza de Ronda equestrian school, founded in 1572 for the Spanish aristocracy to learn to ride and fight. They did this by challenging bulls in an arena, and thus was born the first bullfight.

Legend has it that one of these fights went awry when a nobleman fell from his horse and risked being gored to death. Without hesitation, local hero Francisco Romero (1700–63) leapt into the ring and distracted the bull by waving his hat. By the next generation, Francisco's son, Juan, had added the *cuadrilla* (the matador's supporting team), consisting of two to three *banderilleros* (who work on foot) and two to three picadors (who work on horseback with pike poles). Juan's son Pedro Romero (1754–1839) invented the rules and graceful ballet-like movements of the modern bullfight, introducing the *muleta* (a variation on his grandfather's hat), a red cape used to attract the bull's attention.

In 1932 Ronda birthed one of Spain's greatest 20th-century bullfighters, the charismatic Antonio Ordóñez, who was immortalised by Hemingway in *The Dangerous Summer*.

Ronda

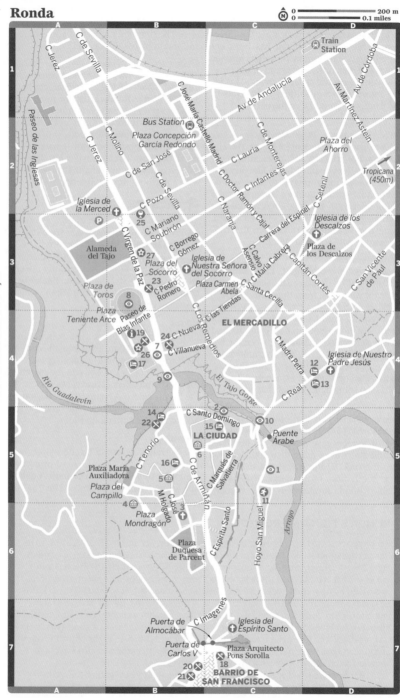

Ronda I, which climbs up the gorge for 56m, is rated difficult. The **Tajo de Ronda II**, which parallels it, is considered easy and ideal for beginners. Various companies, including **Al Andalus Activa** (☑626 364822; www.alandalusactiva.com), offer guided via ferrata climbs from around €30.

✨ Festivals & Events

Ronda Guitar Festival   MUSIC
(www.rondaguitarfestival.com;   ☺Jun) Introduced in 2016 and based at the relatively new Ronda Guitar House, this five-day affair celebrates that most emblematic of Spanish instruments. Concerts, conferences, wine tasting and a guitar maker's exhibition characterise proceedings, which encompass far more than flamenco.

🛌 Sleeping

Ronda has some of the most atmospheric, historically interesting and well-priced accommodation in Málaga province – in fact, in all of Spain. In the first half of May and from July to September, you must book ahead.

★Aire de Ronda   BOUTIQUE HOTEL €€
(☑952 16 12 74; www.airederonda.com; Calle Real 25; r from €125; [P][🛜]) Located in a particularly tranquil part of town, this hotel is one of those old-on-the-outside, supermodern-on-the-inside places that Spain does so well. Smart minimalist rooms come in punchy black and white, and fabulous bathrooms have shimmering silver- or gold-coloured mosaic tiles, walk-in showers and, in one romantic couples' room, a glass partition separating the shower from the bedroom.

★Hotel San Gabriel   HOTEL €€
(☑952 19 03 92; www.hotelsangabriel.com; Calle José M Holgado 19; s/d incl breakfast €72/130; [❄][🛜]) This heavyweight historic hotel is filled with antiques and faded photographs that offer an insight into Ronda's history – bullfighting, celebrities and all. Ferns hang down the huge mahogany staircase, and there's a billiard room, a cosy living room stacked with books, and a DVD-screening room with 10 velvet-covered seats rescued from Ronda's theatre.

★Enfrente Arte   HOTEL €€
(☑952 87 90 88; www.enfrentearte.com; Calle Real 40; r incl breakfast from €99; [❄][@][🏊]) If you hate off-the-rack, middle-of-the-road hotels, you'll love this place. The first hint of its personality greets you at the reception desk: the front of a sawn-in-half Spanish SEAT car. And that's before you've even got to the cosmically colourful rooms, which are as comfortable as they're quirky. Rates include all drinks, to which you help yourself, and a sumptuous buffet breakfast.

Hotel Ronda   BOUTIQUE HOTEL €€
(☑952 87 22 32; www.hotelronda.net; Ruedo Doña Elvira; s/d €53/70; [❄][🛜]) With its geranium-filled window boxes and whitewashed *pueblo* exterior, Hotel Ronda offers relatively simple (for Ronda) contemporary rooms painted in vivid colours and accentuated by punchy original abstracts. Several rooms overlook the beautiful Mina gardens across the way. It's a bargain for the price.

MÁLAGA PROVINCE RONDA

Ronda

Parador de Ronda
HOTEL €€€

(☑ 952 87 75 00; www.parador.es; Plaza de España; r €134-150; P ✳ @ ☎ ⊠) Acres of shining marble and deep-cushioned furniture give this modern *parador* a certain appeal, but really it's all about the views. The terrace is a wonderful place to drink in the sight of the gaping gorge with your coffee or wine, especially at night.

Hotel Montelirio
HOTEL €€€

(☑ 952 87 38 55; www.hotelmontelirio.com; Calle Tenorio 8; s/d €122/140; ✳ ☎ ⊠) Hugging El Tajo gorge, the Montelirio has magical views. The converted *palacio* has been sensitively refurbished and rooms are sumptuous. The lounge has retained its gorgeous Mudéjar ceiling and opens onto a terrace complete with plunge pool. The on-site Albacara restaurant is similarly excellent.

✗ Eating

Typical Ronda food is hearty mountain fare, with an emphasis on stews (called *cocido*, *estofado* or *cazuela*), *trucha* (trout), *rabo de toro* (oxtail stew) and game such as *conejo* (rabbit), *perdiz* (partridge) and *codorniz* (quail). Any Ronda insider will tell you that the food is better in the old town, particularly in the cluster of restaurants around Ruedo Alameda just outside the Puerta de Carlos V.

Bodega San Francisco
TAPAS €

(www.bodegasanfrancisco.com; Calle Ruedo Alameda; raciones €6-10; ⊙1.30-5pm & 8pm-1am Wed-Mon) With three dining rooms and tables spilling onto the narrow pedestrian street, this is one of Ronda's cheapest and most Spanish tapas bars, located in a little *barrio* just south of the old town gate. The menu is vast – including nine-plus salad choices – and contains standards like *revuelto de patatas* (scrambled eggs with potatoes and peppers). Fast-moving waiters are positively athletic.

Tragatá
TAPAS €

(☑ 952 87 72 09; www.tragata.com; Calle Nueva 4; tapas €2-3; ⊙1.15-3.45pm & 8-11pm; ☎) A small outpost for Ronda's new gourmet guru, Benito Gómez, who runs the nearby Bardal, Tragatá allows you to sample some of the same *cocina alta* (haute cuisine) at a fraction of the price. Get ready for an eruption of flavours in an interesting menu of small bites, such as cod sandwiches and (believe it or not) pig's ear.

Casa María
ANDALUCIAN €€

(☑ 951 08 36 63; Plaza Ruedo Alameda 27; menú €20; ⊙noon-3.30pm & 7.30-10.30pm Thu-Tue; ☑) Walk straight through Ronda's old town and out of the Carlos V gate and the crowds mysteriously melt away, leaving just you and a few locals propping up the bar at Casa María. Lap it up. Set menus include dishes featuring the likes of steak, scallops, salmon, cod and asparagus.

Tropicana
ANDALUCIAN €€

(☑ 952 87 89 85; cnr Avenida Málaga & Calle Acinipo; mains €12-20; ⊙12.30-3.30pm & 7.30-10pm Wed-Sun) A little off the trail in Ronda's new town, the Tropicana has nonetheless garnered a strong reputation for its certified-organic food, served in a small but handsome restaurant with the feel of a modern bistro.

★ Almocábar
ANDALUCIAN €€€

(☑ 952 87 59 77; Calle Ruedo Alameda 5; tapas €2, mains €15-30; ⊙12.30-4.30pm & 8-11pm Wed-Mon) Tapas here include *montaditos* (small pieces of bread) topped with delicacies like duck breast and chorizo. Mains are available in the elegant dining room, where meat dominates – rabbit, partridge, lamb and beef cooked on a hot stone at your table. There's a bodega upstairs, and wine tastings and dinner can be arranged for a minimum of eight people (approximately €50 per person).

Bardal
GASTRONOMY €€€

(☑ 951 48 98 28; Aparicio 1; tasting menu €60-77; ⊙1-3.30pm & 8-10.30pm Tue-Sat, 1-3.30pm Sun) The once famed Tragabuches restaurant has been replaced by the equally ambitious Bardal (with some staff crossover), where you'll need to reserve ahead in order to enjoy the astounding 15- to 20-course menu, a whistle-stop tour through oyster stew, yellow tomato gazpacho, frozen apple water, monkfish foie gras and other such uncommon dishes. Hold onto your hat – and fork.

Restaurante Pedro Romero
ANDALUCIAN €€€

(☑ 952 87 11 10; www.rpedroromero.com; Calle Virgen de la Paz 18; mains €18-25; ⊙noon-4.30pm & 7.30-11pm) Eating *rabo de toro* (oxtail) in a restaurant named after a famous bullfighter (p183) that sits opposite Spain's most legendary bullring and has bull's heads on the wall might not be everybody's idea of fine dining. But the Romero has a place. This, after all, is rugged Ronda. The vegetarian-unfriendly menu features partridge stew with dried fruit, rabbit confit, and pork in mustard sauce.

Restaurante Albacara
INTERNATIONAL €€€

(☑ 952 16 11 84; www.hotelmontelirio.com; Calle Tenorio 8; mains €18-25; ⊙12.30-4pm & 7.30-11pm) One of Ronda's best restaurants, the Albacara is in the old stables of the Montelirio palace and teeters on the edge of the gorge. It serves up delicious meals – try the beef stroganoff or the classic magret of duck. Be sure to check out the extensive wine list. Reserve ahead.

🍷 Drinking & Entertainment

Ronda's traditionally low-key flamenco scene has risen in the last few years with the opening of several distinctly different venues.

Entre Vinos   WINE BAR
(Calle Pozo; ⊙ 12.30-4.30pm & 8-11pm Tue-Sat, 8-11pm Mon; 🐾) A stylish small wine bar with exposed brick and wood panelling, frequented mainly by locals. A good place to taste local Ronda wines, as they feature heavily on the wine list. Creative tapas are also served.

Ronda Guitar House   CONCERT VENUE
(📋 951 91 68 43; www.rondaguitarhouse.com; Calle Mariano Soubirón 4; tickets €15; ⊙ concerts 7pm) A little different to the standard flamenco venues, this small performance space offers guitar recitals rather than full-blown shows, using talented musicians who cover a multitude of acoustic genres: classical, flamenco, jazz or a fusion of all three.

El Quinqué   LIVE PERFORMANCE
(📋 633 778181; www.elquinqueronda.com; Paseo de Blas Infante; tickets €8-15; ⊙ shows 2pm & 8.30pm Tue-Sun) For a traditional flamenco show employing a three-pronged attack of voice, guitar and dance, come to El Quinqué. Entry prices are very reasonable for the short 40-minute lunchtime shows. Evening shows are double the length. Food and drink are available at the on-site bar-restaurant.

ℹ️ Information

Tourist Office (www.turismoderonda.es; Paseo de Blas Infante; ⊙ 10am-6pm Mon-Fri, to 7pm Sat, to 2.30pm Sun) Helpful staff with a wealth of information on the town and region.

ℹ️ Getting There & Around

BICYCLE
You can rent a bike from **CenterBikes** (📋 952 87 78 14; www.cyclexronda.com; Calle Sevilla 50; bike hire half/full day €15/20; ⊙ 10am-2pm & 5-8.30pm Mon-Fri, 10am-2pm Sat).

BUS
From the town's **bus station** (Plaza Concepción García Redondo 2), **Comes** (📋 956 29 11 68; www.tgcomes.es) runs services to Arcos de la Frontera (€9.50, two hours, one to two daily), Jerez de la Frontera (€13, three hours, one to three daily) and Cádiz (€18, two hours, one to

three daily). **Los Amarillos** (📋 902 21 03 17; www.samar.es) goes to Seville via Algodonales and Grazalema. **Portillo** (📋 952 87 22 62; www.portillo.avanzabus.com) has four daily buses to Málaga (€12.25, 2¾ hours) and five to Marbella (€6.50, 1¼ hours).

CAR & MOTORCYCLE
There's a number of underground car parks, and some hotels have parking deals for guests. Parking charges are about €1.50 per hour, or €18 to €25 for 14 to 24 hours.

TRAIN
Ronda's **train station** (📋 952 87 16 73; Avenida de Andalucía) is on the line between Bobadilla and Algeciras. Trains run to Algeciras (€30, 1½ hours, five daily) via Gaucín and Jimena de la Frontera. This train ride is one of Spain's finest and worth taking just for the views. Other trains depart for Málaga (€10, two hours, one daily), Madrid (€69, four hours, three daily) and Granada (€20, three hours, three daily). For Seville, change at Bobadilla or Antequera-Santa Ana.

It's less than 1km from the train station to most accommodation. A taxi will cost around €7.

Serranía de Ronda

Curving around Ronda's south and southeast, the Serranía de Ronda may not be the highest or most dramatic mountain range in Andalucía, but it's certainly among the prettiest. Any of the roads through the range between Ronda and southern Cádiz province, Gibraltar or the Costa del Sol make a picturesque route. Cortes de la Frontera, overlooking the Guadiaro Valley, and Gaucín, looking across the Genal Valley to the Sierra Crestellina, are among the most beautiful spots.

To the west and southwest of Ronda stretch the wilder Sierra de Grazalema and Los Alcornocales natural parks. There are plenty of walking and cycling possibilities. The region has developed nearly a dozen vie ferrate (p39), making it one of the best areas in Spain for fixed-protection climbing. Ronda's tourist office can provide details of outdoor activities as well as maps.

Acinipo   ARCHAEOLOGICAL SITE
(⊙ 9am-3pm Tue-Sat, 8am-2pm Sun) FREE North of Ronda, off the A374, is the relatively undisturbed Roman site of Acinipo at Ronda la Vieja. Although ruined, with the exception of its partially reconstructed theatre, it's a wonderfully wild site with fantastic views of the surrounding countryside. You can happily while away a few hours wandering among the fallen stones and trying to guess the location of various baths and forums.

GAUCÍN

Gaucín (pop 1620) is a picturesque whitewashed village located on the edge of the Serranía de Ronda mountain range with views to Gibraltar and Morocco. The village was impoverished until the late 1970s, from which time it was gradually discovered by a group of footloose bohemians and artists, mainly from chilly northern-European climes. Since then Gaucín has continued to grow as an artists colony, now hosting the **Art Gaucín** (www.art gaucin.com; ⊙May) festival. Gaucín is also an excellent spot for birdwatchers; look skywards and you may spy vultures and booted eagles circling above. Gaucín is on the Ronda–Algeciras bus route operated by Comes (p187) that runs once a day in either direction. Alternatively, you can take a train from Ronda (€6.05, 45 minutes, three daily).

La Fructuosa (☑617 692784; www.lafructuosa.com; Calle Luís de Armiñán 67; s/d incl breakfast €80/90; ⊙Mar-Nov; ❋ 🖥) Ask to look at the photo album that documents the fascinating restoration of this exquisite small hotel. Original features have been retained as far as possible, and exposed stone, original beams, terracotta tiles and dark-wood antiques complete the high-end rustic look. The restaurant is housed in the former bodega and there's a glorious terrace with bucolic valley views.

Casa Antonia (Plaza del Santo Niño 10; mains €7-10; ⊙9am-11pm Tue-Sun) Set in Gaucín's square, with its sprawl of tables and views over the rooftops to the coast, the Antonia is a classic. It has barrel tables outside and offers staunchly local dishes, plus one or two nods towards the discerning foreign visitors who come this way, with goat's cheese and quail eggs also on the menu.

The site is 20km northwest of Ronda. There's no public transport. You can rent a bike from CenterBikes (p187) in Ronda.

⭐ **El Molino del Santo** HOTEL €€
(☑952 16 71 51; www.molinodelsanto.com; Estación de Benaoján, Benaoján; d/ste incl breakfast €132/217; ⊙Mar-Nov; 🅿❋🏊) Located near the well-signposted Benaoján train station, this British-owned hotel has a stunning setting next to a rushing stream; the main building is a former olive mill. Rooms are set amid pretty gardens and have private terraces or balconies. The restaurant is popular with locals and serves contemporary international cuisine.

El Chorro

Fifty kilometres northwest of Málaga, the Río Guadalhorce carves its way through the awesome **Garganta del Chorro** (El Chorro gorge). Also called the Desfiladero de los Gaitanes, the gorge is about 4km long, as much as 400m deep and sometimes just 10m wide. Its sheer walls, and other rock faces nearby, are a magnet for rock climbers, with hundreds of bolted climbs snaking their way up the limestone cliffs.

While Ardales (population 2700) is the main town in the area, most people use the hamlet of El Chorro, with its train station, hiking trails and decent hotel, as a base.

Lying 6km west is the serene **Embalse del Conde del Guadalhorce**, a huge reservoir that dominates the landscape and is noted for its carp fishing. This is also the starting point for the legendary and recently revitalised Caminito del Rey (p190) path. The whole area is protected in a natural park.

◉ Sights & Activities

Bobastro RUINS
(⊙guided tours 10am-2pm Fri-Sun) **FREE** Bobastro was the hilltop redoubt of 9th-century rebel Omar ibn Hafsun, who led a prolonged revolt against Córdoban rule. At one stage he controlled territory from Cartagena to the Strait of Gibraltar. It's thought that he converted from Islam to Christianity (thus becoming what was known as a Mozarab) before his death in 917 and was buried here. When Córdoba conquered Bobastro in 927, the poor chap's remains were taken for grisly posthumous crucifixion outside Córdoba's Mezquita. At the top of the hill, 2.5km further up the road and with unbelievable views, are faint traces of Ibn Hafsun's rectangular *alcázar* (Muslim-era fortress).

From El Chorro village, follow the road up the far (western) side of the valley and after 3km take the signed Bobastro turnoff. Nearly 3km up here, an 'Iglesia Mozárabe' sign indicates a 500m path to the remains of a remarkable little Mozarabic church cut from the rock. You can hike 4km to Bobastro from

El Chorro village. Take the road downhill from the station, cross the dam and turn left after 400m at the GR7 trail signpost.

Climbing

Andalucia Aventura (www.andalucia-aventura. com) organises rock climbing and abseiling in El Chorro for various levels of skill, from a one-day taster (€55) to a four-day course (from €250 excluding accommodation). Its website has a calendar showing upcoming courses. Book online.

The new Via Ferrata de los Albercones (fixed-protection climbing route) can be found near the southern exit of the Caminito del Rey (p190). It's rated 'medium' difficulty and comes with a couple of Himalayan-style bridges and a short zip line. You can rent gear and ask about guided trips at Finca La Campana.

Hiking

The most thrilling hike in the area (and probably the whole of Spain) is the vertigo-inducing Caminito del Rey (p190).

A couple of easy circular hikes start from the Conde del Guadalhorce reservoir next to Bar-Restaurante El Kiosko (☑952 11 23 82; Parque de Ardales; mains €7.50-13; ☉8.30am-midnight), including the 4.2km Sendero del Guaitenejo, which offers the opportunity to branch off on a spur path leading up to a good viewpoint over the Chorro gorge.

The GR248 path south to the town of Álora (17.5km) passes through El Chorro and is clearly signposted from the train station.

🛏 Sleeping & Eating

Finca La Campana   HOSTEL, HOTEL €
(☑626 96 39 42; www.fincalacampana.com; camping per person €9, dm/d €14/34, 2-/3-/4-person

cottages €48/62/78; ℗ 🛈 ⚟) A 2km uphill hike from the train station, but worth it, La Campana is a favourite for outdoor types, especially climbers. There are various sleeping configurations, including dorms, doubles, campsites and cottages, plus a pool, a kitchen and even a small climbing wall.

Complejo Turístico Rural
La Garganta   HOTEL €€
(☑952 49 50 00; www.lagarganta.com; r/incl half-board €105/175; ℗ ✳ @ 🛈 ⚟) It's amazing what you can make out of an old flour mill. La Garganta sits right next to El Chorro station, its former milling installations now hosting a pleasant rural hotel with pool, restaurant and comfortable rooms. A diamond in the rough.

Antequera

POP 41,000 / ELEV 577M

Known as the crossroads of Andalucía, Antequera sees plenty of travellers pass through but few lingering visitors. But those who choose not to stop are missing out. The town's foundations are substantial: two Bronze Age burial mounds guard its northern approach and Moorish fables haunt its grand Alcazaba. The undoubted highlight here, though, is the opulent Spanish baroque style that gives the town its character and that the civic authorities have worked hard to restore and maintain. There's also an astonishing number of churches – more than 30, many with wonderfully ornate interiors. It's little wonder that Antequera is often referred to as the 'Florence of Andalucía'.

MÁLAGA PROVINCE ANTEQUERA

OFF THE BEATEN TRACK

CUEVA DE LA PILETA

Twenty kilometres southwest of Ronda la Vieja are some of Andalucía's most ancient and fascinating caves, Cueva de la Pileta (☑952 16 73 43; www.cuevadelapileta.org; Benaoján; adult/child €8/5; ☉tours 10.30am, 11.30am, 1pm, 4.30pm & 6pm Mon-Fri, 10am, 11am, noon, 1pm, 4pm & 5pm Sat & Sun; 🅿). Torchlit guided tours into the dark belly of the cave system reveal Stone Age paintings of horses, goats and fish from 20,000 to 25,000 years ago. Beautiful stalactites and stalagmites add to the effect. The tours are given by members of the Bullón family, who discovered the paintings in 1905 and who speak some English.

Benaoján village is the nearest you can get to the Cueva de la Pileta by public transport. The caves are 4km south of the village, about 250m off the Benaoján–Cortes de la Frontera road; you'll need your own transport from the village, or you can walk. The turn-off is signposted. Benaoján is served by two Los Amarillos buses (from Monday to Friday) and up to four daily trains to/from Ronda. Walking trails link Benaoján with Ronda and villages in the Guadiaro valley.

DON'T MISS

EL CAMINITO DEL REY

El Caminito del Rey (www.caminitodelrey.info; €10; ☺10am-5pm Tue-Sun Apr-Oct, to 3pm Tue-Sun Nov-Mar) is also called the King's Path – so named because Alfonso XIII walked along it when he opened the Guadalhorce hydroelectric dam in 1921 – and consists of a 2.9km boardwalk that hangs 100m above the Río Guadalhorce and snakes around the cliffs, affording breathtaking views at every turn. Required walks to/from the northern and southern access points make the total hiking distance 7.7km.

The *caminito* had fallen into severe disrepair by the late 1990s, and it became known as the most dangerous pathway in the world; it officially closed in 2000 (though some daredevils still attempted it). Following an extensive €5.5-million restoration, it reopened in March 2015 and is now safe and open to anyone with a reasonable head for heights.

The boardwalk is constructed with wooden slats; in some sections the old crumbling path can be spied just below. The walk can only be done in one direction (north–south), and it's highly advisable to book a timeslot online. Buses (€1.55, 20 minutes) leave on the half-hour from El Chorro train station to the starting point, where there's a couple of restaurants. From here you must walk 2.7km to the northern access point of the *caminito*, where you'll show your ticket and be given a mandatory helmet to wear. At the end of the *caminito* there's another 2.1km to walk from the southern access point back to El Chorro. Allow about four hours for the walk, as the views are made for savouring.

The most convenient public transport to the area is the train from Málaga, which leaves twice daily to El Chorro station (42 minutes, €4.85). If you're driving, you can park at either end and use the bus to make your connection.

◉ Sights

The substantial remains of the Alcazaba, a Muslim-built hilltop castle, dominate Antequera's historic quarter and are within easy (if uphill) reach of the town centre.

★ **Antequera**

Dolmens Site ARCHAEOLOGICAL SITE
(☺9am-6pm Tue-Sat, to 3pm Sun) FREE Antequera's two earth-covered burial mounds – the Dolmen de Menga and the Dolmen de Viera – were built out of megalithic stones by Bronze Age people around 2500 BC. When they were rediscovered in 1903, they were found to be harbouring the remains of several hundred bodies. Considered to be some of the finest Neolithic monuments in Europe, they were named a Unesco World Heritage site in 2016.

Prehistoric people of the Bronze Age transported dozens of huge slabs from the nearby hills to construct these burial chambers. The stone frames were covered with mounds of earth. The engineering implications for the time are astonishing. Menga, the larger, is 25m long, 4m high and composed of 32 slabs, the largest of which weighs 180 tonnes. In midsummer the sun rising behind the Peña de los Enamorados hill to the northeast shines directly into the chamber mouth. The dolmens are located 1km from the town centre in a small, wooded park beside the road

that leads northeast to the A45. Head down Calle Encarnación from the central Plaza de San Sebastián and follow the signs. A third chamber, the Dolmen del Romeral (Cerro Romeral; ☺9am-6pm Tue-Sat, to 3pm Sun) FREE, is 4km further out of town.

Alcazaba FORTRESS
(adult/child incl Colegiata de Santa María la Mayor €6/3; ☺10am-7pm Mon-Sat, 10.30am-3pm Sun) Favoured by the Granada emirs of Islamic times, Antequera's hilltop Moorish fortress has a fascinating history and covers a massive 62,000 sq metres. The main approach to the hilltop is from Plaza de San Sebastián, up the stepped Cuesta de San Judas and then through an impressive archway, the Arco de los Gigantes, built in 1585 and formerly bearing huge sculptures of Hercules. All that's left today are the Roman inscriptions on the stones. The admission price includes a multilingual audioguide, which sets the historical scene as you meander along tidy pathways, flanked by shrubs and some archaeological remains of a Gothic church and Roman dwellings from the 6th century AD. Climb the 50 steps of the Torre del Homenaje for great views, especially towards the northeast and of the Peña de los Enamorados (Rock of the Lovers), about which there are many legends.

Admission to the Colegiata de Santa María la Mayor is included in the price.

Don't miss the ruins of **Roman baths** dating from the 3rd century AD, which can be viewed from Plaza Santa María, outside the church entrance. Although the site is a tad overgrown, you can clearly see the layout, aided by an explanatory plaque.

Colegiata de Santa María la Mayor   CHURCH
(Plaza Santa María; adult/child incl Alcazaba €6/3; ☺10am-7pm) Just below the Alcazaba is the large 16th-century Colegiata de Santa María la Mayor. This church-college played an important part in Andalucía's 16th-century humanist movement, and flaunts a beautiful Renaissance facade, lovely fluted stone columns inside and a Mudéjar *artesonado* (a ceiling of interlaced beams with decorative insertions). It also plays host to some excellent musical events and exhibitions.

Museo Conventual
de las Descalzas   MUSEUM
(Plaza de las Descalzas; compulsory guided tour €3.30; ☺10am-2pm & 5-7.30pm Tue-Sat, 9am-12.30pm Sun) This museum, in the 17th-century convent of the Carmelitas Descalzas (barefoot Carmelites), approximately 150m east of the town's Museo Municipal, displays highlights of Antequera's rich religious-art heritage. Outstanding works include a painting by Lucas Giordano of St Teresa of Ávila (the 16th-century founder of the Carmelitas Descalzas), a bust of the Dolorosa by Pedro de Mena and a *Virgen de Belén* sculpture by La Roldana.

Museo de la Ciudad de Antequera   MUSEUM
(Museo Municipal; Plaza del Coso Viejo; compulsory guided tour €3; ☺10am-2pm & 4.30-6.30pm Tue-Fri, 9.30am-2pm Sat, 4.30-6.30pm Sat, 9am-12.30pm Sun) An elegant and athletic 1.4m bronze statue of a boy, *Efebo,* is the pride and joy of the town-centre Museo Municipal. Discovered on a local farm in the 1950s, *Efebo* is possibly the finest example of Roman sculpture found in Spain. The museum also displays some pieces from a Roman villa in Antequera, where a superb group of mosaics was discovered in 1998. The collection includes a repository of religious items, containing so much silver that you can only visit by guided tour on the half-hour.

Iglesia del Carmen   CHURCH
(Plaza del Carmen; €2; ☺11am-1.30pm & 4.30-5.45pm Tue-Fri, 11am-2pm Sat & Sun) Only the most jaded would fail to be impressed by the Iglesia del Carmen and its marvellous 18th-century Churrigueresque *retablo* (altarpiece). Magnificently carved in red pine

by Antequera's own Antonio Primo, it's spangled with statues of angels by Diego Márquez y Vega, and saints, popes and bishops by José de Medina. While the main altar is unpainted, the rest of the interior is a dazzle of colour and design, painted to resemble traditional tilework.

Festivals & Events

Semana Santa   RELIGIOUS
(Holy Week; ☺Mar) One of the most traditional celebrations in Andalucía; items from the town's treasure trove are used in the religious processions.

Real Feria de Agosto   FAIR
(☺mid-Aug) Ccelebrates the harvest with bullfights, dancing and street parades.

Sleeping

Hotel Coso Viejo   HOTEL €
(☑952 70 50 45; www.hotelcosoviejo.es; Calle Encarnación 9; s/d incl breakfast €45/55; P❈☎) This converted 17th-century neoclassical palace is right in the heart of Antequera, opposite Plaza Coso Viejo and the town museum. The simply furnished rooms are set around a handsome patio with a fountain, and there's an excellent tapas bar and restaurant next door.

Parador de Antequera   HISTORIC HOTEL €€
(☑952 84 02 61; www.parador.es; Paseo García del Olmo; s/d incl breakfast €85-120; P❈☎☒) This *parador* is in a quiet area of parkland north of the bullring, near the bus station. It's comfortably furnished and has pleasant gardens with wonderful views, especially at sunset.

Eating

Antequera specialties include *porra antequerana* (a thick and delicious garlicky soup that's similar to gazpacho), *bienmesabe* (literally 'tastes good to me'; a sponge dessert) and *angelorum* (a dessert incorporating meringue, sponge and egg yolk).

Baraka   TAPAS €
(☑951 21 50 88; Plaza de las Descalzas; tapas €2-4; ☺8am-2am Wed-Sat & Mon, 10am-2am Sun) Sombreros off to the brave staff at Baraka, who cross a busy road, trays loaded, risking life and limb to serve punters sitting in a little park opposite. Like all good Antequera restaurants, Baraka doesn't stray far from excellent local nosh (*porra antequerana* calls loudly), although it does a nice sideline in *pintxos* (Basque tapas) and serves heavenly bread.

Santiago
BAKERY, CAFE €

(☎952 84 33 01; Calle Calzada 19; snacks €2-5; ⏰8am-midnight) This multifaceted place serves as bakery, cafe, bar and ice-cream shop all in one. It's particularly good for breakfast and popular with churros addicts, who can be found dipping the thin doughnuts in thick chocolate early in the morning. Decor is contemporary with a neo-industrial look. Service is fast and polite.

⭐ Arte de Cozina
ANDALUCIAN €€

(www.artedecozina.com; Calle Calzada 27-29; mains €14-17, tapas €2.50; ⏰1-11pm) It's hard not to notice the surrounding agricultural lands as you approach Antequera, and this fascinating little hotel-restaurant combo is where you get to taste what they produce. Slavishly true to traditional dishes, it plugs little-known Antequeran specialities such as gazpacho made with green asparagus or *porra* with oranges, plus meat dishes that include *lomo de orza* (preserved pork loin).

It also organises food theme nights with intriguing titles like 'food in the time of Cervantes'. The adjacent tapas bar serves unusual light bites such as snails in a spicy almond sauce or river crab with chilli and peppers. There are plenty of dessert choices, which is unusual in these parts.

Reina Restaurante
ANDALUCIAN €€

(☎952 70 30 31; Calle San Agustín 1; mains €14-18, menú €14; ⏰1-4pm & 8-11pm Tue-Sun) Located in a pretty restaurant-flanked cul-de-sac off Calle Infante Don Fernando, this restaurant also runs a cooking school, La Espuela, so it knows what it's doing. The menu includes a fine selection of Antequeran specialities, such as chicken in almond sauce and partridge pâté, along with more daring dishes like strawberry gazpacho with goat's cheese.

ℹ️ Information

Municipal Tourist Office (☎952 70 25 05; www.antequera.es; Plaza de San Sebastián 7; ⏰9.30am-7pm Mon-Sat, 10am-2pm Sun) A helpful tourist office with information about the town and region.

ℹ️ Getting There & Around

BICYCLE

Bikes are a good way of getting around town or – if you're fit – up into the mountains of El Torcal . Rent bikes from **Ciclos 2000** (www.ciclos2000. com; Calle San José 6; ⏰10am-2pm & 5-9pm Sun-Fri, 10am-2pm Sat).

BUS

The **bus station** (Paseo García del Olmo) is 1km north of the centre. Alsa (p173) runs buses to Seville (€14, 2½ hours, five daily), Granada (€9, 1½ hours, five daily), Córdoba (€11, two hours 40 minutes, one daily), Almería (€23, six hours, one daily) and Málaga (€6, one hour, five daily).

CAR & MOTORCYCLE

A toll road (AP-46), running from Torremolinos to Las Padrizas (€5), is located around 21km southeast of Antequera. There's underground parking on Calle Diego Ponce north of Plaza de San Sebastián (per hour €1.50, 12 to 24 hours €18).

TAXI

Taxis (☎952 84 55 30) (€6 to €7 per 2km to 3km) wait halfway along Calle Infante Don Fernando, or you can call one.

TRAIN

Antequera has two train stations. **Antequera-Ciudad train station** (www.renfe.com; Avenida de la Estación) is 1.5km north of the town centre. At research time, bus transfers were being offered to Seville, Granada and Almería while work was being done on a new high-speed train line.

The **Antequera-Santa Ana train station**, 18km northwest of the town, has high-speed AVE trains to and from Málaga (€26, 30 minutes, 12 daily), Córdoba (€33, 30 minutes, 15 daily) and Madrid (€75, 2½ hours, 12 daily), as well as services to Granada and Seville via Córdoba.

A bus runs roughly three times a day from the Santa Ana station into Antequera (€5), or you can take a taxi (from €25).

Paraje Natural Torcal de Antequera

South of Antequera are the weird and wonderful rock formations of the Paraje Natural Torcal de Antequera. This 12-sq-km area of gnarled, serrated and pillared limestone formed as a sea bed 150 million years ago and now rises to 1336m (El Torcal). Not surprisingly, this other-worldly landscape fanned by fresh mountain breezes was declared a Unesco World Heritage site, along with Antequera's dolmens (p190), in 2016.

The park has an impressive **visitor centre** (☎952 24 33 24; www.torcaldeantequera.com; ⏰10am-7pm Apr-Oct, to 5pm Nov-Mar), which is the starting point for various hiking routes and has a *mirador* (lookout) nearby.

🏃 Activities

Hiking

There are three marked walking trails that you can do unguided. The 1.5km **Ruta Verde** (Green Route) and the 3km **Ruta**

Amarilla (Yellow Route) both start and end at the Centro de Visitantes and take in the full sweep of rocky surrealism. Be prepared for plenty of rock-hopping. The 3.7km **Ruta Naranja** (Orange Route) runs between the upper and lower car parks, tracking below the road. Gentler options are the miradors (lookouts) near the Centro de Visitantes and about 500m down the road.

Several guided hikes are organised on the more restricted routes. These last for approximately three hours and cover 3km; the cost is €10 per person. The park website (www.torcaldeantequera.com) prints a regularly updated itinerary. Book in advance, and wear shoes with good tread as the trails are rocky.

Climbing

The park contains Andalucía's oldest via ferrata, known as the **Camorro route**. Laid out in 1999, it actually consists of four separate vie ferrate: Escalenuela, Alto Antigua, Crestera and Techo. Various companies, including Andalucia Aventura (p189), offer guided climbs. Book in advance.

❶ Getting There & Away

There's no public transport to El Torcal. If you're travelling by car, leave central Antequera along Calle Picadero, which soon joins the Zalea road. After 1km or so you'll see signs on the left to Villanueva de la Concepción. Take this road and, after 12km (before entering Villanueva), turn right and head 3.75km uphill to the information centre.

By bike it's a tough uphill cycle, but a joy coming down, with killer views. Rent bikes from Ciclos 2000 in Antequera.

Laguna de Fuente de Piedra

About 25km northwest of Antequera, just off the A92 *autovía* (toll-free dual carriageway), is the Laguna de Fuente de Piedra. When it's not dried up by drought, this is Andalucía's biggest natural lake and one of Europe's two main breeding grounds for the greater flamingo (the other is in the Camargue region of southwestern France). After a wet winter as many as 20,000 pairs of flamingos breed at the lake.

The birds arrive in January or February, and the chicks hatch in April and May. The flamingos stay until about August, when the lake, which is rarely more than 1m deep, no longer contains enough water to support

them. They share the lake with thousands of other birds of some 170 species.

The small village of Fuente de Piedra sits at the northeastern corner of the lake and has a useful **visitor centre** (☑ 952 71 25 54; www.visitasfuentepiedra.es; ⏰ 10am-2pm & 5-7pm), where you can rent binoculars.

A couple of short trails lead out from the visitor centre to various lookouts and observatories. The longest trail is the 2.5km **Sendero de las Albinas**.

❶ Getting There & Away

Alsa (☑ 952 52 15 04; www.alsa.es) buses stop in the village of Fuente de Piedra, an easy 1.5km walk from the visitor centre. There are three daily buses to Seville (€12, 2¼ hours) and two to Málaga (€8, 1½ hours) via Antequera (€2.50, 30 minutes).

EAST OF MÁLAGA

The coast east of Málaga (the Costa del Sol Oriental) is less developed than its western counterpart. Málaga's sprawl extends through a series of unremarkable seaside towns before culminating in more attractive Nerja. This area's main redeeming feature is the rugged mountain region of La Axarquía, almost as beautiful as Granada's Las Alpujarras yet less known. The Parque Natural Sierras de Tejeda, Almijara y Alhama protects 407 sq km of these mountains.

La Axarquía

The Axarquía region is riven by deep valleys lined with terraces and irrigation channels that date to Islamic times – nearly all the villages dotted around the olive-, almond- and vine-planted hillsides were founded in this era. The wild inaccessible landscapes, especially around the Sierra de Tejeda, made it a stronghold of *bandoleros* who roamed the mountains without fear or favour. Nowadays, its chief attractions include fantastic scenery; pretty white villages; strong, sweet wine made from sun-dried grapes; and good walking in spring and autumn.

The 'capital' of La Axarquía, **Vélez Málaga**, 4km north of Torre del Mar, is a busy but unspectacular town, although its restored hilltop castle is worth a look. **Cómpeta** is the best base in La Axarquía.

Some of the most dramatic La Axarquía scenery is up around the highest villages of **Alfarnate** (925m) and **Alfarnatejo** (858m), with towering, rugged crags such as Tajo de Gomer and Tajo de Doña Ana rising to their south.

You can pick up information on La Axarquía at the tourist offices in Málaga (p173), Nerja (p199), Torre del Mar or Cómpeta (p196). Prospective walkers should ask for the leaflet on walks in the Parque Natural Sierras de Tejeda, Almijara y Alhama. Good maps for walkers are *Mapa topográfico de Sierra Tejeda* and *Mapa topográfico de Sierra Almijara* by Miguel Ángel Torres Delgado, both at 1:25,000. You can also follow the links at www.axarquia.es for walks in the region.

Comares

POP 1350

Comares sits like a snowdrift atop its lofty hill. The adventure really is in getting there: you see it for kilometre after kilometre, before a final twist in an endlessly winding road lands you below the hanging garden of its cliff. From a little car park you can climb steep, winding steps to the village. Look for ceramic footprints underfoot and simply follow them through a web of narrow, twisting lanes past the Iglesia de la Encarnación and eventually to the ruins of Comares' castle and a remarkable summit cemetery.

The village has a history of rebellion, having been a stronghold of Omar ibn Hafsun, but today there is a tangible sense of contented isolation, enjoyed by locals and many newcomers. Visitors are often of the adventurous variety. The village has established itself as a nexus for climbing and hiking excursions and has what is reputedly Andalucía's longest zip line (1/2 rides €15/20). Book rides through an activity company like Vive Aventura.

🏃 Activities

Comares has three vie ferrate, all located in close proximity to each other on the northern side of the village close to the zip line. The easiest is the Fuente Gorda, which takes about 45 minutes and involves 50m of ascent. Slightly more difficult are the Cueva de la Ventana, which includes a 25m-long zip line,

---

OFF THE BEATEN TRACK

ACEBUCHAL: A VILLAGE LOST & FOUND

Etched like a splash of white paint at the head of a steep-sided valley halfway between Cómpeta and Frigiliana, tiny Acebuchal is a one-time 'ghost village' that got a second chance.

Founded as a pit stop on an old mule trail between Granada and the coast in the 17th century, Acebuchal got into trouble during the civil war when it was suspected of harbouring Republican resistance fighters working against Franco's forces. When Franco took power in 1939, the resistance went underground, forming a guerrilla group called the Maquis that operated in mountainous areas like the Axarquía where it could find safe cover and an element of local support. Suspected of collaboration, Acebuchal was targeted in a government-led mopping-up campaign that resolved that the best way to root out Maquis opposition was to evacuate Acebuchal entirely and pack its 200 or so inhabitants off to Cómpeta, Frigiliana and beyond.

Cleared in 1948, the village quickly fell into ruin, a decline that appeared to be terminal. But when democracy returned to Spain in the 1980s, some of the old families, feeling homesick for their mountain nirvana, began planning a return. The dream became reality in 1998 when a former inhabitant named Antonio 'El Zumbo' came back with his family and rebuilt one of Acebuchal's derelict houses as a bar practically with his bare hands. Inspired by his example, more families followed. Electricity and water mains were connected to Acebuchal in 2003, and in 2005 the village celebrated its first Mass in 60 years in its refurbished chapel. By the 2010s discerning tourists had begun to trickle into the former ghost village, most of them on foot, as the settlement isn't on a paved road.

Today Acebuchal is a vibrant hub of rural Spanish life, with all 30-plus of its houses renovated (some as holiday rentals) and Antonio's bar (now run by his son) thriving once again as one of the best mountain pit stops in Andalucía.

The opening of the wonderful Bar-Restaurante El Acebuchal (☑661 214834; mains €8-12; ⊙10am-5pm) in 2005 was an important step in the rehabilitation of Acebuchal. It's now a favoured stop for walkers and lovers of rural tranquillity and plies some of the best food in Málaga province. It's worth hiking in for the homemade bread alone, not to mention the cakes.

and the **Puerta del Agua**, which has a couple of wire 'tightrope' bridges with hand supports. Guided climbs with correct equipment can be organised with **Vive Aventura** (☑697 218289; www.viveaventura.com).

The crags north of Comares have more than two dozen marked climbing routes, graded 6a+ to 8a+.

🛏️ Sleeping & Eating

Hotel Atalaya   HOTEL €
(☑952 50 92 08; Calle las Encinillas; s/d €25/45; P🖥️) Friendly, if simple, rural-style hotel on the southern approach to hilltop Comares. There's an on-site restaurant and sweeping views, and it's highly economical for what you get.

❶ Getting There & Away

Bus M-360 leaves Málaga bus station (p173) for Comares at 6pm and starts back at 7am the next morning (one way €3.20, 1½ hours). There's no service on Sunday.

Cómpeta

POP 3700

This instantly attractive village, with its panoramic views, steep, winding streets and central bar-lined plaza overlooking a 16th-century church, has long attracted a large, mixed, foreign population. This has contributed to an active cultural scene, and Cómpeta is home to one or two above-*pueblo*-average restaurants serving contemporary cuisine. The village also has a couple of charity shops (rare in Spain) and a big following among organised walking groups. Not surprisingly, Cómpeta is a good base for hiking and similar adrenalin-fuelled activities.

🏃 Activities

The Cómpeta region is walking heaven and has become increasingly popular in recent years with nature-seeking visitors (especially Brits), who come here on organised walking holidays. There's even a **walking festival** in September.

Free guided walking tours of the town set out every Saturday at 10.30am from the tourist office (p196). For more information on guided and self-guided walks in the area, check out www.walkspain.co.uk.

El Lucero   WALKING
An exhilarating long walk from Cómpeta is up the dramatically peaked El Lucero (1779m), from whose summit, on a clear day, you can see both Granada and Morocco. This is a demanding full-day return walk from Cómpeta, but it's possible to drive as far up as Puerto Blanquillo pass (1200m) via a slightly hairy mountain track from Canillas de Albaida. From Puerto Blanquillo a path climbs 200m to another pass, the Puerto de Cómpeta. One kilometre down from there, past a quarry, the summit path (1½ hours), marked by a signboard, diverges to the right across a stream bed. Total return walking time to the summit from Puerto Blanquillo is 4½ to five hours. The mountain is also sometimes known as Raspón de los Moriscos.

Salamandra   OUTDOORS
(☑952 55 34 93; www.malaga-aventura.es; Avenida de Sayalonga 13; potholing/kayaking/canyoning per person from €25/20/45; ☺10am-2pm & 5-7pm; 🚴) This is a one-stop centre that organises a wide range of activities, including guided hikes, potholing, canyoning and kayaking, plus themed tours, such as orchid trips in spring, mushroom picking and historical routes. The routes include the former merchants' pathway linking Cómpeta with Játar and covering some 20km (on foot).

Los Caballos del Mosquín   HORSE RIDING
(☑608 658108; www.horseriding-andalucia.com; Canillas de Albaida; half-day trek €70-80) Specialises in guided horse-riding treks in the mountains of La Axarquía ranging from one hour to three days (including full board and accommodation). Located up a steep road between Cómpeta and Canillas de Albaida.

✸ Festivals & Events

Noche del Vino   WINE
(Night of the Wine; ☺15 Aug) Cómpeta has some of the area's best local wine, and the popular Noche del Vino features a program of flamenco and *sevillano* music and dance in the central and pretty Plaza Almijara, plus limitless free wine.

🛏️ Sleeping

⭐**Finca El Cerrillo**   HOTEL €€
(☑952 03 04 44; www.hotelfinca.com; Canillas de Albaida; s/d €90/100; P🍴🖥️🏊) The kind of cathartic rural retreat that'll make you want to up sticks and come and live in Andalucía, British-run El Cerrillo inhabits an old olive-oil mill on the northern side of Canillas de Albaida (4km from Cómpeta) and attracts both groups and indie travellers.

Rooms are comfortable without sacrificing authenticity, there's a stately lounge, and you'll spend 10 minutes admiring the cool pool on its flowery terrace before you jump in. There's ample space around the rambling building to do yoga, paint, take in the view or just sun-lounge. Dinner is available most nights (and breakfast daily).

Hotel Balcón de Cómpeta HOTEL €€
(☑952 55 36 62; www.hotel-competa.com; Calle San Antonio 75; s/d incl breakfast €54/77; ※ 🕿 🐾) A great hotel for such a small town, the Balcón has a wide range of facilities, including tennis court, pool and decent on-site restaurant. It's located at the top of the village with panoramic views over the mountain foothills. Rooms are colour coordinated and up to date, with charcoal greys and raspberry pinks contrasting with cool pastels and whites. Friendly service, too.

🍴 Eating

**Taberna-Tetería
Hierbabuena** MOROCCAN, INTERNATIONAL €
(☑951 70 76 38; Avenida de la Constitución 35; mains €6-13; ☺9am-11pm Tue-Sun) Though it has its share of low-slung tables, shapely lampshades and silver teapots, the Hierbabuena isn't your average *tetería* (teahouse): it offers English breakfasts, 'curry nights' and mushy peas, as well as teas and tagines. The combination seems to satisfy the food urges of its largely expat clientele.

⭐El Pilón INTERNATIONAL €€
(☑951 55 35 12; www.restaurantelpilon.com; Calle Laberinto; mains €13-18; ☺7-11pm; 🖋🍴) This former carpenter's workshop is the village's most popular restaurant – and rightly so. Dishes are created using locally sourced ingredients whenever possible, and the eclectic options include tandoori chicken, swordfish with olive tapenade and some truly creative vegetarian dishes. There's a cocktail lounge with sweeping views, regular entertainment, and sticky toffee pudding for homesick Brits.

**Taberna-Restaurante
Casa Paco** ANDALUCIAN €€
(☑952 51 60 77; www.casapacotapas.es; Plaza Almijara 6; mains €12-23; ☺9am-11pm) One of three restaurants with alfresco seating under a cluster of umbrellas in the main square, Paco – the one nearest to the church – is the best of the trio, with strong coffee, traditional tapas, speedy wait staff and a good line in crêpes.

ℹ Information

Tourist Office (☑952 55 36 85; Avenida de la Constitución; ☺10am-3pm Mon-Sat, to 2pm Sun) Beside the bus stop at the foot of the village.

ℹ Getting There & Away

Loymer runs three daily buses from Málaga to Cómpeta (€4.50, 1½ hours), stopping in Torre del Mar. The buses stop next to the tourist office in Avenida de la Constitución.

Frigiliana

POP 3000

In the beauty pageant of Spanish villages, Frigiliana, 7km north of Nerja, has won plenty of awards – and no wonder. With its multicultural history, handsome, well-looked-after civic buildings and pretty, whitewashed houses kept impeccably clean by a proud populace, it's far from an ugly duckling.

But, like all beauty, the prettiness here comes with a price: you won't have the place to yourself. Coaches pull up daily and disgorge their cargo into the sinuous streets adorned with pots of blood-red geraniums.

Like most small Andalucian towns, Frigiliana is split into two parts: old and new. The steeply banked old town is scattered with pictorial signage directing you from castle to church to fountain. However, the real exhibit is the town itself. Wander around. Get lost. Find yourself.

The **tourist office** (www.frigiliana.es; Plaza del Ingenio; ☺9am-8pm Mon-Fri, 10am-1.30pm & 4-8pm Sat & Sun) is next to the bus stop.

◉ Sights & Activities

The old town's sturdy 16th-century Renaissance palace, **El Ingenio**, today processes molasses from sugar cane.

El Fuerte, the hill that climbs above the village, was the scene of the final bloody defeat of the *moriscos* (Muslim converts to Christianity) of La Axarquía in their 1569 rebellion, and where they reputedly plunged to their death rather than be killed or captured by the Spanish. You can walk up here if you follow the streets to the top of the town and then continue along the dusty track.

Frigiliana is on the GR249 long-distance footpath. You can walk south down to the Cueva de Nerja (p197; 14.6km) or head north into the Almijara Mountains and Cómpeta. Another shorter route heads to Cómpeta via the recently repopulated village of Acebuchal (p194; 7km).

❶ Getting There & Away

Regular buses link Frigiliana with Nerja (€1, 15 minutes, 12 daily). They leave from the taxi rank next to the tourist office.

Nerja

POP 21,200

Nerja, 56km east of Málaga with the Sierra Almijara rising behind it, has succeeded in rebuffing developers, allowing its centre to retain a low-rise village charm despite the proliferation of souvenir shops and the large number of visitors it sees. At its heart is the perennially beautiful Balcón de Europa, a palm-lined promontory built on the foundations of an old fort that offers panoramic views of the cobalt-blue sea flanked by honey-coloured coves.

The town is increasingly popular with package holidaymakers and 'residential tourists', which has pushed it far beyond its old confines. There's significant urbanisation, especially to the east. The holiday atmosphere, and seawater contamination, can be overwhelming from July to September, but the place is more *tranquilo* the rest of the year.

◉ Sights & Activities

The town centres on the delightful **Balcón de Europa**, which juts out over the deep blue Mediterranean and is *the* place for the local *paseo* (promenade) on a languid summer's evening.

★ Cueva de Nerja   CAVE

(www.cuevadenerja.es; adult/child €10/6, incl Museo de Nerja €12, incl train btwn caves & museum €15; ⊘ unguided visit 10am-1pm & 4-5.30pm Sep-Jun, 10am-6pm Jul & Aug, guided visit 1-2pm & 5.30-6.30pm Sep-Jun, 11am-noon & 6.30-7.30pm Jul & Aug) It's hard to imagine the surreal world that lies beneath the mountain foothills 4km east of Nerja, and it's even harder to believe that these vast caverns weren't discovered until five local *chicos* (young men) who had gone out looking for bats stumbled across an opening in 1959. Hollowed out by water around five million years ago and once inhabited by Stone Age hunters, this theatrical wonderland of extraordinary rock formations, subtle shifting colours, and stalactites and stalagmites is evocative of a submerged cathedral. About 14 buses run daily from Málaga and Nerja, except on Sunday. Alternatively you can take a mini tourist train from Nerja's museum, or you can walk (there's pavement all the way).

Playa Burriana   BEACH

(P) This is Nerja's longest and best beach, with plenty of towel space on the sand. You can walk here via the bleached white Calle Carabeo, continuing down the steps to the beach and along to Burriana. The beach is backed by a line of *merenderos* (open-sided restaurants). You can rent kayaks or paddleboards here for €5.50 per hour.

Playa Calahonda   BEACH

This small, pretty cove is just east of the Balcón de Europa. You can rent sunbeds and parasols here, though it does get busy at the height of summer, especially with guests from the nearby Hotel Balcón de Europa (p198).

Playa del Cañuelo   BEACH

East of Nerja the coast becomes more rugged; with your own wheels you can head to some great beaches reached by tracks down from the A7. Playa del Cañuelo, immediately before the border with Granada province, is one of the best, with a couple of summer-only restaurants.

Museo de Nerja   MUSEUM

(☑952 52 72 24; Plaza de España; adult/child €4/2, incl Cueva de Nerja €12, incl train btwn caves & museum €15; ⊘10am-2pm & 4-6.30pm Tue-Sun, to 10pm Jul & Aug) Nerja's museum traces the history of the town from the cave dwellers of Paleolithic times to the tourist-boom years of the '60s, and is well worth a browse (preferably before you visit the Cueva de Nerja). The museum's highlights centre on artefacts found in the caves and range from the thought-provoking skeleton of an adult cave dweller to a fascinatingly mundane prehistoric cheese dish.

Buceo Costa Nerja   DIVING

(☑952 52 86 10; www.nerjadiving.com; Playa Burriana; snorkelling from €30; ⊘9am-7pm) Diving can be especially rewarding here due to the Atlantic stream, which results in highly varied marine life. This reputable outfit organises courses for most levels, from a basic Discover Scuba try-out (€70) to a full-blown Open Water course (€450).

🎎 Festivals & Events

Noche de San Juan   CULTURAL

(⊘23 Jun) Nerja's inhabitants celebrate St John's Day by dusting off their barbecue kits and heading for the beach. There they eat sizzling seafood, drink wine and beer, and stay up until the next morning swimming,

Nerja

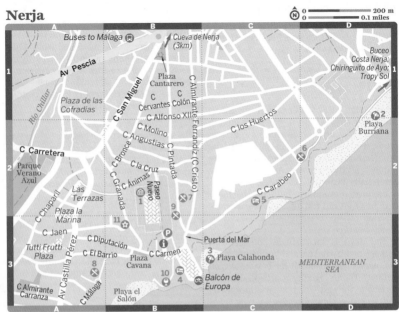

Nerja

dancing, partying and, ultimately, flaking out on the sand.

🛏 Sleeping

Nerja has a huge range of accommodation, but in summer rooms in the better hotels tend to be booked at least two months in advance.

★**Hotel Carabeo** HOTEL €€

(☎952 52 54 44; www.hotelcarabeo.com; Calle Carabeo 34; d/ste incl breakfast from €90/190; ☺Apr-Oct; ❄@☎🐾) Full of stylish antiques and wonderful paintings, this small, family-run seafront hotel is set above manicured terraced gardens. There's also a good restaurant and the pool is on a terrace overlooking the sea. The building is an old schoolhouse and is located on one of the prettiest pedestrian streets in town, festooned with pink bougainvillea.

Hotel Balcón de Europa HOTEL €€

(☎952 52 08 00; www.hotelbalconeuropa.com; Paseo Balcón de Europa 1; s/d €82/115; 🐾) This terraced hotel sticks out on a small promontory like a boat departing for Africa. Outside it's usually mayhem (this is Nerja's popular tourist playground), but inside the mood is surprisingly tranquil, with private room balconies overlooking a snug section of beach lapped by the translucent Mediterranean. A pool, sauna, piano bar and restaurant with a view all add value.

🍴 Eating

Nerja has an abundance of restaurants and bars, most geared towards the undiscerning. In general, avoid any that advertise all-day

English breakfasts or that have sun-bleached posters of the dishes. Playa Burriana, Nerja's best beach, is backed by an animated strip of restaurants and bars.

★ Chiringuito de Ayo   SEAFOOD €

(www.ayonerja.com; Playa Burriana; mains €9-13; ☺9am-midnight; P🅿) The menu is listed in nine languages, but the only word you need to understand at beachside Ayo is 'paella'. They cook the rice dish every day in a huge pan atop an open wood-burning fire right next to the sand. A plateful is yours for €7.50. If you're lucky, you'll be served by Francisco Ortega Olalla (aka Ayo), one of the five *chicos* (young men) who discovered the Cueva de Nerja in 1959. Since it's a *chiringuito*, you're also guaranteed shoals of seafood.

La Piqueta   TAPAS €

(Calle Pintada 8; tapas €2, raciones €4.50-6; ☺10am-midnight Mon-Sat) There are two very good reasons why this is the most popular tapas bar in town: first, the house wine is excellent; second, you get a free tapas with every drink in a tradition that's more Granada than Málaga province. On the menu are sturdy classics such as tripe and *huevos estrellados* (literally, smashed eggs) prepared with ham, garlic, potatoes and peppers.

Lan Sang   THAI, LAO €€

(www.lansang.com; Calle Málaga 12; mains €13-17; ☺1-3pm & 7.30-11pm Tue-Sat, 7-10.30pm Sun) The owner and chef are from Laos, so the dishes here are a subtle combination of Thai and Lao cuisines. As well as curries, stir-fries and soups, there's an emphasis on fresh local fish and seafood, prepared with spices such as tamarind, ginger, kaffir-lime leaves and chilli. Soups and salads are similarly based on delicate, fragrant flavours.

Restaurante 34   EUROPEAN €€€

(☎952 52 54 44; www.hotelcarabeo.com; Hotel Carabeo, Calle Carabeo 34; mains €16-25; ☺1-3pm & 7-11pm Tue-Sun Mar-Nov; 🕿) 🍴 There's a truly gorgeous setting here, both indoors and outside in the garden, which is gently stepped to its furthest section overlooking the sea. Delicious and exotic food combinations are served – roast suckling pig with apple compote is a favourite – and there's an adjacent tapas bar for smaller appetites. Live music Wednesday and Sunday evening.

Oliva   EUROPEAN €€€

(☎952 52 29 88; www.restauranteoliva.com; Calle Pintada 7; mains €21-25; ☺1-4pm & 7-11pm)

Impeccable service, single orchids, a drum-and-bass soundtrack and a charcoal-grey-and-green colour scheme: in short, this place has class. The menu is reassuringly brief and changes regularly according to what's in season. The inventive dishes combine unlikely ingredients – expect the likes of grapes gelée and thyme ice cream, potatoes in vanilla, and black garlic and aubergine purée. Reservations are recommended.

Bakus   BISTRO €€€

(☎952 52 71 79; Calle Carabeo 2; mains €18-24; ☺7-10pm Tue-Sun) The interior combines raspberry pink with charcoal grey, but most people head to the sprawling terrace overlooking pristine Playa Carabello. The menu should suit most discerning diners, ranging from light bites like baked gorgonzola tart and pumpkin soup to meat dishes with sauces that sound decidedly moreish, including tarragon, leek and bacon, truffle cream, and port wine with wild mushrooms.

🍷 Drinking & Entertainment

Cochran's Irish Bar   IRISH PUB

(Paseo Balcón de Europa 6; ☺11.30pm-3am Tue-Sat, 5pm-midnight Sun) Has good Guinness, Murphy's and Jameson's, great live music, and – bonus – a shockingly good view over the Mediterranean from its terrace, which is open during the day. Music kicks off late.

Centro Cultural
Villa de Nerja   LIVE PERFORMANCE

(☎952 52 38 63; Calle Granada 45) This well-run centre organises an ambitious annual program of classical music, theatre, jazz and flamenco, featuring international and Spanish musicians and performers.

ℹ Information

Tourist Office (www.nerja.org; Calle Carmen; ☺10am-2pm & 6-10pm Mon-Fri, 10am-1pm Sat & Sun)

ℹ Getting There & Away

Alsa (p193) runs regular buses to/from Málaga (€4.50, one hour, 23 daily), Marbella (€11, 2¼ hours, one daily) and Antequera (€9, 2¼ hours, two daily). There are also buses to Almería and Granada. There's no bus station, just a ticket office and bus stop on the main roundabout on Carretera N340.

MÁLAGA PROVINCE NERJA

Córdoba Province

Best Places to Stay

➡ Balcón de Córdoba (p214)

➡ Casa Olea (p222)

➡ Viento10 (p214)

➡ Patio del Posadero (p213)

➡ Hotel Zuhayra (p220)

➡ Bed and Be (p213)

Best Places to Eat

➡ Restaurante Zuhayra (p220)

➡ Casa Pepe de la Judería (p215)

➡ Bodegas Campos (p215)

➡ Mercado Victoria (p214)

➡ Restaurante La Fuente (p222)

Why Go?

Once the dazzling beacon of Al-Andalus, the historic city of Córdoba is the main draw of its namesake province. Remnants of the illustrious Caliphate of Córdoba, especially the great Mezquita (Mosque), hold immense historical and architectural interest, and the city around them is full of good food, wine, music and museums, and charming old-fashioned streets, plazas and patios. But there's plenty of territory to explore outside the provincial capital. To the north rises the Sierra Morena, a rolling upcountry expanse of remote villages, ruined castles and protected forests. To the south, olive trees and grapevines carpet the rippling terrain, yielding some of Spain's best oils and the unique sweet Montilla-Moriles wines. Further south, caves and canyons are carved out of the limestone massif of the Sierras Subbéticas, with bustling Priego de Córdoba and crag-perched Zuheros making perfect bases for mountain hiking and dining on homestyle local dishes.

Driving Distances

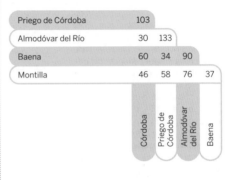

	Córdoba	Priego de Córdoba	Almodóvar del Río	Baena
Priego de Córdoba	103			
Almodóvar del Río	30	133		
Baena	60	34	90	
Montilla	46	58	76	37

CÓRDOBA

POP 294,300 / ELEV 130M

One building alone is reason enough to put Córdoba high on your itinerary: the mesmerising multiarched Mezquita. One of the world's greatest Islamic buildings, the Mezquita is a symbol of the worldly, sophisticated culture that flourished here more than a millennium ago when Córdoba was capital of Islamic Spain and western Europe's biggest, most cultured city. But today's Córdoba is much more than the Mezquita. With a lot to see and do, some charming accommodation, and excellent restaurants and bars, it merits far more than the fleeting visit many travellers give it. Córdoba's real charms unfold as you explore the winding, stone-paved lanes of the medieval city to the west, north and east of the gaudy touristic area immediately around the Mezquita, wandering between wrought-iron balconies and lamps, potted plants, overhanging trees, golden-stone buildings and verdant interior patios, emerging every few minutes on yet another quaint little hidden plaza.

Andalucía's major river, the Guadalquivir, flows just below the Mezquita, and the riverfront streets are home to a band of lively restaurants and bars making the most of the view. The life of the modern city, meanwhile, focuses just to the north of the historic centre, around Plaza de las Tendillas, where you'll find a more local vibe with some excellent bars and restaurants.

Córdoba bursts into life from mid-April to mid-June, when it stages most of its major fiestas. At this time of year the skies are blue, the temperatures are perfect and the city's many trees, gardens and courtyards drip with foliage and blooms. September and October are also excellent weatherwise, but July and August sizzle.

History

The Roman settlement of Corduba was established in the 3rd century BC as a provisioning point for Roman troops. In about 25 BC Emperor Augustus made the city capital of Baetica, one of the three Roman provinces on the Iberian Peninsula, ushering in an era of prosperity and cultural ascendancy that saw Córdoba produce the famous writers Seneca and Lucan. The Roman bridge over the Guadalquivir and the temple on Calle Claudio Marcelo are the most visible remains of this important Roman city, most of whose traces now lie a metre or two below ground. By the 3rd century, when Christianity reached Córdoba, the Roman city was already in decline. It fell to Islamic invaders in AD 711.

The city took centre stage in 756 when Abd ar-Rahman I set himself up here as the emir of Al-Andalus (the Muslim-controlled parts of the Iberian Peninsula), founding the Umayyad dynasty, which more or less unified Al-Andalus for two and a half centuries. Abd ar-Rahman I founded the great Mezquita in 785. The city's, and Al-Andalus', heyday came under Abd ar-Rahman III (r 912–61). Spurred by rivalry with the Fatimid dynasty in North Africa, he named himself caliph (the title of the Muslim successors of Mohammed) in 929, ushering in the era of the Córdoba caliphate.

Córdoba was by now the biggest city in western Europe, with a flourishing economy based on agriculture and skilled artisan products, and a population somewhere around 250,000. The city shone with hundreds of dazzling mosques, public baths, patios, gardens and fountains. This was the famed 'city of the three cultures', where Muslims, Jews and Christians coexisted peaceably and Abd ar-Rahman III's court was frequented by scholars from all three communities. Córdoba's university, library and observatories made it a centre of learning whose influence was still being felt in Christian Europe many centuries later.

Towards the end of the 10th century, Al-Mansur (Almanzor), a ruthless general whose northward raids terrified Christian Spain, took the reins of power from the caliphs. But after the death of Al-Mansur's son Abd al-Malik in 1008, the caliphate descended into anarchy. Berber troops terrorised and looted the city and, in 1031, Umayyad rule ended. Córdoba became a minor part of the Seville *taifa* (small kingdom) in 1069, and has been overshadowed by Seville ever since.

Twelfth-century Córdoba did nevertheless produce the two most celebrated scholars of Al-Andalus – the Muslim Averroës (1126–98) and the Jewish Maimonides (1135–1204), men of multifarious talents most remembered for their efforts to reconcile religious faith with Aristotelian reason. After Córdoba was taken by Castilla's Fernando III in 1236, it declined into a provincial city and its fortunes only looked up with the arrival of industry in the late 19th century. Christian Córdoba did, however, give birth to one of the greatest Spanish poets, Luis de Góngora (1561–1627), still much remembered in the city.

Córdoba Province Highlights

1 Córdoba
(p201) Discovering the marvellous Mezquita and much more in this fascinatingly historic but also buzzing contemporary city.

2 Parque Natural Sierras Subbéticas
(p219) Exploring the mountains, valleys and caves of a picturesque hill-country region.

3 Zuheros
(p219) Taking in this charming white village with a craggy canyon backdrop, good walks and a perfectly perched castle.

4 Montilla wines
(p218) Tasting the province's sweet liquid speciality, found everywhere and ideally experienced at one of the wineries themselves.

5 Priego de Córdoba (p221) Exploring this prosperous market town with baroque fantasy architecture and some of the world's best olive oil.

6 Los Pedroches
(p223) Touring the castles, oak pastures and isolated villages of Andalucía's mysterious 'deep north'.

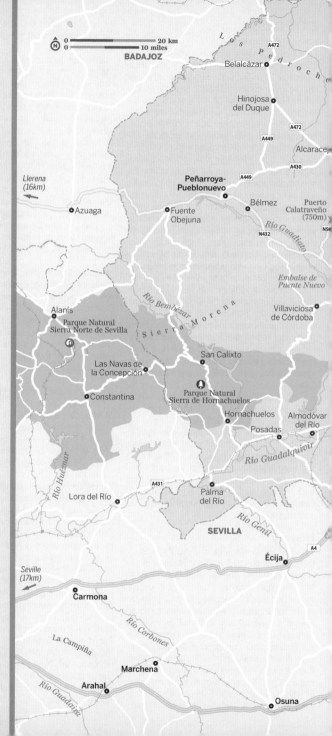

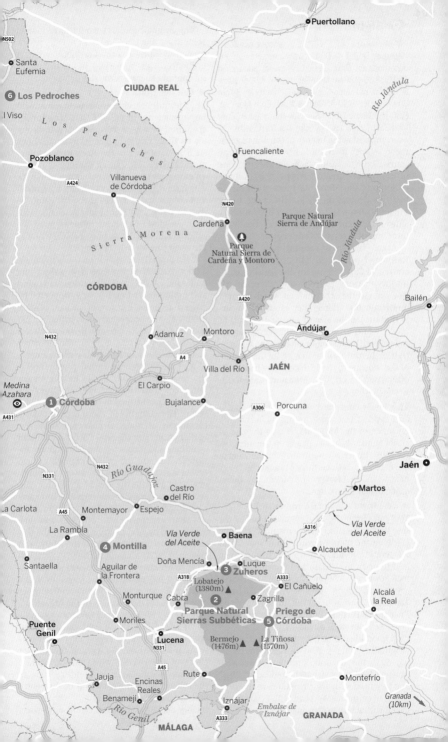

◉ Sights

★ Mezquita
MOSQUE, CATHEDRAL

(Mosque; ☑ 957 47 05 12; www.mezquita-catedral decordoba.es; Calle Cardenal Herrero; adult/child €10/5, 8.30-9.30am Mon-Sat free; ⊘ 8.30-9.30am & 10am-7pm Mon-Sat, 8.30-11.30am & 3-7pm Sun Mar-Oct, 8.30-9.30am & 10am-6pm Mon-Sat, 8.30-11.30am & 3-6pm Sun Nov-Feb, mass 9.30am Mon-Sat, noon & 1.30pm Šun) It's impossible to overemphasise the beauty of Córdoba's great mosque, with its remarkably serene (despite tourist crowds) and spacious interior. One of the world's greatest works of Islamic architecture, the Mezquita hints, with all its lustrous decoration, at a refined age when Muslims, Jews and Christians lived side by side and enriched their city with a heady interaction of diverse, vibrant cultures.

Arab chronicles recount how Abd ar-Rahman I purchased half of the Visigothic church of San Vicente for the Muslim community's Friday prayers, and then, in AD 784, bought the other half on which to erect a new mosque. Three later extensions nearly quintupled the size of Abd ar-Rahman I's mosque and brought it to the form you see today – with one major alteration: a Christian cathedral plonked right in the middle of the mosque in the 16th century (hence the often-used description 'Mezquita-Catedral').

➡ Patio de los Naranjos

This lovely courtyard, with its orange, palm and cypress trees and fountains, forms the entrance to the Mezquita. It was the site of ritual ablutions before prayer in the mosque. Its most impressive entrance is the Puerta del Perdón, a 14th-century Mudéjar archway next to the bell tower. The Mezquita's ticket office is just inside here.

➡ Bell Tower (Torre Campanario)

You can climb the 54m-high bell tower for fine panoramas and an interesting bird's-eye angle on the main Mezquita building. Up to 20 people are allowed up the tower every half hour from 9.30am to 1.30pm and 4pm to 6.30pm (to 5.30pm November to February; no afternoon visits in July or August). Tickets (€2) are sold on the inner side of the Puerta del Perdón, next to the tower: they often sell out well ahead of visit times, so it's a good idea to buy them early in the day. Originally built by Abd ar-Rahman III in 951–52 as the Mezquita's minaret, the tower was encased in a strengthened outer shell and heightened by the Christians in the 16th and 17th centuries. You can still see some caliphal vaults and arches inside.

The original minaret would have looked something like the Giralda in Seville, which was practically a copy. Córdoba's minaret influenced all minarets built thereafter throughout the western Islamic world.

➡ The Mezquita's Interior

The Mezquita's architectural uniqueness and importance lies in the fact that, structurally speaking, it was a revolutionary building for its time. Earlier major Islamic buildings such as the Dome of the Rock in Jerusalem and the Great Mosque in Damascus placed an emphasis on verticality, but the Mezquita was intended as a democratically horizontal and simple space, where the spirit could be free to roam and communicate easily with God – a kind of glorious refinement of the original simple Islamic prayer space (usually the open yard of a desert home).

Men prayed side by side on the *argamasa,* a floor made of compact, reddish slaked lime and sand. A flat roof, decorated with gold and multicoloured motifs, was supported by striped arches suggestive of a forest of date palms. The arches rested on, eventually, 1293 columns (of which 856 remain today). Useful leaflets in several languages are available free just inside the door by which visitors enter.

Abd ar-Rahman I's initial prayer hall – the area immediately inside today's visitor entrance – was divided into 11 'naves' by lines of arches striped in red brick and white stone. The columns of these arches were a mishmash of material collected from the earlier church on the site, Córdoba's Roman buildings and places as far away as Constantinople. To raise the ceiling high enough to create a sense of openness, inventive builders came up with the idea of a two-tier construction, using taller columns as a base and planting shorter ones on top.

Later enlargements of the mosque, southward by Abd ar-Rahman II in the 9th century and Al-Hakim II in the 960s, and eastward by Al-Mansur in the 970s, extended it to an area of nearly 14,400 sq metres, making it one of the biggest mosques in the world. The arcades' simplicity and number give a sense of endlessness to the Mezquita.

The final Mezquita had 19 doors along its north side, filling it with light and a sense of openness. Nowadays, nearly all these doorways are closed off, dampening the vibrant effect of the red-and-white double arches. Christian additions to the building, such as the solid mass of the cathedral in the centre and the 50 or so chapels around the fringes, further enclose and impose on the airy space.

➔ Mihrab & Maksura

Like Abd ar-Rahman II a century earlier, Al-Hakim II in the 960s lengthened the naves of the prayer hall, creating a new *qiblah* wall (indicating the direction of Mecca) and *mihrab* (prayer niche) at the south end. The bay immediately in front of the *mihrab* and the bays to each side form the *maksura,* the area where the caliphs and courtiers would have prayed. The *mihrab* and *maksura* are the most beautifully and intricately decorated parts of the whole mosque.

The greatest glory of Al-Hakim II's extension was the portal of the *mihrab* – a crescent arch with a rectangular surround known as an *alfiz*. For the portal's decoration, Al-Hakim asked the emperor of Byzantium, Nicephoras II Phocas, to send him a mosaicist capable of imitating the superb mosaics of the Great Mosque of Damascus, one of the great 8th-century Syrian Umayyad buildings. The Christian emperor sent the Muslim caliph not only a mosaicist but also a gift of 1600kg of gold mosaic cubes. Shaped into flower motifs and inscriptions from the Quran, this gold is what gives the *mihrab* portal its magical glitter. Inside the *mihrab*, a single block of white marble sculpted into the shape of a scallop shell, a symbol of the Quran, forms the dome that amplified the voice of the imam throughout the mosque.

The arches of the *maksura* are the mosque's most intricate and sophisticated, forming a forest of interwoven horseshoe shapes. Equally attractive are the *maksura*'s skylit domes, decorated with star-patterned stone vaulting. Each dome is held up by four interlocking pairs of parallel ribs, a highly advanced technique for 10th-century Europe.

➔ Cathedral

Following the Christian conquest of Córdoba in 1236, the Mezquita was used as a cathedral but remained largely unaltered for nearly three centuries. But in the 16th century King Carlos I gave the cathedral authorities permission to rip out the centre of the Mezquita in order to construct a new Capilla Mayor (main altar area) and *coro* (choir).

Legend has it that when the king saw the result he was horrified, exclaiming that the builders had destroyed something unique in the world. The cathedral took nearly 250 years to complete (1523–1766) and thus exhibits a range of architectural fashions, from plateresque and late Renaissance to extravagant Spanish baroque. Among the later features are the Capilla Mayor's rich 17th-century jasper and red-marble retable (altar screen), and the fine mahogany stalls in the choir, carved in the 18th century by Pedro Duque Cornejo.

➔ Night Visits

A one-hour sound-and-light show (www.elalmadecordoba.com), in nine languages via audio guides, is presented in the Mezquita twice nightly except Sundays from March to October, and on Friday and Saturday from November to February. Tickets are €18 (senior or student €9).

◎ Around the Mezquita

⭐ **Alcázar de los Reyes Cristianos** FORTRESS
(Fortress of the Christian Monarchs; ☑957 42 01 51; www.alcazardelosreyescristianos.cordoba.es; Campo Santo de Los Mártires; adult/student/child €4.50/2.25/free; ◷8.30am-3pm Tue-Sat, to 2.30pm Sun mid-Jun–mid-Sep, 8.30am-8.45pm Tue-Fri, to 4.30pm Sat, to 2.30pm Sun mid-Sep–mid-Jun; 🚻) Built under Castilian rule in the 13th and 14th centuries on the remains of a Moorish predecessor, this fort-palace was where the Catholic Monarchs, Fernando and Isabel, made their first acquaintance with Columbus in 1486. One hall displays some remarkable Roman mosaics, dug up from Plaza de la Corredera in the 1950s. The Alcázar's terraced gardens – full of fish ponds, fountains, orange trees and flowers – are a delight to stroll around.

At 9pm (except Mondays) there's a popular multimedia show featuring lights, flamenco music and dancing fountains called **Noches Mágicas en el Alcázar** (Magic Nights in the Alcázar; adult/child €6.50/free). While here, it's also interesting to visit the nearby **Baños del Alcázar Califal** (☑608 158893; www.banosdelalcazarcalifal.cordoba.es; Campo Santo de los Mártires; adult/student/child €2.50/1.50/free, free from noon Thu; ◷8.30am-8.45pm Tue-Fri, to 4.30pm Sat & to 2.30pm Sun mid-Sep–mid-Jun, 8.30am-3pm Tue-Sat & to 2.30pm Sun mid-Jun–mid-Sep), the impressive 10th-century bathhouse of the Moorish Alcázar.

Caballerizas Reales STABLES
(Royal Stables; ☑957 49 78 43; www.cordobaecuestre.com; Calle Caballerizas Reales 1; adult/child training €5/1, show €15/10; ◷10am-1.30pm daily plus 4-8pm Tue, 5-8pm Wed-Sat, show 9pm Wed-Sat) These elegant stables were built on orders of King Felipe II in 1570 as a centre for developing the tall Spanish thoroughbred warhorse *(caballo andaluz)*. The centre still breeds these fine horses (47 are here today)

Mezquita

TIMELINE

6th century AD Foundation of a Christian church, the Basilica of San Vicente, on the site of the present Mezquita.

786-87 Salvaging Visigothic and Roman ruins, Emir Abd ar-Rahman I replaces the church with a *mezquita* (mosque).

833-48 Mosque enlarged by Abd ar-Rahman II.

951-2 A new minaret is built by Abd ar-Rahman III.

962-71 Mosque enlarged, and superb new ❶ **mihrab** added, by Al-Hakim II.

991-4 Mosque enlarged for the last time by Al-Mansur, who also enlarged the courtyard (now the ❷ **Patio de los Naranjos**), bringing the whole complex to its current dimensions.

1236 Mosque converted into a Christian church after Córdoba is recaptured by Fernando III of Castilla.

1271 Instead of destroying the mosque, the Christians modify it, creating the ❸ **Capilla de Villaviciosa** and ❹ **Capilla Real**.

1523 Work on a Gothic/Renaissance-style cathedral inside the Mezquita begins, with permission of Carlos I. Legend has it that on seeing the result the king lamented that something unique in the world had been destroyed.

1593-1664 The 10th-century minaret is reinforced and rebuilt as a Renaissance-baroque ❺ **belltower**.

2004 Spanish Muslims petition to be able to worship in the Mezquita again. The Vatican doesn't consent.

TOP TIPS

➡ The Patio de los Naranjos can be enjoyed free of charge at any time.

➡ Entry to the main Mezquita building is offered free every morning, except Sunday, between 8.30am and 9.30am.

➡ Group visits are prohibited before 10am, meaning the building is quieter and more atmospheric in the early morning.

The Mihrab
Everything leads to the mosque's greatest treasure – the beautiful prayer niche, in the wall facing Mecca, that was added in the 10th century. Cast your eyes over the gold mosaic cubes crafted by sculptors imported from Byzantium

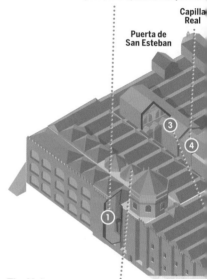

Puerta de San Esteban

Capilla Real

The Maksura
Guiding you towards the mihrab, the *maksura* was the former royal enclosure where the caliphs and their retinues prayed. Its lavish, elaborate arches were designed to draw the eye of worshippers towards the mihrab and Mecca.

Capilla Mayor

A Christian monument inside an Islamic mosque sounds beautifully ironic, yet here it is: a Gothic high chapel sanctioned by Carlos I in the 16th century and planted in the middle of the world's third-largest mosque.

Belltower

Reopened to visitors in 2014 after a 24-year restoration, the 54m-tall belltower has the best views in the city. It was built in the 17th century around and above the remains of the Mezquita's 10th-century minaret.

5

The Mezquita Arches

No, you're not hallucinating. The Mezquita's most defining characteristic is its unique terracotta-and-white striped arches that are supported by 856 pillars salvaged from Roman and other ruins. Glimpsed through the dull light they're at once spooky and striking.

Puerta del Perdón

2

Patio de los Naranjos

Abandon architectural preconceptions all ye who enter here. The ablutions area of the former mosque is a shady courtyard embellished with orange trees that acts as the Mezquita's main entry point.

Capilla de Villaviciosa

Sift through the building's numerous chapels till you find this gem, an early Christian modification which fused existing Moorish features with Gothic arches and pillars. It served as the Capilla Mayor until 1607.

The Cathedral Choir

Few ignore the impressive *coro* (choir), built in the 16th and 17th centuries. Once you've admired the skilfully carved mahogany choir stalls depicting scenes from the Bible, look up at the impressive baroque ceiling.

and trains horses and riders in equestrian disciplines. You can watch training during the daily opening times from Tuesday to Sunday (from 11am in the mornings), or attend the one-hour show that impressively combines horse and rider skills with flamenco dance and music.

Puente Romano
BRIDGE

Spanning the Río Guadalquivir just below the Mezquita, the handsome, 16-arched Roman bridge formed part of the ancient Via Augusta, which ran from Girona in Catalonia to Cádiz. Rebuilt several times down the centuries, it's now traffic-free and makes for a lovely stroll. With the aid of CGI, it not long ago featured as the Long Bridge of Volantis in *Game of Thrones*.

⊙ Judería

The Judería, Córdoba's old Jewish quarter, west and northwest of the Mezquita, is part of the old city's labyrinth of narrow streets and small squares, whitewashed buildings and wrought-iron gates allowing glimpses of plant-filled patios. Some streets here are now choked with gaudy souvenir shops and tourist-oriented restaurants, but others remain quiet and unblemished. The importance of the Jewish community in Moorish Córdoba is illustrated by the Judería's proximity to the Mezquita and the city's centres of power. Spain had one of Europe's biggest Jewish communities, recorded from as early as the 2nd century AD. Persecuted by the Visigoths, they allied themselves with the Muslims following the Arab conquests. By the 10th century they were established among the most dynamic members of society, holding posts as administrators, doctors, jurists, philosophers and poets. One of the greatest Jewish theologians, Maimonides, was born in Córdoba in 1135, though he left with his family at an early age to escape Almohad persecution, eventually settling in Egypt. His magnum opus, the *Mishne Torah,* summarised the teachings of Judaism and systematised all Jewish law.

Sinagoga
SYNAGOGUE

(☑957 74 90 15; www.turismodecordoba.org; Calle de los Judíos 20; EU/non-EU citizen free/€0.30; ☯9am-3pm Tue-Sun mid-Jun–mid-Sep, 9am-8pm Tue-Sat & 9am-3pm Sun mid-Sep–mid-Jun) Constructed in 1315, this small, probably private or family synagogue is one of the best-surviving testaments to the Jewish presence in medieval Andalucía, though it hasn't been used as a place of worship since the expulsion of Jews in 1492. Decorated with extravagant stucco work that includes Hebrew inscriptions and intricate Mudéjar star and plant patterns, it has an upper gallery reserved for women.

Casa de Sefarad
MUSEUM

(☑957 42 14 04; www.casadesefarad.es; cnr Calles de los Judíos & Averroes; €4; ☯10am-7pm Jul-Sep, 11am-7pm Mon-Sat & 11am-2.30pm Sun Oct-Jun) In the heart of the Judería, and once connected by tunnel to the synagogue, the Casa de Sefarad is an interesting museum devoted to the Sephardic (Iberian Peninsula Jewish) tradition. Different rooms cover food, domestic crafts, ritual, music, prominent Jews of Córdoba and the Inquisition. There's also a section on the women intellectuals (poets, artists and thinkers) of Al-Andalus.

⊙ Other Areas

★ Palacio de Viana
MUSEUM

(www.palaciodeviana.com; Plaza de Don Gome 2; whole house/patios €8/5; ☯10am-7pm Tue-Sat & to 3pm Sun Sep-Jun, 9am-3pm Tue-Sun Jul & Aug) A stunning Renaissance palace with 12 beautiful, plant-filled patios, the Viana Palace is a particular delight to visit in spring. Occupied by the aristocratic Marqueses de Viana until 1980, the large building is packed with art and antiques. You can just walk round the lovely patios and garden with a self-guiding leaflet, or take a guided tour of the rooms as well. It's an 800m walk northeast from Plaza de las Tendillas.

★ Centro Flamenco Fosforito
MUSEUM

(Posada del Potro; ☑957 47 68 29; www.centroflamencofosforito.cordoba.es; Plaza del Potro; ☯8.30am-3pm Tue-Sun mid-Jun–mid-Sep, 8.30am-7.30pm Tue-Fri, to 2.30pm Sat & Sun mid-Sep–mid-Jun) **FREE** Possibly the best flamenco museum in Andalucía, the Centro Flamenco Fosforito has exhibits, film and information panels in English and Spanish telling you the history of the guitar and all the flamenco greats. Touch-screen videos demonstrate the important techniques of flamenco song, guitar, dance and percussion – you can test your skill at beating out the *compás* (rhythm) of different *palos* (song forms). Regular free live flamenco performances are held here, too, often at noon on Sundays (listed on the website). The museum benefits from a fantastic location inside the Posada del Potro, a legendary inn that played a part in *Don Quijote,* where Cervantes described it as a 'den of thieves'. The famous square it stands on, once a horse market, features a lovely

16th-century stone fountain topped by a rearing *potro* (colt).

⭐ **Medina Azahara** ARCHAEOLOGICAL SITE
(Madinat al-Zahra; ☑957 10 49 33; www.museos deandalucia.es; Carretera Palma del Río Km 5.5; EU citizen/noncitizen free/€1.50; ☺9am-7pm Tue-Sat Apr–mid-Jun, to 3pm mid-Jun–mid-Sep, to 6pm mid-Sep–Mar, 9am-3pm Sun year-round; Ⓟ) Eight kilometres west of Córdoba stands what's left of Medina Azahara, the sumptuous palace-city built by Caliph Abd ar-Rahman III in the 10th century. The complex spills down a hillside, with the caliph's palace (the area you visit today) on the highest levels overlooking what were gardens and open fields. The residential areas (still unexcavated) were set away to each side. A fascinating modern museum has been installed below the site.

Legend has it that Abd ar-Rahman III built Medina Azahara for his favourite wife, Az-Zahra. Dismayed by her homesickness and yearnings for the snowy mountains of Syria, he surrounded his new city with almond and cherry trees, replacing snowflakes with fluffy white blossoms. More realistically, it was probably Abd ar-Rahman's declaration of his caliphate in 929 that spurred him to construct, as caliphs were wont to do, a new capital. Building started in 940 and chroniclers record some staggering statistics: 10,000 labourers set 6000 stone blocks a day, with outer walls stretching 1518m east to west and 745m north to south.

It is almost inconceivable to think that such a city, built over 35 years, was to last only a few more before the usurper Al-Mansur transferred government to a new palace complex of his own in 981. Then, between 1010 and 1013, Medina Azahara was wrecked by Berber soldiers. During succeeding centuries its ruins were plundered repeatedly for building materials.

From the museum, where you arrive and get tickets for the site (and where you must park if coming in your own vehicle), a shuttle bus (*lanzadera;* adult/child/senior €2.10/1.50/1.50 return) takes you 2km up to the top of the site. The visitors' route then leads down through the city's original northern gate. Highlights of the visitable area are the grand, arched **Edificio Basilical Superior**, which housed the main state admin offices, and the **Casa de Yafar**, believed to have been residence of the caliph's prime minister. The crown jewel of the site, the royal reception hall known as the **Salón de Abd ar-Rahman III** (or Salón Rico), has been closed for restoration since 2009 (with no expected completion date at the time of research). This hall has exquisitely carved stucco work and is said to have been decorated with gold and silver tiles, arches of ivory and ebony, and walls of multicoloured marble.

CÓRDOBA'S PATIOS

Studded with pots of geraniums, with bougainvillea cascading down the walls and a trickling fountain in the middle, the famed patios of Córdoba have provided shade and cool during the searing heat of summer for centuries. The origin of these much-loved courtyards probably lies in the Roman atrium (open spaces inside buildings). The tradition was continued by the Arabs, for whom the internal courtyard was an area where women went about their family life and household jobs. The addition of a central fountain and multitudes of plants heightened the sensation of coolness.

Beautiful patios can be glimpsed – often tantalisingly, through closed wrought-iron gates – in Córdoba's historic centre and other parts of town. They are at their prettiest in spring, and happily dozens of them open up for free public viewing until 10pm for two weeks during the very popular Fiesta de los Patios de Córdoba (p213).

Palacio de Viana This aristocratic palace, visitable year-round, has not one but 12 plant-filled patios.

Asociación de Amigos de los Patios Cordobeses (Calle San Basilio 44; ☺10.30am-1.30pm & 5-8pm) 𝗙𝗥𝗘𝗘 This particularly lovely patio, dripping with vegetation, can be visited free year-round. Colourfulness depends on the season, but you can browse its several craft workshops any time of year.

Patios de San Basilio (www.patiosdesanbasilio.com; €5; ☺10.30am-2pm Wed-Mon mid-Sep–Jun, 10am-1.30pm Wed-Mon Aug–mid-Sep, closed Wed-Thu afternoons Nov-Jan) Offers the chance to visit three patios in the Alcázar Viejo district, about 400m southwest of the Mezquita, outside the festival season.

Córdoba

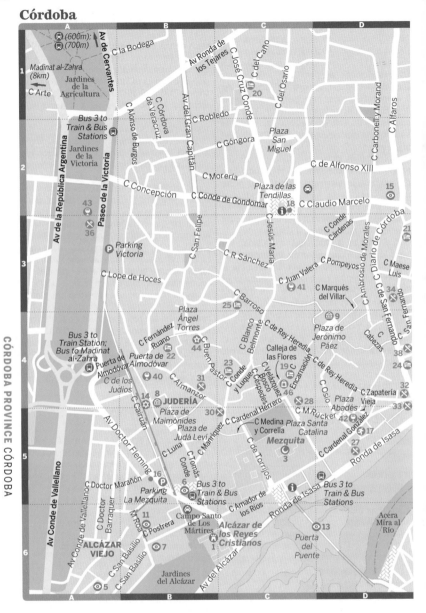

The **museum** takes you through the history of Medina Azahara, with sections on its planning and construction, its inhabitants and its eventual downfall – all illustrated with beautifully displayed pieces from the site and interactive displays, and complemented by flawless English translations.

Drivers should leave Córdoba westward along Avenida de Medina Azahara. This feeds into the A431 road, with the turn-off to Medina Azahara signposted after 6km.

N 0 ___ 200 m
0 ___ 0.1 miles

Plaza de Don Gome | Palacio de Viana 4

C Juan Rufo

C Santa Marta

C Conde de Arenales

C Manchado

C de San Pablo

C Villalones

C Espartería
C Tundidores

C Pedro López
37

Plaza de la Corredera 12
45
Mercado

C Tomillo

C de San Francisco
C R Barros
10
C de Lineros
29
Plaza del Potro
2
39 35
Centro Flamenco Fosforito
C ER de Torres
C de Lucano
Paseo de la Ribera
26

Río Guadalquivir
Puente de Miraflores
Acera Mira al Río

Acera Mira al Río

Río Guadalquivir

Parque de Miraflores

C del Santo Cristo

Feria de Mayo Grounds (500m)

---

day from mid-September to mid-June. You can get tickets on the bus, or in advance at tourist offices. Buying in advance is sensible for weekends and public holidays. The bus starts back from Medina Azahara 3¼ hours after it leaves Córdoba. An interesting alternative way of getting here is on an electric-bicycle tour with Elektrik.es (p217). English- or Spanish-language guided visits with **Córdoba Visión** (☑957 76 02 41, 957 41 92 19; http://cordobavision.es; Calle Doctor Marañón 1; ☉office 9.30am-1.30pm & 5.30-9pm Mon-Fri, 10am-1pm Sat) are offered for €20 (children €10), using the 10.15am bus service; get tickets in advance through its office or tourist offices.

Museo Arqueológico

MUSEUM

(☑957 35 55 17; www.museosdeandalucia.es; Plaza de Jerónimo Páez 7; EU/non-EU citizen free/€1.50; ☉9am-8pm Tue-Sat & 9am-3pm Sun mid-Sep–mid-Jun, 9am-3pm Tue-Sun mid-Jun–mid-Sep) The well-displayed Archaeological Museum traces Córdoba's many changes in size, appearance and lifestyle from pre-Roman to early Reconquista times, with some fine sculpture, an impressive coin collection, and interesting exhibits on domestic life and religion, with explanations in English and Spanish. In the basement, you can walk through the excavated remains of the city's Roman theatre.

Museo Julio Romero de Torres

GALLERY

(Plaza del Potro 1; adult/student/child €4.50/2.25/free; ☉8.30am-3pm Tue-Sat & 8.30am-2.30pm Sun mid-Jun–mid-Sep, 8.30am-8.45pm Tue-Fri, 8.30am-4.30pm Sat & 8.30am-2.30pm Sun mid-Sep–mid-Jun) A former hospital houses this popular museum devoted to much-loved local painter Julio Romero de Torres (1874–1930), who is famed for his paintings expressing his admiration of Andalucian female beauty. He was also much inspired by flamenco and bullfighting.

Templo Romano

TEMPLE

(Calle Claudio Marcelo) Though generally not open to visitors, this 1st-century AD Roman temple can be viewed perfectly well from the street. Its 11 tall white columns make a striking sight, especially when floodlit. Dedicated to emperor worship, the temple is thought to have looked east towards a huge Roman circus (for horse races and other spectacles). The band of cats that hangs out here must be the most photographed cats in Spain.

Plaza de la Corredera

PLAZA

This grand 17th-century square has an elaborate history as a site of public spectacles, including bullfights and Inquisition burnings. Now it's ringed by balconied apartments and

A bus to Medina Azahara (adult/child €9/5 return including the shuttle from museum to site and back) leaves from a **stop** on Glorieta Cruz Roja near Córdoba's Puerta de Almodóvar at 10.15am and 11am Tuesday to Sunday, plus 2.45pm Tuesday to Satur-

Córdoba

is home to an assortment of popular, though culinarily run-of-the-mill, cafes and restaurants. The Mercado de la Corredera (Plaza de la Corredera; ◎8am-3pm Mon-Thu, 8am-3.30pm Fri & Sat) is a busy morning food market selling all kinds of fresh produce.

🏃 Activities

Hammam Baños Árabes　BATHHOUSE
(📞957 48 47 46; http://cordoba.hammamaland alus.com; Calle del Corregidor Luis de la Cerda 51; baths & steam room €28, incl massage from €41; ◎1½hr sessions 10am, noon, 2pm, 4pm, 6pm, 8pm, 10pm & midnight) Follow the lead of the medieval Cordobans and treat yourself to a soak in the warm, hot and cold pools of these beautifully renovated Arab baths, where you can also enjoy an essential-oils massage.

👉 Tours

Oway Tours　TOURS, CULTURAL
(📞688 376581; www.owaytours.com) FREE A vast array of guided tours is available in Córdoba (see www.turismodecordoba.org/seccion/rutas-por-cordoba). Oway does an entertaining free 2½-hour walking introduction to the city, with enthusiastic guides

proffering interesting snippets of history along the way. Find the guides with blue shirts and blue umbrellas in Plaza de las Tendillas at 10.30am daily: participants are divided into English-, Spanish- and French-speaking groups.

🎉 Festivals & Events

Spring and early summer – especially May, when the weather is at its most glorious – are Córdoba's chief festival times.

Semana Santa　RELIGIOUS
(Holy Week; http://hermandadesdecordoba.es; ◎Mar/Apr) Every evening from Palm Sunday to Good Friday, five or six *pasos* (platforms bearing sacred statues from churches) are carried through the city, and into and out of the cathedral in the Mezquita, accompanied by large crowds of the faithful and other onlookers. The thickest crowds gather in the streets around the Mezquita, where most *pasos* arrive between 7pm and 11pm.

Cruces de Mayo　FIESTA
(May Crosses; ◎early May) Crosses adorned with flowers and Manila shawls are set up in about 50 plazas and streets. The plazas too are dec-

orated, drink and tapas stalls are set up, and the whole thing turns into a neighbourhood party with music and dancing. Wednesday to Sunday of the first week of May, peaking on the Friday night and Saturday.

Fiesta de los Patios de Córdoba FIESTA
(http://patios.cordoba.es; ☉ May) This 'best patio' competition sees 50 or more of Córdoba's beautiful private courtyards (p209) open for public viewing till 10pm nightly for two weeks, starting in early May, when the patios are at their prettiest. A concurrent cultural program stages flamenco and other concerts in some of the city's grandest patios and plazas.

Feria de Mayo FERIA
(May Fair; ☉ last week May) A massive week-long party takes over the Arenal area east of the centre, near the river, with music, Sevillana dancing, horses, carriages, traditional dress, fireworks and loads of fun.

★ **Noche Blanca del Flamenco** MUSIC
(http://nocheblancadelflamenco.cordoba.es; ☉ Jun) An all-night fest of top-notch flamenco by leading song, guitar and dance artists of the genre, in picturesque venues around the city such as the Mezquita's Patio de los Naranjos and Plaza del Potro. All performances are free. On a Saturday night around 20 June.

Festival de la Guitarra de Córdoba MUSIC
(www.guitarracordoba.org; ☉ early Jul) A two-week celebration of the guitar, with performances of classical, flamenco, rock, blues and more by top Spanish and international names in Córdoba's theatres.

🛏 Sleeping

Córdoba's budget choices include *hostales* and *pensiones* in characterful old-town houses, plus stylish hostels. In higher price brackets there's a growing number of attractive boutique options as well as plenty of professionally run chain hotels. Room prices are generally at the higher end of their range during the main tourist months of April, May, September and October, and at weekends most of the year. Booking ahead is advisable for these times, and it's essential for Semana Santa, the May festivals and some other national holidays (when prices can reach stratospheric levels). Rates are lower in July, August and the depths of winter.

★ **Bed and Be** HOSTEL €
(☎ 661 420733; www.bedandbe.com; Calle José Cruz Conde 22; incl breakfast dm €17-35, s €30-50, d €49-80; ✷ 🛜) ✎ An exceptional hostel option 300m north of Plaza de las Tendillas. Staff are clued up about what's on in Córdoba, and there's a social event every evening – often a drink on the roof followed by a bar or tapas tour. The shared-bathroom private rooms and four- or eight-bunk dorms are all super clean and as gleaming white as a *pueblo blanco*. Extra value is added by the great two-level roof terrace, bicycle rental (€6/10 per three/six hours), two kitchens and lounge and eating areas.

Option Be Hostel HOSTEL €
(☎ 661 420733; www.facebook.com/optionbecordoba; Calle Leiva Aguilar 1; incl breakfast dm €18-45, d €44-99; ✷ 🛜 ⛱) Option Be is a small, attractive, welcoming, contemporary-design hostel in a quiet old-city street, with a delightful roof terrace and plunge pool. It has just two private rooms (with private bathrooms) and two dorms, plus a bright ground-floor kitchen and neat central patio-lounge area. It's run by the same team as the excellent Bed and Be, and guests can share Bed and Be's nightly social activities.

Hospedería Alma Andalusí HOTEL €
(☎ 957 20 04 25; www.almaandalusi.com; Calle Fernández Ruano 5; r €38-70; ✷ 🛜) This small hotel in a quiet section of the Judería has been brilliantly converted from an ancient structure into a stylish, modern establishment, while rates have been kept sensible. Rooms are small but attractive, with blue-and-white colour schemes, thoughtfully chosen furnishings, appealing large photos of Córdoba's sights and polished-wood or traditional-tile floors – all making for a comfortable base.

Hotel Maestre HOTEL €
(☎ 957 47 24 10; www.hotelmaestre.com; Calle Romero Barros 4-6; s €25-55, d €38-90; P ✷ 🛜) Within easy reach of the Mezquita and some good restaurants, the Maestre is welcoming, efficiently run and well priced. Rooms are medium-sized and fairly plain, but clean and comfy. The three patios, and walls full of art, add light and colour, and there's parking (€10) right on the spot.

★ **Patio del Posadero** BOUTIQUE HOTEL €€
(☎ 957 94 17 33; www.patiodelposadero.com; Call Mucho Trigo 21; r incl breakfast €95-170; ✷ 🛜 ⛱) A 15th-century building in a quiet lane 1km east of the Mezquita has been superbly converted into a welcoming boutique hideaway combining comfort and unique contemporary design with old-Córdoba Moorish style. At its centre is a charming cobble-floored, brick-arched patio, with steps leading up

to a lovely upper deck with plunge pool, where the first-class homemade breakfasts are served.

The handful of rooms, with themes like the Córdoban countryside, flamenco and Moorish culture, have king- or queen-size beds, carved-wood doors and lots of *tadelakt* (a waterproof Moroccan lime plaster).

★ Viento10 BOUTIQUE HOTEL €€

(✆957 76 49 60; www.hotelviento10.es; Calle Ronquillo Briceño 10; s €84-147, d €100-172; ✳🛜) An inspired conversion of a 15th-century hospital building, Viento10 has just eight relaxing, comfortable rooms, in a beautiful, bright, clean-lined style that harmonises perfectly with the ancient stone pillars of its courtyard. A strong sense of light suffuses the property, not least on the roof terrace with its loungers and views over tiled rooftops to the Mezquita. A small spa, affable hosts, and excellent breakfasts (€8), served in the sitting area alongside the patio, add to the happy mix. Viento10 is in a quiet street close to the river, just over 1km east of the Mezquita.

Casa de los Azulejos HOTEL €€

(✆957 47 00 00; www.casadelosazulejos.com; Calle Fernando Colón 5; incl breakfast s €80, d €89-139; ✳🛜♨) Hints of Mexico infuse this stylish eight-room hotel, where the patio is all banana trees, ferns and potted palms bathed in sunlight. The pleasing, uncluttered rooms (named after Mexican plants) feature big beds, walls in lilac, lemon and sky blue, and jazzy bathroom tiles complementing the traditional Spanish floor *azulejos* (tiles) that give the place its name.

Hospedería del Atalia BOUTIQUE HOTEL €€

(✆957 49 66 59; www.hospederiadelatalia.com; Calle Buen Pastor 19; r €50-200; ✳🛜) Entered from a quiet patio in the Judería, the Atalia sports elegant, owner-designed rooms in burgundies, russets and olive greens. Good breakfasts with a wide choice are €6, and there's a big, sunny roof terrace with chairs, tables and a Mezquita view.

★ Balcón de Córdoba BOUTIQUE HOTEL €€€

(✆957 49 84 78; www.balcondecordoba.com; Calle Encarnación 8; incl breakfast s €160-320, d €170-400; ✳🛜) Offering top-end boutique luxury a stone's throw from the Mezquita, the 10-room Balcón is a riveting place with a charming patio, slick rooms and ancient stone relics dotted around as if it were a wing of the nearby archaeological museum. Service doesn't miss a beat and the rooms have tasteful, soothing, contemporary decor with a little art but no clutter.

The roof terrace affords great views across the rooftops to the Mezquita, and the classy restaurant does a great buffet breakfast and a carefully prepared selection of Cordoban-international fusion dishes.

✗ Eating

Restaurants and tapas bars are scattered all over and beyond the old city, including a string of places facing the river along Ronda de Isasa and Paseo de la Ribera.

Córdoba's signature dish is *salmorejo*, a delicious, thick, chilled soup of blended tomatoes, garlic, bread, lemon, vinegar and olive oil, sprinkled with hard-boiled egg and strips of ham. Along with *rabo de toro* (oxtail stew), it appears on every menu. Another meaty Córdoba speciality is the *flamenquín*, a sausage-shaped roll of breaded pork wrapped around slices of ham. Don't miss the sweet local Montilla-Moriles wine.

★ La Bicicleta CAFE €

(✆666 544690; Calle Cardenal González 1; light dishes €4-13; ⊙noon-1am, from 6pm Mon-Thu Jul-Aug; 🛜♪) 🍃 This friendly, informal spot welcomes one and all with an array of drinks – from long, cool multi-fruit juices whizzed up on the spot to cocktails, beer and wine – and tasty light dishes such as hummus, avocado-and-ham toasts and delicious fresh-daily cakes.

★ Mercado Victoria FOOD HALL €

(http://mercadovictoria.com; Paseo de la Victoria; items €2-19; ⊙10am-midnight Sun-Thu, 10am-2pm Fri & Sat) The Mercado Victoria is, yes, a food court – but an unusually classy one, with almost everything, from Argentine empanadas and Mexican burritos to sushi and classic Spanish seafood and grilled meats, prepared fresh before your eyes. The setting is special too – a 19th-century wrought-iron-and-glass pavilion in the Victoria gardens just west of the old city.

Taberna Salinas ANDALUCIAN €

(✆957 48 01 35; www.tabernasalinas.com; Calle Tundidores 3; raciones €8-9; ⊙12.30-4pm & 8-11.30pm Mon-Sat, closed Aug) A historic bar-restaurant (since 1879), with a patio and several rooms, Salinas is adorned in classic Córdoba fashion with tiles, wine barrels, art and photos of bullfighter Manolete. It's popular with tourists (and offers a five-language menu), but it retains a traditional atmosphere and the waiters are very helpful. Not least, the food is very good, from the orange-and-cod salad to the pork loin in hazelnut sauce.

Bar Santos TAPAS €

(Calle Magistral González Francés 3; tapas €2-5; ⏰10am-midnight) This legendary little bar across the street from the Mezquita serves the best *tortilla de patata* (potato omelette) in town – and don't the *cordobeses* know it. Thick wedges (€2.30) are deftly cut from giant wheels of the stuff and customarily served with plastic forks on paper plates to eat outside under the Mezquita's walls. Plenty of other tapas are on offer too. Don't miss it.

La Tinaja ANDALUCIAN €

(☑957 04 79 98; http://latinajadecordoba.com; Paseo de la Ribera 12; raciones €8-18; ⏰1.30-5pm & 7.30pm-1.30am) The food at some river-facing restaurants doesn't live up to the location, but La Tinaja serves reliably good and thoughtful preparations from classic Spanish ingredients, and its terrace is the most romantic of all when candlelit after dark. You might go for the seafood-stuffed leeks, spinach-and-hake ravioli, or the grilled pork with pumpkin hummus. Portions aren't for giant appetites.

Taberna Sociedad de Plateros ANDALUCIAN €

(☑957 47 00 42; Calle de San Francisco 6; tapas €2.25-2.50, raciones €5-12; ⏰noon-4pm & 8pm-midnight Tue-Sat, noon-4pm Sun; 🛜) Run by the silversmiths' guild, this well-loved traditional bar-restaurant serves a selection of generous tapas and *raciones* (full plates of tapas items) in its light, glass-roofed patio. The seafood selection is particularly good, highlighted by such items as *gambas rebozados* (battered shrimps) and *salpicón de mariscos* (shellfish salad), but there's a good choice of meat, fish, eggs, salads and other dishes too.

★**Casa Pepe de la Judería** ANDALUCIAN €€

(☑957 20 07 44; http://restaurantecasapepedela juderia.com; Calle Romero 1; raciones €10-26; ⏰1-4pm & 7.30-11pm; 🛜) Thoughtfully prepared classic Andalucian fare, on a sunny roof terrace or in rooms adorned with traditional and contemporary Cordoban art, keeps Pepe's (first opened in 1920) high in the popularity charts. Dishes range from good *salmorejo*, gazpacho, *flamenquín* (breaded pork loin wrapped with slices of ham) and salads to turbot meunière or lamb shoulder with apple purée. Service remains attentive and friendly even when it's packed out.

★**Bodegas Campos** ANDALUCIAN €€

(☑957 49 75 00; www.bodegascampos.com; Calle de Lineros 32; mains €14-24; ⏰1.30-4.30pm & 8.30-11.30pm Mon-Sat, 1.30-4.30pm Sun) This atmospheric warren of rooms and patios is a Córdoba classic, popular with *cordobeses* and visitors alike. The restaurant and more informal *taberna* (tavern) serve up delicious dishes putting a slight creative twist on traditional Andalucian fare – the likes of cod-and-cuttlefish ravioli or pork tenderloin in grape sauce. Campos also produces its own house Montilla.

La Boca FUSION €€

(☑957 47 61 40; www.facebook.com/restaurante. laboca; Calle de San Fernando 39; dishes €6-15; ⏰noon-4pm & 8pm-midnight Wed-Mon; 🛜) If oxtail tacos, red-tuna *tataki*, or a salad of duck-prosciutto and mango in walnut vinaigrette sound appetising, you'll like La Boca. This inventive eatery serves up global variations in half a dozen appealingly arty, rustic-style '*taberna'* rooms or in its marginally more formal restaurant section. It's very well done, though portions are not large. Reservations advisable at weekends.

Amaltea FUSION, VEGETARIAN €€

(☑957 49 19 68; Ronda de Isasa 10; mains €12-16; ⏰1-4pm & 8-11pm or later Mon-Sat, 1-4pm Sun; 🛜🌱) One of the best of the restaurants along the Ronda de Isasa, Amaltea has a bright, spacious dining room and friendly, relaxed atmosphere, and offers a good mix of Spanish and Mediterranean dishes, plus a few Middle Eastern and Asian options, including plenty of vegetarian and gluten-free fare.

Garum 2.1 ANDALUCIAN €€

(☑957 48 76 73; Calle de San Fernando 122; tapas €3-9, raciones €8-18; ⏰noon-midnight) Garum serves up traditional meaty, fishy and veggie ingredients in creative, tasty concoctions. We recommend the *presa ibérica con patatas al pelotón* (Iberian pork with a juicy potato-onion-capsicum combination). Service is helpful and friendly.

El Churrasco GRILL €€€

(☑957 29 08 19; www.elchurrasco.com; Calle Romero 16; mains €12-28; ⏰1-4pm & 8.30-11.30pm) Famed for its *churrasco cordobés* (pork tenderloin grilled over oak charcoal, with Arabic sauces), this is the place to head for a carnivorous feast, as your nostrils will affirm as you approach. The menu ranges over many meat and fish dishes, up to Galician *chuletón* (a huge beef chop). Dine in a classic Cordoban patio, or the wood-beamed upper room.

🍷 Drinking & Entertainment

Córdoba has a pretty good live music scene, with several venues regularly hosting flamenco, jazz, rock or blues. The Centro Flamenco Fosforito (p208) is one place staging regular flamenco events and is a good place to ask about what else is coming up.

Bodega Guzmán   WINE BAR
(Calle de los Judíos 7; ⊙noon-4pm & 8.30-11.30pm Fri-Wed) This atmospheric, cavern-like Judería drinking spot, frequented by both locals and tourists, is bedecked with bullfighting memorabilia and dispenses Montilla wine from three giant barrels behind the bar: don't leave without trying some *amargoso* (bitter).

Califa   PUB
(www.cervezascalifa.com; Calle Juan Valera 3; ⊙noon-4pm & 7pm-12.30am; 🐾) One of Andalucía's longest-running craft beer pubs, with the ale concocted on the premises. The IPA is very good or you can try the Rubia (blonde), Morena (amber), Sultana (stout) or Trigo Limpio (wheat) varieties. And there are light food items to soak it all up with.

Amapola   BAR
(www.facebook.com/amapolabarcordoba; Paseo de la Ribera 9; ⊙4pm-2.30am or later, from noon Fri-Sun) The artiest bar in the riverside area, with elaborate cocktails and a great terrace looking down to the river. Often DJs or live music on Friday and/or Saturday nights.

El Barón   BAR
(Plaza de Abades 4; ⊙12.30pm-midnight) Set on a traffic-free, orange tree–shaded plaza in the old city, the outside tables at this unassuming local bar are a lovely place for quiet nocturnal drinks. It has Montilla and other wines, *cava* (sparkling wine), craft and other beers, and some good snacks including a very tempting chocolate cake.

Sojo Mercado   BAR, LOUNGE
(http://sojomercado.com; Mercado Victoria, Paseo de la Victoria; ⊙1pm-2am Sun-Thu, to 3am Fri & Sat) Occupying a corner of the Mercado Victoria gastro-market and a roof terrace above, this fashionable spot gets very lively at weekends, with the 20- and 30-something crowd already starting to dance to the pop/electronic/Latin soundtrack by mid-afternoon on Saturdays.

Tablao Cardenal   DANCE, MUSIC
(www.tablaocardenal.es; Calle Buen Pastor 2; admission incl 1 drink €23; ⊙shows 8.15pm Mon-Thu & 9pm Fri & Sat Sep-Jun, 9pm Mon-Sat Jul & Aug) One of Andalucía's top regular flamenco shows, the Cardenal has been staging its professional, authentic, passionate and colourful spectacles of song, dance and music since 1990. You'll be glad you went.

🛍 Shopping

Córdoba's time-honoured craft specialities are colourful embossed leather *(cuero repujado),* silver jewellery and attractive pottery. The leather is also known as *guadamecí* (if it's sheepskin) or *cordobán* (goatskin). Calles Cardenal González and Manríquez have some of the classier craft shops.

Meryan   ARTS & CRAFTS
(📞957 47 59 02; www.meryancor.com; Calleja de las Flores 2; ⊙9am-8pm Mon-Fri, 9.30am-2.30pm Sat) This shop has a particularly good range of embossed leather goods: wallets, bags, boxes, notebooks, leather-covered wooden chests and even copies of Picasso paintings.

❶ Information

Centro de Visitantes (Visitors Centre; 📞902 201774; www.turismodecordoba.org; Plaza del Triunfo; ⊙9am-7pm Mon-Fri, 9.30am-2.15pm Sat & Sun) The main tourist information centre,

BUSES FROM CÓRDOBA

TO	COMPANY	COST	DURATION	FREQUENCY
Almodóvar del Río	Autocares San Sebastián	€2	30min	up to 10 daily
Baena	Autocares Carrera	€5.50	1hr	8 daily
Baeza	Alsa	€12	2¼hr	2 daily
Granada	Alsa	€15	2¾-4hr	7 daily
Hornachuelos	Autocares San Sebastián	€4.45	1¼hr	2-5 daily except Sun
Jaén	Grupo Sepulvedana	€11	2hr	5-6 daily
Madrid	Socibus	€17-23	5hr	8 daily
Málaga	Alsa	€12	3hr	4 daily
Montilla	Autocares Carrera	€3.80	45min	8 or more daily
Priego de Córdoba	Autocares Carrera	€9.20	2hr	3-7 daily
Seville	Alsa	€12	2hr	7 daily
Úbeda	Alsa	€12	2½hr	4 daily
Zuheros	Autocares Carrera	€6.45	1¾hr	2-4 daily

with an exhibit on Córdoba's history, and some Roman and Visigothic remains downstairs.

Córdoba (www.cordobaturismo.es) Tourist information for Córdoba province.

Municipal Tourist Information Kiosk (☑ 902 201774; www.turismodecordoba.org; Plaza de las Tendillas; ☺ 9am-2pm)

Municipal Tourist Information Office (☑ 902 201774; www.turismodecordoba.org; train station; ☺ 9am-2pm & 4.30-7pm) In the station's main entry hall.

ⓘ Getting There & Away

BUS

The **bus station** (☑ 957 40 40 40; www.estacionautobusescordoba.es; Avenida Vía Augusta) is behind the train station, 1.3km northwest of Plaza de las Tendillas.

Alsa (☑ 902 422242; www.alsa.es)

Autocares Carrera (☑ 957 50 16 32; www.autocarescarrera.es)

Autocares San Sebastián (☑ 957 42 90 30; www.autocaressansebastian.es)

Grupo Sepulvedana (☑ 902 119699; www.sepulvedana.es)

Socibus (☑ 902 229292; http://socibus.es)

TRAIN

Córdoba's modern **train station** (☑ 91 232 03 20; www.renfe.com; Plaza de las Tres Culturas), 1.2km northwest of Plaza de las Tendillas, is served both by fast AVE services and by some slower regional trains. The Granada service is due to restart late in 2018.

TO	COST	DURATION	FREQUENCY (DAILY)
Andújar	€8-16	50min	5
Antequera (Santa Ana)	€14-34	30-40min	12-16
Jaén	€15	1¾hr	4
Madrid	€33-63	1¾-2hr	24-33
Málaga	€20-42	1hr	14-18
Seville	€14-30	45-80min	27-39

ⓘ Getting Around

BICYCLE

There are bicycle lanes throughout the city, though they're underused.

Elektrik.es (☑ 671 417814; www.rentabikecordoba.com; Calle María Cristina 5; per 3hr/half-day/full day bicycle €5/9/13, electric bicycle €9/13/18; ☺ shop 9.30am-2pm & 5.30-9pm) Rents bikes for city and out-of-town riding.

BUS

Bus 3 (☑ 957 76 46 76; www.aucorsa.es) (€1.30, every 14 to 20 minutes), from Avenida Vía Augusta (the street between the train and bus stations), runs down Calle Diario de Córdoba and Calle de San Fernando, east of the Mezquita. For the return trip, catch it on Ronda de Isasa near the Puente Romano, or from Campo Santo de los Mártires, Glorieta Cruz Roja or Paseo de la Victoria.

CAR & MOTORCYCLE

Córdoba's one-way system is nightmarish, and cars are banned from the historic centre unless they are going to unload, load or park at hotels, most of which are reasonably well signposted as you approach. There is free, unmetered parking south of the river across the Puente de Miraflores, and a mixture of free and metered parking on Paseo de la Victoria, Avenida Doctor Fleming and streets to their west. Metered zones (with blue lines along the street) are free of charge from 2pm to 5pm and 9pm to 9am, and from 2pm Saturday to 9am Monday.

TAXI

Taxis from the bus or train stations to the Mezquita cost around €7. In the centre, taxis congregate on Campo Santo de los Mártires and just off Plaza de las Tendillas.

SOUTHERN CÓRDOBA PROVINCE

The rolling countryside south of Córdoba, known as the Campiña de Córdoba, is almost entirely covered in olive trees and grapevines, yielding some of Spain's finest olive oils and the unique, sherrylike Montilla-Moriles wines. Back in the 13th to 15th centuries, this region straddled the Islamic-Christian frontier, hence the many towns and villages that cluster around castles set on the higher points of the undulating landscape. Towards the southeast, the mountainous Parque Natural Sierras Subbéticas rises up from the lowlands: 320 sq km of high summits, canyons, caves and wooded valleys surrounded by appealing villages and towns such as Zuheros and Priego de Córdoba, great bases for a scenic natural break.

Baena

POP 17,930 / ELEV 430M

This market town 66km southeast of Córdoba is at the heart of an area producing quality olive oil with its own Denominación de Origen (DO; a quality-certified producing region). If you're passing this way, Baena is worth a stop to visit a working olive-oil mill, an olive-oil museum, a heavily restored castle or a worthwhile archaeological museum.

MONTILLA & ITS WINES

The rolling countryside south of Córdoba is home to the sweet wines of the Montilla-Moriles Denominación de Origen (DO), which you'll find throughout Córdoba province. Endlessly compared to sherry, to the irritation of local vintners, the highly drinkable Montilla-Moriles wines are produced exclusively from the Pedro Ximénez grape. While Jerez wine (sherry) is fortified by the addition of extra alcohol, Montilla wine achieves its own high levels of alcohol (15%-plus) and sweetness from the intense summer temperatures. The wineries in and around the town of Montilla are far less visited than the sherry bodegas of Jerez, but their wines are just as alluring.

This district is a zone of chalky white, moisture-retaining soils, long, hot, dry summers, and sharp day/night temperature changes – disastrous conditions for most grapevines – but not for the Pedro Ximénez. The PX, as it's known (pe equis in Spanish), is a tough one, a vine that thrives on extreme weather – and it's exactly these conditions that yield the unusual flavours of Montilla-Moriles wines.

The most delicate of Montilla wines is the pale, straw-like *fino*; an *amontillado* is a golden-amber wine with a nutty flavour; and the *oloroso* is a darker, full-bodied wine with 18% to 20% alcohol content. Then there's the almost black, super-sweet Pedro Ximénez wine itself – all Montilla-Moriles wines come from PX grapes but wine bearing the name Pedro Ximénez is made from grapes that are put out in the sun to dry, like raisins, before being pressed. Montilla wines go very well with tapas, as predinner drinks or as dessert wines, and the lighter ones nicely accompany soups or seafood starters. If you're feeling brave, try ordering a *fiti* (fifty-fifty), a powerful mix of *fino* and PX!

Montilla's super-enthusiastic and helpful **Oficina de Turismo** (☑957 65 23 54; www.montillaturismo.es; Castillo, off Calle Cuesta del Silencio; ☉9am-2pm & 4-6pm Mon-Fri, 11am-2pm Sat & Sun, hours vary Jun-Sep) is on the ball about winery visits and everything else in the area. The website Ruta del Vino Montilla Moriles (www.turismoyvino.es) is also helpful.

Montilla is a 50km, 45-minute drive south of Córdoba. Eight or more daily buses run to/from Córdoba (€3.80, 45 minutes), and four to/from Málaga (€11, two hours). Autocares Carrera (www.autocarescarrera.es) runs two or three daily buses to/from Priego de Córdoba (€4.70, 1¼ hours).

Bodegas Alvear (☑957 65 29 39; www.alvear.es; Avenida Boucau 6; 1½-hr tours €7-16; ☉tours without reservation 12.30pm Mon-Sat, with reservation Sun or 4.30pm Mon-Sat) The most renowned of Montilla's winemakers and one of Spain's oldest, with a range of PX vintages. Located just south of Montilla's historic core. Tours include tasting of wines and are available in Spanish, English, French or German.

Bodegas Lagar Blanco (☑628 319977; www.lagarblanco.es; Ctra Cuesta Blanca Km 4; tour incl tasting 2/5 wines per person €10/18; ☉1½hr tours Mon-Sat by arrangement; Ⓟ) Owner Miguel Cruz gives excellent tours in English or Spanish at this scenic spot in the Sierra de Montilla, 10km east of town (€10 by taxi). You'll see the vineyards and modern and giant traditional *tinaja* (fermentation vessels) as well as modern winemaking technology. Call or email to book a tour.

Bodegas Pérez Barquero (☑957 65 05 00; www.perezbarquero.com; Avenida de Andalucía 27; 1-1½hr tours in Spanish €5, English, French or German €10; ☉tours by reservation noon daily; Ⓟ) The vast warehouses here are stacked high with oak barrels of highly acclaimed wines, with five wine tastings in an atmospheric former chapel. It's in the western part of Montilla, on the way in from the N331.

Castillo (Calle Cuesta del Silencio; ☉9am-2pm & 4-6pm Mon-Fri, 11am-2pm Sat & Sun, hours vary Jun-Sep) At the panoramic highest point of town, Montilla's once-mighty castle fell into ruin after King Fernando el Católico had its towers demolished in 1508. The building occupying the site today, the Alhorí, was built as a grain store in the 18th century. You can see archaeological remains of the castle in the grounds.

Las Camachas (☑957 65 00 04; Avenida de Europa 3; mains €13-24; ☉1.30-5pm & 9-11.30pm) Montilla's top restaurant, on the western edge of town, offers up delicious local specialities, many prepared with local wines, in several wood-beamed, stone-walled dining halls or outside in the fresh air. It's strong on grilled and roast meats and seafood.

⊙ Sights

Almazara Núñez de Prado WORKSHOP
(☑ 957 67 01 41; Avenida Cervantes 5; ⊙ 9am-2pm
& 4-6pm Mon-Fri mid-Sep–mid-Jun, 9am-3pm Mon-
Fri mid-Jun–mid-Sep; ℗) 🏃 FREE This working
olive-oil mill is run by a family who own
around 100,000 olive trees. Olives are hand-
picked to prevent bruising, then pulped in
ancient stone mills. Núñez de Prado is one
of the few operations in Spain that uses this
traditional pulping method, and is famous
for its *flor de aceite*, the oil that seeps naturally from the crushed olives. Forty-minute
tours are given during opening hours; be
there at least one hour before closing time.

Castillo de Baena CASTLE
(Plaza del Palacio; adult/child & senior €2/1;
⊙9.30am-1.30pm Wed-Mon & 5.30-8.30pm Fri-Sat
May-Sep, 10am-1pm Wed-Mon Oct-Apr; ℗) The
heavily restored 15th- to 16th-century castle-
palace sits right on top of the hill over which
Baena spreads. The construction of water
tanks inside the castle in the 20th century
destroyed nearly all historical structures, but
archaeological work has now revealed some
remains, and there is interesting explanatory
material as well as fine panoramas.

ℹ Information

Tourist Office (☑ 957 67 17 57; www.baena.es;
Calle Virrey del Pino 5; ⊙ 8am-2.30pm Mon-
Wed & 8am-2.30pm & 6-8pm Thu-Sat May-Sep,
9am-2pm Mon-Fri & 10.30am-1.30pm Sat &
Sun Oct-Apr) Has full current information on all
Baena's attractions.

ℹ Getting There & Away

Autocares Carrera (www.autocarescarrera.es)
runs eight daily buses to/from Córdoba (€5.50,
one hour) and three daily to/from Priego de
Córdoba (€4, one hour). Autocares Valenzuela
(www.grupovalenzuela.com) runs three daily
buses to/from Zuheros (€2, 30 minutes). There
are fewer services at weekends, and none at all
for Priego on Saturdays.

Parque Natural Sierras Subbéticas

This 320-sq-km park in the southeast of Córdoba province encompasses a set of craggy,
emerald-green limestone hills pocked with
caves, springs and streams, with some charmingly appealing old villages and small towns
set round its periphery. It makes for lovely
exploring and good hiking among valleys,
canyons and high peaks (the highest is 1570m
La Tiñosa). Most visitors base themselves in

or near picturesque Zuheros or Priego de Córdoba. The ideal months for walking are April,
May, September and October.

The park's visitor centre, **Centro de Visitantes Santa Rita** (☑ 957 50 69 86; Carretera
A339, Km 11.2; ⊙ 9am-2pm Wed-Fri & 9am-2pm &
6-8pm Sat & Sun May-Jun, 9am-2pm Fri-Sun Jul-
Aug, 9am-2pm Wed-Sun Sep, 9am-2pm Wed-Fri &
9am-2pm & 4-6pm Sat & Sun Oct-Apr), is 15km
west of Priego on the Cabra road. The local
tourism website, http://turismodelasubbeti
ca.es, is a useful resource on the area.

An excellent walking guide is *Walking
in the Subbética Natural Park Córdoba* by
local resident Clive Jarman; Zuheros' Hotel
Zuhayra (p220) sells the guide and individual walk sheets.

Zuheros & Around
POP 660 / ELEV 640M

On the northern edge of Parque Natural Sierras Subbéticas, Zuheros sits in a supremely
picturesque location, its white streets and
crag-top castle crouching in the lee of towering hills with olive groves stretching away
below as far as the eye can see. Approached
by twisting roads up from the A318, the village has a delightfully relaxed atmosphere.

⊙ Sights

Castillo de Zuheros CASTLE
(Plaza de la Paz; admission or tour incl Museo Arqueológico adult/child €2/1.25; ⊙10am-2pm & 5-7pm
Tue-Fri, tours 11am, 12.30pm, 2pm, 5pm & 6.30pm
Sat, 6.30pm & holidays, all afternoon times 1hr earlier Oct-
Mar) Set on a picturesque pinnacle, Zuheros'
castle is of 9th-century Moorish origin, but
most of what survives is Christian construction from the 13th and 14th centuries, with
remains of a 16th-century Renaissance palace attached. It's small but panoramic, with
fine views from the top. Visits on weekends
and holidays are guided; other days, visits are
unguided. Tickets are sold at, and include,
the little **Museo Arqueológico** (☑ 957 69 45
45; adult/child incl Castillo €2/1.25; ⊙10am-2pm
Tue-Sun year-round, 5-7pm Tue-Fri Apr-Sep, 4-6pm
Tue-Fri Oct-Mar), just across the square, which
also doubles as Zuheros' tourist office (p221).

Cueva de los Murciélagos CAVE
(Cave of the Bats; ☑ 957 69 45 45; adult/child
€6/5; ⊙ guided tours 12.30pm & 5.30pm Tue-Fri,
11am, 12.30pm, 2pm, 5pm & 6.30pm Sat & Sun, afternoon tours 1hr earlier Oct-Mar; ℗) Carved out
of the limestone massif 4km above Zuheros
is this extraordinary cave. From the vast hall
at the start of the tour, it's a 415m loop walk

(with 700 steps) through a series of corridors filled with fantastic rock formations and traces of Neolithic rock paintings showing abstract figures of goats. Visits are by guided tour only: reserve by phoning or emailing Zuheros' tourist office between 10am and 1.30pm Tuesday to Friday.

🏃 Activities

A number of wonderful walks can be done in the area. A nice stroll of about half an hour round the village's lower periphery is the **Camino Periurbano**, which includes lookout points and a hanging bridge over a small ravine. Hotel Zuhayra can put you in contact with an English-speaking walking guide, **Clive Jarman** (☑669 700763, clivejar man@gmail.com), who lives in Zuheros.

★ Cerro Bramadero Walk   WALKING
Behind Zuheros village lies a dramatic rocky gorge, the Cañón de Bailón. A beautifully scenic circular walk of about four hours takes you up the canyon and round Cerro Bramadero hill then back to Zuheros via the road descending from the Cueva de los Murciélagos. The distance is around 13km, with a total ascent and descent of some 600m.

As well as the rocky canyon and mountain scenery, you'll head through pretty woodlands and alongside mountain streams and pass caves and ruined farmsteads. To start, head down to the bridge over the Río Bailón at the southwest corner of Zuheros. Take the track heading up past the large 'Sendero Río Bailón' signboard and follow it as it winds uphill and then turns left along the slopes above the gorge. The valley opens out between rocky walls and the path descends and crosses the stony bed of the Río Bailón. It then recrosses the river three times in the next 600m.

About 900m past the fourth crossing, a smaller stream enters the Bailón from the left. Cross this and follow the path climbing the hillside roughly parallel to the Bailón. (Cerro Bramadero is the hill up to your left here.) Continue through some beautifully shady woodland to emerge into a clearing. About 100m along the clearing, take a path heading left back into the woods. This leads in about 1km to the Fuente de la Fuenfría water trough in an open area (almost the halfway point of the walk and a good rest spot). From here take the rough vehicle track heading eastward – at first uphill, then levelling off and curving northward and eventually descending to meet the Zuheros–Cueva de los Murciélagos road. It's then 3km down the road to Zuheros, or 1km up it to the Cueva.

Vía Verde del Aceite   CYCLING, HIKING
(www.viasverdes.com; 🚲) 🌿 The area's easiest and best marked path is the *vía verde* (greenway; a disused railway converted to a cycling and walking track), which you can see snaking across the countryside below Zuheros. It runs 128km across Córdoba and Jaén provinces from Camporreal near Puente Genil to Jaén city, skirting the western and northern fringes of the Parque Natural Sierras Subbéticas. With gentle gradients and utilising old bridges, tunnels and viaducts, the greenway makes for a fun outing for travellers of all ages. There are cafes and bike-hire outlets in old station buildings along the route, and informative map-boards – it's impossible to get lost! The section in Córdoba province is also still known by its old name, Vía Verde de la Subbética.

Subbética Bike's Friends (☑672 605088, 691 843532; www.subbeticabikesfriends.com; bikes per half-/full day €9/12, baby seats per day €2; ☉10am-6pm Sat & Sun; 🚲) at Doña Mencía station, 4km west down the hill from Zuheros, rents a range of different bikes, including children's, and can normally provide them any day of the week if you call ahead.

🛏 Sleeping & Eating

★ Hotel Zuhayra   HOTEL €
(☑957 69 46 93; www.zercahoteles.com; Calle Mirador 10; incl breakfast s €42-48, d €52-60; ❋🐾🛜🅿) A short distance below Zuheros' castle, this hotel has breathtaking views of the countryside from every one of its unfussily comfortable rooms, and is an excellent base for exploring the area. The friendly proprietors, the Ábalos brothers (who speak English), offer masses of information about things to see and do.

★ Restaurante Zuhayra   ANDALUCIAN €
(www.zercahoteles.com; Calle Mirador 10; mains & raciones €7-18, medias raciones €4-7.50; ☉1-4pm & 8.30-11pm; 🌿) Hotel Zuhayra's excellent restaurant, open to all, serves uncomplicated but perfectly prepared versions of local and Andalucian favourites, such as its homemade partridge pâté or lamb chops with thyme. Good vegetarian options too: try the *ensalada Zuhayra* with baked vegetables, almonds and caramelised local cheese. In good weather you can sit in a charming patio set beneath a natural rockface.

Mesón Atalaya   ANDALUCIAN €€
(☑957 69 45 28; Calle Santo 58; mains €7-19; ☉1-4pm & 9-11pm Tue-Sun) This family-run establishment at the east end of the village does excellent local fare, with plenty of lamb,

pork, ham, *potajes* and *cazuelas* (types of stew), local cheese and homemade desserts.

ℹ️ Information

Tourist Office (📱 957 69 45 45; http://turismo delasubbetica.es/zuheros; Plaza de la Paz 1; ⏰ 10am-2pm Tue-Sun year-round, 5-7pm Tue-Fri Apr-Sep, 4-6pm Tue-Fri Oct-Mar)

ℹ️ Getting There & Away

BUS

Buses depart from Mesón Atalaya.

Autocares Carrera (p217) Two to four daily buses to/from Córdoba (€6.45, 1¾ hours).

Autocares Valenzuela (📱 956 70 26 09; www. grupovalenzuela.com) Three or more daily buses to/from Doña Mencía (€1.15, 10 to 20 minutes) and two or more to/from Baena (€2, 30 minutes) and Seville (€17, 3¾ hours).

CAR & MOTORCYCLE

There are parking areas near Mesón Atalaya restaurant at the east end of the village: follow 'Cueva de los Murciélagos' signs as you approach Zuheros.

Priego de Córdoba & Around

POP 19,000 / ELEV 650M

Perched on an outcrop above the valley of the Río Salado, Priego de Córdoba is a surprisingly bustling market town in a fertile pocket of the Subbética. Founded in AD 745, it later found itself on the Granada emirate's frontline against its Christian enemies, until its definitive conquest by Alfonso XI in 1341. Priego's cavalcade of fine architecture, including some particularly extravagant baroque churches, is the legacy of a centuries-long run of prosperity, cresting with an 18th-century boom in silk and velvet production.

👁️ Sights

Northeast of the central Plaza de la Constitución, leafy **Plaza Abad Palomino** leads to the original Moorish quarter, the **Barrio de La Villa**. The narrow, geranium-hung lanes of the *barrio* (district) wind through to the clifftop **Paseo del Adarve**, a panoramic promenade looking out over the Salado valley, and the elegant **Paseo de Colombia**, with its fountains, flower beds and pergola.

Opening hours of Priego's churches and other sights have a habit of changing frequently: they are updated weekly on the website of the Oficina de Turismo (p222).

⭐ **Parroquia de la Asunción**   CHURCH
(Plaza Santa Ana 1; €2; ⏰ 11am-1.30pm Tue-Sat, 11am-noon Sun) On the edge of the Barrio de

La Villa, this church represents a high point in Andalucian baroque chiefly thanks to its wonderful Sagrario (Sacristy), where whirls of frothy white stucco work surge upwards to two beautiful cupolas – the work of local artist Francisco Javier Pedrajas in the 1780s. Even if baroque churches normally make you yawn, this is something special. For further lavish church ornamentation, head to the **Iglesia de la Aurora** (Carrera de Álvarez; €1.50; ⏰ 10.30am-1.30pm Tue-Sun) and **Iglesia de San Francisco** (Calle Buen Suceso; ⏰ 10am-1pm & 7-9pm Mon-Fri, 10am-1pm Sat & Sun) 🆓, both rebuilt in baroque style in the 18th century.

Castillo de Priego de Córdoba   CASTLE
(Plaza Abad Palomino; €1.50, Wed free; ⏰ 11am-2pm & 4-7pm Tue-Sat, 11am-2pm Sun) The rectilinear towers of Priego's castle stand proudly alongside Plaza Abad Palomino. Originally an Islamic fortress, it was thoroughly remodelled by the new Christian overlords between the 13th and 15th centuries. You can climb to the top of the keep (Torre del Homenaje) for aerial views of the white town.

Fuente del Rey   FOUNTAIN
(Fountain of the King; Calle del Río; ⏰ 24hr) Southwest of the centre, an entire plaza/park is reserved for this splendid baroque fountain completed in 1803, with its three-tiered basin continually filled with water splashing from 130 spouts. It would be equally at home in the gardens of Versailles. If you take the stairs to the left of the Fuente de la Virgen de la Salud, near the top of the park, you can walk up in about 10 minutes to the Ermita del Calvario (Calvary Chapel), with scenic views of the town and surrounding countryside.

Centro Cultural
Adolfo Lozano Sidro   MUSEUM
(📱 957 54 09 47; Carrera de las Monjas 16; €2, Wed free; ⏰ 10am-2pm & 6-8pm Mon-Fri, 10.30am-2pm & 5-7pm Sat, 10.30am-2pm Sun) You get three museums here: a history museum with four rooms of well-displayed archaeological finds from the Priego area; a gallery with two rooms of modern Spanish landscape paintings; and two floors devoted to painter Adolfo Lozano Sidro (1872–1935), whose family lived in this building. His realistic art covered the spectrum of social life in his era.

🛏️ Sleeping & Eating

⭐ **Casa Olea**   HOTEL €€
(📱 696 748209; www.casaolea.com; Carretera CO7204, near El Cañuelo; s/d incl breakfast €107/121; 🅿️ ❄️ 🐕 🛜 🏊) 🍴 Set in its own little olive grove

12km north of Priego, this British-owned country house has a spacious and relaxed feel. It makes a delightful rural retreat and base for exploring the region, with easy access to walks in the Sierras Subbéticas, mountain bikes to rent (€15 per day), and Córdoba and Granada both within 1½ hours' drive. There's a lovely pool, and excellent dinners (two/three courses €20/25) are available five nights a week. No children under seven.

★ **Casa Baños de la Villa** BOUTIQUE HOTEL €€
(☑957 54 72 74; www.casabanosdelavilla.com; Calle Real 63; incl breakfast s €49-71, d €89-99; P ❄ ☎ ☎) A big draw of this unique and welcoming hotel is that it has its very own *baños árabes*, a Moorish fantasy of baths and arches; room rates include a 90-minute session in its three pools of different temperatures, plus sauna. The rooms are all comfy and individually designed with homey bric-a-brac, and there's a fine roof deck.

La Pianola Casa Pepe ANDALUCIAN €
(Calle Obispo Caballero 6B; raciones €6-12; ☉12.30-4pm & 8pm-12.30am Tue-Sun) Always busy and animated, this smallish local corner restaurant manages to provide good and friendly service at the same time. And the food is excellent – nothing fancy, just expertly prepared local favourites from assorted *revueltos* (scrambled egg dishes) to stuffed artichokes, grilled squid or pork tenderloin in sherry.

★ **Restaurante La Fuente** ANDALUCIAN €€
(Zagrilla Alta; mains €8-21; ☉2-4pm & 8.30pm-midnight) The small village of Zagrilla Alta is 11km northwest of Priego, and well worth the trek for the warm welcome and terrific homestyle cooking you'll receive here. La Fuente is located in a beautiful setting beside a spring and stream just up from the main road.

Great local specialities include *revuelto de collejas* (scrambled eggs with campion leaves, garlic, and ham or shrimps) and *remojón* (chunks of orange, fig and hard-boiled egg with strips of salted cod), or you could go for a heartier *chuletón* or *churrasco* – big slabs of grilled beef.

Balcón del Adarve ANDALUCIAN €€
(☑957 54 70 75; www.balcondeladarve.com; Paseo de Colombia 36; mains €12-19; ☉noon-4.30pm & 8.30pm-midnight Tue-Sun) Overlooking the valley, with a terrace that takes full advantage of its privileged setting, this excellent restaurant brings a touch of elegance to local favourites such as oxtail, partridge pâté and duck breast in Pedro Ximénez wine.

❶ Information

Oficina de Turismo (☑957 70 06 25; www.turismodepriego.com; Plaza de la Constitución 3; ☉10am-2pm & 4.30-7pm Mon-Fri, 10am-2pm & 4.30-6.30pm Sat, 10am-2pm Sun) Very helpful and enthusiastic.

❶ Getting There & Around

BUS

Priego's **bus station** (☑957 70 18 75; Calle Ramón y Cajal) is about 1km west of the centre. Autocares Carrera (p217) runs to Montilla (€4.70, 1¼ hours, two or three daily) and Córdoba (€9.20, two hours, seven times daily Monday to Friday, three times on Saturday and Sunday; some services calling at Baena). Alsa (p217) heads to Granada (€7.40, 1½ to two hours, two to four daily) via Alcalá la Real.

CAR & MOTORCYCLE

There's free parking in the central **Parking Plaza de Abastos** (Calle Doctor Pedrajas; ☉9am-11pm). Also handy to the centre is **Aparcamiento Palenque** (Carrera de las Monjas; per day €1.50; ☉7.30am-9.30pm Mon-Sat).

WESTERN CÓRDOBA PROVINCE

West of Córdoba city unfolds a sparsely inhabited landscape cut through by the Río Guadalquivir and dotted with villages and castles, the most formidable one looming over the whitewashed jumble of Almodóvar del Río. To the north, the pleasant burg of Hornachuelos is the gateway to a remote range of forested hills interspersed with pasturelands and populated by deer, wild boar, otters and large birds of prey.

Parque Natural Sierra de Hornachuelos

The Parque Natural Sierra de Hornachuelos is a 600-sq-km area of rolling hills in the Sierra Morena, northwest of Almodóvar del Río. The park is densely wooded with a mix of holm oak, cork oak and ash, and is pierced by a number of thickly wooded river valleys. It is renowned for its eagles and other raptors, including a colony of rare black vultures.

LOS PEDROCHES

If you like driving empty roads across big landscapes and coming upon the occasional spectacular sight, then Córdoba's isolated far north, known as Los Pedroches, is for you. This is a plateau-like region of long, long vistas, broken up by a few ranges of hills and scattered villages and castles. It's known for its extensive *dehesas* (woodland pastures with acorn-bearing holm oaks) and for its high-quality ham, *jamón ibérico de bellota*, from the black Iberian pigs that feast on the annual acorn (*bellota*) harvest. Salted and cured for six to 12 months, the resulting dark-pink ham is usually served wafer-thin with bread and Montilla wine.

The gateway to Los Pedroches is the Puerto Calatraveño pass, 750m above sea level on the N502 about 55km north of Córdoba. From here the green landscape stretches ahead towards infinity. The first village is Alcaracejos, home to the district tourist office, the Oficina Comarcal de Turismo (☑957 15 61 02; www.turismolospedroches.org; Plaza de Andalucía 1; ⊙9.30am-2.30pm Mon-Fri). Twenty kilometres northwest of Alcaracejos is Hinojosa del Duque with its monumental 16th-century church, the Catedral de la Sierra (Plaza de la Catedral; ⊙11.30am-1.30pm & 8-9.30pm) FREE, whose bell tower is claimed to have been the model for the one on Córdoba's Mezquita. The plaza cafes here are good for refreshments. Hinojosa has a particularly large and impressive Museo Etnológico (Ethnological Museum; ☑957 14 10 56; www.hinojosadelduque.es; Calle Cánovas del Castillo 3; ⊙10am-2pm & 6-9pm Tue-Fri Jun-Aug, 10am-2pm & 5-8pm Tue-Fri Sep-May, 11am-2pm Sat & Sun year-round) FREE, preserving and re-creating country life of the past, from a traditional kitchen and agricultural implements to printing and grocery shops; it also functions as a tourist office.

From Hinojosa it's 9km north to remote Belalcázar whose massive and spooky Castillo de los Sotomayor is visible from far and wide, its top-heavy main tower rising 45m above its hilltop perch. This castle was built in the 15th century by the Knights of Calatrava, a Reconquista crusading order that controlled a huge swath of territory from Córdoba to Toledo and Badajoz. After years of abandonment and closure, a restoration project began in 2017 and the castle may be open to visitors by the end of 2018. Albergue Camino de Santiago (☑617 715129; http://caminodesantiagobelalcazar.blogspot.com.es; Calle Pilar; dm incl breakfast €12, half-board €19.50; P❋☎), just below the castle, is a well-managed hostel intended primarily for walkers following the Camino Mozárabe (one of the Camino de Santiago pilgrim routes to Santiago de Compostela), but is open to all for good-value food and lodging.

The lonely CO9402 heads 27km east across empty countryside to Santa Eufemia, Andalucía's northernmost village. For stupendous 360-degree views over vast swaths of Andalucía and Castilla-La Mancha, head up to the Castillo de Miramontes, a tumbled ruin 2.5km above Santa Eufemia (turn west off the N502 at Bar La Paloma, then turn right at the 'Camino Servicio RTVE' sign after 1km).

Villanueva de Córdoba, a lively market town 50km southeast of Santa Eufemia, makes a good place to bed down for the night; we recommend the cutely contemporary Hotel la Casa del Médico (☑957 12 02 47; http://hotellacasadelmedico.com; Calle Contreras 4; r incl breakfast €85-115; ❋☎☀). Eat and drink at cheerful La Puerta Falsa (Calle Contreras 8; mains €8-17; ⊙8am-midnight or later), with a pretty patio and a good choice of seafood as well as hill-country meat and egg dishes.

Before returning to civilisation, nature lovers can take a wander in the Parque Natural Sierra de Cardeña y Montoro (www.ventanadelvisitante.es), 384 sq km of rolling hills and woodland that is home to a few Iberian lynx and wolves, plus otters and birds of prey. Paths branch out from Aldea del Cerezo, 6km east of Cardeña village. Head to the Centro de Visitantes Venta Nueva (☑957 33 65 03; Junction N420 & A420; ⊙9am-2pm Wed-Fri & 9am-2pm & 6-8pm Sat & Sun May & Jun, 9am-2pm Sat & Sun Jul-Sep, 9am-2pm Wed-Fri & 9am-2pm & 4-6pm Sat & Sun Oct-Apr), 1km south of Cardeña, for information.

Autocares San Sebastián (www.autocaressansebastian.es) provides bus service between Córdoba and Los Pedroches.

WORTH A TRIP

CASTILLO DE ALMODÓVAR

Almodóvar's monumental and sinister-looking castle, **Castillo de Almodóvar** (☑957 63 40 55; www.castillodealmodovar.com; Calle del Castillo, Almodóvar del Río; adult/senior/child €8/6/4; ⊙11am-2.30pm & 4-8pm Mon-Fri, 11am-8pm Sat & Sun, to 7pm Oct-Mar; ℗), dominates the view from far and wide, rising almost sheer above the Río Guadalquivir with just enough room for the AVE high-speed railway to squeeze in between. It was founded in the 8th century but owes most of its present appearance to post-Reconquista rebuilding. Because the castle had never been taken by force, Pedro I ('the Cruel') used it as a treasure store. Its sense of impregnability is still potent within the massive walls.

You can climb up several of the nine towers, the mightiest being the Torre del Homenaje (Tower of Homage), which also contains the dungeon, where medieval conditions are re-created by a mannequin tableau. A film on the castle's history, with English subtitles, is screened in the chapel.

There is parking below the castle, or you can drive up the driveway and park just below the entrance, saving a 600m uphill walk.

The pleasant small town of Hornachuelos on the park's southern fringe, standing above a small reservoir on the Río Bembézar, makes the obvious base for enjoying the park's quiet charms.

🏃 Activities

Walking trails start from both the village and natural park visitors centre, 1.5km north.

Sendero de Los Ángeles WALKING
This path runs 4km from the foot of Hornachuelos village up beside the Bembézar reservoir to a huge, abandoned seminary, the Seminario de los Ángeles (entry prohibited). You may well spy griffon vultures from a colony a little further up the valley.

Sendero Guadalora WALKING
(⊙closed Jun-Sep) This moderately demanding but rewarding walk starts 2.5km northwest of the visitors centre (you can drive that far), then wends its way 6km (about 2½ hours) through evergreen oaks and olive trees and down a thickly wooded river valley to emerge on the CO5310 road. Walkers must obtain a free permit, quickly and easily available at the visitors centre. From the CO5310, you must retrace your steps, if you haven't organised a taxi.

🛏 Sleeping & Eating

Hostal El Álamo HOSTAL €
(☑957 64 04 76; http://complejoelalamo.com; Carretera A3151, Km 8; s/d incl breakfast €45/60;

❄🖝🏊) Motel-style El Álamo, on the main road passing through Hornachuelos, sports a faux *cortijo* (farmhouse) style, with tiled roofs and wagon wheels strewn about. The **cafe/bar/restaurant** (mains €8-21; ⊙1-4pm & 8-11.30pm) is a popular gathering place. Ask for a room away from the road, which can be noisy.

ℹ Information

Centro de Visitantes Huerta del Rey (☑957 57 96 56; Carretera Hornachuelos-San Calixto Km 1.5; ⊙9am-2pm Wed-Sun plus 6-8pm Sat & Sun May-Jun, 9am-2pm Fri-Sun Jul & Aug, 9am-2pm Wed-Sun Sep, 9am-2pm Wed-Sun plus 4-6pm Sat & Sun Oct-Apr) The natural park visitors centre has interesting displays and information for visitors (including a set of six detailed walk leaflets costing €2).

Oficina de Turismo (☑957 64 07 86; http://turismohornachuelos.es; Recinto Ferial; ⊙10am-2pm Tue-Sun) Hornachuelos' helpful tourist office is in the feria grounds off Carretera San Calixto (the A3151 passing through the west side of town).

ℹ Getting There & Away

Autocares San Sebastián (www.autocaressan sebastian.es) runs buses to/from Córdoba (€4.45, 1¼ hours, five daily Monday to Friday, two on Saturday). Buses leave from Carretera San Calixto (the A3151), just below the police station.

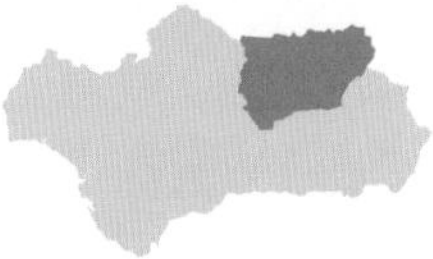

Jaén Province

Includes ➜

Best Places to Stay

➜ Afán de Rivera (p241)

➜ Parador Castillo de Santa Catalina (p230)

➜ Las Casas del Cónsul (p241)

➜ Casa Rural Los Parrales (p247)

➜ Parador de Úbeda (p241)

Best Places to Eat

➜ Palacio de Gallego (p237)

➜ Misa de 12 (p241)

➜ Cantina La Estación (p241)

➜ Casa Antonio (p230)

➜ El Tranco (p248)

Why Go?

For anyone who loves culture, nature, history or good food, this relatively little-visited province turns out to be one magical combination. Endless lines of pale-green olive trees – producing one-sixth of all the world's olive oil – carpet much of the landscape. Castle-crowned hills are a reminder that this was once a frontier zone between Christians and Muslims, while the gorgeous Renaissance architecture of Unesco World Heritage towns Úbeda and Baeza showcases the wealth amassed by the Reconquista nobility.

Beyond the towns and olive groves, Jaén has wonderful mountain country. The Parque Natural Sierras de Cazorla, Segura y Las Villas, Spain's biggest protected area, is a highlight of Andalucía for nature lovers, with rugged mountains, deep green valleys, prolific wildlife and dramatically perched villages – and good lodgings, roads and trails to help you make the most of it.

Driving Distances

	Úbeda	Jaén	Baeza	Cazorla
Jaén	60			
Baeza	16	50		
Cazorla	44	102	58	
Santa Elena	72	79	65	116

Jaén Province Highlights

① **Úbeda** (p237) Indulging the senses with inspired architecture and cuisine.

② **Parque Natural Sierras de Cazorla, Segura y Las Villas** (p245) Roaming

the green valleys, craggy mountains and scenic villages by vehicle or on foot, with an eye open for the plentiful wildlife.

③ **Baeza** (p233) Investigating the tangle of stone lanes lined with beautiful Renaissance buildings.

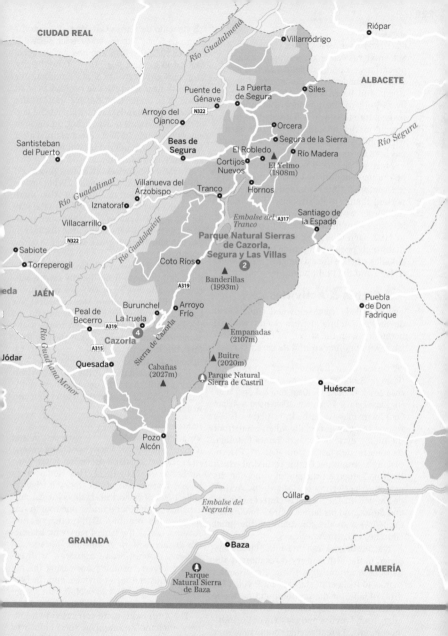

4 Cazorla (p242)
Experiencing the sights and atmosphere of this lively foothill town backed by lofty escarpments and crag-top castles.

5 Alcalá la Real (p232)
Climbing up to a fascinating hilltop castle and medieval town, still under excavation.

6 Jaén (p228) Exploring traditional tapas bars and a historic castle and cathedral.

JAÉN

POP 111,000 / ELEV 575M

Set amid vast olive groves, upon which its precarious economy depends, Jaén is somewhat overshadowed by the beauty of nearby Úbeda and Baeza, and is often passed over by visitors to the province. But once you make it into town you will discover a charming, if mildly dilapidated, historic centre with hidden neighbourhoods, excellent tapas bars and a grandiose cathedral.

Muslim Yayyan was a significant city before its conquest by Castilla in 1246. For 2½ centuries Christian Jaén remained important thanks to its strategic location near the border with Nasrid Granada – until the Muslims were finally driven out of Granada in 1492. Jaén then sank into a decline with many of its people emigrating to the Spanish colonies – hence the existence of other Jaéns in Peru and the Philippines.

◉ Sights & Activities

The wooded, castle-crowned hill Cerro de Santa Catalina defines Jaén's western boundary, with the streets of the old Moorish town huddling around its base.

★ Catedral de la Asunción CATHEDRAL

(Plaza de Santa María; adult incl audio guide €5, child/senior €1.50/2; ◐10am-2pm & 4-8pm Mon-Fri, 10am-2pm & 4-7pm Sat, 10am-noon & 4-7pm Sun) Jaén's massive cathedral still dwarfs the rest of the city, especially when seen from the hilltop eyrie of Cerro de Santa Catalina. Its construction lasted from 1540 to 1724, replacing a crumbling Gothic cathedral which itself had stood on the site of a mosque. Its perceived perfection of design – by Andrés de Vandelvira, the master architect of Úbeda and Baeza, and his father Pedro – made Jaén Cathedral a model for many of the great churches of Latin America.

The facade on Plaza de Santa María, completed in the 18th century, owes more to the baroque tradition than to the Renaissance, thanks to its host of statuary by Seville's Pedro Roldán. But the predominant aesthetic is Renaissance – particularly evident in its huge, round arches and clusters of Corinthian columns. A great circular dome rises over the crossing before the main altar. From the sacristy antechamber, south of the crossing, a 57-step staircase leads up to corridors along the cathedral's south and west sides yielding impressive views down into the cathedral.

★ Castillo de Santa Catalina CASTLE

(Cerro de Santa Catalina; adult/senior, student & child €3.50/1.50, 3-6pm Wed free; ◐10am-6pm Mon-Sat, to 3pm Sun; ℗ ♿) High above the city, atop cliff-girt Cerro de Santa Catalina, this fortress's near-impregnable position is what made Jaén important during the Muslim and early Reconquista centuries. At the end of the ridge stands a large cross, on the spot where Fernando III had a cross planted after Jaén finally surrendered to him in 1246; the views are magnificent.

The Moorish fortress here was revamped after the Christian conquest. What exists today is only about one-third of what there was – the rest was demolished to make way for the adjacent *parador* (state-owned luxury hotel) in the 1960s. Inside, the displays in English and Spanish give a good sense of the castle's history.

If you don't have a vehicle for the circuitous 5km drive up from the city centre, you can take a taxi (€7), or you can walk up in about 40 minutes from the cathedral via Calles Maestra, Parrilla and Buenavista. At the top of Buenavista, go 50m to the right along the Carretera de Circunvalación, then take the track up to the left and walk up through the trees.

If you aren't staying at the *parador,* drop in for a drink to see the extraordinary vaulted, decorative ceilings in the main salon and restaurant.

Palacio de Villardompardo BATHHOUSE, MUSEUM

(Centro Cultural Baños Árabes; www.bañosarabesjaen.es; Plaza de Santa Luisa de Marillac; ◐9am-10pm Tue-Sat, to 3pm Sun) FREE This Renaissance palace houses one of the most intriguing collections of historical, archaeological and artistic exhibits found under one roof in Andalucía: the beautiful 11th-century **Baños Árabes**, one of the largest surviving Islamic-era bathhouses in Spain; the **Museo de Artes y Costumbres Populares**, with extensive, diverse exhibits showcasing the life of pre-industrial Jaén province; and the **Museo Internacional de Arte Naïf** with a large collection of colourful and witty Naïve art.

The Arab baths were converted into a tannery after the Reconquista, then built over completely when the Conde de Villardompardo constructed his handsome palace over them in the 16th century. They were rediscovered in 1913. Of their four rooms (two cold, one warm, one hot), the warm room, with its multiple horseshoe arches, is the finest. On the way out, glass flooring

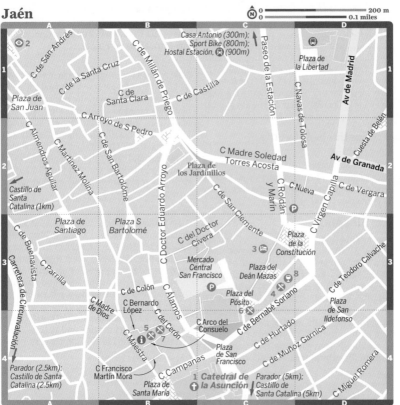

Jaén

reveals part of a Roman street. A 10-minute film with English subtitles helps explain all about the baths. The Museo de Artes y Costumbres Populares, spread over several floors, covers everything from horse carts to pig-slaughtering *(matanza)*. There's an antique doll's house and a recreation of rooms from an early-20th-century rural home, but perhaps most evocative are the photos of country life a century ago, showing just how tough and basic it was. The Naïve art museum is based on the work of its founder, Manuel Moral. You can spend a long time lost in the everyday detail so playfully depicted in these works.

Vía Verde del Aceite   CYCLING, WALKING
(Olive Oil Greenway; www.viasverdes.com; 🚲) Some 120km of disused railway, including three tunnels, 13 viaducts and 12 old stations, running across the olive-strewn countryside of southern Jaén and Córdoba provinces (and close to Córdoba's Sierras Subbéticas moun-

Jaén

tains), have been converted to a well-surfaced cycling and walking track, with gentle gradients and refreshment stops en route making for an enjoyable extended ride.

The track starts at the Polideportivo Las Fuentezuelas sports centre on the northwest edge of Jaén city. This is one of over 120 such *vías verdes* (greenways) around Spain, and the website has maps and plentiful information. **Sport Bike** (☑ 676 539998, 953 27 44 76; www.sportbikejaen.com; Calle San Francisco Javier 14; per day €15; ⊘ 10am-1.30pm & 5-8.30pm Mon-Fri, to 1.30pm Sat), near Jaén train station, rents 24-speed mountain bikes.

🎊 Festivals & Events

Semana Santa   HOLY WEEK
(www.cofradiasjaen.org; ⊘ Mar/Apr) The week leading up to Easter Sunday sees statue-bearing processions through the old city by 30 *cofradías* (brotherhoods).

🛏 Sleeping

Hostal Estación   HOSTAL €
(☑ 953 27 46 14; www.hostalestacionjaen.com; Plaza Jaén por la Paz; s/d/tr/q incl breakfast €42/52/66/76; ⓟ✳ 🛜) It's 1.5km north of the centre, in the railway station building, but after a complete makeover, this *hostal* presents neat, clean rooms in uncluttered modern style, with writing desks and sky-blue bathroom tiles. The welcome is friendly, parking is free, and bus 19 (€0.90) runs to/from the central Plaza de la Constitución.

Hotel Xauen   HOTEL €
(☑ 953 24 07 89; www.hotelxauenjaen.com; Plaza del Deán Mazas 3; incl breakfast s €52-56, d €56-82; ✳ @ 🛜 🌡) The Xauen has a superb location in the centre of town. Communal areas are decorated with large colourful photos on a random range of themes, while the rooms are a study in brown and are moderately sized, but comfy and well cared for. The rooftop sun terrace has stunning cathedral views. Parking nearby is €11.

★ Parador Castillo de Santa Catalina   LUXURY HOTEL €€
(☑ 953 23 00 00; www.parador.es; Cerro de Santa Catalina; r €100-180; ⓟ✳ @ 🛜 🌡) Next to the castle high on the Cerro de Santa Catalina, Jaén's *parador* has an incomparable setting and theatrically vaulted halls. Rooms are luxuriously dignified with plush furnishings, some with four-poster beds. There is also an excellent restaurant and a bar with panoramic terrace seating.

🍴 Eating & Drinking

There aren't many fancy restaurants in Jaén, but one of Andalucía's best tapas zones is here, north of the cathedral, along and between Calles Maestra and Cerón. Here, and throughout Jaén province, bars will give you a free tapa with every drink. You only pay for any extra tapas you order.

El Gorrión   ANDALUCIAN €
(Calle Arco del Consuelo 7; tapas from €2, raciones €8-18; ⊘ 1.30-4pm Tue-Sun & 8.30pm-12.30am Fri & Sat) Lazy jazz plays in the background, old newspaper cuttings and lopsided paintings hang from the walls, and it feels as though local punters have been propping up the bar ever since 1888 (when it opened). But all ages from near and far drop in to sample the atmosphere, the local wine and food offerings such as pepper sausage and seafood-stuffed artichokes.

Taberna La Manchega   ANDALUCIAN €
(Calle Bernardo López 12; bocadillos €2-2.50, platos combinados & raciones €6-12; ⊘ 10am-5pm & 8pm-1am Wed-Mon) La Manchega has been in action since the 1880s; apart from enjoying the *bocadillos* (long bread rolls with fillings including five types of *tortilla*) and *raciones* (full plates of tapas items) such as *chorizo de ciervo* (venison chorizo), *conejo al ajillo* (rabbit in garlic) and *solomillo* (pork tenderloin), you can drink wine and practise your Spanish with the old-time bartenders.

Colombia 50 Café   CAFE €
(Calle de Bernabé Soriano 23; light dishes €3-8; ⊘ 8am-9pm Sun-Thu, to 2am Fri-Sat; 🛜) A large cafe with a sort of tropical-colonial ambience, Colombia is busy most of the day and a fine place for breakfast. Try one of their *blankitas* (toasted bread with assorted toppings, including partridge-and-tomato), along with one of the global range of coffees (including Jamaica Blue Mountain). They do crêpes, croissants, salads and burgers too.

Panaceite   SPANISH €€
(Calle de Bernabé Soriano 1; tapas €3-5.50, raciones €7.50-22; ⊘ kitchen 11am-12.30am) Always packed, this corner bar near the cathedral has a semicircle of outside tables. It serves some seriously good tapas and *raciones*, such as pork tenderloin with a choice of four sauces, or aubergines in sugar-cane syrup, as well as salads, *bocadillos* and wines by the glass.

★ Casa Antonio   SPANISH €€€
(☑ 953 27 02 62; www.casantonio.es; Calle Fermín Palma 3; mains €19-24; ⊘ 1-4pm & 8.30-11.30pm Tue-Sat, 1-4pm Sun, closed Aug) This elegant little restaurant, in an unpromising street off Parque de la Victoria, prepares top-class Spanish fare rooted in local favourites, such as partridge in *escabeche* (an oil-

BUSES FROM JAÉN

DESTINATION	COMPANY	COST	DURATION	FREQUENCY
Baeza	Alsa	€4.50	1hr	10-16 daily
Cazorla	Alsa	€9.25	2½hr	3 daily
Córdoba	Sepulvedana	€11	2hr	6-9 daily
Granada	Alsa	€8.90	1¼hr	11-14 daily
Madrid	Samar	€20	4-5hr	3-4 daily
Málaga	Alsa	€20-24	2¾-4½hr	4 daily
Úbeda	Alsa	€5.40	1-1¾hr	10-17 daily

vinegar-wine marinade), lamb chops or roast shoulder of goat kid. There's also excellent seafood. Nothing overcomplicated, just top ingredients expertly prepared. Service is polished and attentive. They also have a pleasant terrace under the trees outside with a separate menu including some smaller tapas-type dishes.

Deán BAR
(www.facebook.com/dean.plazabar; Plaza del Deán Mazas; ⊗noon-3am) The interior is small and cramped with punters spilling out on to the leafy square, but Deán has a pulsating late-night vibe with its industrial-steel piping and pumping music. During the day it's more of a cafe, with chairs on the square and light eats such as hummus and *tostas* (toast with toppings).

ⓘ Information

Oficina de Turismo (☑ 953 19 04 55; www.turjaen.org; Calle Maestra 8; ⊗9am-7.30pm Mon-Fri, 10am-3pm & 5-7pm Sat, to 3pm Sun) Combined city and regional tourist office with helpful multilingual staff.

ⓘ Getting There & Around

BUS

Alsa (☑ 902 422242; www.alsa.es), **Grupo Sepulvedana** (☑ 902 119699; www.lasepulvedana.es) and **Autocares Samar** (☑ 902 257025; www.samar.es) run services from the **bus station** (☑ 953 23 23 00; www.epassa.es/autobus; Plaza de la Libertad).

CAR & MOTORCYCLE

Jaén's one-way system is no fun, but the way to most hotels is well signposted. There are a couple of central underground car parks: **Parking Constitución** (Calle Roldán y Marín; per 24hr €16; ⊗24hr) and **Parking San Francisco** (Calle de las Flores; per 24hr €16; ⊗24hr).

TRAIN

Jaén's **train station** (www.renfe.com; Plaza Jaén por la Paz) has four trains a day to Cádiz

(€38, five hours) via Córdoba (€15, 1¾ hours) and Seville (€28, three hours), and four to Madrid (€35, 3¾ hours).

NORTHWEST JAÉN PROVINCE

North of Jaén you pass across indifferent countryside until the Sierra Morena appears on the horizon. This range of rolling, green wooded hills stretching along Andalucía's northern border is little visited, but has a mysterious, lonely magic all its own.

Desfiladero de Despeñaperros & Santa Elena

The Desfiladero de Despeñaperros, a dramatic gorge cutting through the Sierra Morena, is straddled by the hilly and beautiful Parque Natural Despeñaperros (www.ventanadelvisitante.es; Ⓟ) 🅿. The gorge is traditionally considered the main gateway to Andalucía from the north. The A4 highway and the Madrid–Jaén railway zip quickly through its viaducts and tunnels. To get a better look at its rocky pinnacles, take the old N-IVa road, which has a mirador and restaurant where you can stop and take in the scenery. From the north, take exit 243 from the A4 and follow 'Parque Natural Despeñaperros' signs; from the south, take exit 257 into Santa Elena town then head out past the signposted Camping, and from the bottom of the gorge follow 'Venta de Cárdenas' signs. For information on the *parque natural* and walking routes, visit the Centro de Visitantes Llano de las Amé (☑ 953 36 88 00; Carretera JA7102, Km 2 2pm Thu, Fri & Sun, 10am-2pm & 4-6 Jun, 8am-2pm Sat Jul-Aug), 2km we towards Miranda del Rey.

⊙ Sights

**Museo Batalla de las
Navas de Tolosa** MUSEUM
(☑953 10 44 35; www.museobatallanavas.es; Carretera JA7102, Santa Elena; adult/child & senior €4/3; ☉10am-2pm Tue-Sun plus 4-7pm Tue-Sat Oct-May, 5-8pm Tue-Sat, 3.30-6.30pm Sun Jun-Sep; P) The course of Spanish history changed 2km west of Santa Elena on 16 July 1212, when Christian armies defeated the Muslim Almohad army in the battle of Las Navas de Tolosa, which opened the doors of Andalucía to the Reconquista. This museum, a few hundred metres west from A4 exit 257, tells the fascinating story and has a viewing tower from which you can see the (now-overgrown) battle site. After the battle the Christians are believed to have tossed Muslim captives off the cliffs of the Desfiladero de Despeñaperros. It's commonly believed this is the origin of the name Despeñaperros, which means 'overthrow of the dogs'.

✕ Eating

El Mesón Despeñaperros ANDALUCIAN €€
(www.elmesondespeñaperros.es; Avenida Andalucía 91, Santa Elena; mains €10-20; ☉noon-midnight) A good choice for refreshments, with a contemporary twist on local fare in some of its dishes including venison burgers, partridge paté and charcoal-grilled meats. Simple rooms (singles/doubles including breakfast from €30/40) are available in the attached hotel.

❶ Getting There & Away

Between two and five daily buses run from Jaén to Santa Elena (€6, 1½ hours), but your own vehicle is by far the easiest way of getting to and around the area.

Parque Natural Sierra de Andújar

This large (748-sq-km) natural park north of Andújar town has the biggest expanses of natural vegetation in the Sierra Morena as well as plenty of bull-breeding ranches. It's an exciting destination for wildlife-spotters, with numerous large mammals and birds found here including five emblematic endangered species: the Iberian lynx, wolf, black vulture, black stork and Spanish imperial eagle. The Iberian lynx population is the largest in the world, with around 200 lynxes here and in the neighbouring Parque Natural Sierra de Cardeña y Montoro (Córdoba province). There are also 25 breeding pairs of Spanish imperial eagle in the Andújar park (one-tenth of the total population of this mighty bird, found only in the Iberian Peninsula).

⊙ Sights & Activities

Staff at the park visitors centre, the **Centro de Visitantes Viñas de Peñallana** (☑953 53 96 28; Carretera A6177, Km 13; ☉10am-2pm Thu-Sun plus 3-6pm Fri-Sun, closed afternoons mid-Jun–mid-Sep, closed Thu Jul & Aug), 13km north of Andújar town, can tell you the best areas for wildlife sightings, though you also need luck on your side. The best months for spotting lynxes are December and January, the mating season. Local guiding outfits can take you out on private land where sighting prospects are often higher: they include **Iberus Birding&Nature** (☑680 468098; www.iberusmedioambiente.com; Centro de Visitantes Viñas de Peñallana, Carretera A6177, Km 13), **IberianLynxLand** (☑636 984515, English 626 700525; www.iberianlynxland.com) and **Turismo Verde** (☑628 709410; www.lasierrade andujar.com). A full-day outing costs around €150/250 for two/four people.

**Santuario de la
Virgen de la Cabeza** CHAPEL
(Carretera A6177, Km 31, Cerro del Cabezo; P) On a hilltop in the heart of the park, 31km up the A6177 from Andújar, this chapel is the focus of one of Spain's biggest religious events, the **Romería de la Virgen de la Cabeza**, on the last weekend in April. The *romería* sees many tens of thousands of people converge to form a huge, festive tent city around the *santuario*, and witness a small statue of the Virgin Mary – known as La Morenita (Little Brown One) – being carried around the Cerro del Cabezo for several hours from 11am on the Sunday. The original 13th-century shrine here was destroyed during the civil war, when it was seized by pro-Franco troops and then captured by the Republicans after eight months of determined bombardment.

🛏 Sleeping & Eating

La Caracola HOTEL €
(☑640 758273; www.lacaracolahotelrural.com; Carretera A6177, Km 13.8; s/d incl breakfast €40/60; P 🐾 🏊) A great base for wildlife watchers, La Caracola sits among woodlands and offers bright, contemporary rooms, comfortable common areas and good meals (lunch or dinner €15). They'll serve breakfast as early as you like, or make you a picnic. It's 1.4km off the A6177: the signed turnoff is 800m north of the park visitors centre.

ALCALÁ LA REAL

From a distance the **Fortaleza de la Mota** (www.tuhistoria.org; Alcalá la Real; adult/child €6/3; ☺10.30am-7.30pm Apr–mid-Oct, 10am-5.30pm mid-Oct–Mar; P ♿) looks more like a city than a mere fort, with its high church tower and doughty keep rising above the surrounding walls. And in a sense that's what it was, for back in the Middle Ages this fortified hill now looming over the town of Alcalá la Real *was* Alcalá la Real. It's a marvellous stop if you're heading along the Granada–Córdoba road across southwestern Jaén province, and well worth a detour even if you're not.

The modern town below only came into being in the 17th century, when fortified towns on hills had passed their use-by date. Today the fortress is as much archaeological site as monument, for what were houses, palaces, stables and streets are now lines of low ruins. The fortress was founded around AD 1000 then largely rebuilt after being wrested from Nasrid Granada by Castilla's Alfonso XI in 1341. One of the most remarkable features is the inside of the church, where the floor has been removed to lay bare dozens of graves carved out of the rock beneath.

If you're here on a Saturday, Sunday or public holiday, budget an extra half-hour and €2 per person for a tour of the Ciudad Oculta (Hidden City), a system of tunnels cut inside the rock for access to an all-important well. The story goes that the fortress only fell to Alfonso XI after the besieging Christians found the way to this well and poisoned it with animal carcasses.

❶ Getting There & Away

Andújar town is served by several daily trains and buses from Jaén and Córdoba, and by buses from Baeza and Úbeda. There are buses to the sanctuary on Saturday and Sunday.

EASTERN JAÉN PROVINCE

This part of the region is where most visitors spend their time, drawn by the allure and Renaissance architecture of the Unesco World Heritage towns of Baeza and Úbeda, and the picturesque villages, mountains and hiking trails of the Parque Natural Sieras de Cazorla, Segura y Las Villas, Spain's biggest protected area, for which Cazorla town makes a great starting point.

Baeza

POP 15,400 / ELEV 760M

The World Heritage–listed twin towns of Baeza (ba-*eh*-thah) and Úbeda, 9km apart, scupper any notion that there is little of architectural interest in Andalucía apart from Moorish buildings. These two remote country towns guard a treasure trove of superb Christian Renaissance buildings from a time when a few local families managed to amass huge fortunes and spent large parts of them beautifying their home towns. Baeza, the smaller of the two, can be visited in a day trip from Úbeda, though it has some good accommodation of its own. Here a handful of wealthy, fractious families, rich from grain-growing and cloth and leather production, left a marvellous catalogue of perfectly preserved Renaissance churches and civic buildings. Baeza was one of the first Andalucian towns to fall to the Christians (in 1227), and little is left today of the Muslim town of Bayyasa after so many centuries of Castilian influence.

◉ Sights

Baeza's main sights mostly cluster in the narrow streets south of the central Plaza de España and the broad Paseo de la Constitución (once Baeza's marketplace and bullring).

★**Catedral de Baeza** CATHEDRAL
(Plaza de Santa María; adult/child €4/1.50; ☺11am-2pm & 4-7pm Mon-Fri, 10am-7pm Sat, to 6pm Sun) As was the case in much of Andalucía, the Reconquista destroyed Baeza's mosque and in its place built a cathedral. It's a stylistic melange, though the predominant style is 16th-century Renaissance, visible in the facade on Plaza de Santa María and in the basic design of the three-nave interior (by Andrés de Vandelvira).

You can climb the tower for great views over the town and countryside. The tower's base dates from the 11th century and was part of the minaret of the mosque. The cathedral's next oldest feature is the 13th-century Gothic-Mudéjar Puerta de la Luna (Moon Doorway) at its western end (now the visitor

Baeza

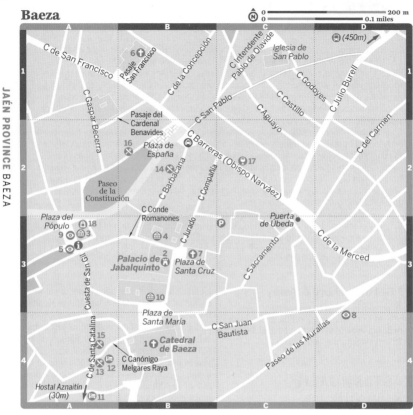

entrance) which is topped by a 14th-century rose window. Inside, there's a clear transition from the nave's two easternmost bays, which are Gothic, with sinuous ceiling tracery, pointed arches and gargoyled capitals, to the Renaissance-style bays further west with their Corinthian capitals and classical square and circle designs. Audio guides in several languages are available for €1. The broad Plaza de Santa María was designed to be a focus of Baeza's religious and civic life. On its north side you can look into the main patio of the 17th-century **Seminario de San Felipe Neri** (Plaza de Santa María; ⊙9am-2pm Mon-Fri) **FREE**, a former seminary, which now houses part of the Universidad Internacional de Andalucía, teaching postgraduate courses.

⭐**Palacio de Jabalquinto** PALACE
(Plaza de Santa Cruz; ⊙9am-2pm Mon-Fri, 10am-2pm & 4-8pm Sat-Sun) **FREE** Baeza's most flamboyant palace was probably built in the late 15th century for a member of the noble

Benavides clan. Its chief glory is the spectacular facade in decorative Isabelline Gothic style, with a strange array of naked humans clambering along the moulding over the doorway; above is a line of shields topped by helmets topped by mythical birds and beasts. The patio has a two-tier Renaissance arcade with marble columns, an elegant fountain, and a magnificent carved baroque stairway. Today the palace is the seat of the Baeza campus of the Universidad Internacional de Andalucía, which runs postgraduate courses in a variety of disciplines. Across the square, the 13th-century **Iglesia de Santa Cruz** (Plaza de Santa Cruz; ⊙11am-1pm & 4-6pm) **FREE** was one of the first churches built in Baeza. With its round arches and semicircular apse, it's a very rare example in Andalucía of Romanesque architecture.

Plaza del Pópulo SQUARE
(Plaza de los Leones) This handsome square is surrounded by elegant 16th-century build-

Baeza

ings. The central **Fuente de los Leones** (Fountain of the Lions) is made of carvings from the Ibero-Roman village of Cástulo and topped by a statue said to represent Imilce, a local princess who became one of the wives of the famous Carthaginian general Hannibal.

The **Puerta de Jaén** on the plaza's west side was originally a city gate of Muslim Bayyasa, though it was reconstructed in 1526. Joined to it is the **Arco de Villalar**, erected by Carlos I the same year to commemorate the crushing of a serious insurrection in Castilla that had threatened to overthrow him. On the southern side of the square is the lovely 16th-century **Casa del Pópulo**, formerly a courthouse and now housing Baeza's tourist office. It was built in the plateresque style, an early phase of Renaissance architecture noted for its decorative facades. Today the role of courthouse is played by the **Antigua Carnicería** (Old Butchery), from 1547, on the eastern side of the square, which must rank as one of the world's most elegant ex-butcheries, with the shield of Carlos I emblazoned on its facade.

Antigua Universidad   HISTORIC BUILDING
(Old University; Calle del Beato Juan de Ávila; ⊙10am-2pm & 4-7pm) FREE Baeza's historic university was founded in 1538. It became a font of progressive ideas that generally conflicted with Baeza's conservative dominant families, often causing scuffles between the highbrows and the well-heeled. Since 1875 the building has housed a secondary school. The main patio, with elegant Renaissance arches, is open to visitors, as is the preserved early-20th-century classroom of the famed poet Antonio Machado, who taught French here from 1912 to 1919.

Paseo de las Murallas   STREET
Heading southwest from Plaza del Pópulo, then looping back northeastward along the escarpment at the edge of town, this street and pedestrian promenade affords superb views across the olive groves to the distant mountains of the Sierra Mágina (south) and Sierra de Cazorla (east).

Convento de San Francisco   CHAPEL
(Calle de San Francisco; ⊙10am-2pm & 4-7pm Wed-Sun, 10am-2pm Mon) FREE This 16th-century monastery suffered grievously from an earthquake and Napoleonic sacking in the early 19th century. The main point of interest is the roofless **Capilla de Benavides** at the northeast end of its church – one of Andrés de Vandelvira's masterpieces, built in the 1540s as the funerary chapel of Baeza's powerful Benavides family. An arrangement of curved girders, erected during a semirestoration in the 1980s, traces the outline of the chapel's majestic dome.

⚑ Festivals & Events

Semana Santa   RELIGIOUS
(www.semanasantabaeza.com; ⊙Mar/Apr) Baeza's Easter processions are solemn, grand and rooted very deep in the town's traditions. Evenings from Palm Sunday to Good Friday.

Feria   FERIA
(⊙mid-Aug) The summer fair starts with a big Carnaval-style procession of *gigantones* (papier-mâché giants) and other colourful figures, and continues with five days of fireworks, a huge funfair, concerts and bullfights.

🛌 Sleeping

Hostal Aznaitín
HOSTAL €€

(☑ 953 74 07 88; www.hostalaznaitin.com; Calle Cabreros 2; incl breakfast s €50-75, d €60-85; ❊❄❅❆) 🅿 Welcoming, bright Aznaitín is a far cry from the dreary *hostales* of old. Rooms are stylish and well sized, with good mattresses and large, appealing photos of Baeza sights. Reception has plenty of information and ideas on what to see and do in and around Baeza.

Hotel Puerta de la Luna
HERITAGE HOTEL €€

(☑ 953 74 70 19; www.hotelpuertadelaluna.com; Calle Canónigo Melgares Raya 7; s €70-130, d €70-139; P❊@❆❅) There is no doubt where Baeza's Renaissance-era nobility would stay if they were to return today. This luxurious hotel in a 17th-century mansion sports orange trees and a pool on its elegant patio, and beautifully furnished salons with welcoming fireplaces. The spacious rooms are enhanced by classical furnishings and art, and good big bathrooms. Buffet breakfast costs €15.

🍴 Eating

Paseo de la Constitución and Plaza de España are lined with bar-cafe-restaurants that are great for watching local life, but most of the best finds are tucked away in the narrow old-town streets. As throughout the province, you'll get a free tapas with drinks in almost every bar.

Bar Pacos
SPANISH €

(Calle de Santa Catalina; tapas & medias raciones €4.50-12; ⊙ 1.30-4pm & 8.30pm-midnight) Frequently thronged with locals and visitors, Pacos prepares a big array of well-presented, creative taste experiences – mostly larger than your average tapas. The crêpes (with fillings such as pork and fried egg) are one speciality, but there are dozens of other tempting choices such as spinach with prawns, or beef tartare with an apple sauce.

DON'T MISS

OLIVE OIL: THE FACTS

You can't fail to notice that in the province of Jaén, the *olivo* (olive tree) rules. Over 60 million olive trees carpet a full 40% of the landscape, and the aroma of the oil perfumes memories of any visit. In an average year these trees yield about 500,000 tonnes of olive oil, meaning that Jaén produces 40% of Spain's, and 17% of the entire world's, production. Almost the whole population depends, directly or indirectly, on this one crop.

Olives are harvested from October until about February. They are taken straight to oil mills to be mashed into a pulp that is then pressed to extract the oil, which is then decanted to remove water. Oil that's good enough for consumption without being refined is sold as *aceite de oliva virgen* (virgin olive oil), and the best of that is *virgen extra*. Plain *aceite de oliva* – known in the trade as *lampante* (lamp oil) – is oil that has to be refined before it's fit for consumption. Oils are tested for chemical composition and tasted in International Olive Council laboratories before they can be labelled virgin or extra virgin.

Jaén is proud of its high-quality olive oil: many restaurants will offer you a few different types to try, soaked up with bread. Quality oil is sold in specialist shops and good groceries, and direct at some mills.

Oleícola San Francisco (☑ 953 76 34 15; www.oleoturismojaen.com; Calle Pedro Pérez, Begíjar; 1½hr tours €5; ⊙ tours 11am & 5pm) 🅿 These fascinating tours of a working oil mill near Baeza will teach you all you could want to know about the process of turning olives into oil, how the best oil is made and what distinguishes extra virgin from the rest. At the end you get to taste a few varieties, and you'll probably emerge laden with a bottle or two of San Francisco's high-quality product. Tours can be given in English or French (ring ahead to ensure availability). To get there, head west out of Baeza on the old Jaén road (A6109, formerly A316), turn right at the Begíjar signpost just before Km 5, then right again after 1.4km, immediately after the petrol station.

Centro de Interpretación Olivar y Aceite (www.centrodeolivaryaceite.com; Corredera de San Fernando 32; adult/child €3.50/free; ⊙ 10am-1pm & 6-9pm Tue-Sat, to 1pm Sun Jun-Sep, 11am-2pm & 5-8pm Tue-Sat, to 2pm Sun Oct-May) Úbeda's olive-oil interpretation centre explains all about the area's olive-oil history, and how the oil gets from the tree to your table, with the help of models, mill equipment and videos in English and Spanish. You get the chance to taste different oils, and to buy from a broad selection.

El Arcediano   TAPAS €
(Calle Barbacana 4; montaditos €3-7, raciones €7-12; ⏱ 8.30pm-midnight Thu, 2-4pm & 8.30pm-midnight Fri-Sun) A quirky spot with dangling chandeliers and a grapevine painted on the ceiling, plus tables out on the narrow pedestrian lane. El Arcediano serves up excellent large *montaditos* (slices of toasted bread with toppings) with anything from pork to anchovies, assorted cheeses, or classic mashed tomato and olive oil.

⭐ **Palacio de Gallego**   SPANISH €€
(📞 667 760184; www.palaciodegallego.com; Calle de Santa Catalina 5; mains €15-30; ⏱ 8pm-midnight Wed, 1-4pm & 8pm-midnight Thu-Mon) In the atmospheric setting of a 16th-century house, with tables on the delightful patio as well as in an old wood-beamed dining room, the Gallego serves up superb meat and fish dishes, barbecued and otherwise. There's a list of well over 100 Spanish wines, and you won't come across many starters better than their goat's cheese, orange and walnut salad.

Service is friendly as well as professional and efficient.

Xavi Taberna   SPANISH €€
(Portales Tundidores 8, Paseo de la Constitución; raciones €8-18; ⏱ 12.30-4pm & 7.30-11.30pm Thu-Tue) On the quieter northern side of the *paseo*, Xavi's has a more contemporary style than the more touristic joints on the south side, and the meat and seafood – classic Spanish ingredients with a few creative twists – are reliably good, with the octopus a standout.

🍷 Drinking & Nightlife

⭐ **Café Teatro Central**   BAR
(www.facebook.com/cafeteatrocentral; Calle Barreras 19; ⏱ 4pm-3am; 📶) The most original and consistent nightspot in the province, with fascinatingly eclectic decor and determined support for live music, the Central fills up around midnight Thursday to Saturday with an arty-indie crowd from other towns as well as Baeza. Live acts play to enthusiastic crowds amid the Buddha statues, historic instruments and coloured lighting every Thursday and most Fridays from October to June. A delightful patio, complete with bubbling fountain and languid goddess statues, adds to the fun.

🛍 Shopping

La Casa del Aceite   FOOD
(www.casadelaceite.com; Paseo de la Constitución 9; ⏱ 10am-2pm & 5-8.30pm Mon-Sat, 10am-2pm &

4-6pm Sun) Sells a big range of quality olive oil, plus other intriguing local products such as wild-boar or partridge pâté, olives and olive-based cosmetics.

ℹ Information

Tourist Office (📞 953 77 99 82; www.andalucia.org; Plaza del Pópulo; ⏱ 9am-7.30pm Mon-Fri, 9.30am-3pm Sat & Sun) Housed in the 16th-century Casa del Pópulo.

ℹ Getting There & Around

BUS

Alsa (p231) runs services from the **bus station** (📞 953 74 04 68; Avenida Alcalde Puche Pardo), 900m northeast of Plaza de España.

TO	COST	DURATION	FREQUENCY
Cazorla	€4.85	1¼-1½hr	3 daily
Córdoba	€11.50	2½hr	2 daily
Granada	€13	2½hr	7-9 daily
Jaén	€4.50	45min-1hr	7-14 daily
Úbeda	€1.15	15min	12-19 daily

CAR & MOTORCYCLE

Street parking in the centre is fairly restricted, but there's an **underground car park** (Calle Compañía; per 1/24hr €1.10/10; ⏱ 7.30am-11.30pm).

TRAIN

The nearest station is Linares–Baeza (www.renfe.com), 13km northwest of town, with a few daily trains to Almería, Córdoba, Jaén, Madrid and Seville. An Alsa (p231) bus leaves Baeza bus station for the train station (€2.70, one hour) at 5.30pm, and two come back, at 7.10am and 3.45pm. There are more buses from Úbeda. A taxi costs €24.

Úbeda

POP 33,600 / ELEV 760M

Beautiful Renaissance buildings grace almost every street and plaza in the *casco antiguo* (old quarter) of World Heritage–listed Úbeda (*oo*-be-dah). Charming hotels in several historic mansions, and some top-class restaurants and tapas bars, make a stay here an all-round delight.

Úbeda's aristocratic lions jockeyed successfully for influence at the Habsburg court in the 16th century. Francisco de los Cobos y Molina became state secretary to King Carlos I, and his nephew Juan Vázquez de Molina succeeded him in the job and kept it under Felipe II. High office exposed these men to the Renaissance aesthetic just then reaching Spain from Italy. Much of the wealth that they and a flourishing agriculture generated was invested in some of Spain's purest examples of Renaissance architecture. As a result, Úbeda (like its little sister Baeza) is one of the few places in Andalucía boasting stunning architecture that was *not* built by the Moors.

◉ Sights

Most of Úbeda's splendid buildings are in the web of narrow, winding streets and expansive squares that make up the *casco antiguo*, on the southern side of the mostly drab modern town. The old town is particularly beautiful at night with its wonderful plateresque facades floodlit gold against inky black skies.

◉ Plaza Vázquez de Molina

The lovely **Plaza Vázquez de Molina** is the monumental heart of Úbeda's old town. An early case of Andalucian urban redevelopment, the plaza took on its present aspect in

the 16th century when Úbeda's nobility decided to demolish existing buildings to make way for an assemblage of grand Renaissance buildings befitting their wealth and importance. Before 1507, the nobility had resided in Úbeda's Alcázar, a fortress-walled area immediately south of Plaza Vázquez de Molina, but this was demolished on Queen Isabel la Católica's orders to defuse power strggles involving the town's quarrelsome aristocrats.

★ **Sacra Capilla de El Salvador**   CHAPEL
(Sacred Chapel of the Saviour; www.fundacionmedinaceli.org; Plaza Vázquez de Molina; adult/child incl audio guide €5/2.50; ⊙9.30am-2.30pm & 4.30-7.30pm Mon-Sat, 11.30am-3pm Sun, plus 4-6pm Sun Oct-Apr) This famous chapel, built between 1536 and 1559, is the flagship of Úbeda Renaissance architecture. Commissioned by Francisco de los Cobos y Molina as his family's funerary chapel, it presents a marked contrast between the relatively sober proportions of the interior (by Diego de Siloé, architect of

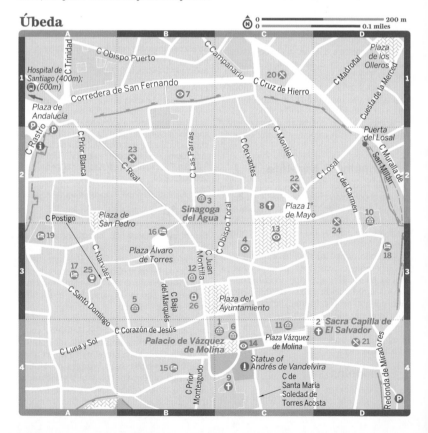

Úbeda

Granada's cathedral) and the more decorative western facade. The facade, a pre-eminent example of plateresque style, was designed by Andrés de Vandelvira, one of Siloé's stonemasons, who took over the project in 1540.

The chapel thus represents the first architectural commission obtained by Vandelvira, who went on to endow Úbeda, Baeza and Jaén with most of their outstanding Renaissance buildings. He worked in tandem with the French sculptor Esteban Jamete, who carved an orgy of classical sculpture depicting Greek gods on the underside of the facade arch, and scattered numerous skulls among the facade's decoration in a reminder that the building is a funerary chapel. Classical figures are also prominent in the sacristy (accessed from the northeast corner of the interior), another Vandelvira creation, but are absent from the main body of the chapel – where the Capilla Mayor sits beneath a stately dome painted in gold, blue and red, and features a grand 1560s altarpiece sculpture of the transfiguration by Alonso de Berruguete.

The Cobos family tombs lie beneath the floor of the chapel and aren't open to visitors. The chapel is still privately owned by the Seville-based Medinaceli ducal family, descendants of the Cobos. The audio guide is full of interesting information and anecdotes and well worth listening to as you go round the chapel. Next to the chapel stands what was originally its chaplain's residence, the **Palacio del Deán Ortega** – another Vandelvira creation. The mansion is now Úbeda's luxurious *parador* (p241).

★**Palacio de Vázquez de Molina**   HISTORIC BUILDING
(Plaza Vázquez de Molina; ☺8am-8pm Mon-Fri, 10am-2pm & 5-7.30pm Sat & Sun) FREE Úbeda's *ayuntamiento* (town hall) is undoubtedly one of, if not the, most beautiful town halls in Spain. It was built by Vandelvira in about 1562 as a mansion for Juan Vázquez de Molina, whose coat of arms surmounts the doorway. The perfectly proportioned, deeply Italian-influenced facade is divided into three tiers by slender cornices, with the sculpted caryatids on the top level continuing the lines of the Corinthian and Ionic pilasters on the lower tiers. Two storeys of elegant arches surround the interior courtyard. In the basement is the **Centro de Interpretación Andrés de Vandelvira** (☺10am-2pm & 5-7.30pm Wed-Sun) FREE – mainly photos but with some background on the great architect's work and life.

Iglesia de Santa María de los Reales Alcázares   CHURCH
(www.santamariadeubeda.es; Plaza Vázquez de Molina; adult/child €4/1.50; ☺10.30am-1.30pm & 5-8pm) Úbeda's grand parish church, founded in the 13th century on the site of Islamic Úbeda's main mosque, is a conglomerate of Gothic, Mudéjar, Renaissance, baroque and neoclassical styles. The main portico, facing Plaza Vázquez de Molina, is a beautiful late-Renaissance composition dating from 1604–12, with a relief sculpture showing the adoration of the shepherds. Inside, the intricate Mudéjar-style *artesonado* (ceiling of interlaced beams) is the fruit of restoration work.

JAÉN PROVINCE ÚBEDA

Úbeda

⊙ Other Areas

★ Sinagoga del Agua   HISTORIC BUILDING
(📞953 75 81 50; www.sinagogadelagua.com; Calle Roque Rojas 2; tours adult/child €4.50/3.50; ⊙ tours every 45min 10.30am-1.30pm & 5-7.15pm, 5.45-8pm Jul & Aug) The medieval Sinagoga del Agua was discovered in 2006 by a refreshingly ethical property developer who intended to build apartments here, only to discover that every swing of the pickaxe revealed some tantalising piece of an archaeological puzzle. The result is this sensitive re-creation of a centuries-old synagogue and rabbi's house, using original masonry whenever possible. Features include the women's gallery, a bodega with giant storage vessels, and a *miqvé* (ritual bath).

There is evidence of a sizeable Jewish community in medieval Islamic Úbeda, cohabiting peacefully with the considerably larger Muslim population. Tours are in Spanish, with printed translations available in English, French, German and Italian.

Casa Museo Andalusí   MUSEUM
(📞953 75 40 14; Calle Narváez 11; €4; ⊙11am-2pm & 5.30-8pm) This fascinating private museum comprises a 16th-century house that was inhabited by *conversos* (Jews who converted to Christianity) and a huge, diverse collection of antiques assembled by owner Paco Castro. The informal guided tours make it all come alive. The first hint that this is somewhere special is the original 16th-century heavy carved door. Ring the bell if it's closed.

Palacio Vela de los Cobos   HISTORIC BUILDING
(Calle Juan Montilla; tours €4; ⊙tours noon or 1.15pm & 6.30pm or 7.15pm Tue-Sat, noon or 1.15pm Sun) This fascinating Vandelvira-designed 16th-century mansion, elegantly restored in the 19th century, is still a private home, fully furnished and replete with paintings, antiques and books. The owner guides tours himself: get tickets at Semer (📞953 75 79 16; www.semerturismo.com; Calle Juan Montilla 3; ⊙9.30am-1.30pm & 6-7.30pm, closed afternoons Aug), across the street.

Plaza 1° de Mayo   PLAZA
Broad Plaza 1º de Mayo was originally Úbeda's market square and bullring. It was also the grisly site of Inquisition burnings, which local bigwigs used to watch from the gallery of the Antiguo Ayuntamiento (Old Town Hall) in the southwestern corner. The Iglesia de San Pablo (Plaza 1º de Mayo; donation €1; ⊙11am-1pm & 6-8pm Tue-Sat, to 1pm Sun), on the square's north side, has a particularly elaborate late-Gothic portal from 1511.

Museo de San Juan de la Cruz   MUSEUM
(📞953 75 06 15; www.sanjuandelacruzubeda.com; Calle del Carmen 13; admission incl audio guide €3.50; ⊙11am-1pm & 5-7pm Tue-Sun) This sizeable museum, part of the Convento de San Miguel, is devoted to the famous mystic and religious reformer St John of the Cross, who died here in 1591. The many memorabilia and relics include some of St John's bones and his rosary, kept in the upper choir of one of the monastery's churches, and a reconstructed monk's cell with a lifelike figure of St John writing at a table he used.

Hospital de Santiago   HISTORIC BUILDING
(Avenida Cristo Rey; ⊙7am-2.30pm & 3.30-9.30pm Mon-Fri, 10am-2pm & 5-9.30pm Sat & Sun, closed Sat Aug, closed Sun Jul & Aug) FREE Andrés de Vandelvira's last architectural project, completed in 1575, has been dubbed the Escorial of Andalucía in reference to the famous monastery outside Madrid, built in a similarly grand, austere late-Renaissance style. The finely proportioned building, which stands outside the old town, 500m west of Plaza de Andalucía, has a broad, two-level, marble-columned patio, and a wide staircase with colourful original frescoes.

JAÉN'S RENAISSANCE MASTER BUILDER

Most of the finest architecture that you see in Úbeda, Baeza and Jaén is the work of one man: Andrés de Vandelvira (1509–75), born in Alcaraz, Castilla-La Mancha, 150km northeast of Úbeda. Thanks largely to the patronage of Úbeda's Cobos and Molina families and the Benavides of Baeza, Vandelvira was able to endow Jaén province with some of Spain's finest Renaissance buildings. His work spanned all three main phases of Spanish Renaissance architecture – the ornamental early phase known as plateresque, as seen in Úbeda's Sacra Capilla de El Salvador (p238); the purer line and classical proportions which emerged in the later Palacio de Vázquez de Molina (p239); and the austere late-Renaissance style (called Herreresque) of his last building, the Hospital de Santiago. Relatively little is known about Vandelvira's life, but his legacy is a jewel of Spanish culture.

✿ Festivals & Events

Semana Santa   RELIGIOUS
(☺Mar/Apr) Eighteen solemn brotherhoods carry sacred church statues through the town in atmospheric processions during the week leading up to Easter Sunday. Thursday and Friday see processions during the daytime as well as after dark.

🛏 Sleeping

Hotel El Postigo   HOTEL €
(☏953 79 55 00; www.hotelelpostigo.com; Calle Postigo 5; s/d Sun-Thu €51/56, Fri & Sat €73/78; ❄@🅿🛅) A smallish modern hotel on a quiet street, El Postigo provides spacious, comfy rooms in red, black and white. Staff are welcoming, and there's a pleasant courtyard as well as a large sitting room with Spotify music, and a log fire in winter. Breakfast €6.50 per person.

★ Las Casas del Cónsul   HERITAGE HOTEL €€
(☏953 79 54 30; www.lascasasdelconsul.es; Plaza del Carmen 1; d Sun-Thu €65-70, Fri & Sat €80-90; ❄🅿🛅) An attractive Renaissance mansion conversion, the welcoming 'Consul's Houses' has elegant, predominantly white rooms with old-time touches, and spacious common areas centred on a two-storey pillared patio, but what sets it apart from similar hotels is the fabulous panoramic terrace (with pool) gazing over the olive groves to the distant mountains of Cazorla.

★ Afán de Rivera   HERITAGE HOTEL €€
(☏953 79 19 87; www.hotelafanderivera.com; Calle Afán de Rivera 4; s/d/tr incl breakfast Sun-Thu €45/69/89, Fri & Sat €52/108/130; ❄🅿) This superb small hotel lies inside one of Úbeda's oldest buildings, predating the Renaissance. Expertly run by the amiable Jorge, it has beautifully historic common areas, and comfortable rooms that offer far more than is usual at these prices: shaving kits, fancy shampoos and tastefully eclectic decor combining the traditional and the contemporary.
Breakfast is a locally sourced feast that makes staying here even more of a pleasure.

Hotel Álvaro de Torres   BOUTIQUE HOTEL €€
(AT Hotel; ☏953 75 68 50; www.hotelat.es; Plaza Álvaro de Torres 2; s €66, d €83-99, breakfast €6; ❄🅿) In a 16th-century mansion set round a stone-pillared patio open to the sky, this is one of the best of Úbeda's ancient-meets-modern hotels. It's on a smallish, personal scale, with just eight all-different rooms that combine thick old stone walls with stylish contemporary fittings and comforts, including spacious walk-in showers.

Palacio de la Rambla   HISTORIC HOTEL €€
(☏953 75 01 96; www.palaciodelarambla.com; Plaza del Marqués de la Rambla 1; s/d incl breakfast €90/120; ☺closed Jul-Aug; ❄🅿) The lovely Palacio de la Rambla gives you a genuine aristocratic mansion experience. The ivy-clad patio is suitably romantic, there are two beautiful salons, one opening to a garden-patio, and the eight rooms are clad in precious art and antiques, with a comfortable, if old-fashioned, style like an aristocratic home of years gone by.

Parador de Úbeda   HISTORIC HOTEL €€€
(Parador Condestable Dávalos; ☏953 75 03 45; www.parador.es; Plaza Vázquez de Molina; r €95-200; ❄🅿) One of Spain's original *paradors* (opened in 1930) and an inspiration for many that were to follow, this plush hotel occupies a historic monument, the Palacio del Deán Ortega (p239), on the wonderful Plaza Vázquez de Molina. It has been comfortably modernised in period style and the rooms and common areas are appropriately luxurious. Breakfast costs €17.

🍴 Eating & Drinking

Úbeda is the culinary hotspot of Jaén province; its talented *andaluz*-fusion chefs are one reason why Spaniards flock here for weekend breaks.

★ Misa de 12   ANDALUCIAN €€
(www.misade12.com; Plaza 1º de Mayo 7; raciones €10-24; ☺1-4pm & 8.30pm-midnight Wed-Sun) From the tiny cooking station in this little corner bar, a succession of truly succulent platters magically emerges – slices of *presa ibérica* (a tender cut of Iberian pork) grilled to perfection, juicy fillets of *bacalao* (cod), or *revuelto de pulpo y gambas* (eggs scrambled with octopus and shrimp).
Staff are attentive and efficient even when run off their feet, which they often are due to the place's popularity.

★ Cantina La Estación   ANDALUCIAN €€
(☏687 777230; www.facebook.com/cantinalaestacion; Cuesta Rodadera 1; mains €17-21; ☺1-4pm & 8pm-midnight Thu-Mon, 1-4pm Tue; 🅿) The charming originality here starts with the design – three rooms with railway themes (the main dining room being the deluxe carriage). It continues with the seasonal array of inspired fusion dishes, such as wild boar in red-wine sauce, or octopus with garlic chips and paprika. Do sample an anchovy or two with the 'false olive' of cheese as an aperitif. Every dish is made with a different olive oil,

and food presentation is a true art form here. Service is welcoming and attentive.

Zeitúm
ANDALUCIAN, FUSION €€

(www.zeitum.com; Calle San Juan de la Cruz 10; mains €10-16, menú €25; ☺1-4pm & 8.30-11.30pm Tue-Sat, 1-4pm Sun) Zeitúm is housed in a headily historic 14th-century building, where staff will show you the original well, and the stonework and beams bearing Jewish symbols. Olive-oil tastings (selected oils to soak into bread) are a feature here, along with top-class preparation of a diverse, frequently changing menu – the likes of venison and tuna sashimi, trout tartare, or pork tenderloin in wild-mushroom sauce.

Llámame Lola
ANDALUCIAN €€

(Calle Baja del Salvador 5; mains & raciones €9-15; ☺12.30pm-midnight; ✐) With an inviting location under the trees near the Sacra Capilla de El Salvador, Lola serves up good, creative *andaluz* fare with less fanfare than some other places and at slightly lower prices. The *solomillo ibérico* (pork tenderloin), the octopus and the *revueltos* (scrambled-egg dishes) are all very tasty.

Restaurante Antique
ANDALUCIAN €€

(✐953 75 76 18; www.restauranteantique.com; Calle Real 25; mains €15-20, raciones €9-19; ☺noon-4pm & 8pm-midnight) Antique is not at all 'antique', but puts a contemporary, high-quality twist on traditional raw materials – try its vegetable wok with partridge and rice noodles, or the mini-brochette of seafood marinated in soy, olive oil and spiced yoghurt. Decor is fittingly simple but stylish.

La Beltraneja
BAR

(Calle Alcolea 6; ☺4pm-3am Sun-Thu, to 4am Fri & Sat; ☏) Hidden away in the old town's backstreets, La Beltraneja combines an interior of exposed stone, flowery wallpaper and pop-art murals with an ample open-air courtyard. Music moves from rock/soul/blues in the afternoon to indie and pop for dancing at night; it's quite a party on Saturdays.

🛍 Shopping

Alfarería Tito
CERAMICS

(Plaza del Ayuntamiento 12; ☺9am-2pm & 4-8pm) Juan Tito's distinctive style veers away from the classic green glaze, with intricate patterns and bright colours, especially blue. His large old-town showroom/workshop displays and sells a big range of very covetable wares. You're looking at €30 or more for a decorative plate; the dazzling designs and artisanship are well worth it.

❶ Information

Oficina de Turismo (✐953 75 04 40; www.turismodeubeda.com; Plaza de Andalucía 5; ☺9am-7.30pm Mon-Fri, 9.30am-3pm & 5-7.30pm Sat, 9.30am-3pm Sun) Helpful place on the northwest edge of the old town.

❶ Getting There & Around

BUS

Alsa (p231) runs services from the **bus station** (✐953 79 51 88; Calle San José 6), which is in the new part of town, 700m west of Plaza de Andalucía.

TO	COST	DURATION	FREQUENCY
Baeza	€1.15	15min	11-17 daily
Cazorla	€4.25	1hr	3-5 daily
Córdoba	€12	2½hr	4 daily
Granada	€13	2¼-3hr	6-10 daily
Jaén	€5.40	1-1¼hr	9-15 daily

CAR & MOTORCYCLE

Parking in the old town is free, but hard to find; the best bet is the car park on **Redonda de Miradores** (free; ☺24hr). The underground **Parking Plaza** (Plaza de Andalucía; per 1/24hr €1.50/17.50; ☺7.30am-11.30pm) is fairly convenient.

TRAIN

The nearest station is **Linares–Baeza** (www.renfe.com), 21km northwest, which you can reach on four daily buses (€2.10, 30 minutes).

TO	COST	DURATION	FREQUENCY
Almería	€20-28	3¼hr	3 daily
Córdoba	€14-20	1¾hr	1 daily
Jaén	€6	45min	3-4 daily
Madrid	€21-33	3-4hr	5-7 daily
Seville	€20-29	3hr	1 daily

Cazorla

POP 7265 / ELEV 800M

This picturesque, bustling white town sits beneath towering crags just where the Sierra de Cazorla rises up from a rolling sea of olive trees, 45km east of Úbeda. It makes the perfect launching pad for exploring the beautiful Parque Natural Sierras de Cazorla, Segura y Las Villas, which begins dramatically among the cliffs of Peña de los Halcones (Falcon Crag) directly above the town.

◉ Sights

The heart of town is Plaza de la Corredera, with busy bars and the elegant *ayuntami-*

ento, in a 400-year-old former monastery, looking down from its southeast corner. Canyonlike streets lead south to the **Balcón de Zabaleta**. This little viewpoint is like a sudden window in a brick wall, with stunning views over the white houses up to the picturesque Castillo de la Yedra and the mountains beyond. From here another narrow street leads down to Cazorla's most picturesque square, **Plaza de Santa María**, dominated by the shell of the 16th-century Iglesia de Santa María.

★ **Castillo de La Iruela**   CASTLE
(Cuesta Santo Domingo, La Iruela; €1; ☺10.30am-2pm & 6.30-10pm, earlier evening hours approx Oct-Mar) In a stunningly picturesque perch on a rocky pinnacle towering over pretty La Iruela village, this ancient fortification is well worth the 3km drive or 1.5km uphill walk from central Cazorla. It was founded in early Islamic times though the keep and much of the walls date from after the castle's conquest by the Archbishop of Toledo in 1231. Adjoining is the shell of the 16th-century Iglesia de Santo Domingo, torched by Napoleonic troops two centuries ago.

★ **Castillo de la Yedra**   CASTLE
(Museo del Alto Guadalquivir; EU/non-EU citizen free/€1.50; ☺9am-3pm Tue-Sun mid-Jun–mid-Sep, 9am-8pm Tue-Sat, to 3pm Sun mid-Sep–mid-Jun) Cazorla's dramatic Castle of the Ivy, a 700m walk above Plaza de Santa María, has great views and is home to the interesting Museum of the Upper Guadalquivir, whose diverse collections include traditional agricultural and kitchen utensils, religious art, models of an old olive mill, and a small chapel featuring a life-size Romanesque-Byzantine crucifixion sculpture. The castle is of Muslim origin, comprehensively rebuilt in the 14th century after the Reconquista.

Iglesia de Santa María   CHURCH
(Plaza de Santa María; church admission free, tour €2; ☺9.30am-1.30pm & 4-8pm Tue-Sun Apr-Oct, to 7pm Nov-Mar) This picturesque shell of a grand church, attributed to the great 16th-century Renaissance architect Andrés de Vandelvira, was wrecked by Napoleonic troops in reprisal for Cazorla's tenacious resistance. It houses Cazorla's tourist office (p245), which offers interesting half-hour tours through the *bóvedas* (vaults) that channel the Río Cerezuelo underneath the church.

🏃 **Activities**

There are some great walks straight out of Cazorla town – all uphill to start with, but your reward is beautiful forest paths and fabulous panoramas of cliffs, crags and circling vultures. Agencies here offer a host of other activities locally, including canyoning in the *parque natural* and an exciting via ferrata for climbers at the neighbouring village of La Iruela.

Good maps and information in anything except Spanish are hard to come by, but the main routes are well signposted and waymarked. Editorial Alpina's *Sierra de Cazorla* map is useful and sold in some Cazorla shops. A few shops, including **Alma Gaia** (www.almagaia.es; Calle Dr Muñoz 13; ☺shop 10am-2pm & 5.30-8.30pm Mon-Sat), sell outdoor gear.

Sendero del Gilillo   WALKING
(PRA313) The best walk for the fit and energetic is this full-day 21km loop (eight to nine hours) from Cazorla up to the Puerto del Gilillo pass (1100m higher than the town and with stupendous views) and back via Loma de los Castellones ridge, Puerto del Tejo pass, Prado Redondo forest house and the Ermita de la Virgen de la Cabeza chapel.

The route ascends from Cazorla's Iglesia de Santa María via the Ermita de San Sebastián chapel (2.2km, about 1½ hours return) and the Riogazas picnic area (3.5km, about three hours return), either of which makes a scenic there-and-back walk if you fancy something shorter. From the Puerto del Gilillo pass a short detour south to the 1848m summit of Gilillo (15 minutes from the pass) provides even more spectacular vistas. From the pass you can, if you like, return to Cazorla the way you came up, which takes about an hour less than the full loop route.

The route is well marked (despite occasionally being numbered PRA312 instead of PRA313) nearly all the way. Just note that when leaving the Puerto del Gilillo your route heads north, passing to the left of a ruined stone hut; and at the Puerto del Tejo you go left, initially downhill and curving to the right, instead of following GR247.3 and PRA314 signs to the right (which would bring you to the Parador de Cazorla). When you reach the Ermita de la Virgen de la Cabeza, follow the paved road downhill to meet another paved road opposite the Mirador Merenderos de Cazorla, then take the downhill path to the right of the mirador, leading down to Cazorla town.

Sendero de Ermitas y Monasterios WALKING
(SLA7) An 11km loop passing isolated chapels and monasteries in the hills, the SLA7 follows the PRA313 (Sendero del Gilillo) from Cazorla

for 4km before continuing along the La Iruela–El Chorro road, then descending back to town via the Monasterio de Montesión. The route begins from Cazorla's Iglesia de Santa María and takes about 3½ hours.

Via Ferrata La Mocha
CLIMBING

(La Iruela) This high-adrenaline challenge is a set of steel ladders, steps, cables and chains fixed into the precipitous rocky cone, La Mocha, above La Iruela village just outside Cazorla. Established in 2016, it ascends 130m and includes a 'Tibetan bridge' – a set of horizontal cables strung across a precipice. **Tierraventura** (📞 953 71 00 73; www.aventura cazorla.com; Carretera A319, Km 16.5, La Iruela; ⏲ 10am-2pm & 5-8pm Mon-Sat) offers guided climbs (€36 per person, about three hours).

☞ Tours

Turisnat
WILDLIFE WATCHING

(📞 953 72 13 51; www.turisnat.es; Calle Martínez Falero 11; half-day tours per person €30-39; ⏲ office 10am-2pm & 5-8pm Mon-Sat, to 2pm Sun) 🏃 This highly experienced agency is a good option for 4WD trips along the forest tracks of the *parque natural*, with an emphasis on wildlife-spotting. English- or French-speaking guides are available at no extra cost. There's a minimum of five people per trip (they can put people together to make up numbers), and they can normally pick you up anywhere between Cazorla and the Centro de Visitantes Torre del Vinagre.

✹ Festivals & Events

Bluescazorla
MUSIC

(www.bluescazorla.com; ⏲ Jul) Cazorla has a surprisingly cosmopolitan vibe for a remote country town and demonstrates it with this annual three-day blues fest, which sees international musicians and several thousand fans packing into town.

⊟ Sleeping

Hotel Guadalquivir
HOTEL €

(📞 953 72 02 68; www.hguadalquivir.com; Calle Nueva 6; s/d incl breakfast €43/57; ❄🏠) Welcoming, family-run Guadalquivir has well-kept, comfy rooms with pine furniture, though no memorable views. It's well run, just a few steps from central Plaza Corredera, and serves up a decent breakfast. It all equals straightforward, good value for money.

Molino La Farraga
CASA RURAL €€

(📞 953 72 12 24, 696 697390; www.molinolafarraga. com; Camino de la Hoz; d incl breakfast €70-100; 🏠🐾) A charming property built around an old water-driven flour mill on the edge of town in the verdant valley of the tinkling Río Cerezuelo. The nine comfy, good-sized rooms have suitably rustic wooden furnishings, but what's really special is the beautiful big garden with fruit and nut trees, organic vegies, rabbits, a fish-and-lily pond – and a large open-air pool. Breakfast includes homemade baked goods and jams, and the PRA313 and SLA7 footpaths go past the door. To get there, go 250m from Plaza de Santa María up the street towards the Castillo de la Yedra, then fork left for 150m along a narrow lane. You have to walk this last bit but owner Manolo can carry luggage up on his quad bike – look for him in his shop, La Alacena de la Abuela, on Plaza de Santa María.

Casa Rural Plaza de Santa María
CASA RURAL €€

(📞 953 72 20 87; www.plazadesantamaria.com; Callejón Plaza Santa María 5; incl breakfast s €39-44, d €55-77; ❄🏠🐾) This multilevel house is set round a lovely garden-patio with a fish pond. Its terraces and a couple of the rooms enjoy superb views over Plaza de Santa María, Cazorla's castle and the mountains beyond. The attractive rooms are all different, in yellows, oranges and blues, with a variety of folksy styles.

✕ Eating

Bar Las Vegas
TAPAS €

(Plaza de la Corredera; tapas €1, raciones €4-12; ⏲ 10am-4pm & 8pm-midnight Tue-Sat, 10am-4pm Sun) It's tiny but it's the best of Cazorla's central bars, with barrel tables outside (and it gets packed inside when the weather's poor). They do great tapas including one called *gloria bendita* (blessed glory – scrambled eggs with prawns and capsicum), as well as *raciones* of local favourites such as cheese, ham, venison and *lomo de orza* (spiced pork).

Mesón Leandro
SPANISH €€

(www.mesonleandro.com; Calle Hoz 3; mains €9-19; ⏲ 1.30-4pm & 8.30-11pm Wed-Mon) Leandro is a step up in class from most other Cazorla eateries – professional but still friendly service in a bright dining room with lazy music, and only one set of antlers on the wall. The broad menu of nicely presented dishes ranges from partridge-and-pheasant pâté to *fettuccine a la marinera* and a terrific *solomillo de ciervo* (venison tenderloin).

La Cueva de Juan Pedro
ANDALUCIAN €€

(Plaza de Santa María; raciones & mains €8-20, menú €13; ⏲ noon-10pm; 🏃) The ancient, wood-beamed bar has antlers and boar heads protruding from the walls, and there's a dining room adjoining, plus outdoor tables on the plaza just below. It's a place for no-frills traditional Cazorla fare including meaty grills (lamb, pork, rabbit, wild boar, venison), trout and *rin-rán* (a mix of salted cod, potato and dried red peppers). They also do a reasonable number of vegetarian options.

ℹ Information

Oficina Municipal de Turismo (☑ 953 71 01 02; www.cazorla.es/turismo; Plaza de Santa María; ⊙10am-1pm & 4-8pm Tue-Sun Apr-Oct, to 7pm Nov-Mar) Inside the remains of Santa María church, with some information on the natural park as well as the town.

Punto de Información Cazorla (☑ 953 72 13 51; Calle Martínez Falero 11; ⊙10am-2pm & 5-8pm Mon-Sat, 10am-2pm Sun) Good for information on the *parque natural* as well as the town and surrounds.

ℹ Getting There & Around

BUS

Alsa (www.alsa.es) runs three to five daily buses to Úbeda (€4.25, one hour), Baeza (€4.85, 1¼ hours), Jaén (€9.25, two to 2½ hours) and Granada (€17.60, 3¾ hours). The bus stop is on Calle Hilario Marco, 500m north of Plaza de la Corredera via Plaza de la Constitución.

CAR & MOTORCYCLE

Driving in the old, central part of town is tricky, but there's free parking around its periphery. If you can wriggle your way down to Plaza de Santa María, there's a free car park just off its northern end. Otherwise, **Parking Plaza de Andalucía** (Calle Cronista Lorenzo Polaino; per 1/24hr €1.25/10; ⊙7am-11pm or later), just down from Plaza de la Constitución at the northern end of the centre, is useful.

Parque Natural Sierras de Cazorla, Segura y Las Villas

One of the biggest drawcards in Jaén province – and, for nature lovers, in all of Andalucía – is the mountainous, lushly wooded Parque Natural Sierras de Cazorla, Segura y Las Villas. This is the largest protected area in Spain – 2099 sq km of craggy mountain ranges, deep, green river valleys, canyons, waterfalls, remote hilltop castles and abundant wildlife, threaded by well-marked walking trails and forest roads, with a snaking, 20km-long reservoir, the Embalse del Tran-

co, in its midst. The abrupt geography, with altitudes varying from 460m up to 2107m at the summit of Cerro Empanadas, makes for dramatic changes in the landscape. The Río Guadalquivir, Andalucía's longest river, rises in the south of the park, and flows northwards into the Embalse del Tranco, before heading west across Andalucía to the Atlantic Ocean.

The best times to visit the park are spring and autumn, when the vegetation is at its most colourful and temperatures pleasant. The park is hugely popular with Spanish tourists and attracts several hundred thousand visitors each year. Peak periods are Semana Santa, July, August, and weekends from April to October.

Exploring the park is far easier if you have a vehicle. The network of paved and unpaved roads and footpaths reaches some remote areas and offers plenty of scope for panoramic day walks or drives. If you don't have a vehicle, you have the option of guided walks, 4WD excursions and wildlife-spotting trips with agencies based in Cazorla (p243) and elsewhere. Bus services are effectively nonexistent.

ℹ Information

Centro de Visitantes Torre del Vinagre (☑ 953 72 13 51; Ctra A319 Km 48; ⊙10am-2pm & 4-7pm, 5-8pm Jul–mid-Sep, 4-6pm Nov-Mar, closed Mon Nov-Mar) The park's main visitors centre is 16km north of Arroyo Frío. It sells maps, guides and souvenirs, and can provide information on walking routes and other attractions, though staff may not speak English.

ℹ Getting There & Away

BUS

Cazorla town is the nearest you can get by bus to the southern part of the park. For the northern part, a Transportes Sierra Segura bus to Segura de la Sierra (€2.60, 45 minutes) leaves **Puente de Génave bus station** (☑ 953 43 53 17; Puente de Génave), just off the N322, at 12.15pm Monday to Friday. The return service departs Segura at 7.30am Monday to Friday.

CAR & MOTORCYCLE

The A319 from Cazorla heads up through the centre of the park past the Embalse del Tranco almost to Hornos, where the A317 heads southeast to Santiago de la Espada. Roads feed into the north of the park from the N322 Úbeda–Albacete road. There are at least seven petrol stations in the park.

The South of the Park

The A319, heading northeast from Cazorla, passes through La Iruela then enters the *parque natural* 6km later at Burunchel, from where it winds 6km up to the 1200m **Puerto de las Palomas** pass. The **mirador** here affords wonderful views northward down the Guadalquivir valley and can be a fine spot for observing raptors gliding the thermals. Three twisting kilometres downhill from here is **Empalme del Valle**, a junction where the A319 turns north to follow the Río Guadalquivir downstream to Arroyo Frío (6km) – the most commercialised of the park's villages, with a rash of restaurants, tour agencies and accommodation.

Past Arroyo Frío, the A319 continues 16km along the valley to the Torre del Vinagre visitors centre and the turn-off for the wonderful Río Borosa walk . After another 10km the **Embalse del Tranco** reservoir opens out beside the road. Several miradors offer panoramas over its waters – often a vivid turquoise colour – as the road continues to the dam holding back the reservoir at Tranco village. From here you have the option of continuing north to Hornos and/ or Segura de la Sierra.

◉ Sights & Activities

Nacimiento del Guadalquivir   SPRING
(Source of the Guadalquivir) An interesting detour from Empalme del Valle will take you past Vadillo Castril village to the Puente de

---

> **ⓘ WALK PREPARED**
>
> The best overall maps for hiking and exploring the park are Editorial Alpina's *Sierra de Cazorla* and *Sierra de Segura*. The website www.sierrasdecazorlase-guraylasvillas.es is a useful resource in English, with walk descriptions and maps. Tourist offices and park information offices can also help, but most handouts are in Spanish only.
>
> When walking, be sure to equip yourself with enough water and appropriate clothes. Temperatures up in the hills are generally several degrees lower than down in the valleys, and the wind can be cutting at any time. In winter the park is often blanketed in snow; summer temperatures can easily reach into the 40°C range.

---

las Herrerías bridge (7km) and then 11km on southward along a good gravel-and-dirt road through the forests to the source of the Guadalquivir, where Andalucía's longest river begins its 657km journey to the Atlantic Ocean as a pool in a shady green nook of the hills.

From here you can, if you like, continue 9km east then south (on similar roads) to Cabañas, which, at 2027m, is one of the highest peaks in the park (it's a 3km round-trip walk of about 1½ hours from the road to the summit and back). Or you can head west then north back to Cazorla (26km) via the Puerto Lorente pass, on good gravel-and-dirt roads most of the way.

Centro de Fauna Silvestre
Collado del Almendral   NATURE RESERVE
(☏680 149028; www.parquecinegeticocollado delalmendral.com; Ctra A319 Km 60; adult/child or senior €9/7; ☉from 10am Tue-Sun; 🅿🚻) You can view ibex, mouflon, deer, eagles, owls and falcons in semi-liberty at this 1-sq-km enclosed animal park. Visits are by mini train along 5km of road through the park, followed by a 1.5km walk taking in three miradors. It's set on a spur of land between the A319 and the Embalse del Tranco, 7km north of Coto Ríos.

Closing times range from 5pm in winter to 9pm from July to September, with last tours starting one hour earlier.

★**Río Borosa Walk**   WALKING
The most popular walk in the Cazorla natural park follows the crystal-clear Río Borosa upstream to its source through scenery that progresses from the pretty to the majestic, via a gorge, two tunnels and a mountain lake. The walk is about 11km each way, with an ascent of about 600m, and takes about seven hours there and back.

To reach the start, turn east off the A319 at the 'Sendero Río Borosa' sign opposite the Centro de Visitantes Torre del Vinagre (p245), and go 1.7km. The first section of the walk criss-crosses the tumbling, beautiful river on a couple of bridges. After just over 3km, where the main track starts climbing to the left, take a path forking right (with a rickety 'Cerrada de Elías' sign at research time). This leads through a lovely 1.5km section where the valley narrows to a gorge, the **Cerrada de Elías**, where the path becomes a wooden walkway. You re-emerge on the dirt road and continue 4km to the **Central Eléctrica**, a small hydroelectric station.

Past the power station, the path crosses a footbridge, after which a 'Nacimiento Aguas Negras, Laguna Valdeazores' sign directs you on and upward. The path winds its way up the valley, through increasingly dramatic scenery and getting gradually steeper. After about an hour, you enter the first of two tunnels cut through the rock for water flowing to the power station. It takes about five minutes to walk the narrow path through the first tunnel (the path is separated from the watercourse by a metal handrail), then there's a short section in the open air before a second tunnel, which takes about one minute to get through. You emerge just below the dam of the **Embalse de los Órganos** (Laguna de Aguas Negras), a small reservoir surrounded by forested hills. Take the leftward path at the dam and in five minutes you reach the **Nacimiento de Aguas Negras**, where the Río Borosa begins life welling out from under a rock. Enjoy your picnic beneath the spreading boughs of a large tree here, then head back down the way you came.

Due to its popularity, it's preferable to do this walk on a weekday! Do carry a water bottle: all the trackside springs are good and drinkable but the last is at the Central Eléctrica. A torch (flashlight) is comforting, if not absolutely essential, for the tunnels.

🛏️ Sleeping & Eating

Casa Rural Los Parrales CASA RURAL €
(📞 699 834049; www.cazorlaturismo.com; Ctra A319 Km 78, Tranco; s/d incl breakfast €40/55; 🅿 ✳ 🛜 ❄) Set on a rise among trees with wonderful views along the Embalse del Tranco, Los Parrales is a great, chilled-out base. The pool and terraced garden enjoy spectacular vistas, and excellent meals emphasising local products are served indoors or outdoors as you prefer. It's 3km north of Tranco village along the A319.

The eight rooms here are cosy with pine furnishings, terracotta-tile floors and

Sierra de Cazorla

WILD THINGS

If you're a wildlife enthusiast, you have to get yourself to the Cazorla natural park. The chances of spotting wildlife are better here than almost anywhere else in Andalucía. Creatures such as red and fallow deer, ibex, wild boar, mouflon (a wild sheep) and red squirrels are all present in good numbers, and are surprisingly visible out on the trails (even along the roads in the case of deer). The autumn mating season (September and October for deer, November for mouflon and wild boar) is a particularly exciting time to observe the big mammals. The park is also home to some 180 bird species, including griffon vultures, golden eagles, peregrine falcons and the majestic *quebrantahuesos* (lammergeier, bearded vulture), which is being reintroduced here after dying out in the 1980s. In short, get walking and keep those binoculars at the ready!

wrought-iron bedheads. The GR247 long-distance footpath passes close by and its 9km section to Hornos runs mostly close to the lake shore.

Hotel Rural La Hortizuela
HOTEL **€**

(☑953 71 31 50; Ctra A319 Km 50.5; s/d/q €35/50/75, Aug & Semana Santa €45/60/85; ☺closed Dec-Feb; **P**🅿🖥) The 24 rooms here are well kept, with splashes of colour, but nothing fancy. What's special is the beautiful natural setting in wooded four-hectare grounds, which are fenced in to protect plants such as wild orchids and wild asparagus. Wildlife, including deer, boar and red squirrels, is plentiful in the surrounding woodlands.

A bar and good-value restaurant (half-board €18 per person) add to the appeal. It's 1km west off the A319, 3km north of Torre del Vinagre visitors centre.

Parador de Cazorla
HOTEL **€€**

(Parador El Adelantado; ☑953 72 70 75; www.para dor.es; Paraje El Sacejo, Sierra de Cazorla; incl breakfast s €87-167, d €104-207; ☺closed Jan; **P**🅿🖥) Built in the 1960s, Parador de Cazorla has that rather staid, old-fashioned atmosphere of many *paradores*, but is certainly a comfortable and spacious abode with a superb setting way out in the forests 25km from Cazorla, and panoramic mountain views (enjoyed by the common areas and about half the 34 bedrooms). A highlight is the expansive lawned garden with large open-air pool.

The *parador* has its own 5km paved approach road off the Empalme del Valle–Vadillo Castril road, and is a possible walking base, with a number of trails passing the entrance, including the SLA8 and GR247.3 from Cazorla. Room rates fluctuate wildly depending on dates and how far ahead you book. The set menu in the restaurant is €29, with individual mains between €12 and €21.

El Tranco
ANDALUCIAN **€€**

(☑953 00 22 76; www.tranco.es; Centro Náutico, Ctra A319, Km 75, Tranco; mains €9-16; ☺1-4pm & 7.30pm-midnight) Highly popular El Tranco is quite avant-garde for this neck of the woods, providing a tasty contemporary take on traditional local ingredients, in generous portions. Dishes include venison in aromatic herb sauce, trout-and-mushroom risotto, some creative salads, baked apple with crumble and olive-oil ice cream, and options like guacamole or sweet-chilli sauce to go with the charcoal-oven grills.

Hornos

POP 410 / ELEV 867M

Like better-known Segura de la Sierra, little Hornos is fabulously located – atop a crag backed by a sweep of mountains, with marvellous views over the shimmering Embalse del Tranco and the lush, green countryside, richly patterned with olive, pine and almond trees and the occasional tossed dice of a farmhouse.

The castle on the crag was built by Christians in the mid-13th century, probably on the site of an earlier Muslim fortification. Don't expect colour-coordinated geraniums, souvenir shops or a tourist office: Hornos' charms lie in exploring the narrow, winding streets and wondering at the view from several strategically placed miradors.

If you want to stride out, there are several trails including two of about 4km each to tiny outlying villages – the PRA152 south down to Hornos El Viejo and the PRA148 east up to La Capellanía – as well as the long-distance GR247 to El Yelmo or Tranco.

To get to Hornos, take the A319 12km north of the Tranco dam to a T-junction; from here the A317 winds 4km up to Hornos village.

Iglesia de la Asunción   CHURCH
(Plaza de la Rueda) The early-16th-century Iglesia de la Asunción has the oldest, albeit crumbling, plateresque portal in the province, plus a vibrant and colourful *retablo* (altarpiece) with nine painted panels dating from 1589.

Cosmolarium   PLANETARIUM
(☑ 688 906165; www.cosmolarium.info; admission €3, incl planetarium €5; ⊙ 11am-2pm & 4.30-7.30pm Thu-Mon Apr-Jun & Sep-Oct, 11am-2pm & 6-9pm Thu-Mon 1st half Jul, 11am-2pm daily mid-Jul-Aug, 11am-2pm & 4-6pm Fri-Sun Nov-Mar) Hornos' panoramic medieval castle now houses, curiously enough, a modern astronomy interpretation centre and planetarium. Exhibits are devoted to the universe, galaxies, the solar system and the history of astronomy, with English or French audio guides included in the ticket price. The planetarium presents projections in Spanish and English on astronomical themes.

Segura de la Sierra
POP 250 / ELEV 1145M

One of Andalucía's most picturesque villages, Segura de la Sierra perches on a steep hill crowned by a Reconquista castle. The village takes some of its character from its five Moorish centuries before the Knights of Santiago captured it in 1214, after which it became part of the Christian front line against the Almohads and then the Granada emirate.

As you drive up into the village, the Puerta Nueva, one of four gates of Islamic Saqura, marks the entrance to the old part of Segura. Signs to the Castillo lead you round to a junction on the northern side by

---

BRINGING BACK THE BONE-BREAKERS

The lammergeier or bearded vulture, once widespread around Andalucía, was finally hunted and poisoned to extinction in the region in 1986 when the last lammergeier disappeared from the Cazorla mountains – at the time, its last refuge in western Europe except the Pyrenees and Corsica. Today this giant bird with its 2.70m-to-2.90-m wingspan, and downy yellowy-white leg and neck feathers, is flying again over the Sierra de Cazorla, thanks to a heartening reintroduction program based at the **Centro de Cría del Quebrantahuesos** (Lammergeier Breeding Centre; ☑ 953 72 09 23; www.gypaetus.org; Nava de San Pedro; tour per person €5; ⊙ tours 5pm Thu, noon & 5pm Fri-Sun, May-Sep) deep in the forests of the Parque Natural Cazorla. A visit to the centre, possible outside the breeding season and with advance reservation, is a fascinating experience for any wildlife lover.

One of the weirdest things about the lammergeier is its main diet – animal bones, which it breaks into small, edible pieces by dropping them from the sky on to rocks below – hence its evocative Spanish name, *quebrantahuesos*, which means bone-breaker.

Reintroduction is a long, painstaking process. The birds typically don't start breeding till they are eight or nine years old. The breeding centre was established in 1996; the first young lammergeiers were released into the wild in 2006; the first chick hatched in the wild in 2015. By 2017 there were two breeding pairs residing in these hills.

On a visit to the breeding centre you'll see several of these spectacular birds (individuals unsuitable for release into the wild) in their large cages, and have the breeding, rearing and release process explained in detail. It's essential to call in advance for a visit. The centre is a 33km drive from Cazorla, the last 7km on a well-surfaced gravel-and-dirt road. Make it known when booking if you'd like a guide who speaks some English; also double-check the location as there's a possibility that it may move.

Lammergeier Movements

During their youth lammergeiers may wander enormous distances, up to 600km a day, roaming all over the Iberian Peninsula and even into France. Our guide at the breeding centre told us they tracked one which flew from the Pyrenees to the Sierra de Cazorla in two days. Where did it stop to rest for the night en route? In Madrid, on the roof of Real Madrid football stadium, of course. You can see monthly updates on the Cazorla birds' movements on the Facebook page of Fundación Gypaetus, which runs the breeding centre.

OFF THE BEATEN TRACK

EL YELMO

El Yelmo (1808m) is one of the highest and most panoramic mountains in the north of the park. A 5.5km road – paved all the way, but single-track in parts – goes right to the summit, which is disfigured by a rash of communications towers but has magnificent 360-degree views. El Yelmo is a favourite take-off point for paragliders and is the focus of a big fiesta of free-flying and other activities, the **Festival Internacional del Aire** (www.fiaelyelmo.com; ⊙ Jun), which attracts thousands of people for three days every June (usually the first weekend of the month). For tandem flights contact **Olivair** (📞 607 301716; www.facebook.com/olivairfly; Calle Francisco Quevedo) in Segura de la Sierra.

To drive to El Yelmo, take the A6305 from Hornos, winding your way east up into the mountain pine forests. Go left (signposted to Segura and Siles) at a junction after 13km, and in 1km you'll see a road taking off to the left, between a ruined building and a smaller intact one (El Campillo walkers' refuge). This is the road up to El Yelmo. If you'd prefer to walk up, take the path signed 'Derivación 2 Bosques del Sur' from the El Campillo refuge. It shortens the climb to 3km (about 1½ hours).

---

the little walled bullring. Turn left here for the castle itself.

Several country roads meet here: the main approach is from the A317 between Cortijos Nuevos and La Puerta de Segura.

⊙ Sights

In the village below the magnificent castle, the sturdy 16th-century **Iglesia de Nuestra Señora del Collado** stands just below the main square, **Plaza de la Encomienda**. In addition to the Arab baths in the castle, there's a set of 12-century **Baños Árabes** (Calle Baño Moro; ⊙ hours variable) **FREE** at the foot of the village. Nearby is the **Puerta Catena**, the best-preserved of Segura's Islamic gates.

★**Castillo de Segura**   CASTLE
(📞 627 877919; adult/child & senior €4/3, audio guide €2.50; ⊙ 10.30am-2pm & 5-8.45pm Jul & Aug, approx 11am-2pm & 4.30-7.45pm Wed-Sun Mar-Jun & Sep-Dec, closed Wed Apr-May; 🚗) This lofty castle dates from Moorish times but was rebuilt after the Christian conquest in the 13th century. Abandoned in the 17th century, it was restored in the 1960s and has now become a 'frontier territory' interpretation centre. The ticket office is also Segura's main tourist information point. You can see the original Arab steam baths (with a video on the history of Segura and the castle), visit the 13th-century Mudéjar chapel, climb the tower and walk round the battlements for a bird's-eye view of El Yelmo, 5km south, and the rocky crags and olive-tree-strewn lowlands all around.

It's a minimum 400m walk, plus 80 steps, from the nearest parking place to the castle entrance, though vehicles are allowed to drop passengers near the entrance then go back down to park. Note: the castle's opening hours are complicated; it's advisable to call ahead to check the schedule.

🛏 Sleeping & Eating

La Mesa Segureña   APARTMENT €
(📞 953 48 21 01; Calle Cruz de Montoria; incl breakfast 2-person apt €45-55, 4-person apt €80; ❄🛜) Seven cosy apartments just below Segura castle, with great views, a touch of bright art, cast-iron trimmings, fireplaces and minikitchens.

Mirador de Peñalta   ANDALUCIAN €€
(📞 953 48 20 71; Calle San Vicente 29; mains €5-18; ⊙ 1.30-4pm & 8-10pm Tue-Sun; 🛜) On the street entering Segura from below, this place caters to hungry travellers with a meaty menu that includes steaks, lamb chops and pork, as well as smoked trout and some sierra specialities such as *ajo atao* (a belly-filling fry-up of potatoes, garlic and eggs).

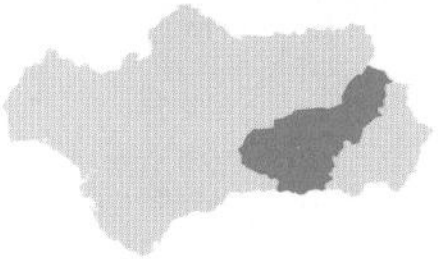

Granada Province

Best Places to Stay

➡ Santa Isabel La Real (p271)

➡ Hotel Real de Poqueira (p285)

➡ Casa Morisca Hotel (p271)

➡ Hotel GIT Abentofail (p278)

➡ Alquería de Morayma (p288)

Best Places to Eat

➡ El Bar de Fede (p273)

➡ La Fábula Restaurante (p273)

➡ Los Geraneos (p291)

➡ Taberna Restaurante La Tapa (p285)

➡ La Bodeguilla (p279)

Why Go?

Nowhere encapsulates the exotic drama of Andalucía's past to more gripping effect than Granada. The capital is home to Spain's single greatest Islamic building, the Alhambra, and it retains a distinct Moorish air with its shadowy *teterías* (teahouses), winding alleyways and whitewashed *cármenes* (mansions with walled gardens, from the Arabic *karm* for garden). Elsewhere, monumental churches tower over teeming tapas bars and garish murals adorn off-the-radar backstreets. For a change of pace, the mighty peaks of the Sierra Nevada provide a magnificent outdoor playground. Hiking possibilities range from summitting mainland Spain's highest mountain to trekking through the gorges and white villages of Las Alpujarras on the range's southern reaches. Skiers can take to the pistes at Europe's most southerly ski resort.

Further afield, you can soak up the sun on Costa Tropical beaches, explore cave houses in Guadix, and bone up on prehistory in Granada's haunting Altiplano (high plain).

Driving Distances

	Granada	Guadix	Almuñécar	Trevélez
Guadix	52			
Almuñécar	80	132		
Trevélez	74	76	65	
Pampaneira	58	92	49	16

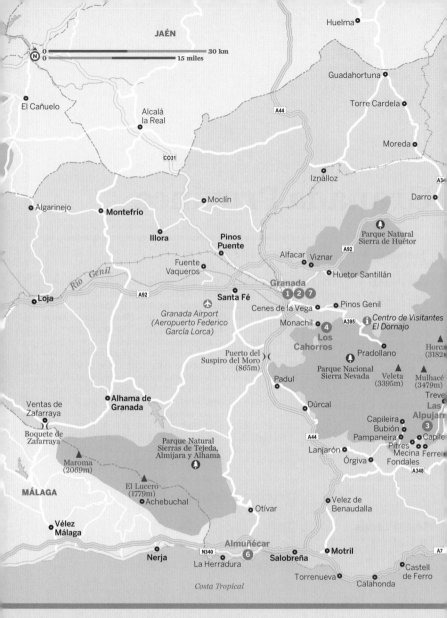

Granada Province Highlights

1 **Alhambra** (p254) Basking in the majesty of Spain's most spectacular monument, a masterpiece of exquisite Islamic architecture and horticultural landscaping.

2 **Mirador San Nicolás** (p262) Snapping those sunset shots of the Alhambra from this viewing balcony in Granada's atmospheric Albayzín district.

3 **Las Alpujarras** (p282) Hiking through the villages and canyons of the Sierra Nevada's southern slopes.

4 **Los Cahorros** (p281) Exploring the rocky gorges

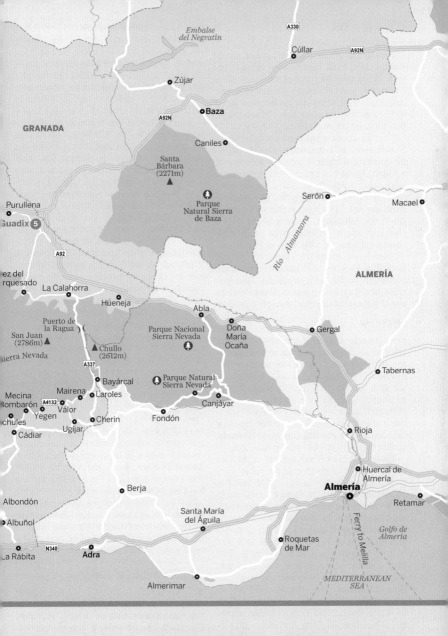

of this enchanting and often overlooked corner of the Sierra Nevada.

5 **Guadix** (p278) Going underground for a glimpse of cave life in this lively provincial town, packed with authentic tapas bars.

6 **Almuñécar** (p290) Hitting the beach for a day of unashamed loafing at this attractive resort on the Costa Tropical.

7 **Granada** (p272) Bar-crawling for free tapas and calling it dinner.

GRANADA

POP 234,760 / ELEV 680M

Drawn by the allure of the Alhambra, many visitors head to Granada unsure what to expect. What they find is a gritty, compelling city where serene Islamic architecture and Arab-flavoured street life go hand in hand with monumental churches, old-school tapas bars and counterculture graffiti art.

The city, sprawled at the foot of the Sierra Nevada, was the last stronghold of the Spanish Moors and their legacy lies all around: it's in the horseshoe arches, the spicy aromas emanating from street stalls, the *teterías* (teahouses) of the Albayzín, the historic Arab quarter. Most spectacularly, of course, it's in the Alhambra, an astonishing palace complex whose Islamic decor and landscaped gardens are without peer in Europe.

There's an energy to Granada's streets, packed as they are with bars, student dives, bohemian cafes and intimate flamenco clubs, and it's this as much as the more traditional sights that leaves a lasting impression.

History

From its origins as a 5th-century-BC Iberian settlement, Granada grew to become one of the medieval world's great Islamic cities. The Muslims first arrived in 711 but it wasn't until the 13th century that the city really started to flourish. As Córdoba (1236) and Seville (1248) fell to Catholic armies, a minor potentate named Mohammed ibn Yusuf ibn Nasr founded an independent emirate in Granada, paving the way for a 250-year golden age.

Under the Nasrid sultans, the Alhambra was developed into a spectacular palace-fort, and Granada, the last bastion of Al-Andalus, blossomed into one of Europe's richest cities, its streets teeming with traders and artisans. Two centuries of artistic and scientific splendour peaked under Yusuf I (r 1333–54) and Mohammed V (r 1354–59 and 1362–91).

It all began to go pear-shaped in the late 15th century: the economy stagnated and court politics turned violent as rival factions argued over the throne. One faction supported the emir Abu al-Hasan and his Christian concubine, Zoraya, while another backed Boabdil (Abu Abdullah), Abu al-Hasan's son by his wife Aixa – even though Boabdil was still just a child. In 1482 civil war broke out and, following Abu al-Hasan's death in 1485, Boabdil won control of the city. It proved a pyrrhic victory, though, and with the emirate weakened by infighting, the Catholic monarchs pounced in 1491. After an eight-month siege, Boabdil agreed to surrender the city in return for the Alpujarras valleys, 30,000 gold coins, and political and religious freedom for his subjects. Boabdil hiked out of town – letting out the proverbial 'Moor's last sigh' as he looked over his shoulder in regret – and on 2 January 1492, Isabel and Fernando entered Granada.

What followed was a period of religious persecution as the Christian authorities sought to establish Catholic rule on the city and former Moorish territories. The Jews were expelled from Spain in 1492 and, after a series of Muslim rebellions, Spain's *moriscos* (Muslims who had converted to Christianity) were thrown out in 1609.

This brutal expulsion backfired, however, and Granada – once the prize jewel of the Reyes Católicos (Catholic Monarchs) – sank into a deep decline from which it only began to emerge in the mid-19th century. Interest aroused by the Romantic movement, and in particular by Washington Irving's 1832 *Tales of the Alhambra,* helped pave the way for the restoration of the city's Islamic heritage and its resurrection as a tourist destination.

However, Granada suffered another dark period when Nationalists took the city at the start of the Spanish Civil War: an estimated 4000 *granadinos* with left or liberal connections were killed, among them Federico García Lorca, the city's most famous writer.

◉ Sights

Most sights are concentrated in the city's central neighbourhoods, which can mostly be covered on foot. To the north of Plaza Nueva, Granada's main square, the Albayzín district is demarcated by Gran Vía de Colón and the Río Darro. Over the river is the Alhambra hill whose southwestern slopes are occupied by the Realejo, Granada's former Jewish quarter. To the west of this, the Centro is home to the cathedral and a series of vibrant plazas, most notably Plaza Bib-Rambla.

◉ Alhambra & Realejo

★ **Alhambra**   ISLAMIC PALACE
(Map p258; ☑ 958 02 79 71, tickets 858 95 36 16; http://alhambra-patronato.es; adult/12-15yr/under 12yr €14/8/free, Generalife & Alcazaba adult/under 12yr €7/free; ⊙ 8.30am-8pm Apr–mid-Oct, to 6pm mid-Oct–Mar, night visits 10-11.30pm Tue-Sat Apr–mid-Oct, 8-9.30pm Fri & Sat mid-Oct–Mar)
The Alhambra is Granada's – and Europe's – love letter to Moorish culture. Set against a backdrop of brooding Sierra Nevada peaks, this fortified palace complex started life as

a walled citadel before going on to become the opulent seat of Granada's Nasrid emirs. Their showpiece palaces, the 14th-century Palacios Nazaríes, are among the finest Islamic buildings in Europe and, together with the gorgeous Generalife gardens, form the Alhambra's great headline act.

As one of Spain's most high-profile attractions, the Alhambra can draw up to 6000 daily visitors. Tickets sell out quickly so to avoid disappointment it pays to book ahead, either online or by phone. Note that when you buy a ticket you'll be given a time to enter the Palacios Nazaríes, admission to which is strictly controlled. For more information, see Alhambra Practicalities.

The origins of the Alhambra, whose name derives from the Arabic *al-qala'a al-hamra* (the Red Castle), are mired in mystery. The first references to construction in the area appear in the 9th century but it's thought that buildings may already have been

ALHAMBRA PRACTICALITIES

The Alhambra is Spain's most visited tourist attraction, drawing almost 2.5 million visitors a year. To ease your visit, it pays to book ahead and know the ropes.

Tickets

Some parts of the Alhambra can be visited free of charge, but for the main areas, you'll need a ticket. There are several types:

General (€14) Covers all areas.

Gardens (€7) Gives entry to all areas except the Palacios Nazaríes.

Night Visit Palacios Nazaríes (€8) For year-round night visits to the Nasrid Palaces.

Night Visit Gardens & Generalife (€5) Available from April to May and September to mid-October.

Dobla de Oro (€11.65 to €19.65) Covers admission to the Alhambra and several sites in the Albayzín neighbourhood.

How to Buy a Ticket

You can buy **tickets** (☏ 858 95 36 16; https://tickets.alhambra-patronato.es) from two hours to three months in advance, online or by phone, or at the Alhambra ticket office. Depending on the number of tickets reserved in advance, a limited number of same-day tickets are available at the ticket office. These sell out quickly, so get in early.

➡ If you've booked a ticket, you can either print it yourself or pick it up at the ticket office at the Alhambra Entrance Pavilion (p258) or the Corral del Carbón (p265) where there's a ticket machine.

➡ All children's tickets must be collected at the Alhambra ticket office as you'll need to prove your kids' ages – take their ID documents or passports.

➡ All tickets are named and nontransferable.

➡ Admission to the Alhambra is covered by the Granada Card (p270).

On-Site Facilities

➡ Audio guides are available for €6.

➡ No outside food is allowed, but there's a cafe-bar at the Parador de Granada (p272) and a kiosk in front of the Alcazaba. You'll also find vending machines by the ticket office and in a services pavilion by the Puerta del Vino.

➡ Strollers and prams are not permitted in the Palacios Nazaríes. You can leave them at the services pavilion.

Getting There

By foot, walk up the Cuesta de Gomérez from Plaza Nueva through the woods to the **Puerta de la Justicia** (Map p258; ☏ 958 02 79 71; http://alhambra-patronato.es; ⊙ 8.30am-8pm Apr–mid-Oct, to 6pm mid-Oct–Mar, night visits 10-11.30pm Tue-Sat Apr–mid-Oct, 8-9.30pm Fri & Sat mid-Oct–Mar) FREE. Enter here if you already have your ticket, otherwise continue to the ticket office.

Bus C3 (€1.20) runs to the ticket office from a bus stop (Map p264) just off Plaza Isabel la Católica.

Alhambra

A TIMELINE

900 The first reference to *al-qala'a al-hamra* (the Red Castle) atop Granada's Sabika Hill.

1237 Founder of the Nasrid dynasty, Mohammed I, moves his court to Granada. Threatened by belligerent Christian armies he builds a new defensive fort, the ❶ **Alcazaba**.

1302–09 Designed as a summer palace-cum-country estate for Granada's foppish rulers, the bucolic ❷ **Generalife** is begun by Mohammed III.

1333–54 Yusuf I initiates the construction of the ❸ **Palacios Nazaríes**, still considered the highpoint of Islamic culture in Europe.

1350–60 Up goes the ❹ **Palacio de Comares**, taking Nasrid lavishness to a whole new level.

1362–91 The second coming of Mohammed V ushers in even greater architectural brilliance, exemplified by the construction of the ❺ **Patio de los Leones**.

1527 The Christians add the ❻ **Palacio de Carlos V**. Inspired Renaissance palace or incongruous crime against Moorish art? You decide.

1829 The languishing, half-forgotten Alhambra is 'rediscovered' by American writer Washington Irving during a protracted sleepover.

1954 The Generalife gardens are extended southwards to accommodate an outdoor theatre.

TOP TIPS

➡ Reserve tickets either by phoning ☏858 95 36 16 or online http://alhambra-patronato.es.

➡ You can visit the general areas of the palace free of charge any time by entering through the Puerta de la Justicia.

➡ Two fine hotels are housed on the grounds if you wish to stay over: Parador de Granada (pricey) and Hotel América (more economical).

CHOI HYEKYUNG / SHUTTERSTOCK ©

Sala de la Barca
Throw your head back in the anteroom to the Comares Palace, where the gilded ceiling is shaped like an upturned boat. Destroyed by fire in the 1890s, it has been painstakingly restored

Mexuar

Patio de Machuca

Palacio de Carlos V
It's easy to miss the stylistic merits of this Renaissance palace, added in 1527. Check out the ground-floor Museo de la Alhambra for artefacts directly related to the palace's history.

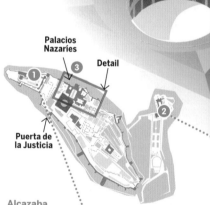

Palacios Nazaríes

❸

Detail

❶

❷

Puerta de la Justicia

Alcazaba
Find time to explore the towers of the original citadel, the most important of which – the Torre de la Vela – takes you, via a winding staircase, to the Alhambra's best viewpoint.

EMPERORCOSAR / SHUTTERSTOCK ©

Palacio de Comares

The neck-ache continues in the largest room in the Comares Palace, renowned for its rich geometric ceiling. A negotiating room for the emirs, the Salón de los Embajadores is a masterpiece of Moorish design.

JOSE IGNACIO SOTO / SHUTTERSTOCK ©

atio de los Arrayanes

only you could linger longer beside the rows of *rrayanes* (myrtle bushes) that border this calming *ctangular pool. Shaded porticos with seven armonious arches invite further contemplation.

Salón de los Embajadores

Baños Reales

Washington Irving Apartments

Sala de Dos Hermanas

Focus on the *dos hermanas* – two marble slabs either side of the fountain – before enjoying the intricate cupola embellished with 5000 tiny moulded stalactites. Poetic calligraphy decorates the walls.

④

Patio de los Arrayanes

Patio de la Lindaraja

⑤

Sala de los Reyes

Palacio del Partal

Sala de los Abencerrajes

Jardines del Partal

eneralife

coda to most people's visits, the 'architect's arden' is no afterthought. While Nasrid in origin, e horticulture is relatively new: the pools and cades were added in the early 20th century.

Patio de los Leones

Count the 12 lions sculpted from marble, holding up a gurgling fountain. Then pan back and take in the delicate columns and arches built to signify an Islamic vision of paradise.

FOTOGRAFIECOR NL / SHUTTERSTOCK ©

standing since Roman times. In its current form, it largely dates to the 13th and 14th centuries when Granada's Nasrid rulers transformed it into a fortified palace complex. Following the 1492 Reconquista (Christian reconquest), its mosque was replaced by a church and the Habsburg emperor Charles V had a wing of palaces demolished to make space for the huge Renaissance building that still bears his name. Later, in the early 19th century, French Napoleonic forces destroyed part of the palace and attempted to blow up the entire site. Restoration work began in the mid-1800s and continues to this day.

➡ **Palacio de Carlos V**

From the **entrance pavilion**, a signposted path leads into the core of the complex, passing a couple of notable religious buildings. The first is the **Convento de San Francisco**, now the Parador de Granada hotel (p270), where the bodies of Isabel and Fernando were laid to rest while their tombs were being built in the Capilla Real (p263). A short walk further on brings you to the **Iglesia de Santa María de la Alhambra** (⊙10am-1pm Tue-Sun & 4-6pm Tue-Sat), a 16th-century church on the site of the Alhambra's original mosque.

Beyond the church, the **Palacio de Carlos V** clashes spectacularly with the style of its surroundings. The hulking palace, begun in 1527 by Toledo architect Pedro Machuca, features a monumental facade and a two-tiered circular courtyard ringed by 32 columns. This circle inside a square is the only Spanish example of a Renaissance ground plan symbolising the unity of heaven and earth.

Inside the palace are two museums: the **Museo de la Alhambra** (☑958 02 79 00; ⊙8.30am-8pm Wed-Sat, to 2.30pm Sun & Tue Apr–mid-Oct, 8.30am-6pm Wed-Sat, to 2.30pm Sun & Tue mid-Oct–Mar) **FREE**, which showcases an absorbing collection of Islamic artefacts, including the door from the Sala de Dos Hermanas; and the **Museo de Bellas Artes** (Fine Arts Museum; ☑958 56 35 08; EU/non-EU citizens free/€1.50; ⊙9am-3pm Tue-Sat mid-Jun–mid-Sep, to 8pm Apr–mid-Jun & mid-Sep–mid-Oct, to 6pm Jan-Mar & mid-Oct–Dec, 9am-3pm Sun year-round), home to a collection of 15th- to 20th-century artworks.

➡ **Alcazaba**

Occupying the western tip of the Alhambra are the martial remnants of the **Alcazaba**, the site's original 13th-century citadel. The **Torre de la Vela** (Watchtower) is famous as the tower where the cross and banners of the Reconquista were raised in January 1492. A winding staircase leads to the top where you can enjoy sweeping views over Granada's rooftops.

Alhambra

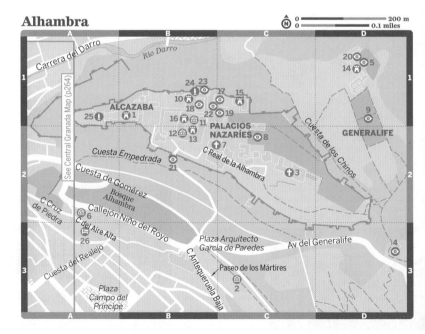

➡ Palacios Nazaríes

The Alhambra's stunning centrepiece, the palace complex known as the **Palacios Nazaríes** (Nasrid Palaces), was originally divided into three sections: the Mexuar, a chamber for administrative and public business; the Palacio de Comares, the emir's official private residence; and the Palacio de los Leones, a private area for the royal family and harem. Entrance is through the **Mexuar**, a 14th-century hall where the council of ministers would sit and the emir would adjudicate citizens' appeals. Two centuries later, it was converted into a chapel, with a prayer room at the far end. Look up here to appreciate the geometrically carved wood ceilings.

From the Mexuar, you pass into the **Patio del Cuarto Dorado**, a courtyard where the emirs gave audiences, with the **Cuarto Dorado** (Golden Room) on the left. Opposite the Cuarto Dorado is the entrance to the **Palacio de Comares** through a beautiful facade of glazed tiles, stucco and carved wood. A dogleg corridor (a common strategy in Islamic architecture to keep interior rooms private) leads through to the **Patio de los Arrayanes** (Court of the Myrtles). This elegant patio, named after the myrtle hedges around its rectangular pool, is the central space of the palace that was built in the mid-14th century as Emir Yusuf I's official residence.

The southern end of the patio is overshadowed by the walls of the Palacio de Carlos V. To the north, in the 45m-high **Torre de Comares** (Comares Tower), the **Sala de la Barca** (Hall of the Blessing) leads into the **Salón de los Embajadores** (Chamber of the Ambassadors), where the emirs would have conducted negotiations with Christian emissaries. The room's marvellous domed marquetry ceiling contains more than 8000 cedar pieces in an intricate star pattern representing the seven heavens of Islam.

The Patio de los Arrayanes leads into the **Palacio de los Leones** (Palace of the Lions), built in the second half of the 14th century under Muhammad V. The palace rooms branch off the **Patio de los Leones** (Lion Courtyard), centred on an 11th-century fountain channelling water through the mouths of 12 marble lions. The courtyard layout, using the proportions of the golden ratio, demonstrates the complexity of Islamic geometric design – the 124 slender columns that support the ornamented pavilions are placed in such a way that they are symmetrical on numerous axes.

Of the four halls around the patio, the southern **Sala de los Abencerrajes** is the most impressive. Boasting a mesmerising octagonal stalactite ceiling, this is the legendary site of the murders of the noble Abencerraj family, whose leader, the story goes, dared to dally with Zoraya, Abu al-Hasan's favourite concubine. The rusty stains in the fountain are said to be the victims' indelible blood.

At the eastern end of the patio is the **Sala de los Reyes** (Hall of the Kings) with a leather-lined ceiling painted by 14th-century Christian artists. The hall's name comes from the painting on the central alcove, thought to depict 10 Nasrid emirs.

GRANADA PROVINCE GRANADA

Alhambra

Granada

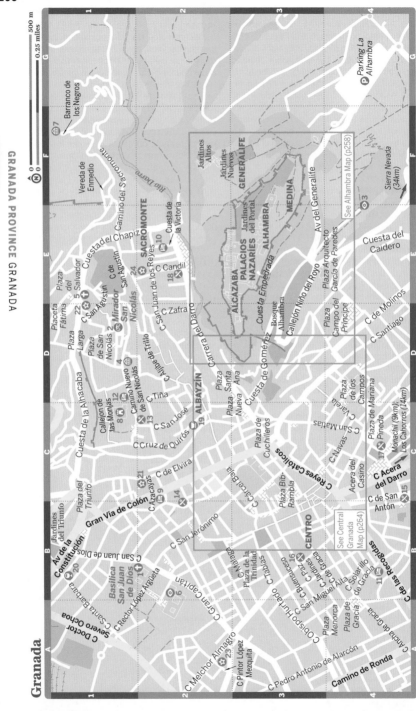

500 m
0.25 miles

Barranco de los Negros

7

Vereda de Enmedio

SACROMONTE

Camino del Sacromonte

Río Darro

GENERALIFE

Jardines Altos

Jardines Nuevos

Parking La Alhambra

Sierra Nevada (34km)

3

See Alhambra Map (p258)

MEDINA

ALHAMBRA

Cuesta de la Victoria

Cuesta del Chapiz

Cuesta del Caidero

Plaza del Salvador

C de San Agustín

Placeta Fátima

22 5

C San Agustín

Mirador San Nicolás

24

C de San Agustín

C San Juan de los Reyes

C Candil

18

C Zafra

10

Jardines del Portal

ALCAZABA

PALACIOS NAZARIES

Cuesta Empedrada

Bosque Alhambra

Av del Generalife

Plaza Arquitecto García de Paredes

C de Molinos

C Santiago

Plaza Larga

Plaza de San Nicolás

2

4

Cuesta de la Alhacaba

Camino Nuevo de San Nicolás

C de Trillo

C Tiña

C San José

13

ALBAYZIN

19

Carrera del Darro

Callejón de las Monjas

8 12

C Cruz de Quirós

Plaza Santa Ana

Plaza Nueva

Cuesta de Gomérez

Callejón Niño del Royo

Plaza Campo del Príncipe

Plaza de los Campos

C de Molinos

Jardines del Triunfo

Plaza del Triunfo

21

9

C de Elvira

14

Plaza de Cuchilleros

C Varela

San Matías

Plaza de Mariana Pineda

Monachil (9km); Los Cahorros (14km)

17

Av de la Constitución

Gran Vía de Colón

C Azacayas

C San Jerónimo

Cárcel Baja

C Reyes Católicos

C Navas

Acera del Casino

Plaza Bib-Rambla

Plaza Bib

See Central Granada Map (p264)

CENTRO

C de San Antón

15

C Acera del Darro

C de San Antón

Basílica San Juan de Dios

C San Juan de Dios

C Rector López Argüeta

C Gran Capitán

23

6

20

C Doctor Severo Ochoa

C Santa Bárbara

C Melchor Almagro

C Pintor López Mezquita

C Málaga

Plaza de la Trinidad

C Tablas

16

C Buensuceso

C San Miguel Alta

C Obispo Hurtado

C Solarillo de Gracia

Plaza Menorca

Plaza de Gracia

11

C Angosto de Gracia

Camino de Ronda

C Pedro Antonio de Alarcón

On the patio's northern side is the richly decorated **Sala de Dos Hermanas** (Hall of Two Sisters), probably named after the slabs of white marble flanking its fountain. It features a dizzying *muqarnas* (honeycomb-vaulted) dome with a central star and 5000 tiny cells, reminiscent of the constellations. This may have been the room of the emir's favourite paramour. The carved wood screens in the upper level enabled women (and perhaps others involved in palace intrigue) to peer down from hallways above without being seen. At its far end, the tile-trimmed **Mirador de Daraxa** (Daraxa lookout) was a lovely place for palace denizens to look onto the garden below.

From the Sala de Dos Hermanas, a passageway leads through the **Estancias del Emperador** (Emperor's Chambers), built for Carlos I in the 1520s, and later used by American author Washington Irving. From here descend to the **Patio de la Reya** (Patio of the Grille) and the **Patio de la Lindaraja**, where,

in the southwest corner you can peer into the bathhouse lit by star-shaped skylights.

You eventually emerge into the **Jardines del Partal**, an area of terraced gardens laid out at the beginning of the 20th century. Here a reflecting pool stands in front of the **Palacio del Partal**, a small porticoed building with its own tower (the Torre de las Damas) dating to the early 14th century. Leave the Partal gardens by a gate facing the Palacio de Carlos V, or continue along a path to the Generalife.

➡ Generalife

The Generalife, the sultans' gorgeous summer estate, dates to the 14th century. A soothing ensemble of pathways, patios, pools, fountains, trees and, in season, flowers of every imaginable hue, it takes its name from the Arabic *jinan al-'arif,* meaning 'the overseer's gardens'.

A string of elegant rectangular plots, the **Jardines Nuevos**, leads up to the white-washed **Palacio del Generalife**, the emirs' summer palace. The courtyards here are particularly graceful – in the second one, the **Patio del Ciprés de la Sultana**, the trunk of a 700-year-old cypress tree suggests the delicate shade that would once have graced the area. Beyond the courtyard, a staircase known as the **Escalera del Agua** is a delightful work of landscape engineering with water channels running down the shaded steps.

Fundación Rodríguez-Acosta MUSEUM
(Map p258; ☑958 22 74 97; www.fundacion rodriguezacosta.com; Callejón Niño del Royo 8; guided tour adult/reduced €5/4; ⊙10am-6.30pm Apr–mid-Oct, to 4.30pm mid-Oct–Mar) On the Realejo hill, the so-called 'Carmen Blanco' houses the Rodríguez-Acosta foundation in a building built by the Granada-born modernist artist, José María Rodríguez-Acosta, in 1914. It's an unusual and whimsical place that borrows from several architectural genres including art deco, Nasrid, Greek and baroque. The one-hour guided tour includes a walk through the house's subterranean tunnels, and entry to a well-curated museum containing works by Francisco Pacheco, Alonso Cano and Francisco de Zurbarán.

Casa-Museo Manuel de Falla MUSEUM
(Map p258; ☑958 22 21 88; www.museomanuel defalla.com; Paseo de los Mártires; adult/reduced €3/1; ⊙10am-5pm Tue-Sat, to 3pm Sun) Arguably Spain's greatest classical composer and an artistic friend of Lorca, Manuel de Falla (1876–1946) was born in Cádiz, but spent the key years of his life in Granada until

the civil war forced him into exile. You can learn all about the man at this attractive *carmen* (traditional house with walled garden) where he lived and composed, and which has been preserved pretty much as he left it. Ring the bell to get in.

Carmen de los Mártires GARDENS
(Map p260; Paseo de los Mártires; ⊙10am-2pm & 6-8pm Mon-Fri, 10am-8pm Sat & Sun) FREE A peaceful oasis, these romantically dishevelled 19th-century gardens sprawl around a restored mansion on the hillside south of the Alhambra. It's a great spot to escape the evening crowds and enjoy uplifting views of the city and surrounding mountains.

Centro de la Memoria Sefardí MUSEUM
(Map p264; ☑610 060255; Placeta Berrocal 5; guided tour €5; ⊙10am-2pm Sun-Fri year-round, plus 5-8.30pm winter, 4-8pm winter) Since being expelled en masse in 1492, there are very few Sephardic Jews left in Granada. But this didn't stop one enterprising couple from opening a museum to their memory in 2013, the year the Spanish government began offering Spanish citizenship to any Sephardic Jew who could prove their Iberian ancestry. The museum is tiny, but the selected artefacts make excellent props to the passionate and fascinating history related by its owners.

◉ Plaza Nueva & Around

Baños Árabes El Bañuelo BATHHOUSE
(Map p264; Carrera del Darro 31; ⊙9am-2.30pm & 5-8.30pm summer, 10am-5pm winter) FREE Located by the river on Carrera del Darro is this well-preserved, 11th-century Islamic bathhouse. Its bare brick rooms feature columns, capitals and marble-tiled floors.

Iglesia de Santa Ana CHURCH
(Map p264; Plaza Santa Ana; €1.50; ⊙10.30am-1.30pm Tue-Fri) Extending from the northeast corner of Plaza Nueva, Plaza Santa Ana is dominated by the Iglesia de Santa Ana, a 16th-century Mudéjar church whose bell tower incorporates the minaret of the mosque over which it stands.

Archivo-Museo San Juan de Dios MUSEUM
(Map p264; ☑958 22 21 44; www.museosanjuandedios.es; Calle Convalecencia 1; €3; ⊙10am-1pm Mon-Sat) This small museum occupies the aristocratic Casa de los Pisa where Granada's resident saint, San Juan Robles (San Juan de Díos), died in 1550. The house was subsequently bought by the Hospitaller Order of St John of God and today houses the Order's archives and a small collection of

religious art. Visits are by 45-minute guided tour (Spanish and English).

◉ Albayzín

The Albayzín, Granada's old Muslim quarter, is sprawled over a hill facing the Alhambra. Ideal for aimless wandering – you'll almost certainly get lost at some point – it's a fascinating district of steep cobblestone streets, *teterías* (teahouses) and whitewashed *cármenes*. The area is served by bus C1, which runs a circular route from Plaza Nueva, departing approximately every eight minutes between 7am and 11pm.

★ Mirador San Nicolás VIEWPOINT
(Map p260; Plaza de San Nicolás) This is the place for those classic sunset shots of the Alhambra sprawled along a wooded hilltop with the dark Sierra Nevada mountains looming in the background. It's a well-known spot, accessible via Callejón de San Cecilio, so expect crowds of camera-toting tourists, students and buskers. It's also a haunt of pickpockets and bag-snatchers, so keep your wits about you as you enjoy the views.

Palacio de Dar-al-Horra PALACE
(Map p260; Callejón de las Monjas; €5, Sun free; ⊙9am-2.15pm & 5-8.15pm mid-Mar–mid-Oct, 10am-5pm mid-Oct–mid-Mar) Up in the Albayzín – down a short lane off Callejón del Gallo – this 15th-century Nasrid palace was home to the mother of Boabdil, Granada's last Muslim ruler. It's surprisingly intimate, with rooms set around a central courtyard and fabulous views over the surrounding neighbourhood and over to the Alhambra.

Carmen Museo Max Moreau MUSEUM
(Map p260; ☑958 29 33 10; Camino Nuevo de San Nicolás 12; ⊙10.30am-1.30pm & 6-8pm Tue-Sat) FREE Most of the Albayzín's *cármenes* are true to their original concept – quiet, private houses with high walls that hide beautiful terraced gardens. But you can get a rare (and free) glimpse of one of these secret domains at the former home of Belgium-born portrait painter and composer Max Moreau. His attractive house has been made into a museum displaying his former living quarters and work space, along with a gallery showcasing his best portraits.

Calle Calderería Nueva STREET
(Map p264) Linking the upper and lower parts of the Albayzín, Calle Calderería Nueva is a narrow street famous for its *teterías*. It's also a good place to shop for slippers, hookahs, jewellery and North African pottery

from an eclectic cache of shops redolent of a Moroccan souk.

Colegiata del Salvador CHURCH

(Map p260; ☑958 27 86 44; Plaza del Salvador; admission €1; ☉10am-1pm & 4.30-6.30pm Mon-Sat) Plaza del Salvador, near the top of the Albayzín, is dominated by this 16th-century church on the site of the Albayzín's former mosque, the patio of which still survives at the church's western end.

Palacio de los Olvidados MUSEUM

(Map p264; ☑958 10 08 40; www.palaciodelos olvidados.es; Cuesta de Santa Inés 6; adult/reduced €5/4.50; ☉10.30am-9pm) The 16th-century 'palace of the forgotten' in the Albayzín is home to a gruesome exhibition of torture instruments used by the Spanish Inquisition. The top floor, however, is given over to the city's Jewish history – Jews played a vital role in the Nasrid Emirate of Granada from the 1200s to 1492 – with display cabinets exhibiting scrolls, costumes and artefacts.

◎ Centro

★Capilla Real HISTORIC BUILDING

(Royal Chapel; Map p264; ☑958 22 78 48; www.capil larealgranada.com; Calle Oficios; adult/student/child €5/3.50/free; ☉10.15am-6.30pm Mon-Sat, 11am-6.30pm Sun) The Royal Chapel is the last resting place of Spain's Reyes Católicos (Catholic Monarchs), Isabel I de Castilla (1451–1504) and Fernando II de Aragón (1452–1516), who commissioned the elaborate Isabelline-Gothic-style mausoleum that was to house them. It wasn't completed until 1517, hence their interment in the Alhambra's Convento de San Francisco (p258) until 1521.

Their monumental marble tombs (and those of their heirs) lie in the chancel behind a gilded wrought-iron screen, created by Bartolomé de Jaén in 1520.

However, the tombs are just for show as the monarchs actually lie in simple lead coffins in the crypt beneath the chancel. Also there are the coffins of Isabel and Fernando's unfortunate daughter, Juana the Mad, her husband, Philip of Flanders; and Miguel, Prince of Asturias, who died as a boy.

The sacristy contains a small but impressive museum, with Fernando's sword and Isabel's sceptre, silver crown and personal art collection, which is mainly Flemish but also includes Botticelli's *Prayer in the Garden of Olives*. Felipe de Vigarni's two early-16th-century statues of the Catholic Monarchs at prayer are also here.

Catedral de Granada CATHEDRAL

(Map p264; ☑958 22 29 59; www.catedralde granada.com; Plaza de las Pasiegas; adult/reduced €5/3.50; ☉10am-6.30pm Mon-Sat, 3-6pm Sun) From street level it's difficult to appreciate

---

LORCA'S LEGACY

Spain's greatest poet and playwright, Federico García Lorca (1898–1936), epitomised many of Andalucía's potent hallmarks – passion, ambiguity, exuberance and innovation. Born in Fuente Vaqueros, a village 17km west of Granada, he won international acclaim in 1928 with *El romancero gitano* (Gypsy Ballads), a collection of verses on Roma themes, full of startling metaphors yet crafted with the simplicity of flamenco song. Between 1933 and 1936 he wrote the three tragic plays for which he's best known: *Bodas de sangre* (Blood Wedding), *Yerma* (Barren) and *La casa de Bernarda Alba* (The House of Bernarda Alba) – brooding, dramatic works dealing with themes of entrapment and liberation.

Lorca was killed at the start of the civil war in August 1936. Although the whereabouts of his remains has proven elusive, it's generally held he was executed by military authorities loyal to Franco for his perceived left-wing political views and his homosexuality.

Lorca's summer house, the **Huerta de San Vicente** (☑958 25 84 66; www.huerta desanvicente.com; Calle Virgen Blanca; €3, Wed free; ☉9.30am-5pm Tue-Sun mid-Sep–May, 9am-2pm Tue-Sun Jun–mid-Sep), is now a museum in the city's southern suburbs. Back in the centre, the **Centro Federico García Lorca** (Map p264; ☑958 27 40 62; www.centro federicogarcialorca.es; Plaza de la Romanilla; ☉11am-2pm & 5-8pm Tue-Sat, 11am-2pm Sun) FREE houses the Lorca foundation and provides a modern setting for exhibitions and cultural events.

In Fuente Vaqueros, the **Museo Casa Natal Federico García Lorca** (☑958 51 64 53; www.patronatogarcialorca.org; Calle Poeta Federico García Lorca 4; €1.80; ☉guided visits hourly 10am-1pm Tue-Sat year-round & 4-5pm Oct-Mar, 5-6pm Apr-Jun & Sep) displays photos, posters and costumes for the writer's plays. Hourly **Ureña** (☑953 22 01 71) buses serve the village (€1.70, 20 minutes) from Avenida de Andaluces near the bus station in Granada.

GRANADA PROVINCE GRANADA

the immensity of Granada's cavernous cathedral. It's too boxed in by other buildings to stand out, but it's nonetheless a monumental work of architecture. Built atop the city's former mosque, it was originally intended to be Gothic in appearance, but over the two centuries of its construction (1523–1704) it underwent major modifications. Most notably, architect Diego de Siloé changed its layout to a Renaissance style, and Alonso Cano added a magnificent 17th-century baroque facade.

Cano was also responsible for two wooden busts of Adam and Eve on the altar in the Capilla Mayor (main chapel). The cathedral's interior is vast with a series of 20 huge white piers rising from a black-and-white tiled floor to a ceiling capped by a 30m-high dome.

Plaza Bib-Rambla   PLAZA

(Map p264) A picturesque, pedestrian-only square ringed by 19th-century townhouses, lime trees, kiosks and cafes. Ornamental lampposts stand around the plaza's baroque centrepiece, a 17th-century fountain whose rather underwhelming statue of Neptune stands atop an obelisk-like structure, itself balanced on a disk supported by grotesque figures, the so-called *gigantones*.

Central Granada

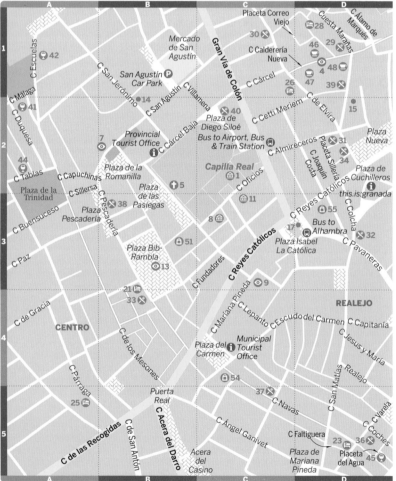

Palacio de la Madraza HISTORIC BUILDING

(Map p264; 958 24 12 99; Calle Oficios; guided tour €2; 10.30am-7.45pm) La Madraza, easily recognisable by the trompe l'oeil on its facade, was founded in 1349 by Sultan Yusuf I as a school and university – and it still belongs to Granada University. Since an extensive renovation in the early 2010s, it's possible to view its interesting, and sometimes contradictory, mix of Arabic, Christian, Mudéjar and baroque architecture. Highlights include an elaborate *mihrab* (prayer niche), a baroque dome and some coloured stucco. Student guides take you through the details.

Corral del Carbón COURTYARD

(Map p264; Calle Mariana Pineda; 9am-8pm) Just east of Calle Reyes Católicos, an elaborate horseshoe arch leads through to the 14th-century Corral del Carbón, a cobbled courtyard surrounded by two storeys of brick galleries. Initially, this was a Nasrid-era corn exchange, but in subsequent centuries it was used as an inn for coal dealers (hence its modern name, Coal Yard) and later as a theatre.

Centro José Guerrero GALLERY

(Map p264; 958 22 01 09; www.centroguerrero.org; Calle Oficios 8; 10.30am-2pm Tue-Sun & 4.30-9pm Tue-Sat) FREE An exhibition space and gallery named after the Granada-born abstract painter (1914–91) who went to live in the US. Exhibitions are temporary and with a modernist bent, though the gallery keeps a roomful of Guerrero's characteristically vibrant works in a permanent collection.

⊙ Outside the Centre

★ Basílica San Juan de Dios BASILICA

(Map p260; www.sjdgranada.es; Calle San Juan de Dios 19; €4; 10am-1.30pm Mon-Sat, 4-6.45pm Sun) Head to this historic basilica, built between 1737 and 1759, for a blinding display of opulent baroque decor. Barely a square inch of its interior lacks embellishment, most of it in gleaming gold and silver. Frescos by Diego Sánchez Sarabia and the Neapolitan painter Corrado Giaquinto adorn the ceilings and side chapels, while up above, the basilica's dome soars to a height of 50m. The highlight, however, is the extraordinary gold altarpiece in the Capilla Mayor (main chapel). Once you've taken in the head-spinning details, search out a staff member to accompany you up the stairs behind the altar to where St John of God's remains are set deep in a niche surrounded by gold, gold and yet more gold.

Monasterio de San Jerónimo MONASTERY

(Map p260; 958 27 93 37; Calle Rector López Argüeta 9; €4; 10am-1.30pm & 4-7.30pm) This 16th-century monastery, complete with cloisters and a lavishly decorated interior, is one of Granada's most stunning Catholic buildings. The church, a mix of late Gothic and Renaissance styling, boasts a profusion of painted sculptures and vivid colours, most spectacularly on the apse's immense eight-level gilt retable.

Gonzalo Fernández de Córdoba, the Reyes Católicos' (Catholic Monarchs') military man known as *El Gran Capitán,* is entombed in the church, at the foot of the

Central Granada

steps, and figures of him and his wife stand on either side of the retable.

Monasterio de la Cartuja   MONASTERY
(☑958 16 19 32; Paseo de la Cartuja; €5; ⊙10am-8pm) Built between the 16th and 18th centuries by the Carthusian monks themselves, this monastery features an imposing sandstone exterior and some incredibly lavish baroque decor. A highlight is the *sagrario* (sanctuary) behind the main altar in the church, a dizzying ensemble of coloured marble, columns and sculpture capped by a beautiful frescoed cupola. To get to the monastery, take bus LAC or N7 from the city centre.

🏃 Activities

Hammam Al Ándalus   HAMMAM
(Map p264; ☑902 33 33 34; www.granada.ham mamalandalus.com; Calle Santa Ana 16; bath/bath & massage €30/45; ⊙10am-midnight) With three pools of different temperatures, plus a steam room and the option of skin-scrubbing massages, this is the best of Granada's Arab-style baths. Its dim, tiled rooms are suitably sybaritic and relaxing. Reservations required.

📖 Courses

Escuela Delengua   LANGUAGE
(Map p264; ☑958 20 45 35; www.delengua.es; Calle Calderería Vieja 20; individual lessons €36, 2-week course €260) With a massive student population, Granada is an ideal place to learn Spanish. This school in the heart of the Albayzín runs a range of courses, as well as offering individual lessons and loads of extracurricular activities, including guided tours and tapas nights. It can also arrange accommodation.

☞ Tours

Play Granada   CULTURAL
(Map p264; ☑958 16 36 84; www.playgranada. com; Calle Santa Ana 2; tours from €20) On foot, by electric bike, on a Segway – this outfit offers a choice of tours, taking in the city and its historic quarters, as well as packages for

the Alhambra (p254). Reckon on €20 for a two-hour 8km Segway ride, and from €60 for a guided tour of the Alhambra.

Pancho Tours WALKING

(Map p264; ☑ 664 64 29 04; www.panchotours.com) FREE The guys in orange T-shirts lead excellent free tours of the city. The walks, which depart daily at 10.30am from Plaza Isabella la Católica, last around 2½ hours. Also available are tours of the Albayzín and Sacromonte (€13 per person) and skip-the-line entry to the Alhambra (p254) combined with an Albayzín tour (€134). Book online.

Cicerone Cultura y Ocio WALKING

(Map p264; ☑ 958 56 18 10; www.ciceronegranada. com; Calle San Jerónimo 10) Offers a range of individual and group walking tours, as well as thematic itineraries and excursions out of the city to Las Alpujarras and the Costa Tropical. Reckon on €18 to join a two-hour city walk.

Festivals & Events

Semana Santa RELIGIOUS

(Holy Week; ⊘ Mar/Apr) The two most striking events in Granada's Easter week are Los Gitanos (Wednesday), when members of the *fraternidad* (brotherhood) parade to the Abadía de Sacromonte, lit by bonfires, and El Silencio (Thursday), when the street lights are turned off for a silent candlelit march.

Día de la Cruz RELIGIOUS

(Day of the Cross; ⊘ 3 May) Squares, patios and balconies are adorned with floral crosses, beginning three days of revelry.

Feria del Corpus Christi RELIGIOUS

(Corpus Christi Fair; ⊘ May/Jun) The most spectacular of Andalucía's Corpus Christi celebrations, this is Granada's big annual party. Held approximately 60 days after Easter,

it involves a week of bullfighting, dancing, street parades and processions. Events are held across town and in fairgrounds near the bus station. Bullfighting has deep cultural roots in Andalucía but there is opposition to it and visitors may wish to avoid the fights, held in the Plaza de Toros north of the city centre.

Festival Internacional de Música y Danza MUSIC

(www.granadafestival.org; ⊘ Jun & Jul) For three weeks in June and July, first-class classical and modern performances are staged at the Alhambra and other historic sites.

Sleeping

Granada has plenty of hotels and hostels, many in the compact area around the cathedral. Some of the prettiest lodgings are in the Albayzín district, though these might call for some hill-walking, and many aren't accessible by taxi. The few hotels near the Alhambra are scenic but a hassle for sightseeing elsewhere. Rates are highest in spring and autumn, spiking over Easter.

Alhambra & Realejo

Carmen de la Alcubilla del Caracol HISTORIC HOTEL €€

(Map p258; ☑ 958 21 55 51; www.alcubilladelcara col.com; Calle del Aire Alta 12; r €100-180; ⊘ closed mid-Jul–Aug; ❄ ⊗) This much-sought-after small hotel inhabits a traditional white-washed *carmen* on the slopes of the Alhambra. It feels more like a B&B than a hotel with its elegant homey interiors and seven quietly refined rooms washed in pale pastel colours. Outside, you can bask in views from the spectacular terraced garden.

GRANADA PROVINCE GRANADA

SACROMONTE

Sacromonte, Granada's historic *gitano* (Roma) neighbourhood, sits northeast of the Albayzín (p262). Renowned for its flamenco traditions, it draws tourists to nightclubs and aficionados to music schools yet still feels like the fringes of the city. This despite the fact that some of the caves dug out of the hillside date back to the 14th century.

The area, centred on the Camino del Sacromonte, is good for an idle stroll, yielding some great views, particularly from the Vereda de Enmedio, which overlooks the Alhambra and Albayzín. For some local insight, stop off at the **Museo Cuevas del Sacromonte** (Map p260; ☑ 958 21 51 20; www.sacromontegranada.com; Barranco de los Negros; €5; ⊘ 10am-8pm mid-Mar–mid-Oct, to 6pm mid-Oct–mid-Mar) where you can see what a traditional cave home once looked like. The diligent can then press on to the **Abadía de Sacromonte** (€4; ⊘ 10am-1pm Mon-Sat, 11am-1pm Sun & 5-7.30pm daily summer, 4-6pm winter) at the top of the hill, to explore some catacombs and underground cave chapels.

Note that it's not considered safe for lone women to wander around the uninhabited parts of the area, day or night.

ALEKSANDAR TODOROVIC/SHUTTERSTOCK ©

1. Bathhouse, Córdoba (p201) 2. Tearoom, Granada (p254)
3. Hammam Al Ándalus (p266), Granada 4. Mint tea

MATYAS REHAK/AKA/SHUTTERSTOCK ©

Teterías & Hammams

More so than in other parts of Spain, the Moorish era in Andalucía had a sense of destiny and permanence. The region spent nearly eight centuries (AD 711 to 1492) under North African influence, and exotic reminders flicker on every street corner, from the palatial Alhambra to the tearooms and bathhouses of Córdoba and Málaga.

Moorish Tearooms

Moorish-style *teterías* (tearooms), carrying a whiff of Fez, Marrakesh or even Cairo in their ornate interiors, have been revived in Andalucía as a result both of North African migration and a local interest in the Moorish side of their heritage. Calle Caldelería Nueva in Granada's Albayzín (p262) kicked off the trend some years back. Today even Torremolinos has a couple! Look out for dimly lit, cushion-filled, fit-for-a-sultan cafes where pots of herbal tea accompanied by plates of Arabic sweets arrive at your table on a silver salver.

Arabic Bathhouses

Sitting somewhere between a Western spa and a Moroccan *hammam*, Andalucía's modern bathhouses possess enough old-fashioned elegance to satisfy a latter-day emir with a penchant for Moorish-era opulence. You can recline in candlelit subterranean bliss sipping mint tea, and experience the same kind of bathing ritual – successive immersions in cold, tepid and hot bathwater – that the Moors did. Seville, Granada, Almería, Córdoba and Málaga all have excellent Arabic-style bathhouses, with massages also available.

BEST TETERÍAS

Tetería Nazarí (p275), Granada

La Tetería (p172), Málaga

Tetería Almedina (p297), Almería

Tetería La Jaima (p127), Jerez de la Frontera

Tetería Dar Ziryab (p275), Granada

ⓘ GRANADA CARD

This city pass comes in two forms, both available for pre-purchase or to buy in Granada:

Granada Card Básica (€37) Valid for three days, it provides admission to 10 monuments, including the Alhambra, Catedral, and Capilla Real, and covers five trips on local city buses.

Granada Card Plus (€40) Valid for five days, it covers admission to the same monuments as the basic card plus nine trips on local buses and a single tour on a tourist train.

Kids passes (€10.50) Available for children aged between three and 11. These must be associated with a regular adult card and there's a maximum of three passes per adult.

Further details, along with online booking, are available at www.granadatur.com or by phoning ☑858 88 09 90. Note that when you buy a pass you have to specify a start date as admission to parts of the Alhambra are regulated and require you to visit at a set time.

Hotel Molinos　　　　　　　　HOTEL €€

(Map p264; ☑958 22 73 67; www.hotelmolinos.es; Calle Molinos 12; s €35-53, d €39-85; ❋🛜) Don't let the 'narrowest hotel in the world' moniker put you off – and yes, it actually is, with a certificate from *Guinness World Records* to prove it – there's plenty of breathing space in Molinos' attractively fashioned rooms. Situated at the foot of the Realejo, it's an economical central option.

Hotel Palacio de Los Navas　　HISTORIC HOTEL €€

(Map p264; ☑958 21 57 60; www.hotelpalacio delosnavas.com; Calle Navas 1; s €65-130, d €70-165; ❋🛜) This 16th-century building, set around a classic columned patio, has attractive rooms with lots of cool creams, wrought-iron headsteads and terracotta-tiled floors. Location-wise, it's well placed for tapas action on Calle Navas, one of Granada's quintessential bar streets.

Parador de Granada　　　HISTORIC HOTEL €€€

(Map p258; ☑958 22 14 40; www.parador.es; Calle Real de la Alhambra; r €220-436; 🅿❋@🛜) Few hotels can claim a more impressive setting than this luxury *parador* (state-run hotel), housed in a 15th-century convent in the Alhambra. Book here if you're looking for romance or want to revel in the history of its surrounds. Reserve ahead; it's mega-popular – obviously.

🛏 Plaza Nueva & Around

Hotel Palacio de Santa Inés　　HOTEL €€

(Map p264; ☑958 22 23 62; www.palaciosan taines.es; Cuesta de Santa Inés 9; d €85-125; ❋🛜) A Moorish-era house, extended in the 16th and 17th centuries, with a fetching double patio around which rooms, some with Alhambra views, are arranged on three levels. The interior resembles a coaching inn, its decor a mix of burnt sienna tiles, old timber beams and heavy furniture.

🛏 Albayzín

Oasis Backpackers' Hostel　　HOSTEL €

(Map p264; ☑958 21 58 48; https://hostels oasis.com/granada-hostels/oasis-granada; Placeta Correo Viejo 3; dm €11-23; ❋@🛜) Budget digs in a bohemian quarter, the friendly Oasis is seconds away from the *teterías* and bars on Calle Elvira. The first in what is now a chain of Oasis hostels, it has beds in six- to 10-person dorms, both mixed and women only, and a long list of facilities including a fully equipped kitchen and rooftop terrace.

Hotel Posada del Toro　　　　HOTEL €

(Map p264; ☑958 22 73 33; www.posadadeltoro. com; Calle de Elvira 25; s/d/ste from €45/49/71; ❋🛜) A lovely little hotel in the lively Albayzín quarter. Bullfighting posters line a small passageway that leads to the main body of the hotel where tasteful rooms are decked out with parquet floors, Alhambra-style stucco and rustic furniture. Rates are a bargain considering its central location.

Hotel Casa del Capitel Nazarí　　HISTORIC HOTEL €€

(Map p264; ☑958 21 52 60; www.hotelcasaca pitel.com; Cuesta Aceituneros 6; s €52-100, d €65-125; ❋@🛜) Another slice of Albayzín magic in a Renaissance palace that's as much architectural history lesson as midrange hotel. The sound of trickling water follows you through the columned courtyard to traditional, low-ceilinged rooms clad in tiles, bricks and heavy wood. It scores for its location too, just off Plaza Nueva.

Hotel Zawán del Darro　　HISTORIC HOTEL €€

(Map p264; ☑958 21 57 30; http://hotelzawan deldarro.com; Carrera del Darro 23; s €50-70, d €65-99; ❋@🛜) In the buzzy riverside area of the Albayzín, this pleasant three-star occupies a tastefully restored 16th-century mansion.

Expect stone floors, wood beams and 13 character-filled rooms, the best of which have Alhambra views. There are plenty of eating and drinking options nearby, hence a bit of evening noise.

★**Santa Isabel La Real**   BOUTIQUE HOTEL €€€
(Map p260; ☑958 29 46 58; www.hotelsanta isabellareal.com; Calle de Santa Isabel La Real 19; r €119-199; ❋@🛜) Up in hilltop Albayzín, this welcoming small hotel occupies a white-washed 16th-century building. Many original architectural features endure, including marble columns and flagged stone floors, while a fireplace and sofa add a homey touch in the communal area. The guest rooms, which are set around a central patio, are individually decorated with embroidered pictures and hand-woven rugs.

Go for room 11 if you can, for its Alhambra views.

★**Casa Morisca Hotel**   HISTORIC HOTEL €€€
(Map p260; ☑958 22 11 00; www.hotelcasamor isca.com; Cuesta de la Victoria 9; d €129-175, ste €231; ❋🛜) Live like a Nasrid emir in this late-15th-century mansion in the historic Albayzín quarter. Atmosphere and history are laid on thick in the form of timber-beamed ceilings, brick columns and an enchanting tiled courtyard. Rooms, the best of which have Alhambra views, are attractive and simply furnished.

Hotel Casa 1800 Granada   BOUTIQUE HOTEL €€€
(Map p264; ☑958 21 07 00; www.hotelcasa1800. com; Calle Benalúa 11; r €75-425, ste €155-800; ❋🛜) Elegantly ensconced in a venerable 16th-century building, this classy hotel charms with its delightful old-world decor: beds with gilded headboards, coffered ceilings, a lovely central courtyard overlooked by wood-balustraded balconies. Service is warm and efficient, and complimentary high tea is offered to guests each afternoon.

🛏 Centro

Hotel Párragasiete   HOTEL €€
(Map p264; ☑958 26 42 27; www.hotelparra gasiete.com; Calle Párraga 7; s €36-65, d €48-150; ❋🛜) With its blond-wood floors, severe furniture and clean modern lines, this smart hotel seems more Scandinavia than southern Spain. However, Granada appears in the form of wall sketches of local monuments and a sleek downstairs bar-restaurant called Vitola – ideal for breakfast or tapas.

Hotel Los Tilos   HOTEL €€
(Map p264; ☑958 26 67 12; www.hotellostilos.com; Plaza Bib-Rambla 4; s/d €45/75; ❋) If you're after a strategically sited bolt-hole, this unpretentious hotel fits the bill. It's on ever-lively Plaza Bib-Rambla in the heart of the historic centre and offers plain, decent-sized rooms whose double-glazed windows keep out most of the late-night racket. Alhambra views can also be enjoyed from a small panoramic rooftop terrace.

Hotel Hospes Palacio de Los Patos   LUXURY HOTEL €€€
(Map p260; ☑958 53 57 90; www.hospes.com/en/ granada-palacio_patos; Solarillo de Gracia 1; d €140-420, ste €344-1456; ▣❋🛜🏊) In a palatial 19th-century building, this is one of Granada's top hotels. Its sharply designed minimalist rooms, all in clean whites and pearl greys, are spread over the original building and a contemporary new wing. To relax, drinks are served in a delightful Arabian garden or you can sign up for a massage in the spa.

AC Palacio de Santa Paula   LUXURY HOTEL €€€
(Map p260; ☑958 80 57 40; www.palaciodesanta paula.com; Gran Vía de Colón 31; d €117-250, ste €202-277; ▣❋🛜) The modern grey frontage of this central five-star gives no hint of what lies behind. A cobbled cloister forms the elegant centrepiece of what was once a

---

DON'T MISS

GRANADA'S STREET ART

While the UK has Banksy, Granada has El Niño de las Pinturas (real name Raúl Ruíz), a street artist whose creative graffiti has become a defining symbol of the city. Larger-than-life, lucid and thought-provoking, El Niño's murals, many of which are in the Realejo neighbourhood, often juxtapose vivid close-ups of human faces with short poetic stanzas written in highly stylised lettering. Over the last two decades, El Niño has become a famous underground personality in Granada and has sometimes been known to give live painting demonstrations at the university. Although he risks criticism and occasional fines for his work, most *granadinos* agree that his street art brings creative colour and a contemporary edge to their ancient city.

16th-century convent but is now a slick, luxury hotel with good-looking contemporary-styled rooms, an in-house restaurant, fitness centre, sauna and Turkish bath.

Eating

Eating out in Granada is largely about the joys of tapas and traditional Andalucian fare. The city boasts a good mix of restaurants and batteries of bars and cafes, many catering to locals as much as tourists and out-of-towners. It also excels in Moroccan cuisine with a number of authentic places in the Albayzín quarter.

Alhambra & Realejo

Hicuri Art Restaurant   VEGAN €
(Map p264; ☑858 98 74 73; www.restaurante hicurivegan.com; Plaza de los Girones 3; mains €7.50-10, menú del día €14; ☺11am-11pm Mon-Fri, noon-11pm Sat, to 4.30pm Jul & Aug; ☑) Granada's leading graffiti artist, El Niño de las Pinturas, has been let loose inside Hicuri, creating a psychedelic backdrop to the vegan food served at this friendly, laid-back restaurant. Zingy salads, tofu, and curried seitan provide welcome alternatives to the traditional meat dishes that dominate so many city menus.

La Botillería   SPANISH €€
(Map p264; ☑958 22 49 28; www.labotilleriagra nada.es; Calle Varela 10; mains €11-18; ☺12.30pm-1am Wed-Sun) Since opening in 2013, La Botillería has established a fine local reputation thanks to its elegantly presented food and thoughtful wine list. It's smart in a modern, casual way, with a bar area for tapas and a back restaurant where you can dine on starters of Cantabrian anchovies and creative mains such as *milhoja de presa ibérica* (millefeuille with pork and avocado).

Los Diamantes   TAPAS, SEAFOOD €€
(Map p264; www.barlosdiamantes.com; Calle Navas 26; raciones €10-14; ☺12.30-4.30pm & 8.30pm-midnight) A Granada institution, this scruffy old-school joint is one of the best eateries on bar-lined Calle Navas. Always busy, it's generally standing room only but the seafood – the first tapas comes free with your drink – is excellent and there's usually a wonderful sociable vibe. There's a second, smarter branch on Plaza Nueva.

Carmela Restaurante   SPANISH €€
(Map p264; ☑958 22 57 94; www.restaurantecar mela.com; Calle Colcha 13; tapas €7, mains €7.50-17; ☺8am-midnight, kitchen noon-midnight) Tra-

ditional tapas updated for the 21st century are the star turn at this smart all-day cafe-restaurant at the jaws of the Realejo quarter. Bag a table in the cool brick-lined interior or on the outdoor terrace and bite into croquettes with black pudding and caramelised onion, or tuna *tataki* with soy reduction.

Parador de Granada   INTERNATIONAL €€€
(Map p258; ☑958 22 14 40; Calle Real de la Alhambra; mains €16-26; ☺1-4pm & 8-10.30pm) As much as the food – mainly contemporary Andalucian – a meal at the Parador de Granada hotel (p270) restaurant is all about its unique Alhambra setting. The terrace, which it shares with the hotel's all-day bar-cafe, is a magical spot for a formal dinner or a post-sightseeing snack. The location does, however, bump up the prices a fair bit.

Plaza Nueva & Around

Bodegas Castañeda   TAPAS €
(Map p264; ☑958 21 54 64; Calle Almireceros 1; tapas €2-5; ☺11.30am-4.30pm & 7.30pm-1.30am) Eating becomes a contact sport at this traditional tapas bar where crowds of hungry punters jostle for food under hanging hams. Don't expect any experimentation nonsense here, just classic tapas (and *raciones*) served lightning-fast with booze poured from big wall-mounted casks.

Greens & Berries   FAST FOOD €
(Map p264; Plaza Nueva 1; snacks from €2.50; ☺9am-10pm; ☑) Fast food, Granada style. This hole-in-the-wall joint is ideal for a quick pit stop, serving a range of toasties, wraps, *bocadillos* (filled baguettes), salads and fresh smoothies made with juicy, sun-kissed fruit. Benches on the plaza provide the seating.

Ruta del Azafrán   INTERNATIONAL €€
(Map p260; ☑958 22 68 82; www.rutadelaza fran.es; Paseo del Padre Manjón 1; mains €17-21; ☺1-11.30pm) At this hit riverside restaurant, modern design goes hand in hand with Alhambra views and an eclectic menu of international dishes. Moroccan starters pave the way for Asian-inspired tuna creations and hearty Andalucian staples such as pork cheeks slow-cooked in red wine.

Albayzín

Babel World Fusion   TAPAS €
(Map p264; ☑958 22 78 96; Calle de Elvira 41; beer & tapas €2, mains from €6.50; ☺12.30-4.30pm & 6pm-2am; ☑) A laid-back eatery loved by foreign students, Babel stands out from its more

traditional neighbours on the bar-lined Calle de Elvira. It takes an international approach to the tapas concept, cooking up falafels, Mexican fajitas and Thai noodles alongside more regular Andalucian creations.

Arrayanes
MOROCCAN €€

(Map p264; ✏958 22 33 53, 619 076862; www.rest-arrayanes.com; Cuesta Marañas 4; mains €9-16; ⊘1.30-4.30pm & 7.30-11.30pm Wed-Mon; ✍) The Albayzín quarter is the place to sample Moroccan food, and this well-known restaurant has a reputation as one of the neighbourhood's best. Ceramic tiles, ornate latticework arches and crimson seats set the stage for classic North African staples such as *bisara* soup, made with split beans, rich, fruity tagine casseroles, and flaky *pastelas* (stuffed pastries). Note that alcohol isn't served.

El Ají
SPANISH €€

(Map p260; ✏958 29 29 30; Plaza San Miguel Bajo 9; mains €12-20; ⊘1-11pm) With alfresco seating on a charming hilltop plaza in the Albayzín, this cosy neighbourhood restaurant offers a warm welcome and a something-for-everyone menu. There are pastas if you fancy Italian, delicious chargrilled steaks, and inventive fish dishes such as prawns with tequila and honey, or cod in lime sauce.

Samarkanda
LEBANESE €€

(Map p264; Calle Calderería Vieja 3; mains €8-12; ⊘1-4.30pm & 7.30-11.30pm Thu-Tue; ✍) Despite the rather tired decor, this friendly family-run Lebanese restaurant is a sound choice, cooking up a menu of traditional mainstays in the backstreets of the Albayzín. Kick off with hummus and *mutabal* (aubergine and tahini-based dip) before digging into a bowl of *kafta* (ground beef baked and served with potatoes and a sesame sauce).

✖ Centro

Poë
TAPAS €

(Map p260; www.barpoe.com; cnr Calles Paz & Verónica de la Magdalena; tapas €1.50, raciones €5; ⊘8pm-12.30am) Friendly Poë offers an inviting multicultural vibe and international favourites such as Brazilian *feijoada* (black bean and pork stew) and spicy-hot Thai chicken. It doesn't look much from the outside, but like Dr Who's Tardis, it's a whole different world once you walk through the door.

Gran Café Bib-Rambla
CAFE €

(Map p264; Plaza Bib-Rambla 3; hot chocolate & churros €3.90-4.40; ⊘8am-midnight summer, to 10pm winter; ✍) One of a string of cafes and restaurants on Plaza Bib-Rambla, this

1907-vintage cafe is reckoned to serve some of Granada's best *churros* (fried dough strips). Check for yourself, ideally by dipping them into ultra-thick hot chocolate.

★ El Bar de Fede
INTERNATIONAL €€

(Map p260; ✏958 28 88 14; Calle Marqués de Falces 1; raciones €7.50-16; ⊘9am-2am Mon-Thu, to 3am Fri & Sat, 11am-2am Sun) The 'Fede' in the name is hometown poet Federico García Lorca, whose free spirit seems to hang over this hip, gay-friendly bar. It's a good-looking spot with patterned wallpaper and high tables set around a ceramic-tiled island, and the food is a joy. Standouts include chicken pâté served with orange sauce and heavenly melt-in-your mouth grilled squid.

Siloé Café & Grill
INTERNATIONAL €€

(Map p264; ✏958 22 07 52; http://siloebarygrill.com; Plaza de Diego Siloé; mains €10-20; ⊘10am-11pm) Tucked in behind the cathedral, the Siloé is as good for a relaxed coffee as for a full-blown lunch or dinner. In summer, its pleasant outdoor terrace is the place to be, while in the cooler months diners take to the modern interior to enjoy the likes of burgers and barbecued wings.

Oliver
SEAFOOD €€

(Map p264; ✏958 26 22 00; www.restaurante oliver.com; Plaza Pescadería 12; mains €12-22; ⊘12.30-3.30pm & 8-11.30pm Mon-Sat) One of the best of the seafood bar-restaurants that throng Plaza Pescadería in central Granada. Well-dressed office folk pack in alongside street-sweepers to devour *raciones* of garlicky shrimps and fried treats at the mobbed bar, while families and tourists dine in comfort at the calmer outside tables.

★ La Fábula Restaurante
GASTRONOMY €€€

(Map p260; ✏958 25 01 50; www.restaurantela fabula.com; Calle de San Antón 28; mains €24-28, tasting menus €75-90; ⊘1-4pm & 8.30-11pm Tue-Sat) It's hard to avoid the pun, Fábula is pretty fabulous. A formal fine-dining restaurant set in the refined confines of the Hotel Villa Oniria, it's the domain of chef Ismael Delgado López whose artfully composed plates of contemporary Spanish cuisine are sure to impress. Be sure to book.

🍷 Drinking & Nightlife

From old-school tapas bars to historic cafes, traditional wine bars and Arabian Nights teahouses, Granada is well stocked with drinking options. Hot spots include the rather scruffy Calle de Elvira, the Río Darro at the base of the Albayzín, Calle Navas, and

FREE TAPAS

Granada is one of the last bastions of the highly civilised practice of serving a free tapas with every drink. Place your drink order at the bar and, hey presto, a plate will magically appear with a generous portion of something delicious-looking on it. Order another drink and another plate will materialise. The process is repeated with every round you buy. As many bars serve only small glasses of beer (*cañas* measure just 250ml) it's just about possible to fill up on free tapas over the course of an evening without getting totally legless. Indeed, some people 'crawl' from bar to bar getting a drink and free tapas in each place. Packed shoulder-to-shoulder with tapas institutions, Calle de Elvira and Calle Navas are good places to start.

the area to the north of Plaza de Trinidad where you'll find several cool, edgy bars.

Taberna La Tana WINE BAR
(Map p264; ☑958 22 52 48; Placeta del Agua 3; ☺12.30-4pm & 8.30pm-midnight) With bottles stacked to the rafters, hanging strings of garlic, and a small wood-and-brick interior, friendly La Tana is a model wine bar. It specialises in Spanish wines, which it backs up with some beautifully paired tapas. Ask the bartender about the 'wines of the month' and state your preference – a *suave* (smooth) red, or something more *fuerte* (strong).

El Bar de Eric BAR
(Map p264; ☑958 27 63 01; Calle Escuelas 8; ☺10am-2am Mon-Thu, to 3am Fri, 1.30pm-3am Sat, 1pm-2am Sun) Strewn with old gig posters and photos of musical heroes, from Debbie Harry to Jim Morrison, this laid-back bar is the creation of Spanish drummer Eric Jiménez of band Los Planetas. Get into the swing with some fusion tapas and a jar of sangria.

Botánico BAR
(Map p264; ☑958 27 15 98; www.botanicocafe.es; Calle Málaga 3; ☺1pm-1am Mon-Thu, to 2am Fri & Sat, to 6pm Sun) Dudes with designer beards, students finishing off their Lorca dissertations, and bohemians with arty inclinations hang out at Botánico, a casual eatery by day, a cafe at *merienda* time (5pm to 7pm), and a buzzing bar come the evening.

Mundra BAR
(Map p264; Plaza de la Trinidad; ☺8.30pm-2am Mon-Thu, to 3am Fri & Sat) One of the best bars on leafy Plaza de Trinidad, Mundra has something of a New Age feel with its exposed brick walls, Buddha statues and chill-out sounds. There are outdoor tables, great for people-watching, and a decent choice of tapas and platters to share.

Boogaclub CLUB
(Map p260; www.boogaclub.com; Calle Santa Barbara 3; ☺2am-6am Mon-Wed, 11pm-6am Thu &

Sun, to 7am Fri & Sat) A historic club, good for full-on dance sessions. Chill to soulful house, funk and electro then kick off to international DJs spinning rock, soul, Latin and reggae. Also hosts jam sessions and regular gigs. Check the website for upcoming events.

La Candela BAR
(Map p264; Calle Santa Escolástica 9; ☺1-4pm & 9pm-1am) A cosy neighbourhood bar in the hip Realejo quarter, home to local street artist El Niño de las Pinturas whose murals adorn the bar's shutters. Its welcoming vibe, low-key ambient tunes and steady supply of beer and tapas draw a convivial crowd of locals and out-of-towners.

☆ Entertainment

Granada is a great place to catch a flamenco performance, with a number of intimate clubs staging nightly shows. Elsewhere, you can foot-tap to jazz, brush up on your tango turns and catch a stage play at the theatre.

Peña La Platería FLAMENCO
(Map p260; ☑958 21 06 50; www.laplateria.org.es; Placeta de Toqueros 7) Peña La Platería claims to be Spain's oldest flamenco club, founded in 1949. Unlike other more private clubs, it regularly opens its doors to nonmembers for performances on Thursday nights at 10pm. Tapas and drinks are available. Reservations recommended.

Jardines de Zoraya FLAMENCO
(Map p260; ☑958 20 62 66; www.jardinesdezora ya.com; Calle Panaderos 32; ticket €20, dinner from €29; ☺shows 8pm & 10.30pm) In a restaurant in the Albayzín district, this appears, at first, to be a touristy *tablao* (choreographed flamenco show). But reasonable entry prices, talented performers and a highly atmospheric patio make it a worthwhile stop for any aficionado.

Casa del Arte Flamenco FLAMENCO
(Map p264; ☑958 56 57 67; www.casadelarte flamenco.com; Cuesta de Gomérez 11; tickets €18;

⊙shows 7.30pm & 9pm) A small flamenco venue that is neither a *tablao* (choreographed flamenco show) nor a *peña* (private club), but something in between. The performers are invariably top-notch, managing to conjure a highly charged mood in the intimate space.

Le Chien Andalou   FLAMENCO
(Map p264; ☑717 709100; www.lechienandalou. com; Carrera del Darro 7; tickets €10-12; ⊙shows 7.30pm, 9.30pm & 11.30pm) Small cavernous bar that was once a cistern, but now hosts three nightly flamenco shows for half the price of the bigger places. Performances can be hit or miss, but at this price, it's probably worth the gamble.

Eshavira   JAZZ, FLAMENCO
(Map p260; ☑958 29 08 29; https://eshaviraclub. wordpress.com; Calle Postigo de la Cuna 2; €6-15; ⊙10pm-4am) Just off Calle Azacayas, this is one of Granada's historic jazz and flamenco haunts, staging a regular program of gigs, jam sessions and flamenco performances – check its website for upcoming dates. It's a late-starter though, and events rarely kick off much before 11pm with the partying continuing throughout the night.

La Tertulia   LIVE PERFORMANCE
(Map p260; ☑958 29 17 96; www.tertuliagranada. com; Calle Pintor López Mezquita 3; ⊙9pm-3am Tue-Sat) In Spain, a *tertulia* is an artistic gathering, and that's what you generally get at this bohemian bar where the emphasis is less on beer and more on what's happening on stage – film screenings, poetry jams, book presentations and, every Tuesday, tango sessions.

🛍 Shopping

Many shops in Granada play on the city's Moorish heritage. A local craft speciality to look out for is *taracea* (marquetry) – the best work has shell, silver or mother-of-pearl inlay, applied to boxes, tables, chess sets and more.

La Oliva   FOOD & DRINKS
(Map p264; ☑958 22 57 54; Calle Rosario 9; ⊙11am-2.30pm Mon-Sat & 7-10pm Mon-Fri) By day, La Oliva is a small food shop, stocking a selection of fine Spanish wines, olive oils and gourmet treats. By night, the tables come out and owner Francisco welcomes a few guests – bookings necessary – to dine on his €38.50 tasting menu.

Artesanías González   ARTS & CRAFTS
(Map p264; Cuesta de Gomérez 12; ⊙11am-8.30pm) Specialising in the art of marquetry since 1920, this artisan shop is a great place to pick up a memento or small gift. There's a good selection of handcrafted inlaid boxes, as well as coasters, chess sets and beautiful backgammon boards.

GRANADA'S TEAHOUSES

Granada's *teterías* (teahouses) have proliferated in recent years, but there's still something invitingly exotic about their dark atmospheric interiors, stuffed with lace veils, stucco and low cushioned seats. Most offer a long list of aromatic teas and infusions, along with a selection of sticky Arabic sweets. Many still permit their customers to puff on *cachimbas* (hookah pipes). Calle Calderería Nueva in the Albayzín is Granada's most celebrated '*tetería* street'.

Abaco Té (Map p260; ☑958 22 19 35; Calle Álamo de Marqués 5; ⊙3-9.30pm Mon-Thu, 1.30-11.30pm Fri-Sun) Abaco's Arabian minimalist interior is a soothing spot to bask in Alhambra views from a comfy-ish floor mat. You can choose from an encyclopaedic list of teas and medicinal infusions or keep it fruity with a fresh juice or shake. Excellent cakes and a small menu of mainly vegetarian snacks will fend off the munchies.

Tetería Nazarí (Map p264; Calle Calderería Nueva 13; ⊙2pm-midnight) The best of the teahouses on this touristy stretch of the Albayzín. Plonk yourself on a stool at a small elaborately painted table and choose from the decent selection of teas, perhaps a mint and cinnamon infusion accompanied by a sweet, honey-based pastry.

Tetería Dar Ziryab (Map p264; ☑655 446775; Calle Calderería Nueva 11; ⊙1pm-1am) Duck into the dimly lit interior, adorned with tiling, cushions and typical Moorish latticework arches, to puff on a *cachimba* and drink herb tea from ornately decorated glasses.

Tetería Kasbah (Map p264; Calle Calderería Nueva 4; ⊙noon-1am) Wispy curtains, stuccoed arches and low lighting set the scene for a relaxed tea break – service can be slow – in Calle Calderería Nueva's largest and busiest *tetería*. A full food menu is also available.

DEAD POETS SOCIETY

Intellectual debate has long flourished in Granada's bars, cafes and *teterías*. It's a tradition that harks back to the early 1920s, when a group of poets, writers and musicians came together in a *tertulia* (a Spanish artistic/literary gathering) known as El Rinconcillo in the Café Alameda. Regularly holding court was Federico García Lorca, who had returned to Granada in 1921 after a period studying in Madrid, and classical composer Manuel de Falla, who had moved to the city from Cádiz the previous year. They were joined by the likes of classical guitarist Andrés Segovia, painter Ismael González de la Serna, poet Miguel Pizarro, Lorca's brother Francisco, and many others.

Fascinated by flamenco and inspired by the baroque poetry of Luis de Góngora, El Rinconcillo wanted to celebrate the authenticity of Andalucian culture while also vanquishing the overly picturesque vision of Spain expounded by outsiders. In 1922 the group was instrumental in organising the Concurso de Cante Jondo, a flamenco singing competition staged in the Alhambra that aimed to save the art from over-commercialisation. Five years later they reappeared at an event organised by the Ateneo de Sevilla, a Sevillan cultural society, to celebrate the 300th anniversary of Góngora's death, the first unofficial gathering of what later became known as the Generación del '27 (an influential group of Spanish writers, film-makers and artists that included Salvador Dalí and Luis Buñuel).

Granada still exudes an edgy literary air in its diverse drinking establishments, although the Café Alameda is no longer in business. Its former digs are now occupied by the **Restaurante Chikito** (Map p260; ☑958 22 33 64; www.restaurantechikito.com; Plaza Campillo 9; mains €17-29; ☉12.30-3.30pm & 7.30-11.30pm Thu-Tue), which in February 2015 placed a statue of El Rinconcillo's most famous member, Lorca, in its front bar, in the very corner where he and his compatriots once met, drank and sought to reinvent Spanish culture.

Tienda Librería de la Alhambra
BOOKS

(Map p264; ☑958 22 78 46; www.alhambratienda.es; Calle Reyes Católicos 40; ☉9.30am-8.30pm) This is a fabulous shop for Alhambra aficionados, with a great collection of books dedicated to the monument, its art and history. You'll find everything from simple guidebooks to glossy coffee-table tomes on Islamic art, as well as a selection of quality gifts, including hand-painted fans, stationery and stunning photographic prints, which you select from a vast digital library.

Granada Vinos
WINE

(Map p264; Calle Navas 29; ☉10am-1.45pm & 5.30-9pm Mon-Fri; 10am-3pm & 5-10pm Sat) This bottle shop has an excellent selection of local vintages, including organic wines from around Andalucía, as well as wines from the rest of Spain and New World producers.

Alcaicería
GIFTS & SOUVENIRS

(Map p264; Calle Alcaicería; ☉10am-9pm) Laden with everything from leather satchels and Moroccan-style slippers to gaudy ceramic wares, cheap jewellery, scarves and Swiss Army knives, the brazen stalls on this narrow street are all that remain of what was once Granada's great bazaar. Try to get in early before the coach parties arrive.

Gil de Avalle
MUSIC

(Map p264; ☑958 22 16 10; www.gildeavalle.com; Plaza del Realejo 15; ☉5-8pm Mon-Fri, 10am-1.30pm Sat) The workshop of master guitar-maker Daniel Gil de Avalle is a paradise for aficionados with a range of exquisite handmade flamenco and classical guitars, as well as castanets and sheet music. To visit on a weekday morning, phone ahead for an appointment.

ℹ Information

Alhambra Tourist Information Point (☑958 02 79 71; www.granadatur.com; Calle Real de la Alhambra Granada, Alhambra; ☉8.30am-8.30pm)

Municipal Tourist Office (Map p264; ☑958 24 82 80; www.granadatur.com; Plaza del Carmen 9; ☉9am-8pm Mon-Sat, to 2pm Sun)

Provincial Tourist Office (Map p264; ☑958 24 71 28; www.turgranada.es; Cárcel Baja 3; ☉9am-8pm Mon-Fri, 10am-7pm Sat, 10am-3pm Sun) Information on Granada province.

Regional Tourist Office (Map p264; ☑958 57 52 02; www.andalucia.org; Calle Santa Ana 2; ☉9am-7.30pm Mon-Fri, 9.30am-3pm Sat & Sun) Covers the whole Andalucía region.

this.is:granada (Map p264; ☑958 21 02 39; www.thisisgranada.com; Plaza de Cuchilleros; ☉9.30am-2pm & 4-7pm Mon-Sat, to 6pm Sun) An agency selling tickets for flamenco shows, city tours and buses.

⚙ Getting There & Away

AIR

Granada airport (Aeropuerto Federico García Lorca; ☑ 902 40 47 04; www.aena.es) is 17km west of the city, near the A92. Direct flights connect with Madrid, Barcelona, Bilbao, Palma de Mallorca, and, outside Spain, London, Manchester and Milan. It's served by international airlines such as easyJet, Vueling, Iberia and British Airways.

BUS

Granada's **bus station** (☑ 958 18 54 80; Avenida Juan Pablo II; ⊙ 6.30am-1.30am) is 3km northwest of the city centre. To get into the centre, take city bus SN1 for the Gran Vía de Colón (Map p264).

Alsa (☑ 902 42 22 42; www.alsa.es) runs buses in the province and across the region, and has a night bus direct to Madrid's Barajas airport (€47.85, 6¼ hours).

TO	COST	DURATION	FREQUENCY
Almuñécar	€8.34	1¼-2hr	9 daily
Córdoba	€15	2¼-4hr	8 daily
Guadix	€5.50	1hr	14 daily
Jaén	€8.87	1¼hr	15 daily
Lanjarón	€4.27	1-1½hr	9 daily
Málaga	€10-14	1¾hr	17 daily
Seville	€23-29	3hr	8 daily

TRAIN

The **train station** (☑ 958 27 12 72; Avenida de Andaluces) is 1.5km northwest of the centre. For the centre, walk straight ahead to Avenida de la Constitución and turn right to pick up bus SN1 to Gran Vía de Colón.

TO	COST	DURATION	FREQUENCY
Algeciras	€30	4¼-5hr	3 daily
Almería	€20	2½hr	4 daily
Barcelona	€40-59	7¾hr	2 daily
Córdoba	€23-37	2¼-3hr	7 daily
Madrid	€28-39	4hr	5 daily
Seville	€30	3¼hr	4 daily

⚙ Getting Around

TO/FROM THE AIRPORT

Alsa bus 245 runs to the city centre (€2.90, 40 minutes) at 6am and then at least hourly between 9.15am and 11.30pm. It stops at various points, including Gran Vía de Colón near the cathedral. Get tickets on board. A taxi to the bus station will cost around €20 to €24.

BUS

One-way tickets, which can be bought on buses (cash only), cost €1.40. Useful bus lines:

C1 From Plaza Nueva up to the Albayzín.

C2 From Plaza Nueva up to Sacramonte.

C3 From Plaza Isabel II to the Alhambra via the Realejo quarter.

SN1 Connects the bus and train stations with Via Gran Vía de Colón in the centre.

CAR & MOTORCYCLE

Driving in central Granada – as in most large Andalucian cities – can be frustrating and should be avoided if possible. Park your car on the outskirts and use public transport; there are plenty of options. If you have to drive, there are several central car parks: **Parking La Alhambra** (☑ information 902 44 12 21; Paseo de la Sabika; per hr/day €2.70/18.40; ⊙24hr), **Parking San Agustín** (Calle San Agustín; per hr/day €1.70/25; ⊙24hr) and **Parking Plaza de los Campos** (Plaza de los Campos 4; per hr/day €1.95/19.50; ⊙8am-1am Mon-Sat, 8.30am-11pm Sun).

METRO

Opened in September 2017, Granada's lmetro – in fact more a light rail link as all but a 3km stretch is overground – runs between Albolote in the north and Armilla in the southwest. It serves 26 stations, running from 6.30am to 11pm Mondays to Thursdays, to 2am on Fridays, from 7.30am to 2am on Saturdays and 7.30am to 11pm on Sundays. Single tickets cost €1.35.

TAXI

Taxis congregate in Plaza Nueva and at the train and bus stations. To call a taxi, contact **Tele-Radio Taxi Granada** (☑ 958 28 00 00; www.granadataxi.com).

LA VEGA & EL ALTIPLANO

Surrounding Granada is a swath of fertile land known as La Vega, a patchwork of woods, shimmering poplar groves and cultivated farmlands. To the northeast of the city, the landscape becomes increasingly hilly and arid until it tops out in a highland plain known as El Altiplano. This vast tract of barren semidesert is a hauntingly scenic place, made all the more dramatic by the mighty Sierra Nevada peaks looming on the southern horizon.

To access the area, the A92 runs from near Granada through the Parque Natural Sierra de Huétor to Guadix, a handsome provincial town famed for its cave houses. Continuing

WORTH A TRIP

CASTILLO DE LA CALAHORRA

The forbidding landmark **Castillo de la Calahorra** (☏958 67 70 98; €3; ⏰10am-1pm & 4-6pm Wed) guards access to the Sierra Nevada from a hilltop position outside the sleepy village of La Calahorra. Built between 1509 and 1512, its four cylindrical towers and blank outer wall enclose an elegant Renaissance courtyard with a staircase of Italian marble.

The lavish Renaissance interior was built at the behest of the the Marqués Rodrigo de Mendoza, the aristocrat commander of the surrounding plains, whose tempestuous love life included a spell in Italy unsuccessfully wooing Lucrezia Borgia.

Visits to the castle, which is about 20km southeast of Guadix, are by guided tours (in Spanish only), which take about 30 minutes. For guided tours outside of regular hours, contact the caretaker Antonio Trivaldo on the castle phone number. To drive up to the castle, turn onto the dirt road opposite La Hospedería del Zenete in La Calahorra and take the winding route uphill. If you're in a hire car you might prefer to park in the town plaza and walk up the stone footpath.

northeast brings you to Baza and the Altiplano proper. Although sparsely populated, Granada's 'High Plain' has supported human life since prehistoric times and is well known for its palaeontological riches.

Guadix

POP 18,800

Guadix (gwah-deeks), a lively provincial town near the foothills of the Sierra Nevada, is best known for its cave dwellings, many of which are still occupied by local townsfolk. Caves apart, the town boasts a handsome historic core centred on an imposing Renaissance-baroque cathedral. The *accitanos* (from the town's Moorish name, Wadi Acci) also enjoy some excellent, tourist-free tapas bars.

◉ Sights

Guadix's best-known drawcard is its cave district, on the southern fringes of town. Back in the centre, the cathedral is an imposing sight and the old quarter an attractive place for a wander with its own distinctive architecture, much of it rendered in warm sandstone.

Cathedral   CATHEDRAL
(☏958 66 51 08; Paseo de la Catedral; adult/reduced €5/3.50; ⏰10.30am-2pm & 4-6pm Mon-Sat Oct-Mar, 4.30-6.30pm Mon-Sat Apr-May, 5-7.30pm Mon-Sat Jun-Sep, 10.30am-2.30pm Sun year-round & 5-7.30pm Sun Jun-Sep) With its flamboyant sandstone exterior set against the rich blue sky, Guadix's cathedral is an impressive spectacle. Built between the 16th and 18th centuries on the site of the town's former main mosque, it incorporates a mix of Gothic, Renaissance and baroque styles. Inside, a small museum displays a series of books dating from the 15th to 18th centuries.

Plaza de la Constitución   PLAZA
Guadix's showcase square is a fine example of late 16th-century Renaissance urban design. Overlooked by the town's striking town hall, it's centred on a rectangular area flanked by arched porticoes, under which cafe tables are put out each day.

Barrio de las Cuevas   AREA
Guadix's main cave district is said to contain some 2000 dwellings burrowed into the rocky terrain. Some 1.2km south of the centre (about 20 minutes' walk), it's a weird, almost otherworldly place where stumpy chimneys, antennae and white walls emerge from a series of undulating yellow-brown hillocks. For a grandstand view of the area, head up to the signposted Mirador Padre Poveda.

Centro de Interpretación
Cuevas de Guadix   MUSEUM
(☏958 66 55 69; Plaza del Padre Poveda; admission €2.60; ⏰10am-2pm daily & 4-6pm Mon-Sat) This small museum re-creates cave life of years past, with an audiovisual presentation and displays of traditional housewares and furnishings, including ox yokes, clay water pots, woven esparto grass, and wooden furniture.

🛏 Sleeping

★**Hotel GIT Abentofail**   BOUTIQUE HOTEL €€
(☏958 66 92 81; www.hotelabentofail.com; Calle Abentofail; s €40-63, d €48-73; ❉🐾) Boutique style at bargain prices, this elegant hideaway is one of the best deals in town. Discreetly located a short hop from Plaza de la Constitución, it offers stylish modern rooms, set above a columned patio and furnished with quiet taste. Guests are also given a voucher for a drink at the adjacent **El Búho** restaurant, itself a smart choice for lunch or dinner.

✖ Eating

No need for a sit-down meal in Guadix – you can feed yourself well, and meet the locals, at the wonderful tapas bars around town. At most places, you'll pay about €1 to €4 for a tapa, with *raciones* costing from around €6.

★ La Bodeguilla   TAPAS €
(Calle Doctor Pulido 4; tapas €1-4; ☺ 9am-3.30pm & 7pm-midnight Mon-Sat, 11am-3.30pm & 7-11pm Sun) No frills, no gourmet cuisine, precious few tables, this old-school hang-out off Avenida Medina Olmos is one of the best tapas bars in town, as well as the oldest (1904). Here, old boys in flat caps line the bar tucking into plates of olives and cured meats, accompanied by *fino* (sherry) direct from the stacked-up barrels lining the wall.

Bodega Calatrava   TAPAS €
(Calle La Tribuna 2; drink & tapa €1.70, raciónes €6; ☺ 8.30am-5pm & 7.30pm-1am Mon-Sat) A cosy wood-beamed bar tucked down a side street in the centre of town. It specialises in simple tapas like juicy fried prawns and *montaditos* (mini-baguettes), as well as more substantial *raciónes*.

❶ Information

Tourist Office (☎ 958 66 28 04; Plaza de la Constitución 15; ☺ 9am-2pm & 4-6pm Mon-Fri, 10am-2pm & 4-6pm Sat, 10am-2pm Sun) Very helpful office on Guadix's showcase square.

❶ Getting There & Away

BUS
Buses run to Granada (€5.50, one hour, up to 12 daily), Almería (€9.37, two hours, three daily), and Málaga (€18, three to 3½ hours, four daily). The **bus station** (☎ 958 66 06 57; Santa Rosa) is off Avenida Medina Olmos, about 700m southeast of the centre.

TRAIN
There are four trains daily to Granada (€9.50, one hour) and six to Almería (€10.55, 1¼ hours). The station is off the Murcia road, about 2km northeast of the town centre.

SIERRA NEVADA

Providing Granada's dramatic backdrop, the Sierra Nevada range extends about 75km from west to east. Its wild snowcapped peaks boast the highest point in mainland Spain (Mulhacén, 3479m) and Europe's most southerly ski resort at Pradollano. The lower southern reaches, peppered with picturesque white villages, are collectively known as Las Alpujarras (p282).

Some 859 sq km are encompassed by the Parque Nacional Sierra Nevada. Spain's largest national park, this protected area is home to 2100 of Spain's 7000 plant species, including unique types of crocus, narcissus, thistle, clover, poppy and gentian, as well as

GRANADA PROVINCE SIERRA NEVADA

WORTH A TRIP

ORCE

Orce, a dusty outpost on Granada's parched Altiplano, and its environs are of huge importance to palaeontologists, and make an interesting stop on the drive between Granada and Los Vélez (p313) in Almería province. Fossils, bones and tools have been found at three sites – Barranco León, Fuente Nueva and Venta Micena – attesting to human activity more than a million years ago and local fauna that once included mammoths, sabre-toothed tigers, hyenas and elephants.

In 1982, palaeontologist Josep Gibert made international headlines when he unearthed a human skull fragment at Venta Micena. He put its age at between 0.9 and 1.6 million years old, making it potentially the oldest such fragment ever discovered in Europe. However, subsequent studies threw doubt on his claims, holding that the fragment was more likely from a horse or donkey – turning Orce Man into Orce Donkey.

A second major find was made in 2002 when archaeologists working at Barranco León discovered a child's milk tooth they reckoned to be 1.4 million years old. If this age proves true, it would make the Orce molar the oldest human remain ever found in Western Europe. Alsa (p277) runs a daily bus between Orce and Granada (€12.84, 2½ hours).

A fossilised human tooth, stone tools dating back some 1.3 million years, and bones of mammoths and other long-extinct beasts are among the palaeontological treasures showcased at the modern, purpose-built **Centro de Interpretación Primeros Pobladores de Europa 'Josep Gibert'** (Camino de San Simón; admission €2; ☺ 11am-2pm Tue-Thu & Sun, 4-7pm Fri, 11am-2pm & 4-6pm Sat). Wall illustrations and a skeletal reproduction of a sabre-toothed tiger add colour.

Sierra Nevada & Las Alpujarras

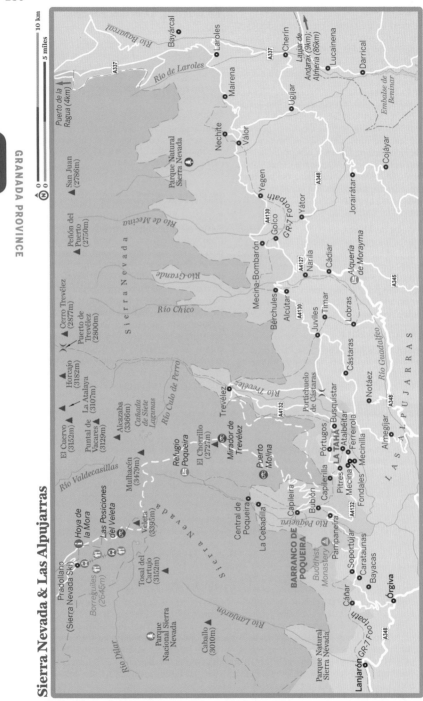

Andalucía's largest ibex population. Bordering the national park at lower altitudes is the Parque Natural Sierra Nevada.

From July to early September, the higher mountains offer wonderful multiday trekking and day hikes. Outside of this period, there's a risk of inclement weather, but the lower Alpujarras are always welcoming, with most snow melted by May.

Los Cahorros

The area known as Los Cahorros, accessible via the small village of Monachil some 8km southeast of Granada, provides some fantastic walking. Trails run through the wooded terrain that flanks the Río Monachil as it cuts through a dramatic, rocky gorge. A popular route – the Cahorros Altos – starts just east of Monachil and follows the river upstream, passing over a hanging bridge and alongside sheer, and in some places overhanging, rock faces. These walls are also popular with rock climbers.

Hotel Rural Huerta del Laurel   HOTEL €
(☑ 958 50 18 67; www.huertadellaurel.com; Calle Madre Trinidad Carreras 2, Monachil; s €40-50, d €45-55, tr €60-70; P ❋ ☎ 🏊) Largely overlooked by the majority of visitors to the Sierra Nevada, the riverside village of Monachil is a lovely place for an overnight stay. The Hotel Rural Huerta del Laurel extends a warm welcome, offering warm, woody rooms and a terrific terrace restaurant.

ℹ Getting There & Away

Bus 183 runs from Paseo del Salón in Granada to Monachil (€2.90, 30 minutes). Services are hourly between 8.15am and 11.10pm on weekdays, less frequently on Saturday afternoons and Sundays.

Pradollano

Around 33km from Granada, the modern village of Pradollano (2100m) is home to Sierra Nevada Ski (☑ 902 70 80 90; www.sierranevada. es; Pradollano; one-day ski pass adult €36.50-48, child €24-35; 🚠), Europe's most southerly ski resort. Some 107km of pistes plunge down the surrounding mountains, many on the flanks of the mighty Veleta (3395m). Gear rental is available at the resort for about €25 per day. Away from the slopes, action is focused on the central Plaza de Andalucía, with an information kiosk (open daily from 9.15am to 6.30pm). From late June to early September, skiing gives way to mountain biking in the Sierra Nevada Bike Park (http://sierranevadabikepark.com; Pradollano; 1-day pass €21; ☺ lifts 9.45am-6pm).

ℹ Getting There & Away

In winter Tocina (☑ 958 46 50 22; www.auto carestocina.es) operates three daily buses (four on the weekend) to Pradollano from Granada's bus station (€5, one hour). Outside the ski season there's just one daily bus (9am from Granada, 5pm from the ski station). A taxi from Granada costs about €60.

WORTH A TRIP

CLIMBING MULHACÉN & VELETA

To climb Mulhacén and Veleta from the north, take the shuttle bus (☑ 671 564407; one way/return €6/10; ☺ 8am-6pm Jun-Oct) from the Albergue Universitario at Hoya de la Mora, 3km above Pradollano. This drops you at the Posiciones del Veleta (3100m), from where it's a 4km trek (1½ hours) to the top of Veleta or 14km (four to five hours) to the summit of Mulhacén. To tackle Mulhacén from the south side, base yourself in Capileira (p285). From the village's Servicio de Interpretación de Altos Cumbres (p286) you can catch a summer shuttle bus to the Mirador de Trevélez, from where it's around a three-hour hike to the summit (6km, 800m ascent).

To make the trip into an overnight excursion, you can bunk down at the Refugio Poqueira (☑ 958 34 33 49; www.refugiopoqueira.com; per person €17.50), which sits at 2500m below the southwestern face of Mulhacén. The loop to Mulhacén from the Mirador de Trevélez incorporating the refugio takes six to seven hours. Book in advance.

It's always best to phone ahead and check availability on the shuttle buses.

The routes described here are suitable for walkers of good to moderate fitness. However, in winter they should only be attempted by experienced mountaineers or with a guide. Always check on weather forecasts beforehand and be prepared for changing conditions and possible high winds. A good source of information is http://sierranevada guides.co.uk/information-about-the-sierra-nevada.

Mulhacén & Veleta

The Sierra Nevada's two highest peaks are Veleta (3395m) and Mulhacén which, at 3479m, is the highest mountain in mainland Spain. Both are on the western end of the range, and both can be summitted (p281) from a national park post at Hoya de la Mora (2512m) on the mountains' northern flank. The post, accessible by road from Granada and the Pradollano ski resort, sits by the entrance to a mountain pass that runs over to the Alpujarran village of Capileira on the southern side. However, the top road is closed to private vehicles and the mountains' upper reaches can only be accessed by a national park shuttle bus that's operational between late June and October (snow permitting). For more information on the area, stop off at the **Centro de Visitantes El Dornajo** (☑958 34 06 25; A395, Km 23; ☺10am-5pm Wed-Sun) on the A395, about 23km from Granada.

LAS ALPUJARRAS

Las Alpujarras is a 70km stretch of valleys and deep gorges on the southern flank of the Sierra Nevada. A mix of rocky, arid slopes, woods, and terraced farmlands made fertile by melted snow water, it's best known for its picturesque white villages. These cling to the verdant hillsides, their Berber-style flat-roofed houses recalling the area's past as a refuge for Moors escaping the Christian conquest of Granada. These days, the villages host a mixed population of locals and expats, while towns in the lower reaches simmer with spiritual seekers, long-term travellers and rat-race dropouts. Well-trod footpaths criss-cross the hills, linking the villages and offering superlative hiking.

Lanjarón

POP 3590

A popular day-trip destination, Lanjarón is the main gateway to the western Alpujarras. An attractive, leafy mountain town, it's best known for its therapeutic spa waters, which have long been a major source of local income and still today draw coach-loads of visitors. It also profits from its pure spring water, which is bottled and sold across Spain, and its air-cured *jamón serrano* (ham) which enjoys pride of place on many local menus.

🏃 Activities

Caballo Blanco Trekking Centre   HORSE RIDING
(☑627 794891; www.caballoblancotrekking.com; 2/4hr rides €40/70, full day plus picnic €95) Just east of Lanjarón, this well-established outfit offers horse-riding lessons and treks into the surrounding hills and mountains. English, Spanish, German and a little French are spoken. Book in advance.

Balneario de Lanjarón   SPA
(☑958 77 04 54; www.balneariodelanjaron.com; Avenida de Madrid 2; baths from €18) Lanjarón's thermal waters have been a major draw to the town for centuries. To test their medicinal properties, this spa – now part of a four-star hotel complex – offers a range of bathing options, massages and beauty treatments.

🍴 Eating & Drinking

El Arca de Noé   SPANISH €€
(☑958 77 00 27; Avenida de la Alpujarra 38; mains €6-18; ☺10am-3pm daily, plus 6.30-10.30pm Mon-Sat) The orderly rows of hanging hams and shelves laden with wine bottles, conserves and marinated goodies give the game away. This deli-eatery is the place to sample the celebrated local *jamón,* as well as a smorgasbord of regional delicacies: spicy sausages, goat's cheese, pâtés and tomato salads.

Cafetería Denebola   CAFE
(☑958 77 22 78; Avenida de Andalucía 38; ☺9am-1.30pm & 4-8pm) A bright and breezy cafe on the main drag through town, Denebola is a top spot for a Spanish breakfast – perhaps *café con leche* (coffee with milk) and a *tostada* (toasted baguette) with the traditional topping of crushed tomato and olive oil.

LAS ALPUJARRAS BUSES FROM GRANADA

TO	COST	DURATION	FREQUENCY
Bérchules	€9.50	3¾hr	2 daily
Bubión	€6	2¼hr	3 daily
Cádiar	€9	2¾hr	3 daily
Capileira	€6	2½hr	3 daily
Lanjarón	€4.50	1–1½hr	6–9 daily
Mecina Bombarón	€9.50	3hr	2 daily
Órgiva	€5	1½–1¾hr	6–9 daily
Pampaneira	€6	2hr	3 daily
Pitres	€7	2¾hr	3 daily
Trevélez	€8	3¼hr	3 daily
Válor	€10.50	3½hr	2 daily
Yegen	€10	3¼hr	2 daily

ⓘ Information

Tourist Office (☑ 958 77 04 62; http://
turismo.lanjaron.es; Avenida de Madrid 3;
⊙ 10am-2pm, 4.30-8.30pm Thu-Tue) At the
western entrance to town.

ⓘ Getting There & Away

Lanjarón, 45km south of Granada, is served by
Alsa (p277) buses from Granada (€4.27, one to
1½ hours, up to nine daily), Málaga (€12.66, 3¼
hours, one daily Monday to Saturday), and Motril
(€4.02, 1¼ hours, two daily Monday to Friday,
one Saturday).

Órgiva

The main town of the western Alpujarras,
Órgiva is a bit scruffier and considerably
larger than neighbouring villages. A hippie
scene has long been fertile here – the alternative lifestyle community of Benefício is
nearby and its inhabitants regularly come
into town to sell their wares or busk at the
Thursday market. British visitors might
recognise the town from Chris Stewart's
best-selling book, *Driving Over Lemons*.

🛏 Sleeping & Eating

Casa Rural Jazmín   CASA RURAL €€
(☑ 958 78 47 95; www.casaruraljazmin.com; Calle
Ladera de la Ermita; d €53-70; P❋🛜🏊) A
warm welcome awaits at this peaceful sanctuary in the upper part of town. It's a cosy
set-up with four homey guest rooms, each
decorated in a different style and some larger than others. Outside, there's a bountiful
garden where breakfast is served in summer
and you can splash around in a pool.

Casa Santiago   ANDALUCIAN €
(Plaza García Moreno 13; mains €8.50-12;
⊙ 9am-midnight Mon-Sat) Authentic regional
food served in a rustic bricks-and-beams
interior; this is the real deal. Don't expect
anything fancy, just favourites like tortillas,
morcilla (black pudding), and *migas* (fried
breadcrumbs with ham, garlic and onions).

Tetería Baraka   INTERNATIONAL €€
(☑ 958 78 58 94; www.teteria-baraka.com; Calle
Estación 12; mains €10-15; ⊙ 10am-11pm Mon-Wed,
Fri & Sat, 9am-11pm Thu, 11am-11pm Sun) A much-
loved local haunt, especially on Thursdays
when the market crowds flock here from
mid-morning. Its laid-back vibe comes with
an eclectic menu featuring Moroccan tagines, couscous, doner kebabs, wraps and natural juices. You'll find it above the municipal
car park in the upper part of town.

ⓘ SIERRA NEVADA MAPS

The best maps for the Sierra Nevada
and Las Alpujarras are Editorial Alpina's
Sierra Nevada, La Alpujarra (1:40,000)
and Editorial Penibética's *Sierra Nevada*
(1:40,000). Both come with booklets
describing walking, cycling and skiing
routes; both are available at the Centro
de Visitantes El Dornajo near Pradollano.

🛍 Shopping

Tara   FASHION & ACCESSORIES
(Avenida González Robles 19; ⊙ 10am-2pm & 5.30-
8pm Mon-Sat) In keeping with Órgiva's hippie
spirit, Tara can sort out your wardrobe with
a choice of subcontinental-styled clothes,
drapes, bags and jewellery. You can also pick
up joss sticks in a range of exotic aromas.

ⓘ Information

Tourist Office (☑ 958 78 42 66; https://org
ivaturismo.wordpress.com; Plaza de la Alpujarras; ⊙ 10am-2pm Tue-Sun & 6-8pm Tue-Sat
summer, 9am-2pm & 5-7pm Tue-Sat, 10am-2pm
Sun winter) In the upper part of town.

Barranco de Poqueira

The Barranco de Poqueira (Poqueira Gorge)
is home to three of Las Alpujarras' most celebrated, and most visited, villages: Pampaneira, Bubión and Capileira, respectively 14km,
18.5km and 20km northeast of Órgiva. Seen
from a distance they resemble flecks of white
paint flicked Jackson Pollock–style on the
vertiginous green landscape. Up close, they're
textbook models of the steeply stacked white
villages for which the Alpujarras are famous.

The valley is also known for its handi-
crafts and you'll find shops selling leather
goods, woven rugs and tilework, all made
according to age-old methods. You can also
fill up on foodie treats such as locally produced ham, jam, cheese, honey, mushrooms
and grapes. For more active pursuits, hiking
trails link the villages and most are perfectly
doable in a day.

Pampaneira

POP 320

The lowest of the three villages in the Barranco de Poqueira, Pampaneira is also the most
obviously tourist-driven. Its white centre, set
around Plaza de la Libertad, is packed with
bars, restaurants and handicraft shops selling
coarsely woven Alpujarran rugs.

DON'T MISS

LAS ALPUJARRAS WALKING TRAILS

The ridges and valleys of Las Alpujarras are criss-crossed with a network of mule paths, irrigation ditches and hiking routes, providing a near-infinite number of walks between villages or into the wild. The best periods are April to mid-June and mid-September to early November, when the temperatures are just right and the flora is at its most colourful.

The three villages in the Barranco de Poqueira – Pampaneira, Bubión and Capileira – are the most popular starting points, but even there, you'll rarely pass another hiker on the trail. Colour-coded routes, ranging from 4km to 23km (two to eight hours), run up and down the gorge, and you can summit Mulhacén from Capileira. Get maps and advice at the Nevadensis office in Pampaneira, or you can make do with the Editorial Alpina map (p283), which shows most of the trails.

Of the long-distance footpaths that traverse Las Alpujarras, the GR7 follows the most scenic route – you can walk it from Lanjarón to Válor in around five days staying in Pampaneira, Pitres, Trevélez, and Bérchules en route. Buses serve all these villages, allowing you to split it into shorter day walks. The Bubión–Pitres section makes a good afternoon outing.

Another trail, the GR240 (better known as the *Sulayr*) runs in a 300km circuit around the Sierra Nevada at a higher altitude than the GR7. Divided into 19 stages, it's relatively well signposted and takes 15 to 19 days to walk in its entirety, although you can easily join it for just a stage or two.

To escape the day trippers, paths fan out from the village, including a 9km trail known as the **Sendero Pueblos de Poqueira**, which runs up the gorge to Bubión and Capileira.

◉ Sights & Activities

O Sel Ling   MONASTERY
(☑958 34 31 34; www.oseling.com; ⊙3.30-6pm Oct-Jun, 5-7.30pm Aug & Sep) Opposite Pampaneira village, 2km up the western side of the Poqueira gorge, you can just make out the stupa of the small stone Buddhist monastery, established as a retreat centre by a Tibetan monk in 1982. It makes a good destination for a hike.

Nevadensis   OUTDOORS
(☑958 76 31 27; www.nevadensis.com; Plaza de la Libertad; ⊙10am-2pm & 5-7pm Tue-Sat, to 3pm Sun & Mon) The most all-encompassing outdoor adventure specialists in the Alpujarras have an office in Pampaneira's main square – signposted as the 'Info Point', it effectively serves as a local tourist information hub. They offer a huge range of activities, from mountaineering courses and canyoning to guided hikes and 4WD tours.

🛏 Sleeping & Eating

Estrella de las Nieves   HOTEL €€
(☑958 76 39 81; www.estrelladelasnieves.com; Calle Huertos 21; s/d/ste €50/75/100; P🅿🛜❄) This dazzling white complex at the top of the village offers elegant, understated modern rooms with terraces overlooking the rooftops and surrounding mountains. It also

has pleasant gardens and the twin perks of a pool and car park (€5 per day).

Bodega El Lagar   ANDALUCIAN €
(☑673 636394; Calle Silencio; raciones €10; ⊙11am-5pm & 8pm-midnight daily) Hidden on a winding side street behind Plaza de la Libertad, this tiny bodega is one of the village's best eateries. Decked out in classic rustic fashion – picture rough white walls adorned with farm tools and wicker baskets – it cooks up huge helpings of reassuring farmhouse food, including wonderful chargrilled steaks.

Restaurante Casa Diego   ANDALUCIAN €
(☑958 76 30 15; Plaza de la Libertad 3; menú del día €10, mains €10-18; ⊙10am-5pm & 7pm-midnight) Bag a table on the quaint upstairs terrace and gaze over Pampaneira's 16th-century stone church as you dine on traditional dishes such as *choto al ajillo,* kid goat in garlic sauce, and *migas alpujarreñas,* a sort of couscous paired with garlic, green pepper and bacon.

🛍 Shopping

Abuela Ili Chocolates   CHOCOLATE
(http://abuelailichocolates.com; Plaza de la Libertad 1; ⊙9am-2pm & 3-6pm Mon-Fri, 9am-8pm Sat & Sun) Chocoholics take note – there are loads of free samples here, and most of them are fabulous. All the chocolate sold in this basement shop is made on the premises and you'll find plenty of weird and wacky flavours such as choc with goat's cheese or pepper, alongside the traditional stuff. Information panels in the entrance hallway explain the manufacturing process.

El Jardín
FOOD & DRINKS

(Calle Aguilla 11; ⊙10am-9pm) To take the taste of the Alpujarras home with you, this tempting shop sells a range of local delicacies, all produced by the owner's family: jars of honey and jam, bottles of wine, fruity liqueurs and sticky cakes.

Bubión

POP 290

Bubión is the smallest and quietest of the villages in the Barranco de Poqueira. There are few sights, but it's a picturesque spot with its Moorish backstreets, arches, and white, flat-roofed houses. The GR7 cross-continental footpath bisects the village.

◉ Sights

Casa Alpujarreña
MUSEUM

(Calle Real; €1.80; ⊙11am-2pm Sun, Mon, Wed & Thu, 11am-2pm & 5-7pm Fri, Sat & holidays) Located in the lower village beside the church, this folk museum occupies a typical mountain house, giving a glimpse of bygone Alpujarran life through its display of household utensils, farming tools and traditional furnishings.

⊨ Sleeping & Eating

Las Terrazas de la Alpujarra
HOSTAL €

(☑958 76 30 34; www.terrazasalpujarra.com; Plaza del Sol 7; s/d €26/36, 2-/4-/6-person apt €45/55/72; 🐾) This friendly, old-school *hostal* makes a pleasant base for the area. Rustic and homey, it offers basic, unassuming rooms and three self-catering apartments, as well as fabulous views from its garden terrace. It's located below the main road in the heart of the village.

Teide
ANDALUCIAN €

(Calle Carretera 1; mains €7-15; ⊙10am-10.30pm Wed-Mon) A large, easy-to-find restaurant on the main road at the bottom end of the village. With outdoor tables and a large wood-beamed dining hall, it serves a comprehensive menu of Alpujarran dishes, along with additions like consommé and spag bol.

Estación 4
INTERNATIONAL €

(☑651 831363; Calle Estación 4; mains €9-15; ⊙7-11pm Mon, Tue, Thu & Fri, 1-4pm & 7-11pm Sat & Sun) Wind your way down from the main road to find this lovely, rustic restaurant. Its snug dining room is a charming spot to dig into classic local staples such as air-cured *jamón serrano*, pastas and Moroccan-inspired lamb dishes.

Capileira

POP 520

Capileira, the highest, largest and prettiest village in Las Alpujarras, sports the best stash of restaurants and accommodation options, and has a long tradition of producing top-quality leather goods. It's also the departure point for high-altitude hikes up and around Mulhacén.

◉ Sights

Casa Museo Pedro Antonio de Alarcón
MUSEUM

(☑958 76 30 51; Calle Mentidero; €1; ⊙11am-2pm Sat & Sun) A house-museum exhibiting local farming and living utensils, and illustrating the life and work of Guadix-born novelist Pedro Antonio de Alarcón, whose 1872 book *La Alpujarra* detailed his travels in the region.

⊨ Sleeping & Eating

★**Hotel Real de Poqueira**
HOTEL €€

(☑958 76 39 02; www.hotelpoqueira.com; Doctor Castillas 11; s €40-50, d €60-70; 🕸🐾🏊) Occupying a typical old house opposite Capileira's lily-white church, this terrific three-star is one of several village hostelries run by the same family. But with its modern, boutique-like rooms, designer bathrooms and small swimming pool, this is the pick of the crop.

Finca Los Llanos
HOTEL €€

(☑958 76 30 71; www.hotelfincalosllanos.com; Carretera de Sierra Nevada; s €56 d €60-89; 🅿🐾🏊) In the upper part of the village, this is an attractive chalet-style hotel with 45 rustic rooms spread over three buildings. It also has a decent restaurant and, outside, a pool and panoramic terrace, ideal for a summer drink.

★**Taberna Restaurante La Tapa**
SPANISH, MOROCCAN €€

(☑618 30 70 30; Calle Cubo 6; mains €9-18; ⊙noon-4pm & 8pm-midnight; 🍴) Las Alpujarras is a culinary micro-region with its own distinct flavours and, at La Tapa, they're skillfully melded with the area's Moorish past in dishes such as wild boar casserole and vegetable couscous. The restaurant, which is snugly ensconced in a classic whitewashed house, is tiny, so book ahead if you want to guarantee a table.

El Corral del Castaño
INTERNATIONAL €€

(Plaza del Calvario 16; mains €8-21; ⊙1-4pm & 7.30-10pm Thu-Tue) Enjoy a lovely setting on a quaint plaza and excellent food at this welcoming village restaurant. Take your pick from the extensive selection of traditional

DON'T MISS

L'ATELIER

Set in a traditional house in the hamlet of Mecina Fondales, **L'Atelier** (☑ 958 85 75 01; www.facebook.com/lateliervegres taurant; Calle Alberca 21, Mecina Fondales; mains €10-14; ☺ 1-4pm & 7-10pm; ☑) is a tiny, candlelit restaurant presenting an array of globetrotting vegetarian and vegan dishes (tabbouli, Moroccan tagine, miso soup). It also has a couple of **B&B rooms** (d/q €50/56; ☎).

Alpujarran classics or opt for something more inventive such as skewered chicken with citrus fruit and ginger. Alternatively, go Italian with a pizza or focaccia.

🛍 Shopping

Piel J Brown   FASHION & ACCESSORIES
(☑ 958 76 30 92; www.jbrowntallerdepiel.com; Calle Doctor Castilla 7; ☺ 10am-1.30pm & 5-8pm Mon-Fri, to 1.30pm Sat) Don't miss the excellent leatherwork on show here, including bags, belts and Western-style hats, all handcrafted by artisan José Manuel Moreno. Bank on at least €70 for a bag and €40-plus for hats.

ℹ️ Information

Servicio de Interpretación de Altos Cumbres (☑ 671 564406; picapileira@oapn.mma. es; Carretera de Sierra Nevada; ☺ 10am-2pm & 5-8pm) For information about the Sierra Nevada national park and Las Alpujarras in general. Next to the bus stops in Capileira.

La Tahá

In La Tahá, the valley east of the Barranco de Poqueira, life slows and the number of tourists drops. The area consists of Pitres and outlying villages – Mecina Fondales, Capilerilla, Mecinilla, Ferreirola and Atalbéitar – in the valley below. Ancient paths (marked with signposts labelled 'Sendero Local Pitres–Ferreirola') link the hamlets, wending their way through woods and orchards, while running water provides the soundtrack. About 15 minutes' walk below Mecina Fondales, an old Moorish-era bridge spans the deep gorge of the Río Trevélez.

🛏 Sleeping

Sierra y Mar   CASA RURAL €
(☑ 958 76 61 71; www.sierraymar.com; Calle Albaicín, Ferreirola; s/d incl breakfast €42/69; P ☎) With guestrooms in several houses set around a lush terraced garden, this *casa rural* complex has been welcoming guests to tiny Ferreirola since 1985. There's nothing fancy about the place but its white walls, simple country decor and uplifting mountain views combine to make a wonderfully relaxing base.

Hotel La Capilerilla   HOTEL €€€
(☑ 958 76 62 92; www.hotellacapilerilla.com; Calle Fuente Escarda 5, Capilerilla; d €140-180; P ❄ ☎ ☒) Total tranquillity, huge mountain views and charming rustic rooms await at this hilltop hotel in the hamlet of Capilerilla, up an alarmingly steep road from Pitres. And with a swimming pool and adjacent restaurant, you're well set for a relaxing, self-sufficient stay.

Trevélez

POP 780

To gastronomes, Trevélez is celebrated for its *jamón serrano,* one of Spain's finest cured hams, which matures perfectly in the village's rarefied mountain air. To hikers it's the gateway to a cobweb of high mountain trails, including one of the main routes up Mulhacén, mainland Spain's highest peak. To statisticians it's the second-highest village in Spain after Valdelinares in Aragón. Sited at 1476m on the almost treeless slopes of the Barranco de Trevélez, the village is divided into two sections: the *alto* (high) part, which is older, more labyrinthine, and commands the best views; and the *bajo* (low) part, which has the bulk of the tourist facilities.

🏃 Activities

Trevélez is a spaghetti junction of hiking paths. The GR7 passes through the village and it's a starting point for one of the longer ascents of Mulhacén via Siete Lagunas, possible in around 12 hours if you're mega-fit (you can descend via the Mirador de Trevélez to make a circuit). An easier hike follows the Trevélez river valley from the top of town.

🛏 Sleeping & Eating

Hotel La Fragua II   HOTEL €
(☑ 958 85 86 26; www.hotellafragua.com; Calle Posadas; d/tr/q €62/78/85; ☎ ☒) La Fragua is something of a mini-chain with two hotels – this and the more modest **Hotel La Fragua I** (Calle San Antonio 4; s/d/tr/q €38/50/65/70; ☎) – and a cosy restaurant. La Fragua II sports a smart alpine look with a white-and-stone exterior adorned with potted flowers, and spacious, sun-filled rooms. Outside, you can revel in mountain views as you laze in the pool.

Camping Trevélez   CAMPGROUND €

(☏958 85 87 35; www.campingtrevelez.net; Carretera Trevélez-Órgiva, Km 32.5; adult/tent/car/cabin €5/5.25/4/29; ⊘closed Jan–mid Feb; P🛜🏊) On a leafy, terraced hillside 1km southwest of Trevélez, this is a family-run campsite offering tent pitches, wooden cabins, bungalows and wonderful views. Facilities include an on-site bar-restaurant, shop and pool.

Mesón La Fragua   ANDALUCIAN €

(Calle San Antonio; mains €8-14; ⊘12.30-4pm & 8-10.30pm; 🍴) At the very top of the village, this cosy restaurant is worth searching out for its hunky chargrilled meats and vegetarian wonders such as garlic and almond soup. As you eat, either in the wood, chalet-style interior, or the small open-air terrace, the distant mountains provide a terrific backdrop.

Mesón Joaquín   ANDALUCIAN €€

(☏958 85 85 14; http://jamonestrevelez.com; Carretera Laujar Órgiva, Km 22; mains €8-20; ⊘12.30-4.30pm) Starters of thinly sliced *jamón*, vermicelli soup with ham and eggs, and trout capped by ham. No prizes for spotting the star ingredient at this casual restaurant by the village's southern entrance. As if to reinforce the point, scores of cured hams hang from the ceiling in the ceramic-tiled interior.

🛍 Shopping

Jamones Cano González   FOOD

(☏958 85 86 32; www.jamonescanogonzalez.com; Calle Pista del Barrio Medio 18; ⊘10am-2pm & 5-7pm Mon-Fri, 11am-2pm & 4-8pm Sat, 11am-2pm Sun) Load up on Trevélez's celebrated ham at this small shop bursting with ham, cured meats and other local gourmet treats.

Eastern Alpujarras

The central and eastern reaches of the Granada Alpujarras reveal a harsher, barer landscape. Their small villages – Bérchules, Cádiar, Mecina Bombarón, Yegen, Válor, Mairena – provide oases of greenery but for the main part this is tough mountain country. Significantly fewer tourists make it this far, and those who do are often on long, solitary hiking expeditions – the long-distance GR7 path traverses the area. Much of the pleasure in travelling here lies in enjoying the local food at casual restaurants and inns.

Bérchules

POP 730

Surrounded by chestnut trees and terraced fields watered by flowing streams, Bérchules

is one of the highest villages in the Alpujarras, sitting at 1350m. There's not a lot to do in the village itself other than investigate the steep streets and enjoy the views, but there's wonderful walking in the surrounding hills.

Mirador Era de la Platera   VIEWPOINT

(Calle Platera) This viewing platform at the top of the village commands huge views over the surrounding hills down to the white town of Cádiar. The terrace was once used by local farmers for threshing and wind-winnowing, two traditional techniques for separating grain from the chaff.

Hotel Los Bérchules   HOTEL €

(☏958 85 25 30; www.hotelberchules.com; Carretera de Granada 20; s €42 d €59-64; P🛜🏊) This large family-run hotel makes an ideal base for walking tours of the area. It's well placed on the western entrance to the village and offers warm Alpujarran hospitality along with simply attired rooms and uplifting views of the surrounding slopes. Extras include a large pool and a cosy **restaurant** (fixed-price dinner menu €19; ⊘by reservation).

Mecina Bombarón

This white mountain village is generally overlooked by all but the most dedicated walkers. Located on the GR7 path, 7km west of Yegen and 5km east of Bérchules, it was the birthplace and final refuge of Aben Aboo, the last leader of the Moors in Spain. His death in 1571 signalled the end of the Moorish rebellion and the beginning of their expulsion. On the eastern side of the village, just below the GR7, you'll find a 13th-century medieval bridge. This was once part of the 'camino real', a one-time royal path connecting Granada and Almería.

Restaurante Casa Joaquin   ANDALUCIAN €

(☏628 670113; Avenida Jose Antonio 65; mains €10; ⊘7am-midnight) After a hike in the hills, reward yourself with an ice-cold beer and no-nonsense *plato alpujarreño* (spicy sausage, black pudding, bacon, a fried egg, chips and fried green pepper) at this no-frills bar-restaurant on the main through road.

Cádiar

POP 1530

Cádiar is one of the bigger Alpujarras villages, down in the lowlands by the Río Guadalfeo. Early October is a good time to visit as the town celebrates its four-day annual **feria** (Plaza de la Iglesia; ⊘early Oct) by opening the taps on its *Fuente del Vino* (Wine

Fountain), unleashing a flow of wine that you're welcome to fill up on. Cádiar is 8km south of Bérchules on the A348.

★ **Alquería de Morayma** CASA RURAL €€
(☑958 34 32 21; www.alqueriamorayma.com; Ctra A348, Km 50; d €70, 4-person apt €120; P⛅) Set in its own 40-hectare estate of vineyards and woodland 2km south of Cádiar, this is a gorgeous rural retreat. The centre of operations is the main farmstead, with its heavy wood-beamed ceilings, stone-flagged floors, **restaurant** (mains €10-16; ⓧ1.30-4.30pm & 7.30-11pm) and small library, but there are also rooms and apartments in outlying buildings.

Yegen

The 400-strong village of Yegen is best known as the home of British writer Gerald Brenan, a peripheral Bloomsbury Group member whose *South from Granada* depicted life here in the 1920s. A plaque marks Brenan's house, just off the fountain plaza below the main road, while the Sendero Gerald Brenan retraces his steps through a nearby gorge.

Sendero Gerald Brenan WALKING
Walkers can explore the dramatically eroded red landscape around Yegen on the Sendero Gerald Brenan, a 1.9km signposted trail – there's a map of the route on the main plaza. The walk might only take an hour or so but it provides a workout as it plunges into a gorge towards the Peñón del Fuerte, a giant rock platform that once supported an 11th-century fortress, and back up the other side.

El Rincón de Yegen ANDALUCIAN €€
(☑958 85 12 70, 638 190390; Calle de las Eras 2; mains €14-20; ⓧ1-4pm & 8pm-midnight) On the eastern edge of the village, this is a cosy country restaurant with tables set around a stone fireplace in a quaint wood-beamed dining room. Dishes reflect the setting, featuring local specialities such as trout topped by Trevélez ham. If you fancy overnighting in the village, El Rincón has two-person mini apartments for €55 per night.

Válor

POP 670

Now a typical Alpujarras village, Válor has an important history. It was the birthplace of Aben Humeya, a *morisco* (Muslim who converted to Christianity) who led a 1568 rebellion against Felipe II's repressive policies banning Arabic names, dress and even language. Two years of guerrilla mountain warfare ended only after Don Juan de Aus-

tria, Felipe's half-brother, was brought in to quash the insurrection and Aben Humeya was assassinated by his cousin Aben Aboo. To re-create the historical clash, Válor musters a large *Moros y Cristianos* (Moors and Christians) **festival** (ⓧ12-15 Sep), with colourfully costumed 'armies' battling it out. Válor is 5km northeast of Yegen along the A4130.

Hostal Las Perdices HOSTAL €
(☑958 85 18 21; www.hlasperdices.com; Ctra Trevélez; d €47; ✴⛅) For basic digs in the village, this roadside *hostal* does the job nicely. It's a fairly modest affair but there's a relaxed, easygoing family atmosphere and the plainly furnished rooms are comfortable enough.

Bar Azahara ANDALUCIAN €
(Calle Aben Humeya; mains €7-15, menú del día €10; ⓧ8am-2am) As authentic as it gets, this local bar heaves on Saturday nights as locals come for their weekend meal out or just to chat with friends over beers and tapas. Sitting outside you can just see over the road to the distant mountains as you munch on vibrant seafood tapas or more substantial offerings such as pizzas and *solomillo* (sirloin) steaks.

Restaurante Aben Humeya ANDALUCIAN €
(☑958 85 18 10; Calle Los Bolos; mains €9-15; ⓧ9am-1am) The village of Válor is known for its olive oil, goat's cheese and partridge, all of which you can sample at this cosy bar-restaurant, downhill of the main road. Its menu features seasonal treats, such as local mushrooms, along with regional staples like *conejo al ajillo* (rabbit in a garlic-spiked sauce) and delicate *croquetas* (croquettes).

Mairena

Even in this silent mountain country, Mairena feels remote. A tiny white village, it sits above the main A4130 road through the Alpujarras, offering inspiring views and a timeless sense of calm. By car, Mairena is 7km east of Válor off the A4130. Continuing past the village you can access the Sierra Nevada via the A337 and the 2000m Puerto de la Ragua pass which leads down to La Calahorra.

Las Chimeneas CASA RURAL €€
(☑958 76 03 52; www.alpujarra-tours.com; Calle Amargura 6; d €90; ✴@⛅) In an 800-year-old village house, this charming bolt-hole makes a wonderful base for walking in the area. Its guest rooms exude character with antiques, timber beams and wood-framed windows, while the **restaurant** (menu €25; ⓧ7-11pm) serves up earthy mountain fare made with organic produce from the owners' *finca* (farm).

The British owners are a mine of local information and happily share their expertise.

COSTA TROPICAL

There's a hint of Italy's Amalfi Coast about the Costa Tropical, Granada province's 80km coastline. Named for its subtropical microclimate, it's far less developed than the Costa del Sol to the east and often dramatically beautiful, with dun-brown mountains cascading into the sea and whitewashed villages nestled into coves and bays. The main resorts of Almuñécar and Salobreña are popular summer destinations with long beaches, hilltop castles and handsome historic centres.

Salobreña

POP 12,400

Like a number of coastal towns, Salobreña is split into two distinct poles: the main town with its attractive hillside centre, white-cube houses and formidable Islamic castle, and, about a kilometre away, the seafront district centred on a long grey-sand beach. For much of the year, the town is a fairly quiet, low-key place but come August it bursts into life as the summer holiday season kicks into gear.

◉ Sights

Casco Antiguo   OLD TOWN
(Old Town) Salobreña's historic centre, comprising the *barrios* that once huddled inside its medieval walls, is the town's most characteristic and picturesque area. Skinny cobbled lanes snake past pristine white houses as they lead up the steep hillside to the Arab castle, 110m above sea level. There are several viewpoints, including seaward-facing **Mirador de Enrique Morente**, and the **Mirador del Postigo**, which looks inland across the valley to the distant hills.

The Casco is to the west of the modern town centre, easily accessible on foot.

Castillo Árabe de Salobreña   CASTLE
(Calle Andrés Segovia; adult/reduced €4/2; ⊙10am-2pm year-round & 5.30-9pm mid-Jun–Aug, reduced hours rest of year) Crowning the white old town, Salobreña's landmark Arab castle dates to the 1100s, though the site was fortified as early as the 10th century. It served as the summer residence for the Granada emirs, but legend has it that Emir Muhammad IX had his three daughters – Zaida, Zoraida and Zorahaida – held captive here. Washington Irving relates the story in his *Tales of the Alhambra*.

Playa de la Charca   BEACH
Salobreña's main beach is about 1km from the centre of town along Avenida del Mediterráneo. Overlooked by a rocky outcrop known as El Peñón, the lengthy strip of grey sand is backed by a road and palm-lined pavement.

🛏 Sleeping & Eating

Hostal San Juan   HOSTAL €
(☑958 61 17 29; www.hostalsanjuan.com; Calle Jardines 1; s €37-44, d €45-64, f €65-80; ⊙closed Nov-Feb; ❄🐾🛜) A lovely tiled and plant-filled patio-lounge welcomes guests at this friendly, family-run *hostal* on a quiet street about 400m from the tourist office. It's a modest affair but its bright rooms, ceramic tiles and sunny roof terrace make for an appealing package. As well as 14 regular rooms, there are also a couple of two-person apartments.

Aráis Restaurante Bar   TAPAS, SPANISH €€
(☑958 61 17 38; Calle Granada 11; bar mains €9-20, restaurant mains €15-26; ⊙9am-midnight Tue-Thu, to 1am Fri & Sat) Take your pick: tapas-style food in the laid-back bar or contemporary cuisine in the sharply designed fine-dining restaurant. The bar, a good-looking local haunt, serves a menu of creative international dishes, including a superlative guacamole with fat, sweet mussels, while the more formal restaurant impresses with its artfully presented culinary compositions.

Mesón de la Villa   ANDALUCIAN €€
(☑958 61 24 14; Plaza Francisco Ramírez de Madrid; mains €9-17.50; ⊙noon-midnight Thu-Tue; 🐾) Housed in a crimson-red villa on a quiet palm-filled plaza, this good-looking restaurant is a hit with locals for its rustic regional fare such as *rabo de toro* (oxtail stew) served in a warm, candlelit room – ideal if you're in town before the summer heat kicks in. There are also plenty of vegetarian options, including a selection of filling salads.

ℹ Information

Tourist Office (☑958 61 03 14; www.turismo salobrena.com; Plaza de Goya; ⊙10am-2pm & 5-8pm daily Jul & Aug, 10am-2pm Mon-Fri Sep-Jun) This helpful tourist office is in the modern part of town on Plaza de Goya.

ℹ Getting There & Around

Alsa (☑902 422 242; www.alsa.es) runs buses to/from Almuñécar (€1.33, 15 minutes, 16 daily), Nerja (€4.03, one hour, 12 daily), Órgiva (€3.28, one hour, one daily Monday to Saturday), Málaga (€8.54, one hour, five daily), Granada (€6.71, 1¼ to two hours, eight daily), and Almería (€10, 2½ to 3¼ hours, two daily). The buses stop just off Plaza de Goya. The number 1 local bus (€1.10) runs a circular route from the main town (Plaza Goya) to the beaches, departing almost every hour between 9.25am and 8.25pm.

By car, Salobreña is just off the N340 between Motril and Almuñécar.

Almuñécar & La Herradura

POP 27,400

The main resort town on the Costa Tropical, Almuñécar heaves in summer as crowds of Spanish holidaymakers and northern European sunseekers flock to its long pebble beaches and palm-fringed esplanade. Back from the seafront, it's not an obviously attractive place, but look beyond the dreary high-rises and you'll discover a picturesque *casco antiguo* (historic town centre) with narrow lanes, bar-flanked plazas and a striking hilltop castle. Some 7km to the west, the neighbouring village of La Herradura maintains a more castaway feel, catering to a younger crowd of windsurfers and water-sports fans.

◉ Sights

Life in Almuñécar is very much centred on its two main beaches: Playa de San Cristóbal to the west, and Playa Puerta del Mar to the east. Elsewhere, the town's few sights are mostly in and around the historic centre, a tangle of narrow alleyways wedged in between Avenidas de Europa and Juan Carlos I.

Castillo de San Miguel   CASTLE
(🔲958 83 86 23; Explanada del Castillo; adult/child €2.35/1.60; ⊙10am-1.30pm & 6.30-9pm Tue-Sat Jul–mid-Sep, reduced hours Tue-Sat Apr-Jun & mid-Sep–Oct, 10am-1.30pm & 4-6.30pm Tue-Sat Nov-Mar, 10am-1pm Sun year-round) Crowning the town, Almuñécar's impressive hilltop castle was built over Islamic and Roman fortifications by the conquering Christians in the 16th century. The hot, circuitous climb up to the entrance rewards with excellent views and an informative little museum. Don't forget to check out the skeleton in the dungeon: it's a reproduction of human remains discovered here.

Peñón del Santo   VIEWPOINT
(⊙7am-midnight May-Sep, to 10pm Oct-Apr) A rocky outcrop crowned by a large crucifix, the Peñón del Santo commands sweeping views of the town's seafront. To the west, the Playa de San Cristóbal is the best of Almuñécar's beaches, a strip of grey pebbles that catches the sun well into the evening. On the other side, Playa Puerta del Mar is the main eastern beach, backed by high-rise tower blocks.

Parque Botánico El Majuelo   PARK
(Avenida de Europa, Almuñécar; ⊙8am-10pm) FREE A lush park built around the remains of a Carthaginian and Roman fish-salting workshop, where the sauce called *garum* was produced. Subtropical plants flourish, shading a series of free-standing modern sculptures by Syrian artists.

Museo Arqueológico
Cueva de Siete Palacios   MUSEUM
(🔲958 83 86 23; Calle San Joaquín, Almuñécar; adult/child €2.35/1.60; ⊙10am-1.30pm & 6.30-9pm Tue-Sat Jul–mid-Sep, reduced hours rest of year, 10am-1pm Sun year-round) This small museum

---

WORTH A TRIP

THE MOOR'S SIGH

If driving from Almuñécar to Granada, the obvious route is the A44. A more spectacular alternative is the A4050, a snaking mountain road known as the Carretera del Suspiro del Moro. Straight through, the drive takes about two hours. From the N340 in Almuñécar, turn northwest out of the main roundabout, following a sign to Otívar.

In Otívar, note your car's odometer reading. The road ascends sharply. Where it finally levels off, after 13km, the landscape is limestone studded with pine trees. Just over 16km from Otívar, you'll find the trailhead of the Sendero Río Verde on the left side of the road. The path descends nearly 400m into the deep valley of the Río Verde, offering the chance of spotting an ibex. The full loop is 7.4km (about 3½ hours), but as this requires you walk back to your car along the road, you may prefer to double back when you reach the Fuente de las Cabrerizas, a water pump near the bottom of the gorge.

Back on the road, and descending the other side of the mountain, 43.5km from Otívar you'll see a road signed 'Suspiro del Moro' heading to the left. Follow this to take the pass where, legend has it, the emir of Granada, Boabdil, looked back and let out a regretful sigh as he left the city in 1492. Follow the Granada signs to continue 12km to the city.

WATER SPORTS IN LA HERRADURA

If you're craving a more remote beach scene than Almuñécar, or more activity, head 7km west to the small, horseshoe-shaped bay at La Herradura, where a younger crowd of wind-surfers and water-sports enthusiasts congregate. On the beach, **Windsurf La Herradura** (☑958 64 01 43; www.windsurflaherradura.com; Paseo Andrés Segovia 34, La Herradura; wind-surf rent/lesson €20/30; ☺school 10.30am-8pm Easter-Oct, shop 10.30am-2pm & 5.30-8.30pm year-round) is a good point of reference, providing equipment rental, courses and lessons.

The waters around La Herradura offer good diving, with a varied seabed of seagrass, sand and rock flecked with caves, crevices and passages. **Buceo La Herradura** (☑958 82 70 83; www.buceolaherradura.com; Puerto Marina del Este; dive plus equipment €48; ☺10.30am-4.30pm Mon, Wed-Fri, 9.30am-4.30pm Sat & Sun) is a reliable dive outfit, operating out of the marina at Punta de la Mona between Almuñécar and La Herradura.

is set in a series of 1st-century underground stone cellars, built at a time when the town was ruled by the Romans and known as Sexi (yes, really). On display are finds from local Phoenician, Roman and Islamic sites plus a 3500-year-old Egyptian amphora.

🛏 Sleeping

Hotel Casablanca HOTEL €€
(☑958 63 55 75; www.hotelcasablancaalmunecar.com; Plaza de San Cristóbal 4; s €35-86, d €42-96; ❄☎) Convenient for both the beach and Almuñécar's lively centre, this hotel sports a distinctive Al-Andalus look and offers handsomely decorated rooms, some with sea views. For breakfast, available for about €7, or a relaxed afternoon drink, there's a ground-floor bar with tables outside on the plaza.

🍴 Eating

Almuñécar harbours an inordinate number of tapas bars, particularly in the streets around Plaza Kebila.

La Italiana Cafe CAFE €
(☑649 881601; www.laitalianacafe.com; Hurtado de Mendoza 5, Almuñécar; pastries from €2.20; ☺8am-10pm; ☎) With its gaudy Italianate decor – chandeliers, ceiling frescoes, mirrors and elaborately gilded pillars – La Italiana is a favourite late-afternoon hang-out. Locals and visitors stop by for a coffee and sweet snack, perhaps a pastry, crêpe or ice cream.

★**Los Geráneos** ANDALUCIAN €€
(☑958 63 40 20; Placeta de la Rosa 4, Almuñécar; menú del día €15; ☺1-5pm & 7.30-11pm Mon-Sat) With tables on a sunny cobbled plaza or be-neath a low wood-beamed ceiling in the rus-tic interior, Los Geráneos makes a good first impression. Things only get better when the food arrives: zingy salads, fresh grilled fish

tasting magically of the sea, and sweet, ripe melons. And all for €15 – magnificent.

La Ventura ANDALUCIAN €€
(☑958 88 23 78; Calle Alta del Mar 18; lunch menu €10, tasting menu €30; ☺1-4pm & 8-11.30pm Wed-Sun) A bit of a flamenco secret in Almuñécar and all the better for it, Ventura is best visit-ed on Thursday, Friday or Sunday evenings when music and dance inflame the atmos-phere, providing a memorable accompani-ment to solidly traditional Andalucian fare.

ℹ Information

Information Kiosk (☑958 61 60 70; Paseo del Altillo; ☺10am-1pm & 6.30-9pm Jul–mid-Sep, reduced hours winter) Just back from Almuñé-car's seafront.

La Herradura Tourist Office (☑958 61 86 36; Centro Cívico La Herradura; ☺10am-1pm & 5.45-8.15pm Tue-Sun Jul–mid-Sep, reduced hours winter)

Main Tourist Office (☑958 63 11 25; www.turismoalmunecar.es; Avenida Europa; ☺10am-1pm & 6.30-9pm Jul–mid-Sep) A block back from the seafront, in Almuñécar's pink neo-Moorish Palacete de la Najarra. Shorter hours in winter.

ℹ Getting There & Away

Almuñécar Bus Station (☑958 63 01 40; Avenida Juan Carlos I 1) is north of the town centre. Alsa (p277) services run to/from Gra-nada (€8.34, 1½ hours, up to 12 daily), Málaga (€7.43, 1¾ to two hours, up to eight daily), and Almería (€12, 3½ hours, five daily).

There are also buses to La Herradura (€1.16, 15 minutes, up to 17 daily), Salobreña (€1.33, 15 minutes, 16 daily), and Nerja (€2.91, 30 minutes, up to 17 daily).

For Las Alpujarras, a single daily bus goes to Órgiva (€4.68, 1¼ hours, one daily) departing at 4.45pm Monday to Saturday.

Almería Province

Best Places to Stay

➡ Plaza Vieja Hotel & Lounge (p296)

➡ MC San José (p308)

➡ Cortijo de la Alberca (p302)

➡ Hostal El Olivar (p312)

➡ MiKasa (p310)

Best Places to Eat

➡ 4 Nudos (p308)

➡ Restaurante La Villa (p310)

➡ Casa Puga (p300)

➡ Tito's (p312)

Why Go?

Silent mountain valleys, sublime beaches and vast tracts of semidesert scrubland – Almería province is an area of haunting natural beauty. Despite this, and despite enjoying 3000 hours of annual sunshine, it remains relatively unknown outside of Spain. Its obvious drawcard is its glorious coastline, most notably the thrilling beaches of the Parque Natural de Cabo de Gata-Níjar, and the lively, good-time resort of Mojácar. But venture inland, and you'll discover plenty to explore in its sparsely populated and often other-worldly hinterland. Tour the spaghetti-western badlands of the Desierto de Tabernas and discover underground treasures in the Sorbas caves. Further north, the wooded peaks of Los Vélez provide a majestic backdrop for mountain walking. After so much nature, the port city of Almería offers a welcome blast of urban energy with its impressive monuments, handsome centre and buzzing tapas bars.

Driving Distances

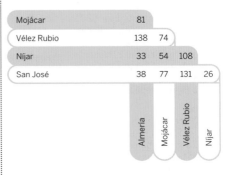

	Almería	Mojácar	Vélez Rubio	Níjar
Mojácar	81			
Vélez Rubio	138	74		
Níjar	33	54	108	
San José	38	77	131	26

ALMERÍA

POP 165.180

An energetic port city with an illustrious past, Almería is one of Andalucía's emerging destinations. Until fairly recently the city was generally overlooked by travellers, but recent efforts to spruce it up are beginning to pay dividends. It has a handsome centre, punctuated by palm-fringed plazas and old churches, several interesting museums and a plethora of fantastic tapas bars. Best of all – and reason alone for a visit – is its spectacular Moorish Alcazaba (fortress).

History

Founded in AD 955 by the Córdoba caliph Abd ar-Rahman III, Almería quickly became the largest and richest port in Moorish Spain and the headquarters of the Umayyad fleet. Its streets thronged with merchants from Egypt, Syria, France and Italy, who came to buy silk, glass, marble and glazed ceramics in Al-Andalus. It eventually lost its trading supremacy during a Christian occupation from 1147 to 1157 but it remained a significant Moorish city until conquered by the Catholic Monarchs in 1489. It subsequently went into rapid decline – a 1658 census counted only 500 inhabitants – due to devastating earthquakes, the expulsion of Andalucía's Muslim population and attacks by Barbary pirates. In the late 20th century its fortunes took a turn for the better as agriculture and tourism flourished in the surrounding region.

⊙ Sights

Almería's top sights are the Alcazaba and the cathedral, both of which can be explored in a morning, but there are plenty of interesting additional distractions in the city's meandering streets. Orientate yourself from Paseo de Almería, the city's main drag, which runs north–south through the historic centre.

★ Alcazaba   FORTRESS
(☑950 80 10 08; Calle Almanzor; ⊙9am-8pm Tue-Sat Apr–mid-Jun, to 3pm Tue-Sat mid-Jun–mid-Sep, to 6pm Tue-Sat mid-Sep–Mar, to 3pm Sun year-round) FREE A looming fortification with great curtain-like walls rising from the cliffs, Almería's Alcazaba was founded in the mid-10th century and was one of the most powerful Moorish fortresses in Spain. It's survived in good shape and while it lacks the intricate decoration of Granada's Alhambra, it's still a magnificent sight. Allow about 1½ hours to explore everything. Pick up a guide leaflet at the kiosk inside the four-arch entrance gate.

The Alcazaba is divided into three distinct *recintos* (compounds). The lowest, the Primer Recinto, was residential, with houses, streets, wells, baths and other necessities – now replaced by lush gardens and water channels. From the battlements, you can look over the city's huddled rooftops and down to the Muralla de Jayrán, a fortified wall built in the 11th century to defend the outlying northern and eastern parts of the city.

Further up in the Segundo Recinto you'll find the ruins of the Muslim rulers' palace, built by the *taifa* ruler Almotacín (r 1051–91), under whom medieval Almería reached its peak, as well as a chapel, the Ermita de San Juan, which was originally a mosque. The highest section, the Tercer Recinto, is a castle added by the Catholic Monarchs.

★ Catedral de la Encarnación   CATHEDRAL
(☑950 23 48 48; www.catedralalmeria.com; Plaza de la Catedral 8, entrance Calle Velázquez; €5, 8.30-9am Mon-Sat & 10.30-11.30am Sun free; ⊙10am-7pm Mon-Fri, 10am-2.30pm & 3.30-7pm Sat, 1.30-7pm Sun Apr-Jun, 10am-8.30pm Mon-Fri, 10am-2.30pm & 3.30-7pm Sat, 1.30-7pm Sun Jul-Sep, shorter hours Oct-Mar) Almería's formidable, six-towered cathedral, begun in 1525, was conceived both as a place of worship and a refuge for the population from frequent pirate raids from North Africa. It was originally Gothic-Renaissance in style, but baroque and neoclassical features were added in the 18th century. The Gothic interior, entered through a fine neoclassical cloister, is an impressive spectacle with its sinuous, ribbed ceiling, 16th-century walnut choir stalls and monumental Capilla Mayor (Chancel). On the building's exterior, note the cute stone lions around the northwest tower and the exuberant Sol de Portocarrero, a 16th-century relief of the sun (now serving as the city's symbol) on the cathedral's eastern end.

Museo de Almería   MUSEUM
(Museo Arqueológico; ☑950 17 55 10; www.museosdeandalucia.es; Calle Azorín; ⊙9am-3pm Tue-Sun & 6-9.30pm Wed-Sat mid-Jun–mid-Sep, 9am-8pm Tue-Sat, 9am-3pm Sun mid-Sep–mid-Jun) FREE Almería's excellent archaeology museum, housed in a spacious modern building, focuses on two local prehistoric cultures – Los Millares (3200–2250 BC; probably the Iberian Peninsula's first metalworking culture), and El Argar (2250–1550 BC), which ushered in the Bronze Age. Artefacts from these important sites are well displayed and accompanied by informative explanatory panels in English and Spanish. Up on the 3rd floor, you'll

Almería Province Highlights

1 Parque Natural de Cabo de Gata-Níjar (p305) Hopping around the heavenly beaches and plunging cliffs of Andalucía's southeastern coastline.

2 Alcazaba (p293) Patrolling Almería's formidable hilltop fort, once one of the most powerful in Moorish Spain.

3 Cuevas de Sorbas (p303) Going underground in this otherworldly cave complex.

4 Los Vélez (p313) Taking to the remote forests and rocky peaks of the Sierra de María in the province's far north.

5 Desierto de Tabernas (p301) Touring the cinematic Wild West landscapes of this barren semidesert.

6 Mojácar (p310) Soaking up the *playa*'s summer beach vibe, and basking in sweeping vistas from the quaint hilltop *pueblo* (village).

7 Tapas Crawl (p297) Eating and drinking your way around Almería's ever-popular tapas bars.

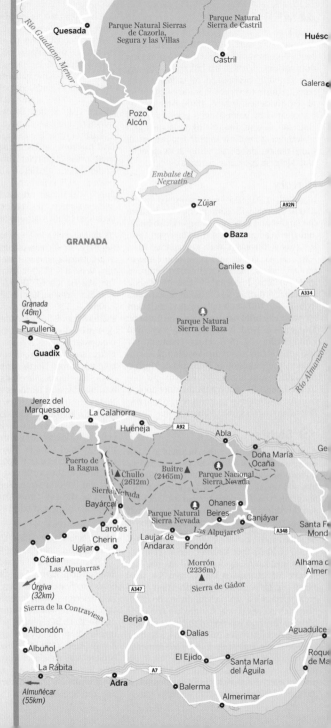

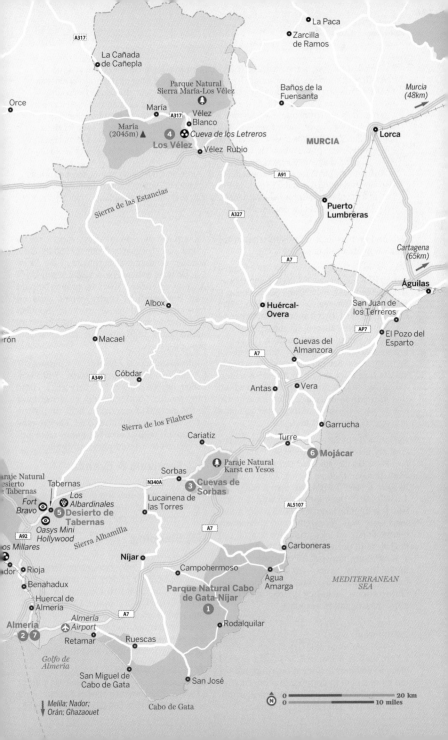

THE OLD MEDINA

Sprawled at the foot of the Alcazaba (p293), the maze-like Almedina is one of Almería's most atmospheric neighbourhoods. This was the area occupied by the original Almería – a walled medina (city), bounded by the Alcazaba to the north, the sea to the south, and what are now Calle de la Reina and Avenida del Mar to the east and west. At its heart was the city's main mosque – whose *mihrab* (a prayer niche indicating the direction of Mecca) survives inside the **Iglesia de San Juan** (Calle General Luque; ⊕ open for Mass 8pm Apr-Sep, 7pm Oct-Mar, closed Tue & Fri) FREE – with the commercial area of markets and warehouses spread around it. Calle de la Almedina still traces the line of the old main street running diagonally across the medina.

An excellent place for refreshment is Tetería Almedina, a friendly teahouse-restaurant. Also worth seeking out is the **Plaza de Pavía market** (Plaza de Pavía; ⊕ 9am-2pm Mon-Sat), at its liveliest on Saturdays, with stalls selling everything from cheap shoes to churros (delicious, fat, tubular doughnuts).

also find archaeological finds relating to the area's Roman and Islamic past.

Museo de la Guitarra
MUSEUM

(🖉 950 27 43 58; Ronda del Beato Diego Ventaja; adult/reduced €3/2; ⊕ 10.30am-1.30pm Tue-Sun & 6-9pm Fri & Sat Jun-Sep, 10am-1pm Tue-Sun, 5-8pm Fri & Sat Oct-May) Two important facts before you enter this absorbing museum. First: the word 'guitar' is derived from the Andalucian-Arabic word *qitara*, hinting at its Spanish roots. Second: all modern acoustic guitars owe a huge debt to Almerían guitar-maker Antonio de Torres (1817–92), to whom this museum is dedicated. The museum itself details the history of the guitar and pays homage to Torres' part in it.

Refugios de la Guerra Civil
HISTORIC SITE

(Civil War Shelters; 🖉 950 26 86 96; Plaza de Manuel Pérez García; adult/reduced €3/2; ⊕ tours 10am, 11.30am, 12.30pm, 6pm & 7.30pm Jun-Sep, 10.30am & noon Tue-Sun, plus 5pm & 6.30pm Fri & Sat Oct-May) During the civil war, Almería was the Republicans' last holdout in Andalucía, and was repeatedly and mercilessly bombed. The attacks prompted a group of engineers to design and build the Refugios, a 4.5km-long network of concrete shelters under the city. Visits - by 1¼-hour guided tour, in Spanish only – take you through 1km of the tunnels, including the recreated operating theatre and storerooms.

Centro de Interpretación Patrimonial
MUSEUM

(🖉 671 099981; Plaza de la Constitución; ⊕ 10am-1.30pm Tue-Sun, 6-9pm Fri & Sat) FREE A good place to get your historical bearings and set the city's sights in context, this informative museum has three floors of historical exhibits as well as a panoramic roof terrace.

Centro Andaluz de la Fotografía
GALLERY

(Andalucian Photography Centre; 🖉 950 18 63 60; www.centroandaluzdelafotografia.es; Calle Pintor Díaz Molina 9; ⊕ 11am-2pm & 5.30-9.30pm) FREE Anyone interested in photography should visit this excellent centre, which puts on top-class exhibitions of work by Spanish and international photographers. They vary dramatically in theme but are invariably thought-provoking.

Aljibes Árabes de Jayrán
HISTORIC SITE

(🖉 950 27 30 39; Calle Tenor Iribarne; ⊕ 10.30am-1.30pm Tue-Sun & 6-9pm Fri & Sat) FREE These brick-vaulted underground cisterns, built in the early 11th century to help supply the city's water, are well preserved. They're now a venue for regular events, ranging from guitar recitals to art and photo exhibitions.

🎇 Festivals & Events

Feria de Almería
FIESTA

(www.feriadealmeria.es) Ten days and nights of live music, fairground rides, exhibitions and full-on partying in the second half of August.

🛏 Sleeping

Hotel Nuevo Torreluz
HOTEL €

(🖉 950 23 43 99; www.torreluz.com; Plaza de las Flores 10; r €55-70; 🅿 🌢 🤶) A polished four-star enjoying a superb location on a small square in the historic centre. Carpeted corridors lead to smallish but comfortable rooms sporting parquet floors and modern pearl-grey colours. The hotel also runs a trio of cafes and restaurants around the square.

★ Plaza Vieja Hotel & Lounge
BOUTIQUE HOTEL €€

(🖉 950 28 20 96; www.airehotelalmeria.com; Plaza de la Constitución 5; d €69-150, ste €119-175; 🌢 🤶)

Part of the plush Hammam Aire de Almería, this elegant hideaway is perfectly situated just steps from some of the city's top tapas bars. Its slick, contemporarily attired rooms come with high ceilings, polished wood floors and vast photo-walls of local sights such as the Cabo de Gata.

Hotel Catedral BOUTIQUE HOTEL **€€**
(☑ 950 27 81 78; www.hotelcatedral.net; Plaza de la Catedral 8; r €90-150; ❀ 🛜) In a prime location overlooking the cathedral, this debonair four-star occupies a handsome 1850s building. Inside, the decor slickly marries the old and the new, combining clean contemporary lines with Gothic arches and an *artesonado* (coffered) ceiling in the restaurant. Rooms are large and high-ceilinged, and the roof terrace offers heady cathedral views.

🍴 Eating

Frequented as much by locals as out-of-towners and tourists, many of Almería's top tapas bars (p300) are squeezed into the tight-knit area between Plaza de la Constitución and Paseo de Almería.

La Coquette CAFE, PASTRIES **€**
(Paseo de Almería 34; snacks from €1.80, ice cream €1.80-3.70; ⊗ 8.30am-9.30pm, to 1.30am summer; 🎝) This wonderful patisserie is perfectly sited for a quick pit stop on Almería's central drag. Choose from the tempting array of croissants, brownies, tarts and meringues or go for a creamy Italian-style gelato to take away or linger over at one of the shaded pavement tables.

Mercado Central MARKET **€**
(Circunvalación Ulpiano Díaz; ⊗ 8am-3pm Mon-Sat) Almería's central market occupies a grand 1890s building near the top of Paseo de Almería. Go early to see squid so fresh they're still changing colour, as well as a profusion of fruit and veg grown in greenhouses across the province.

★ **Tetería Almedina** MOROCCAN **€€**
(☑ 629 277827; www.teteriaalmedina.com; Calle Paz 2, off Calle de la Almedina; mains €10-15, fixed-price menus €17-30; ⊗ 1-11pm Tue-Sun; 🎝) For a break from tapas, this welcoming little tearoom-restaurant is the answer. Hidden away in a backstreet below the Alcazaba, it serves a reassuring menu of homestyle Moroccan staples – tagines, tabbouli, couscous and lightly spiced legume soups. To drink, a herbed tea or infusion is the way to go. The restaurant is run by a local group dedicated to revitalising the old town, with its many

Moroccan immigrants, and reviving the culture of Al-Andalus.

El Asador SPANISH **€€€**
(☑ 950 23 45 45; www.elasadoralmeria.com; Calle Fructuoso Pérez 14; mains €18-25; ⊗ 1.30-4.30pm Mon-Sat & 8.30pm-midnight Tue-Sat) Formal and elegantly furnished, El Asador is smarter than most of its tapas-bar neighbours. Tall-backed chairs and starched table settings set the tone for high-end Spanish cuisine that features foie-gras starters and succulent barbecued steaks.

Casa Joaquín SEAFOOD **€€€**
(☑ 950 26 43 59; Calle Real 111; raciones €12-36; ⊗ 1.30-4.30pm & 9-11.30pm Mon-Fri, to 3.30pm Sat) Fresh seafood is the star of this historic Almería bodega, classically attired with hanging hams and rustic clutter. What's on offer depends on the day's catch but regular crowd-pleasers include juicy *gambas rojas* (red prawns) cooked a la plancha (grilled on a hotplate), and fried *calamares* (squid).

🍷 Drinking & Nightlife

The old-town tapas bars (p300) are many people's chosen drinking spots. The city's nightlife epicentre is the Cuatro Calles area around the intersection of Calles Real, Trajano and Eduardo Pérez. Within a couple of blocks you'll find several pubs, bars and clubs, generally with free admission. Note that most places heat up late, often not hitting their stride until around midnight.

HEAVENLY HAMMAMS

Hammam Aire de Almería (☑ 950 28 20 95; www.airedealmeria.com; Plaza de la Constitución 5; 1½hr session €27 Mon-Thu, €29 Fri-Sun; ⊗ 10am-10pm) This luxurious and spacious *hammam* exudes a feeling of tranquillity throughout its marble and warm-brick interior. It offers three baths: the frigidarium (16°C), tepidarium (36°C) and caldarium (40°C), as well as a range of aromatherapy and other massages. Reservations are advisable.

Hammam Almeraya (☑ 950 23 10 10; www.almeraya.info; Calle Perea 9; 1½hr session incl aromatherapy €18; ⊗ 9am-9.30pm Wed-Mon) This small *hammam* has hot and cold baths, a 'Turkish' steam bath and a beautiful marble-and-tiled interior. It also offers massages, and has a relaxing *tetería* (⊗ 9am-2pm & 4pm-midnight Wed-Mon). Reservations required.

ALMERÍA PROVINCE ALMERÍA

Almería

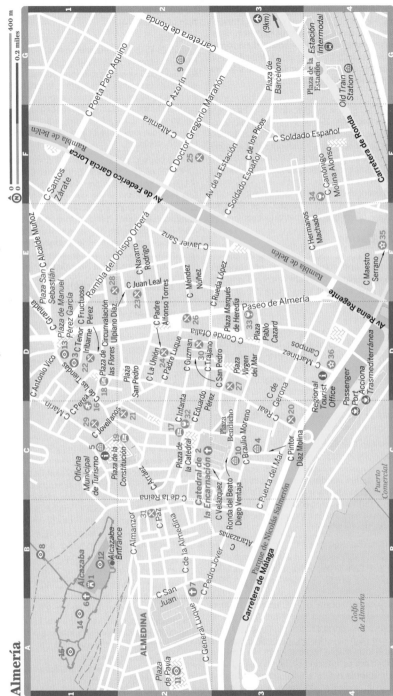

La Cueva
PUB

([phone]950 08 25 21; www.lacueva-almeria.com; Calle Canónigo Molina Alonso 23; ⊙4pm-4am) Craft beer goes hand-in-hand with jam sessions and live music at this laid-back pub. The subdued lighting and walls plastered with posters and concert flyers create an intimate vibe for everything from blues and rock to punk, rap and heavy metal. Gigs are either free or cost around €3 to €5.

Burana
BAR

(Paseo de Almería 56; ⊙3pm-4am) With its terrace in the portals of the neoclassical Teatro Cervantes and a disco-lit interior, this is a fashionable spot for an afternoon coffee or late-night cocktail. The vibe is upmarket trendy, with regular DJ sets at weekends.

☆ Entertainment

Almería has an active cultural scene, with everything from flamenco performances to theatrical drama, classical music concerts, jazz and rock. Check www.almeriaculturaen tradas.es for upcoming events.

Clasijazz
JAZZ

(www.clasijazz.com; Calle Maestro Serrano 9; non-members €2-25) Located in a bland shopping centre, Clasijazz is a thriving music club that stages four or five weekly gigs – ranging from jam sessions to jazz, big band and classical concerts – in a clean, contemporary space. Check the website for upcoming events.

MadChester
LIVE MUSIC

([phone]661 696930; www.facebook.com/madches terclub; Parque Nicolás Salmerón 9; cover €8-16; ⊙11pm-late Fri & Sat, 6-11pm Sun) This club venue hosts Spanish and international DJs and regular gigs by bands playing indie, rock and electronica.

Peña El Taranto
FLAMENCO

([phone]950 23 50 57; www.eltaranto.com; Calle Tenor Iribarne 20) This is Almería's top flamenco club, where local guitar star Tomatito has been known to stroke the strings. Housed in a series of medieval cisterns, it hosts exhibitions, runs courses and puts on occasional recitals and performances.

ⓘ Information

Oficina Municipal de Turismo ([phone]950 21 05 38; www.turismodealmeria.org; Plaza de la Constitución; ⊙10am-2pm & 6-8pm Jul & Aug, 9am-3pm Mon-Fri, 10am-2pm Sat & Sun Sep-Jun)

Regional Tourist Office ([phone]950 17 52 20; www.andalucia.org; Parque de Nicolás Salmerón; ⊙9am-7.30pm Mon-Wed, to 3pm Thu & Fri, 9.30am-3pm Sat & Sun)

Almería

ALMERÍA TAPAS TOUR

The area between Paseo de Almería and Plaza de la Constitución is packed with busy and atmospheric tapas bars. Many maintain the civilised tradition of serving a free tapas with your drink. As a rule, portions are generous, and for the hungry – or to share – almost everywhere offers *raciones* and *medias raciones* (full- and half-sized plates of tapas items).

Casa Puga (www.barcasapuga.es; Calle Jovellanos 7; tapas from €1.70, raciones €8-15; ⊙noon-4pm & 8.15pm-midnight Mon-Sat) Dating to 1870, this is one of Almería's oldest and best-known tapas bars. Its small interior, a cluttered space of hanging hams, yellowing wall pictures and wine bottles, gets very animated as locals and visitors squeeze in to snack on classic, old-school tapas.

Nuestra Tierra (Calle Jovellanos 16; tapas €2.80-5; ⊙7.30am-noon Mon, to midnight Tue-Thu, to 1am Fri, 8.30am-1am Sat, noon-midnight Sun) Head to this good-looking modern eatery on bar-heavy Calle Jovellanos for creative tapas made with seasonal Andalucian ingredients. Showstoppers include garlic lamb with potatoes and octopus grilled to buttery softness.

El Quinto Toro (☑950 23 91 35; Calle Juan Leal 6; tapas from €1.50, raciones €8-15; ⊙noon-5pm Mon-Sat & 8pm-midnight Mon-Fri) Keep it traditional at this old-school bar near the central market. Don't expect culinary fireworks, just tried-and-tested staples such as *chorizo ibérico* (spicy sausage) and *albóndigas* (meatballs) in wine sauce.

La Mala (Calle Real 69; tortillas €8-12, raciones €6-22; ⊙1-5pm & 8.30pm-1.30am) A favourite local hang-out, this buzzing corner bar fills quickly on weekend evenings. With its boho decor and young crowd, it's a great spot to try a genuine Spanish tortilla (omelette), here prepared with everything from tuna to prawns and chilli.

Entrefinos (☑950 25 56 25; www.entrefinos.es; Calle Padre Alfonso Torres 8; tapas €3.50, fixed-price menus €35-50; ⊙1-4pm & 8pm-midnight Mon-Sat) Dressed like a woody wine bar with a timber-beamed ceiling, barrel-top tables and blackboard menus, this ever-popular eatery offers a menu of timeless tapas, such as grilled mushrooms and fried anchovies.

Taberna Postigo (Calle Guzmán; tapas €2.50-3; ⊙11am-5pm & 7pm-midnight Tue, Wed & Sun, to 1am Thu-Sat) Laid-back, friendly and often very busy, this tavern is tucked away in a leafy corner off Paseo de Almería. Grab an outdoor table and dig into crowd-pleasing tapas *a la brasa* (grilled over hot coals), including a flavoursome bacon with *pimientos* (peppers). No credit cards.

ⓘ Getting There & Away

AIR

Almería's small **airport** (☑902 40 47 04; www.aena.es) is 9km east of the city centre.

EasyJet (☑902 59 99 00; www.easyjet.com), **Ryanair** (☑902 05 12 92; www.ryanair.com), and **Thomas Cook Airlines** (☑950 21 39 78; www.thomascookairlines.com) fly direct to/from various English airports (Ryanair also flies from Dublin and Brussels); **Iberia** (☑901 11 13 42; www.iberia.com) and **Vueling** (☑902 80 80 22; www.vueling.com) serve Spanish destinations.

BOAT

Acciona Trasmediterránea (☑902 454645; www.trasmediterranea.es) sails from the **passenger port** (☑950 23 60 33; www.apalmeria.com) to the Moroccan ports of Nador (€62, six hours) and Melilla (€35, eight hours) at least once daily, and to the Algerian cities of Orán (€81, nine hours) and Ghazaouet (€81, nine hours) at least once weekly.

BUS

Buses and trains share the **Estación Intermodal** (☑950 17 36 02; Plaza de la Estación 6), just east of the centre. **Bus Bam** (☑902 227272; www.busbam.com) runs up to six daily buses (one on Sunday) to/from Madrid (€23, 6¾ hours). Most other intercity services are operated by **Alsa** (☑902 42 22 42; www.alsa.es).

TO	COST	DURATION	FREQUENCY
Córdoba	€29	5hr	1 daily
Granada	€14-17.50	2-4¼hr	8 daily
Guadix	€9.50	2hr	2 daily
Jaén	€19.50	4-5hr	3 daily
Málaga	€19-22	2½-5½hr	7 daily
Murcia	€14	2¾-4½hr	7 daily
Seville	€37	5½-8½hr	4 daily

TRAIN

From the Estación Intermodal, there are direct trains to Granada (€20, 2½ hours, four daily), Seville (€41, 5¾ hours, four daily) and Madrid (€33 to €83, 6½ hours, three daily).

❶ Getting Around

TO/FROM THE AIRPORT

Surbus (www.surbus.com) city bus 30 (€1.05, 35 minutes) runs from the airport to the centre, stopping at the main Estación Intermodal, among other places. Services run at least hourly, and often half-hourly, between about 7.15am and 11.20pm (finishing earlier on Sundays).

Taxis between the airport and city centre cost approximately €15 to €20.

CAR & MOTORCYCLE

The A7/E15 runs a large ring around Almería; the easiest access to the centre is along the seafront (Carretera de Málaga) from the west, or the AL12 (Autovía del Aeropuerto) from the east.

Underground car parks dotted around the city centre area cost about €16 for 24 hours.

TAXI

Catch a taxi at ranks on Paseo de Almería, or call **Radio-Taxi Almería** (📞950 22 61 61, 950 22 22 22; www.radiotaxialmeria.com) or **Tele Taxi Almería** (📞950 25 11 11; www.teletaxialmeria.com).

NORTH OF ALMERÍA

Desierto de Tabernas

Travel 30km north of Almería and you enter another world. The Desierto de Tabernas (Tabernas desert) is a strange and haunting place, a vast, sun-baked scrubland of shimmering, dun-coloured hills scattered with tufts of tussocky brush. In the 1960s the area was used as a film location for Sergio Leone's famous spaghetti westerns (*A Fistful of Dollars; For a Few Dollars More; The Good, the Bad and the Ugly;* and *Once Upon a Time in the West*), and still today film-makers come to shoot within its rugged badlands. Many of its 'Western' sets have now been incorporated into Wild West theme parks, which make for a fun family day out. The main town in the area is Tabernas, on the N340A road.

◉ Sights & Activities

Oasys Mini Hollywood   AMUSEMENT PARK
(📞902 53 35 32; www.oasysparquetematico. com; Carretera N340A, Km 464; adult/child €22.50/12.50; ⊙10am-7.30pm Jun & Sep, to 9pm

Jul & Aug, to 6pm Oct-May, closed Mon-Fri Nov-Mar; 🅿🚼) This, the best known and most expensive of Tabernas' Wild West parks, provides good family entertainment. The set itself is in decent condition, and the well-kept zoo has some 800 animals, including lions, giraffes, tigers and hippos. Children usually enjoy the 20-minute shoot-outs, while adults may prefer the clichéd can-can show (or at least the beer) in the saloon. There are also two summer pools, restaurants and cafes. Take sunscreen and a hat: there's little shade.

Malcaminos   TOURS
(📞652 022582; www.malcaminos.com; Avenida de las Angustias, Tabernas) A local outfit running excellent tours of Tabernas' cinematic landscape. The guides are enthusiastic and knowledgeable about the area – not just its filmic geography but also its history and geology. Packages include a two-hour 4WD tour (per adult/child €30/18.50) of the area's movie locations.

✗ Eating

Las Eras Antonio   ANDALUCIAN €
(📞950 36 52 69; www.antoniogazquez.net; Paraje Las Eras, Tabernas; menú del día €12; ⊙1-6pm Mon-Fri; 🅿) This barn-like restaurant, hidden behind a petrol station at the northern entrance to town, is ideal for a filling lunch. It's well known locally and gets very busy as everyone from groups of labourers to smartly dressed office workers stops by for their midday meal. The €12 *menú* includes three courses of homey cooking with soup starters, grilled meat mains and refreshing fruit salads.

Los Albardinales   ANDALUCIAN €€
(📞950 61 17 07; www.losalbardinales.com; Carretera N340A, Km 474; mains €13-22; ⊙9am-6pm Fri-Wed, dinner by reservation only; 🅿) 🌱 Some 2km east of Tabernas, Los Albardinales is an award-winning organic olive-oil producer. At this, their roadside mill, you can see how the oil is pressed and sample it at their excellent farmhouse restaurant. Expect earthy regional cuisine, prepared with locally sourced ingredients, accompanied by fine organic wines.

❶ Getting There & Away

Tabernas is about 35km north of Almería, accessible via the A7 and N340A roads.

Up to six weekday Alsa buses run from Almería to Tabernas (€2.58, 40 minutes). Weekend services are much reduced (one on Saturday, three on Sunday).

Níjar

POP 28,580

Níjar, a pristine white town in the foothills of the Sierra Alhamilla, is best known for its glazed pottery and handwoven rugs known as *jarapas*. These are widely available in shops and showrooms on the main drag, Avenida García Lorca, and in the old potters' quarter, the Barrio Alfarero. Shopping apart, the town has a quaint old town, centred on leafy Plaza La Glorieta, and huge views from its signature monument, the Atalaya watchtower.

◉ Sights

Plaza La Glorieta PLAZA

The central square in Níjar's hilltop centre, delightful Plaza La Glorieta is surrounded by trees and overlooked by the 16th-century Iglesia de Santa María de la Anunciación.

🛏 Sleeping & Eating

★**Cortijo de la Alberca** CASA RURAL €€

(☑ 678 841248; www.cortijolaalberca.com; Camino de Huebro; s €35-90, d €50-120, tr €90-140; P🅿🛜🐾) ✔ In a 250-year-old farmhouse nestled amidst fruit trees, this tranquil refuge promises peace and traditional country accommodation. Its eight thickly walled rooms, each with its own terrace, are spacious and rustic, with Moroccan lamps, wood-and-cane ceilings and tiled floors. Terrific breakfasts are included in the rates.

The Cortijo is 900m from Níjar – follow signs for 'Huebro'.

La Mandila SPANISH €

(Calle Parque 17; mains €7-12, menú €12; ⊙8.30am-midnight) A popular local haunt with pavement seating and a traditional wooden bar, this casual eatery is one of several in the upper part of town. It's good throughout the day, serving everything from breakfast *tostadas* to pizzas, tapas and flavoursome seafood dishes.

🛍 Shopping

Avenida García Lorca is lined with shops selling pottery, woven rugs, esparto-grass baskets and the local *higo chumbo* liquor, produced from the prickly pear cactus (though not all of these goods are made in Níjar). For the workshops and showrooms of local potters, head down Calle Las Eras into the Barrio Alfarero (Potters' Quarter).

La Tienda de los Milagros CERAMICS

(☑ 645 504162; www.latiendadelosmilagros.com; Callejón del Artesano 1; ⊙10am-10pm) This is the workshop of British ceramicist Matthew Weir and Spanish artisan Isabel Hernández, who produces artistic *jarapa* (cotton-rag) rugs. As well as quality ceramics, Matthew makes woodblock prints and works with stoneware and porcelain. The workshop is just off Calle Las Eras in the Barrio Alfarero.

ℹ Information

Oficina Municipal de Turismo (☑ 950 61 22 43; Plaza del Mercado 1; ⊙10am-2pm Tue-Sun & 4-6pm Tue-Sat) Níjar's official tourist office.

Tourist Office (Nijarate; ☑ 950 36 01 23; Plaza García Blanes; ⊙10am-8.30pm) Part shop, part tourist office.

ℹ Getting There & Away

Níjar is 4km north of the A7, 30km northeast of Almería. There are parking bays all the way up Avenida Lorca.

Five Alsa (p300) buses head here from Almería (€1.95, 1¼ to 1½ hours) Monday to Friday, with three on Saturday and two on Sunday.

LIGHTS, CAMERA, ACTION

International film-makers have long been drawn to Almería's harsh desert landscapes. Most famously, director Sergio Leone teamed up with Clint Eastwood et al in the mid-1960s to shoot his 'spaghetti westerns' in the Desierto de Tabernas (p301). But the Italian wasn't the first to film in the area. A few years earlier, David Lean had brought the production of his 1962 epic *Lawrence of Arabia* to the province, filming at various locations including the Playa de los Genoveses (p308). A second beach, the Playa de Mónsul (p308), later featured in *Indiana Jones and the Last Crusade* (1989), serving as the backdrop for a scene in which Sean Connery brings down a plane with a flock of birds.

Almería city has also staged its fair share of drama. It doubled as Palermo and Messina in the WWII classic *Patton* (1970) and has hosted shoots for the sixth season of *Game of Thrones* – the Alcazaba (p293) appears as Sunspear, the capital of Dorne.

Other movies filmed in the province include *Cleopatra* (1963); *2001: A Space Odyssey (1968); Conan the Barbarian* (1982); *Never Say Never Again* (1983); and *The Girl with the Dragon Tattoo* (2009).

SORBAS

Dramatically perched on a rocky gorge overlooking the Río de Adeguar, Sorbas is a small, attractive town known for its traditional pottery. Its main drawcard is its network of caves, the Cuevas de Sorbas, protected as part of the 24-sq-km Paraje Natural Karst en Yesos de Sorbas (Sorbas Gypsum Karst Natural Area).

By road, Sorbas is 60km northeast of Almería, 36km west of Mojácar, and 33km northeast of Níjar. Two daily Alsa (p300) buses run between Almería and Sorbas (€4.75, one hour) except on Saturday, when there's just one.

Cuevas de Sorbas (✆950 36 47 04; www.cuevasdesorbas.com; basic tour adult/child €15/10.50; ◷tours 10am-1pm year-round & 3-7pm summer, 4-6pm spring, 4-5pm winter & autumn; 🅿🚻) These rare and spectacular caves, 2km east of Sorbas, are part of a vast network of underground galleries and tunnels. Guided visits lead through the labyrinthine underworld, revealing glittering gypsum crystals, tranquil ponds, stalactites, stalagmites and dark, mysterious tunnels. The basic tour, suitable for everyone from children to seniors, lasts about 1½ hours. Tours need to be reserved at least one day ahead; English- and German-speaking guides are available.

Centro de Visitantes Los Yesares (✆950 36 45 63; Calle Terraplén; ◷10am-2pm & 4-7pm Tue-Sun Apr-Sep & Wed-Sat Oct, 10am-2.30pm Wed-Sun Mar & Nov, 10am-2.30pm Thu-Sun Feb & Dec) It's worth taking a moment to stop off at this visitor centre at the entrance to Sorbas. As well as providing local information, it has three small exhibition rooms illustrating the area's karstic geology, with panels in English and Spanish and a mock-up of a cave.

Almond Reef (✆950 36 90 97; www.almondreef.co.uk; Calle Los Josefos, Cariatiz; incl breakfast s/d/f/ste €40/60/77/99; 🅿🛜🏊) A tranquil hideaway in the sleepy hamlet of Cariatiz, 8km northeast of Sorbas. Run by an English couple, it's a cosy spot with seven rustic rooms in a whitewashed farmhouse, a small pool, and a four-bed cottage to rent. As well as breakfast, dinner is also available. To get there take the Cariatiz turning off the N340A and follow 'Todas Direcciones' and 'Ecomuseo Cariatiz' signs till you reach the square with the Ecomuseo. Almond Reef is 300m up the road from there.

Un Sitio (✆950 36 48 24; N340A, Paraje El Pocico; tapas €1.50, menú del día €12; ◷10am-5pm & 8pm-midnight Tue-Sat, 10am-10pm Sun) About 1.5km east of town on the main N340A road, this casual roadside eatery is recommended locally. It looks fairly ordinary from outside but the hearty Spanish food – the *conejo* (rabbit) is something of a local speciality – hits the mark nicely, and service is friendly and professional.

LAS ALPUJARRAS DE ALMERÍA

The Almerían part of Las Alpujarras (the Sierra Nevada's southern foothills and valleys) is much less visited than its Granada counterpart (p282) – and admittedly less spectacular – but it's still a very pretty part of the world. White villages, clustered around large churches that are mostly former mosques, are strung along the valley of the Río Andarax between the mountains of the Sierra Nevada to the north and Sierra de Gádor to the south. Approaching from Almería, the landscape is at first rather barren, but the land gradually becomes more lush, with lemon and orange orchards and vineyards producing plenty of Almerian wine.

Los Millares ARCHAEOLOGICAL SITE
(✆677 903404; AL3411; ◷10am-2pm Wed-Sun; 🅿) FREE Los Millares, reckoned one of Europe's most important Copper Age sites, occupies a plateau above the Río Andarax some 20km north of Almería. Dusty and exposed, it contains the scant remains of a fortified metalworking settlement that stood here between 3200 and 2200 BC. Excavations, which began in the early 20th century, have unearthed outlines of defensive walls, stone houses and domed graves. Also of note is a series of recreated huts and workshops.

Before heading onto the site, take a moment to bone up on its history at the small interpretation centre by the entrance (signage is in Spanish, English and German).

The site is 1km off the A348, 3km before Alhama de Almería.

OHANES

The drive up to **Ohanes** – an isolated, whitewashed hamlet wedged into vertiginous, terraced slopes – is as worthwhile as the visit itself. The snaking road up from the A348 winds past stark red rock until it curves around a ridge into the upper Ohanes valley, where the scenery changes completely, to green terraces and flourishing vineyards. Continuing past the village down the steep west side of the valley, you'll enjoy further splendid views of the terraced fields. This route back to the A348 is shorter than the ascent, but slightly more nerve-racking, dwindling to one lane as it zigzags down through the fields. It comes out just west of Canjáyar.

Laujar de Andarax

POP 1550 / ELEV 906M

Overlooked by foreboding hills and surrounded by vineyards, Laujar de Andarax is the 'capital' of the Almería Alpujarras. It was here that Boabdil, the last emir of Granada, settled briefly after losing Granada, and where Aben Humeya, the leader of the doomed 1568–70 *morisco* (Christians converted from Islam) uprising, had his main base. These days, Laujar is a laid-back wine town with a handsome town hall and a formidable 17th-century church, the towering **Iglesia de la Encarnación**.

👁 Sights & Activities

Mirador de Laujar　　　　　　　VIEWPOINT
A hairy drive up a steep, snaking road leads to this terrific viewing platform 3.2km above town. From here you can look down on the full sweep of the valley – and beyond to the remote mountains that curtain it. To get to the site from the western end of town, follow signs to the Recreation Area ('Área Recreativa') and, shortly after, to the Mirador.

Cortijo El Cura　　　　　　　　WINERY
(☑950 52 40 26; www.cortijoelcura.com; ⊗9am-2pm & 4-7pm; 🅿) 🍷 A rare organic vineyard, family-run El Cura produces prize-winning wines from native Alpujarras grapes. To learn more and sample some of their wares, sign up for one of their weekend **guided tours** (check the website for details). The winery, which enjoys a bucolic farmhouse setting, is signposted off the A348, 3km west of Laujar.

Bodega Valle de Laujar　　　　WINERY
(☑950 51 42 00; www.bodegasvallelaujar.es; Carretera AL5402; ⊗8am-2pm & 3.30-7pm; 🅿) **FREE** This established wine producer is a good place to pick up a bottle or two, along with gourmet treats: jams, cheeses, sausages, hams and honey. You'll find it on the western access road into Laujar from the A348.

El Nacimiento Waterfalls　　　WATERFALL
Just east of Laujar's main plaza, a signposted road heads 1.5km north to El Nacimiento, a shaded recreation area set around a series of waterfalls. It's not at its best in high summer – the water flow can dry up then – but for most of the rest of the year it's a popular weekend haunt.

Sendero del Aguadero　　　　　WALKING
The Sendero del Aguadero (PRA37) is a lovely path up through woodlands of alder, pine and chestnut. The whole trail is a circular route of 14km (about five hours), climbing and descending more than 600m, but you can double back whenever you like. Look out for wild boar and hoopoes (black-and-white birds with elaborate orange crests). The path starts around 1km from El Nacimiento waterfalls.

🛏 Sleeping & Eating

Hotel Almirez　　　　　　　　HOTEL **€**
(☑655 573204, 950 51 35 14; www.hotelalmirez.es; Carretera AL5402; s €43, d €52-60, q €100-112; 🅿❄🛜) 🍷 A friendly, family-run hotel set in its own grounds off Laujar's western access road. Its spotless, spacious rooms are plainly furnished but each comes with a terrace offering lovely views of the verdant surrounds.

Fonda Nuevo Andarax　　ANDALUCIAN **€**
(☑950 51 31 13; Calle Villaespesa 43; mains €8-15; ⊗8am-6pm) A no-frills restaurant and bar on the main drag through town, with good valley panoramas from its bright dining room. It's a good bet for *raciones* of *embutidos* (sausages and cured meats) and various local specialities, such as kid goat in almond sauce.

Bar Rodríguez　　　　　ANDALUCIAN **€€**
(☑950 51 31 10; Calle San Miguel 1; mains €7-15; ⊗7am-midnight) This convivial bar near Plaza Mayor is as genuine as they come, the sort of place where locals come to catch up on gossip over a beer and a bite to eat. Its tiny kitchen produces wonderful plates of tradi-

tional food, ranging from spicy *chorizo* sausage to helpings of finger-lickinging good fried squid.

ℹ Information

Centro de Visitantes Laujar de Andarax
(☑ 950 51 55 35; Carretera AL5402; ⏰ 9.30am-2.30pm Thu-Sun & 5-8pm Fri & Sat Apr-Sep, 10am-2.30pm Thu-Sun & 4-6pm Fri & Sat Oct-Mar) On Laujar's western access road, 1.5km from the town centre.

ℹ Getting There & Away

Three Alsa (p300) buses run from Almería to Laujar (€6.36, two to 2¼ hours) Monday to Friday, and one on Saturday and Sunday. To continue on to the Granada Alpujarras you'll have to travel via Berja (€2.10, 40 to 55 minutes, two daily Monday to Friday, one daily Saturday and Sunday), south of Laujar; it's most practical if you start on the 7.50am bus (Monday to Friday only) from Laujar to Berja.

COSTA DE ALMERÍA

Almeria's coastline is one of Andalucia's great natural wonders. Encompassing heavenly beaches, plunging cliffs and wild tracts of arid scrubland, it has largely escaped unsightly development and remains an unspoilt and relatively unexplored part of the region. Hot spots include the Parque Natural de Cabo de Gata-Níjar to the southeast and, to the north, Mojácar, a quaint hilltop *pueblo* with a vibrant beachfront scene.

Parque Natural de Cabo de Gata-Níjar

Extending southeast of Almería, the Parque Natural de Cabo de Gata-Níjar (www.dega ta.com/en) has some of Spain's most flawless and least crowded beaches. The park, which stretches from Retamar in the west up to Agua Amarga in the east, encompasses 340 sq km of dramatic cliff-bound coastline and stark semidesert terrain punctuated by remote white villages and isolated farmsteads. Adding to the often eerie atmosphere are the abandoned mines and bizarre rock formations that litter the landscape.

There is plenty to do in the area besides enjoying the beaches and walking: diving, snorkelling, kayaking, sailing, cycling, horse riding, and 4WD and boat tours are all popular. A host of operators offers these activities from the coastal villages during Easter and from July to September, though only a few carry on year-round.

The park's main hub is San José, a popular resort on the east coast.

☞ Tours

El Cabo a Fondo BOATING
(☑ 637 449170; www.elcaboafondo.es; 1½hr tour adult/child €25/20) Some of the most spectacular views of the Cabo de Gata coast are from the sea – a perspective you'll get on Cabo a Fondo's outings, which start from La Isleta del Moro, Las Negras or La Fabriquilla. Tours

---

ALMERÍA: THE GREENHOUSE OF EUROPE

As much a feature of Almería's landscape as its arid badlands and remote beaches are the plastic-covered *invernaderos* (greenhouses) that sprawl across the province. West of Almería city, for example, the entire 35km-long coastal plain from Roquetas de Mar to Adra is coated in grey-white polythene. Such is the size of this sea of plastic that sunbeams reflected off it are said to have caused the local climate to cool.

Almería province has long supported agriculture. Its mountainsides have been farmed for centuries after the Moors built a complex system of terraces and irrigation channels a millennium or so ago. But it wasn't until the introduction of year-round greenhouse cultivation in the late 20th century that this previously dirt-poor part of Spain started to profit from its agricultural endeavours. Now produce grown in the province accounts for some 37% of Spain's vegetable exports, including around half its tomato sales, with a value of more than €2 billion.

Given this, it's not surprising that tomatoes are a staple on menus across the region. In summer, mountain-grown, sun-ripened tomatoes are delectable. In winter, look out for *tomate Raf*, a greenish heirloom variety with a sweet taste and segmented surface.

But away from the restaurants and supermarkets, there's another, less savoury, side to the story. Reports in the international press have highlighted the plight of greenhouse workers, drawing attention to the exploitation of the largely immigrant labour force and the appalling living and working conditions endured by many labourers.

Parque Natural de Cabo de Gata-Níjar

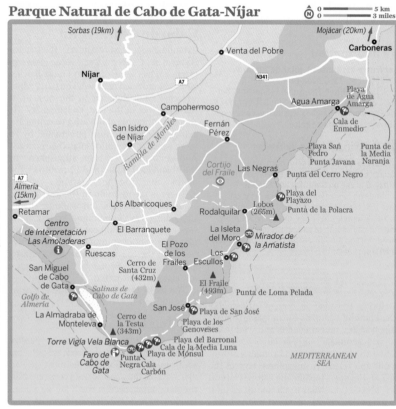

run up to seven times daily and are offered year-round, weather permitting (minimum numbers may be needed in low season). Reservations required.

ℹ Information

Centro de Información (☎950 38 02 99; www. cabodegata-nijar.com; Avenida San José 27; ⊙10am-2pm & 5.30-8.30pm Apr-Oct, to 2pm Nov-Mar) Park information centre in San José.

Centro de Interpretación Las Amoladeras (☎950 16 04 35; Carretera Retamar-Pujaire, Km 7; ⊙10am-2pm Wed-Sun) The park's main visitor centre, 2km west of Ruescas on the main road from Almería.

ℹ Getting There & Away

Alsa (p300) runs at least six daily buses from Almería's Estación Intermodal to San Miguel de Cabo de Gata (€2.90, one hour), and one to Las Negras (€2.90, 1¼ hours) and Rodalquilar (€2.90, 1½ hours).

Autocares Bernardo (☎950 25 04 22; www. autocaresbernardo.com) operates buses from Almería to San José (€2.90, 1¼ hours, two to four daily).

Autocares Frahermar (☎950 26 64 11; www. frahermar.com) runs a single bus from Almería to Agua Amarga (about €5.50, 1¼ hours) daily in July and August, and every day except Tuesday and Thursday for the rest of the year.

San Miguel de Cabo de Gata & Around

Salinas de Cabo de Gata   LAGOON

Southeast of San Miguel de Cabo de Gata, some of Spain's last surviving salt-extraction lagoons draw flocks of migrating flamingos and other waterbirds between spring and autumn: by late August there can be a thousand flamingos there. To spy on them, search out the strategically sited birdwatching hides.

Faro de Cabo de Gata   LIGHTHOUSE

Marking the southwest point of the promontory, this photogenic lighthouse commands stirring views of a jagged volcanic reef known as the **Arrecife de las Sirenas** (Reef of the Mermaids), after the monk seals that used to lounge here. From the site, a side road runs 3km up to the **Torre Vigía Vela Blanca**, an 18th-century watchtower boasting even more coastal vistas.

Camping Cabo de Gata   CAMPGROUND €

(☑ 950 16 04 43; www.campingcabodegata.com; Carretera Cabo de Gata, Cortijo Ferrón; 2 people, tent & car €23-27, bungalows €70-150; P ✻ 🛜 ☎) The excellent Camping Cabo de Gata offers year-round tent pitches and two-to-four-person bungalows – many newly built and equipped with air-con and smart, IKEA-style furniture. Situated about 4km north of San Miguel de Cabo de Gata, it has all the necessary amenities, including a restaurant, shop and swimming pool.

San José

POP 4440

The main beach resort in the Parque Natural de Cabo de Gata-Níjar, San José makes a wonderful base for exploring the area. It's well set up with hotels and restaurants and the surrounding coastline harbours a string of sublime beaches, most within easy striking distance.

🏃 Activities

The cold, clear waters off Cabo de Gata offer superlative diving (and snorkelling), rivalled in southern Spain only by Cabo de Palos in Murcia. The posidonia seagrass meadows are proof of water cleanliness, and along with caves, rocks and canyons they provide a habitat for many marine animals, including eagle rays, sunfish, moray and conger eels, grouper, angelfish and barracuda. A highlight for experienced divers is the wreck *El Vapor,* 1.8km off the Faro de Cabo de Gata.

There are dive centres in San José, La Isleta del Moro, Rodalquilar, Las Negras, Agua Amarga and Carboneras.

Isub   DIVING

(☑ 950 38 00 04; www.isubsanjose.com; Calle Babor 8; ⊙ 8.30am-2pm & 4.30-7pm Mon-Sat, 8.30am-2pm Sun Mar-Dec) PADI-certified Isub runs dives for beginners (€75) and qualified divers (from €33, or €47 with equipment hire) as well as snorkelling outings (€25 to €30). Equipment is available to hire.

MedialunAventura   WATER SPORTS, MOUNTAIN BIKING

(☑ 950 38 04 62; www.medialunaventura.com; Calle del Puerto 7; kayak/SUP per hour €10/12, bike hire per half-day/day €13/18; ⊙ 10am-2pm & 5-8pm year-round, to 10pm summer) This year-round outfit offers a range of activities: kayak and mountain-bike hire and guided trips; SUP (stand-up paddle) rental and tuition; boat trips (two hours with snorkelling €34); and diving (from €75).

🛏 Sleeping

You'll need to book early for the peak periods of Semana Santa, July and August. Many places close for a few months in winter; most offer discounts outside high season.

La Posada de Paco   HOTEL €€

(☑ 950 38 00 10; www.laposadadepaco.com; Avenida de San José 12; d €61-150; ⊙ closed Nov-Feb; P ✻ 🛜 ☎) With a convenient central location, gleaming tiled rooms and a

---

WALKING THE CABO DE GATA COAST

An extensive network of roads and trails runs for about 50km along the coast from San Miguel de Cabo de Gata to Agua Amarga. The full hike requires three days and should only be attempted in spring or, even better, autumn (when the sea is warm), as the summer heat is fierce and there is no shade. But you can embark on sections of the walk for a day or afternoon, using buses to reach some of the beaches you'll pass are otherwise inaccessible.

Southwest from San José it's a fine 9km walk of about 2½ hours (passing some of the best beaches) to the Torre Vigía Vela Blanca, an old lookout tower with superb panoramas. Northeast from San José, there are further views to be enjoyed on the fairly level 8km hike to the tiny beach settlement of **Los Escullos**. The route, which partly follows old mining roads, skirts the ancient volcano **El Fraile**.

Another good stretch is from Rodalquilar to **Playa del Playazo**, then up the coast along cliff edges to **Las Negras** (6km from Rodalquilar). It's another 3km to the real prize: Playa San Pedro (p308) – inaccessible by road – with its small settlement of boho travellers. You can also drive to Las Negras and walk to Playa San Pedro from there.

CABO DE GATA BEACHES

Cabo de Gata's best beaches are strung along the south and east coasts, with some of the most beautiful southwest of San José. A dirt road signposted 'Playas' and/or 'Genoveses/Mónsul' runs to them from San José. However, from mid-June to mid-September, the road is closed to cars once the beach car parks (€5) fill up, typically by about 10am, but a bus (€1 one way) runs from town every half hour from 9am to 9pm.

The first beach outside of San José is **Playa de los Genoveses**, a 1km stretch of sand where the Genoese navy landed in 1147 to help the Christian attack on Almería. A further 2.5km on, pristine **Playa de Mónsul** is another glorious spot – you may recognise the large free-standing rock on the sand from the film *Indiana Jones and the Last Crusade*. Tracks behind the large dune at Mónsul's east end lead down to nudist **Playa del Barronal** (600m from the road). If you bear left just before Barronal, and work your way over a little pass just left of the highest hillock, you'll come to **El Lance del Perro**. This beach, with striking basalt rock formations, is the first of four gorgeous, isolated beaches called the **Calas del Barronal**. Tides permitting, you can walk round the foot of the cliffs from one to the next.

A little west of Playa de Mónsul, paths lead from the road to two other less-frequented beaches, **Cala de la Media Luna** and **Cala Carbón**.

San José has a busy sandy beach of its own, and to the northeast there are reasonable beaches at **Los Escullos** and **La Isleta del Moro**. Much finer is **Playa del Playazo**, a broad, sandy strip between two headlands 3.5km east of Rodalquilar (the last 2km along a drivable track from the main road) or 2.5km south of Las Negras via a coastal footpath.

Las Negras, which has its own part-sandy, part-stony beach, is also a gateway to the fabulous **Playa San Pedro** (Las Negras), 3km to the northeast. Set between dramatic headlands and home to a small New Age settlement, this fabled beach can be reached only on foot or by boat (€12 return) from Las Negras.

Further up the coast, the small resort of **Agua Amarga** is fronted by a popular sandy beach. A short but steep 1.5km trek to the southwest leads to **Cala de Enmedio** (Agua Amarga), a pretty, secluded beach enclosed between eroded rocks.

sunny, summery feel, Paco's scores across the board. Rooms, which come in various sizes and colours, have their own terraces, some of which offer sea views, and there's a decent range of facilities including a spa, gym, breakfast cafe and pool.

Aloha Playa HOSTAL €€
(☎950 61 10 50; www.pensionaloha.com; Calle Cala Higuera; r €60-90; ⊘closed Dec-Feb; ❄❤☁) This friendly, family-run *hostal* is one of the best deals in town. It's a modest place, but its plainly furnished white rooms are light and airy, there's a great pool out back, and it's within easy walking distance of the beach.

⭐**MC San José** BOUTIQUE HOTEL €€€
(☎950 61 11 11; www.hotelesmcsanjose.com; Calle El Faro 2; r incl breakfast €92-220; ⊘closed Nov-Feb; 🅿❄❤☁) The MC offers the best of both worlds – warm family hospitality and a chic, designer look. Inside, it's all sharp modern furniture, cool whites and slate-greys, while outside the plant-lined terrace and small pool are ideal for basking in the sun.

Come the evening, you can relax over a glass of local Almería wine at the bodega, and dine on Mediterranean cuisine at the in-house restaurant.

🍴 Eating & Drinking

⭐**4 Nudos** SEAFOOD €€
(☎620 938160; Club Náutico, Puerto Deportivo; mains €15-20; ⊘9am-5pm & 7.30pm-midnight Tue-Sun) Of San José's various seafood restaurants, the 'Four Knots' is the star performer. Aptly housed in the Club Náutico at the marina, it serves classic Spanish dishes – paella included – alongside more innovative creations such as baby-prawn ceviche and tuna marinated in soy sauce, ginger and rosemary. Reservations advised except at the quietest times.

La Gallineta MEDITERRANEAN €€
(☎950 38 05 01; El Pozo de los Frailes; mains €11-27; ⊘1.30-3.30pm & 9-11pm, closed dinner Sun & Mon) An elegant restaurant in the village of El Pozo do los Frailes, 4km north of San José, La Gallineta is a hit with city escapees who make the drive out for its innovative,

outward-looking cuisine. Menu highlights include ravioli stuffed with foie gras and carpaccio of red prawns. Book two or three days ahead at Easter or in July and August.

Casa Miguel SPANISH €€
(☎950 38 03 29; www.restaurantecasamiguel.es; Avenida de San José 43-45; mains €10-20; ⏲1-4.30pm & 7.30-11.30pm Tue-Sun) Service and food are reliably good at this long-standing San José favourite, one of several places with outdoor seating on the main drag. There's plenty to choose from on the extensive menu but you'll rarely go wrong ordering the grilled fish of the day.

Abacería BAR
(☎950 38 01 73; Calle del Puerto 3; ⏲11am-4pm & 7-11.30pm, closed Tue & Wed winter) Search out this cosy bar for a taste of the local wine. It looks the part with its burgundy walls, blackboards and high wooden stools, and has a decent selection of Almería labels and craft beers – best enjoyed with a side plate of cheese and cured ham.

La Isleta del Moro

Buceo en Cabo de Gata DIVING
(☎664 534200; www.buceoencabodegata.es; Calle Cala Stay 1; ⏲9am-8pm) This outfit based in La Isleta del Moro, 12km northeast of San José, offers a range of dives, costing from €30 per person.

Casa Café de la Loma MEDITERRANEAN, BASQUE €€
(☎950 38 98 31; www.casacafelaloma.com; mains €10-30; ⏲7pm-1am Jul & Aug; ✎) A Mediterranean haven with great sea views, this old *cortijo* (farmstead) is an enchanted spot for a relaxed summer dinner. Fresh fish and local meats are the headline act but the menu also lists creative salads and other vegetarian dishes. Regular jazz and flamenco concerts add to the atmosphere. Look for the turn-off just north of La Isleta del Moro. The 200-year-old house has been restored in Al-Andalus style and offers six simply furnished **rooms** (s €40, d €50-65; P 📶) as well as terrific views.

Rodalquilar

Until not long ago the tiny village of Rodalquilar was a ghost town, its few residents hanging on among the shells of its abandoned gold mines. However, since the 1990s it has undergone something of a makeover, thanks in part to the transfer of the Parque Natural's headquarters here, and nowadays it attracts a steady stream of visitors. Most come to explore its former gold mine but it also has an excellent botanical garden and many buildings sport large murals, lending it something of a bohemian air.

Sights

Mirador de la Amatista VIEWPOINT
(P) On the main road between La Isleta del Moro and Rodalquilar, this high viewpoint commands breathtaking views of the vertiginous, unspoilt coastline. From here the road snakes down into the basin of the Rodalquilar valley.

Gold Mines RUINS
(P) Set amid the Martian red-rock terrain at the top of the village, the skeletal remains of Rodalquilar's gold mines are an eerie sight. The complex, which was fully operational as recently as the mid-20th century, lies abandoned – and you're free to explore its former crushing towers and decantation tanks.

To get an insight into the area's mining history, stop first at **La Casa de los Volcanes** (Calle Apartadero; ⏲10am-2pm Thu-Sat; P) FREE, a small museum with displays on the mines and the geology of Cabo de Gata.

Beyond the mines, a rough dirt road continues through the hills, pocked with abandoned mines and the ruined miners' hamlet of **San Diego**. Rather than attempt this road by car, you'd be better off taking the **Sendero Cerro del Cinto**, an 11km walking trail that traverses the striking postindustrial landscape.

Jardín Botánico El Albardinal GARDENS
(☎971 56 12 26; Calle Fundición; ⏲9am-2pm Tue-Fri, 10am-2pm & 4-6pm Sat & Sun; P) FREE Rodalquilar's extensive botanical gardens showcase the vegetation of Andalucía's arid southeast. It's well planned, with every plant, tree and shrub identified. There's also a charming *huerta* (vegetable garden), complete with jam recipes and a scarecrow.

El Cortijo del Fraile HISTORIC BUILDING
(P) This abandoned farmstead on a windswept plain 6km northwest of Rodalquilar was the scene of the tragic, true-life love-and-revenge story that inspired Federico García Lorca's best-known play, *Blood Wedding*. In 1928, in what's known as El Crimen de Níjar (the Níjar Crime), a woman due to be married here disappeared with another man, who was then shot dead by the brother of the jilted groom. The romantically ruined 18th-century buildings are now fenced off but maintain a suitably doom-laden aura.

To get to the Cortijo, take the ALP824 road (which soon becomes a dirt track) from Los Albaricoques to Rodalquilar and follow it for about 7km.

🛏 Sleeping & Eating

El Jardín de los Sueños
CASA RURAL €€

(☑669 184118, 950 38 98 43; www.eljardindelossue nos.es; Calle Los Gorriones; incl breakfast d €76-98, ste €96-140; 🅿❄🛜🌊) Just outside Rodalquilar, signposted off the main road, this year-round retreat is ideal for getting away from it all. The main farmhouse is surrounded by a beautiful garden of dry-climate plants and fruit trees, some of which contribute to the substantial breakfasts. Inside, the rooms are notable for bright colours, original art, private terraces and the absence of TVs.

Oro y Luz
ANDALUCIAN €€

(☑950 80 88 19; www.oroyluz.com; Paraje Los Albacetes; mains €10-16; ⊙7-10.45pm Mon-Wed, 1-4pm & 8-11.15pm Thu-Sun) This smart resort restaurant impresses with its cool, minimalist white decor, terrace views and modern brand of regional cuisine. Seafood such as marinated squid and tuna *tataki* (seasoned with vinegar and ginger and lightly seared) stars on the menu, alongside a series of rich meaty mains.

Las Negras

Restaurante La Palma
SEAFOOD €€

(☑950 38 80 42; Calle Bahía de Las Negras 21; mains €10-35; ⊙9am-11:30pm) The sound of waves breaking on the pebble beach provides the soundtrack to meals at this jaunty seafront restaurant in Las Negras. Seafood is an obvious highlight, ideally eaten on the outdoor terrace, but you can also dine on roast meats and rice dishes.

Agua Amarga

POP 400

A tiny fishing village turned low-key resort, Agua Amarga is a favourite with Spanish urbanites and Scandinavian sun-seekers. It's a sleepy spot for much of the year but bursts into life in July and August, when holidaymakers flock to its fine, sandy beach and casual seafront restaurants.

🛏 Sleeping & Eating

Hotel Senderos
HOTEL €€

(☑950 13 80 87; www.hotelsenderos.com; Calle Pueblecico 1; s €59-105, d €79-135; ❄🛜🌊) Like everywhere in Agua Amarga, the Senderos hides its charms behind a cool white exterior.

Inside it reveals spacious, light-filled rooms with polished marble floors and big, firm beds. There's public parking just outside and the beach is about two minutes' walk away.

⭐MiKasa
BOUTIQUE HOTEL €€€

(☑950 13 80 73; www.mikasasuites.com; Carretera Carboneras 20; d incl breakfast €130-240; 🅿❄🛜🌊) An enchanting romantic retreat. A few blocks back from the beach (but still within easy walking distance), it's a lovely villa set up with charming, individually styled rooms, two pools, a spa and a beach bar. Room rates drop considerably outside August.

La Palmera
SEAFOOD €€

(☑950 13 82 08; www.hostalrestaurantelapalm era.com; Calle Aguada 4; mains €9-20; ⊙noon-11pm; ❄) Seafood on the beach is one of Agua Amarga's specialities and this breezy, beachfront restaurant is ideally situated to provide it. Bag a table on the terrace and dig into hearty bowls of mussels and grilled cuttlefish. The restaurant also has several simple sea-facing guest rooms (€90).

⭐Restaurante La Villa
MEDITERRANEAN €€€

(☑950 13 80 90; Carretera Carboneras 18; mains €15-25; ⊙8pm-midnight Jun-Sep, closed Mon & Tue Oct-Dec & Mar-May, closed Jan & Feb) La Villa is a sophisticated Agua Amarga restaurant with a romantically lit dining room and an elegant outdoor terrace. Dishes are original and artfully presented, ranging from Tex-Mex starters to steak tartare and gourmet black-Angus burgers. Reservations advised.

Mojácar

POP 6490

Both a massively popular beach resort and a charming hill town, Mojácar is divided into two quite separate parts. Mojácar Pueblo is the attractive historic centre, a picturesque jumble of white-cube houses daubed down an inland hilltop. Some 3km away on the coast, Mojácar Playa is its young offspring, a modern low-rise resort fronting a 7km-long sandy beach. As recently as the 1960s, Mojácar was decaying and almost abandoned. But a savvy mayor managed to resurrect its fortunes by luring artists and travellers to the area with offers of free land – which brought a distinct bohemian air that endures to this day.

◉ Sights

The main sight is Mojácar's hilltop *pueblo*, with its whitewashed houses, charming plazas, bars and cafes. To reach the *pueblo* from

Mojácar Pueblo

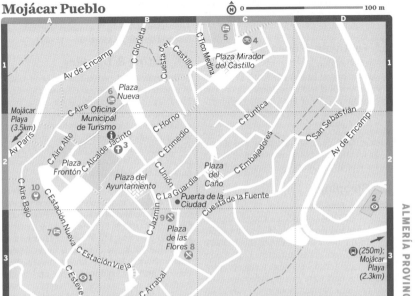

the *playa* turn inland at the roundabout by the Parque Comercial, a large shopping centre towards the north end of the beach. Regular buses also connect the two.

Mirador del Castillo VIEWPOINT

(Plaza Mirador del Castillo, Mojácar Pueblo) Perched on the highest point in town – originally the site of a castle and now home to the hotel El Mirador del Castillo (p312) – this hilltop mirador (viewpoint) looks down to the sea and over a hazy brown-green landscape studded with white buildings and stark volcanic cones just like the one Mojácar occupies.

Iglesia de Santa María CHURCH

(Calle Iglesia, Mojácar Pueblo; ⊙10am-1.30pm & 2.30-7.30pm) The fortress-style Iglesia de Santa María dates from 1560 and may have once been a mosque. Inside, its restrained white interior features a modern 1960s altar mural.

Casa La Canana HOUSE

(☑950 16 44 20; Calle Esteve 6, Mojácar Pueblo; €2.50; ⊙10.30am-2pm & 5.30-10pm Tue-Sat, 11am-3pm Sun) This recently opened house-museum recreates the dwelling of a well-to-do villager from the first half of the 20th century. The layout of the furniture reflects the interior decor of the period, while information panels, tools and model animals illustrate the household habits of the time.

Mojácar Pueblo

Beaches

With some 7km of sands, Mojácar Playa has room for everyone, as well as some excellent beachfront bars and restaurants. The best sands are at the southern end, which also has a pleasant seafront promenade.

To the south of the main beach, a 1.25km stretch of rocks gives onto a second, 1.25km-long beach overlooked by an 18th-century watchtower, the Castillo de Macenas. From the Castillo an unpaved track runs 3km along the coast passing several small coves, some of which have nudist beaches. Along the way you can climb the Torre Pirulico, a 13th-century defensive tower.

✨ Festivals & Events

Moros y Cristianos   CULTURAL
(☺weekend nearest 10 Jun) Mojácar's big annual event sees locals don costumes in dances, processions and other festivities to commemorate the Christian reconquest of the town.

Noche de San Juan   FIESTA
(Mojácar Playa; ☺23 Jun) Bonfires and dawn-to-dusk eating, drinking and dancing at this big beach party to mark the summer solstice.

🛏 Sleeping

★Hostal Arco Plaza   HOSTAL €
(☎950 47 27 77, 647 846275; www.hostalarcoplaza.es; Calle Aire 1, Mojácar Pueblo; d €39-45, tr €45-50; ❄@🤙) In the heart of the action, this friendly, good-value *hostal* has attractive blue rooms with wrought-iron beds and terracotta-tiled floors. The best have private balconies overlooking Plaza Nueva, though you can enjoy the same views from the communal rooftop terrace. The plaza can be noisy in the evening but generally quietens after midnight.

★Hostal El Olivar   HOSTAL €€
(☎950 47 20 02, 672 019767; www.hostalelolivar.es; Calle Estación Nueva 11, Mojácar Pueblo; incl breakfast s €44-59, d €54-89; ❄🤙) A stylish retreat in the historic centre, the Olivar has eight pearl-grey rooms furnished in a cool, modern style. Some overlook a plaza, others the mountains behind the *pueblo*. Breakfast is generous and you can take it on the panoramic roof terrace when the weather is decent.

El Mirador del Castillo   HOTEL €€
(☎694 454768; www.elmiradordelcastillo.com; Plaza Mirador del Castillo, Mojácar Pueblo; r €68-145, ste €136-145; ☺Easter-Oct; ❄🤙🏊) Right at the top of town, this delightful villa hotel offers five characterful rooms and suites with superb views, rustic dark-wood furniture and colourful paintings by local artists. Private terraces lead to a central garden and pool. Minimum stay is two nights.

Hotel El Puntazo   HOTEL €€
(☎950 47 82 65; www.hotelelpuntazo.com; Paseo del Mediterráneo 257, Mojácar Playa; four-star d €84-166, tr €108-190, one-star d €50-90; 🅿❄🤙🏊) A big seafront set-up in Mojácar Playa, El Puntazo is made up of two hotels, one a four-star, the other a more basic one-star. Rooms in the four-star are bright and

spacious, decked out in summery whites and greens; in the one-star they're smaller and more modestly furnished. All have access to the on-site swimming pool.

🍴 Eating & Drinking

Both *pueblo* and *playa* have a good range of eateries serving varied cuisines (Spanish, Mexican, Italian), though some close from about November to March. In summer, especially August, Mojácar nightlife is hopping, with a number of friendly, lively bars tucked into small houses in the *pueblo*. Down at the *playa,* action is centred on the many beach bars and clubs that front the sands.

Tito's Cantina   MEXICAN €
(☎950 47 88 41; www.facebook.com/lacantina.mojacar; Paseo del Mediterráneo, Mojácar Playa; mains €7-12; ☺7pm-midnight summer, 1-4pm & 7pm-midnight Thu-Sun winter; 🍴) 🚭 Sister restaurant to beachside Tito's, the Cantina is the real deal. Tito is from LA so he knows his Tex-Mex cuisine, and the colourful decor and bright craftworks make you feel like you're in…well, Mexico. Expect all the old favourites – enchiladas, quesadillas, fajitas, tacos and guacamole – plus enough tequila and Mexican beer to ensure a grand old time.

La Taberna   ANDALUCIAN €
(☎950 61 51 06; Plaza del Caño, Mojácar Pueblo; raciones €7-13; ☺noon-4pm & 6pm-midnight, closed Wed Sep-Jun) Beside the Puerta de la Ciudad in the heart of the whitewashed centre, La Taberna keeps its diners happy with an extensive selection of salads, tapas and *raciones*. A cosy place, its warren of intimate rooms is often full of chatter and happily full diners.

★Tito's   INTERNATIONAL €€
(☎950 61 50 30; Paseo del Mediterráneo 2, Mojácar Playa; mains €9.50-16; ☺10am-9pm Apr-Oct, to midnight late Jun–Aug; 🤙) Picture the ideal beachside bar and chances are it would look something like Tito's, a cane-canopied hangout set amid palm trees on the southern promenade. It's a wonderfully laid-back spot to sate your thirst on fresh-fruit cocktails and enjoy international, fusion-leaning food.

Arlequino   FUSION €€
(☎950 47 80 37; Plaza de las Flores, Mojácar Pueblo; mains €10-20; ☺1-4pm Wed-Sun & 7pm-2am daily) The mismatched bohemian decor and panoramic rooftop terrace pair well with the fusion Middle Eastern cuisine it serves. Vegetable samosas pave the way for mains such as lightly herbed lamb, elegantly presented on a slate-grey plate, and satisfyingly rich desserts.

Neptuno ANDALUCIAN €€

(☑616 005387; www.neptunomojacar.com; Paseo del Mediterráneo 62E, Mojácar Playa; mains €10-21; ☺10am-5pm & 7pm-midnight, closed evenings Sun-Thu Oct-May) One of the smartest, busiest and best regarded of the *chiringuitos* (beach restaurants) in Mojácar Playa. Specialities of the house are its barbecued meats and fresh fish, but there's also a decent selction of salads and rice dishes.

El Loro Azul BAR

(Plaza Frontón, Mojácar Pueblo; ☺6.30pm-2am Mon-Thu, to 3am Fri & Sat) Tucked into one of the *pueblo's* quirky white houses, the convivial 'Blue Parrot' mixes great mojitos to a jazz, soul, blues and rock 'n' roll soundtrack for an international crowd.

Aku Aku BEACH BAR

(☑950 47 89 81; www.akuakumojacar.com; Paseo del Mediterráneo 30, Mojácar Playa; ☺11am-2am Apr-Oct) The silky sands of Mojácar's beach set the evocative backdrop to free jazz and flamenco concerts at this, one of the many *chiringuitos* strung along the *playa*. Gigs, held in July and August, generally start at 11pm.

ⓘ Information

Oficina Municipal de Turismo (☑950 61 50 25; www.mojacar.es; Plaza Frontón, Mojácar Pueblo; ☺9.30am-2pm & 5-8pm Mon-Fri, 10am-2pm & 5-8pm Sat, 10am-2pm Sun) Up in Mojácar's hilltop *pueblo*.

Tourist Information Point (www.mojacar.es; Playa Villazar, Mojácar Playa; ☺10am-2pm daily & 5-8pm Mon-Sat) Down on the beach in front of the Parque Comercial (shopping centre).

ⓘ Getting There & Around

BUS

Intercity buses stop at various spots around the Parque Comercial roundabout in Mojácar Playa and on Avenida de Andalucía in Mojácar Pueblo.

Alsa (p300) runs buses to/from Almería (€7.67, 1¼ to 1¾ hours, two to four daily) and Murcia (€9.18, 2½ to three hours, three daily). Buy tickets at **Mojácar Tour** (☑950 47 57 57; Centro Comercial Montemar, Avenida de Andalucía; ☺10am-1.30pm & 5.30-8pm), a travel agency at the Parque Comercial in Mojácar Playa.

A local bus (€1.20) runs a circuit from Mojácar Pueblo along the full length of the beach and back again, roughly every half-hour from 9.15am to 11.35pm June to September, and until 9.15pm from October to May.

CAR & MOTORCYCLE

Follow the main road through the *pueblo* to reach two large parking lots on the far edge of town. Avoid the Plaza del Rey car park on Wednesday mornings, when it hosts a weekly market.

TAXI

Taxis wait in the *pueblo's* Plaza Nueva, or call 950 88 81 11.

LOS VÉLEZ

The beautiful mountain landscape of the remote Los Vélez district, in the northernmost part of Almería, is greener and more forested than most of the province. Three small towns – Vélez Rubio, Vélez Blanco and María – nestle in the shadow of the stark Sierra de María range, part of the Parque Natural Sierra María-Los Vélez. There's good walking in the area, as well as some celebrated rock art at the Cueva de los Letreros.

ⓘ Getting There & Away

Alsa (p300) runs one afternoon bus from Almería to Vélez Rubio (€14.75, 2¾ hours), Vélez Blanco (€15.25, three hours) and María (€16, 3¼ hours). The return service starts from María at 6am (6.30pm on Sundays). From Vélez Rubio, Alsa also runs buses to Granada (€14, two to three hours, three to four daily).

PARQUE NATURAL SIERRA MARÍA-LOS VÉLEZ

Encompassing 226 sq km of verdant mountain terrain in the north of Almería province, the Parque Natural Sierra María-Los Vélez is a glorious wilderness. Its rocky peaks are cloaked in forests of pine and holm oaks whilst overhead golden eagles and peregrine falcons patrol the silent skies. The area offers wonderful walking, with waymarked trails at their best in spring or autumn; pick up information at Vélez Blanco's Centro de Visitantes Almacén del Trigo (p314). A good circular trail is the 13km Sendero Solana de Maimón, which runs through the Sierra de Maimón hills southwest of Vélez Blanco.

Just west of the tiny upland town of María, off the A317, the 40-hectare Jardín Botánico Umbría de la Virgen (☺9am-3pm Tue-Sun May-Sep, 10am-4pm Tue-Sun Oct-Apr) FREE highlights the unique flora of the Sierra de María area and the Altiplano of Granada. From here, you can follow the circular, fairly easy 3km Sendero Umbría de la Virgen (about 1¾ hours).

Vélez Blanco

At 1070m, with its scramble of red-roofed houses, fairy-tale castle and sensational valley views, Vélez Blanco is the most appealing base among Los Vélez' three villages. On Wednesday mornings you can browse its lively street market on central Calle Corredera.

Sights

Cueva de los Letreros   CAVE
(☑694 467136; www.hazyenves.es; adult/child €2/1; ☻guided tours 7pm Wed, Sat & Sun Jun-Aug, 4.30pm Wed & Sat, noon Sun Sep-May; ℗) Of the several Unesco-protected cave-painting locations in the area, this Stone Age ceremonial site is the star. The reddish drawings, made before 5500 BC, show animals, a large horned figure dubbed *El Hechicero* (The Witchdoctor) and the *indalo*, a stick-person whose outspread arms are connected by an arc (possibly a bow), among other things. Visits are by guided tour only; these depart from the entrance to Pinar del Rey camping complex, about 1km south of Vélez Blanco off the A317.

Castillo de Vélez Blanco   CASTLE
(☻10am-2pm & 5-8pm Wed-Sun Apr-Sep, 10am-2pm & 4-6pm Oct-Mar; ℗) FREE The Disneyesque castle rising on a pinnacle high above Vélez Blanco's tiled roofs confronts the great sphinx-like butte La Muela (The Molar Tooth) across the valley as if in a bizarre duel. From the outside, the 16th-century castle is all Reconquista fortress, but inside it's pure Renaissance palace – or was until 1904, when the carved marble arcades, columns, doorways, window frames, statues and friezes were sold off by the impoverished owners.

Sleeping & Eating

El Palacil   APARTMENT €€
(☑950 41 50 43; www.elpalacil.com; Calle Molino Cantarería; 2-/4-/6-person apt €70/140/210; ℗❄🐾🍽) Enjoying a tranquil setting beside a running stream in Vélez Blanco, El Palacil offers spacious apartments for up to six people, with rustic homey decor and big kitchens. It also has a decent restaurant serving pizzas, salads, grilled meats and seafood (mains €10 to €20).

Mesón El Molino   SPANISH €€
(☑950 41 50 70; Calle Curtidores 1; mains €10-28; ☻1-4.30pm Mon-Sun, plus 8-11pm Fri & Sat) With its whitewashed walls, rustic timber beams and courtyard seating, this grand rural restaurant creates an atmospheric setting for hearty country fare and interesting local

wines. You'll find it tucked away up a narrow alley in the centre of Vélez Blanco.

ℹ Information

Centro de Visitantes Almacén del Trigo (☑950 41 95 85; Avenida Marqués de Los Vélez; ☻10am-2pm Thu, Fri & Sun year-round, plus 6-8pm Sat Apr-Sep, 4-6pm Sat Oct-Mar) Has useful information on the Parque Natural Sierra María-Los Vélez.

Cuevas del Almanzora

With its formidable, art-rich castle and handsome architecture, the busy agricultural centre of Cuevas del Almanzora merits a brief visit on your way up from Almería's coast to Los Vélez. The town, whose name is a nod to the many caves that pit the surrounding landscape, has ancient origins but took on its current form in the 19th century, when it flourished as a base for the silver mines in the nearby Sierra Almagrera hills.

Sights

Castillo del Marqués de los Vélez   CASTLE
(☑950 54 87 07; Plaza de la Libertad; Campoy museum & Goya gallery €2.50, other parts free; ☻ 9am-2pm Tue-Sat mid-Jun–mid-Sep, 10am-1.30pm & 5-8pm Tue-Sat, 10am-1pm Sun mid-Sep–mid-Jun) This imposing 16th-century castle presides over the old part of Cuevas del Almanzora, housing the **Museo Antonio Manuel Campoy** and one of Andalucía's premier modern art collections. Amassed by the celebrated Spanish art critic, this fascinating selection of paintings and sculpture includes works by the likes of Picasso, Miró and Tàpies. Also of note is the **gallery of Goya lithographs** and the small **archaeology museum** devoted to the El Argar Bronze Age culture.

Cueva Museo   MUSEUM
(Calle El Vergel; €2.50; ☻9am-2pm Tue-Sat mid-Jun–mid-Sep, 10am-1.30pm & 5-8pm Tue-Sat, 10am-1pm Sun mid-Sep–mid-Jun; ℗) People have lived in caves in and around Cuevas del Almanzora for thousands of years. To see an example of a relatively comfortable mid-20th-century dwelling head to the Cueva Museo, which displays a cave-house that was lived in by a family of ten until the 1960s.

ℹ Getting There & Away

By car, Cuevas del Almanzora is just east of the main A7 road, about 24km north of Mojácar.
By public transport, take one of the three daily buses Alsa (p300) runs from Almería (€9.25, 1¾ to 2¼ hours).

Understand
Andalucía

Andalucía Today

In the worst economic crisis that most Spaniards can remember, Andalucía was hit especially hard. It's working its way out of it now, and tourism is booming again. The good times of 12% unemployment (the lowest in memory in this chronically underemployed region) aren't going to come round again any time soon, but there's a jauntier buzz on the streets and in the bars than at any time in the past decade.

Best on Film

Marshland (2014) This story of detectives investigating murders in the Guadalquivir delta scooped 10 Goyas (the Spanish 'Oscars').

The Disappearance of García Lorca (1997) A journalist investigates the death of the great Spanish playwright (played by Andy García).

Living Is Easy with Eyes Closed (2013) It's 1966 and three Spanish music fans search for John Lennon, who's shooting a film in Almería.

South from Granada (2003) Touching screen rendition of Gerald Brenan's classic book.

Best in Print

South from Granada (Gerald Brenan; 1957) A Bloomsbury intellectual tries village life in Las Alpujarras in the 1920s.

Three Plays (Federico García Lorca) Andalucía's, and Spain's, greatest playwright's three great tragedies, written in the 1930s.

The Ornament of the World (María Rosa Menocal; 2002) Examines the tolerance and sophistication of Moorish Andalucía.

Andalus (Jason Webster; 2004) Webster's adventurous travels uncover the modern legacy of the Moorish era.

Driving Over Lemons (Chris Stewart; 1999) An anecdotal bestseller about life on a small Alpujarras farm.

Díaz Pulls the PSOE Through

That Andalucía has always had left-wing leanings is no surprise given its historical legacy of a few rich landowning families and a lot of poor workers. Ever since 1982, when Andalucía got its own parliament and government, the Junta de Andalucía, under democratic Spain's regional autonomy system, the reins of power here have been held by the left-of-centre Partido Socialista Obrero Español (PSOE; Spanish Socialist Workers' Party).

But Spain's political landscape underwent a transformation in the run-up to the Junta election of 2015. Two brand-new national forces born of popular protest movements during the economic crisis burst on to the scene, challenging the traditional might of the PSOE and its conservative rival the Partido Popular (PP; Popular Party). One was the radical, anti-austerity Podemos ('We Can'); the other was the centrist Ciudadanos (Citizens). These two parties won 24 seats in the Andalucian parliament – enough to deny the PSOE, for the first time ever, a parliamentary majority.

The election was, however, hailed as a triumph for the Andalucian PSOE and its popular young working-class leader from Seville, Susana Díaz – for Podemos' and Ciudadanos' gains were mainly at the expense of the PP, while the PSOE held steady. Díaz was able to form a minority government thanks to Ciudadanos' support for her investiture in May 2015. Díaz is also a powerful figure in the PSOE nationally and it's entirely possible that she may one day follow in Felipe González' footsteps as a PSOE prime minister from Seville.

Economy on the Mend, Sort of

Andalucía is on the way back from the economic crisis that shook Spain to its roots following the credit crunch and property crash of 2008. By the end of 2017 Andalucía's unemployment rate was down to 25%, having peaked at a dreadful 36% in 2013. Andalucía's all-time record of 10.6 million foreign tourists in 2016 was very good news, and 2017 was set to beat that. A happy hubbub of vacationers injecting €100 per day each into the local economy is now to be heard throughout spring and summer in the coastal resorts and inland cultural destinations.

But scratch a little below the surface, in the rural areas and urban neighbourhoods where tourists don't go, and the picture is rather different. Andalucía's jobless rate is still the highest in Spain, and one of the highest in Europe. Unemployment among 16- to 24-year-olds remains near an agonising 60%. Indeed, a lot of young Andalucians have left altogether, for Germany, Britain and Latin America, to find work.

The fact is, Andalucía has for centuries been Spain's most impoverished region. Large-scale tourism was launched during the Franco dictatorship to alleviate its distress – and remains a mainstay today. But tourism work is notoriously seasonal and insecure, and the region still lacks much industry. The town of Sanlúcar de Barrameda, in Cádiz province, highlights the gap between rich and poor acutely. Famous for its sherry wineries and as a gateway to Doñana National Park, Sanlúcar is a place where many rich families have holiday homes, and it stages fashionable horse races every August. But it has the second-highest jobless rate (38%) and second-lowest household income (€17,222 a year) of all Spanish towns.

Yet economic poverty sometimes goes hand in hand with cultural riches. it can be hard to reconcile the warmth and colour of the Andalucian atmosphere with the gloom and doom of the news stories. Family bonds are strong and supportive; the 'grey economy' (part-time work for cash) helps; the music still plays; the fiestas go on. With their gregarious, warm nature, their enjoyment of the good things and their optimism, Andalucians have a time-tested recipe for making the best of whatever fate throws at them.

No Separatism Here

Andalucians take much pride in being *andaluz* (Andalucian), but they equally consider themselves to be very much Spanish. They have little sympathy for separatist movements that threaten to break up Spain, such as the Catalonia independence drive of 2017. Hundreds of thousands of Andalucians migrated to work in low-paid jobs in Catalonia during the impoverished decades of the mid-20th century, and the experience didn't leave many Andalucians with huge affection for the northeastern region. If you happen to be in an Andalucian bar when Real Madrid (many Andalucians' favourite football team) is playing Barcelona, you'll get the vibe!

POPULATION: **8.4 MILLION**

AREA: **87,268 SQ KM**

UNEMPLOYMENT RATE: **29%**

HIGHEST PEAK: **MULHACÉN (3479M)**

INTERNATIONAL TOURISTS: **10.6 MILLION (2016)**

IBERIAN LYNX POPULATION: **400**

if Andalucía were 100 people

92 would be Spanish
4 would be other European
2 would be African
2 would be other

belief systems
(% of population)

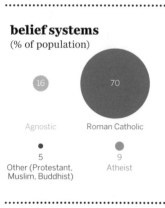

16 — Agnostic
70 — Roman Catholic
5 — Other (Protestant, Muslim, Buddhist)
9 — Atheist

population per sq km

ANDALUCÍA SPAIN UK

≈ 30 people

History

A beacon of culture in medieval Europe, then the hub of a transcontinental empire that declined into a destitute backwater and revived as a booming tourism destination – Andalucía has seen it all. Set at a meeting point of continents and oceans, its countless cross-currents have yielded a culture unique in the world. From Islamic palaces to Christian cathedrals and the rhythms of the flamenco guitar, Andalucía cherishes its heritage, and you will sense the past in the fabric of the present everywhere you go.

Andalucía's Early Innovators

Prehistoric Andalucía

....

Cueva de la Pileta (Benaoján, near Ronda)

....

Dolmen de Menga and Dolmen de Viera (Antequera)

....

Orce

....

Cueva de Nerja

....

Museo de Almería

It was prehistoric Andalucians, especially in the east, who introduced many early technological advances to the Iberian Peninsula, perhaps thanks to contact with more advanced societies around the Mediterranean.

The Cueva de los Letreros near Vélez Blanco, with paintings of animals and human and mythological figures, is among the finest of many Neolithic (New Stone Age) rock-art sites scattered up the Mediterranean side of Spain. The Neolithic reached Spain from Egypt and Mesopotamia around 6000 BC, bringing the revolution of agriculture – the plough, crops, domesticated livestock – and with it pottery, textiles and villages. Some 3500 years later the people of Los Millares, near Almería, learned how to smelt and shape local copper deposits and became Spain's first metalworking culture. Around the same time, people near Antequera were constructing Spain's most impressive dolmens (megalithic tombs, made of large rocks covered in earth), during the same era as the megalithic age in France, Britain and Ireland.

About 1900 BC the people of El Argar (Almería province) learned to make bronze, an alloy of copper and tin that is stronger than copper – ushering the Bronze Age into the Iberian Peninsula.

Earlier, Andalucía may have been home to the last Neanderthal humans. Excavations at Gorham's Cave in Gibraltar show that Neanderthals were probably still hanging on there until at least 26,000 BC. Neanderthals had begun their terminal decline around 35,000 BC as a result of climate change and the arrival of Europe's first Homo sapiens, probably from North Africa. Like 21st-century tourists, early European Homo sapiens gravitated to Andalucía's relatively warm climate, which

TIMELINE	18,000–14,000 BC	1000–800 BC	700–600 BC
	Palaeolithic hunter-gatherers paint quarry such as aurochs, stags, horses and fish in the Cueva de la Pileta (near Ronda), Cueva de Ardales and Cueva de Nerja.	Olives, grapevines and donkeys arrive in Andalucía with Phoenician traders, who establish coastal colonies such as Gadir (Cádiz) and Onuba (Huelva).	Iron replaces bronze as the most important metal around the lower Guadalquivir valley. The Tartessos culture that develops here is later mythologised as a source of fabulous wealth.

permitted varied fauna and thick forests to develop, and made hunting and gathering somewhat easier. Between 20,000 and 16,000 years ago they left impressive rock paintings of some of the animals they hunted in Andalucian caves such as the Cueva de Ardales near Bobastro, the Cueva de la Pileta near Ronda and the Cueva de Nerja.

Traders & Invaders

As history dawned, Andalucía's rich resources and settled societies attracted seafaring traders from around the Mediterranean. Later, the traders were replaced by invaders as imperialistic states emerged in the Mediterranean and sought not just to tap local wealth but also to exert political control. All these newcomers – Phoenicians, Greeks, Carthaginians, Romans and Visigoths – left indelible marks on Andalucian life and identity.

Phoenicians, Greeks & Tartessos

By about 1000 BC, a flourishing culture rich in agriculture, animals and metals arose in western Andalucía. This attracted Phoenician traders (from present-day Lebanon), who came to exchange perfumes, ivory, jewellery, oil, wine and textiles for Andalucian silver and bronze. The Phoenicians set up coastal trading settlements at places such as Cádiz (which they called Gadir), Huelva (Onuba) and Almuñécar (Ex or Sex). As a result Cádiz, founded around 1100 BC, has a good claim to be the oldest continuously inhabited settlement in Europe. In the 7th century BC Greeks arrived, too, trading much the same goods. The Phoenicians and Greeks brought with them the potter's wheel, writing and three quintessential elements of the traditional Andalucian landscape: the olive tree, the vine and the donkey.

The Phoenician- and Greek-influenced culture of western Andalucía in the 8th and 7th centuries BC is known as the Tartessos culture. The Tartessians developed advanced methods of working gold, but it was iron that replaced bronze as the most important metal. Tartessos was described centuries later by Greek, Roman and biblical writers as the source of fabulous riches. Whether it was a city or just a region no one knows. Some argue that it was a trading settlement near Huelva; others believe it may lie beneath the lower Guadalquivir marshes.

Carthage & Rome

A former Phoenician colony in modern Tunisia, Carthage came to dominate trade around the western Mediterranean from the 6th century BC. Unhappily for the Carthaginians, the next new Mediterranean power was Rome. Carthage was defeated by Rome in the First Punic War (264–241 BC), fought for control of Sicily. Later, Carthage occupied southern Spain, and the Second Punic War (218–201 BC) saw Carthaginian general Hannibal march his elephants over the Alps from Spain to threaten Rome.

HISTORY TRADERS & INVADERS

Ancient Andalucía

Museo Arqueológico (Seville)

Museo de Huelva

Museo de la Ciudad (Carmona)

Museo de Cádiz

Museo Arqueológico (Almuñécar)

Roman Andalucía

Itálica (Santiponce, near Seville)

Baelo Claudia (Bolonia)

Necrópolis Romana (Carmona)

Museo de la Ciudad de Antequera

Roman Amphitheatre (Málaga)

Puente Romano (Córdoba)

Museo Histórico Municipal (Écija)

206 BC	100 BC–AD 300	AD 98–138	AD 552
Roman legions under General Scipio Africanus defeat the army of Carthage at Ilipa, near Seville. Itálica, the first Roman town in Spain, is founded near the battlefield.	Andalucía becomes one of the wealthiest, most civilised areas of the Roman Empire, with Corduba (Córdoba) its most important city. Christianity arrives in the 3rd century AD.	The Roman Empire is ruled by two successive emperors from Itálica in Andalucía: Trajan (AD 98–117) and Hadrian (AD 117–138).	Byzantium, capital of the eastern Roman Empire, conquers Andalucía. The Visigoths, a Christian Germanic people now controlling the Iberian Peninsula, drive the Byzantines out in 622.

But the Romans opened a second front by sending legions to Spain, and their victory at Ilipa near modern Seville in 206 BC gave them control of the Iberian Peninsula. The first Roman town in Spain, Itálica, was founded near the battlefield soon afterwards.

As the Roman Empire went from strength to strength, Andalucía became one of its wealthiest and most civilised areas. Rome imported Andalucian crops, metals, fish and *garum* (a spicy seasoning derived from fish, made in factories whose remains can be seen at Bolonia and Almuñécar). Rome brought the Iberian Peninsula aqueducts, temples, theatres, amphitheatres, baths, Christianity, a sizeable Jewish population (Jews spread throughout the Mediterranean areas of the empire) – and the peninsula's main languages (Castilian Spanish, Portuguese, Catalan and Galician are all descended from the colloquial Latin spoken by Roman colonists).

The Visigoths

When the Huns erupted into Europe from Asia in the late 4th century AD, displaced Germanic peoples moved westwards across the crumbling Roman Empire. One group, the Visigoths, took over the Iberian Peninsula in the 6th century, with Toledo, in central Spain, as their capital. The long-haired Visigoths, numbering about 200,000, were, like their relatively sophisticated Hispano-Roman subjects, Christian, but their rule was undermined by strife among their own nobility. Andalucía spent some decades (552 to 622) as an outpost of the Byzantine empire, but then came under Visigothic sway.

Heartland of Islamic Spain

Andalucía was under Islamic rule, wholly or partly, for nearly eight centuries from 711 to 1492 – a time span much longer than the five centuries that have passed since 1492. For much of those eight centuries Andalucía was the most cultured and economically advanced region in a Europe that for most part was going through its 'dark ages'. The Islamic centuries left a deep imprint that still permeates Andalucian life, and a legacy of unique monuments: Granada's Alhambra, Córdoba's great Mezquita and Seville's Alcázar are windows into the splendours of the age and essential Andalucian cultural experiences.

Arabs carried Islam through the Middle East and North Africa following the death of the Prophet Mohammed in 632. Legend has it they were ushered onto the Iberian Peninsula by the sexual exploits of the last Visigothic king, Roderic. Chronicles relate how Roderic seduced young Florinda, the daughter of Julian, the Visigothic governor of Ceuta in North Africa, and how Julian sought revenge by approaching the Arabs with a plan to invade Spain. In reality, Roderic's rivals may just have been seeking support in the endless struggle for the Visigothic throne.

Most if not all of Córdoba's Umayyad rulers had Spanish mothers – concubine slaves from the north. Caliph Abd ar-Rahman III is said to have had red hair and blue eyes, and to have been the grandson of a Basque princess.

711	756–929	785	929–1031
Muslim forces from North Africa thrash the Visigothic army near the Río Guadalete in Cádiz province. Within a few years, the Muslims overrun almost the whole Iberian Peninsula.	The Muslim emirate of Córdoba, under the Umayyad dynasty founded by Abd ar-Rahman I, rules over most of the Iberian Peninsula. The name Al-Andalus is given to Muslim-controlled areas.	The Mezquita (Mosque) of Córdoba, one of the world's wonders of Islamic architecture, opens for prayer.	The caliphate of Córdoba: ruler Abd ar-Rahman III declares himself caliph; Al-Andalus attains its greatest power; and Córdoba becomes Western Europe's biggest city.

PATH OF KNOWLEDGE

Al-Andalus was an important conduit of classical Greek and Roman learning into Christian Europe, where it would exert a profound effect on the Renaissance, which got under way in 14th-century Italy. The Arabs had absorbed the philosophy of Aristotle, the mathematics of Pythagoras, the astronomy of Ptolemy and the medicine of Hippocrates during their conquests in the eastern Mediterranean and Middle East. Al-Andalus was one of the few places where Islamic and Christian worlds met, enabling this knowledge to find its way northward. Particularly influential was the Cordoban Averroës (1126–98), whose commentaries on Aristotle tried to reconcile religious faith with science and reason.

In 711 Tariq ibn Ziyad, the Muslim governor of Tangier, landed at Gibraltar with around 10,000 men, mostly indigenous North African Berbers. They decimated Roderic's army, probably near the Río Guadalete in Cádiz province, and Roderic is thought to have drowned as he fled. Within a few years, the Muslims had taken over the whole Iberian Peninsula except for small areas in the Asturian mountains in the far north. The name given to the Muslim-ruled territories was Al-Andalus. From this comes the modern name of the region that was always the Islamic heartland on the peninsula – Andalucía. Al-Andalus' frontiers shifted constantly as the Christians strove to regain territory, but until the 11th century the small Christian states developing in northern Spain were too weak to pose much of a threat to Al-Andalus.

In the main cities, the Muslims built beautiful palaces, mosques and gardens, opened universities and established public bathhouses and bustling *zocos* (markets). The Moorish (as it's often known) society of Al-Andalus was a mixed bag. The ruling class was composed of various Arab groups prone to factional friction. Below them was a larger group of Berbers, some of whom rebelled on numerous occasions. Jews and Christians had freedom of worship, but Christians had to pay a special tax, so most either converted to Islam or left for the Christian north. Christians living in Muslim territory were known as Mozarabs (*mozárabes* in Spanish); those who adopted Islam were *muwallads (muladíes)*. Before long, Arab, Berber and local blood merged, and many Spaniards today are partly descended from medieval Muslims.

The Cordoban Emirate & Caliphate

The first centre of Islamic culture and power in Spain was the old Roman provincial capital Córdoba. In 750 the Umayyad dynasty of caliphs in Damascus, supreme rulers of the Muslim world, was overthrown by a group of revolutionaries, the Abbasids, who shifted the caliphate to Baghdad. One of the Umayyad family, Abd ar-Rahman, escaped the

Moorish Spain Reads

Moorish Spain (Richard Fletcher; 1992)

The Ornament of the World (María Rosa Menocal; 2002)

Andalus (Jason Webster; 2004)

1091–1140	1160–73	1212	1227–48
The strict Muslim rulers of Morocco, the Almoravids, conquer Al-Andalus and rule it as a colony. Their power crumbles in the 1140s.	The Almoravids' successors in Morocco, the Almohads, in turn take over Al-Andalus, making Seville their capital and promoting arts and learning.	The armies of three northern Spanish Christian kingdoms, Castilla, Aragón and Navarra, defeat a large Almohad force at Las Navas de Tolosa in northeastern Andalucía – the beginning of the end for Al-Andalus.	Castilla's King Fernando III (El Santo, the Saint) conquers the west and north of Andalucía, culminating in the capture of Seville in 1248.

Moorish Andalucía

Alhambra (Granada)

Mezquita (Córdoba)

Albayzín (Granada)

Medina Azahara (Córdoba)

Giralda (Seville)

Castillo de Gibralfaro (Málaga)

Alcazaba (Almería)

Mezquita (Almonaster la Real)

Bobastro (near El Chorro)

slaughter and somehow made his way to Morocco and then to Córdoba, where in 756 he set himself up as an independent emir (prince). Abd ar-Rahman I's Umayyad dynasty kept Al-Andalus more or less unified for over 250 years.

In 929 Abd ar-Rahman I's descendant Abd ar-Rahman III (r 912–961) gave himself the title caliph to assert his authority in the face of the Fatimids, a growing Muslim power in North Africa. Thus he launched the caliphate of Córdoba, which at its peak encompassed three quarters of the Iberian Peninsula and some of North Africa. Córdoba became the biggest, most dazzling and cultured city in Western Europe. Astronomy, medicine, mathematics, philosophy, history and botany flourished, and Abd ar-Rahman III's court was frequented by Jewish, Arabian and Christian scholars.

Later in the 10th century, the fearsome Cordoban general Al-Mansur (or Almanzor) terrorised the Christian north with 50-odd *razzias* (forays) in 20 years. In 997 he destroyed the cathedral at Santiago de Compostela in northwestern Spain – home of the cult of Santiago Matamoros (St James the Moor-Slayer), a key inspiration to Christian warriors. But after Al-Mansur's death, the caliphate disintegrated into dozens of small kingdoms known as *taifas*, ruled by local potentates (often Berber generals).

The Almoravids & Almohads

Seville, in the wealthy lower Guadalquivir valley, emerged as the strongest *taifa* in Andalucía in the 1040s. By 1078 the writ of its Abbadid dynasty ran all the way from southern Portugal to Murcia (southeast Spain), restoring a measure of peace and prosperity to the south.

Meanwhile, the northern Christian states were starting to raise their game. When one of them, Castilla, captured Toledo in 1085, a scared Seville begged for help from the Almoravids, a strict Muslim sect of Saharan Berbers who had conquered Morocco. The Almoravids came, defeated Castilla's Alfonso VI, and ended up taking over Al-Andalus, too, ruling it from Marrakesh as a colony and persecuting Jews and Christians. But the charms of Al-Andalus seemed to relax the Almoravids' austere grip: revolts spread across the territory from 1143 and within a few years it had again split into *taifas*.

In Morocco, the Almoravids were displaced by another strict Muslim Berber sect, the Almohads, who in turn took over Al-Andalus by 1173. Al-Andalus was by now considerably reduced from its 10th-century heyday: the frontier ran from south of Lisbon to north of Valencia. The Almohads made Seville capital of their whole realm and revived arts and learning in Al-Andalus.

In 1195, the Almohad ruler Yusuf Yakub al-Mansur thrashed Castilla's army at Alarcos, south of Toledo, but this only spurred other Christian

1249–1492	1250–80	1350–69	January 1492
The emirate of Granada, ruled by the Nasrid dynasty from the lavish Alhambra palace, sees the final flowering of medieval Muslim culture on the Iberian Peninsula.	Fernando III's son Alfonso X of Castilla, known as El Sabio (the Learned), makes Seville one of his several capitals and launches a cultural revival there.	Castilian king Pedro I, 'El Cruel', creates the most magnificent section of Seville's Alcázar palace, but reputedly has a dozen relatives and friends murdered in his efforts to keep the throne.	After a 10-year war Granada falls to the armies of Castilla and Aragón, which are now united through the marriage of their rulers Isabel and Fernando, the 'Catholic Monarchs'.

kingdoms to join forces with Castilla against him. In 1212 the combined armies of Castilla, Aragón and Navarra routed the Almohads at Las Navas de Tolosa, a victory that opened the gates of Andalucía. With the Almohad state riven by a succession dispute after 1224, Castilla, Aragón and two other Christian kingdoms, Portugal and León, expanded southwards down the Iberian Peninsula. Castilla's Fernando III took strategic Baeza (near Jaén) in 1227, Córdoba in 1236, and Seville, after a two-year siege, in 1248.

The Nasrid Emirate of Granada

The Granada emirate was a wedge of territory carved out of the disintegrating Almohad realm by Mohammed ibn Yusuf ibn Nasr, from whom it's known as the Nasrid emirate. Comprising essentially the modern provinces of Granada, Málaga and Almería, it held out for nearly 250 years as the last Muslim state on the Iberian Peninsula.

The Nasrids ruled from the lavish Alhambra palace in Granada, which witnessed the final flowering of Islamic culture in Spain. Their emirate reached its peak in the 14th century under emirs Yusuf I and Mohammed V, authors of the Alhambra's greatest splendours. The Nasrids' final downfall was precipitated by two things: one was Emir Abu al-Hasan's refusal in 1476 to pay any further tribute to Castilla; the other was the unification in 1479 of Castilla and Aragón, Spain's biggest Christian states, following the marriage of their monarchs Isabel and Fernando. The Reyes Católicos (Catholic Monarchs), as the pair is known, launched the final crusade of the Reconquista (Christian reconquest) against Granada in 1482.

Jewish Andalucía

Centro de Interpretación Judería de Sevilla

Palacio de los Olvidados (Granada)

Sinagoga del Agua (Úbeda)

Casa de Sefarad (Córdoba)

Sinagoga (Córdoba)

Centro de la Memoria Sefardí (Granada)

HISTORY HEARTLAND OF ISLAMIC SPAIN

IN ISLAMIC FOOTSTEPS

The medieval Islamic era left a profound stamp on Andalucía. The great architectural monuments such as Granada's Alhambra and Córdoba's Mezquita are the stars of this Islamic heritage, but the characteristic tangled, narrow street layouts of many towns and villages also date from Islamic times, as do the Andalucian predilections for fountains, running water and decorative plants. Flamenco music, though brought to its modern form by Roma people in more recent times, has clear influences from medieval Andalucian Islamic music.

The Muslims developed Spain's Hispano-Roman agricultural base by improving irrigation and introducing new fruits and crops, many of which are still widely grown, often on the same irrigated terraces created by the Moors. The Spanish language contains many common words of Arabic origin, including the names of some of those new crops – naranja (orange), azúcar (sugar) and arroz (rice). Nowadays you can experience a taste of Moorish life in luxurious hammams – bathhouses with the characteristic three pools of cold, warm and hot water – and Middle Eastern–style teterías (teahouses) that have opened in several Andalucian cities.

April 1492	August 1492	1500	1503
Under the influence of Grand Inquisitor Tomás de Torquemada, Isabel and Fernando expel from Spain all Jews who refuse Christian baptism. Some 200,000 Jews leave for other Mediterranean destinations.	Christopher Columbus, funded by Isabel and Fernando, sails from Palos de la Frontera and after 70 days finds the Bahamas, opening up a whole new hemisphere of opportunity for Spain.	Persecution of Muslims in the former Granada emirate sparks rebellion. Afterwards, Muslims are compelled to adopt Christianity or leave. Most, an estimated 300,000, undergo baptism.	Seville is granted a monopoly on Spanish trade with the Americas and becomes the cosmopolitan hub of world trade, with its population jumping from 40,000 to 150,000 by 1600.

Harem jealousies and other feuds among Granada's rulers degenerated into a civil war that allowed the Christians to push across the emirate. They captured Málaga in 1487, and Granada itself, after an eight-month siege, on 2 January 1492.

The surrender terms were fairly generous to the last emir, Boabdil, who received the Alpujarras valleys, south of Granada, as a personal fiefdom. He stayed only a year, however, before departing to Africa. The Muslims were promised respect for their religion, culture and property, but this didn't last long.

Christians in Control

The relatively uniform culture of modern Andalucía has its roots in the early centuries of Christian rule. In their zeal to establish Christianity in the conquered territories, Andalucía's new rulers enforced increasingly severe measures that ended with the expulsion of two of the three religious groups that had cohabited in Al-Andalus.

In areas that fell under Christian control in the 13th century, Muslims who stayed on (known as Mudéjars) initially faced no reprisals. But in 1264 the Mudéjars of Jerez de la Frontera rose up against new taxes and rules that required them to celebrate Christian feasts and live in ghettos. After a five-month siege they were expelled to Granada or North Africa, along with the Mudéjars of Seville, Córdoba and Arcos.

Large tracts of southern Spain were handed to nobility and knights who had played important roles in the Reconquista. These landowners turned much of their vast estates over to sheep, and by 1300 rural Christian Andalucía was almost empty. The nobility's preoccupation with wool and politics allowed Jews and foreigners, especially Genoese, to dominate Castilian commerce and finance.

Fernando III's son Alfonso X (r 1252–84) made Seville one of Castila's capitals and launched something of a cultural revival there, gathering scholars around him, particularly Jews, who could translate ancient texts into Castilian Spanish. But rivalry within the royal family, and challenges from the nobility, plagued the Castilian monarchy right through till the late 15th century, when the Catholic Monarchs took things in hand.

Persecution of the Jews

After the Black Death and several bad harvests in the 14th century, discontent found its scapegoat in the Jews, who were subjected to pogroms around Christian Spain in the 1390s. As a result, many Jews converted to Christianity (they became known as *conversos*); others found refuge in Muslim Granada. In the 1480s the *conversos* became the main target of the new Spanish Inquisition, founded by the Catholic Monarchs, which accused many *conversos* of continuing to practise Judaism in secret.

The Spanish Inquisition was established by the Reyes Católicos (Catholic Monarchs; Isabel and Fernando) in 1478. Of the estimated 12,000 deaths for which it was responsible in its three centuries of existence, 2000 took place in the 1480s.

1568–70	17th century	19th century	1805
Persecution of the *moriscos* (converted Muslims) leads to a two-year revolt centred on the Alpujarras valleys, south of Granada. *Moriscos* are eventually thrown out of Spain altogether by Felipe III between 1609 and 1614.	The boom engendered by American trade fizzles out as silver shipments slump, and epidemics and bad harvests kill 300,000 Andalucians.	Andalucía sinks into economic depression, with landless labourers and their families making up three-quarters of the population.	In the Napoleonic Wars, Spanish sea power is terminated when a combined Spanish–French navy is defeated by the British fleet, under Admiral Nelson, off Cabo de Trafalgar, south of Cádiz.

In 1492 Isabel and Fernando ordered the expulsion of every Jew who refused Christian baptism. Around 50,000 to 100,000 converted, but some 200,000 left for other Mediterranean destinations – the Sephardic (Iberian Peninsula Jewish) diaspora. A talented middle class was decimated.

Morisco Revolts & Expulsion

The task of converting Granada's Muslims to Christianity was handed to Cardinal Cisneros, overseer of the Inquisition. He carried out forced mass baptisms, burnt Islamic books and banned the Arabic language. As Muslims found their land being expropriated, too, a revolt in Las Alpujarras in 1500 spread right across the former Granada emirate. Afterwards, Muslims were ordered to convert to Christianity or leave. Most converted, becoming known as *moriscos* (converted Muslims), but after the fanatically Catholic King Felipe II (r 1556–98) forbade the Arabic language, Arabic names and *morisco* dress in 1567, a new Alpujarras revolt spread across southern Andalucía and took two years to put down. The *moriscos* were then deported to western Andalucía and more northerly parts of Spain, before being expelled altogether from Spain by Felipe III between 1609 and 1614.

> The Catholic Monarchs, pious Isabel and machiavellian Fernando, united Spain under one rule for the first time since Roman days – a task completed when Fernando annexed Navarra in 1512, eight years after Isabel's death.

Seville & The Americas: Boom & Bust

If Islamic Andalucía's golden age was the 10th-century Cordoban caliphate, its Christian counterpart was 16th-century Seville.

In April 1492 the Catholic Monarchs granted the Genoese sailor Christopher Columbus (Cristóbal Colón to Spaniards) funds for a voyage across the Atlantic in search of a new trade route to the Orient. Columbus found the Americas instead – and opened up a whole new hemisphere of opportunity for Spain, especially for the river port of Seville.

During the reign of Carlos I (r 1516–56), the first ruler of Spain's new Habsburg dynasty, the ruthless but brilliant conquerors Hernán Cortés and Francisco Pizarro subdued the Aztec and Inca empires respectively with small bands of adventurers, and other Spanish conquerors and colonists occupied further vast tracts of the American mainland. The new colonies sent huge quantities of silver, gold and other treasure back to Spain, where the crown was entitled to one-fifth of the bullion (the *quinto real,* or royal fifth).

Seville became the hub of world trade, a cosmopolitan melting pot of money seekers, and remained the major city in Spain until late in the 17th century, even though a small country town called Madrid was named the national capital in 1561. The prosperity was shared to some extent by Cádiz, and less so by inland cities such as Jaén, Córdoba and Granada.

But Spain never developed any strategy for investing the American windfall, spending too much on European wars and opulent palaces,

> **The American Adventure**
>
> Lugares Colombinos (near Huelva)
> ....
> Columbus' Tomb (Seville Cathedral)
> ....
> Archivo de Indias (Seville)
> ....
> Patio de la Montería (Real Alcázar, Seville)

Side tab: HISTORY SEVILLE & THE AMERICAS: BOOM & BUST

1810–12	1873	1891–1919	1923–30
With most of Spain under Napoleonic occupation, Cádiz survives a two-year siege. In 1812 the Cádiz parliament adopts Spain's first constitution, 'La Pepa', proclaiming sovereignty of the people.	During Spain's chaotic, short-lived First Republic, numerous cities and towns declare themselves independent states. Seville and the nearby town of Utrera even declare war on each other.	Impoverished Andalucian rural workers launch waves of anarchist strikes and revolts. Powerful anarchist union the CNT is founded in Seville in 1910 and gains 93,000 members in Andalucía by 1919.	General Miguel Primo de Rivera, from the Andalucian town of Jerez de la Frontera, rules Spain in a moderate military dictatorship. He is dismissed by King Alfonso XIII in 1930.

cathedrals and monasteries, while wasting any chance of becoming an early industrial power. Grain had to be imported, while sheep and cattle roamed the countryside. The ensuing centuries of neglect and economic mismanagement would turn Andalucía into a backwater, a condition from which it didn't start to emerge until the 1960s.

In the 17th century, silver shipments from the Americas shrank disastrously and the lower Río Guadalquivir, Seville's lifeline to the Atlantic, became increasingly silted up. In 1717 control of commerce with the Americas was transferred to the seaport of Cádiz, which enjoyed its heyday in the 18th century.

The Battle of Trafalgar (1805), in which Spanish sea power was terminated by Admiral Nelson's British fleet, was fought off a small headland, Cabo de Trafalgar, in the town Los Caños de Meca (Cádiz province). A plaque commemorating those who died was erected at the cape in 2005, the bicentenary.

The Great 19th-Century Wealth Gap

The 18th century saw a few economic advances in Andalucía such as a new road from Madrid to Seville and Cádiz, new lands planted with wheat and barley, and new settlers from elsewhere in Spain, who boosted Andalucía's population to about 1.8 million by 1787. But Spain's loss of its American colonies in the early 19th century was desperate news for the port of Cádiz, which had been totally reliant on trade with them. As the 19th century wore on, Andalucía declined into one of Europe's most backward, socially polarised regions.

The Disentailments of 1836 and 1855, when church and municipal lands were auctioned off to reduce the national debt, were a disaster for the peasants, who lost grazing lands. At one social extreme were the few bourgeoisie and rich aristocratic landowners; at the other, a very large number of impoverished *jornaleros* – landless agricultural day labourers who were without work for a good half of the year. Illiteracy, disease and

LA PEPA

One of the few places to hold out against the French forces that occupied Spain during the Napoleonic Wars was Cádiz, which withstood a two-year siege from 1810 to 1812. During the siege, the Cortes de Cádiz, a Spanish parliament, convened in the city, and on 19 March 1812 it promulgated Spain's first-ever constitution, the Constitución de Cádiz. This was a notably liberal document for its time, decreeing, among other things, universal male suffrage, a constitutional monarchy and freedom of the press. It didn't last long, being abolished by King Fernando VII on his restoration in 1814, but it remained a touchstone for Spaniards of liberal leanings – and was celebrated with fanfare on its bicentenary in 2012.

Spaniards call the Cádiz Constitution 'La Pepa' – the explanation being that the day of its promulgation, 19 March, is also the Día de San José (St Joseph's Day). None the wiser? The affectionate form of the Spanish name José is Pepe, and since the word *constitución* is of feminine gender, the Cádiz Constitution takes the feminine version of Pepe – so *¡Viva La Pepa!*

1931–36	17 July 1936	1936–37	1936–39
The Second Republic: the king goes into exile and Spain is ruled first by the left, then the right, then the left again, with political violence spiralling.	The Spanish garrison at Melilla (North Africa) revolts against the government, starting the Spanish Civil War. The plot is led by five 'Nationalist' generals, including Francisco Franco.	Western Andalucía falls early in the civil war to the Nationalists, who also take Málaga, with Italian help, in February 1937. Massacres are carried out by both Nationalists and republicans.	Helped by Nazi Germany and fascist Italy, Franco leads the Nationalists to civil-war victory. Much of eastern Andalucía remains in republican hands until the end of the war.

hunger were rife. Andalucian peasants began to stage uprisings, always brutally quashed. Many favoured the anarchist strategy of strikes, sabotage and revolts as the path to spontaneous revolution and a free society, governed by voluntary cooperation. Powerful anarchist union the Confederación Nacional del Trabajo (CNT; National Labour Confederation) was founded in Seville in 1910.

The Civil War

The polarisation of Andalucian society and politics in the 19th century was mirrored in Spain at large. As the 20th century progressed, divisions deepened and a large-scale conflagration looked increasingly inevitable. It came with the devastating Spanish Civil War of 1936–39.

The Prelude: Dictatorship & Republic

In 1923 an eccentric Andalucian general from Jerez de la Frontera, Miguel Primo de Rivera, launched a comparatively moderate military dictatorship with the cooperation of the big socialist union, the Unión General de Trabajadores (UGT; General Union of Workers). Primo was unseated in 1930 as a result of an economic downtown and discontent in the army. When Spain's burgeoning republican movement scored sweeping victories in local elections in 1931, King Alfonso XIII departed for exile in Italy.

The ensuing Second Republic (1931–36) was a tumultuous period of mounting confrontation between left and right. National elections in 1931 brought in a mixed government including socialists, centrists and republicans, but the next elections in 1933 were won by the right. By 1934 violence was spiralling out of control, and the left, including the emerging communists, was calling increasingly for revolution. In the February 1936 elections a left-wing coalition narrowly defeated the right-wing National Front. Violence continued on both sides of the political spectrum, the anarchist CNT had over a million members and the peasants were on the verge of revolution.

But when the revolt came, on 17 July 1936, it came from the other end of the political spectrum. On that day the Spanish military garrison at Melilla in North Africa revolted against the leftist government, followed the next day by some garrisons on the mainland. The leaders of the plot were five generals. The Spanish Civil War had begun.

The War

The civil war split communities, families and friends. Both sides committed atrocious massacres and reprisals, especially in the early weeks. The rebels, who called themselves Nationalists, shot or hanged tens of thousands of supporters of the republic. Republicans did likewise to those

---

In republican-held areas during the civil war, anarchists, communists or socialists ran many towns and cities. Social revolution followed. In Andalucía this was often anarchist-led, with private property abolished and churches and convents wrecked. Large estates were occupied by peasants and around 100 agrarian communes were established.

By most estimates, about 350,000 Spaniards died in the civil war, although some writers put the figure as high as 500,000.

HISTORY THE CIVIL WAR

1939–75	1950–60	1969	1975–78
The Franco dictatorship: his opponents continue to be killed and jailed after the civil war; no political opposition is tolerated; the Catholic Church gains a privileged position in society.	Some 1.5 million Andalucians leave to find work elsewhere in Spain or Europe. New mass tourism on Andalucía's Costa del Sol helps to stimulate some economic recovery.	Andalucía's first national park, the Parque Nacional de Doñana, is declared. By 2017, environmentally protected areas cover 30% of Andalucian territory, the biggest such program in Spain.	Following Franco's death, King Juan Carlos I and Prime Minister Adolfo Suárez engineer a transition to democracy. The 1978 constitution makes Spain a parliamentary monarchy with no official religion.

they considered Nationalist sympathisers, including some 7000 priests, monks and nuns.

The basic battle lines were drawn very early. Cities whose military garrisons backed the rebels (most did) often fell immediately into Nationalist hands, as happened at Cádiz, Córdoba and Jerez. Seville was in Nationalist hands within three days and Granada within a few more. The Nationalists killed an estimated 4000 people in and around Granada after they took the city, including the great writer Federico García Lorca. There was slaughter in republican-held areas, too. An estimated 2500 were murdered in anarchist-controlled Málaga. The Nationalists then executed thousands in reprisals when they and their fascist Italian allies took the city in February 1937. Eastern Andalucía remained in republican hands until the end of the war.

By late 1936 General Francisco Franco emerged as the undisputed Nationalist leader, calling himself Generalísimo (Supreme General). The republicans had the support of some Soviet planes, tanks, artillery and advisers, and 25,000 or so French soldiers fought with them, along with a similar number of other foreigners in the International Brigades – but the scales of the war were tipped in the Nationalists' favour by weapons, planes and 92,000 troops from Nazi Germany and fascist Italy.

The republican government moved from besieged Madrid to Valencia in late 1936, then to Barcelona in 1937. The USSR withdrew from the war in 1938, and the Nationalists took Barcelona in January 1939 and Madrid in March. Franco declared the war won on 1 April 1939.

Franco's Spain

After the civil war, instead of reconciliation, more bloodletting ensued and an estimated 100,000 Spaniards were killed or died in prison. Franco ruled absolutely. He was commander of the army and leader of the only political party, the Movimiento Nacional (National Movement). Army garrisons were maintained outside every large city, strikes and divorce were banned, and church weddings became compulsory.

Spain stayed out of WWII but afterwards suffered a UN-sponsored trade boycott that helped turn the late 1940s into the *años de hambre* (years of hunger) – particularly in poor areas such as Andalucía where, at times, peasants subsisted on soup made from wild herbs.

In an effort to relieve Andalucian poverty, mass foreign tourism was launched on the Costa del Sol in the late 1950s. But 1.5 million hungry people still left Andalucía in the 1950s and '60s to look for work in Madrid, northern Spain and other countries. By the 1970s many Andalucian villages still lacked electricity, reliable water supplies and paved roads, and the education system was pathetically inadequate. Today a surprising number of rural Andalucians over 50 are still illiterate.

A few communists and republicans continued their struggle after the civil war in small guerrilla units in Andalucía's mountains and elsewhere. *Between Two Fires* (2011) by David Baird is a fascinating chronicle of their activity around Frigiliana (near Nerja) in 1940–50.

1982–96	1982	1992	1996–2004
Sevillan Felipe González, of the left-of-centre Partido Socialista Obrero Español (PSOE), enjoys 14 years as Spain's prime minister, presiding over an economic boom after Spain joins the EU in 1986.	Under Spain's new regional autonomy system, Andalucía gets its own parliament (in Seville). Over the next 10 years, PSOE government at national and regional level eliminates the worst of Andalucian poverty.	Hundreds of thousands of people visit Expo '92 in Seville, and the superfast AVE (Alta Velocidad Española) Madrid–Córdoba–Seville rail link opens. Andalucian roads get a major upgrade, too.	Spain is governed by the right-of-centre Partido Popular (PP). Andalucian unemployment nearly halves (to 16%), thanks to a construction boom, tourism and industrial growth, and EU subsidies.

The New Democracy

Spain, and Andalucía, have come a very long way in the four decades since Franco died in 1975. Democracy has taken root, society has been liberalised beyond recognition, and living standards, despite the knock they took from the post-2008 economic crisis, have climbed. High-speed trains, fast highways, shiny shopping malls, one-child families, gay marriage, thinly populated churches and heavily populated universities are just a few of the things that would amaze 1970s Andalucians today if they returned after being away for 40 years.

Franco's chosen successor, Alfonso XIII's grandson Prince Juan Carlos, took the throne two days after Franco's death. Much of the credit for Spain's transition to democracy goes to Juan Carlos and his prime minister, Adolfo Suárez. A new parliamentary system was introduced, and political parties, trade unions and strikes were all legalised. Spain enjoyed a rapid social liberation: contraceptives, homosexuality and divorce were legalised, adultery was decriminalised, and a wave of hedonism was unleashed.

In 1982 Spain made a final break with the Franco era by voting the left-of-centre Partido Socialista Obrero Español (PSOE; Spanish Socialist Workers' Party) into power. The PSOE's leader, Felipe González, a young lawyer from Seville, was to be prime minister for 14 years, and his party's young, educated leadership included several other Andalucians. The PSOE made improvements in education, launched a national health system and basked in an economic boom after Spain joined the European Community (now the EU) in 1986.

The PSOE has dominated Andalucía's regional government in Seville, the Junta de Andalucía, ever since it was inaugurated in 1982. It eradicated the worst of Andalucian poverty in the 1980s and early 1990s with grants, community works schemes and a relatively generous dole system. It also gave Andalucía Spain's biggest network of environmentally protected areas.

The PSOE lost power nationally in 1996 to the centre-right Partido Popular (PP; People's Party), which presided over eight years of economic progress – and the economic sun continued to shine after the PSOE regained national power in 2004. By 2007 Andalucía had never had it so good. A decade-long boom in construction and property prices, massive EU funds for agriculture, and a constant flow of tourists saw unemployment down to 13%, the lowest in memory (albeit still the highest in Spain). Instead of Andalucians emigrating for jobs, hundreds of thousands of immigrants were coming to work in Andalucía.

Then everything fell apart in 2008 when the global economic crisis hit Europe, a blow from which Andalucía is only now recovering.

Andalucía's regional government, the Junta de Andalucía, controls many policy areas and services including health, schools, environment, town planning and agriculture. It has an annual budget of over €30 billion and more than 250,000 direct employees, about 80% of those being teachers or health workers.

2000–10	2004	2008–13	2014
Hundreds of thousands of northern and eastern Europeans, Africans and Latin Americans migrate to Andalucía. Some are sun seekers, more are job seekers. The official foreign population grows to a record 700,000.	The PSOE wins the Spanish national and Andalucian regional elections, days after the Madrid train bombings by Islamic extremists, which kill 191 people and injure 1800.	Andalucía is savaged by economic recession; unemployment leaps from 13% to 36%. The PP returns to power nationally in 2011 with an austerity program to tackle the crisis.	King Juan Carlos abdicates, with his health and the monarchy's popularity declining, making way for his son, Felipe VI.

Andalucian Architecture

From the noble Renaissance palaces of Úbeda and Baeza to the finely carved stucco work that beautifies the Alhambra, Andalucía's architecture is a study in grace, skilled artisanship and unique cultural interchange. Hybridisation is almost a hobby here. Wander the region's towns and cities, and you'll see mosques converted into churches, Moorish arches held up by Roman columns, and minarets refashioned as belfries. Spared the carpet bombing that plagued other European cities in WWII, Andalucía's historic buildings are remarkably well preserved.

Moorish Factor

Islamic
Fortresses
....
Alcazaba (Almería)
....
*Alcazaba
(Antequera)*
....
*Alhambra
(Granada)*
....
*Castillo de Gibral-
faro (Málaga)*
....
*Castillo de los
Guzmán (Tarifa)*
....
*Torre del Oro
(Seville)*

Architecturally speaking, Spain – and in particular Andalucía – is different from the rest of Europe. The reason? The Moorish factor. The conquering Christian armies may have disposed of the emirs and government of Al-Andalus (the Muslim-controlled parts of the Iberian Peninsula) by 1492, but, tellingly, they didn't have the heart to flatten all of its most iconic buildings. While they knocked down some mosques and replaced them with churches, other mosques were simply repurposed for the new religion. Fortresses, palaces and mansions were often re-used and adapted as the centuries went by. Córdoba's Mezquita still stands, as do Seville's Giralda and Granada's Palacios Nazaríes. As a result, Andalucía's architecture is a story of layers, hybrids and Christian–Moorish intermixing. Even today, 500 years since the fall of Granada, the impact of the Islamic centuries is never far from the surface. In villages across the region, and in the hearts of cities (as in Granada's Albayzín), intricate tangles of streets are redolent of North African medinas. Similarly, the Islamic love of ornate, scented gardens with flowing or trickling water – hidden inner sanctums that safeguarded residents from prying eyes – can be seen in patios, courtyards and the carefully manicured greenery that embellishes Andalucía's Moorish-influenced houses and palaces. The resulting picture is as inspiring as it is complicated. Indeed, one might even come to the conclusion that European architectural design reached its highpoint in the 1350s in a palace complex at the foot of the Sierra Nevada called the Alhambra.

In more recent times, architects have often sought to emulate the glories of the Moors by regularly revisiting Islamic form and vision. One of the more spectacular results can be seen in Seville's Plaza de España, constructed in the 1920s.

Islamic Architecture

The period of Islamic architectural dominance began with the Umayyads, the Muslim invaders who kick-started eight centuries of Islamic rule in 711 and ushered in an era that bequeathed the region, more than anywhere else in Europe, a strong sense of the exotic. Elaborate monuments on an unprecedented scale – Córdoba's Mezquita and Granada's Alhambra, for example, which stand like bookends to the Moorish era – were the means by which the rulers of Al-Andalus brought architectural sophistication to Europe. They remain the most visible legacy of Andalucía's Islamic past.

Umayyads

When the Umayyad caliphs of Damascus were overthrown by the revolutionary Abbasids in 750, one young member of the Umayyad clan, Abd ar-Rahman ibn Muawiya, managed to escape the carnage and flee to Morocco and then Spain. In 756 he set himself up as an independent emir, Abd ar-Rahman I, in Córdoba, launching a dynasty that lasted until 1031 and made Al-Andalus, at the western extremity of the Islamic world, the last outpost of Umayyad culture.

Mezquita of Córdoba

Abd ar-Rahman I was responsible for founding Córdoba's Mezquita in AD 784, a building that was – and still is – the epitome of Islamic architecture's grace and pleasing unity of form. This sense of harmony is all the more remarkable given the significant alterations carried out over the centuries. Zealous Christian architects darkened the original light-filled interior by building thick outer walls, and in the middle of the 16th century an incongruous Christian cathedral was plonked right in the middle of the former mosque.

In its original form, the Mezquita was a square split into two rectangular halves: a covered prayer hall, and an open courtyard where the faithful performed their ritual ablutions before entering the prayer hall. This early structure drew on the essential elements of Umayyad architecture. It maintained, for example, the 'basilical' plan of some early Islamic buildings by having a central 'nave' of arches, broader than the others, leading to the *mihrab*, the niche indicating the direction of Mecca (and thus of prayer) that is key to the layout of any mosque. But the Mezquita's prayer hall drew away from the verticality of earlier landmark Umayyad buildings, such as the Great Mosque of Damascus and the Dome of the Rock in Jerusalem. Instead, it created a broad horizontal space that evoked the yards of desert homes that formed the original Islamic prayer spaces. It also conjured visions of palm groves with mesmerising lines of two-tier, red-and-white-striped arches in the prayer hall.

As Córdoba grew into its role as the increasingly sophisticated capital of Al-Andalus, later emirs left their personal stamp on Al-Andalus' landmark building. Later enlargements extended the lines of arches to cover an area of nearly 120 sq metres, making it one of the biggest of all mosques. These arcades afford ever-changing perspectives, vistas disappearing into infinity and interplays of light and rhythm that rank among the Mezquita's most arresting features.

It was the caliph Al-Hakim II (r 961–76) who endowed the Mezquita with its most splendid flourishes. Al-Hakim II created a magnificent new *mihrab*, decorated with superb Byzantine mosaics that imitate those of the Great Mosque of Damascus. In front of the *mihrab* Al-Hakim II added a new royal prayer enclosure, the *maksura*, whose multiple interwoven

HORSESHOE ARCH

The Visigoths are an often-overlooked civilisation who on the Iberian Peninsula had the historical misfortune to fall between the Romans and the Moors. But they did contribute at least one indelible architectural legacy: the horseshoe arch – so called because it curves inwards at the bottom like a horseshoe and unlike pure semicircle arches. The horseshoe arch was taken up by the Umayyads; the Mezquita in Córdoba displays the best early arches, but the style endured to become a hallmark of Spanish Islamic architecture, passed down through the Almoravids, Almohads and Nasrids and ultimately to Mudéjar architects employed by the Christians.

MEDINA AZAHARA

The Córdoba caliphate's 'brilliant city', the Medina Azahara, was as architecturally lavish as it was ephemeral. The pet project of Caliph Abd ar-Rahman III, it was conceived as the caliphate's new capital and laid out from scratch 8km west of the city of Córdoba, starting in AD 940. Naming it after his favourite wife, Az-Zahra, the caliph planned his retreat as a royal residence, palace and seat of government, set away from the hubbub of the city in the same manner as the Abbasid royal city of Samarra, north of Baghdad. Its chief architect was Abd ar-Rahman III's son, Al-Hakim II, who later embellished the Córdoba Mezquita so superbly. Although it was wrecked during the collapse of the Córdoba caliphate less than a century after it was built, the remaining imposing horseshoe arches, exquisite stucco work and extensive gardens demonstrate how large and lavish it was.

arches and lavishly decorated domes were much more intricate and technically advanced than anything previously seen in Europe. The *maksura* formed part of a second axis to the building, an aisle running along in front of the wall containing the *mihrab* – known as the *qiblah* wall because it indicates the *qiblah*, the direction of Mecca. This transverse axis creates the T-plan that features strongly in many mosques. In its 'final' 10th-century form the Mezquita's roof was supported by 1293 columns.

The Almohads

As the centuries wore on, competing North African dynasties turned their attention to the glittering prize of Al-Andalus. Some, such as the Almoravids – a Berber dynasty from Morocco from the late 11th to mid-12th centuries – created few notable buildings in Spain. But the second wave of Moroccan Berbers to conquer Al-Andalus, the Almohads, more than made up for the Almoravids' lack of architectural imagination.

Late in the 12th century, the Almohads made a priority of building huge Friday mosques in the main cities of their empire, with Seville especially benefiting from their attention. The design of the mosques was simple and purist, with large prayer halls conforming to the T-plan of the Córdoba Mezquita, but the Almohads introduced some important and beautiful decorative innovations. The bays where the naves meet the *qiblah* wall were surmounted by cupolas or by stucco *muqarnas* (stalactite or honeycomb vaulting composed of hundreds or thousands of tiny cells or niches), an architectural style with its origins in Iran or Syria. On walls, large brick panels with designs of interwoven lozenges were created. Tall, square, richly decorated minarets were another Almohad trademark.

The Giralda, the minaret of Seville's Great Mosque, is the masterpiece of surviving Almohad buildings in Spain, with its beautiful brick panels. The mosque's prayer hall was demolished in the 15th century to make way for the city's cathedral, but its ablutions courtyard (the Patio de los Naranjos), and its northern gate, the handsome Puerta del Perdón, survive.

With defence a primary preoccupation due to Christian advances in the north, the Almohads went on a fortress-building spree in the 12th and early 13th centuries. Cities with bolstered defences included Córdoba, Seville and Jerez de la Frontera. Seville's primary Almohad creation – aside from its mosque – was the river-guarding Torre del Oro, still standing today. Another survivor is Jerez' Alcázar – the tall, austere brick building is based on an unusual octagonal plan inscribed within a square; inside its walls the Almohad mosque was later turned into a church, while its minaret became a bell tower. Further outstanding Almohad-era creations are Tarifa's Castillo de los Guzmán and the city walls of historic Niebla in Huelva province.

Nasrids

With the armies of the Reconquista (Christian reconquest) continuing their seemingly inexorable march south, the last emirate of Islamic Al-Andalus, the Nasrid emirate of Granada (1249–1492), could have been forgiven for having its mind on nonarchitectural matters. But in a recurring theme that resonates down through Andalucian history, it was the architecture that emerged from this period that best captured the spirit of the age. The Alhambra is at once an expansive fortification that reflected uncertain times and an extraordinary palace of last-days opulence.

Alhambra

Granada's magnificent palace-fortress, the Alhambra, is the only surviving large medieval Islamic palace complex in the world. It's a palace-city in the tradition of Córdoba's Medina Azahara, but it's also a fortress, with 2km of walls, 23 towers and a fort within a fort, the Alcazaba. Within the Alhambra's walls were seven separate palaces, mosques, garrisons, houses, offices, baths, a summer residence (the Generalife) and exquisite gardens.

The Alhambra's designers were supremely gifted landscape architects, integrating nature and buildings through the use of pools, running water, meticulously clipped trees and bushes, vista-framing windows, carefully placed lookout points, interplays between light and shadow, and contrasts between heat and cool. The juxtaposition of fountains, pools and gardens with domed reception halls reached a degree of perfection suggestive of the paradise described in the Quran. In keeping with the Alhambra's partial role as a sybarite's delight, many of its defensive towers also functioned as miniature summer palaces.

A huge variety of densely ornamented arches adorns the Alhambra. The Nasrid architects refined existing decorative techniques to new heights of delicacy, elegance and harmony. Their media included sculptured stucco, marble panels, carved and inlaid wood, epigraphy (with endlessly repeated inscriptions of 'There is no God but Allah') and colourful tiles. Plaited star patterns in tile mosaic have since covered walls the length and breadth of the Islamic world, and Nasrid Granada is the dominant artistic influence in the Maghrib (northwest Africa) even today.

Mudéjars & Mozarabs

Islam's architectural legacy lived on even after Christian conquest. Gifted Muslim artisans were frequently employed by Christian rulers and the term Mudéjar – from the Arabic *mudayan* (domesticated) – which was used to describe Muslims who stayed on in areas reconquered by the Christians, came to stick as an architectural label. One hallmark of the style is geometric decorative designs in brick or stucco, often further embellished with tiles. Elaborately carved timber ceilings are also a mark of the Mudéjar hand. *Artesonado* is the word used to describe ceilings with interlaced beams leaving regular spaces for decorative insertions. True Mudéjar *artesonados* generally bear floral or simple geometric patterns.

You'll find Mudéjar or part-Mudéjar churches and monasteries all over Andalucía (Mudéjar is often found side by side with the Christian Gothic style). Andalucía's classic Mudéjar building is the exotic Palacio de Don Pedro, built in the 14th century inside the Alcázar of Seville for the Christian king Pedro I of Castilla. Pedro's friend, Mohammed V, the Muslim emir of Granada, sent many of his best artisans to work on Pedro's palace and, as a result, the Palacio de Don Pedro is effectively a Nasrid building, and one of the best of its kind. Nowhere is this more evident than in the beautiful Patio de las Doncellas at its heart, with its sunken garden surrounded by exquisite arches, tiling and plasterwork.

The term Mozarab, from *musta'rib* (Arabised), refers to Christians who lived, or had lived, in Muslim-controlled territories in the Iberian

---

The Mezquita at Almonaster la Real in Huelva province is like a miniature version of Córdoba's Mezquita, with rows of arches forming five naves, the central one leading to a semicircular *mihrab*.

Although strongly associated with Andalucía, Mudéjar architecture originated in Castilla and Aragón during the 12th and 13th centuries. The best Andalucian Mudéjar buildings are in Seville.

Peninsula. Mozarabic architecture was much influenced by Islamic styles and includes, for instance, the horseshoe arch. The majority of Mozarabic architecture is found in northern Spain; the most significant remaining Mozarabic structure in Andalucía is the rock-cut church at Bobastro.

Christian Architecture

Alonso Cano (1601–67) was a sculptor, architect and painter from Granada whose creative talents were as vivid as his famous temper. He's sometimes called the Spanish Michelangelo, and his most celebrated work is the elaborate baroque facade of Granada's cathedral.

The churches and monasteries built by the Christian conquerors, and the palaces and mansions of their nobility, are a superb part of Andalucía's heritage. But there is, as always, a uniquely Andalucian twist: after the Christian reconquest of Andalucía (1214–1492), Islamic buildings were often simply repurposed for Christian ends. Many Andalucian churches occupy converted mosques (most famously at Córdoba), several church towers began life as minarets, and the zigzagging streets of numerous old towns – such as Granada's Albayzín district – originated in labyrinthine Islamic-era street plans.

Andalucian Gothic

Christian architecture reached northern and western Andalucía with the Reconquista during the 13th century. The prevailing architectural style throughout much of Christian Europe at the time was Gothic, with its distinctive pointed arches, ribbed ceilings, flying buttresses and fancy window tracery. Dozens of Gothic or part-Gothic churches, castles and mansions are dotted throughout Andalucía. Some of these buildings combine Gothic with Mudéjar style, while others have Gothic mixed with later styles and so have ended up as a stylistic hotchpotch.

The final flourish of Spanish Gothic was Isabelline Gothic, from the time of Queen Isabel la Católica. Isabelline Gothic features sinuously curved arches and tracery, and facades with lacelike ornament and low-relief sculptures (including lots of heraldic shields).

Clean Lines of the Renaissance

The Renaissance in architecture was an Italian-originated return to classical ideals of harmony and proportion, dominated by columns and shapes such as the square, circle and triangle. Many Andalucian Renaissance buildings feature elegant interior courtyards lined by two tiers of wide, rounded arcades. Whereas the Gothic period left its most striking mark on church architecture, the Renaissance period was an era in which the gentry built themselves gorgeous urban palaces with delightful patios surrounded by harmonious arched galleries. Many such mansions now serve as beautifully located museums or hotels.

Spanish Renaissance architecture had three phases. First came plateresque, taking its name from the Spanish for silversmith, *platero,* because it was primarily a decorative genre, with effects resembling those of silverware. Round-arched portals were framed by classical columns and stone sculpture. Next came a more purist style, the ultimate expres-

---

BOOKS ON ANDALUCIAN ARCHITECTURE

➡ *Moorish Architecture in Andalusia* (Marianne Barrucand and Achim Bednorz; 1992) Wonderfully illustrated with a learned but readable text.

➡ *Houses & Palaces of Andalusia* (Patricia Espinosa de los Monteros and Francesco Venturi; 1999) A coffee-table tome full of beautiful photography.

➡ *The Alhambra* (Robert Irwin; 2004) Challenges the myths that have coalesced around this most famous of Spanish buildings and brings the place to life.

➡ *Art & Architecture: Andalusia* (Brigitte Hintzen-Bohlen; 2010) A stunning overview of the subject, combining a comprehensive photographic record with informative text.

sion of which is the Palacio de Carlos V within Granada's Alhambra, while the last and plainest phase was Herreresque, after Juan de Herrera (1530–97), creator of the austere palace-monastery complex of El Escorial, near Madrid, and Seville's Archivo de Indias.

All three phases of Renaissance architecture were spanned in Jaén province by the legendary master architect Andrés de Vandelvira (1509–75), who gave the town of Úbeda one of the finest ensembles of Renaissance buildings in Spain. Vandelvira was much influenced by Burgos-born Diego de Siloé (1495–1563), who was primarily responsible for the cathedrals of Granada, Málaga and Guadix.

Baroque Backlash

An inevitable reaction to Renaissance sobriety came in the colours and dramatic sense of motion of baroque. This style really seemed to catch the Andalucian imagination, and Andalucía was one of the places where baroque blossomed most brilliantly, reaching its peak of elaboration in the 18th century.

Baroque style was at root classical, but it specialised in ornamental facades crammed with decoration, and interiors chock-full of ornate stucco sculpture and gilt paint. *Retablos* (retables) – the large, sculptural altarpieces that adorn many Spanish churches to illustrate Christian stories and teachings – reached extremes of gilded extravagance. The most hyperbolic baroque work is termed Churrigueresque after a Barcelona family of sculptors and architects named Churriguera.

Before full-blown baroque there was a kind of transitional stage, exemplified by more sober works such as Alonso Cano's 17th-century facade for Granada's cathedral.

Seville has probably more baroque churches per square kilometre than any city in the world. However, the church at Granada's Monasterio de La Cartuja, by Francisco Hurtado Izquierdo (1669–1725), is one of the most lavish baroque creations in all Spain, with its multicoloured marble, golden capitals and profuse sculpture. Hurtado's followers also adorned the small town of Priego de Córdoba with seven or eight baroque churches.

Modern Andalucian Architecture

In the 19th century, Andalucía acquired some neo-Gothic and neobaroque architecture, but most prevalent were neo-Mudéjar and neo-Islamic styles, harking back to an age that was now catching the fancy of the Romantic movement. Mansions such as the Palacio de Orleans y Borbon in Sanlúcar de Barrameda, and public buildings ranging from train stations in Seville to markets in Málaga and Tarifa, were constructed in colourful imitation of past Islamic architectural styles. For the 1929 Exposición Iberoamericana, fancy buildings in almost every past Andalucian style were concocted in Seville, chief among them the gaudy Plaza de España ensemble by local architect Aníbal González.

During the Franco dictatorship, drab Soviet-style blocks of workers' housing were erected in many cities, while Andalucía's decades-long tourism boom engendered, for the most part, architecture that ranged from the forgettable to the downright hideous. The 21st century has sparked a little more imagination, most notably in Seville, where a trio of big architectural projects – the Metropol Parasol, the Cajasol tower and the Pabellon de la Navegación – has added culture *and* controversy to the urban framework.

Andalucía's architects have demonstrated greater flair in restoring older edifices to serve as hotels, museums or other public buildings. Projects such as Málaga's Museo Picasso and Jaén's Palacio de Villardompardo are both 16th-century urban palaces that have been turned into top-class modern museums.

ANDALUCIAN ARCHITECTURE MODERN ANDALUCIAN ARCHITECTURE

Landscape & Wildlife

Andalucía is better known internationally for its history and culture than its wilderness. That 30% of the land is environmentally protected comes as a surprise to many visitors, who end up wishing they'd planned their trips with more nature in mind. Icons to rival the Alhambra include the snowcapped Sierra Nevada and the precious Doñana wetlands, both national parks. These stellar landscapes are backed up by 240 more protected areas and sites, most of them eminently accessible and enjoyable.

Landscape

Andalucía contains both Spain's wettest town (Grazalema in Cádiz province, with up to 200cm of rain annually) and its driest area (the Desierto de Tabernas in Almería province, with a mere 14cm annually).

Andalucía has mountains in abundance, from the relatively low hills of the Sierra Morena to the heights of the Sierra Nevada. The Sierra Morena, which rarely rises higher than 1000m, rolls across the north of Andalucía like the last outpost of rugged southern Spain before it yields to the sweeping flat lands and distant horizons of Spain's central *meseta* (plateau). Very sparsely populated, the Sierra Morena is extremely beautiful in its own subtle way, divided between evergreen oak woodlands, scrub, rough grazing pasture, river valleys and scattered old stone villages.

Closer to the coast, the Cordillera Bética was pushed up by the pressure of the African tectonic plate on the Iberian subplate 15 to 20 million years ago. This band of jagged mountains widens out from its beginnings in southwestern Andalucía to a breadth of 125km or so in the east. It includes the 75km-long Sierra Nevada southeast of Granada, with several 3000m-plus peaks (including 3479m Mulhacén, the highest mountain in mainland Spain). The cordillera continues east from Andalucía across Spain's Murcia and Valencia regions, before re-emerging from the Mediterranean as the Balearic islands of Ibiza and Mallorca. Much of it is composed of limestone, yielding some wonderful karstic rock formations.

Apart from the coastal plain, which varies in width from 50km in the far west to virtually nothing in parts of Granada and Almería provinces, the fertile valley of the 660km-long Río Guadalquivir is Andalucía's other major geographical feature. The Guadalquivir, rises in the Cazorla mountains of Jaén province, flows westward through Córdoba and Sevilla, and enters the Atlantic at Sanlúcar de Barrameda. Before entering the ocean, the river splits into a marshy delta known as Las Marismas del Guadalquivir, which includes the Parque Nacional de Doñana.

Andalucía's Main Parks & Protected Areas

Andalucía has the biggest environmental-protection program in Spain. More than 240 areas, covering some 27,000 sq km, are included within regional, national or international protection networks, amounting to 30% of Andalucian territory. All this habitat conservation, as well as some specific recovery programs, has helped bring about a highly encouraging recovery in the numbers of some iconic endangered species such as the Iberian lynx and the black vulture. Ventana del Visitante (Visitor's Window; www.juntadeandalucia.es/medioambiente/servtc5/ventana) is the comprehensive and very useful official website for information about visiting Andalucía's protected areas, with much of the information in English as well as Spanish.

Parques Nacional & Natural de Doñana

The Doñana national park and its *parque natural* buffer, in the Guadalquivir delta, embrace most of Europe's largest wetlands, a crucial area for over 350 migratory and resident bird species and 37 types of mammal, including the rare Iberian lynx and big herds of deer and wild boar. A range of 4WD, horse-riding and walking trips enables you to get into either or both parks.

Parque Nacional & Natural Sierra Nevada

The national park covers the upper reaches of mainland Spain's highest mountain range – a great summer hiking and winter skiing challenge – while the surrounding *parque natural* includes timeless white villages and many walking, mountain-biking and horse-riding routes on the Sierra Nevada's lower slopes, especially in the Alpujarras valleys on the southern side.

Parque Natural Sierra de Andújar

A medium-sized park in the Sierra Morena in the northwest of Jaén province, Andújar is notable for its rare mammals and birds. It contains Andalucía's largest population of Iberian lynx, endangered black vultures, black storks and Spanish imperial eagles.

Parque Natural de Cabo de Gata-Níjar

Flamingo colonies, volcanic cliffs and sandy beaches make for a combination unlike any other protected area in Andalucía. One of the region's driest corners, the eastern park showcases a semidesert terrain, and promises a range of activities, including swimming, birdwatching, walking, horse riding, diving and snorkelling.

Parque Natural Sierras Subbéticas

Consisting of a set of craggy, green hills and canyons in Córdoba province, and sprinkled with caves, springs and streams, this park offers good hiking and some charming old villages and country hotels around its periphery. The best bases are Zuheros and Priego de Córdoba.

Donaña, established in 1969, was Spain's sixth national park; the Sierra Nevada, established in 1999, was the 12th.

PARKS & PROTECTED AREAS

Andalucía's protected areas fall into two main categories.

Parques nacionales (national parks) are areas of exceptional importance for their fauna, flora, geomorphology or landscape, and their conservation is considered to be in the national interest. These are the most strictly protected areas and may include reserve areas closed to the public, or restricted areas that can only be visited with permission. Spain has just 15 *parques nacionales*; two of them – Doñana and Sierra Nevada – are in Andalucía.

Parques naturales (natural parks) are intended to protect cultural heritage as well as nature, and to promote economic development (including tourism) that's compatible with conservation. There are 24 *parques naturales* in Andalucía; they account for most of its protected territory and include nearly all of its most spectacular country.

Other types of protected areas in Andalucía include *parajes naturales* (natural areas; there are 32 of these) and *reservas naturales* (nature reserves, numbering 28). These are generally smaller, little-inhabited areas, with much the same goals as natural parks. There are also 49 *monumentos naturales* (natural monuments), protecting specific features such as waterfalls, forests or dunes.

Then there are areas protected under various international agreements, which often overlap with the regionally or nationally protected areas. They include 226 sites in the Natura 2000 European network of conservation areas, and 25 Ramsar wetland areas; Ramsar is an international treaty that focuses on wetlands conservation.

Parque Natural Sierra de Grazalema

Ibex, griffon vultures and other species inhabit this beautiful, damp, hilly region that is notable for its vast sweeps of Mediterranean woodlands and stands of rare Spanish firs. Archetypal white Andalucian villages serve as gateways to fantastic hiking trails, and you can also climb, canyon and paraglide to your heart's content.

Parque Natural Sierra de las Nieves

Spectacular vistas and deep valleys characterise this mountain region deep in the interior of Málaga province. With iconic examples of Andalucian flora (stands of Spanish firs) and fauna (ibex), as well as other species, the park is a good choice for hiking in off-the-beaten-track Andalucian wilds.

Parque Natural Sierra de Aracena y Picos de Aroche

Woodlands, evergreen oak pastures, old stone villages and imposing castles populate this charming tract of the Sierra Morena in far western Andalucía. An extensive network of well-maintained walking trails provides some of the most delightful rambling in Andalucía.

Parque Natural Sierras de Cazorla, Segura y las Villas

Abundant, easily visible wildlife, craggy mountains, deep valleys and thick forests – it's difficult to overestimate the charms of this beautiful park, Spain's largest (2099 sq km), in Jaén province. Red and fallow deer, wild boar, mouflon and ibex provide the wildlife interest. Hike or explore on horseback or by 4WD.

Paraje Natural Torcal de Antequera

The mountain La Veleta, in the Sierra Nevada, sports Europe's highest paved road, which climbs to an altitude of 3380m, just 15m below the summit. The road is not, however, open to private vehicles.

Striking limestone formations are what most visitors remember about this mountainous natural area close to Antequera in Málaga province. It contains some of the strangest landforms in Andalucía and has a handful of walking trails. It also draws climbers.

Parque Natural Sierras de Tejeda, Almijara y Alhama

Popular with walkers, this park encompasses a large area of mountains and valleys not far back from the coast of Málaga and Granada provinces. Ibex roam the higher altitudes and wild boar the valleys. Nerja, Cómpeta and Almuñécar all make good bases.

Wildlife

Andalucía is a haven for wildlife that is hard or impossible to find elsewhere, and wildlife enthusiasts, if they know where to look, are unlikely to return home disappointed.

Signature Mammals

Several large mammal species that once roamed across Western Europe are now confined to small, isolated populations surrounded by an ever-expanding sea of humanity. That they survive in Andalucía is thanks to the region's varied, often untamed terrain, and admirable nature-conservation policies, but even here they remain at risk.

Andalucía's most celebrated mammal, the Iberian lynx, has been recovering well in the last decade thanks to a successful captive breeding and release program. The species is still endangered, but, with patience and a bit of luck, it's no longer impossible to see a lynx in the wild.

Wolves (lobos) are in a far more precarious situation, possibly down to single figures (or none at all), in and around Jaén province's Parque Natural Sierra de Andújar. Wolf numbers have increased in recent years in Spain as a whole, to about 2000, but almost all of these are in the northwest of the country.

Hunting throughout the 20th century, and traps and poison put out by livestock farmers, are among the reasons that lynx and wolf populations declined so alarmingly.

One of the region's most easily spotted mammals is the ibex *(cabra montés)*, a stocky wild mountain goat whose males have distinctive long, curved horns. Probably more than 30,000 ibex live in Andalucía, with the largest populations found in the Sierra Nevada; the Parque Natural Sierras de Cazorla, Segura y las Villas; and the Sierras de Tejeda, Almijara, Mágina, Grazalema and Nieves (all protected as *parques naturales*). It's in no apparent danger of extinction, although its numbers sometimes plummet due to outbreaks of scabies.

One of Spain's most unusual wildlife-watching experiences is the sight of Barbary apes, the only wild primates in Europe, clambering around Gibraltar's heights.

Whales *(ballenas)* and dolphins *(delfines)* are more often associated with the open waters of the Atlantic than with the Mediterranean. Even so, the Bahía de Algeciras and Strait of Gibraltar harbour plenty of common, striped and bottlenose dolphins, as well as some pilot, killer and even sperm whales. You can get close to them on whale-and-dolphin-watching trips from Tarifa.

More common, less iconic mammals abound. Although some are nocturnal, those you may come across once you leave behind well-trodden trails include wild boar *(jabalí)*, red deer *(ciervo)*, roe deer *(corzo)*, fallow deer *(gamo)*, genets *(gineta)*, Egyptian mongooses *(meloncillo)*, red squirrels *(ardilla)*, badgers *(tejón)* and otters *(nutria)*.

The Parque Natural Sierras de Cazorla, Segura y las Villas, at 2099 sq km, is the largest protected area in Spain and the second largest in Europe.

LANDSCAPE & WILDLIFE WILDLIFE

Endangered Lynx

The Iberian (or pardel) lynx (*lince ibérico* to Spaniards; *Lynx pardina* to scientists) – a separate species from the larger Eurasian lynx found elsewhere in Europe – is, at the time of writing, a remarkable success story. The species once ranged across almost the whole Iberian Peninsula (the Hispanic Legions of the Roman Empire wore breastplates adorned with it) and a century ago there were perhaps 100,000 Iberian lynx in the wild. So plentiful was the lynx that the Spanish government classed it as vermin, encouraging hunters to kill it. By 1960 there were only an estimated 500 left. By 1973, the species was officially protected, but this did little to slow the lynx's precipitous decline, prompting fears that it would become the first cat species to become extinct since the sabre-toothed tiger, 10,000 years ago.

By the early 21st century, numbers were down to little over 100, chiefly in two separate areas of Andalucía – in and around the Parque Nacional de Doñana, and in the Sierra Morena in northern Jaén province – with a few more in the Montes de Toledo of Castilla-La Mancha. Since then a captive breeding program, initially launched at El Acebuche in Doñana in 1992 and later extended to other centres in Andalucía, with young lynx being released into the wild, has proved a big success. By 2015 numbers had risen to about 400 and the Iberian lynx was taken off the International Union for Conservation of Nature's 'critically endangered' list. In 2017 there were estimated to be some 500 Iberian lynx in the wild, 400 of them in Andalucía – about 300 in the Parque Natural Sierra de Andújar and other areas of the Sierra Morena in Jaén and Córdoba provinces, and around 100 in the Doñana area. Lynx have also been released in the Montes de Toledo, the south of Extremadura and southern Portugal.

The Iberian lynx still faces threats from road accidents and epidemics that kill off large numbers of rabbits (its main prey), but its future certainly looks far rosier than it did a decade ago.

Live film of lynx in the breeding program is displayed on a screen at Doñana's El Acebuche visitor centre, though the breeding centre itself is closed to the public. Chances of sighting a wild lynx are highest in the Parque Natural Sierra de Andújar.

Birdwatcher's Paradise

Andalucía is something of a last refuge for several highly endangered raptor species. When it comes to migratory bird species, however, Andalucía is a veritable superhighway.

Andalucía has 13 resident raptor species, as well as a handful of summer visitors from Africa. The rare and vulnerable black vulture *(buitre negro)* – Europe's biggest bird – has established a stronghold in the Sierra Morena, with around 400 pairs (doubled since 2001) scattered from Huelva's Sierra Pelada to Jaén's Sierra de Andújar. As this is probably the world's biggest population of black vultures, the bird's survival here is critical to the viability of the species.

An excellent English-language source of information on Andalucian fauna and flora is Iberianature (www.iberia nature.com).

More easily spotted and just as impressive is the 2.5m-wingspan griffon vulture *(buitre leonado)*, which numbers well over 2000 breeding pairs in Andalucía (out of about 18,000 in Spain). You are virtually guaranteed sightings in places such as the Garganta Verde in the Parque Natural Sierra de Grazalema, the Peñón de Zaframagón near Olvera, and the hills around the town of Cazorla.

Also emblematic and very rare is the Spanish imperial eagle *(águila imperial ibérica)*, found in no other country. Its total numbers have increased from about 50 nesting pairs in the 1960s to over 500 by 2016, helped by an active government protection plan operative since 2001. About 110 pairs are in Andalucía – mostly in the Sierra Morena, with about nine pairs in the Doñana area.

The bearded vulture or lammergeier *(quebrantahuesos)*, with its majestic 2.7m to 2.9m wingspan, disappeared from Andalucía – its last refuge in Spain except for the Pyrenees – in 1986. But a breeding centre was established in the Parque Natural Sierras de Cazorla, Segura y las Villas in 1996; the first young lammergeiers were released into the wild in 2006; the first chick hatched in the wild in 2015; and in 2017 there were two breeding pairs residing in the Cazorla mountains.

Other large birds of prey in Andalucía include the golden eagle *(águila real)* and the Egyptian vulture *(alimoche)*, all found in mountain regions.

If Andalucía's raptors lend gravitas to birdwatching here, the waterbirds that visit Andalucía add a scale rarely seen in Europe, mainly thanks to extensive wetlands along the Atlantic coast. Hundreds of thousands of migratory birds, including an estimated 80% of Western Europe's wild ducks, winter in the Doñana wetlands of the Guadalquivir delta, and many more call in during spring and autumn migrations.

Laguna de Fuente de Piedra, near Antequera, sees as many as 20,000 greater flamingo *(flamenco)* pairs rearing chicks in spring and summer. This beautiful pink bird can also be seen in several other places, including San Miguel de Cabo de Gata, El Rocío on the edge of the Parque Nacional de Doñana, and the Paraje Natural Marismas del Odiel; these last two have extensive wetlands that serve as a haven for many other waterbirds.

The large, ungainly white stork *(cigüeña blanca)*, actually black and white, nests from spring to summer on electricity pylons and in trees and towers (sometimes right in the middle of towns) across western Andalucía. Much rarer and less sociable is the black stork *(cigüeña negra)*, which prefers cliff ledges. Both birds are mainly migrant visitors, crossing the Strait of Gibraltar from Africa to breed in Spain.

For more information on Andalucía's bird life, check out SEO/BirdLife (www.seo.org) and the Andalucia Bird Society (www.andaluciabird society.org).

Arts & Culture

For significant parts of Spanish history, Andalucía has stood at the forefront of the nation's artistic and cultural life. Halcyon eras have come and gone, often ebbing and flowing with the power of Spain in world affairs. Though all the arts are well represented, the region has produced a particularly rich seam of talented painters, including Diego Velázquez and Pablo Picasso. Meanwhile, flamenco – reflective but uplifting, raw but layered, pure yet loaded with historical and emotional complexity – is proudly and unequivocally a product of Andalucía.

Arts

Córdoba Caliphate

The most populous and culturally vibrant city in Europe at the time, the Córdoba of the 8th to 11th centuries was an intellectual powerhouse, replete with libraries, schools and a university that competed with the rival caliphate of Baghdad to promote the global spread of ideas. Emir Abd ar-Rahman II (r 822–52) was a strong patron of the arts who maintained a close relationship with the influential Arabic poet and musician Ziryab; Abd ar-Rahman III (r 912–61) filled his city Medina Azahara with the finest Islamic art, crafts and mosaics, much of it copied from Byzantine artists; while Al-Hakim II (r 961–76) was an avid reader who collected and catalogued hundreds of thousands of books. Many of the great works of Greek philosophy were later translated and reinterpreted in medieval Córdoba by scholarly polymaths such as Averroës (1126–98), Maimonides (1135–1204) and Ibn Tufail (1105–85).

Though Córdoba's influence declined after its reconquest by the Christians in 1236, the invaders from the north subtly absorbed many of the city's ideas. It was partly through this intellectual inheritance that Western Europe attained the know-how and inspiration that sparked the Renaissance in Italy two centuries later.

> The Seville studio of painter Francisco Pacheco (1564–1644) was the centre of a humanist circle that influenced most of the leading Andalucian artists of the Golden Age, including Velázquez (who married Pacheco's daughter), Zurbarán and Alonso Cano. Pacheco advised his pupils to follow nature for everything.

Nasrid Flowering

The Nasrid emirate established in Granada in 1232 was more of a defensive entity than an outward-looking culture-spreader in the mould of Córdoba. However, its foppish rulers were vociferous appreciators of the arts, in particular poetry. Several of the emirate's sultans became acclaimed poets, most notably the yearningly romantic Yusuf III (r 1408–17). The high point of the Granadan flowering came during the illustrious reigns of Yusuf I (1333–54) and Mohammed V (1354–91), the two great builders of the Alhambra. Both sultans established literary circles in their courts. Yusuf employed Arabic poet and historian Ibn al-Khatib (1313–74), whose verse was set to music and whose lyrical poems remain inscribed on the walls of Alhambra's palaces and fountains. Mohammed V installed al-Khatib as his *vizier* (political adviser), a position that stoked much political controversy at the time and possibly cost al-Khatib his life: in 1374, according to one version of the story, al-Khatib's student and fellow poet Ibn Zamrak (1333–93) hired assassins to kill him. Ibn Zamrak subsequently became court poet to Mohammed V, during an era when poetry and cultural exchange with Morocco and Egypt had created a healthy cross-continental flow of ideas.

Golden Age

For a glittering 50 years during Spain's artistic Siglo de Oro (Golden Age), which ran from the late 16th to late 17th centuries, Andalucian painters pretty much defined world art. The mantle rested chiefly on the shoulders of three Sevillan giants. Bartolomé Esteban Murillo (1617–82) was a baroque master with a delicate touch and a penchant for documentary and religious painting. The mystically inclined Francisco de Zurbarán (1598–1664), born in Extremadura but resident in and around Seville for most of his life, was a more restrained exponent of the Italian art of chiaroscuro (the technique of contrasting light and dark elements in a painting to create a dramatic effect). Diego Velázquez (1599–1660) was known as an artist's artist; his exacting methods and subtle use of colour and tone ultimately opened the door to Impressionism. He was born and started his artistic career in Seville but moved to Madrid to become a court painter in 1623. Velázquez' most celebrated work, *Las meninas* (Maids of Honour), is a revolutionary masterpiece of viewpoint in which the artist depicts himself contemplating his invisible subjects, King Felipe IV and Queen Mariana of Spain, whose faces appear reflected in a mirror. *Las meninas* hangs today in Madrid's El Prado. Three centuries after Velázquez' death, an enamoured Picasso made 58 abstract attempts to reinterpret this great work.

Both Velázquez and Zurbarán were employed by the royal court of Felipe IV, while Murillo was favoured by the Catholic Church. Murillo painted several works for Seville's cathedral and produced dozens of depictions of the Virgin Mary's immaculate conception.

Velazquez' friend Alonso Cano (1601–72), from Granada, was a gifted painter, sculptor and architect noted for an uncontrollable temper. In the course of his turbulent life he also found work at Felipe IV's court. Much of his best work hangs in Seville's Museo de Bellas Artes, along with strong representations of Zurbarán's and Murillo's art.

Generation of '98

The Andalucian art scene dimmed in the 18th and 19th centuries as Spain lost its overseas empire and position as a global power. Spain's humiliation in the Spanish-American War of 1898, when it lost its last colonies, was the event around which revolved a group of critical writers known as the Generación de '98. Their writings, flecked with rebellion and realism, aimed to offset the cultural malaise and re-establish the nation's literary prominence. The circle's leading poet, Seville-born Antonio Machado (1875–1939), chided the nation for being asleep, adrift in a sea of mediocrity. Machado spent most of his adult life outside Andalucía, except for a few years as a teacher in Baeza, where he completed *Campos de Castilla*, a set of poems evoking the landscape of Castilla and ruminating on the national malaise. Machado's friend Juan Ramón Jiménez (1881–1958), from Moguer near Huelva, touchingly and amusingly brought to life his home town in *Platero y Yo* (Platero and I), a prose poem telling of his childhood wanderings with his donkey and confidant, Platero. Winner of the 1956 Nobel literature prize, Juan Ramón stands as a kind of bridge between the Generation of '98 and the next great wave of Andalucian writers in the Generation of '27.

Around the same time, classical music found a cohesive Iberian voice in a group of four Spanish composers, two of whom were from Andalucía. Both Manuel de Falla (1876–1946) from Cádiz and Joaquín Turina (1882–1949) from Seville used influences absorbed from Parisian Impressionists Debussy and Ravel to craft operas, ballet scores, songs and

Lord Byron first visited Andalucía in 1809. Inspired by the experience, he wrote his mock-epic poetic masterpiece *Don Juan*, based on the famous Spanish fictional hero, in the early 1820s.

Miguel de Cervantes, creator of Don Quijote, was not Andalucian, but he did spend 10 troubled years in the region procuring oil and wheat for the Spanish navy and as a collector of unpaid taxes. Some of his short *Novelas ejemplares* (Exemplary Novels) chronicle life in turbulent 16th-century Seville.

chamber music that resonated with echoes of Andalucian folklore. Falla, in particular, was fascinated by flamenco; along with poet and playwright Federico García Lorca, he organised the famous flamenco-revival event the Concurso de Cante Jondo (p347) in Granada in 1922.

Generation of '27

Spain's great literary blossoming took place during the relatively calm 1920s dictatorship of Primo de Rivera, between the social unrest of the early 20th century and the tumultuous years leading to the Spanish Civil War in the 1930s. In 1927 in Seville, a key group of 10 poets came together to mark the 300th anniversary of the death of lyrical baroque Córdoba master Luis de Góngora. Of the 10, six were born in Andalucía, including the peerless Federico García Lorca (from Granada), the romantic turned polemicist poet Rafael Alberti (from El Puerto de Santa María) and the surrealist wordsmith Vicente Aleixandre (from Seville).

Unlike the more pessimistic Generación de '98, which had criticised the conformism of Spain after the restoration of the monarchy in 1874, the 27ers were less damning of what had gone before in their exploration of classic themes such as love, death, destiny and the beauty of images. Obsessed by the work of Góngora, they espoused wider poetic expressionism and free verse, combining elements of the new surrealism with echoes from Spain's ancient folkloric tradition (in particular, flamenco). The movement was ultimately shattered and dispersed by the civil war, an event that killed Lorca and exiled many of the others.

The last surviving member of the Generación de '27, Francisco Ayala from Granada, died in 2009 aged 103. Ayala spent many years in exile in Argentina and Puerto Rico after his father and brother were murdered by Nationalists in the civil war.

Lorca – Man of Many Talents

Andalucía's (and arguably Spain's) greatest writer, Granada-born Federico García Lorca (1898–1936), is best known for his poems and plays and – more tragically – his senseless murder at the hands of Spanish fascists at the start of the civil war. But Lorca's talents went beyond writing. He was an accomplished pianist, an actor with a rural theatre troupe, a director of his own and other people's plays, and a deft cultural organiser – along with classical composer Manuel de Falla, he was instrumental in conceiving flamenco's Concurso de Cante Jondo (p347) in 1922. In collusion with Falla, Lorca also co-composed an opera – sadly, unfinished – called *Lola, la Comedianta;* inspired by another friend, Salvador Dalí, he demonstrated his skill for art. Lorca once even drafted a surrealistic film screenplay entitled *Viaje a la luna* (Trip to the Moon, which wasn't filmed until 1998).

ARTS & CULTURE ARTS

The 2008 British-Spanish film *Little Ashes (Cenicitas)* is based on longstanding rumours of a 1920s love affair between Federico García Lorca and Salvador Dalí.

PICASSO RECLAIMED

Born in Málaga in 1881 to Don José Ruíz y Blasco (also an artist) and María Picasso y López, Pablo Picasso lived in Málaga until he was 10. In 1891 he moved with his family to A Coruña in Galicia and then, in 1895, to Barcelona, where he ultimately established his artistic reputation. Since he never returned permanently to Málaga, Picasso's connection with Andalucía was long underemphasised; you'll find better exhibitions of his art in Barcelona and Paris. But with Málaga undergoing a cultural awakening in recent decades, the city took steps to reclaim him. The Picasso Foundation was established in 1988 in his Casa Natal (birth house) in Plaza de la Merced, and, in 2003, after 50 years of on-off planning, the excellent Museo Picasso Málaga was opened in a 16th-century palace.

Dead by the age of 38, Lorca squeezed his achievements into a fertile two decades between 1918 and 1936, when he was shot and slung into an unmarked grave just outside Granada. Not surprisingly, his legacy is massive and regularly refuelled by the ongoing search for his remains. They are thought to lie somewhere near the village of Viznar, beneath the pastoral Vega he loved so dearly.

Flamenco

Basics

One of the beauties of flamenco is its lack of straightforwardness, though a handful of basic points offer some clarity. First, flamenco is an expressive art, incorporating more than just music. In the early days it was a realistic reflection of the lives of those who sang it – the oppressed – and they carried it with them everywhere: in the fields, at work, at home and in their famed *juergas* (Roma parties). Second, it is very much a 'live' spectacle and – for purists, at least – a necessarily spontaneous one. The preserve of the Roma until the 19th century, performances were never rehearsed or theatrical, and the best ones still aren't. Third, flamenco hinges on the interaction between its four basic elements: the *cante* (song), the *baile* (dance), the *toque* (guitar), and an oft-forgotten fourth element known as the *jaleo* (handclaps, shouts and audience participation/appreciation). The *cante* sits centre stage, as the guide. In its earliest incarnations, flamenco didn't have regular dancers, and guitars weren't added until the 19th century. Some flamenco forms, such as *martinetes* and *carceleras*, remain voice only. In traditional flamenco performances, players warm up slowly, tuning their guitars and clearing their throats while the gathered crowd talk among themselves. It is up to the dancers and musicians to grab the audience's attention and gradually lure them in.

> Saetas are religious laments that are often included under the name 'flamenco'. You'll still hear them sung unaccompanied from upper-floor balconies during Semana Santa processions as the float passes beneath.

Flamenco Palos (Musical Forms)

The purist expression of flamenco is known as *cante jondo* (literally 'deep song'), a primitive collection of *palos* (musical forms) that includes *soleares* (a quintessential form with a strong, strict rhythm), the tragic and expressive *siguiriyas*, and *tientos*, *martinetes* and *carceleras*. *Cante jondo* is considered to be the main building block of flamenco and good singers – whose gravelly, operatic voices can sound like a cross between Tom Waits and Pavarotti – are required to sing as if their lives depended upon it, and leave a piece of their soul in every stanza. The ideal is to inspire *duende* – the musical spirit that reaches out and touches your soul during an ecstatic live performance. But *duende* can be elusive. The poet Federico García Lorca, in his many commentaries on the subject, often alluded to its intangibility. Thus, it is up to the singer to summon it up, amalgamating yearning, superstition, anguish and fervour into a force that is both intimate and transcendental.

> **Best Peñas**
>
> Peña de la Platería, Granada
>
> Peña Flamenca La Perla, Cádiz
>
> Peña Juan Breva, Málaga
>
> Peña Flamenca Tomás El Nitri, El Puerto de Santa María
>
> Centro Cultural Flamenco Don Antonio Chacón, Jerez de la Frontera

Cantes Chicos

The other main grouping of flamenco songs is called *cantes chicos* (little songs), *palos* that are more light-hearted and accessible derivatives of *cante jondo*. Popular *cantes chicos* are the upbeat *alegrías* from Cádiz, descended from sailor's jigs; the fast but tongue-in-cheek *bulerías* from Jerez; and the ubiquitous *tangos* made popular by the great Sevillan singer La Niña de los Peines.

Cantes Andaluces

A third, more nebulous, group of *palos* (sometimes called *cantes andaluces*) exists outside what most aficionados would call 'pure' flamenco.

This consists mainly of *fandangos* that are descended from Spanish folk music, with each region broadcasting its own variation. The most famous are the strident *fandangos de Huelva*, enthusiastically danced during the Romería del Rocío religious pilgrimage. *Verdiales*, an ancient Arabic-style song/dance, are a type of *fandango* from Málaga, a province that also concocted the freer and easier (and undanced) *malagueñas*. *Granaínas* are an ornamental and introspective *fandango* offshoot from Granada with no set rhythm; *tarantas* are an earthier, sparser version of the form from the mining communities of the Levante (Almería).

Historical Roots

The long-time preserve of marginalised and culturally oppressed people (most of whom were illiterate), flamenco was neither written about nor eulogised in its early days. Instead, the music was passed through bloodlines by word of mouth. No published testimonies exist before 1840.

The genesis of the art as we now know it took place in Andalucía some time in the early 15th century, among disparate groups of Roma, Jews, Moors and perhaps other Spaniards. Anthropological evidence suggests that the Roma had begun a 400-year westward migration from the Indian subcontinent in the 11th century, settling all over Europe, with a southern contingent reaching Andalucía in the early 15th century. The Roma brought with them a dynamic form of musical expression – a way of performing that encouraged embellishment, virtuosity and improvisation – and they blended this rich musicality with the songs and melodies of the regions in which they settled. In Andalucía, they found natural allies among the Jews and Moors recently disenfranchised by the Reconquista (Christian reconquest). The collision of these three distinct cultures and the subsequent marinating of their music and culture over three or four centuries resulted in what we now know as *cante jondo*, or pure flamenco.

The Ortegas are one of the great Roma families. They have produced such flamenco singers as El Fillo (Francisco Ortega Vargas) and El Caracol ('The Snail'; Manuel Ortega Juárez), as well as legendary bullfighters such as Joselito 'El Gallo' ('The Rooster'; José Gómez Ortega).

ARTS & CULTURE FLAMENCO

FLAMENCO LEGENDS

El Planeta (1785–1850) Legendary Roma blacksmith who purportedly invented many unaccompanied *cantes* (songs).

El Fillo (1829–78) Protégé of El Planeta and famed for his gravelly voice, dubbed the *voz afillá*.

Silverio Franconetti (1831–89) Non-Roma who met El Fillo in Morón de la Frontera. Became an accomplished singer and set up Spain's most famous *café cantante* in Seville.

Antonio Chacón (1869–1929) Non-Roma singer with a powerful voice. Hired by Franconetti to sing in his Seville *café cantante* in the 1890s.

Ramón Montoya (1880–1949) Accompanist to Chacón from 1922 onwards – he put the guitar centre stage in flamenco.

La Niña de los Peines (1890–1969) Dynamic Roma singer from Seville who sang with Chacón and provided a vital link between the golden age and the 1950s revivalists.

El Caracol (1909–73) Discovered at age 12 at the Concurso de Cante Jondo in 1922. Went on to become one of the greatest, yet most self-destructive, flamenco singers of all time.

Carmen Amaya (1913–63) Her dynamic dancing and wild lifestyle made her the Roma dance legend of all time. From Barcelona.

Camarón de la Isla (1950–92) Performed in a club owned by El Caracol; this modern flamenco 'god' from San Fernando (La Isla) lived fast, died young and dabbled in bold experimentation.

Paco de Lucía (1947–2014) Guitar phenomenon from Algeciras who became Camarón's main accompanist, and successfully crossed over into jazz and classical music.

Best Festivals

························

*Festival de Jerez,
Jerez de la
Frontera*

························

*Noche Blanca del
Flamenco, Córdoba*

························

*Bienal de
Flamenco, Seville*

A Tale of Three Cities

Flamenco's documented history begins in the early 19th century and is essentially a tale of three cities in western Andalucía: Seville, Cádiz and Jerez de la Frontera, and their respective Roma neighbourhoods. Jerez has often been called the 'cradle of flamenco', primarily because its densely packed Roma quarters of Santiago and San Miguel have produced so many great artists. Today, the city is home to Andalucía's main flamenco centre/school and hosts two major festivals: the Festival de Jerez (in February or early March) and the Fiestas de Otoñõ (in September). Flamenco in Cádiz grew up in the Santa María neighbourhood, while in Seville its font was the riverside Roma district of Triana. A few other towns with strong flamenco traditions lie in Sevilla province: Morón de la Frontera, Utrera and Lebrija. Together with Seville, Jerez and Cádiz, they make up Andalucía's so-called 'flamenco triangle'.

The first real flamenco singer of note was the mysteriously named El Planeta (Antonio Monge Rivero), a Roma blacksmith born in either Jerez or Cádiz around 1785. El Planeta wasn't a performer in the modern sense, but he soon became well known for his passionate singing voice, which gave birth – allegedly – to such early flamenco *palos* as *martinetes* and *livianas*. El Planeta sits at the head of a flamenco family tree of interrelated singers, musicians and dancers that has carried on to the present day. His immediate heir was El Fillo (Francisco Ortega Vargas), whose naturally gravelly voice became the standard against which all others were compared, and whose name lived on in the term used to describe that type of voice – *voz afillá*.

Golden Age

Flamenco's 'golden age' began in the late 1840s and lasted until around 1915. In the space of 70 years, the music metamorphosed from an esoteric Roma art practised spontaneously at raucous *juergas* into a professional and increasingly popular form of public entertainment that merged *cante jondo* with other forms of Spanish folkloric music. It was during this fertile epoch that the modern musical forms took shape. Other innovations included the more complex choreography of flamenco dance and the emergence of the guitar as the de rigueur accompanying instrument.

The catalysts for change were the famous *cafés cantante* that took root in many Spanish cities, especially in Andalucía, and became the engine rooms of a dramatic musical cross-fertilisation. The first cafe opened in Seville in 1842, and the establishments gradually spread, reaching their apex in the 1880s with prestigious venues such as the Café Silverio in Seville. Presiding over this conflation was Silverio Franconetti, proprietor of Seville's Café Silverio and soulful inheritor of El Fillo's hoarse, cracked *voz afillá*. Yet, despite his lifelong penchant for *siguiriyas* and *soleares*, Franconetti couldn't stop the bastardisation of the music he loved as it moved from the *juergas* into the cafes, substituting tragic harshness for tuneful palatability. Unwittingly, he had created the conditions for flamenco's jump from music of the Roma to popular property.

Slide into Decadence

By 1920 pure flamenco, threatened by changing public tastes and impending political crises, was an endangered species. Fearing oblivion, Andalucian aesthetes Federico García Lorca and Manuel de Falla organised a competition in Granada in 1922 to try to save the art – the Concurso de Cante Jondo. But with the civil war approaching, the die was cast. The music entered an era known as *ópera flamenco*, when *cante jondo* was diluted further by folk music, greater commercialisation and influences from Latin America. The controversial figure of the era was Pepe Marchena (1903–76), flamenco's first well-paid superstar, who broke with

CONCURSO DE CANTE JONDO, 1922

On an ethereal summer's evening in June 1922, a little-known Andalucian poet named Federico García Lorca welcomed 4000 guests to the Concurso de Cante Jondo (competition of 'deep song'), a flamenco singing contest he had organised at Granada's Alhambra in collusion with the distinguished Spanish classical composer Manuel de Falla.

Between them, these two great avant-garde artists had struggled relentlessly to elevate flamenco – and in particular *cante jondo* – into a serious art form, a dynamic cultural genre of half-forgotten Andalucian folkloric traditions, in the face of a growing popular penchant for watered-down forms of flamenco 'opera'.

Amassed inside the atmospheric confines of the Alhambra was an impressive array of intellectuals, writers, performers, musicians and flamenco purists. One 72-year-old *cantaor* (singer) named Tio Bermúdez had walked 100km from his village to be there, and stunned the audience with his interpretations of old-style *siguiriyas*. Another, an old blind woman of Roma stock, hunted down by Lorca, sang an unaccompanied *liviana*, a flamenco form long thought to be dead. A 12-year-old boy named Manolo Ortega, aka 'El Caracol' ('The Snail'), so impressed the judges that he walked off with first prize. Young men swapped guitar *falsetas* (riffs), ladies stood up and danced *soleares*, while others listened to the virtuosity of established stars such as Ramón Montoya and Manuel Torre.

Whether the *concurso* ultimately 'saved' flamenco is open to debate. While the music gained some short-lived prestige, and sporadic recordings and revivals ensued, its golden age was over. An era of decadence followed, hastened by the onset of the civil war and the repressive Franco dictatorship that followed. Flamenco's modern rebirth ultimately had to wait for a second *concurso* in Córdoba in 1956, and the subsequent rise of more ground-breaking innovators over a decade later.

---

tradition by singing lighter *fandangos* and *cantes de ida y vuelta* (musical forms sugar-frosted with Latin American influences before being 'returned' to Spain), often backed by an orchestra. Just below the radar, *cante jondo* survived, in part because it was still performed by Roma singers such as Manuel Torre and La Niña de los Peines, the greatest male and female voices of their age.

Rebirth

By the 1950s, the re-evaluation of *cante jondo* fell to Antonio Mairena (1909–83), an impassioned Roma *cantaor* (singer) from Sevilla province and the first real flamencologist to historically decipher the art. Mairena insisted on singing only old forms of *palos,* such as *siguiriyas* and *martinetes,* many of which he rescued from almost certain extinction. Through his stubborn refusal to pander to commercial tastes, he provided a lifeline between the golden age and the revival that was to come.

By the 1960s, nascent *tablaos* – nightclubs staging professional flamenco shows – had filled the vacuum left by the closure of the *cafés cantante* in the 1920s. Some *tablaos,* particularly those in the new resort towns on the coast, were fake and insipid, while others played a role in re-establishing *cante jondo* alongside the newer *palos.* Flamenco's ultimate revival was spearheaded, however, not by venues but by the exciting performers who frequented them. Two in particular stood out. Paco de Lucía from Algeciras was a guitarist so precocious that by age 14 he had absorbed everything any living musician could teach. His muse and foil was Camarón de la Isla, a Roma singer from the town of San Fernando (known as La Isla), who by the early 1970s had attained the kind of godlike status normally reserved for rock stars and bullfighters. Between them, Camarón and de Lucía took flamenco to a different level, injecting it with out-of-the box innovations (such as electric guitars and keyboards) while, at the same time, carefully safeguarding its purity.

Best Tablaos

Tablao Cardenal, Córdoba

Jardines de Zoraya, Granada

Puro Arte, Jerez de la Frontera

Tablao El Arenal, Seville

La Cava, Cádiz

Modern Flamenco

In the 1970s musicians began mixing flamenco with jazz, rock, blues, rap and other genres. The purists loathed these changes, but this *nuevo flamenco* greatly broadened flamenco's appeal. The seminal recording was a 1977 flamenco-folk-rock album, *Veneno* (Poison), by the group of the same name centred on Kiko Veneno and Raimundo Amador, both from Seville.

The group Ketama, whose key members were all from Granada's Montoya flamenco family, was crucial in bringing flamenco to a younger audience in the 1980s and '90s, mixing the music with African, Cuban, Brazilian and other rhythms. *Songhai* (1987) and *Songhai II* (1995) – collaborations with Malian *kora* (harp) player Toumani Diabaté – were among their best albums.

Flamenco today is as popular as it has ever been and probably more innovative. New generations continue to increase flamenco's audience. Among the most popular are José Mercé from Jerez, whose big-selling albums have included *Lío* (Entanglement; 2002) and *Mi Única Llave* (My Only Key; 2012), and El Barrio, a 21st-century urban poet from Cádiz.

Some say that Madrid-born Diego El Cigala (b 1968) is Camarón de la Isla's successor, although he turns his talent as much to flamenco-Latin crossover as to pure flamenco. This powerful singer launched himself onto the big stage with the extraordinary *Lágrimas negras* (2003), a wonderful collaboration with Cuban virtuoso Bebo Valdés that mixes flamenco with Cuban influences.

Another innovative singer, whose untimely death in 2010 was mourned by a generation of flamenco aficionados, was Granada's Enrique Morente (1942–2010). While careful not to alienate flamenco purists, Morente, through numerous collaborations across genres, helped lay the foundations for *nuevo flamenco*. His daughter Estrella Morente (internationally best known for being the 'voice' behind the 2006 film *Volver*) has also carved out a niche in the first rank of performers.

Flamenco dance has reached its most adventurous horizons in the person of Joaquín Cortés, born in Córdoba in 1969. Seemingly indefatigable, Cortés fuses flamenco with contemporary dance, ballet and jazz in spectacular shows all over the world with music at rock-concert amplification. Top-rank, more purist dancers include Sara Baras and Antonio Canales.

On the guitar, modern virtuosos include Manolo Sanlúcar from Cádiz, Tomatito from Almería (who used to accompany Camarón de la Isla) and Vicente Amigo from Córdoba. A rising guitar star, from Málaga, is Daniel (Dani) Casares (b 1980).

The traditional flamenco costume – shawl, fan and long, frilly *bata de cola* (tail gown) for women, and flat Cordoban hats and tight black trousers for men – is based on Andalucían fashions in the late 19th century.

Bullfighting

There is no more controversial activity in Spain than bullfighting. Already effectively banned in three of the country's autonomous communities (Catalonia and the Balearic and Canary Islands), this deeply rooted traditional activity has faced mounting opposition in recent years. It's unlikely, however, that Andalucía will cave in any time soon, as this is the region where modern bullfighting was invented, and it has produced the lion's share of the nation's legendary matadors.

For & Against

Supporters of bullfighting emphasise its historical legacy and high-profile place in Spanish culture. Some claim that *corridas* (bullfights) are less cruel than slaughterhouses; fighting bulls, they argue, live longer in better conditions than domestic beasts. For its opponents, however, bullfighting is an intolerably cruel, violent spectacle that sees many thousands of bulls slowly and painfully killed in public every year, and it is a blight on Spain's conscience in these supposedly more enlightened times.

A national opinion poll in December 2015 found that only 19% of Spaniards aged between 16 and 65 supported bullfighting, while 58% opposed it. Among 16- to 24-year-olds, the level of support was just 7%. But the anti-bullfighting lobby is bigger and more influential in northern Spain than it is in Andalucía, Madrid, Castilla y León or Castilla-La Mancha, and the pro-bullfighting lobby is powerful. The governing Partido Popular explicitly supports bullfighting as part of Spain's cultural heritage.

That there is a debate at all about the morality of bullfighting owes much to Spain's growing integration with the rest of Europe since its return to democracy in the late 1970s. Much of the anti-bullfighting impetus has come from groups beyond Spanish shores, among them PETA (www.peta.org.uk) and World Animal Protection (www.worldanimalprotection.org.uk). But home-grown Spanish anti-bullfighting, animal rights organisations are ever more active, including a political party, PACMA (www.pacma.es), the parliamentary grouping APDDA (www.apdda.es), the vets-against-bullfighting association AVATMA (www.avatma.org) and the animal-rights NGO ADDA (www.addaong.org).

An *espontáneo* is a bullfight spectator who illegally jumps into the ring and attempts to fight the bull. Famous matador 'El Cordobés' controversially launched his career this way. Ironically, years later, one of his own fights was interrupted by a less lucky *espontáneo* who was fatally gored.

History

Some historical testimonies suggest that it was Roman emperor Claudius who introduced bullfighting to Spain. However, it was the Moors who refined what was then an unregulated spectacle by adding ritualistic moves and the use of horses. The practice was largely the preserve of the horse-riding nobility until the early 18th century, when an Andalucian from Ronda named Francisco Romero got down from his mount, feinted a few times with a cape and killed the bull with a sword. Francisco's methods quickly gained popularity and he became the first professional bullfighter and head of Ronda's famous Romero dynasty. His son Juan Romero evolved bullfighting further by adding the *cuadrilla* (bullfighting team). Third in line, Pedro (Francisco's grandson) remains the most celebrated bullfighter of all time, with more than 5000 bulls slain in a 60-year career.

The most celebrated Andalucian matador today is Juan José Padilla, born in Jerez in 1973. He is known as El Pirata (the Pirate) for the eyepatch he wears after losing an eye to a bull's horn. Other stars, from elsewhere in Spain, include José Tomás, El Juli and Enrique Ponce.

Pedro introduced theatrics to bullfighting and established it as a serious pursuit. His methods remained commonplace for nearly a century.

Bullfighting's 'golden age' came in the 1910s, when it was transformed into a breathtaking show of aesthetics and technicality with a minuscule margin for error. The change was prompted by two famous matadors: Juan Belmonte and Joselito 'El Gallo'. Regarded as the two greatest bullfighters in history, they were born within three years of each other in Sevilla province. Juan Belmonte (1892–1962) had deformed legs, so, unable to move like other matadors, he elected to stand bolt upright and motionless in the ring until the bull was nearly upon him. This startling new technique kept the audience's hearts in their mouths and resulted in Belmonte getting gored more than 20 times; yet he lived. Joselito (1895–1920) was a child prodigy who adapted Belmonte's close-quarter methods; the two quickly became rivals and their duels between 1914 and 1920 are unlikely to be replicated. The rivalry came to an end when Joselito was fatally gored in 1920.

Doused in tradition, bullfighting has changed little in essentials since Joselito's demise. Manolete (1917–47), a notoriously serious bullfighter from Córdoba, added some of the short, close passes with the *muleta* (matador's cape) that are now common, while his fellow Cordoban 'El Cordobés' combined flamboyance inside the ring with equally flamboyant antics outside it.

The Fight

The number of bullfights in Spanish bullrings has fallen dramatically, from 3651 in 2007 to 1598 in 2016 (of which 260 took place in Andalucía), according to government figures. The bullfighting industry attributes the decline partly to economic recession.

If you do plan to attend a bullfight, it's important to understand what you're about to witness. The bull's back and neck are repeatedly pierced by lances and harpoon-like prods, resulting in a lot of blood, as well as considerable pain and distress for the animal. The bull gradually becomes weakened through blood loss before the matador delivers the final sword thrust. If this is done properly, the bull dies instantly. If the *coup de grâce* is not delivered well, the animal dies a slow death. When this happens, the scene can be extremely disturbing.

Bullfights usually begin at about 6pm and, as a rule, in a professional *corrida* (bullfight) three different matadors will fight two bulls each. Each fight takes about 20 minutes.

The matador (more often called the *torero* in Spanish) is the star of the team. Adorned in his glittering *traje de luces* (suit of lights), it is his fancy footwork, skill and bravery before the bull that has the crowd in raptures or in rage, depending on his (or very occasionally her) performance. A complex series of events takes place in each clash. *Peones* (the matador's 'footmen') dart about with grand capes in front of the bull to test its strength; horseback picadors drive lances into the bull's withers; and *banderilleros* (flagmen) charge headlong at the bull in an attempt to stab its neck. Finally, when the bull seems tired out, the matador, facing the animal head-on, aims to sink a sword cleanly into its neck for an instant kill – the *estocada*. A skilful, daring performance followed by a clean kill will have the crowd on its feet, perhaps waving handkerchiefs in an appeal to the fight president to award the matador an ear of the animal.

Survival Guide

Directory A–Z

Accommodation

During peak season (ie around Easter, Christmas and in July and August), it is best to book accommodation in advance. While most travellers use online sites like booking.com to reserve rooms, you can often save money by booking directly with the property.

Hostales Small family-run hotels ranked from one to three stars.

Casa Rurales Rural houses run as B&Bs, or independent longer-term lets.

Hotels From modern chains in big cities to opulent *paradores* (luxury state-owned hotels) in historic buildings.

Hostels Cheap backpacker accommodation with dorm rooms.

Hostels & Hostales

In Spain, it is important to make a distinction between hostels and *hostales*. Hostels offer standard backpacker accommodation with dorm beds, kitchen facilities, communal lounges, shared bathrooms and local information for budget travellers. Prices vary according to room size and, to a lesser extent,

season, but start at around €16 for a shared dorm room. Dorms can have four, six, eight or 10 beds, and many offer double rooms and/or family rooms as well, usually with shared bathrooms. *Hostales* are small family-run hotels where basic but adequate facilities are provided in single, double or triple rooms rather than dorms. Double rooms rarely go for more than €60. Travellers can usually expect private bathrooms and more personal service.

In Andalucía, hostels are normally confined to the main cities such as Seville, Granada and Málaga, although there's a handful of Hostelling International (HI) hostels in smaller villages such as El Bosque (in the Parque Natural Sierra de Grazalema), Cortes de la Frontera and Cazorla. The privately run **Oasis Hostels** (www.hosteloasis.com) is an excellent non-HI bet. It runs hostels in Granada and Málaga, as well as two in Seville (one of which is in an old palace). All are centrally located and offer heaps of freebies such as tapas tours, drink vouchers, bike hire and pancake breakfasts.

For more information on hostels or to make online bookings, see www.hostelworld.com, www.hostelbookers.com or **Andalucia Youth Hostels** (☑902 510000; www.inturjoven.com).

Hotels

Andalucía's hotels range from spruce business-style operations to the state-run *parador* chain of luxury hotels inhabiting old historic buildings. Boutique hotels are well on the rise; in Andalucía they often cleverly combine historical features with dynamic contemporary design. Seville, Granada and Córdoba host some of the finest boutique hotels, though a number of *pueblos blancos* (white villages) also have spectacular options, particularly Vejer de la Frontera.

Campgrounds

Andalucía has approximately 150 campgrounds, accommodating both caravans and tents. Cádiz province leads the way with 32 facilities, while Sevilla province has a select five. Rural areas offer the most idyllic camping spots. Highlights include the Costa de la Luz, with more than 20 campgrounds; the areas abutting the Parque Nacional de Doñana marshes; the steep Las Alpujarras valleys in the Sierra Nevada; the Cazorla mountains; and the Cabo de Gata coastline. Campgrounds in Spain are graded 1st class, 2nd class or 3rd class, and facilities are generally very good. Even a 3rd-class campground will have hot showers, electrical hook-ups and a cafe; top-notch places, meanwhile, often have minimarkets and swimming pools.

Campgrounds normally charge separately per adult, child and car. Average prices are rarely higher than €7.50, €5 and €6 respectively. Many facilities also rent cabins or bungalows from approximately €50 a night depending on size and season.

The **Federación Españo-la de Clubes Campistas** (FECC; www.guiacamping fecc.com) is Spain's main camping club. Its website is an excellent information resource; from it you can access the websites of individual campgrounds, and most allow you to make reservations online and provide further contact info. It also publishes the annual *Guía Camping*, available in bookshops in Spain.

Self-Catering Apartments & Casas Rurales

Self-catering apartments and houses are relatively easy to procure in Andalucía and are particularly popular in coastal resort areas. Basic one-bedroom apartments start at around €30 per night, while a luxury pad with a swimming pool somewhere like Marbella will set you back up to €400 a night for four people.

Casas rurales are usually old renovated farmhouses run as B&Bs or as more independent short-term holiday lets. They exist predominantly in smaller towns and villages. Prices for double rooms run from €50 to €100, though many people opt for longer-term bookings, thus saving money. Agencies include the following:

Escapada Rural (www.escapadarural.com)

Owners Direct (www.owners direct.co.uk)

Ruralka (www.ruralka.com)

Rustic Rent (www.rusticrent.com)

Secret Places (www.secretplaces.com)

Customs Regulations

Duty-free allowances for travellers entering Spain from outside the EU include 2L of wine (or 1L of wine and 1L of spirits), and 200 cigarettes or 50 cigars or 250g of tobacco.

There are no restrictions on the import of duty-paid items into Spain from other EU countries for personal use. You *can* buy VAT-free articles at airport shops when travelling between EU countries.

Discount Cards

At museums, never hesitate to ask if there are discounts for students, young people, children, families or seniors.

Senior cards Reduced prices for people over 60, 63 or 65 (depending on the place) at various museums and attractions (sometimes restricted to EU citizens) and occasionally on transport.

Student cards Discounts (usually half the normal fee) for students. You will need some kind of identification (eg an International Student Identity Card; www.isic.org) to prove student status. Not accepted everywhere.

Youth cards Travel, sights and youth-hostel discounts with the European Youth Card (www.euro26.org), known as the Carnet Joven in Spain.

PARADORES: HISTORIC LUXURY

The state-run *parador* hotels were founded by King Alfonso XIII in the 1920s. There are 16 of them in Andalucía, all rated three or four stars. Prices range from €100 to €370, but check the www.parador.es website for significant discounts. Occupying some astounding locations, these are possibly the best accommodation options around if you're up for a splurge. The following all occupy fine historical buildings:

➡ Parador de Arcos de la Frontera (p137)

➡ Parador de Granada (p270)

➡ Parador Castillo de Santa Catalina (p230)

➡ Parador Málaga Gibralfaro (p170)

➡ Parador de Ronda (p186)

➡ Parador de Úbeda (p241)

Electricity

Type C
230V/50Hz

Type F
230V/50Hz

Health

For emergency treatment, go straight to the *urgencias* (casualty) section of the nearest hospital, or call 061 for an ambulance. Good health care is readily available and *farmacias* (pharmacies) offer valuable advice and sell over-the-counter medication. In Spain, a system of *farmacias* *de guardia* (duty pharmacies) operates so that each district has one open all the time. When a pharmacy is closed, it posts the name of the nearest open one on the door.

Tap water is generally safe to drink in Spain, but in the city of Málaga many people prefer to play it safe by drinking bottled water. Do not drink water from rivers or lakes as it may contain harmful bacteria.

Health Insurance

If you're an EU citizen, or a citizen of Norway, Iceland, Liechtenstein or Switzerland, the free **EHIC** (European Health Insurance Card; www. ehic.org.uk) covers you for most medical care in Spain, including maternity care and care for chronic illnesses such as diabetes (though not for emergency repatriation). However, you will normally have to pay for medicine bought from pharmacies, even if prescribed, and perhaps for some tests and procedures. The EHIC does not cover private medical consultations and treatment in Spain; this includes most dentists, and some better clinics and surgeries. For more info on applying for an EHIC, see the European Commission site (http:// ec.europa.eu/social/main. jsp?catId=563). Non-EU citizens should find out if there is a reciprocal arrangement for medical care between their country and Spain.

Insurance

A travel-insurance policy to cover theft, loss and medical problems is a good idea. Travel agents will be able to make recommendations.

Climate

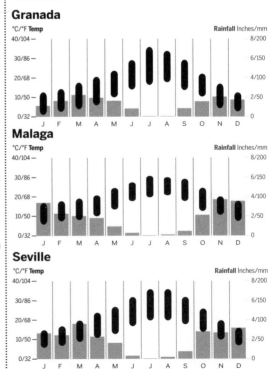

Granada

Malaga

Seville

GIBRALTAR PRACTICALITIES

Border Crossings The border is open 24 hours. Bag searches at **customs** (☎20046729; Customs House; ⊗24hr) are usually perfunctory.

Electricity Electric current is the same as in Britain: 220V or 240V, with plugs of three flat pins. You'll need an adaptor (available from electronics shops on Main St) to use your Spanish-plug devices.

Emergency ☎190, 112

Money Currencies are the interchangeable Gibraltar pound (£) and pound sterling. You can spend euros, but conversion rates are poor. Change unspent Gibraltar currency before leaving. Banks (mostly on Main St) open weekdays from 8.30am to 4pm.

Telephone To phone Gibraltar from other countries, dial the international access code, then 350 (Gibraltar's country code) and the eight-digit local number. To call Spain from Gibraltar, dial 0034, then the nine-digit number.

Visas & Documents To enter Gibraltar, you need a passport or EU national identity card. American, Canadian, Australian, New Zealand and EU passport holders are among those who do not need visas for Gibraltar. For further information, contact Gibraltar's **Civil Status and Registration Office** (☎20070071; www.gibraltar.gov.gi; 6 Convent Pl).

Check the small print: some policies specifically exclude 'dangerous activities', which can include scuba diving, motorcycling or even trekking. Strongly consider a policy that covers you for the worst possible scenario, such as an accident requiring an ambulance or emergency flight home. Find out in advance if your insurance plan will make payments to doctors or hospitals directly, rather than your having to pay on the spot and claim later. The former option is generally preferable, as it doesn't leave you out of pocket. If you have to claim later, make sure you keep all documentation.

Buy travel insurance as early as possible. If you buy it in the week before you leave home, you may find, for example, that you are not covered for delays to your trip caused by strikes. Paying for your airline ticket with a credit card often provides limited travel-accident insurance, and you may be able to reclaim payment if the operator doesn't deliver.

Worldwide travel insurance is available at www.lonelyplanet.com/travel-insurance. You can buy, extend and claim online any time – even if you're already on the road.

Internet Access

Nearly all hotels in Andalucía offer free wi-fi, and signal strength has improved in recent years. Many cafes offer free wi-fi, as do airports, libraries and other public buildings.

Internet cafes exist but are no longer ubiquitous. They generally charge between €1 and €1.50 per hour.

Language Courses

Privately run language schools are scattered all over Spain and many of them are excellent. But, with most courses requiring a minimum of one week's study, it's important to find the right location. Seville is a beautiful city in which to linger for a week or two and has an abundance of top-notch language schools. If you'd prefer a slightly smaller city with instant access to history and beaches, try Cádiz, where a couple of good schools are located in the old quarter. For a more rural experience in a diminutive hilltop town close to the coast, you can't beat Vejer de la Frontera.

The best schools running language courses:

CLIC (International House; Map p58;☎954 50 21 31; www.clic.es) Schools in Seville and Cádiz.

Escuela Delengua (Map p264; ☎958 20 45 35; www.delengua.es; Calle Calderería Vieja 20; individual lessons €36, 2-week course €260) Centre in student-heavy city of Granada.

K2 Internacional (Map p116; ☎956 21 26 46; www.k2internacional.com; Plaza Mentidero 19) School in Cádiz.

La Janda (☎956 44 70 60; http://lajanda.org; Avenida San Miguel 19; per 20hr week €190) Family-run school in Vejer de la Frontera.

EATING PRICE RANGES

The following price ranges refer to a main course at dinner, excluding drinks. The service charge is included in the price.

€ less than €12

€€ €12–€20

€€€ more than €20

Legal Matters

➡ Spain has some of Europe's more liberal laws on marijuana, but note that the drug is legal for personal use only – which means very small amounts. Public consumption of any drug is illegal. It would be very unwise to smoke cannabis in hotel rooms or guesthouses. Travellers entering Spain from Morocco, especially with a vehicle, should be prepared for intensive drug searches.

➡ Spain's drink-driving laws are relatively strict: the blood-alcohol limit is 0.05%, or 0.01% for new drivers.

➡ Under the Spanish constitution, anyone who is arrested must be informed immediately, in a manner understandable to them, of their rights and the grounds for the arrest. Arrested people are entitled to the assistance of a lawyer (and, where required, an interpreter) during police inquiries or judicial investigations. For many foreign nationals, including British citizens, the police are also obliged to inform an arrested person's consulate immediately. Arrested people may not be compelled to make a statement. Within 72 hours of arrest, the person must be brought before a judge or released.

Police

Spain has three main types of police:

Policía Nacional (National Police; ☏091) Covers cities and bigger towns, sometimes forming special squads dealing with drugs, terrorism and the like. A further contingent is to be found in police stations called *comisarías*.

Policía Local (Local Police; ☏092) Also known as Policía Municipal; is controlled by city and town halls and deals mainly with minor matters such as parking, traffic and by-laws. Officers wear blue-and-white uniforms.

Guardia Civil (Civil Guard; ☏062) The responsibilities of the green-uniformed Guardia Civil include roads, the countryside, villages and international borders.

If you need to go to the police (for example, if you're the victim of petty theft), any of these services will do, but your best bets are the Policía Nacional or Policía Local.

LGBTIQ Travellers

Spain is one of the most progressive countries in the world for LGBTIQ travellers. Openly gay people have been able to serve in the Spanish military since 1979, antidiscrimination laws were introduced in the 1990s, and in 2005 Spain became the third country in the world to legalise same-sex marriage.

Andalucía's liveliest gay scene is in Torremolinos, closely followed by the scenes in Málaga, Seville and Granada, but there are gay- and lesbian-friendly bars and clubs in all major cities. Some cities produce special leaflets and maps advertising gay-specific sights. Ask at tourist-information offices.

Websites such as www.travelgayeurope.com and www.patroc.com have helpful listings of gay and gay-friendly accommodation, bars, clubs, beaches, cruising areas, health clubs and associations. Patroc has special sections for the cities of Seville and Granada.

The **Federación Andaluza Arco Iris** (☏951 38 39 62; www.federacionarcoiris.blogspot.com) is an organisation based in Málaga that campaigns for equal opportunities for LGBTIQ people.

Maps

Michelin's 1:400,000 *Andalucía* (No 578) is excellent for planning and touring. It's widely available in and outside Andalucía; find it at petrol stations and bookshops.

Maps provided by tourist offices are often adequate for finding your way around cities and towns. For something more comprehensive, most cities are covered by one of the Spanish series such as Telstar, Escudo de Oro, Alpina or Everest, all with street indexes; they're available in bookshops. Be sure to check the publication dates.

Local availability of maps is patchy, so it's a good idea to try to obtain them in advance. Stanfords (www.stanfords.co.uk) has a good range of Spain maps and you can order them online.

Walking Maps

If you're going to do any walking in Andalucía you should arm yourself with the best possible maps, as trail markings can be patchy.

Spain's **Centro Nacional de Información Geográfica** (CNIG; www.cnig.es), the publishing arm of the Instituto Geográfico Nacional (IGN), produces a useful *Mapa Guía* series of national and natural parks, mostly at 1:25,000. The CNIG also covers Andalucía in its 1:50,000 *Mapa Topográfico Nacional* maps, most of which are up to date. Andalucia's eight provinces can be studied separately in the *mapas provinciales* series (1:200,000). CNIG maps may be labelled CNIG, IGN or both.

The CNIG website lists where you can buy CNIG maps (click on 'Puntas de Venta') or you can buy online. There are sales offices in Seville, Granada, Málaga, Almería and Jaén.

Good commercially published series, all usually accompanied by guide booklets, come from **Editorial Alpina** (www.editorialalpina.com), **Editorial Penibética** (www.penibetica.com) and Britain's **Discovery Walking Guides** (www.dwgwalking.co.uk).

The **Junta de Andalucía** (www.juntadeandalucia.es), Andalucía's regional government, also publishes a range of Andalucía maps, including a *Mapa Guía* series of natural and national parks. These have been published recently and are widely available, although they're perhaps better for vehicle touring than for walking, with a scale of 1:75,000. The covers are predominantly green, as opposed to the CNIG *Mapas Guías* that are mainly red or pink. Other Junta maps include 1:10,000 and 1:20,000 maps covering the whole of Andalucía – they're good maps, but there are few sales outlets for them.

Money
ATMs

Many credit and debit cards can be used for withdrawing money from *cajeros automáticos* (ATMs) that display the relevant symbols, such as Visa, MasterCard, Cirrus etc. There's usually a withdrawal charge of 1.5% to 2%.

Cash

Most banks and building societies will exchange major foreign currencies and offer the best rates. Ask about commissions and take your passport.

Credit & Debit Cards

You can generally get by very well in Andalucía with a credit or debit card enabling you to make purchases and withdraw euros from ATMs.

Not every establishment accepts payment by card, but most do. You should be able to make payments by card in midrange and top-end accommodation and restaurants, and larger shops, but you cannot depend on this elsewhere. When you pay by card, you may occasionally be asked for ID such as your passport. Don't forget to memorise your PIN, as you may have to key it in as you pay, and keep a note of phone numbers to call for reporting a lost or stolen card.

American Express (Amex) cards are much less widely accepted than Visa and MasterCard.

Tipping

Restaurants A service charge is usually included in the bill, but most people leave some small change if they're satisfied – 5% is usually plenty.

Hotels Tip porters around €1.
Taxis Tipping isn't necessary, but a little rounding up won't go amiss.

Taxes & Refunds

In Spain, value-added tax (VAT) is known as IVA (ee-ba; *impuesto sobre el valor añadido*). Visitors are entitled to a refund of the 21% IVA on purchases costing more than €90.16 from any shop, if they are taking them out of the EU within three months. Ask the shop for a cash-back (or similar) refund form showing the price and IVA paid for each item, and identifying the vendor and purchaser. Present the refund form to the customs booth for IVA refunds at the airport, port or border when you leave the EU.

Post

Stamps are sold at *estancos* (tobacconist shops with 'Tabacos' in yellow letters on a maroon background) as well as at *oficinas de correos* (post offices; www.correos.es). Mail to or from other Western European countries normally arrives within a week; to or from North America within 10 days; and to or from Australia and New Zealand within two weeks.

Public Holidays

Everywhere in Spain has 14 official holidays a year – some are holidays nationwide, some only in one village. The list of holidays in each place may change from year to year. If a holiday date falls on a weekend, sometimes the holiday is moved to the Monday or replaced with another at a different time. If a holiday falls on the second day following a weekend, many Spaniards take the intervening day off, too. The two main holiday periods are Semana Santa (Holy Week, leading up to Easter Sunday) and the six weeks from mid-July to the end of August. At these times accommodation in resorts can be scarce and transport heavily booked.

There are usually nine official national holidays:

Año Nuevo (New Year's Day) 1 January

Viernes Santo (Good Friday) 19 April 2019, 10 April 2020

Fiesta del Trabajo (Labour Day) 1 May

La Asunción (Feast of the Assumption) 15 August

Fiesta Nacional de España (National Day) 12 October

Todos los Santos (All Saints' Day) 1 November

Día de la Constitución (Constitution Day) 6 December

La Inmaculada Concepción (Feast of the Immaculate Conception) 8 December

Navidad (Christmas) 25 December

In addition, regional governments normally set three holidays. In Andalucía they are usually the following:

Epifanía (Epiphany) or **Día de los Reyes Magos** (Three Kings' Day) 6 January

Día de Andalucía (Andalucía Day) 28 February

Jueves Santo (Holy Thursday) Easter

The following are often selected as holidays by local councils:

Corpus Christi Around two months after Easter

Día de San Juan Bautista (Feast of St John the Baptist, King Juan Carlos II's saint's day) 24 June

Día de Santiago Apóstol (Feast of St James the Apostle, Spain's patron saint) 25 July

Safe Travel

Most visitors to Andalucía never feel remotely threatened, but a sufficient number have unpleasant experiences to warrant an alert. Be careful, but don't be paranoid.

➡ The main thing to be wary of is petty theft (which may of course not seem so petty if your passport, cash, travellers cheques, credit card and camera go missing). Keep a close eye on your bag(s) in busy public areas, especially parks, plazas and bus/train stations.

➡ Beware of extreme heat and always carry water when hiking in the high summer.

Government Travel Advice

The following government websites offer travel-advisory services and information for travellers:

Department of Foreign Affairs and Trade (www.smartraveller. gov.au) Australia.

Global Affairs Canada (www. voyage.gc.ca)

Ministère de l'Europe et des Affaires étrangères (www.diplo matie.gouv.fr/fr/conseils-aux-vo yageurs) France.

Auswärtiges Amt, Länder und Reiseinformationen (www. auswaertiges-amt.de/de/) Germany.

Ministero degli Affari Esteri e della Cooperazione Internazi-

onale (www.viaggiaresicuri.mae. aci.it) Italy.

Ministerie van Buitenlandse Zaken (www.rijksoverheid.nl/ ministeries/ministerie-van -buitenlandse-zaken#ref-min buza.nl) Netherlands.

Ministry of Foreign Affairs and Trade (www.safetravel.govt.nz) New Zealand.

Foreign & Commonwealth Office (www.gov.uk/foreign -travel-advice) UK.

Department of State (www. travel.state.gov) US.

Telephone

Local SIM cards can be used in European/Australian phones. Other phones must be set to roaming to work – be wary of roaming charges, although these should no longer apply if you have an EU phone. Calling from your computer using an internet-based service such as Skype or from your mobile phone using Whatsapp is generally the cheapest option.

Mobile Phones

Spain uses GSM 900/1800, which is compatible with the rest of Europe and Australia but not with the North American system – unless you have a GSM/GPRS-compatible phone (some AT&T and T-Mobile cell phones may work) – or the system used in Japan. From those countries, you will need to travel with a tri-band or quadric-band phone.

You can buy SIM cards and prepaid time in Spain for your mobile phone, provided you own a GSM, dual- or tri-band cellular phone. This only works if your national phone hasn't been code-blocked; check before leaving home.

All the Spanish mobile-phone companies (Telefónica's MoviStar, Orange and Vodafone) offer *prepagado* (prepaid) accounts for mobiles. The SIM card costs from €10, to which you add some prepaid phone time. Phone outlets are scattered across the

country. You can then top up in their shops or by buying cards in outlets, such as *estancos* (tobacconists) and newspaper kiosks.

There is now EU-wide roaming, so call and data plans for mobile phones from any EU country should be valid throughout Spain without extra roaming charges. If you're from elsewhere, check with your provider for information on roaming charges.

Phone Codes & Useful Numbers

Spain has no telephone area codes. Every phone number has nine digits and for any call within Spain you just dial all those nine digits. The first digit of all Spanish fixed-phone numbers is 9. Numbers beginning with 6, 7 or 8 are mobile-phone numbers. Phone numbers in Gibraltar have eight digits.

Calls to Spanish numbers starting with 900 are free. Numbers starting with 901 to 906 are pay-per-minute numbers and charges vary. For a rundown on these numbers, visit www.andalucia. com/travel/telephone/num bers.htm.

International access code ☏00

Spain's country code ☏34

Phonecards

Cut-rate prepaid phonecards can be good value for international calls. They can be bought from *estancos*, small grocery stores, *locutorios* (private call centres) and newsstands in the main cities and tourist resorts. If possible, try to compare rates. Many private operators offer better deals than those offered by Telefónica. *Locutorios* that specialise in cut-rate overseas calls have popped up all over the place in bigger cities.

Time

➡ Mainland Spain is on GMT/UTC plus one hour during winter, and GMT/UTC plus two hours during the country's daylight-saving period, which runs from the last Sunday in March to the last Sunday in October.

➡ Most Western European countries have the same time as Spain year-round, the major exceptions being Britain, Ireland and Portugal. Add one hour to these three countries' times to get Spanish time.

➡ Morocco is on GMT/UTC year-round, so it's two hours behind Spain during Spanish daylight-saving time, and one hour behind at other times.

Toilets

➡ Public toilets are almost nonexistent; the exceptions are some tourist offices, large tourist-oriented beaches (eg Torremolinos) and all bus and train stations.

➡ It's OK to use the toilet at bars and cafes, but you're usually expected to order something.

➡ It's worth carrying some toilet paper with you, as many toilets lack it.

Tourist Information

All cities and many smaller towns and villages in Andalucía have at least one *oficina de turismo* (tourist office). Staff are generally knowledgeable and increasingly well versed in foreign languages; they can help with everything from town maps and guided tours to opening hours for major sights and, sometimes, bus timetables. Offices are usually well stocked with printed material. Opening hours vary widely (and seasonally).

Tourist offices may be operated by the local town hall, by local district organisations, by the government of whichever province you're in or by the Junta de Andalucía (regional government). There may also be more than one tourist office in larger cities: in general, regional tourist offices offer information on the city and the wider region,

while municipal offices deal just with the city and immediate surrounds. The Junta de Andalucía's Consejería de Medio Ambiente (environmental department) also has visitor centres located in many environmentally protected areas (*parques naturales* and so on). Many present interesting displays on local flora and fauna and carry info on hiking routes.

Travellers with Disabilities

Accessibility in Andalucía is improving as new buildings (including hotels) meet regulations requiring them to have wheelchair access. Many midrange and top-end hotels are now adapting rooms and creating better access for wheelchair users; accessibility is poorer at some budget accommodation options. If you call a taxi and ask for a 'eurotaxi', you should be sent one adapted for wheelchair users.

International organisations can usually offer advice (sometimes including Andalucía-specific info):

Accessible Travel & Leisure (☑01452-729739; www. accessibletravel.co.uk) Claims to be the biggest UK travel agent specialising in travel for people with a disability, and encourages independent travel.

Mobility International (☑541-343-1284; www.miusa.org; 132 E Broadway, Suite 343; ⏰9am-4pm Mon-Fri) Advises travellers with disabilities on mobility issues and runs an educational exchange program.

Visas

Spain is one of 26 member countries of the Schengen Agreement, under which 22 EU countries (all but Bulgaria, Croatia, Cyprus, Ireland, Romania and the UK) plus Iceland, Norway, Liechtenstein and Switzerland have abolished checks at common borders. Bulgaria, Croatia, Cyprus and Romania are all

legally obliged to become a part of the Schengen Area in the near future.The visa situation for entering Spain is as follows:

➡ For citizens or residents of EU and Schengen countries, no visa is required.

➡ For citizens or residents of Australia, Canada, Israel, Japan, New Zealand and the USA, no visa is required for tourist visits of up to 90 days.

➡ For other countries, check with a Spanish embassy or consulate.

➡ To work or study in Spain a special visa may be required; contact a Spanish embassy or consulate before travel.

➡ Remember that Gibraltar is not part of Schengen and if you do not have permission to enter the UK, you may not enter Gibraltar.

Women Travellers

Women travellers in Spain will rarely experience harassment, although you may find yourself subjected to stares, catcalls and comments from time to time. Skimpy clothes are the norm in many coastal resorts, but people tend to dress more modestly elsewhere. Some women travellers have reported feeling more comfortable at the front of public transport. Remember the word for help (*socorro*) in case you need to use it.

Each province's national police headquarters has a special Servicio de Atención a la Mujer (SAM; literally 'Service of Attention to Women'). The national **Comisión para la Investigación de Malos Tratos a Mujeres** (Commission for Investigation into Abuse of Women; ☑emergency 900 100009; www. malostratos.org; ⏰9am-9pm) maintains an emergency line for victims of physical abuse anywhere in Spain. In Andalucía the **Instituto Andaluz de la Mujer** (☑900 20 09 99; www.juntadeandalucia.es/institutodelamujer; ⏰24hr) also offers help.

Transport

GETTING THERE & AWAY

Andalucía is a top European holiday destination and is well linked to the rest of Spain and Europe by air, rail and road. Regular hydrofoils and car ferries run to and from Morocco, and there are also ferry links to Algeria. Flights, tours and rail tickets can be booked online at lonelyplanet.com/bookings.

Entering the Region

Immigration and customs checks usually involve a minimum of fuss, although there are exceptions. Spanish customs look for contraband duty-free products designed for illegal resale in Spain, in particular from people arriving from Morocco. Expect long delays at this border, especially in summer.

Passport

Citizens of other EU member states as well as those from Norway, Iceland, Liechtenstein and Switzerland can travel to Spain with their national identity card alone. If such countries do not issue ID cards – as in the UK – travellers must carry a valid passport. All other nationalities must have a valid passport.

In the aftermath of the UK's decision to leave the EU, the future requirements for UK citizens travelling in Spain and the rest of the EU remains unclear – check with your local Spanish embassy or consulate for the latest rules.

By law you are supposed to carry your passport or ID card with you in Spain at all times.

Air

Getting to Andalucía by air from the rest of Europe is easy. Dozens of regular and charter airlines fly into the region's five airports from elsewhere in Europe, especially the UK, and a couple also fly from the UK to Gibraltar. Andalucía's busiest airport, Málaga, also has flights from Morocco. The region is well connected by domestic flights to other Spanish cities. From outside Europe, you'll normally need to change planes en route, usually at Madrid or Barcelona or in another European country. A couple of charters connect Málaga with Montreal in Canada and, seasonally, with JFK in New York.

High season is generally mid-June to mid-September, although flights can also be fully booked (and prices higher) during Semana Santa (Holy Week; the week leading up to Easter Sunday).

Airports

Málaga Airport (AGP; ☎952 04 88 38; www.aena.es) is the main international airport in Andalucía and Spain's fourth

---

CLIMATE CHANGE & TRAVEL

Every form of transport that relies on carbon-based fuel generates CO_2, the main cause of human-induced climate change. Modern travel is dependent on aeroplanes, which might use less fuel per kilometre per person than most cars but travel much greater distances. The altitude at which aircraft emit gases (including CO_2) and particles also contributes to their climate change impact. Many websites offer 'carbon calculators' that allow people to estimate the carbon emissions generated by their journey and, for those who wish to do so, to offset the impact of the greenhouse gases emitted with contributions to portfolios of climate-friendly initiatives throughout the world. Lonely Planet offsets the carbon footprint of all staff and author travel.

busiest, with almost 60 airlines connecting the city to Spain, Europe and beyond.

Seville (Aeropuerto de Sevilla; ☑ 902 404704; www.aena.es; A4, Km 532), **Granada** (Aeropuerto Federico García Lorca; ☑ 902 404704; www.aena.es), **Jerez de la Frontera** (☑ 956 15 00 00; www.aena.es; Carretera A4) and **Almería** (☑ 902 404704; www.aena.es) also have connections to other Spanish and European cities, although apart from flights to and from Seville, the choices are far more limited. To see which airlines fly into the airport you're hoping to start your journey in, visit www.aena.es, choose the airport from the pull-down menu, then click on 'Airlines' for a full list. The website also has detailed information on facilities at each airport.

Gibraltar (Map p155; ☑ 20 012345; www.gibraltarairport.gi) also receives a small number of flights direct from the UK and Morocco.

Land

If you're coming from Morocco, journey times are increased by a couple of hours by border formalities, which are notoriously strict at the ferry departure and arrivals terminals. There are usually long queues at customs on both sides of the Strait of Gibraltar.

Bus

Andalucía is well connected by bus with the rest of Spain. Although there are direct bus services from many European countries, it rarely works out cheaper than flying and takes a whole lot longer.

Places from where taking a bus may work out to be more economical include Lisbon and Morocco. **Alsa** (www.alsa.es) has regular daily services to Seville from Lisbon (seven hours). Alsa also runs several weekly buses between Moroccan cities such as Casablanca, Marrakesh and Fès, and Andalucian destinations such as Seville, Marbella, Málaga, Granada, Jerez de la Frontera and Almería, via the Algeciras–Tangier ferries. As an indication of time, the Málaga–Marrakesh trip takes 19 to 20 hours.

Buses run to most Andalucian cities and medium-sized towns from elsewhere in Spain, with the largest selection leaving from Madrid's **Estación Sur de Autobuses** (www.estacionautobusesmadrid.com). The trip from Madrid to Seville, Granada or Málaga takes around six hours. There are also services down the Mediterranean coast from Barcelona, Valencia and Alicante to Almería, Granada, Jaén, Córdoba, Seville, Málaga and the Costa del Sol. The best bus companies serving Andalucía from other parts of Spain are Alsa and **Secorbus/Socibus** (☑ 902 229292; www.socibus.es).

Car & Motorcycle

Drivers can reach Andalucía from just about anywhere in Spain in a single day on the country's good-quality highways. The main routes run down the centre of the country from Madrid and along the Mediterranean coast from Barcelona. Popular vehicle ferries run from the UK to Bilbao and Santander in northern Spain, from where you can drive to Andalucía via Madrid. Ferry routes also connect Andalucía with Tangier and Nador in Morocco and with Ceuta and Melilla, the Spanish enclaves on the Moroccan coast.

The main highway from Madrid to Andalucía is the

A4/AP4 to Córdoba, Seville and Cádiz. For Jaén, Granada, Almería or Málaga, turn off at Bailén. In the east, the AP7/A7 leads all the way down the Mediterranean side of Spain from La Jonquera on the French border as far as Algeciras.

If you just want to drive once you get to Andalucía, it usually works out cheaper (and quicker) to fly and hire a car there. In the UK, further information on driving in Europe is available from the AA (www.theaa.com).

Train

Renfe (Red Nacional de los Ferrocarriles Españoles, Spanish National Railways; ☑ 902 240202; www.renfe.es) is the excellent national Spanish train system that runs services in Andalucía. It has benefited from massive investment in recent years, meaning journeys are fast, efficient and comfortable.

IN SPAIN

The fastest train to Andalucía is the 280km/h Alta Velocidad Española (AVE) from Madrid, operated by Renfe. These trains connect Madrid to Córdoba (one way from €62, 1¾ hours), Seville (from €76, 2½ hours) and Málaga (from €80, 2¾ hours) in not much more time than travelling by plane. Multigauge Alvia trains also run direct between Madrid and Cádiz three or four times daily. From most other parts of Spain you can reach Andalucía by train in one day, usually with a connection in Madrid or Barcelona.

Most long-distance trains have *preferente* (1st-class) and *turista* (2nd-class) carriages. They go under various names indicating standards of comfort and time of travel:

Daytime trains Consist of AVEs on the Madrid–Seville and Madrid–Córdoba–Málaga routes, Alvia on the Madrid–Cádiz and Huelva routes, and Altaria on the Madrid–Granada and Ronda–Algeciras routes.

Overnight trains Comfortable Trenhotels (with seats, couchettes and sleeping compartments) run between Barcelona and Granada.

Buy your ticket in advance as trains can get fully booked, especially in July and August. You can buy tickets in English by phone and online. Phone-booked tickets must be collected and paid for at a Renfe ticket office within 72 hours of booking and more than 24 hours before the train's departure. Internet tickets can be paid for online. The first time tickets are purchased online by credit card, they must be picked up at a Renfe ticket office at least one hour before the train's departure; subsequent tickets with the same card can be printed online.

Some fare discounts are available:

➜ Return fares on long-distance trains are 20% less than two one-way fares.

➜ Children aged under four travel free (except on high-speed trains, where they pay the four- to 13-year-old rate).

➜ Children aged four to 13 get 40% off the cost of seats and couchettes.

➜ The European Youth Card (www.euro26.org) entitles holders to 20% or 25% off long-distance and regional train fares.

OUTSIDE SPAIN

If you're coming from elsewhere in Europe and can afford to take at least a day to arrive, there are rail routes to Andalucía, always involving a change of train. The best routing is through Barcelona Sants station (roughly 5½ hours from Málaga and Seville), where you can catch direct trains to Paris. In Paris there are connections on to Amsterdam, the UK and Germany. Alternatively, take a train from Barcelona to Geneva (changing in Valence), where there are connections to Ita-

ly. For more details on these and other routes, check **The Man in Seat 61** (www.seat61.com).

Sea

You can sail to Andalucía from the Moroccan ports of Tangier and Nador, as well as Ceuta or Melilla (Spanish enclaves on the Moroccan coast), and Oran and Ghazaouet (in Algeria). The routes are: Melilla–Almería, Nador–Almería, Oran–Almería, Ghazaouet–Almería, Melilla–Málaga, Tangier–Algeciras, Ceuta–Algeciras and Tangier–Tarifa.

All routes usually take vehicles as well as passengers and the most frequent sailings are to/from Algeciras. Usually at least 12 sailings a day ply the routes between Algeciras and Tangier (1½ hours), and 10 run between Algeciras and Ceuta (one hour). Extra services are added at busy times, especially during the peak summer period (mid-June to mid-September), when hundreds of thousands of Moroccan workers return home from Europe for holidays. If you're taking a car, book well ahead for July, August or Easter travel, and expect long queues and customs formalities.

The following are the main ferry companies; there's little price difference between them.

Acciona/Trasmediterránea (www.trasmediterranea.es)

Inter Shipping (www.intershipping.es)

FRS (www.frs.es)

GETTING AROUND

Air

There are barely any regular flights between airports within Andalucia. The one

exception is the daily flight between Seville and Almería with Air Nostrum, a franchise of Iberian Airines.

Bicycle

Andalucía is good biking territory, with wonderful scenery and varied terrain. While some mountain roads (such as those through the Sierra de Grazalema or Sierra Nevada) are best left to professional cyclists, there aren't too many corners of Andalucía that keen and reasonably fit cyclists can't reach. Plenty of lightly trafficked country roads, mostly in decent condition, enable riders to avoid the busy main highways. Road biking here is as safe as anywhere in Europe, provided you make allowances for some drivers' love of speed. Day rides and touring by bike are particularly enjoyable in spring and autumn, as you'll avoid weather extremes.

➜ It's often possible to take your bike on a bus (you'll usually just be asked to remove the front wheel).

➜ You can take bikes on overnight sleeper trains (not long-distance daytime trains), and on most regional and suburban trains; check at the train station for any special conditions before buying tickets.

➜ Bicycles are available for hire in main cities, coastal resorts, and inland towns and villages that attract tourism. They're often *bicis todo terreno* (mountain bikes). Prices range from €10 to €20 a day. Seville is easily the region's most cycle-friendly city.

➜ Bike lanes on main roads are rare, but cyclists are permitted to ride in groups up to two abreast.

➜ Helmets are obligatory outside built-up areas.

Boat

There's a regular catamaran service (p120) between Cádiz and El Puerto de Santa María.

Bus

Buses in Andalucía are mostly modern, comfortable and inexpensive, and run almost everywhere – including along some unlikely mountain roads – to connect remote villages with their nearest towns. The bigger cities are linked to each other by frequent daily services. On the quieter routes, services may be reduced (or nonexistent) on Saturday and Sunday.

➡ Alsa's luxurious 'Supra' buses have wi-fi, free drinks and snacks, toilets and single seats available.

➡ Larger towns and cities usually have one main *estación de autobuses* (bus station) where all out-of-town buses stop. In smaller places, buses tend to operate from a particular street or square, which may be unmarked. Ask around; locals generally know where to go.

➡ During Semana Santa (Holy Week) and July and August it's advisable to buy most bus tickets a day in advance.

➡ On a few routes, a return ticket is cheaper than two singles.

➡ Travellers aged under 26 should ask about discounts on intercity routes.

➡ Buses on main intercity routes average around 70km/h, and cost around €1.20 per 14km.

Car & Motorcycle

Andalucía's excellent road network and inexpensive rental cars make driving an attractive and practical way of getting around.

Bringing Your Own Vehicle

Bringing your own car to Andalucía is possible. Roads are generally good, although driving and finding parking in cities can be tiresome. Petrol (around €1.20 to €1.25 per litre in Spain) is widely available. In the event of breakdowns, every small town and many villages will have a garage with mechanics on site.

If the car is from the UK or Ireland, remember to adjust the headlights for driving in mainland Europe (motor-accessory shops sell stick-on strips that deflect the beams in the required direction).

Driving Licence & Documentation

All EU countries' licences (pink or pink and green) are accepted in Spain. Licences from other countries are supposed to be accompanied by an International Driving Permit, but in practice your national licence will suffice for renting cars or dealing with traffic police. The International Driving Permit, valid for 12 months, is available from automobile clubs in your country.

When driving a private vehicle in Europe, proof of ownership (a Vehicle Registration Document for UK-registered vehicles), driving licence, roadworthiness certificate (MOT), and either an insurance certificate or a Green Card should always be carried. Also ask your insurer for a European Accident Statement form, which can greatly simplify matters in the event of an accident.

Hire

If you plan to hire a car in Andalucía, it's a good idea to organise it before you leave home. As a rule, local firms at Málaga airport or on the Costa del Sol offer the cheapest deals. You can normally get a four-door, air-con, economy-class car from local agencies for around €150 a week in August or €120 a week in January. Many local firms offer internet booking and have a desk in or just outside the airport. In general, rentals away from the holiday *costas* (coasts) are more expensive.

Well-established local firms with branches at Andalucian airports and/or major rail stations (such as Málaga

MAIN BUS COMPANIES

COMPANY	WEBSITE	TELEPHONE	MAIN DESTINATIONS
Alsa	www.alsa.es	☎902 422242	Almería, Córdoba, Granada, Jaén, Málaga, Seville
Casal	www.autocarescasal.com	☎954 999290	Carmona, Seville
Comes	www.tgcomes.es	☎902 199208	Algeciras, Cádiz, Granada, Jerez, Málaga, Ronda, Seville
Damas	www.damas-sa.es	☎959 256900	Ayamonte, Huelva, Seville
Los Amarillos	www.losamarillos.es	☎902 210317	Cádiz, Jerez, Málaga, Ronda, Seville
Portillo	www.ctsa-portillo.com	☎902 143144	Algeciras, Costa del Sol, Málaga, Ronda
Autocares Carrera	www.autocarescarrera.es	☎957 500302	Córdoba province

and Seville) include the following:

Centauro (☏902 104103; www.centauro.net)

Crown Car (☏952 17 64 86; www.crowncarhire.com)

Helle Hollis (☏952 24 55 44; www.hellehollis.com)

Niza Cars (☏952 23 61 79; www.nizacars.es)

Pepecar.com (☏807 414243; www.pepecar.com)

Major international rental companies are also usually available:

Avis (☏902 135531; www.avis.com)

Europcar (☏913 43 45 12; www.europcar.com)

Hertz (☏917 49 90 69; www.hertz.es)

Enterprise (☏902 100101; www.enterprise.es)

To rent a car you need to be aged at least 21 (23 with some companies) and to have held a driving licence for a minimum of one year (sometimes two years).

Under-25s have to pay extra charges with many firms.

Insurance

Third-party motor insurance is a minimum requirement throughout Europe. If you live in the EU, your existing motor insurance will probably provide automatic third-party cover throughout the EU if you're travelling in your own vehicle. Check with your insurer if you will also be covered for medical or hospital expenses or accidental damage to your vehicle. You might have to pay an extra premium if you want the same protection abroad as you have at home. A European breakdown-assistance policy is a good investment, providing services such as roadside assistance, towing, emergency repairs and 24-hour telephone assistance in English.

If you're renting a vehicle in Andalucía, the routine insurance provided may not go beyond basic third-party requirements. For cover

against theft or damage to the vehicle, or injury or death to driver or passengers, you may need to request extra coverage. Always read the fine print and don't be afraid to ask.

Parking

Street parking can be hard to find in larger cities during working hours (about 9am to 2pm Monday to Saturday and 5pm to 8pm Monday to Friday). You'll often have to use underground or multistorey car parks, which are common enough in cities, and well-enough signposted, but not cheap (typically around €1 per hour or €10 to €15 for 24 hours). City hotels with their own parking usually charge for the right to use it, at rates similar to or slightly cheaper than those of underground car parks.

Blue lines along the side of the street usually mean you must pay at a nearby meter to park during working hours (typically around €0.50 to €1 an hour). Yellow lines mean

Train Destinations

no parking. A sign with a red line through a blue backdrop also indicates that parking is prohibited. It's inadvisable to park in prohibited zones, even if other drivers have (you risk your car being towed and paying at least €60 to have it released).

Road Rules

➡ As elsewhere in continental Europe, drive on the right and overtake on the left (although the latter is just as often honoured in the breach).

➡ The minimum driving age is 18 years.

➡ Rear seatbelts, if fitted, must be worn and children under three must sit in child safety seats.

➡ The blood-alcohol limit is 0.05% (0.01% for drivers with a licence less than two years old) and breath-testing is carried out on occasion.

➡ The police can – and do – carry out spot checks on drivers, so it pays to have all your papers in order. Nonresident foreigners may be fined on the spot for traffic offences. For any questions relating to traffic-violation tickets, phone 902 508686.

➡ The speed limit is 50km/h in built-up areas, between 80km/h and 100km/h outside built-up areas, and 120km/h on *autopistas* (toll highways) and *autovías* (toll-free highways).

➡ In Spain it's compulsory to carry two warning triangles (to be placed 100m in front of and 100m behind your vehicle if you have to stop on the carriageway), and a reflective jacket, which must be donned if you get out of your vehicle on the carriageway or hard shoulder outside built-up areas.

➡ It's illegal to use hand-held mobile phones while driving.

Taxi

Taxis are plentiful in larger places, and most villages have a taxi or two. Fares are reasonable – a €3 to €3.50 start rate and then around €1.05 per kilometre, with airport runs costing a bit extra. You don't have to tip taxi drivers, but rounding up the change is always appreciated.

Train

Renfe (Red Nacional de los Ferrocarriles Españoles, Spanish National Railways; ☑902 240202; www.renfe.es) has an extensive and efficient rail system in Andalucía that links most of the main cities and many smaller places. Trains are at least as convenient, quick and inexpensive as buses on many routes.

➡ High-speed AVE trains run between Córdoba and Málaga, Córdoba and Seville, and Seville and Málaga.

➡ Generally, more frequent services between Andalucian destinations are provided by the cheaper (but slower) one-class *regional* and *cercanía* trains. *Regionales*, some of which are known as Andalucía Exprés, run between Andalucian cities, stopping at many towns en route. *Cercanías* are commuter trains that link Seville, Málaga and Cádiz with their suburbs and nearby towns.

➡ Train tickets can be booked online with Renfe, which also lists full up-to-date timetables.

➡ Reservations are necessary on high-speed AVE trains but less important on shorter, slower routes.

➡ Regional trains average around 75km/h, for a cost of around €1 per 15km.

➡ Return fares on many routes operated by Renfe (but not its *cercanía* services) are 20% less than two one-way fares.

Language

Spanish (*español*) – also called Castilian (*castellano*) – is spoken throughout Andalucia.

Most Spanish sounds are pronounced the same as their English counterparts. If you read our coloured pronunciation guides as if they were English, you'll be understood. Note that the kh is a throaty sound (like the 'ch' in Scottish *loch*), r is strongly rolled, ly is pronounced as the 'lli' in 'million' and ny as the 'ni' in 'onion'. If you travel outside the region, you'll also notice that the 'lisped' th sound, which is typical of the pronunciation in the rest of Spain, is pronounced as s in Andalucia. In our pronunciation guides, the stressed syllables are in italics.

Where necessary in this chapter, masculine and feminine forms are marked as 'm/f', while polite and informal options are indicated by the abbreviations 'pol' and 'inf'.

BASICS

Hello.	Hola.	o·la
Goodbye.	Adiós.	a·dyos
How are you?	¿Qué tal?	ke tal
Fine, thanks.	Bien, gracias.	byen gra·syas
Excuse me.	Perdón.	per·don
Sorry.	Lo siento.	lo syen·to
Yes.	Sí.	see
No.	No.	no
Please.	Por favor.	por fa·vor
Thank you.	Gracias.	gra·syas

WANT MORE?

For in-depth language information and handy phrases, check out Lonely Planet's *Spanish Phrasebook*. You'll find it at **shop.lonelyplanet.com**, or you can buy Lonely Planet's iPhone phrasebooks at the Apple App Store.

You're welcome.	De nada.	de na·da
My name is ...		
Me llamo ...		me lya·mo ...

What's your name?

| ¿Cómo se llama Usted? | ko·mo se lya·ma oo·ste (pol) |
| ¿Cómo te llamas? | ko·mo te lya·mas (inf) |

Do you speak English?

| ¿Habla inglés? | a·bla een·gles (pol) |
| ¿Hablas inglés? | a·blas een·gles (inf) |

I don't understand.

| No entiendo. | no en·tyen·do |

ACCOMMODATION

hotel	hotel	o·tel
guesthouse	pensión	pen·syon
youth hostel	albergue juvenil	al·ber·ge khoo·ve·neel
I'd like a ... room.	Quisiera una habitación ...	kee·sye·ra oo·na a·bee·ta·syon ...
single	individual	een·dee·vee·dwal
double	doble	do·ble
air-con	aire acondicionado	ai·re a·kon·dee·syo·na·do
bathroom	baño	ba·nyo
bed	cama	ka·ma
window	ventana	ven·ta·na

How much is it per night/person?

| ¿Cuánto cuesta por noche/persona? | kwan·to kwes·ta por no·che/per·so·na |

Does it include breakfast?

| ¿Incluye el desayuno? | een·kloo·ye el de·sa·yoo·no |

DIRECTIONS

Where's ...?

| ¿Dónde está ...? | don·de es·ta ... |

What's the address?
¿Cuál es la dirección?   kwal es la dee·rek·*syon*

Can you please write it down?
¿Puede escribirlo,   pwe·de es·kree·*beer*·lo
por favor?   por fa·*vor*

Can you show me (on the map)?
¿Me lo puede indicar   me lo pwe·de een·dee·*kar*
(en el mapa)?   (en el *ma*·pa)

at the corner	*en la esquina*	en la es·*kee*·na
at the traffic lights	*en el semáforo*	en el se·*ma*·fo·ro
behind ...	*detrás de ...*	de·*tras* de ...
far away	*lejos*	*le*·khos
in front of ...	*enfrente de ...*	en·*fren*·te de ...
left	*izquierda*	ees·*kyer*·da
near	*cerca*	*ser*·ka
next to ...	*al lado de ...*	al *la*·do de ...
opposite ...	*frente a ...*	*fren*·te a ...
right	*derecha*	de·*re*·cha
straight ahead	*todo recto*	*to*·do *rek*·to

EATING & DRINKING

What would you recommend?
¿Qué recomienda?   ke re·ko·*myen*·da

What's in that dish?
¿Que lleva ese plato?   ke *lye*·va e·se *pla*·to

I don't eat ...
No como ...   no *ko*·mo ...

Cheers!
¡Salud!   sa·*loo*

That was delicious!
¡Estaba buenísimo!   es·*ta*·ba bwe·*nee*·see·mo

Please bring us the bill.
Por favor, nos trae   por fa·*vor* nos *tra*·e
la cuenta.   la *kwen*·ta

I'd like to book a table for ...	*Quisiera reservar una mesa para ...*	kee·*sye*·ra re·ser·*var* oo·na *me*·sa pa·ra ...
(eight) o'clock	*las (ocho)*	las (*o*·cho)
(two) people	*(dos) personas*	(dos) per·*so*·nas

Key Words

appetisers	*aperitivos*	a·pe·ree·*tee*·vos
bar	*bar*	bar
bottle	*botella*	bo·*te*·lya
bowl	*bol*	bol
breakfast	*desayuno*	de·sa·*yoo*·no
cafe	*café*	ka·*fe*

To get by in Spanish, mix and match these simple patterns with words of your choice:

When's (the next flight)?
¿Cuándo sale   *kwan*·do sa·le
(el próximo vuelo)?   (el *prok*·see·mo *vwe*·lo)

Where's (the station)?
¿Dónde está   *don*·de es·*ta*
(la estación)?   (la es·ta·*syon*)

Where can I (buy a ticket)?
¿Dónde puedo   *don*·de pwe·do
(comprar   (kom·*prar*
un billete)?   oon bee·*lye*·te)

Do you have (a map)?
¿Tiene (un mapa)?   *tye*·ne (oon *ma*·pa)

Is there (a toilet)?
¿Hay (servicios)?   ai (ser·*vee*·syos)

I'd like (a coffee).
Quisiera (un café).   kee·*sye*·ra (oon ka·*fe*)

I'd like (to hire a car).
Quisiera (alquilar   kee·*sye*·ra (al·kee·*lar*
un coche).   oon *ko*·che)

Can I (enter)?
¿Se puede (entrar)?   se pwe·de (en·*trar*)

Can you please (help me)?
¿Puede (ayudarme),   pwe·de (a·yoo·*dar*·me)
por favor?   por fa·*vor*

Do I have to (get a visa)?
¿Necesito   ne·se·*see*·to
(obtener   (ob·te·*ner*
un visado)?   oon vee·*sa*·do)

(too) cold	*(muy) frío*	(mooy) *free*·o
dinner	*cena*	*se*·na
food	*comida*	ko·*mee*·da
fork	*tenedor*	te·ne·*dor*
glass	*vaso*	*va*·so
highchair	*trona*	*tro*·na
hot (warm)	*caliente*	ka·*lyen*·te
knife	*cuchillo*	koo·*chee*·lyo
lunch	*comida*	ko·*mee*·da
main course	*segundo plato*	se·*goon*·do *pla*·to
market	*mercado*	mer·*ka*·do
(children's) menu	*menú (infantil)*	me·*noo* (een·fan·*teel*)
plate	*plato*	*pla*·to
restaurant	*restaurante*	res·tow·*ran*·te
spoon	*cuchara*	koo·*cha*·ra
supermarket	*supermercado*	soo·per·mer·*ka*·do
vegetarian food	*comida vegetariana*	ko·*mee*·da ve·khe·ta·*rya*·na

| with | con | kon |
| without | sin | seen |

Meat & Fish

beef	carne de vaca	kar·ne de va·ka
chicken	pollo	po·lyo
cod	bacalao	ba·ka·la·o
duck	pato	pa·to
lamb	cordero	kor·de·ro
lobster	langosta	lan·gos·ta
pork	cerdo	ser·do
prawns	camarones	ka·ma·ro·nes
salmon	salmón	sal·mon
tuna	atún	a·toon
turkey	pavo	pa·vo
veal	ternera	ter·ne·ra

Fruit & Vegetables

apple	manzana	man·sa·na
apricot	albaricoque	al·ba·ree·ko·ke
artichoke	alcachofa	al·ka·cho·fa
asparagus	espárragos	es·pa·ra·gos
banana	plátano	pla·ta·no
beans	judías	khoo·dee·as
beetroot	remolacha	re·mo·la·cha
cabbage	col	kol
(red/green) capsicum	pimiento (rojo/verde)	pee·myen·to (ro·kho/ver·de)
carrot	zanahoria	sa·na·o·rya
celery	apio	a·pyo
cherry	cereza	se·re·sa
corn	maíz	ma·ees
cucumber	pepino	pe·pee·no
fruit	fruta	froo·ta
grape	uvas	oo·vas
lemon	limón	lee·mon

lentils	lentejas	len·te·khas
lettuce	lechuga	le·choo·ga
mushroom	champiñón	cham·pee·nyon
nuts	nueces	nwe·ses
onion	cebolla	se·bo·lya
orange	naranja	na·ran·kha
peach	melocotón	me·lo·ko·ton
peas	guisantes	gee·san·tes
pineapple	piña	pee·nya
plum	ciruela	seer·we·la
potato	patata	pa·ta·ta
pumpkin	calabaza	ka·la·ba·sa
spinach	espinacas	es·pee·na·kas
strawberry	fresa	fre·sa
tomato	tomate	to·ma·te
vegetable	verdura	ver·doo·ra
watermelon	sandía	san·dee·a

Other

bread	pan	pan
butter	mantequilla	man·te·kee·lya
cheese	queso	ke·so
egg	huevo	we·vo
honey	miel	myel
jam	mermelada	mer·me·la·da
oil	aceite	a·sey·te
pepper	pimienta	pee·myen·ta
rice	arroz	a·ros
salt	sal	sal
sugar	azúcar	a·soo·kar
vinegar	vinagre	vee·na·gre

Drinks

beer	cerveza	ser·ve·sa
coffee	café	ka·fe
(orange) juice	zumo (de naranja)	soo·mo (de na·ran·kha)
milk	leche	le·che
red wine	vino tinto	vee·no teen·to
tea	té	te
(mineral) water	agua (mineral)	a·gwa (mee·ne·ral)
white wine	vino blanco	vee·no blan·ko

EMERGENCIES

| Help! | ¡Socorro! | so·ko·ro |
| Go away! | ¡Vete! | ve·te |

Call ...!	*¡Llame a ...!*	*lya·*me a ...
a doctor	*un médico*	oon me·dee·ko
the police	*la policía*	la po·lee·*see·*a

I'm lost.
Estoy perdido/a. es·*toy* per·*dee·*do/a (m/f)

I'm ill.
Estoy enfermo/a. es·*toy* en·*fer·*mo/a (m/f)

It hurts here.
Me duele aquí. me dwe·le a·*kee*

I'm allergic to (antibiotics).
Soy alérgico/a a soy a·*ler·*khee·ko/a a
(los antibióticos). (los an·tee·*byo·*tee·kos) (m/f)

Where are the toilets?
¿Dónde están los *don·*de es·*tan* los
servicios? ser·*vee·*syos

SHOPPING & SERVICES

I'd like to buy ...
Quisiera comprar ... kee·*sye·*ra kom·*prar* ...

I'm just looking.
Sólo estoy mirando. so·lo es·*toy* mee·*ran·*do

Can I look at it?
¿Puedo verlo? pwe·do *ver·*lo

I don't like it.
No me gusta. no me *goos·*ta

How much is it?
¿Cuánto cuesta? *kwan·*to *kwes·*ta

That's too expensive.
Es muy caro. es mooy *ka·*ro

Can you lower the price?
¿Podría bajar un po·*dree·*a ba·*khar* oon
poco el precio? *po·*ko el *pre·*syo

There's a mistake in the bill.
Hay un error en ai oon e·*ror* en
la cuenta. la *kwen·*ta

ATM	*cajero*	ka·*khe·*ro
	automático	ow·to·*ma·*tee·ko
credit card	*tarjeta de*	tar·*khe·*ta de
	crédito	*kre·*dee·to
internet cafe	*cibercafé*	see·ber·ka·*fe*
post office	*correos*	ko·*re·*os
tourist office	*oficina*	o·fee·*see·*na
	de turismo	de too·*rees·*mo

TIME & DATES

What time is it?	*¿Qué hora es?*	ke o·ra es
It's (10) o'clock.	*Son (las diez).*	son (las dyes)
Half past (one).	*Es (la una)*	es (la *oo·*na)
	y media.	ee me·dya
At what time?	*¿A qué hora?*	a ke o·ra
At ...	*A la(s) ...*	a la(s) ...

morning	*mañana*	ma·*nya·*na
afternoon	*tarde*	*tar·*de
evening	*noche*	*no·*che
yesterday	*ayer*	a·*yer*
today	*hoy*	oy
tomorrow	*mañana*	ma·*nya·*na

Monday	*lunes*	*loo·*nes
Tuesday	*martes*	*mar·*tes
Wednesday	*miércoles*	*myer·*ko·les
Thursday	*jueves*	*khwe·*bes
Friday	*viernes*	*vyer·*nes
Saturday	*sábado*	*sa·*ba·do
Sunday	*domingo*	do·*meen·*go

January	*enero*	e·*ne·*ro
February	*febrero*	fe·*bre·*ro
March	*marzo*	*mar·*so
April	*abril*	a·*breel*
May	*mayo*	*ma·*yo
June	*junio*	*khoo·*nyo
July	*julio*	*khoo·*lyo
August	*agosto*	a·*gos·*to
September	*septiembre*	sep·*tyem·*bre
October	*octubre*	ok·*too·*bre
November	*noviembre*	no·*vyem·*bre
December	*diciembre*	dee·*syem·*bre

TRANSPORT

Public Transport

boat	*barco*	*bar·*ko
bus	*autobús*	ow·to·*boos*
plane	*avión*	a·*vyon*
train	*tren*	tren
tram	*tranvía*	tran·*vee·*a
first	*primer*	pree·*mer*
last	*último*	*ool·*tee·mo
next	*próximo*	*prok·*see·mo

QUESTION WORDS

How?	*¿Cómo?*	*ko·*mo
What?	*¿Qué?*	ke
When?	*¿Cuándo?*	*kwan·*do
Where?	*¿Dónde?*	*don·*de
Who?	*¿Quién?*	kyen
Why?	*¿Por qué?*	por ke

NUMBERS

1	uno	oo·no
2	dos	dos
3	tres	tres
4	cuatro	kwa·tro
5	cinco	seen·ko
6	seis	seys
7	siete	sye·te
8	ocho	o·cho
9	nueve	nwe·ve
10	diez	dyes
20	veinte	veyn·te
30	treinta	treyn·ta
40	cuarenta	kwa·ren·ta
50	cincuenta	seen·kwen·ta
60	sesenta	se·sen·ta
70	setenta	se·ten·ta
80	ochenta	o·chen·ta
90	noventa	no·ven·ta
100	cien	syen
1000	mil	meel

I want to go to (Córdoba).
Quisiera ir a (Córdoba).   kee·sye·ra eer a (kor·do·ba)

At what time does it arrive/leave?
¿A qué hora llega/sale?   a ke o·ra lye·ga/sa·le

Is it a direct route?
¿Es un viaje directo?   es oon vya·khe dee·rek·to

Does it stop at (Granada)?
¿Para en (Granada)?   pa·ra en (gra·na·da)

Which stop is this?
¿Cuál es esta parada?   kwal es es·ta pa·ra·da

Please tell me when we get to (Seville).
¿Puede avisarme   pwe·de a·vee·sar·me
cuando lleguemos   kwan·do lye·ge·mos
a (Sevilla)?   a (se·vee·lya)

I want to get off here.
Quiero bajarme aquí.   kye·ro ba·khar·me a·kee

a ... ticket	un billete de ...	oon bee·lye·te de ...
1st-class	primera clase	pree·me·ra kla·se
2nd-class	segunda clase	se·goon·da kla·se
one-way	ida	ee·da
return	ida y vuelta	ee·da ee vwel·ta
aisle/window seat	asiento de pasillo/ ventana	a·syen·to de pa·see·lyo/ ven·ta·na

bus/train station	estación de autobuses/ trenes	es·ta·syon de ow·to·boo·ses/ tre·nes
cancelled	cancelado	kan·se·la·do
delayed	retrasado	re·tra·sa·do
platform	plataforma	pla·ta·for·ma
ticket office	taquilla	ta·kee·lya
timetable	horario	o·ra·ryo

Driving & Cycling

I'd like to hire a ...	Quisiera alquilar ...	kee·sye·ra al·kee·lar ...
4WD	un todo- terreno	oon to·do- te·re·no
bicycle	una bicicleta	oo·na bee·see·kle·ta
car	un coche	oon ko·che
motorcycle	una moto	oo·na mo·to

child seat	asiento de seguridad para niños	a·syen·to de se·goo·ree·da pa·ra nee·nyos
diesel	gasóleo	ga·so·le·o
helmet	casco	kas·ko
mechanic	mecánico	me·ka·nee·ko
petrol	gasolina	ga·so·lee·na
service station	gasolinera	ga·so·lee·ne·ra

How much is it per day/hour?
¿Cuánto cuesta por   kwan·to kwes·ta por
día/hora?   dee·a/o·ra

Is this the road to (Malaga)?
¿Se va a (Málaga)   se va a (ma·la·ga)
por esta carretera?   por es·ta ka·re·te·ra

(How long) Can I park here?
¿(Por cuánto tiempo)   (por kwan·to tyem·po)
Puedo aparcar aquí?   pwe·do a·par·kar a·kee

The car has broken down (at Cádiz).
El coche se ha averiado   el ko·che se a a·ve·rya·do
(en Cádiz).   (en ka·dees)

I have a flat tyre.
Tengo un pinchazo.   ten·go oon peen·cha·so

I've run out of petrol.
Me he quedado sin   me e ke·da·do seen
gasolina.   ga·so·lee·na

Are there cycling paths?
¿Hay carril bicicleta?   ai ka·reel bee·see·kle·ta

Is there bicycle parking?
¿Hay aparcamiento   ai a·par·ka·myen·to
de bicicletas?   de bee·see·kle·tas

GLOSSARY

alameda – *paseo* lined (or originally lined) with *álamo* (poplar) trees
alcázar – Islamic-era fortress
artesonado – ceiling with interlaced beams leaving regular spaces for decorative insertions
autopista – toll highway
autovía – toll-free dual carriageway
AVE – Alta Velocidad Española; the high-speed train between Madrid and Seville
ayuntamiento – city or town hall
azulejo – tile

bahía – bay
bailaor/a – flamenco dancer
bandolero – bandit
barrio – district or quarter (of a town or city)
bodega – winery, wine bar or wine cellar
buceo – scuba diving
bulería – upbeat type of flamenco song
buzón – postbox

cajero automático – automated teller machine (ATM)
calle – street
callejón – lane
cambio – currency exchange
campiña – countryside (usually flat or rolling cultivated countryside)
campo – countryside, field
cantaor/a – flamenco singer
cante jondo – 'deep song', the essence of flamenco
capilla – chapel
capilla mayor – chapel containing the high altar of a church
carnaval – carnival; a pre-Lent period of fancy-dress parades and merrymaking
carretera – road, highway
carta – menu
casa rural – a village house or farmhouse with rooms to let
casco – literally 'helmet'; used to refer to the old part of a city (*casco antiguo*)
castellano – Castilian; the language also called Spanish

castillo – castle
caza – hunting
centro comercial – shopping centre
cercanía – suburban train
cerro – hill
cervecería – beer bar
chiringuito – small, often makeshift bar or eatery, usually in the open air
Churrigueresque – ornate style of baroque architecture named after the brothers Alberto and José Churriguera
cofradía – see *hermandad*
colegiata – collegiate church, a combined church and college
comedor – dining room
comisaría – station of the Policía Nacional (National Police)
converso – Jew who converted to Christianity in medieval Spain
cordillera – mountain chain
coro – choir (part of a church, usually in the middle)
corrida de toros – bullfight
cortes – parliament
cortijo – country property
costa – coast
coto – area where hunting rights are reserved for a specific group of people
cruce – cross
cuenta – bill (check)
cuesta – sloping land, road or street
custodia – monstrance (receptacle for the consecrated Host)

dehesa – woodland pastures with evergreen oaks
Denominación de Origen (DO) – a designation that indicates the unique geographical origins, production processes and quality of wines, olive oil and other products
duende – the spirit or magic possessed by great flamenco performers
duque – duke
duquesa – duchess

embalse – reservoir
ermita – hermitage or chapel

escalada – climbing
estación de autobuses – bus station
estación de esquí – ski station or resort
estación de ferrocarril – train station
estación marítima – passenger port
estanco – tobacconist
estrella – literally 'star'; also class of overnight train with seats, couchettes and sleeping compartments

farmacia – pharmacy
faro – lighthouse
feria – fair; can refer to trade fairs as well as to city, town or village fairs
ferrocarril – railway
fiesta – festival, public holiday or party
finca – country property, farm
flamenco – means flamingo and Flemish as well as flamenco music and dance
frontera – frontier
fuente – fountain, spring

gitano – the Spanish word for Roma people
Guardia Civil – Civil Guard; police responsible for roads, the countryside, villages and international borders. They wear green uniforms. See also *Policía Local, Policía Nacional.*

hammam – Arabic-style bathhouse
hermandad – brotherhood (which may include women), in particular one that takes part in religious processions; also *cofradía*
hospedaje – guesthouse
hostal – simple guesthouse or small place offering budget hotel-like accommodation

infanta – daughter of a monarch but not first in line to the throne
infante – son of a monarch but not first in line to the throne

jardín – garden

judería – Jewish barrio in medieval Spain

Junta de Andalucía – executive government of Andalucía

lavandería – laundry

librería – bookshop

lidia – the modern art of bullfighting on foot

lucio – pond or pool in the Doñana *marismas* (wetlands)

madrugada/madrugá – the 'early hours', from around 3am to dawn; a pretty lively time in some Spanish cities

marismas – wetlands, marshes

marisquería – seafood eatery

marqués – marquis

medina – Arabic word for town or inner city

mercadillo – flea market

mercado – market

mezquita – mosque

mihrab – prayer niche in a mosque indicating the direction of Mecca

mirador – lookout point

morisco – Muslim converted to Christianity in medieval Spain

moro – 'Moor' or Muslim (usually in a medieval context)

movida – the late-night bar and club scene that emerged in Spanish cities and towns after Franco's death; a *zona de movida* or *zona de marcha* is an area of a town where people gather to drink and have a good time

mozárabe – Mozarab; Christian living under Islamic rule in medieval Spain

Mudéjar – Muslim living under Christian rule in medieval Spain; also refers to their decorative style of architecture

muelle – wharf, pier

muladí – Muwallad; Christian who converted to Islam, in medieval Spain

nazareno – penitent taking part in Semana Santa processions

nieve – snow

nuevo – new

oficina de correos – post office

oficina de turismo – tourist office

olivo – olive tree

palacio – palace

palo – literally 'stick'; also refers to the categories of flamenco song

panadería – bakery

papelería – stationery shop

parador – one of the Paradores Nacionales, a state-owned chain of luxurious hotels, often in historic buildings

paraje natural – natural area

parque nacional – national park

parque natural – natural park

paseo – avenue or parklike strip; walk or stroll

paso – literally 'step'; also the platform an image is carried on in a religious procession

peña – a club; usually for supporters of a football club or flamenco enthusiasts *(peña flamenca)*, but sometimes a dining club

pensión – guesthouse

pescadería – fish shop

picadero – riding stable

pícaro – dice trickster and card sharp, rogue, low-life scoundrel

pinsapar – forest of *pinsapo*

pinsapo – Spanish fir

piscina – swimming pool

plateresque – early phase of Renaissance architecture noted for its decorative facades

playa – beach

plaza de toros – bullring

Policía Local – Local Police; also known as Policía Municipal. Controlled by city and town halls, they deal mainly with minor matters such as parking, traffic and bylaws. They wear blue-and-white uniforms. See also *Guardia Civil, Policía Nacional.*

Policía Municipal – Municipal Police; see *Policía Local*

Policía Nacional – National Police; responsible for cities and bigger towns, some of them forming special squads dealing with drugs, terrorism and the like.

preferente – 1st-class carriage on a long-distance train

provincia – province; Spain is divided into 50 of them

pueblo – village, town

puente – bridge

puerta – gate, door

puerto – port, mountain pass

puerto deportivo – marina

puerto pesquero – fishing port

punta – point

rambla – stream

Reconquista – the Christian reconquest of the Iberian Peninsula from the Muslims (8th to 15th centuries)

refugio – shelter or refuge, especially a mountain refuge with basic accommodation for hikers

regional – train running between Andalucian cities

reja – grille; especially a wrought-iron one over a window or dividing a chapel from the rest of a church

Renfe – Red Nacional de los Ferrocarriles Españoles; Spain's national rail network

reserva – reservation, or reserve (eg nature reserve)

reserva nacional de caza – national hunting reserve

reserva natural – nature reserve

retablo – retable (altarpiece)

ría – estuary

río – river

romería – festive pilgrimage or procession

ronda – ring road

sacristía – sacristy, the part of a church in which vestments, sacred objects and other valuables are kept

salina – salt lagoon

Semana Santa – Holy Week; the week leading up to Easter Sunday

sendero – path or track

sevillana – a popular Andalucian dance

sierra – mountain range

Siglo de Oro – Spain's cultural 'Golden Century', beginning in the 16th century and ending in the 17th century

taberna – tavern

tablao – flamenco show

taifa – one of the small kingdoms into which the Muslim-ruled parts of Spain were divided during parts of the 11th and 12th centuries

taquilla – ticket window

taracea – marquetry

tarjeta de crédito – credit card

tarjeta telefónica – phonecard

teléfono móvil – mobile telephone

terraza – terrace; often means an area with outdoor tables at a bar, cafe or restaurant

tetería – Middle Eastern–style teahouse with low seats around low tables

tienda – shop, tent

tocaor/a – flamenco guitarist

torre – tower

trenhotel – sleek, expensive, sleeping car–only train

turismo – means both tourism and saloon car; *el turismo* can also mean the tourist office

turista – second-class carriage on a long-distance train

valle – valley

zoco – large market in Muslim cities

Behind the Scenes

SEND US YOUR FEEDBACK

We love to hear from travellers – your comments keep us on our toes and help make our books better. Our well-travelled team reads every word on what you loved or loathed about this book. Although we cannot reply individually to your submissions, we always guarantee that your feedback goes straight to the appropriate authors, in time for the next edition. Each person who sends us information is thanked in the next edition – the most useful submissions are rewarded with a selection of digital PDF chapters.

Visit **lonelyplanet.com/contact** to submit your updates and suggestions or to ask for help. Our award-winning website also features inspirational travel stories, news and discussions.

Note: We may edit, reproduce and incorporate your comments in Lonely Planet products such as guidebooks, websites and digital products, so let us know if you don't want your comments reproduced or your name acknowledged. For a copy of our privacy policy visit lonelyplanet.com/privacy.

OUR READERS

Many thanks to the travellers who used the last edition and wrote to us with helpful hints, useful advice and interesting anecdotes:

Alfonso Iturbe, David Drouet, David Martin, Denise Komen, Ewelina Miklas, Joseph Stanik, Kuro Kurosaka, Marlies Van Hoef, Melanie Staes, Ron Stewart

WRITER THANKS

Isabella Noble

In Andalucía, thanks to Jack, Dan, Annie, Pepi, Helen, Eugenia, Monika, Tessa, and the Grazalema and Tarifa tourism teams. Extra special *gracias* to my fabulous co-writers, John, Gregor, Duncan and Brendan.

Gregor Clark

Muchísimas gracias to the many Spaniards and resident expatriates who shared their love of country and local knowledge with me, especially Isabella, Eneida, Nigel, Emma, Domingo, Lucy, Ángel, Peter Jan, Monica, Charles, Justine, Aideen and Marcel. Back home, *besos y abrazos* to Gaen, Meigan and Chloe, who always make coming home the best part of the trip.

Duncan Garwood

I owe a lot of thanks, starting with my favourite travel companions Lidia, Ben and Nick. Thanks also to fellow writer John Noble for his generous advice and Tom

Stainer for his support at Lonely Planet. In Spain, *gracias* to Carmen Prado, Vincente del Moral, María April, Paco Parra, Antonia Requena, Yolanda Magán, Encarni Gutiérrez, Carmen Plazas, Mercedes Aguilar Pérez, Paula, Alcayada García, Irene Godoy, Paula Dominguez and the team at Mojácar tourist office.

John Noble

Thanks to so many people for their help but extra special thanks to Isabella Noble, Iain Colquhoun, Colin Richardson, Pablo and Manolo Canosa, Adrián Costa García and the Liñares family.

Brendan Sainsbury

Muchas gracias to all the bus drivers, tourist information staff, hoteliers, chefs, hiking guides and innocent passers-by who helped me, unwittingly or otherwise, on my research trip.

ACKNOWLEDGEMENTS

Climate map data adapted from Peel MC, Finlayson BL & McMahon TA (2007) 'Updated World Map of the Köppen-Geiger Climate Classification', Hydrology and Earth System Sciences, 11, 1633–44.

Cover photograph: Andalucian horses, photo muguette/Getty Images ©

Illustrations pp54–5, 206–7 & 256–7 by Javier Zarracina

THIS BOOK

This 9th edition of Lonely Planet's *Andalucía* guide was researched and written by Isabella Noble, Gregor Clark, Duncan Garwood, John Noble and Brendan Sainsbury. The previous edition was written by Isabella Noble, John Noble, Josephine Quintero and Brendan Sainsbury. This guidebook was produced by the following:

Destination Editor
Tom Stainer

Product Editors Kate James, Kathryn Rowan

Senior Cartographer
Anthony Phelan

Assisting Cartographer
James Leversha

Book Designer
Mazzy Du Plessis

Assisting Editors Sarah Bailey, Andrew Bain, Michelle Coxall, Samantha Forge, Emma Gibbs, Carly Hall, Trent Holden, Gabby Innes, Anita Isalska, Ali Lemer, Jodie Martire, Rosie Nicholson, Chris Pitts, Sarah Reid, Gabrielle Stefanos, Sam Wheeler

Cover Researcher Naomi Parker

Thanks to Joe Bindloss, Gemma Graham, Tanya Parker, Alison Ridgway, Fiona Flores Watson

Index

Map Legend

Sights

- Beach
- Bird Sanctuary
- Buddhist
- Castle/Palace
- Christian
- Confucian
- Hindu
- Islamic
- Jain
- Jewish
- Monument
- Museum/Gallery/Historic Building
- Ruin
- Shinto
- Sikh
- Taoist
- Winery/Vineyard
- Zoo/Wildlife Sanctuary
- Other Sight

Activities, Courses & Tours

- Bodysurfing
- Diving
- Canoeing/Kayaking
- Course/Tour
- Sento Hot Baths/Onsen
- Skiing
- Snorkelling
- Surfing
- Swimming/Pool
- Walking
- Windsurfing
- Other Activity

Sleeping

- Sleeping
- Camping
- Hut/Shelter

Eating

- Eating

Drinking & Nightlife

- Drinking & Nightlife
- Cafe

Entertainment

- Entertainment

Shopping

- Shopping

Information

- Bank
- Embassy/Consulate
- Hospital/Medical
- Internet
- Police
- Post Office
- Telephone
- Toilet
- Tourist Information
- Other Information

Geographic

- Beach
- Gate
- Hut/Shelter
- Lighthouse
- Lookout
- Mountain/Volcano
- Oasis
- Park
- Pass
- Picnic Area
- Waterfall

Population

- Capital (National)
- Capital (State/Province)
- City/Large Town
- Town/Village

Transport

- Airport
- Border crossing
- Bus
- Cable car/Funicular
- Cycling
- Ferry
- Metro station
- Monorail
- Parking
- Petrol station
- S-Bahn/Subway station
- Taxi
- T-bane/Tunnelbana station
- Train station/Railway
- Tram
- Tube station
- U-Bahn/Underground station
- Other Transport

Routes

- Tollway
- Freeway
- Primary
- Secondary
- Tertiary
- Lane
- Unsealed road
- Road under construction
- Plaza/Mall
- Steps
- Tunnel
- Pedestrian overpass
- Walking Tour
- Walking Tour detour
- Path/Walking Trail

Boundaries

- International
- State/Province
- Disputed
- Regional/Suburb
- Marine Park
- Cliff
- Wall

Hydrography

- River, Creek
- Intermittent River
- Canal
- Water
- Dry/Salt/Intermittent Lake
- Reef

Areas

- Airport/Runway
- Beach/Desert
- Cemetery (Christian)
- Cemetery (Other)
- Glacier
- Mudflat
- Park/Forest
- Sight (Building)
- Sportsground
- Swamp/Mangrove

Note: Not all symbols displayed above appear on the maps in this book

OUR STORY

A beat-up old car, a few dollars in the pocket and a sense of adventure. In 1972 that's all Tony and Maureen Wheeler needed for the trip of a lifetime – across Europe and Asia overland to Australia. It took several months, and at the end – broke but inspired – they sat at their kitchen table writing and stapling together their first travel guide, *Across Asia on the Cheap*. Within a week they'd sold 1500 copies. Lonely Planet was born.

Today, Lonely Planet has offices in Franklin, London, Melbourne, Oakland, Dublin, Beijing and Delhi, with more than 600 staff and writers. We share Tony's belief that 'a great guidebook should do three things: inform, educate and amuse'.

OUR WRITERS   31901064234638

Isabella Noble

Cádiz Province, Gibraltar English-Australian on paper but Spanish at heart, Isabella has been wandering the globe since her first round-the-world trip as a one-year-old. Having grown up in a whitewashed Andalucian village, she is a Spain specialist travel journalist, but also writes extensively about India, Thailand, the UK and beyond for Lonely Planet, the *Daily Telegraph* and others. Find Isabella on Twitter and Instagram (@isabellamnoble). Isabella also wrote the Plan section.

Gregor Clark

Huelva Province Gregor Clark is a US-based writer whose love of foreign languages and curiosity about what's around the next bend have taken him to dozens of countries on five continents. Since 2000, Gregor has regularly contributed to Lonely Planet guides, with a focus on Europe and the Americas. He lived in California, France, Spain and Italy prior to settling with his wife and two daughters in his current home state of Vermont.

Duncan Garwood

Sevilla Province, Granada Province, Almería Province From facing fast bowlers in Barbados to sidestepping hungry pigs in Goa, Duncan's travels have thrown up many unique experiences. These days he largely dedicates himself to Spain and Italy, his adopted homeland, where he's lived since 1997. He's worked on more than 30 Lonely Planet titles, including guidebooks to Rome, Sardinia, Sicily, Bilbao and San Sebastián. He's also written on Italy for newspapers, websites and magazines.

John Noble

Jaén Province, Córdoba Province John has been travelling for Lonely Planet since the 1980s. The number of LP titles he's written is well into three figures, on numerous countries scattered across the globe. He's still as excited as ever about heading out to unfamiliar destinations, especially off-the-beaten-track ones. Above all, he loves mountains, from the Pyrenees to the Himalaya. See his pics on Instagram: @johnnoble11. John also wrote the Understand section.

Brendan Sainsbury

Málaga Province Born and raised in the UK, Brendan spent the holidays of his youth caravanning in the English Lake District and didn't leave Blighty until he was 19. Making up for lost time, he's since squeezed 70 countries into a sometimes precarious existence as a writer and professional vagabond. In the last 11 years, he has written more than 40 books for Lonely Planet from Castro's Cuba to the canyons of Peru. Brendan also wrote the Survival Guide section.

Published by Lonely Planet Global Limited
CRN 554153
9th edition – Jan 2019
ISBN 978 1 78657 2752
© Lonely Planet 2019   Photographs © as indicated 2019
10 9 8 7 6 5 4 3 2 1
Printed in China